Global Social Issues

Volume Two

Global
Social Issues
An Encyclopedia

Volume Two

Christopher G. Bates and James Ciment, Editors

SHARPE REFERENCE

an imprint of M.E. Sharpe, Inc.

SHARPE REFERENCE

Sharpe Reference is an imprint of M.E. Sharpe, Inc.

M.E. Sharpe, Inc.
80 Business Park Drive
Armonk, NY 10504

© 2013 by M.E. Sharpe, Inc.

Cover images (clockwise from top left) were provided by: Patrik Stollarz/AFP/Getty Images; Heng Sinith/AP Images; AFP/Getty Images; STR/AFP/Getty Images; Roberto Schmidt/AFP/Getty Images; Mark Wilson/Getty Images.

Library of Congress Cataloging-in-Publication Data

Global social issues : an encyclopedia / Christopher G. Bates and James Ciment, editors.
     v. ; cm.
Includes bibliographical references and index.
ISBN 978-0-7656-8292-5 (alk. paper)
1. Social problems—Encyclopedias. I. Bates, Christopher G. II. Ciment, James.

H41.G56 2013
361.003—dc23   2012021425

Printed and bound in the United States

The paper used in this publication meets the minimum requirements of
American National Standard for Information Sciences—Permanence of
Paper for Printed Library Materials,
ANSI Z 39.48.1984.

EB (c) 10 9 8 7 6 5 4 3 2 1

Publisher: Myron E. Sharpe
Vice President and Director of New Product Development: Donna Sanzone
Vice President and Production Director: Carmen Chetti
Executive Development Editor: Jeff Hacker
Project Manager: Angela Piliouras
Program Coordinator: Cathleen Prisco
Editorial Assistant: Lauren LoPinto
Cover Design: Jesse Sanchez
Typesetter: Nancy Connick

CONTENTS

VOLUME 2

Gambling 365

Gastrointestinal Disease 373

Gay, Lesbian, Bisexual, and Transgender Issues 381

Genetically Engineered Crops and Foods 390

Government Corruption and Transparency 398

Health Care 408

Hepatitis 416

Homelessness 422

Housing Costs, Finance, and Affordability 427

Human Rights 435

Hunger and Malnutrition 447

Identity Fraud 456

Immigration, Illegal and Irregular 461

Indigenous Peoples' Rights 469

Inequality, Income and Wealth 478

Infant Mortality 487

Influenza 495

Infrastructure 501

Intellectual Property Rights 508

Kidnapping and Hostage-Taking 514

Land Mines 522

Law, Rule of 527

Literacy 536

Marriage and Divorce 543

Mental Health 550

Migrant Labor 557

Mining Issues 563

Money Laundering and Illegal Transfers 571

Mosquito-borne Disease 575

Natural Disasters, Preparedness and Response 582

Neurological Disease 591

Nuclear Energy 599

Nuclear Proliferation 607

Obesity and Eating Disorders 616

Oil, Economic and Political Aspects 624

Oil, Environmental and Health Aspects 632

Organ and Tissue Trade 641

Parasitic Disease 645

Pesticides and Artificial Fertilizers 653

Pharmaceuticals: Availability, Cost, Efficacy, and Safety 660

Piracy, Maritime 669

Police Corruption and Brutality 676

Polio 682

Pollution, Air 688

Pollution, Water 695

Population Growth and Demographic Issues 703

Poverty 711

Press, Freedom of 719

Prisoners and Prisoner Rights 727

Privacy 734

Privatization 741

Protectionism and Free Trade 749

Public Health 756

GAMBLING

Gambling is an activity in which two or more parties bet money or goods on an event whose outcome is uncertain and is dictated, at least in part, by chance. Those bettors who pick the correct outcome win their original bet back, along with additional money or goods.

There are many different ways to bet: on card games, dice rolls, horse races, lotteries, slot machines, and sporting events, among other options. Some gambling is legal (for example, participation in state-run lotteries, bets at licensed casinos or racetracks), but the majority—whether among friends or acquaintances or with a "bookie" or other unlicensed operation—is illegal. The appeal of extralegal gambling is significant—it allows for home poker games, sports pools, and other types of social betting; it affords gaming opportunities in places where casinos and other legal options are sparse or nonexistent; and, in the cases of professional gamblers or very large wagers, it facilitates tax evasion.

The benefits of gambling include the entertainment it provides for participants, as well as the financial boost it brings to local and national economies. At the same time, gambling, especially when done to excess, is linked to a host of social ills, including alcoholism, crime, homelessness, and increased rates of suicide. Further, municipalities that choose to limit or prohibit gambling are often drained of significant capital by neighboring municipalities where the activity is legal.

The most recent estimates suggest that legal gambling is a $350 billion a year industry worldwide. Illegal gambling involves considerably more revenue than this, though it is difficult to ascertain how much more, since it is by nature underground and undocumented. Analysts estimate the figure to be anywhere from $2 trillion to $10 trillion annually.

History

Gambling is one of humankind's oldest leisure activities. Archaeologists have found astralagi—a form of dice made from the bones of dogs or sheep—at sites that date back 40,000 years, sometimes accompanied by cave paintings that depict gaming.

Most ancient civilizations appear to have had some form of gambling. The Chinese played a tile-based game of chance that dates back to at least 2300 B.C.E. Greek soldiers enjoyed dice games, and Greek mythology taught that the gods Zeus, Hades, and Poseidon divided up the world among heaven, hell, and the seas by casting lots. The Egyptians, Persians, and Indians also enjoyed dice games—indeed, the Indian epic *Mahabharata*, which dates to 1500 B.C.E., begins with a dice match. On the other side of the world, Native Americans played games of chance with special stones painted white or black.

Playing cards, an essential component of modern gaming, were first developed in Asia around the year 700 C.E. Exactly which Asian nation can claim the honor is in dispute. Some scholars believe it was Korea; others point to China. In any event, playing cards slowly worked their way westward to India and Persia and Europe, with the number of suits, ranks, and total cards varying widely. For almost a thousand years, cards remained the province of social elites because they had to be made by hand and so were quite expensive. It was not until the development of the printing press in the 1400s that playing cards became inexpensive enough to be within the means of the general public. It was also around that time that the French developed the basic deck configuration most commonly used today: four suits—clubs, diamonds, hearts, and spades—with two being the lowest ranking card and king the highest ranking. Aces were added starting in the 1500s, with jokers rounding out the deck in the mid-1800s.

Just as gambling itself has a long history, so, too, do antigaming laws. Throughout history, most governments have regarded gambling as a cause for concern for a number of reasons: because it distracted citizens from more important tasks, promoted general immorality and lawlessness, or reduced the flow of tax revenue to the government. The laws of ancient China, Greece, India, Persia, and Rome all strictly limited—or even prohibited—gaming, as do the Jewish Talmud, the Muslim Koran, and the Buddhist Tripitaka. The penalties for violating these prohibitions could be severe: forced labor in many cases, execution in others.

Antigaming laws generally were not very effective, however, since they tended to be poorly enforced. For example, Henry VIII of England outlawed most forms of gambling in 1541 because he felt that his soldiers were spending too little time honing their martial skills. He seems to have done little to implement the decree, however, and he himself was an inveterate gambler. Certainly, he looked the other way when Englishmen wagered on the outcome of his wife Anne Boleyn's trial for treason and incest. Those who wagered that she would be executed got 10-to-1 odds, and so a handsome return on their investments.

The 1700s witnessed the advent of modern sports betting, which started with wagers on horse and dog racing and eventually expanded to boxing and other contests involving human participants. New games were also invented, notably roulette in the 1790s. State-run lotteries were commonplace during this time and served as an important source of financing for national governments, particularly those that lacked other options. The funding for the Continental Army during the Revolutionary War was largely paid by lotteries, for example, as were the costs for the construction of Washington, D.C. The rebels behind the French Revolution also took advantage of this method. However, state-run lotteries largely fell out of favor in the mid-1800s, having become a product of widespread corruption and fraud. The rise of evangelical Christianity as well contributed to their unpopularity.

Although reformers held the line against gambling in some parts of the United States and Europe in the nineteenth century, they were not able to stem the tide completely. In the American West, riverboats and other gambling operations flourished, and they gave rise to the games of poker (around 1830) and craps (which evolved from a game called "hazard" around 1840) as well as to slot machines (around 1890). In Europe, the first great casino resorts opened for business, notably the Hotel de Paris in Monte Carlo in 1864. Sports betting continued to grow in prominence, expanding to newly created team sports such as baseball (in the 1860s) and football (in the 1890s).

In the twentieth century, particularly following World War II, gambling experienced another leap forward. Beginning in 1946, the small desert town of Las Vegas, Nevada, was transformed into a mecca for casino goers, aided both by rapid innovations in slot machine technology and by the financial resources of organized crime. Atlantic City, New Jersey, followed Las Vegas's lead in 1977. In subsequent decades, many nations—even those predominated by religions that frown on gambling—decided to embrace the casino business. Today, a list of the world's leading casinos includes not only those in Las Vegas and Monte Carlo but also Argentina, Australia, Egypt, Germany, Italy, Japan, Macao, South Africa, Spain, and the United Kingdom. The latter decades of the twentieth century also witnessed the resurgence of government-run lotteries, which now generate more money than any other form of legal gambling (though casinos are not far behind).

Gambling Today

Gambling today is a massive worldwide industry. Some analysts believe that it is the leading form of entertainment spending in the world; others rank it second behind alcohol. Spending on gambling, not surprisingly, generally correlates with wealth—in North America, legal gambling is an estimated $120 billion a year industry, followed by Europe (just over $100 billion) and Asia and the Middle East (about $75 billion together). From there, the decrease is pronounced: about $18 billion in Latin America, less than $17 billion in Oceania, and less than $5 billion in Africa. Among individual nations, the United States is far and away the world's leader in income generated from legal gambling, with an estimated $95 billion annually, followed by Japan ($35 billion), Italy ($18 billion), the United Kingdom (just over $15 billion), and Hong Kong/Macao (just under $14.8 billion).

The U.S. lead over other countries is due, in part, to its great wealth and population size; however, it is also due to the fact that the American model of casino management is very different from the European model. American casinos are aggressively marketed, boldly decorated with lights and other glitzy touches, and often built in clusters. European casinos are not advertised, are understated, and tend to be monopolies—there is only one casino per municipality. Further, American casinos entice gamblers with loose credit, free or inexpensive alcohol, and vast numbers of slot machines. In European casinos,

The Venetian Macao (*center*), Four Seasons Hotel (*left*), and Galaxy Macau (*right*), all on the Cotai Strip, have helped make Macao the world's largest gambling market and top casino travel destination. Most visitors come from mainland China and Hong Kong. *(Jerome Favre/Bloomberg via Getty Images)*

by contrast, credit is not extended, alcoholic drinks are rare, and table games, which generally offer better odds than slots, are predominant. The European model is utilized across most of the world, though the American model is beginning to achieve broader currency, particularly because many American operators have opened foreign subsidiaries in recent years. For example, the world's largest casino—the Venetian Macao, with 6,000 slot machines and 870 table games—is located in Asia but operated by the Las Vegas Sands Corporation.

Because illegal gambling is poorly documented, it is more difficult to be confident about its prevalence on a regional or national basis. Generally speaking, experts believe that there is a fairly strong correlation between the amount of legal gambling and the amount of illegal gambling that occurs in a particular place. Put another way, there is a presumption that North America in general, and the United States in particular, leads the world by a large margin in money spent on illegal gambling. One should recall, however, that this covers a wide range of activities. Two friends

who bet $20 on the outcome of a baseball game are technically breaking the law. So, too, is an individual who places a $10,000 wager with a bookmaker employed by an organized crime organization. There is considerable difference between these two acts, and yet both fall under the rubric of "illegal gambling."

In any event, gambling—particularly legalized gambling—offers tangible benefits. On an individual level, betting can be an enjoyable form of recreation with a relatively high return on investment. One can spend multiple hours in a home poker game, or wagering on sporting events, or playing low-cost slot machines, and come out ahead or behind by only $20 or $30. This compares favorably to the cost of attendance at a movie, a sporting event, or a music concert. Studies have also indicated the value of sports pools, lottery pools, and other forms of communal betting in creating team spirit and workplace cohesion.

On a societal level, the capacity for gambling to transform and revitalize local economies is well documented. The state of Nevada is, of course, the best-known success story of this sort. Suffering terribly from the straits imposed by the Great Depression, Nevada legalized casino wagering in 1931. The state's economy slowly recovered thereafter and then took off after World War II owing to the postwar boom and the rise of Las Vegas. In the early 2010s, just over 60 percent of all revenue in the state comes from gambling. Similarly, impoverished Native American tribes in the United States and Canada and declining industrial towns like Manchester in England and Gary and Detroit in the United States have benefited enormously from legalized gaming. In the United States alone, the gambling industry provides more than 600,000 jobs.

The downsides to gambling are significant as well, especially for those who bet recklessly or compulsively (properly known as "ludomania"). Problem gamblers are vastly more likely to have substance abuse problems than the general populace, are twice as likely to get divorced, and are three times as likely to commit suicide. Most have credit problems and struggle to pay their bills. One in four problem gamblers will declare bankruptcy, and one in five will spend time living on the streets. In response to these financial issues, problem gamblers are vastly more likely to commit crimes than the general populace. Nearly half will steal—primarily by embezzling from their employers—to cover their gambling losses.

Because the criteria for what constitutes problem gambling are imprecise and are still debated, and because those who bet compulsively tend to hide their behavior, calculating the prevalence of problem gambling presents a challenge. The best estimates place the figure at about 3 percent of the gambling population of the United States (or about 2 million people in all), 1 percent in Western Europe, and somewhere between those two figures for most of the rest of the world (with Asia, at about 2.5 percent, closest to the United States in terms of prevalence). There are also a few outliers: the area with the highest incidence of problem gambling in the world is Hong Kong, at 5 percent of the betting populace, while the nations of Scandinavia have the lowest rates among those countries that have been studied, hovering around 0.3 percent.

Needless to say, when individual problems are multiplied by hundreds of thousands or millions of people, they also become societal problems. Of particular concern to critics of gambling is the extent to which it promotes criminal activity. On top of the thefts perpetrated by problem gamblers, reckless betting also facilitates crime against those who lose money, as unsavory figures attempt to collect debts that result from lost bets. Further, the rise of Las Vegas and other gambling operations was notoriously accompanied by all manner of violent crime. Today, gaming is much more tightly regulated, though casinos remain a focal point for money laundering.

Another criticism is that certain forms of legalized gambling, particularly state-run lotteries, effectively serve as a hidden form of taxation. For example, most individuals are reluctant to pay more taxes, but many of them are willing to gamble on lotteries—effectively handing over their money to the government. Beyond the inherent duplicity that this represents, these "lottery taxes," as they are often called, are highly regressive. That is to say, lotteries are get-rich-quick schemes, and so they primarily attract the dollars of poor people, who can least afford to pay.

Coping with Gambling

Among individual bettors, gambling imposes far and away the greatest burden on those who are problem gamblers; however, these people can be difficult to identify. Because of shame or a desire to hide crimes and other misdeeds, there is a strong tendency toward duplicity and denial. To aid in diagnosis, clinicians often use screening tools, such as brief surveys designed to pinpoint problematic patterns of behavior. The best known of these is the South Oaks Gambling Screen, which is in use around the world. Still, only one problem gambler in 10 seeks treatment once confronted with his or her illness.

Even when a problem gambler has been identified and has agreed to accept assistance, there is no consensus among health care professionals about what the next step should be. Some organizations—the Illinois Institute for Addiction Recovery, for example—argue that problem gambling is a biochemical addiction like alcoholism and should therefore be diagnosed and treated in a similar fashion. A majority—including, notably, the American Psychological Association—regard problem gambling as an impulse control disorder, like kleptomania (compulsive desire to steal) or pyromania (compulsive desire to set fires), that primarily requires counseling.

The lack of consensus has significant implications for individuals who want assistance with their gambling behavior. To start, there are no pharmaceutical aids available to help problem gamblers in the way that there are for alcohol, tobacco, or heroin addicts. Beyond that, treatment programs are far less common, and they are much less likely to be paid for by health insurance. Consequently, the most common "cure" for problem gambling—beyond a brief course of counseling—is attendance at a support group such as Gamblers Anonymous (GA). Modeled on the 12-step program, such as that of Alcoholics Anonymous, GA provides information, peer support, and other assistance. Unfortunately, it appears to be ineffective more often than not, with some studies putting its success rate at as low as 8 percent.

Problem gambling, then, is a vexing issue for individuals to confront. Governments that wish to address problem gambling also find themselves in something of a bind. To start, they may not always have the legal power to control casinos and other betting operations. In many circumstances, local governments find themselves trumped by national laws or national governments find themselves compelled to defer to local laws. For example, a number of U.S. states, notably California, have attempted to impose limits on the size and number of Native American casinos. The Indian tribes have responded by taking the matter to federal courts, consistently emerging triumphant.

Further, controls on gambling are often impractical from an economic standpoint. When there are neighboring cities, states, or countries where one offers legalized gambling and the other does not, it is invariably the case that gamblers will travel from the locality that does not have gambling to the one that does. The result for the nongambling locality is that it loses a great deal of money to its neighbor while still bearing many of the social ills that result from problem gambling—embezzlement, higher divorce rates, increased alcoholism, and so forth.

As the country where gaming is most prevalent, the United States provides an instructive example of this phenomenon. In 1980, gambling was legal in only three states—Nevada, New Hampshire, and New Jersey. Neighboring states were having so much money drained from them—particularly California from Nevada—that they felt compelled to embrace some form of legal gambling to protect themselves. Over the course of the next three decades, all but two states in the entire country ultimately eliminated some restrictions on gaming. The exceptions are Hawaii, which has no bordering states and so is not subject to the flight of capital, and Utah, where the predominant Mormon Church vigorously opposes gambling. Indeed, Utah is the exception that proves the rule—the five locations that sell the most lottery tickets of any retailer in the United States are all located along the Utah border.

Finally, and perhaps most significantly, if human history has shown anything in regard to betting, it is that citizens will gamble whether their leaders allow them to do so or not. This is the ultimate trump card for proponents of gambling—if betting is legally prohibited, it will not go away. It will simply be forced underground, leading to an increase in crime and a decrease in tax revenue.

The Future

In the world of gambling, the dominant story of the twenty-first century has been the rise of Internet casinos—more than 1,400 by the early 2010s. Online operations allow small or remote nations the opportunity to participate in the cash bonanza that gaming represents, and they also afford bettors access to services—sports wagering, for example, or poker games—that are highly convenient and require no investment of travel time or that are unavailable in their locale.

For several years, online casinos were something of an afterthought, but their gross revenues exceeded $20 billion in 2008 and $25 billion in 2011. Consequently, the governments of many nations—with the United States taking the lead—have launched aggressive efforts intended to shut down or curtail the operations of these online casinos. Whether these actions are designed to protect innocent citizens or simply to keep tax revenues flowing into government coffers is open to debate. What is less arguable is that this is a fight the online casinos are eventually going to win. No less an authority than the *Economist* opined in 2010, "Attempts to ban online gaming are doomed to fail." The only real question is how long failure will take.

Of course, as opportunities to gamble become more ubiquitous and more convenient, the consequences that gambling entails will become more pronounced. In particular, experts predict that problem gambling is poised to skyrocket, with the British medical journal *Lancet* suggesting in 2011 that the number of problem gamblers worldwide may double by 2020. Gambling, then, is a social issue that is becoming more profound without any clear solutions in sight.

Christopher Bates and Jeffrey Gold

See also: Credit and Debt, Personal and Business; Money Laundering and Illegal Transfers.

Further Reading

Castellani, Brian. *Pathological Gambling: The Making of a Medical Problem.* Albany: State University of New York Press, 2000.

Cooper, Andrew F. *Internet Gambling Offshore: Caribbean Struggles over Casino Capitalism.* London: Palgrave Macmillan, 2011.

Hoffer, Richard. *Jackpot Nation: Rambling and Gambling Across Our Landscape of Luck.* New York: Harper, 2007.

Kingma, Sytze. *Global Gambling: Cultural Perspectives on Gambling Organizations.* New York: Routledge, 2009.

Meyer, Gerhard, Tobias Hayer, and Mark Griffiths, eds. *Problem Gambling in Europe: Challenges, Prevention, and Interventions.* New York: Springer, 2008.

Pavalko, Ronald M. *Problem Gambling and Its Treatment: An Introduction.* Springfield, IL: Charles C. Thomas, 2001.

Reith, Gerda, ed. *Gambling: Who Wins? Who Loses?* Amherst, NY: Prometheus Books, 2003.

Schwartz, David G. *Roll the Bones: The History of Gambling.* New York: Gotham, 2006.

Thompson, William N. *Gambling in America: An Encyclopedia of History, Issues, and Society.* Santa Barbara, CA: ABC-CLIO, 2001.

Vaughan-Williams, Leighton. *The Economics of Gambling.* New York: Routledge, 2002.

Whelan, James P., Andrew W. Meyers, and Timothy A. Steenbergh. *Problem and Pathological Gambling.* Toronto: Hogrefe & Huber, 2007.

Web Sites

Center for Gaming Research: http://gaming.unlv.edu

Gamblers Anonymous: www.gamblersanonymous.org

Global Betting and Gaming Consultancy: www.gbgc.com

Global Gambling Guidance Group: www.gx4.com

Institute for the Study of Gambling and Commercial Gaming: http://business.unr.edu/gaming

National Council on Problem Gambling: www.ncpgambling.org

Problem Gambling Guide: www.problemgamblingguide.com

Documents

Document 1: "The Discourse to Sigala," Sutta Pitaka, Fourth Century B.C.E.

The Sutta Pitaka is the second of "three baskets" that make up the basic collection of scriptures embraced by the Theravada Buddhist tradition. It is a collection of more than 10,000 suttas (teachings) attributed to the Buddha. The following selection, from the Digha Nikaya *(the first of five collections that make up the Sutta Pitaka), recounts a conversation between the Buddha and one of his followers, warning against the evils of gambling.*

On one occasion, the Buddha was living near the town of Rajagaha at a spot in the Bamboo Grove called the Squirrel's Feeding Place.

At that time a young householder named Sigalaka arose early and set out from Rajagaha with freshly washed clothes and hair. With palms together held up in reverence, he was paying respect towards the six directions: that is east, south, west, north, lower and upper.

Meanwhile the Buddha dressed himself in the early morning, took his bowl and robe and went in to Rajagaha on alms round. On the way, he saw Sigalaka worshipping the six directions. Seeing this, the Buddha said to him: "Young man, why have you risen in the early morning and set out from Rajagaha to worship in such a way?"

"Dear sir, my father on his deathbed urged me, 'My son, you must worship the directions.' So, dear sir, realizing, honoring, respecting, and holding sacred my father's request, I have risen in the early morning and set out from Rajagaha to worship in this way."

"But, young man, that is not how the six directions should be worshipped according to the discipline of the noble ones."

"Then how, dear sir, should the six directions be worshipped according to the discipline of the noble ones? I would appreciate it if you would teach me the proper way this should be done."

"Very well, young man, listen and pay careful attention while I tell you."

"Yes, dear sir," agreed Sigalaka.

The Buddha said this:

"Young man, by abandoning the four impure actions, a noble disciple refrains from harmful deeds rooted in four causes and avoids the six ways of squandering wealth. So, these fourteen harmful things are removed. The noble disciple, now with the six directions protected, has entered upon a path for conquering both worlds, firmly grounded in this world and the next. At the dissolution of the body after death, a good rebirth occurs in a heavenly world.

"What four impure actions are abandoned? The harming of living beings is an impure action, taking what is not given is an impure action, sexual misconduct is an impure action, and false speech is an impure action. These four are abandoned."

That is what the Buddha said.

"What are the four causes of harmful deeds? Going astray through desire, hatred, delusion, or fear, the noble disciple does harmful deeds. But, young man, not going astray through desire, hatred, delusion, or fear, the noble disciple does not perform harmful deeds . . ."

"And what six ways of squandering wealth are to be avoided? Young man, heedlessness caused by intoxication, roaming the streets at inappropriate times, habitual partying, compulsive gambling, bad companionship, and laziness are the six ways of squandering wealth . . .

"These are the six dangers inherent in compulsive gambling: winning breeds resentment; the loser mourns lost property; savings are lost; one's word carries no weight in a public forum; friends and colleagues display their contempt; and one is not sought after for marriage, since a gambler cannot adequately support a family . . ."

Summing up in verse, the sublime teacher said:

Some are drinking buddies,
Some say, 'Dear friend! Dear friend!'
But whoever in hardship stands close by,
That one truly is a friend.

Sleeping late, adultery,
Hostility, meaninglessness,
Harmful friends, utter stinginess:
These six things destroy a person.

Bad friends, bad companions,
Bad practices—spending time in evil ways,
By these, one brings oneself to ruin,
In this world and the next.

Seduction, gambling, drinking, singing, dancing,
Sleeping by day, wandering all around untimely,
Harmful friends, utter stinginess:
These things destroy a person.

They play with dice; they drink spirits;
They consort with lovers dear to others.
Associating with low-life and not the esteemed,
They come to ruin like the waning moon.

Whoever is a drunkard, broke, and destitute,
Dragged by thirst from bar to bar,
Sinking into debt like a stone in water
Into bewilderment quickly plunges.

When sleeping late becomes a habit
And night is seen as time to rise,
For one perpetually intoxicated,
A home life cannot be maintained.

'Too cold! Too hot!
Too late!': they say.
Having wasted work time this way,
The young miss out on opportunities.

For one regarding cold and hot
As not more than blades of grass,
Doing whatever should be done,
Happiness will not be a stranger.

Source: accesstoinsight.org

Document 2: "The South Oaks Gambling Screen," 1987

The South Oaks Gambling Screen, developed by Drs. Henry Lesieur and Sheila Blume and first appearing in a 1987 issue of the American Journal of Psychiatry, *"offers a convenient means to screen clinical populations of alcoholics and drug abusers, as well as general populations, for pathological gambling." Lesieur and Blume developed the test based on their work with 1,616 subjects: 867 people with diagnoses of substance abuse and pathological gambling, 213 members of Gamblers Anonymous, 384 university students, and 152 hospital employees.*

1. Please indicate which of the following types of gambling you have done in your lifetime. For each type, mark one answer: "Not at All," "Less than Once a Week," or "Once a Week or More."

Please check one answer for each statement:

		Not at all	Less than once a week	Once a week or more
a.	Played cards for money.			
b.	Bet on horses, dogs, or other animals (at OTB, the track, or with a bookie).			
c.	Bet on sports (parlay cards, with bookie, at Jai Alai).			
d.	Played dice games, including craps, over and under or other dice games.			
e.	Went to casinos (legal or otherwise).			
f.	Played the numbers or bet on lotteries.			
g.	Played bingo.			
h.	Played the stock and/or commodities market.			
i.	Played slot machines, poker machines, or other gambling machines.			
j.	Bowled, shot pool, played golf, or some other game of skill for money.			
k.	Played pull tabs or "paper" games other than lotteries.			
l.	Some form of gambling not listed above (please specify):			

2. What is the largest amount of money you have ever gambled with on any <u>one day</u>?

_____ Never Gambled
_____ $ 1.00 or less
_____ More than $1.00 up to $10.00
_____ More than $10.00 up to 100.00
_____ More than $100.00 up to $1,000
_____ More than $1,000 up to $10,000
_____ More than $10,000

3. Check which of the following people in your life has (or had) a gambling problem.

_____ Father
_____ Brother/Sister
_____ My child(ren)
_____ A friend or someone important in my life
_____ Mother
_____ My spouse/partner
_____ Another relative

4. When you gamble, how often do you go back another day to win back money you have lost?

_____ Never
_____ Some of the time (less than half of time I lose)
_____ Most of the time
_____ Every time that I lose

5. Have you ever claimed to be winning money gambling, but weren't really? In fact you lost?

_____ Never
_____ Yes, less than half the time I lost
_____ Yes, most of the time

6. Do you feel you have ever had a problem with betting or money gambling?

_____ No _____ Yes _____ Yes, in the past, but not now.

7. Did you ever gamble more than you intended to?

_____ Yes _____ No

8. Have people criticized your betting or told you that you had a problem, regardless of whether or not you thought it was true?

_____ Yes _____ No

9. Have you ever felt guilty about the way you gamble, or what happens when you gamble?

_____ Yes _____ No

10. Have you ever felt like you would like to stop betting money or gambling, but did not think that you could?

_____ Yes _____ No

11. Have you ever hidden betting slips, lottery tickets, gambling money, IOUs, or other signs of betting or gambling from your spouse, children, or other important people in your life?

_____ Yes _____ No

12. Have you ever argued with people you live with over how you handle money?

_____ Yes _____ No

13. (If you answered "yes": to question 12) Have money arguments ever centered on your gambling?

_____ Yes _____ No

14. Have you ever borrowed from someone and not paid them back as a result of your gambling?

_____ Yes _____ No

15. Have you ever lost time from work (or school) due to betting money or gambling?

_____ Yes _____ No

16. If you borrowed money to gamble or to pay gambling debts, who or where did you borrow from (check "Yes" or "No" for each):

a. From household money	_____ Yes	_____ No
b. From your spouse/partner	_____ Yes	_____ No
c. From relatives or in-laws	_____ Yes	_____ No
d. From banks, loan companies, or credit unions	_____ Yes	_____ No
e. From credit cards	_____ Yes	_____ No
f. From loan sharks	_____ Yes	_____ No
g. You cashed in stocks, bonds or other securities	_____ Yes	_____ No
h. You sold personal or family property	_____ Yes	_____ No
i. You borrowed on your checking accounts (passed bad checks)	_____ Yes	_____ No
j. You have (had) a credit line with a bookie	_____ Yes	_____ No
k. You have (had) a credit line with a casino	_____ Yes	_____ No

Source: Illinois Institute for Addiction Recovery.

GASTROINTESTINAL DISEASE

Gastrointestinal (GI) disease affects a growing percentage of the world's population and has become an increasing global concern. Billions of cases of GI disease occur annually, with moderate to severe symptoms (including death), loss of quality of life, and enormous costs to patients' pocketbooks and national health-care systems.

Although one in five people worldwide suffers from some type of gastrointestinal disorder each year, little is known about the actual causes of many of these disorders. That is to say, while these illnesses account for some of the most common complaints among children and adults alike, much about them is still unknown. The term "gastrointestinal disease" includes diseases that affect any of the hollow organs within the digestive system, beginning at the mouth and continuing through the system to the rectum. Gastrointestinal diseases also include afflictions of the liver, gallbladder, and pancreas. These diseases vary as greatly as the organs they affect in the symptoms they present, the rate at which they occur, and the speed with which they spread through the body and through populations at large. Many people who suffer from GI diseases lead normal lives, while others suffer acute loss of mobility.

History

Systematic study of gastrointestinal disease did not begin until the latter half of the twentieth century. Prior to that time, only occasional reports of GI illnesses were published. Although historians and physicians have documented GI disorders throughout history, the first known published report appeared only 200 years ago. Until recently, reports were sporadic and given little attention because of the absence of an organizational system with which to categorize and understand them as well as the lack of a distinguishable pathology. Owing to progressive scientific advancements in both understanding and treating GI disease, physicians and researchers now better understand the manifestations and epidemiology of all types of GI disease. Researchers continue to explore the causation of the various GI disorders, yet much is still unknown and theories vary greatly.

Gastrointestinal Disease Today

Symptoms of both acute and chronic GI diseases range from fairly common complaints to serious, life-threatening manifestations that greatly interfere with a sufferer's quality of life. Moreover, symptoms of the various diseases within the gastrointestinal category not only vary but also overlap significantly, and they therefore require careful investigative skills for proper diagnosis. Despite the variation in symptoms for individual diseases, there are some clear early-warning signals that, experts say, should always prompt sufferers to seek medical attention, including any changes in bowel habits, blood in the stool, severe abdominal pain, unexplained weight loss, and recurring heartburn not relieved by simple remedies, such as over-the-counter antacids. Treatments for GI disease, in fact, are no more uniform than the symptoms of the individual diseases. Although many people suffering from a gastrointestinal disease fail to get medical attention, doctors routinely treat patients suffering from various GI disorders with success.

Because of the extreme discomfort and pain that they associate with eating, many people with gastrointestinal disease develop severe weight loss. This development may progress to anorexic behavior and consequently to serious nutritional deficiencies in essential minerals, protein, and vitamins, which may further amplify GI symptoms.

Global statistics on GI diseases are scarce, but in the United States, a not atypical developed world country, approximately 60 million to 70 million people are affected each year, or about one in five Americans. Of these, some 250,000 persons die annually. Gastrointestinal illnesses result in 14 million hospitalizations annually and about 6 million in-patient diagnostic and therapeutic treatments, or about 12 percent of all inpatient procedures. They also result in roughly one in three of all outpatient surgeries. Altogether it is estimated that the costs of GI illnesses in the United States run to $150 billion annually, including about $100 billion in direct medical costs. In Canada it is estimated that about 30,000 persons die annually from digestive disorders and that the combined health-care and lost-productivity costs amount to $20 billion annually.

Upper Gastrointestinal Diseases

Gastrointestinal disease may affect both the upper GI tract and the intestines. Of the former, the main diseases are gastroesophageal reflux disease, laryngopharyngeal reflux disease, esophageal motility disorder, celiac disease, peptic ulcer disease, and pyloric stenosis.

Gastroesophageal Reflux Disease

Gastroesophageal reflux disease (GERD), also known as acid reflux disease, affects a growing number of people yearly. Currently GERD affects approximately 20 percent of Americans weekly, and the rising prevalence of symptomatic GERD in Canada, India, Europe, Asia, and South America is gaining worldwide attention. The condition occurs when the lower esophageal sphincter opens spontaneously, causing stomach contents to rise up from the stomach into the esophagus. In adults the main symptom of GERD frequently is heartburn. Also called indigestion, or acid indigestion, heartburn is so-named because of the burning-type pain, which appears in the midchest area. Other symptoms of GERD include nausea, vomiting, difficulty swallowing, asthma symptoms, and, occasionally, dry cough.

The causes of GERD are still unclear, but some that have been identified include hiatal hernias, abnormal esophageal contractions, abnormally slow emptying of the stomach, and an abnormal lower esophageal sphincter. Additionally, research indicates several factors that may contribute to this disease as well as other triggers that can worsen reflux symptoms. Obesity, pregnancy, and smoking appear to contribute to GERD, according to research. Factors contributing to increased symptom severity include consumption of caffeinated drinks, fatty and deep-fried foods, garlic,

spicy foods, citrus fruits, chocolate, and tomato-based sauces.

Treatment for GERD often begins with over-the-counter antacids or other reflux medications. When symptoms continue for more than three weeks despite this treatment, medical attention is recommended. Medications for GERD include antacids, H2 blockers, proton pump inhibitors, and prokinetics, but the condition is considered serious and in some cases may lead to surgery.

Laryngopharyngeal Reflux Disease

Also known as extraesophageal reflux disease (EERD), laryngopharyngeal reflux disease (LPRD) is similar to GERD but primarily causes respiratory and laryngeal symptoms. These extraesophageal symptoms are caused by the retrograde flow of the gastric juices into the upper aerodigestive tract.

Symptoms of LPRD often include hoarseness, postnasal drip, sore throat, wheezing, chronic cough, difficulty swallowing, and chronic throat clearing. Many adults with LPRD complain of an acrid, bile-like taste in the back of the throat. Treatment and advice for those suffering from LPRD are essentially the same for those with GERD

Esophageal Motility Disorder

Esophageal motility disorder occurs when peristalsis—the esophagus's involuntary sequenced wavelike motions—fails and ingested food cannot pass freely from the throat to the stomach. (A related condition, achalasia, occurs when the lower esophageal sphincter fails to relax.) The food passes partway down the esophagus, but it then cannot easily enter the stomach. This condition is quite rare and difficult to diagnose and treat, and research indicates that most esophageal motility disorders are difficult to differentiate from GERD and other more common esophageal disorders.

Celiac Disease

Celiac disease, sometimes called sprue, involves an immune reaction to gluten, a protein found in wheat, barley, and rye. Eating gluten, for a celiac, disrupts the absorption of nutrients in the small intestine. The gluten-triggered immune response in the small intestine actually damages or destroys the villi—the tiny, fingerlike protrusions that line the small intestine. Since villi allow absorption of most nutrients through the walls of the small intestine into the bloodstream, without healthy villi, nutrients are not absorbed. Consequently, patients often suffer from severe malnutrition. People with celiac disease experience moderate to severe bloating; abdominal pain; chronic diarrhea; vomiting or constipation, or both; pale, foul-smelling, or fatty stools; and unexplained weight loss.

Once considered rare and affecting fewer than one in 2,000 persons, celiac disease is now believed to affect one out of every 150 or so persons in developed world countries, or about 3 million people in the United States each year. At the same time, it is also one of the most difficult diseases to diagnosis, with just one in 4,700 cases in the United States accurately diagnosed each year.

The only effective treatment for celiac disease is a gluten-free diet: elimination of all forms of wheat, rye, barley, and triticale. Celiac disease is not a food allergy; it is an autoimmune disease. The cause of celiac disease remains unknown, but research indicates that it is hereditary.

Peptic Ulcer Disease

Peptic ulcer disease (PUD) is the most common GI tract ulcer, affecting at any given time approximately 10 to 15 percent of the population of both developing and developed world countries. Occurring in the lining of the stomach or in the duodenum, the first part of the small intestine, the peptic ulcer is a breakdown of the protective lining of the stomach or the duodenum. The inflammation that results from this breakdown normally causes ulceration in the first layer of the lining, but if the peptic ulcer goes untreated, a perforation of the entire lining may occur. This results in a medical crisis usually requiring emergency surgery.

Early signs of peptic ulcer disease include stomach pain, nausea, and heartburn. When the ulcers are more advanced, symptoms can include sudden weight loss, severe pain, vomiting blood (vomit will look like coffee grounds), and black, tarry stool (due to bleeding). In severe cases doctors may recommend an upper endoscopy to gain additional information. This involves inserting a narrow, lighted tube down the throat and into the stomach. *Helicobacter pylori* (*H. pylori*), a spiral-shaped bacterium that thrives in the acidic stomach environment, is the primary cause of most peptic ulcers. These can be effectively treated with antibiotics. Another frequent cause of peptic ulcers is the use of nonsteroidal anti-inflammatory drugs or agents/analgesics (NSAID) such as aspirin, naproxen, and ibuprofen. These create excess acid that eats away at the inner surface of the stomach, the small intestine, or the esophagus. In addition to antibiotics for *H. pylori*–caused ulcers, treatments for peptic ulcers include acid-blocking medications.

Pyloric Stenosis

Pyloric stenosis, a rare condition involving a narrowing of the opening from the stomach into the small intestine, affects newborns and infants. The muscles of the pylorus (the pyloric sphincter) become abnormally large and block food from entering the infant's small intestine.

Infants with pyloric stenosis often experience projectile vomiting, severe dehydration, constipation, stomach contractions, and weight loss (or failure to thrive). These babies may seem to be always hungry, because they are not retaining much of the food they ingest. Pyloric stenosis in infants can be corrected with surgery, and doctors recommend early and prompt treatment to avoid serious complications.

Intestinal Diseases

Along with upper gastrointestinal system disorders, there are those of the intestines themselves. These include Crohn's disease, diverticular disease, and—the most common and deadly, especially for children—diarrheal disease.

Inflammatory Bowel Disease

Diseases involving the chronic, or recurring, immune response and inflammation of the GI tract are classified under the broad term "inflammatory bowel disease" (IBD). Crohn's disease, which is autoimmune in nature, falls into this category and normally occurs in people between ages 15 and 35. Ulcerative colitis is similar to Crohn's disease, but its symptoms are limited to the top layers of the colon (large bowel).

Flare-ups of Crohn's disease often result in fever, fatigue, loss of appetite, pain with passing stool, abdominal pain, water diarrhea or constipation, fistulas (usually around the rectal area), joint pain and swelling, rectal bleeding, and bloody stools. Complications can include severe ulceration anywhere in the GI tract, ruptures in the small or large intestine, and increased risk of cancer. Symptoms of ulcerative colitis involve abdominal pain and cramping, fatigue, and diarrhea, often with severe bleeding. Eating small amounts of food throughout the day and drinking plenty of water ease symptoms for some people who suffer from IBD, and people often learn to avoid certain foods that trigger their diarrhea or gas flare-ups. No specific diet has been shown to improve or worsen symptoms for Crohn's disease. Medications sometimes relieve Crohn's symptoms, but occasionally surgery is required to remove damaged sections of the small or large intestine.

In the United Kingdom, approximately 90,000 persons suffer from Crohn's disease at any one time, with approximately 8,000 new cases each year. Meanwhile, it is estimated that in the United States and Canada, approximately 400,000 to 600,000 persons suffer from the disease, or more than one in 1,000.

Diarrheal Disease

Worldwide, diarrheal disease is the second-leading cause of death in children under five years old and in general a significant cause of sickness and death. Left untreated, excessive, continuing, or recurring diarrhea can result in severe dehydration and lead to death. This poses a particular challenge in less-developed countries because of their inability to stop the spread of disease-causing germs and a lack of resources to treat the disease. Diarrheal disease treatments are well under control in the United States, yet millions of Americans still suffer from this aggravating illness.

Symptoms of diarrheal disease are no surprise—diarrhea is the main presenting sign—but the illness can be surprisingly serious. Fevers, bloating, and severe cramping also may accompany diarrheal disease.

The sources of diarrheal disease are many: multiple viral, parasitic, and bacterial organisms cause diarrheal diseases. Contaminated water and food supplies, ineffective hand-washing techniques, and lack of access to water and soap all contribute to the prevalence of diarrheal disease. Effective treatments include antibiotics when the diarrheal disease is caused by bacteria, over-the-counter antidiarrheal medications, and rehydration therapy to alleviate dehydration symptoms. Gastrointestinal diseases caused by viruses and parasites are, of course, not responsive to antibiotics; for them, various treatments are used.

While diarrheal disease affects persons in both the

Diarrhea Deaths Among Children Under Age Five, Top 15 Countries, 2007

Country	Number of deaths	Percentage of world total
India	386,600	25.8
Nigeria	151,700	10.1
Congo, Democratic Republic of	89,900	6.0
Afghanistan	82,100	5.5
Ethiopia	73,700	4.9
Pakistan	53,300	3.6
Bangladesh	50,800	3.4
China	40,000	2.7
Uganda	29,300	2.0
Kenya	27,400	1.8
Niger	26,400	1.8
Burkina Faso	24,300	1.6
Tanzania	23,900	1.6
Mali	20,900	1.4
Angola	19,700	1.3
Total, Top 15	1,100,000	73.3
Total, World	1,500,000	100.0

Sources: UNICEF; World Health Organization.

developed and developing worlds, with over 2 billion cases annually, it tends to have higher morbidity rates in the latter, since the simple treatments used to deal with it are often unavailable. The disease takes an estimated 2.2 million lives annually, accounting for roughly one in 25 of all deaths, and 5 percent of health loss to disability. It is particularly hard on the very young, killing about 1.5 million children annually, most of them under the age of two. Diarrhea is also the leading cause of malnutrition in children under the age of five.

Diverticular Disease

Diverticular disease occurs primarily in the large intestine or colon when pouches (diverticula) become inflamed. Although diverticulosis (the presence of many diverticula) occurs throughout the world, it is more commonly found in countries where the diet is largely low in fiber. Diverticulitis occurs when one or more of the diverticula become inflamed.

Symptoms for diverticulosis and diverticulitis may be as innocuous as irregularities in bowel habits. Some people with diverticular disease experience fever, rectal bleeding, nausea, vomiting, excessive gas, and bloating. More serious symptoms include fistulas, which can result in severe infection and peritonitis.

In the United States, about 2.5 million people are affected annually by diverticular disease, resulting in approximately 400,000 hospitalizations and just under 2,000 deaths.

Diseases of the Accessory Glands

Health experts usually classify diseases of accessory glands to the digestive system as gastrointestinal-related illnesses. These include diseases affecting the liver, gallbladder, and pancreas.

Liver Disease

Liver diseases include autoimmune hepatitis; the viral infections hepatitis A, hepatitis B, hepatitis C, hepatitis D, and hepatitis E; hemochromatosis; liver disease associated with alcohol; and Reye syndrome, a liver function disorder without any known cause. "Hepatitis" means inflammation of the liver, but the types are distinct diseases that affect the liver in different ways. The hepatitis A infection rarely requires treatment and does not lead to long-term liver malfunctions. Hepatitis B is more serious and requires treatment, and hepatitis C is the most symptomatic and damaging to the liver of these three most prevalent viral hepatitis diseases. Hepatitis B and C cause the greatest concern because they are the most common causes of liver cirrhosis and cancer. Hemochromatosis, an inherited condition, occurs when the body absorbs too much iron from ingested food.

One of the first signs indicating liver disease is jaundice—a yellowing of the eyes or skin. This telltale yellowing often sends people to a medical facility, where they undergo liver-function tests to determine the cause. Abdominal pain also frequently accompanies liver disease. More specific signs of hepatitis B include flulike symptoms such as muscle aches, fever, headache, nausea, vomiting, diarrhea, and extreme fatigue. Hepatitis C involves more extensive liver damage and sometimes dark (cola-colored) urine. Treatment for liver diseases is specific to the disease. Treatment for hepatitis B usually includes mild antiviral medications to prevent liver damage. Treatment for hepatitis C is much lengthier and more involved; it can include long-term antiviral medications and, sometimes, a liver transplant. Hemochromatosis is one of the few diseases that actually stood to benefit from the early medical practice of bloodletting; effective treatment of the disease includes removing blood from the affected individual's body to lower the level of iron.

Various contributing factors lead to liver diseases. Hepatitis A and E, for example, are usually caused by ingestion of contaminated food or water, while hepatitis B, C, and D normally occur as the direct result of contact with infected body fluids. The virus that causes hepatitis B is commonly spread through unprotected sexual contact, but it can also be transmitted from a mother to her baby at birth. Hepatitis C is commonly spread through sharing needles, being exposed to blood already contaminated with the hepatitis C virus, or, less commonly, having unprotected sex with an infected partner. Hereditary hemochromatosis symptoms usually appear in one's thirties, although that can vary. Signs include joint pain, excessive fatigue, abdominal pain, and impotence. The body stores the excess iron that it absorbs as a result of hemochromatosis in the liver, heart, and pancreas, and that stored iron can also lead to cancer, heart disease, and liver disease.

Altogether, it is estimated that nearly one in three persons globally are exposed, at some point in their life, to one or both of the viruses causing hepatitis B and C. In addition, the World Health Organization estimates that 500 million persons, or one out of every 14 persons globally, was infected with hepatitis B or C, with some 1.5 million persons dying annually in the late 2000s.

Gallbladder Disease

The most common gallbladder diseases include cholelithiasis (gallstones in the biliary tract) and choledocholithias (gallstones in the bile ducts) as well as biliary dyskinesia and cholecystitis. In the latter two diseases, gallstones are not present but acute pain or inflammation, or both, are. The gallstones, derivatives of bile, are tiny pebblelike deposits made up of calcium, cholesterol, or bilirubin that can obstruct bile from draining out of the liver. These gallbladder intruders may be as small as a grain of sand or as large as a walnut. Gallstones are much more common in Hispanics, Scandinavians, and American Indians, and in women.

Gallbladder disease symptoms also include jaundice, in severe cases, and debilitating pain, nausea, and fever in more common cases; however, many patients experience little to no pain with gallstones. They discover their presence through a routine X-ray. When pain accompanies gallstones, the pain is usually sharp and sudden, in the upper-right or middle-right abdomen. Nausea and vomiting may be involved, and some people have clay-colored stools. Medication can sometimes dissolve some types of gallstones, but others require surgery. To remove a diseased gallbladder or one with problematic gallstones, physicians use a technique called a laparoscopic cholecystectomy. This laparoscopic procedure allows smaller surgical cuts than did the former, invasive gallbladder surgery, and most patients recovery rapidly.

Gallstones can form when the gallbladder does not empty completely or often enough. Other causes for gallstones are not fully understood. Research indicates that gallstones occur if an imbalance of cholesterol, bilirubin, or bile salts exists in the gallbladder, but the reason for such imbalances is unknown.

In the United States, it is estimated that gallstones will affect one in 10 Americans at some point in their lives. Each year, there are approximately 800,000 hospitalizations due to gallstones and about 500,000 persons undergo surgery for the condition. Some 3,000 deaths annually also are attributed to gallstones.

Pancreatitis

Although merely a small gland located behind the stomach, the pancreas plays a key role in the digestive system and, when infected, wreaks havoc in the body. Pancreatitis is a potentially serious digestive disease in which the pancreas becomes inflamed. The initial stage of the disease is characterized by a gradual or sudden severe pain that begins in the abdomen and moves around to the back. Some people describe it as feeling as if they were "knifed."

Although often life threatening, pancreatitis is usually treated successfully with intravenous fluids, pancreatic enzyme pills, and pain medications. Patients are advised to stop drinking alcoholic beverages and to adopt a low-fat diet. Pancreatitis is normally caused by heavy use of alcohol over a period of time, but the condition may also be caused by gallstones. Less frequently, the pancreas becomes inflamed from certain medications, trauma, metabolic disorders, or infection. In about 10 to 15 percent of people with acute pancreatitis, the cause remains unknown.

Some 80,000 persons are affected by pancreatitis each year in the United States, while globally the condition is believed to affect about 1.5 million persons.

Surgical Issues

Of the gastrointestinal conditions that primarily require surgical procedures to remedy them, the two most common are hernias and appendicitis.

Hernias

A hernia is a bulge or protrusion of an organ through a weak area of a muscle or connective tissue in the abdomen. Anything that causes an increase in the pressure in the abdomen can cause a hernia, including heavy lifting, constipation, diarrhea, obesity, and persistent coughing and sneezing. Severe cases require surgical repair to prevent further damage. It is estimated that some 2.5 million persons in China alone suffer from hernias annually, while the figure for the United States is just over 500,000.

Appendicitis

Appendicitis, the infection of the appendix, is considered a medical emergency that requires immediate medical attention. A patient with appendicitis will usually have sharp pain, abdominal swelling, fever, and nausea or vomiting, or both. If left untreated, the appendix will rupture or perforate, leading to a serious infection that can be fatal. When the appendix is surgically removed, the patient will normally recover thoroughly.

Each year in the United States, approximately 700,000 persons develop the kind of acute appendicitis that requires surgery, although fewer than 500 persons annually die from the condition.

Global Concerns and the Future

Although global statistics for gastrointestinal illness are hard to come by, the overall figure is estimated at more than 1 billion persons affected annually, making development of effective treatment for digestive diseases a critical health priority, say experts. But different conditions prevail in various parts of the world, requiring targeted approaches. For example, stomach disease and colorectal cancers are relatively uncommon in sub-Saharan Africa, yet duodenal ulcers are frequently found. India has seen an alarming increase in the incidence of GI disease, and China has seen an increase in the prevalence of gastroesophageal reflux disease but a marked decrease in the prevalence of peptic ulcer disease. Of greater concern, diarrheal disease alone is one of the major causes of death in the developing world. Bacterial GI diseases spread rapidly, regardless of borders and ordinary precautions.

Understanding global concerns is crucial. Steps are

being taken to reduce and prevent the occurrences of gastrointestinal diseases while at the same time improving treatments of the same diseases. Treating disease is the least effective method of alleviating the global effects of GI disease, however. Approximately 40 percent of the global population lacks access to basic sanitation. Efforts are under way to provide clean water, basic waste disposal facilities, and food safety education throughout the world, but the integration of knowledge, technology, and labor is required. Long-term research goals include determining the genetic, molecular, and integrated physiological bases of intestinal water, nutrient, and electrolyte transport in order to better understand and prevent gastrointestinal disease worldwide, as well as developing clinically useful imaging and diagnostic techniques to examine digestive processes and abnormalities in GI diseases such as diarrheal and malabsorptive diseases. By improving early screening, diagnosis, prevention, and treatment of the gastrointestinal diseases, people suffering from these illnesses should experience quicker relief and a better quality of life.

Virginia Payne Dow

See also: Environmental Illnesses; Hunger and Malnutrition; Infant Mortality; Obesity and Eating Disorders; Pollution, Water; Public Health; Water Supply and Access; Waterborne Disease.

Further Reading

Erceg, Danijel, and Pero Milojeviae, eds. *Ulcers: Causes, Diagnosis, and Treatment*. Hauppauge, NY: Nova Science, 2009.

Feldman, Mark, and Lawrence S. Friedman, eds. *Sleisenger and Fordtran's Gastrointestinal and Liver Disease: Pathophysiology, Diagnosis, Management*. 2 vols. Philadelphia: Saunders, 2010.

Fenoglio-Preiser, Cecilia M., et al. *Gastrointestinal Pathology: An Atlas and Text*. Philadelphia: Wolters Kluwer/ Lippincott Williams & Wilkins, 2008.

Jones, Rory, and Peter H.R. Green. *Celiac Disease: A Hidden Epidemic*. New York: William Morrow, 2010.

Miskovitz, Paul F. *The Doctor's Guide to Gastrointestinal Health: Preventing and Treating Acid Reflux, Ulcers, Irritable Bowel Syndrome, Diverticulitis, Celiac Disease, Colon Cancer, Pancreatitis, Cirrhosis, Hernias, and More*. Hoboken, NJ: John Wiley, 2005.

Modlin, Irvin M., and George Sachs. *Acid Related Diseases: Biology and Treatment*. Philadelphia: Lippincott Williams & Wilkins, 2004.

Ogunlesi, Tinuade A. *Types and Causes of Childhood Diarrhea*. Hauppauge, NY: Nova Science, 2010.

Talley, Nicholas J., G. Richard Locke III, and Yuri Saito, eds. *GI Epidemiology*. Malden, MA: Blackwell, 2010.

Windelspecht, Michael. *The Digestive System*. Westport, CT: Greenwood, 2004.

Yamada, Tadataka, ed. *Principles of Clinical Gastroenterology*. Hoboken, NJ: Wiley-Blackwell, 2008.

Web Sites

Association of Gastrointestinal Motility Disorders: www.agmd-gimotility.org

Centers for Disease Control and Prevention: www.cdc.gov/nchs/fastats/digestiv.htm

National Commission on Digestive Diseases: http://ncdd.niddk.nih.gov

National Institutes of Health, National Digestive Diseases Information Clearinghouse: http://digestive.niddk.nih.gov/statistics/statistics.aspx

World Health Organization, Health Topics: Diarrhoea: www.who.int/topics/diarrhoea/en

Document

Document: *Diarrhoea: Why Children Are Dying and What Can Be Done* (excerpt), UNICEF and World Health Organization, 2009

In 2009, the United Nations Children's Fund (UNICEF) and World Health Organization (WHO) published Diarrhoea: Why Children Are Dying and What Can Be Done, *the most comprehensive report ever published on what the report noted was the number two killer of young children around the world, after pneumonia. In the report, the organizations offered a multipronged approach for what they called "comprehensive diarrhoea control" globally.*

Section 4: A 7-point plan for comprehensive diarrhoea control

Treatment package

The treatment package focuses on two main elements, as outlined in a 2004 joint statement from UNICEF and WHO: 1) fluid replacement to prevent dehydration and 2) zinc treatment. Oral rehydration therapy—which has been heralded as one of the most important medical advances of the 20th century—is the cornerstone of fluid replacement. New aspects of this approach include low-osmolarity oral rehydration salts (ORS), which are more effective at replacing fluids than the original ORS formulation, and zinc treatment, which decreases diarrhoea severity and duration. Important additional components of the package are continued feeding, including breastfeeding, during diarrhoea episodes and the use of appropriate fluids available in the home if ORS are not available, along with increased fluids in general.

Prevention package

The prevention package highlights five main elements that require a concerted approach in their implementation. The package includes: 3) rotavirus and measles vaccinations, 4) promotion of early and exclusive breastfeeding and vitamin A supplementation, 5) promotion of handwashing with soap, 6) improved water supply quantity and quality, including treatment and safe storage of household water, and 7) community-wide sanitation promotion.

New aspects of this approach include vaccinations for rotavirus, which is estimated to cause about 40 percent of hospital admissions due to diarrhoea among children under five worldwide. In terms of community-wide sanitation, new approaches to increase demand to stop open defecation have proven more effective than previous strategies. It has been estimated that 88 percent of diarrhoeal deaths worldwide are attributable to unsafe water, inadequate sanitation and poor hygiene.

Actions needed to take interventions to scale

In many countries, progress has been made in the delivery or promotion of several of these interventions, particularly vitamin A supplementation and exclusive breastfeeding. However, a substantial reduction in the diarrhoea burden will require greater emphasis on the following actions:

- Ensure wide availability of low-osmolarity ORS and zinc, which could have a profound impact on child deaths from diarrhoea if scaled up immediately. Possible strategies to increase their uptake and availability could include the development of smaller ORS packets and flavoured formulas, as well as delivering zinc and low-osmolarity ORS together in diarrhoea treatment kits.
- Include rotavirus vaccine in national immunization programmes worldwide, which was recently recommended by the World Health Organization. Accelerating its introduction, particularly in Africa and Asia, where the rotavirus burden is greatest, should be an international priority.
- Develop and implement behaviour change interventions, such as face-to-face counselling, to encourage exclusive breastfeeding.
- Ensure sustained high levels of vitamin A supplementation, such as by combining its delivery, where effective, with other high-impact health and nutrition interventions.
- Apply results of existing consumer research on how

to motivate people to wash their hands with soap to increase this beneficial and cost-effective health practice. Handwashing with soap has been shown to reduce the incidence of diarrhoeal disease by over 40 percent.
- Adopt household water treatment and safe storage systems, such as chlorination and filtration, in both development and emergency situations to support reductions in the number of diarrhoea cases.
- Implement approaches that increase demand to stop community-wide open defecation. As with handwashing, the new approach employs behavioural triggers, such as pride, shame and disgust, to motivate action, and leads to greater ownership and sustainability of programmes.

We know what works to immediately reduce deaths from childhood diarrhoea. We also know what actions will make a lasting contribution to reducing the toll of diarrhoeal diseases for years to come. But strengthened efforts on both fronts must begin right away.

The following actions are needed to take the 7-point plan to scale:

- Mobilize and allocate resources for diarrhoea control.
- Reinstate diarrhoea prevention and treatment as a cornerstone of community-based primary health care.
- Ensure that low-osmolarity ORS and zinc are adopted as policy in all countries.
- Reach every child with effective interventions.
- Accelerate the provision of basic water and sanitation services.
- Use innovative strategies to increase the adoption of proven measures against diarrhoea.
- Change behaviours through community involvement, education and health-promotion activities.
- Make health systems work to control diarrhoea.
- Monitor progress at all levels, and make the results count.
- Make the prevention and treatment of diarrhoea everybody's business.

There is no better time than now. Political momentum is building to address the leading causes of child deaths, including pneumonia and diarrhoea, to achieve measurable gains in child survival. The year 2008 marked the 30th anniversary of the Alma-Ata Declaration, with reinvigorated calls to focus on primary health care. Lessening the burden of childhood diarrhoea fits squarely with this emphasis, and is essential for achieving Millennium Development Goal 4: reduce child mortality, whose target date is now only six years away.

Sources: UNICEF; World Health Organization.

GAY, LESBIAN, BISEXUAL, AND TRANSGENDER ISSUES

Gay, lesbian, bisexual, and transgender issues run the gamut of social concerns, from equality before the law to personal safety to the right to participate openly in the institutions of society.

There is much debate about whether homosexuality and other alternative sexual identities are innate or the result of environmental influences. This question is more than a purely academic one, in that it either undergirds or diminishes the calls of the lesbian, gay, bisexual, and transgender (LGBT) community for equal treatment before the law.

Whatever the reason for a person's sexual identity, the historical record reveals that homosexuality has existed throughout history. Indeed, a certain amount of scientific evidence shows that homosexual acts occur among other sentient creatures. But attitudes toward, and treatment of, homosexuals or, more precisely, homosexual acts, have varied widely, from open acceptance to hostility and persecution.

Prospects for the future are mixed, with gay rights and acceptance likely to be further expanded in the developed world and certain parts of the developing world, but likely to remain unchanged or even reversed in many parts of the developing world, particularly those countries where religion is becoming a more important component of people's identity and national politics.

For the sake of clarity, this chapter uses the term "homosexual" in its technical sense, to refer to people of both sexes whose sexual preferences are for those of the same sex. Male homosexuals are referred to as "gays" and female homosexuals as "lesbians." The term "bisexual" refers to people of either sex whose preferences run to both sexes. The term "transgender" refers to several categories of individuals: those whose gender self-identity does not correspond to their biological or socially defined sex; those individuals who by birth have strong characteristics of both sexes (intersexuals); and those individuals who have undergone surgery or other medical procedures to alter their primary (sexual organs) or secondary (facial hair, voice timbre, and other nonreproductive characteristics) biological sexual characteristics, in order to align them with their own gender identification. Finally, readers should note that due to the nature of the subject, explicit sexual imagery and terminology are used in this chapter.

Nature Versus Nurture Debate

Although humans have long engaged in homosexual acts, homosexuality as an identity is of much more recent vintage, dating in Western culture to the nineteenth century. With that new definition arose questions about why some people had this identity and others did not.

As with so much else about human behavior, the question comes down to one of nature versus nurture or a combination of the two. Almost every great breakthrough in both human psychology and physiology over the past 150 years or so has asked this question. For those who believe that homosexuality is innate, the biological factors can be broken down into two basic categories—the theory that homosexuality, and, for that matter, heterosexuality, is imprinted in a person's genetic makeup and the theory that sexual preference arises because of hormonal or other influences during gestation. According to these views, such primary biological causes then affect various mechanisms and systems within the body, such as brain structure or hormones.

Although earlier ideas about homosexuality as a mental illness have been discarded by virtually all members of the scientific and medical communities—the American Psychiatric Association declassified it as a mental disorder in 1973—psychological and environmental causes of homosexuality continue to be explored by researchers and clinicians, usually focusing on relationships between parents and children and, more recently, on the birth order of male offspring.

Whether biological, psychological, or environmental, the source of a person's homosexuality has important political and social repercussions. If a person's sexual identity is either biologically predetermined, established by environmental factors at a young age, or caused by an epigenetic combination of the two—in which genetic factors are then triggered by environmental factors—it can be argued that homosexuals are as deserving of equal protection and social acceptance as any other minority or oppressed group, such as African Americans or women, whose identity is predetermined. Some gay rights activists dismiss the importance of causation, arguing that a person's sexual activities, as long as they are between consenting adults, are no one else's business and that homosexuals are entitled to the same rights as heterosexuals simply because they are human beings and citizens.

At the same time, many opponents of gay rights—especially those who regard homosexuality as a sin against God and a crime against nature—argue that homosexuality is a choice and that the lifestyle choices of those who practice it, including sexual acts, should not be protected by the law, and that the privileges and rights extended to heterosexuals—such as marriage, the right to adopt, and the right to serve openly in the military—should not be extended to homosexuals.

History

Although scientists continue to grapple with the question of what factors lead to homosexuality and, for that matter, any sexual identity, the historical record reveals the presence of homosexual men and women, along with bisexuals and transgender people, and homosexual practices in virtually all cultures in all eras. Moreover, historical writings reveal that attitudes toward alternative sexual identities vary widely across cultures and eras.

Within the Western tradition, the earliest references to homosexuality come from ancient Greece. Historians argue that the Greeks did not conceive of homosexuality in the same way as modern societies do, in that the person's sex was less important than the role played in the sexual act. One was either active (the penetrator) or passive (the person being penetrated), regardless of whether one was a male or a female. The Greeks associated the act of penetration with the socially determined male attributes of aggression and dominance, as well as high social status and maturity, while the act of being penetrated was associated with female attributes, such as passivity and subservience, as well as lower social status and immaturity. Although homosexual relations between adults of either sex were generally frowned upon, the Greeks did commonly engage in the more controversial practice, at least to modern sensibilities, of pederasty, particularly between adult and teenage males.

Like many cultures, both ancient and modern, Greek culture designated a period during puberty for rites of passage. In preliterate tribal Greece, this consisted of having male youths go into the wilderness with adult males to be taught the customs, roles, and practices associated with male adulthood, including sexual practices. After the rise of the city-state, the journey portion of the rite was abandoned, as male youths simply paired up with male adults for this kind of education. Similar kinds of pairings also occurred in the various militaries of the Greek city-states. Female youths in tribal times underwent a similar initiation with adult females in communities known as *thiasoi*, though these were not as formally ritualized. Perhaps the best known accounts of these come from the island of Lesbos, largely as a result of the writings of the seventh-century B.C.E. poet Sappho. The *thiasoi* disappeared after the development of the city-state and the formalization of marriage as the ideal institution for women.

In parallel with so much else in their culture, the ancient Romans adopted many of their ideas about homosexual relationships from the Greeks. Again, a person's sex was less important in defining the sexual partner than the act engaged in by the partner. As long as the older or higher-status male performed penetration and the younger, lower-status male was penetrated, homosexual acts were deemed acceptable. Although the Romans did not practice formalized rites of passage involving sexuality, most homosexual acts occurred between adult and teenage Roman males. Finally, because most males in ancient Greece and Rome were also expected to engage in heterosexual acts, it is perhaps more accurate to speak of the civilizations as having a culture that accepted bisexuality rather than homosexuality as it is understood today.

Historical evidence abounds of an acceptance of homosexual behavior, particularly between males, in non-Western cultures. (The absence of female homosexuality in the literature has more to do with women's lower status and, hence, absence from the written record.) Chronicles of Chinese emperors going back to the Han dynasty of the seventh century B.C.E. refer repeatedly to youthful male consorts, while writings about everyday life talk of both homosexual relations between adult males and the presence of male prostitutes. The imperial Japanese court followed customs similar to that of China. In *The Tale of Genji*, the great epic of medieval Japanese literature, a passage speaks of the eponymous hero being rejected by a lady and then opting to sleep with her more sexually willing younger brother. In India, the tradition of the *hijra*, or males dressing like females and adopting female roles and engaging in sex with other men, is mentioned in the *Kama Sutra*, a collection of writings about sexuality composed and collected between the fourth century B.C.E. and second century C.E. And in pre-Columbian North America, some native peoples also had special castes of males who took on feminine roles.

These relatively accepting attitudes toward homosexuality continued in Asian cultures well into the medieval and even early modern era, but a more unforgiving stance emerged in the West with the rise of the main monotheistic faiths, Judaism, Christianity, and Islam. The Old Testament, a holy scripture for all three faiths, contains several proscriptions against acts of male homosexuality, most notably in Leviticus 18:22, in which they are condemned as an "abomination." The Jewish rabbinate declared male homosexuality a sin worthy of death. The early Christian Church was more ambivalent. The New Testament contains no explicit condemnation of homosexuality—indeed, the topic is not even mentioned in the Gospels—and Jesus declared many of the proscriptions in the Old Testament, not applicable to his followers. Corinthians does say that "fornicators," which would apply to homosexuals, are guilty of grave sin. Thus, it was not until the Middle Ages that the Christian Church explicitly declared sodomy a crime worthy of death. Early Muslim scholars, following in the Judaic tradition, were quicker to condemn homosexuality as a crime punishable by death. Since then, homosexuality has remained taboo in Muslim culture and, in some Muslim countries, remains punishable by death.

By the early modern era in European history, homosexuality was widely condemned and remained punishable by death in most jurisdictions—a view and response that carried into the colonies established by Europeans in the Americas. The Enlightenment initiated an easing of penalties against homosexual acts, part of the overall trend away from the death penalty except for the most heinous of crimes. However, homosexuality remained disdained, outlawed, and subject to corporal punishment and, later, long prison sentences. It remained a capital crime in some countries, including Britain, which did not lift the sanction until 1861. In all these cultures and crimes, lesbian sexual acts, while condemned, were not subject to such severe sanctions and did not seem to preoccupy the attention of authorities, secular or sacred, to the degree that male homosexual acts did.

However severe the penalties, they were directed at homosexual acts rather than homosexuals. That is, until the nineteenth century, there was no real concept of homosexuality as a way of life or as an identity in the Western tradition, though, as noted above, the *hijras* of India and the feminized male castes of North America indicate that such an identity was accepted in some non-Western cultures into the modern era. According to some historians in gay studies, what gave birth to that identity, at least among men in Western societies, was the Romantic idealization of male friendship and bonding in such subcultures as the military, boarding schools, and, in the United States, in the nearly all-male societies on the Western frontier.

By the early twentieth century, a homosexual subculture had emerged in many European countries and North America, particularly in large and socially liberal metropolises, such as New York City and interwar Berlin. Because of their cafes and nightspots that catered to a homosexual clientele, these cities attracted homosexuals from across their respective countries, offering a sanctuary from moral strictures and a gathering place to discuss and write about issues of concern to them. This subculture included both homosexual men and women.

Homosexuals, like other groups targeted for extinction by the Nazis, especially suffered in World War II, but the war also provided the impetus for changes in their status after its conclusion. They were subject to the same sort of distinctive markings on their clothing, mass incarceration in concentration camps, and murder as the other targeted groups in Germany and other parts of Europe occupied by the Nazis. At the same time, the mass mobilization of young men and women into the various Allied armed forces introduced many with a homosexual orientation to this subculture, either as they traveled to such cities as New York, San Francisco, and London on their way to deployment overseas or by encountering others like themselves in a largely single-sex context. The war, which included as one of its aims a crusade against the intolerance and authoritarianism of fascist regimes, nurtured new concerns about civil and human rights around the world. As members of a much despised and persecuted minority, it was only natural that homosexuals would begin to move beyond merely establishing an identity and subculture of their own into avenues of activism that would gain them acceptance, both in public opinion and before the laws of the state.

Most scholars of gay studies pinpoint the 1969 Stonewall riots—in which patrons of a gay bar of the same name in New York City fought back against a routine police raid—as the beginning of the gay and lesbian political movement. From that time on, demands for justice and equality became more overt and forceful in much of the Western world. This kind of political activism against state-sanctioned repression and discrimination was augmented by a gay and lesbian cultural revolution, both at the society-wide level and in more intimate settings. The former included public celebrations of gay, lesbian, bisexual, and transgender identities and ways of life, most notably in gay pride parades in cities around the world. At the same time, homosexuals began to declare their sexuality to family, colleagues, and heterosexual friends, a process known as "coming out of the closet," which helped to promote the idea that homosexuals were not all that different from heterosexuals and thus deserved to gain acceptance in the arena of public opinion.

Such progress did not come without resistance and setbacks. The outbreak of the AIDS epidemic in the 1980s hit gay communities in the Western world particularly hard, causing much suffering and adding to the public stigma against male homosexuality. A backlash against granting homosexuals equal rights and social acceptance emerged in many countries, often affiliated with conservative religious organizations, which cited scriptural proscriptions against homosexuality and declared AIDS a punishment from God. In many developing countries, particularly in sub-Saharan Africa, the backlash against homosexuality, which was often viewed as a corrupting Western import, became extremely harsh, as a number of countries imposed harsh laws against homosexual acts, particularly between males.

Despite such setbacks, the gay, lesbian, bisexual, and transgender communities had made what seem like irreversible advances in much of the developed world by the early twenty-first century, eliminating legal sanctions, gaining rights, and winning broader acceptance among the public, particularly among youth and young adults.

Issues

The struggle for acceptance and equality among gays, lesbians, bisexuals, and transgender individuals that began after World War II became more overt in the wake of the Stonewall riots and continues. It revolves around a number of critical issues, though these differ between societies in which strict sanctions against homosexuality remain the norm and those where opinions have become more liberal and where laws against homosexual acts have been overturned. In the former, the lifting of such sanctions remains the prime objective, as it is often a matter of sheer survival. In more liberal countries—most Western countries and developing countries with less-harsh traditions against homosexuality, such as those in parts of Asia—recent political efforts have been aimed primarily at gaining equality on a broad array of fronts: freedom from violence; an end to discriminatory laws and the homophobia, or fear and loathing of homosexuals, that gives birth to them; the right to serve openly in the military; and the right to marry, with all the concomitant rights and privileges that come with that right.

Violence Against Gays

Violence against people with alternative sexual identities comes in two forms. The first is state-sanctioned violence, such as the whippings administered as punishment for homosexual acts in a number of predominantly Muslim and sub-Saharan countries and the death penalty in seven predominantly Muslim countries (Afghanistan, Iran, Mauritania, Saudi Arabia, Sudan, United Arab Emirates, and Yemen) and parts of two other countries (the part of Somalia still controlled by the government in Mogadishu, and several predominantly Muslim states in northern Nigeria). Although these countries have been under international pressure to change their laws, the authoritarianism of most of these regimes, along with generally harsh public attitudes toward homosexuality, mitigate against the prospect

Gay activists in Rio de Janeiro, Brazil, demonstrate against laws in Iran, Saudi Arabia, and other countries that call for the death penalty for acts of consensual gay and lesbian sex. In scores of other countries, homosexuality is criminal but carries lesser penalties. *(Agencia Estado via AP Images)*

that internal political activism will succeed in ending such punishments.

Of more widespread concern in the developed world are attacks on LGBT individuals by members of the public, acts widely referred to as "gay bashing." These attacks can occur in countries where homosexual acts are illegal and in countries where they are legal. For example, in Brazil, a country with relatively liberal attitudes toward sexuality, with an openly gay community, and where homosexuality is not a crime, the country's leading gay rights organization has estimated that, between 1980 and 2009, 190 homosexuals were murdered, in incidents in which homophobia was proven to be a factor. Further, the organization indicated that this number is probably low, as many of the other roughly 3,000 murders of homosexuals in the country could have had a homophobic element to them.

Even in the many developed-world countries with hate-crime legislation—and which include homophobia as an official motivation for a hate crime—members of the LGBT community, particularly gay men, are violently attacked. Canadian authorities, for example, estimated that about 6 percent of all violent hate crimes in the country in 2008 were motivated by homophobia. The U.S. Federal Bureau of Investigation, which compiles national hate-crime statistics, cited more than 1,600 hate crimes of varying severity in which the sexual orientation of the victim was a factor in 2008, compared with about 4,700 cases in which the race of the victim was the chief factor.

Discrimination and Homophobia

According to recent surveys, 74 of the world's 196 countries have laws that consider homosexual acts a crime, though in many cases the legislation only prohibits such acts for men. In several instances, the laws allow for the imposition of capital punishment for those found guilty of engaging in homosexual acts. Yet even in countries where such draconian measures are not allowed, the state has taken a harsh approach to homosexuality. In Zimbabwe, for example, citizens have been asked to report homosexuals to police. In general, in countries where homosexual acts are prohibited, gays, lesbians, and others with alternative sexual identities or practices are frequently banned from teaching in schools and have no legal recourse if they are dismissed from a job or evicted from housing because of their sexual identity or practices. In many of these countries, homosexual gathering places, such as bars and cafes, are routinely raided by police.

In democratic developed-world countries, gays and lesbians enjoy far more protections and far less official discrimination, but this has only been achieved in recent decades. Moreover, many homosexuals continue to face de facto discrimination by employers, landlords, and others. Much of this discrimination is motivated by homophobia, which might have psychological and social roots—in fears that homophobes might have about their own sexuality, from peer pressure, or because of a particular subculture's negative feelings about homosexuals. Young gays and lesbians

Countries or Territories in Which Same-Sex Activity Is Prohibited by Law, 2008

Country or territory	Illegal in all cases	Illegal in some sub-jurisdictions	Illegal for males only
Africa, sub-Saharan			
Angola	X		
Botswana	X		
Burundi	X		
Cameroon	X		
Comoros	X		
Eritrea	X		
Ethiopia	X		
Gambia	X		
Guinea	X		
Kenya			X
Lesotho			X
Liberia	X		
Malawi			X
Mauritius			X
Namibia	X		
Nigeria*		X	X
Senegal	X		
Seychelles			X
Sierra Leone			X
Somalia*	X		
Somaliland	X		
South Sudan	X		
Swaziland			X
Tanzania	X		
Togo	X		
Uganda	X		
Western Sahara	X		
Zambia			X
Zimbabwe			X
Americas			
Antigua and Barbuda	X		
Barbados	X		
Belize			X
Dominica	X		
Grenada			X
Guyana			X
Jamaica			X
Saint Kitts and Nevis			X
Saint Lucia			X
Saint Vincent and Grenadines	X		
Trinidad and Tobago	X		
Asia, East and Southeast			
Brunei	X		
Malaysia	X		
Myanmar (Burma)	X		
Philippines		X	
Singapore			X
Asia, South			
Afghanistan*	X		X
Bangladesh	X		X
Bhutan	X		
Pakistan	X		
Former Soviet Union			
Turkmenistan			
Uzbekistan			
Middle East and North Africa			
Algeria	X		
Egypt	X		
Iran*	X		
Kuwait	X		
Lebanon	X		
Libya	X		
Mauritania*	X		
Morocco	X		
Oman	X		
Palestinian Territories (Gaza)			X
Qatar	X		
Saudi Arabia*	X		
Sudan	X		
Syria	X		
Tunisia	X		
United Arab Emirates*	X		
Yemen*	X		
Oceania			
Cook Islands			X
Kiribati			X
Nauru			X
Palau			X
Papua New Guinea	X		
Samoa	X		
Solomon Islands	X		
Tonga			X
Tuvalu			X

*Punishment includes possible execution.
Source: International Lesbian and Gay Association.

are often the targets of smear campaigns and bullying by schoolmates, sometimes on social networking and other Internet sites, leading victims to feel shame and, in some cases, to commit suicide.

Military Service

As gay rights activists note, homosexuals have always served in the military, for the simple reason that there have always been gays and lesbians and that there have always been armies and navies in which they have served. In some ancient cultures, such as the city-states of first-millennium B.C.E. Greece, homosexual relations were an accepted part of military life. In modern times, however, homosexuals have had to serve without revealing their sexual identity. Along with the overall push for homosexual rights in other aspects of life has come a push to allow gays and lesbians to serve in the military without concealing their sexual identity or orientation.

In some countries, such a change has met with resistance from policymakers, military officials, and some members of the general public who say that allowing gay service members to serve openly would affect morale and lead to sexual relationships that undermine military readiness and effectiveness. But advocates have countered that gays and lesbians already serve in the military and that given the more relaxed attitudes about homosexuality among younger service members—the bulk of the troops in most militaries—such fears about morale

Countries Where Gays and Lesbians Are Allowed to Serve Openly in the Military, 2011

Country	Year allowed
Albania	2008
Argentina	2009
Australia	1992
Austria	Not indicated
Bahamas	1998
Belgium	Not indicated
Canada	1992
Colombia	2002
Croatia	No explicit ban
Czech Republic	No explicit ban
Denmark	1981
Estonia	No explicit ban
Finland	Not indicated
France	2000
Germany	2000
Greece	2002
Ireland	1993
Israel	1993
Italy	Not indicated
Japan	Not indicated
Lithuania	No explicit ban
Luxembourg	Not indicated
Malta	No explicit ban
Netherlands	1974
New Zealand	1993
Norway	1979
Peru	2009
Philippines	2010
Poland	Not indicated
Romania	Not indicated
Russia	2003
Serbia	2010
Slovenia	No explicit ban
South Africa	1994
Spain	2009
Sweden	Not indicated
Switzerland	Not indicated
Taiwan	2002
Thailand	2005
United Kingdom	2000
United States	2011
Uruguay	2009

Source: Human Rights Watch.

and effectiveness are outdated. Such arguments are prevailing, particularly in the developed world, but also in many developing countries, as more than 40 countries now allow gays and lesbians to serve openly in the military.

Marriage and Civil Union

Even more controversial than the right of gays and lesbians to serve openly in the military has been the right to same-sex marriage, as this topic goes to the heart of religious beliefs and social customs, and affects far more people. The question of same-sex marriage incorporates two broad issues: the definition and meaning of marriage itself; and the rights and privileges that most countries give to people who are legally married, including the right to adopt children, a privileged tax status, inheritance rights, and health-care decision making.

As to the first issue—the definition and meaning of marriage—most gay and lesbian rights advocates argue that civil unions are insufficient beyond the realm of practical matters. That is, by denying homosexuals the right to marry the person of their choice and have that marriage officially recognized and publicly acknowledged, governments relegate homosexuals to second-class citizenship in a matter that is central to everyday life and dignity. Opponents of same-sex marriage, even those who support civil unions, often defer to tradition to justify their position, saying that marriage has always been between a man and a woman, that religions and tradition sanction such a definition, and that allowing homosexuals to marry will undermine the institution of heterosexual marriage, though exactly how this can occur is often not made clear. They also offer the slippery-slope argument, saying that if same-sex marriage is permitted, there is no reason for government to deny other forms of marriage that may seem offensive to large segments of the population, such as polygamous marriage and marriage to children.

Concerning the second issue, many countries and subjurisdictions, such as some U.S. states, have opted for the middle ground of sanctioning same-sex "civil unions." Short of formal marriage, civil unions satisfy some of the demands of same-sex couples to receive legal treatment that is equal to that of heterosexual married couples, guaranteeing them the same rights, privileges, and benefits. But many same-sex marriage advocates argue that civil unions are not equal to marriage in that so much in common and statutory law, as well as regulations about the provision of government and private benefits, is connected to married status. Thus, they say, civil unions will inevitably fall short in guaranteeing same-sex couples the full equality before the law that they seek. Opponents of same-sex unions focus more on the alleged effect that they have on social cohesion and the rights of those who oppose homosexuality as a sin or as an aberration of nature. They contend that legalization of civil unions puts a government imprimatur on the legitimacy and even morality of homosexuality while forcing those who are opposed to it to pay taxes that will go to homo-

Countries That Allow or Recognize Same-Sex Marriages, 2011

Country	Same-sex marriage legal	Same-sex marriage legal in some jurisdictions	Same-sex marriage recognized but not permitted
Argentina	X		
Belgium	X		
Brazil		X	
Canada	X		
Iceland	X		
Israel			X
Mexico		X	X
Netherlands	X		
Norway	X		
Portugal	X		
South Africa	X		
Spain	X		
Sweden	X		
United States		X	

Source: JURIST, University of Pittsburgh, School of Law.

sexual couples. Many of those who object also say that allowing civil unions is to the first step toward the legalization of same-sex marriage.

As of early 2012, same-sex marriage and even civil unions have received less international acceptance than having gays and lesbians serve openly in the military. Although more than 40 countries allowed open service, just 10 legalized gay marriage, though some jurisdictions recognized marriages performed and legally sanctioned elsewhere.

The Future

Prospects for further advances in the status, rights, and security of lesbians, gays, bisexuals, and transgender people appear mixed. On the one hand, in much of the developed world and certain countries in the developing world, the rights of homosexuals and their acceptance by the public seem likely to be further consolidated and expanded. Evidence for this prospect can be found in public opinion polls, which consistently find that the younger the respondent is, the more likely he or she is to accept homosexuals and other people with an alternative sexual identity as equals, deserving of social acceptance and full civil rights. Eventually, the argument goes, such opinions will become the majority sentiment, if they are not already.

At the same time, gays, lesbians, and transgender individuals in many parts of the developing world are likely to face continued discrimination, persecution, and violence, say homosexual rights advocates. The rise of religious fundamentalism—both Muslim and Christian—is increasing the level of intolerance toward homosexuals, with all of the social and legal consequences of such intolerance.

James Ciment

See also: AIDS/HIV; Human Rights; Marriage and Divorce.

Further Reading

Badgett, Lee, and Jeff Rank, eds. *Sexual Orientation Discrimination: An International Perspective.* New York: Routledge, 2007.

Browne, Kath, Jason Lim, and Gavin Brown, eds. *Geographies of Sexualities: Theory, Practices, and Politics.* Burlington, VT: Ashgate, 2007.

Burg, B.R., ed. *Gay Warriors: A Documentary History from the Ancient World to the Present.* New York: New York University Press, 2002.

Davidson, James. *The Greeks and Greek Love: A Bold New Exploration of the Ancient World.* New York: Random House, 2007.

Fone, Byrne. *Homophobia: A History.* New York: Picador, 2001.

Freeman, Elizabeth. *Time Binds: Queer Temporalities, Queer Histories.* Durham, NC: Duke University Press, 2010.

Jacobsen, Joyce, and Adam Zeller, eds. *Queer Economics: A Reader.* New York: Routledge, 2008.

Johnson, William Stacy. *A Time to Embrace: Same-Sex Relationships in Religion, Law, and Politics.* Grand Rapids, MI: W.B. Eerdmans, 2012.

Love, Heather. *Feeling Backward: Loss and Politics of Queer History.* Cambridge, MA: Harvard University Press, 2007.

Meem, Deborah T., Michelle A. Gibson, and Jonathan F. Alexander. *Finding Out: An Introduction to LGBT Studies.* Los Angeles: Sage, 2010.

Web Sites

Amnesty International, LGBT Rights: www.amnestyusa.org/our-work/issues/lgbt-rights/

Human Rights Campaign: www.hrc.org.

Human Rights Watch, LGBT Rights: www.hrw.org/en/category/topic/lgbt-rights/

International Gay & Lesbian Human Rights Commission: www.iglhrc.org

Documents

Document 1: *Araxes: A Call to Free the Nature of the Urning from Penal Law* (excerpt), Karl Heinrich Ulrichs, 1870

Born in the kingdom of Hanover in 1825, Karl Heinrich Ulrichs is widely considered by scholars in gay and lesbian studies to be the first significant advocate of gay rights in the modern era. Using a German variant of the ancient Greek term "Uranian," or a female psyche trapped in a male body, to describe himself, he came out as a homosexual to family and friends at the age of 47. Eight years later, he published a pamphlet titled Araxes: A Call to Free the Nature of the Urning from Penal Law, *in which he argued that homosexuality is innate in certain individuals and, therefore, is a natural right that no government has the right to persecute or legislate against.*

The Urning, too, is a person. He, too, therefore, has inalienable rights. His sexual orientation is a right established by nature. Legislators have no right to veto nature; no right to persecute nature in the course of its work; no right to torture living creatures who are subject to those drives nature gave them.

The Urning is also a citizen. He, too, has civil rights; and according to these rights, the state has certain duties to fulfill as well. The state does not have the right to act on whimsy or for the sheer love of persecution. The state is not authorized, as in the past, to treat Urnings as outside the pale of the law.

To be sure, legislators do have the right to make laws to contain certain expressions of the Uranian drive, just as lawmakers are empowered to legislate the behavior of all citizens. Accordingly, they may prohibit Urnings from:

    (a) seduction of male minors;
    (b) violation of civil rights (by force, threat, abuse of unconscious people, etc.);
    (c) public indecency.

The prohibition of the expression of the sex drive, i.e., between consenting adults in private, lies outside the legal sphere. All grounds for legal prosecution are lacking in this case. Legislators are hindered from doing this by human rights and the principle of the constitutional state. The legislator is hindered by the laws of justice, which forbid applying a double standard. As long as the Urning respects guidelines (a), (b), and (c) above, the legislator may not prohibit him from following the rightful law of nature to which he is subject.

Within these guidelines Uranian love is in any instance no real crime. All indications of such are lacking. It is not even shameful, decadent or wicked, simply because it is the fulfillment of a law of nature. It is reckoned as one of the many imagined crimes that have defaced Europe's law books to the shame of civilized people. To criminalize it appears, therefore, to be an injustice officially perpetrated.

Just because Urnings are unfortunate enough to be a small minority, no damage can be done to their inalienable rights and to their civil rights. The law of liberty in the constitutional state also has to consider its minorities.

And no matter what the legislators have done in the past, the law of liberty knows of no limitation.

Legislators should give up hope at the beginning of uprooting the Uranian sexual drive at any time. Even the fiery pyres upon which they burned Urnings in earlier centuries could not accomplish this. Even to gag and tie them up was useless. The battle against nature is a hopeless one. Even the most powerful government, with all the means of coercion it can bring to bear, is too weak against nature. On the other hand, the government is capable of controlling the battle. The reasoning and consciousness of the Urning's own sense of morality offer the government wholehearted cooperation toward this goal.

Source: Karl Heinrich Ulrichs, *Araxes: A Call to Free the Nature of the Urning from Penal Law,* 1870.

Document 2: "Discriminatory Laws and Practices and Acts of Violence Against Individuals Based on Their Sexual Orientation and Gender Identity," Report of the UN High Commissioner for Human Rights, 2011

In June 2011, the United Nations Human Rights Council issued a resolution expressing "grave concern" at acts of violence against persons based on their sexual orientation, and asked that a report be drawn up to examine the issue. This marked the first time that a UN body indicated a willingness to add sexual orientation as a possible human rights issue. While non-binding, the message of the report, which was issued in November 2011 was forceful, calling upon member states to repeal anti-homosexual laws and institute measures to combat violence against persons based on their sexual orientation.

http://globalequality.files.wordpress.com/2011/12/a-hrc-19-41_english.pdf

Source: The Council for Global Equality.

GENETICALLY ENGINEERED CROPS AND FOODS

Humans have been manipulating the crops that they grow for millennia, dating as far back as ancient Mesopotamia 10,000 years ago. The techniques used include grafting (inserting the tissues of one plant into those of another plant so that they combine), controlled pollination (manipulating the reproductive cycle of plants), and selective breeding (allowing only the most desirable plants to reproduce). The goal of these methods is to create hybrids (new species, like the boysenberry, loganberry, or pluot) or to grow plants with particular traits (like larger size or resistance to cold). Because of human intervention, many of today's plants are dramatically different from their ancestors. Domesticated corn, for example, bears little resemblance to the tiny ears familiar to our ancient ancestors.

In some ways, the concept of genetically engineered crops simply takes this long history of crop manipulation one step further, but in other ways it is a sharp break with past practices, a leap into a new frontier of agricultural techniques unlike anything possible before. These new crops are known by several names: genetically modified (GM), genetically engineered (GE), transgenic, biotech, bioengineered, and recombinant DNA (rDNA) crops; although some experts see differences among these terms, they are, for the most part, used interchangeably.

Unlike grafting or seed selection, genetic modification of crops introduces traits from one species into another wholly unrelated species using genetic material. Critics often call the crops derived from such work "Frankenfoods"—an allusion to Frankenstein's monster, a collection of mismatched parts put together into something unnatural and potentially dangerous. Although genetic engineering certainly does bring together disparate parts to form something never seen before, the debate is over whether these new crops are, in fact, dangerous or offer mankind new opportunities undreamed of by earlier agriculturalists.

Among the traits currently being sought through genetic engineering are insect resistance, weed control, and improved nutritional content. Such improvements, proponents argue, could revolutionize farming, combating poverty and malnutrition. Critics worry, however, that genetically engineered crops could infiltrate fields of conventionally grown crops with unforeseen consequences or could harm the animals and humans who consume the crops. Thus, whether such techniques bring with them a blessing or a danger is still under debate; the full answer will likely not be known for some time.

History

Genes carry the hereditary information of a species, encoded in deoxyribonucleic acid (DNA). Genetic modification of crops differs from older methods of crop modification in its use of this genetic material to create desired changes in plants. Unlike grafting or selective breeding, genetic engineering involves physically taking DNA from one species and introducing it into another. In grafting, the two plants being combined must be closely related, but in genetic engineering this is no longer a requirement. Thus desired traits from one species can be introduced into another, completely unrelated species. A less common technique for genetic modification involves removing or turning off a particular gene already present in an organism.

The U.S. government has largely approached this new science by treating it much the same way as it does traditional food production. In 1987, the National Academy of Sciences determined that the use of genetically modified crops posed no greater risks than any other sort of crop production, and so GM crops would be subject to the same kind of regulation as all other crops, with no specific additional limitations placed on them. The only caveat was that any plant that produced a pesticide would also fall under the scrutiny of the Environmental Protection Agency (EPA).

In 1994, the first genetically engineered crop was approved for commercial sale. Known as the Flavr Savr tomato, this was a variety that could be picked when ripe, rather than when green, and would retain its freshness during transport. By inhibiting the plant's natural levels of ethylene, an organic compound responsible for ripening, its makers were able to slow the ripening process. Although the Flavr Savr itself was not commercially successful, due to cost, flavor, and transport issues, it paved the way for future endeavors in GM crops.

A short time after the Flavr Savr became available, another genetically modified crop—the Roundup Ready soybean—was approved. Developed by Monsanto, Roundup Ready was modified to include resistance to the herbicide Roundup (also developed by Monsanto). The purpose was to allow for fields to be sprayed liberally with the pesticide, which would kill weeds and other unwanted plants, while leaving the soybeans unharmed. This, in turn, would greatly reduce the labor involved in weed removal, keep weeds from choking the soybean plants, reduce the need for repeated spraying of herbicides, and (ideally) would reduce potential toxicity in the soybeans grown.

Additional transgenic crop innovations quickly followed, including Bt corn and Bt cotton in 1996. Both of these varieties carry a soil bacterium *Bacillus thuringiensis* (or Bt), which is used in pesticides and is insect resistant. What Roundup Ready soybeans were intended to do for weed control, Bt crops were meant to do for insect control. The idea was to greatly reduce the labor involved for the farmer, to decrease the amount of harmful pesticides that needed to be sprayed onto fields, to decrease loss from insect damage, and thus to increase yield.

Bt crops also reduce the risk of insect-caused fungal growth, particularly the growth of mycotoxins, which cause health problems in many parts of the world where the people rely on a diet heavy in corn, such as the poorer regions of South America. Bt varieties are now the most widely planted GM crops in the world. And in contrast to standard pesticides, thus far there has been no evidence that insects are developing resistance to Bt crops, though some observers are concerned that such resistance will develop eventually.

Among the more recent GM crops to spark great excitement and optimism among researchers is "golden rice." In as many as 100 countries in the developing world, rice is the main staple food, often forming the bulk of the diet of the world's poorest residents. Because rice lacks many nutrients, residents of these areas often suffer from a deficiency of beta-carotene. The body converts beta-carotene, which comes primarily from vegetables, into vitamin A, a nutrient essential for the health of the eyes as well as overall. Consequently, among people who subsist on a diet high in rice and low in vegetables, blindness and other health problems are commonplace. Further, as many as 8 million children under school age die every year as a result of vitamin-A deficiency.

To combat this, genetic engineers have inserted beta-carotene synthesized genes from daffodils and the bacteria *Erwinia uredovora* into ordinary rice; the result is a pale yellow rice that they hope will help ward off blindness and other health problems in these impoverished areas. Golden rice has been held up by development and regulatory delays, but the Philippines has cleared the way for its introduction there in 2013.

Twenty-First Century

During the second half of the 1990s, genetically engineered crops became accepted rapidly in the United States, Mexico, South America, Europe, Japan, and Australia. This early widespread acceptance, however, proved short lived. By the end of the 1990s, many mainstream newspapers and other media were questioning whether GM crops posed a public hazard. Although some studies suggesting potential problems have since been dismissed by experts, the concerns raised by the media attracted public attention and raised more general fears that this was an uncontrolled and possibly dangerous branch of science.

The European Union, for example, has put in place regulations that require labeling of genetically modified organisms (GMOs, the term favored in Europe for modified crops). They also have distinct and rigorous regulations for the approval of such organisms. Unlike in the United States, in Europe authorities can deny approval of genetically engineered crops without any proof of harm to consumers or the environment. As a result of strict labeling guidelines, a reluctance to authorize new transgenic plant strains, and widespread public resistance to such crops, Europeans have largely rejected these products.

Greenpeace activists in 2009 call on the European Union to ban genetically modified foods. The EU had passed strict limits on imports and suspended the approval of new organisms, but opponents advocated an outright ban to avoid environmental damage. *(Georges Gobet/AFP/Getty Images)*

Other countries have followed the Europeans' lead in taking a cautious, even oppositional, approach to GM crops. Countries that have close economic ties to Europe are particularly reluctant to accept the new technology. In Africa, for instance, just three countries allowed GM crops to be grown in 2009: Burkina Faso, Egypt, and South Africa. By contrast, close ties to the United States account for the willingness of other countries to embrace these crops. The Philippines—once a U.S. territory—is the only Asian country to permit the growing of GM maize (a crop closely related to corn).

Because of concerns that this technology is too new for its full ramifications to be understood yet, genetically engineered crops are accepted by just a handful of governments today. In 2008, more than 90 percent of acreage planted with such crops was located in just five countries: the United States, Argentina, Brazil, Canada, and India. Half the world's GM crops are grown in the United States. But while U.S. authorities have been much more accepting of GM products, they have still been greeted with considerable public resistance. As a result, much of the emphasis is on non-food crops, such as cotton, or those intended for animal feed, such as yellow corn and soybeans. Most staple food crops—wheat and rice, for example—thus far are not produced using genetic modification. The same is largely true in the other countries that have embraced GM crops.

As of 2010, about 95 percent of soybeans and 60 percent of corn produced in the United States were genetically modified. One estimate places the amount of processed food containing at least some GM components in the country at 70 to 75 percent. Most of these ingredients, however, appear in very small amounts and usually have been highly processed, as in the case of corn processed into high fructose corn syrup, leaving little trace of the original transgenic material.

The Debate

Despite extensive research into the safety of this technology, thus far no scientific proof has been found that genetically engineered crops pose any health or environmental risks. Critics point out that the technology is too new, that risks may be obvious only after it is too late to reverse any negative impact, and that the lack of evidence of harm is not the same as evidence of harmlessness.

One concern of GM opponents is the potential dangers of pollen drift, the possibility that pollen from transgenic crops could drift on the wind and contaminate regular crops, or that they could self-sow in new areas and become invasive species. Experts consider both scenarios extremely unlikely, as domesticated crops generally do not behave this way, genetically modified or not. Weeds may be sown by the wind, but desired crops generally require human intervention to succeed. Moreover, a close relative to the GM crop would be necessary for either scenario to play out. For example, Bt corn could only potentially reproduce with another strain of corn, not with any other kind of plant.

In places where there are concerns about contamination, farmers keep a distance between GM and non-GM varieties of the same species to avoid this possibility. In January 2012, the U.S. Department of Agriculture approved the use of Roundup Ready alfalfa, asserting that the risk of contamination appeared to be negligible. Still, the potential that a more robust form of transgenic plant could become an invasive species because of its superior traits is believed to be among the more valid concerns about GM crops. Thus far, scientists are watching carefully for signs, but have not yet seen any indication that this is occurring.

Critics have cited a number of scientific studies that they claim demonstrate other risks involved with GM crops. One such study—which has done more than any other to spark opposition to GM crops—indicated that monarch butterfly larvae could be killed by pollen from Bt corn. Subsequent studies have shown that the levels needed to kill the larvae are not present in current Bt corn crops. Another study indicated that rats fed on genetically modified potatoes suffered ill effects. The Royal Society of London for Improving Natural Knowledge, known as the Royal Society, later denounced the study as having been flawed, and no study since has been able to replicate the negative findings.

There has also been nervousness about the possibility that these transgenic crops could eventually cause the development of herbicide-resistant weeds or pesticide-resistant insects. Other concerns include the fear that GM crops might lead to antibiotic resistance in humans, that they might trigger retroviruses similar to HIV, and that they could lead to lower fertility rates. Although no reliable scientific proof has been offered for any of these claims, public officials and consumers in many countries have been sufficiently frightened by these suggestions that they have rejected genetic modification of all crops. Additional concerns focus on effects of GM crops that would not be observable for years or even decades, such as the potential for allergic reactions to transgenic material or other genetic modifications that would eventually affect those who consume GM foods over long periods.

An entirely different set of concerns centers on the fact that these technologies, even individual crop varieties, can be patented. Although such patents apply only in certain countries, the fact that much of the innovation in GM crops has come from Monsanto, a U.S. chemical powerhouse, is cited as a major issue. Opponents charge that to have such a powerful corporation holding the patents for GM technology invites an agricultural monopoly. Some critics go further, suggesting that such a corporate entity cannot be trusted to behave responsibly, or to act in the public's best interests when profits are at stake, and that they would thus withhold information of health threats created by their products.

Also impeding general acceptance is the fact that thus far there have been few, if any, obvious benefits to consumers from the production of GM crops. Savings in farm labor have not been realized, for example, and GM food is not demonstrably more nutritious or better tasting. Companies such as Monsanto have clearly profited from the adoption of their patented varieties, but the public has seen little direct evidence that these crops benefit them in any way. This being the case, it is easy for consumers to question whether such meddling with nature is worth the perceived potential risks.

Several factors have combined to keep genetically engineered crops from making a substantial impact on world poverty. One impediment is resistance from governments. Even in places where hunger is a major concern, such as parts of Africa and Asia, opposition to and fear of GM foods overwhelm consideration of the potential benefits. Many authorities simply do not consider the purported dangers as worth the risk.

Another obstacle is the fact that currently most technology has been applied to large, commercial crops such as soybeans, corn, and cotton. Most of the crops grown by African farmers for local consumption—cassava, for example, or yams—have not yet been developed as GM products, largely because the profitability of major commercial crops is so much greater, but also because of the high levels of opposition to the technology. The companies that have pioneered genetic engineering have thus far focused their attention on those crops for which the market is greatest. Furthermore, the seeds for GM crops are priced beyond the means of most small subsistence farmers. Golden rice may prove the exception, as it will potentially be made available to the poorest farmers at no cost. Critics argue, however, that the introduction of this "humanitarian" crop is merely a public relations tactic to encourage more widespread acceptance of transgenic technologies.

The Future

Genetic engineering itself is not universally questioned. Some genetic modifications have inarguably benefited humankind and have faced much less opposition; for example, many genetically modified medicines have been developed (starting with insulin in 1977) and for the most part have been accepted much more readily and widely than GM crops have been. Part of the greater willingness to accept genetically engineered drugs might derive from the fact that genetic manipulation in the making of pharmaceuticals does not pose the same potential dangers of pollen drift and contamination, since drugs are produced within controlled laboratory settings. It also seems to be the case that the food we eat produces much more anxiety and faces much greater scrutiny than the drugs we take.

Nevertheless, after more than a decade of consumption of GM foods, no scientific evidence has been found that it is harmful to humans. Even so, some experts who admit that no evidence of harm exists advise caution and continued study as more transgenic crops are introduced and planted. Other experts herald this as a powerful new weapon in the millennia-long effort to bend nature to the will of humankind. The final verdict on transgenic crop technology thus is awaited.

Julie Turner

See also: Farm Policy; Food and Drug Safety; Pesticides and Artificial Fertilizers

Further Reading

Cobb, Allan B. *Scientifically Engineered Foods: The Debate Over What's on Your Plate.* New York: Rosen, 2003.

Conko, Gregory, and Henry I. Miller. "The Rush to Condemn Genetically Modified Crops." *Policy Review* 165 (February/March 2011): 69–82.

Fiechter, Armin, and Christof Sautter. *Green Gene Technology: Research in an Area of Social Conflict.* New York: Springer, 2007.

Grumet, Rebecca, et al., eds. *Environmental Safety of Genetically Engineered Crops.* East Lansing: Michigan State University Press, 2011.

Paarlberg, Robert. *Food Politics: What Everyone Needs to Know.* New York: Oxford University Press, 2010.

Pinstrup-Andersen, Per, and Ebbe Schioler. *Seeds of Contention: World Hunger and the Global Controversy over GM Crops.* Baltimore: Johns Hopkins University Press, 2001.

Ronald, Pamela. "Foreign 'Invaders': Genetically Modified Crops and Plant Diversity." *Harvard International Review* 31:2 (Summer 2009): 58–60.

Ronald, Pamela, and Raoul Adamchak. *Tomorrow's Table: Organic Farming and the Future of Food.* New York: Oxford University Press, 2008.

Taylor, Iain E.P., ed. *Genetically Engineered Crops: Interim Policies, Uncertain Legislation.* New York: Haworth Food and Agricultural Products, 2007.

Web Sites

Center for Food Safety: www.centerforfoodsafety.org/campaign/genetically-engineered-food/crops

Food and Agriculture Organization: www.fao.org

Green Facts: www.greenfacts.org/en/gmo/index.htm

United States Department of Agriculture: www.ers.usda.gov/Data/BiotechCrops

Documents

Document 1: "Genetically Modified Organisms in Food and Agriculture: Where Are We? Where Are We Going?" Speech by Louise O. Fresco, September 2001

At the time of this address, Louise O. Fresco was serving as assistant director-general for agriculture of the Food and Agriculture Organization (FAO) of the United Nations. In the speech, she argues that the debate over whether or not to have genetically modified crops and foods has reached its end and that the focus should shift to understanding the implications of these organisms and developing ways to regulate them.

Genetically modified organisms (GMOs) are here to stay. Scientists in both public and private sectors clearly regard genetic modification as a major new set of tools, while industry sees GMOs as an opportunity for increased profits. Yet the public in many countries distrusts GMOs, often seeing them as part of globalization and privatization, as being "anti-democratic" or "meddling with evolution." In turn, governments often lack coherent policies on GMOs, and have not yet developed and implemented adequate regulatory instruments and infrastructures.

As a result, there is no consensus in most countries on how biotechnology, and GM crops in particular, can address key challenges in the food and agricultural sector. FAO recognizes both the great potential, and the complications, of these new technologies. We need to move carefully, with a full understanding of all factors involved. In particular, we need to assess GMOs in terms of their impact on food security, poverty, biosafety and the sustainability of agriculture. GMOs cannot be seen in isolation, simply as technical achievements.

Nor can we talk intelligently about GMOs if debate remains at the level of generalities. For this reason, FAO has been conducting a worldwide inventory of agricultural biotechnology applications and products, with special reference to developing countries. Preliminary findings indicate that the total area cultivated with GMO crops stands at about 44.2 million hectares, up from 11 million hectares just three years ago. About 75% of this area is in industrialized countries. Substantial plantings largely concern four crops: soybean, maize, cotton, and canola. About 16% of the total area planted to these crops is now under GM varieties, and two traits—insect resistance and herbicide tolerance—dominate. There are also small areas of potato and papaya, with inserted genes for delayed ripening and virus-resistance.

Only seven developing countries cultivate GMO crops commercially, with most of the areas involved (except in Argentina and China) being smaller than 100,000 hectares. Here again, the dominant crops are soybean and cotton, and the traits are herbicide tolerance and insect resistance. Only China is using a locally developed and commercialized GM crop (cotton)—other countries have obtained genetic constructs or varieties from industrialized countries. The FAO survey also found that several forest tree species—including conifers, poplar, sweet gum and eucalypts—have been transformed using recombinant DNA technology, but have not been released for commercial purposes. Tropical fruit tree species seem to have been largely neglected.

FAO's conclusion is that current GMO crop releases are still very narrow in terms of crops and traits and have not addressed the special needs of developing countries. But what is in the pipeline? Throughout the world, several thousand GMO field tests have been conducted or are under way, again mostly in industrialized countries. Some 200 crops are currently under field testing in developing countries, the vast majority (152) in Latin America, followed by Africa (33) and Asia (19). Many more countries are involved than the seven that have already released GMOs, and many more crop-trait combinations are being investigated, with greater focus on virus resistance, quality and, in some cases, tolerance to abiotic stresses.

It can therefore be expected that the number of GMOs ready for commercial release in these countries will expand considerably in the next few years. However, many important crops—such as pulses, vegetables, and fodder, and industrial crops and certain traits—such as drought- and aluminum-tolerance—are still almost entirely neglected.

As the portfolio of GM applications increases, the international community needs to ensure that GM crops make an optimal contribution to world food security, to food safety and food quality, and to sustainability, and that they remain available to the public at large. However, despite some hopeful signs, FAO's inventory suggests that genomics and related research are not being directed to meeting these key challenges.

Indeed, the perceived profit potential of GMOs has already changed the direction of investment in research and development, in both the public and private sectors, away from systems-based approaches to pest management, and towards a greater reliance on monocultures. The possible long-term environmental costs of such strategies should not be overlooked.

Developing transgenic crops implies massive investments, and the need for massive returns. The small number of GM technologies currently in use suggests that there is a real danger that the scale of the investment may lead to selective concentration on species and problems of global importance, and concomitant capital inertia. At the same time, there is a growing use of "hard" intellectual property rights over seeds and planting material and the tools of genetic engineering. This changes the relationship between the public and private sectors, to the detriment of the former.

A policy question that governments must take up, in both the national and international contexts, is how to ensure that public research does not become a "poor relation." In developing countries in particular, it is important for the public sector to retain enough capacity, resources and freedom of action to provide the services on which their national private sectors can build. They will also need to build their policy and regulatory capacities with regard to transgenic crops that originate elsewhere. In this area, the International Plant Protection Convention (IPPC) is establishing practical cooperation with the Convention on Biological Diversity and its Biosafety Protocol. It is also developing a detailed standard specification for an International Standard for Phytosanitary Measures that identifies the plant pest risks associated with Living Modified Organisms, and ways of assessing these risks.

Another issue of concern to FAO is access to research and new technologies for developing countries, poor producers and consumers. Biotechnology in agriculture is applied to genetic resources that are the fruit of selection and development by farmers throughout the world since the Neolithic age. This poses the immediate question of how to guarantee continued access by farmers and breeders.

A major step forward is the International Undertaking on Plant Genetic Resources, which aims at creating a multilateral system of facilitated access and benefit-sharing for the world's key crops. Multilateral access provides multilateral benefit-sharing, which includes the sharing of the benefits arising from the commercialization of materials from the multilateral system through a mandatory payment. The access of breeders to genetic material for further breeding—which becomes ever more difficult with GM crops under patents—is a public good that needs to be protected. On this issue, FAO is involved in discussions on food and agriculture and IPRs in association with the World Intellectual Property Organisation.

While genetic modification has increased production in some crops, the evidence suggests that the technology has so far addressed too few challenges, in few crops of relevance to production systems in developing countries. Even in developed countries, a lack of perceived benefits for consumers, and uncertainty about their safety, have limited their adoption. The scale of investment involved, and the attraction of advanced science, may distort research priorities and investment.

Genetic modification is not a good in itself, but a tool integrated into a wider research agenda, where public and private science can balance each other. Steering research in the right direction and developing adequate, international agreements on safety and access is a difficult and responsible task. While we are more aware than ever of the need to manage international public goods responsibly, the political tools to do so are weak, and, in a globalized economy, the voices of small countries and poor producers and consumers often go unheard.

If research is to address the challenges in agriculture, we need to put genetic modification in context, and realize that it is but one of the many elements of agricultural change. Scientists must not be blinded by the glamour of cutting-edge molecular science for its own sake. Governments must not let this glamour, or private industry's perception of major profit opportunities, draw investment away from research in other, more traditional fields, such as water and soil management or ecology, and from public sector research. At the same time, the best science is developed in a climate of intellectual freedom without much direct government interference. It will be a difficult balance to strike!

Source: Food and Agriculture Organization of the United Nations.

Document 2: "Genetically Engineered Foods Will Not Feed The World," Press Release by the Center for Food Safety, 2012

The Center for Food Safety has taken the lead in resisting the spread of genetically engineered foods. In this press release, dated January 25, 2012, the Center reiterates some of its main objections to the technology.

WASHINGTON, D.C.—January 25, 2012—The Center for Food Safety (CFS) pushed back today against longtime biotech crop supporter, the Bill and Melinda Gates Foundation, over its announcement that it has invested nearly $2 billion in a campaign to fund the development of genetically engineered (GE) crops in an attempt to address global hunger. The Gates Foundation has been widely criticized

by food security and public interest groups for promoting GE crops in developing countries rather than investing in organic and sustainable local models of agriculture.

"The biotech industry has exploited the image of the world's poor and hungry to advance a form of agriculture that is expensive, input-intensive, and of little or no relevance to developing country farmers," said Andrew Kimbrell, Executive Director for the Center for Food Safety. "It's long past time that the Gates Foundation redirect its investments in biotech companies like Monsanto, and its funding of dead-end GE crop projects, to promote agroecological techniques with a proven record of increasing food production in developing countries."

Since their introduction in the mid-90s, developers of GE crops have claimed their crops will reduce agriculture's environmental footprint, provide benefits to farmers, and meet the needs of a hungry planet. Yet across the board GE crops have failed to deliver results. GE crops have remained an industrial tool dependent upon costly inputs, such as patented seeds and synthetic pesticides and fertilizers, that farmers in the most food insecure regions can ill-afford. For instance, 5 out of every 6 acres of GE crops worldwide are herbicide-resistant varieties designed explicitly to increase dependence on expensive herbicides, and this remains the major R&D focus of the industry.

In contrast, the emerging consensus of international development experts is that real solutions to addressing global hunger must be inexpensive, low-input and utilize local/regional resources as much as possible—all areas where GE crops fail to deliver. For instance, the UN and World Bank's 2008 International Assessment of Agricultural Knowledge, Science and Technology for Development (IAASTD), which engaged some 400 experts from multiple disciplines, concluded that biotech crops have very little potential to alleviate poverty and hunger. Instead, IAASTD recommended support for agroecological approaches and food sovereignty.

In 1998, African scientists at a United Nations conference strongly objected to Monsanto's promotional GE campaign that used photos of starving African children under the headline "Let the Harvest Begin." The scientists, who represented many of the nations affected by poverty and hunger, said gene technologies would undermine the nations' capacities to feed themselves by destroying established diversity, local knowledge and sustainable agricultural systems.

Developing nations also object to seed patents, which give biotech firms the power to criminalize the age-old practice of seed-saving as "patent infringement." Thousands of U.S. farmers have been forced to pay Monsanto tens of millions of dollars in damages for the "crime" of saving seed. Loss of the right to save seed through the introduction of patented GE crops could prove disastrous for the 1.4 billion farmers in developing nations who depend on farm-saved seed.

It is increasingly understood that poverty, inadequate access to land and food, and unfair trade policies are the major causes of hunger in the world, rather than absolute shortage of food. Additional factors contributing to food insecurity include declining investments in infrastructure (storage facilities, roads to markets) and increased diversion of food crops for biofuels and animal feed. The UN World Food Program notes many farmers in developing countries cannot afford seed or other materials for crop production, so GE seeds, which cost twice to over six times the price of conventional seed, are even less affordable.

Source: Center for Food Safety.

GOVERNMENT CORRUPTION AND TRANSPARENCY

Government corruption and transparency have emerged as key issues in debates on good governance in recent years, with a growing consensus among policymakers and academics that corruption is one of the biggest obstacles to national development. The fact that "corruption" can refer to a wide range of social practices and mean different things in different contexts has not deterred many attempts at a definition. The noted Harvard political scientist Joseph Nye defined corruption as "behavior that deviates from the formal duties of a public role (elective or appointive) because of private-regarding (personal, close family, private clique) wealth or status gains; or violates rules against the exercise of certain types of private-regarding influence." A more succinct definition widely used today is "the abuse of public office for private gain." Both definitions can accommodate a wide range of practices, including bribery, extortion, collusion, vote rigging, embezzlement, fraud, patronage, and nepotism. And in both definitions given above, the emphasis is specifically on the abuse of *public* office.

Given that corruption thrives in environments characterized by secrecy and information asymmetries, transparency is one of the most frequently prescribed solutions to the syndrome of problems associated with corruption. As with corruption, no single definition of transparency exists. It is described by the International Monetary Fund's Working Group on Transparency and Accountability as "the process by which information about existing conditions, decisions and actions is made accessible, visible and understandable." The nongovernmental organization Transparency International defines it as "a principle that allows those affected by administrative decisions, business transactions or charitable work to know not only the basic facts and figures but also the mechanisms and processes." Considered by many to be a core principle of good governance, the Access Initiative writes that transparency "allows stakeholders to gather information that may be critical to uncovering abuses and defending their interests."

The complexity of corruption and the multitude of factors contributing to its proliferation render it impossible for any single remedy to work effectively in its prevention or mitigation. That includes transparency in public administration, which as a principle and practice needs to be part of a wider, multipronged strategy to reduce the opportunities and incentives to engage in corrupt behavior.

Historical Background

The rise of corruption to prominence in the policymaking agenda of the international development community, and the proliferation of organizations working on the issue, are relatively recent. That corruption is as old as government itself is evidenced by recorded history. In third century B.C.E., the Indian statesman and philosopher Kautilya detailed in a famous treatise "forty ways of embezzlement" for officers who handle money and valuables. Fourteenth-century Arab historian and scholar Ibn Khaldun noted that the demands of people and their disposition toward pleasure and indulgence induce a gradual corruption that endangers social cohesion. References to corruption and moral decay, and the threat they pose to political order, can also be found in the works of such Western philosophers as Aristotle (384–322 B.C.E.), Plato (424–324 B.C.E.), Niccolò Machiavelli (1469–1527), Montesquieu (1689–1755), and Jean-Jacques Rousseau (1712–1778).

Incidents and allegations of specific corrupt practices run throughout history. In China, they litter the annals from the very first Xia dynasty (2070–1600 B.C.E.) to the last Chinese dynasty, the Qing (1644–

1911), often couched in terms of the concept and practice of *guanxi* (using personal networks of influence). The prosecution of Roman governor Gaius Verres by Cicero in first century B.C.E. on charges of corruption and extortion is emblematic of the corruption prevalent in the Roman Empire. Indeed, several historical accounts of the decline and fall of great empires, or of the impetus for revolutions, center on corruption as a symptom, cause, or motivation.

Despite the frequent appearance of corruption in historical records, there are few comprehensive historical works on the subject, partly on account of the discreet nature of corruption and the definitional and measurement challenges involved in such undertakings. In his seminal 1984 work *Bribes*, John T. Noonan divides the history or the evolution of the "idea" of bribes (as one form of corruption) into four discernible stages:

- *3000 B.C.E.–1000 C.E.:* The idea that favors must not be exchanged between supplicants and those in positions of power struggled against deeply held assumptions of reciprocity as the basis for all social exchange;
- *1000–1550:* The notion of antibribery emerged in religious, legal, and literary works and its enforcement was attempted through successive reformations.
- *Sixteenth to Eighteenth Century:* Among English-speaking people, the period started with the domestication of the idea of bribes in bibles, plays, and laws, and ended with antibribery being proclaimed as a "norm."
- *Late Nineteenth Century (American Stage):* The antibribery norm is implemented by the heirs of successive reformations and spreads to the rest of the world under the American influence and the general expansion of Western moral tradition.

Of course, the gradual evolution of antibribery norms did not necessarily affect or reflect the prevalence of corruption during the periods over which these ideals developed. With successive waves of democratization and the birth of the modern idea of the state, the idea of public office as private property fell out of favor, and certain corrupt practices in Western Europe and America began to decline, relatively speaking. However, electoral corruption, the sale of public office, cronyism, and other such practices were rampant throughout the eighteenth and nineteenth centuries in these places, and there continued to be patches of systemic corruption in most countries well into early twentieth century.

Despite the annals of history being replete with incidents of, and references to, corruption, academic and policy-oriented empirical research on the subject is relatively new. It first emerged as a focus of a significant number of scholars in the 1960s, within the fields of economics and political science. Between then and the early 1990s, most of the scholarly work treated corruption as a domestic problem, with a focus on individual incentives and the functional, economic, and moral dimensions of the issue. This period was marked by definitional debates centering on whether corruption was "sand in the wheels" of development or instead "greased the wheels" in inefficient and overcentralized, rigid systems. Others focused on the ethical dimensions of corruption. Empirical data on the subject was limited, and most of the analyses suggesting how corruption could be reduced emphasized eliminating inefficient regulation and strengthening law enforcement.

On the policy front, proactive governments enacted laws delineating and criminalizing corrupt practices, and specialized institutions known as anticorruption agencies, modeled on the lines of successful models in Singapore and Hong Kong, began sprouting up in many developing countries. Just a handful of developed countries had freedom of information laws during this period.

It was only in the early 1990s that the subject of corruption erupted within the development discourse. These years are considered the watershed years for the global anticorruption campaigns that have marked the decades since.

Corruption as a Global Social Issue

The foundations of much of our current understanding of corruption were laid during the 1990s. During this decade, the study of corruption became increasingly oriented toward giving practical policy advice. The renewed attention to the subject was an outcome of several political and economic trends that characterized the period:

- The end of the Cold War facilitated a relative decline in superpower support to corrupt regimes.
- The democratization that followed opened up discussions on how transitioning polities should be governed.

- The information revolution taking place at the time, coupled with the rise of transnational civil society organizations, put accountability and transparency at the center of the emerging global governance agenda.
- Transparency International, founded by a former World Bank official in 1983 and perhaps the first transnational corruption-oriented NGO, was wildly successful in stimulating debate and raising awareness about the issue, not least through the introduction of its Corruption Perceptions Index (CPI) in 1995, marking the first time countries had been formally ranked on some corruption-related indicator.

These trends converged with donor-aided free market reforms, based in large part on the principle of leveling economic playing fields and developing shared norms and practices to underpin international economic governance. In 1996, James Wolfensohn, then president of the World Bank (which had heretofore largely avoided the topic of corruption as a sensitive political issue), made his groundbreaking "cancer of corruption" speech, and anticorruption reform soon began to feature more prominently in the policy prescriptions and conditions that accompanied donor funds. Fueled partly by the terrorist attacks on the U.S. homeland in September 2001, corrupt institutions in developing countries also came to be seen as posing a potential national security threat. Against this backdrop, exponentially growing resources were dedicated to understanding and eliminating corruption, giving rise to an entire "global anticorruption industry" composed of researchers and policymakers engaged in analytical and policy advisory work aimed at corruption control.

Types of Corruption

Recognizing that corruption finds multiple channels of expression and that not all forms have the same effects, researchers have suggested ways of defining and categorizing the phenomenon.

The two most widely used distinctions are those between "petty" and "grand" corruption, and between "opportunistic" and "systemic" corruption. Petty corruption, also known as "administrative corruption," is the collusion of a public official with a member of the public to subvert the system over relatively small transactions. Grand corruption, or state capture, pervades the highest levels of government, leading to the erosion of confidence in the policymaking process and rule of law in a country.

Corruption is said to be opportunistic or "incidental" when it represents individual deviant acts in a system where formal institutions are sufficiently free of corruption to be able to play their constraining roles. In contrast, corruption is "systemic" when the formal institutions themselves are compromised and corrupt practices entrenched.

In an earlier stream in the literature, David Osterfeld distinguished between "expansive" and "restrictive" corruption. The former encompassed activities that resulted in enhanced competitive exchange and market flexibility (for instance, by mitigating effects of excessive regulation), while the latter was used to describe those activities that limited opportunities for mutually beneficial exchange (for instance, by redistributing wealth in favor of certain individuals or groups). However, there is a general agreement among most scholars today that the short-term benefits of any expansive corruption are outweighed by the long-term costs it imposes on the economy. Consequently, the use of this classification has declined in recent years.

Measures of Corruption

The hidden nature of corruption makes it extremely difficult to measure. However, with the advance of empirical studies on parameters of governance, several individuals and organizations have taken up the challenge of measuring the prevalence and costs of corruption. The following are the main types of corruption indicators, according to the United Nations Development Programme.

Objective indicators quantify certain types of corrupt practices, or the administrative or judicial handling thereof. They are based on information that is, in principle, verifiable (though subject to the possibility of distortion or mismeasurement in practice). Examples of such indicators might be the number of corruption cases filed, the number of convictions, or the actual amount of leakage from project funds, and so on.

Perception-based indicators rely on subjective opinions of corruption among experts or stakeholder groups. Transparency International pioneered this field with its index, the CPI. An example of a composite indicator that draws data from multiple sources, the CPI ranks countries on the basis of the degree of corruption which is perceived to exist among public officials. The perceived level of corruption in each

Corruption Perception Index,* Top- and Bottom-Ranking Countries, 2011

Rank	Country
1	New Zealand
2	Denmark
2	Finland
4	Sweden
5	Singapore
6	Norway
7	Netherlands
8	Australia
8	Switzerland
10	Canada
11	Luxembourg
12	Hong Kong
13	Iceland
14	Germany
14	Japan
16	Austria
16	Barbados
16	United Kingdom
19	Belgium
19	Ireland
21	Bahamas
22	Chile
22	Qatar
24	United States
25	France
25	Saint Lucia
25	Uruguay
154	Central African Republic
154	Congo Republic
154	Côte d'Ivoire
154	Guinea-Bissau
154	Kenya
154	Laos
154	Nepal
154	Papua New Guinea
154	Paraguay
154	Zimbabwe
164	Cambodia
164	Guinea
164	Kyrgyzstan
164	Yemen
168	Angola
168	Chad
168	Democratic Republic of the Congo
168	Libya
172	Burundi
172	Equatorial Guinea
172	Venezuela
175	Haiti
175	Iraq
177	Sudan
177	Turkmenistan
177	Uzbekistan
180	Afghanistan
180	Myanmar
182	Korea (North)
182	Somalia

*Published by Transparency International, the CPI ranks almost 200 countries by their perceived levels of corruption, as determined by expert assessments and opinion surveys. These surveys and assessments include questions related to the bribery of public officials, kickbacks in public procurement, embezzlement of public funds, and the effectiveness of public sector anticorruption efforts.

Source: Transparency International.

country is measured through a composite index that aggregates data collected from two sources of information—business opinion surveys and country assessments by experts. Another commonly used composite perception-based indicator is the World Bank's World Governance Indicators (WGI). One of the six dimensions measured by the WGI is Control of Corruption. The WGI compiles and summarizes information from thirty existing data sources. The aggregate control of corruption indicator is constructed through a weighted average of the rescaled data from the individual sources.

Experience-based indicators rely on actual reported experiences of individuals and organizations in paying and being offered bribes, as assessed through self-reported surveys. The need for experience-based indicators has been emphasized time and again in the literature on corruption. However, experience-based indicators can be time- and resource-intensive to construct. Transparency International's Global Corruption Barometer, which is a public opinion survey, is in part experience-based. Along with assessing citizens' perception of corruption, it probes the frequency of bribe-paying, reasons for paying bribes, and attitudes toward reporting incidents of corruption.

Proxy indicators seek to measure corruption indirectly, by aggregating different signals of corruption or the absence thereof. Most proxy indicators measure the opposite of corruption: anticorruption or good governance measures. Global Integrity, an independent nonprofit organization, uses integrity indicators to assess the strengths and weaknesses of countries' public sector anticorruption mechanisms by collecting data on the legal anticorruption framework, as well as on its practical implementation.

Despite the proliferation of indicators, measuring corruption still remains a challenge. The perception-based and proxy indicators that dominate the field today are of questionable validity and reliability—the hallmarks of good indicators. (Reliability refers to the consistency or the repeatability of a measuring instrument while validity refers to the extent to which a measure accurately depicts what it claims to measure.) The clandestine nature of corruption makes a shift toward more objective and experience-based indicators a complex task.

Causes of Corruption

Precisely identifying and isolating the underlying causes of corruption is not easy given its multifaceted nature and the diverse contexts it thrives in. However, theoretical and empirical research has yielded several insights into why some countries might be more corrupt than others. Four groups of causes are commonly posited in the literature.

Economic Development

High levels of corruption have been found to correlate closely with low levels of economic development (usually measured by gross domestic product, or GDP, per capita); in short, developing countries tend to have higher levels of corruption. Low levels of personal income have also been found to be associated with higher levels of corruption, fuelling a proposed distinction between "need" and "greed" corruption. Economies dependent on natural resources have richer opportunities for (illegal) rent extraction. Economies with low levels of openness to foreign trade usually tend to have burdensome regulations. Highly unequal societies tend to be more corrupt than more equal ones. However, the direction of causation between the above features and corruption is complex and forms the subject of much of the current debate on how corruption should be tackled.

Institutional Development

In general, weak institutions have been found to provide fertile ground for corruption. Systems in which public officers enjoy, by law or by default, high levels of discretion in exercising regulatory authority have been found to be particularly prone to corruption. Such discretionary authority, when coupled with a lack of competition in the provision of essential services and low levels of accountability, make it easier for corrupt officials to impose ad hoc restrictions and engage in rent-seeking behavior. A lack of transparency in decision making, inadequate provision of public information pertaining to laws and regulations, ineffective institutional controls, and weak law enforcement further compound the problem.

Political Structures

The emphasis on accountability and transparency has led to several assertions about the relationship between corruption and democracy. Some believe that nondemocratic systems, with their lack of checks and balances, a free press, and independent civil soci-ety organizations, are more likely to be corrupt than democratic systems. But the econometric evidence supporting this claim is mixed, not least because of the huge range of variation within the categories of "democratic" and "nondemocratic" systems. Similarly, there is mixed evidence for centralization as a cause of corruption. Some studies suggest that decentralized systems may increase competition between jurisdictions and allow for greater oversight by citizens, reducing vulnerabilities to corruption. Others posit that decentralized systems may be *more* corruptible as rules are harder to enforce in fragmented systems, and as the corrupters have more frequent and intimate access to corrupt (local) public officials. Presidential systems, especially those with closed-list proportional representation systems, are found in some studies to be correlated with a higher incidence of corruption than parliamentary systems as a result of the difficulties involved in identifying and monitoring corrupt acts of individual leaders.

Historical and Cultural Factors

Historical and cultural variables have also been introduced to explain why some countries are more corrupt than others. Studies have asserted linkages between colonial history and present-day corruption. Former British colonies, for example, have been found to have a lower propensity for corruption than French, Spanish, or Portuguese ones owing to differences in legal and institutional traditions that have continued in the post-colonial period.

Some scholars argue that societies that are highly fragmented on ethno-linguistic grounds are likely to be more corrupt than homogenous ones because of the unequal access to power generated in these societies. Others argue that a culture of distrust and suspicion gives rise to corruption because of the perceived uncertainty of entering into legitimate transactions with strangers. Predominantly Protestant countries tend to have lower levels of corruption than those dominated by other religions. The prevalence of particular traditions and customs, such as gift giving and certain patterns of personal network usage, are also associated with higher levels of corruption. There are arguments to suggest that such practices must be taken into context before applying a so-called Western lens of corruption to such countries.

It is important to note once again that virtually all of the above assertions are subject to varied interpretations and disagreements in the literature, particularly with respect to the tricky question of what exactly is causing what. This obviously complicates the effort to draw clear policy conclusions from these studies.

Tackling Corruption

In response to increasing concerns about corruption's debilitating effects, the early 1990s witnessed the emergence of sweeping reform proposals intended to target the roots of corruption. These strategies were guided by several assumptions about the causes of corruption, especially the concentration of regulatory power in the hands of unaccountable public officials and weaknesses in institutional and legal frameworks. Alongside overarching reform programs such as democratization and privatization, specific reforms targeting corruption included changes to procurement practices, deregulation, legal development, the launch or strengthening of anti-corruption agencies, public education, and the direct participation of civil society organizations in monitoring government practices and advocating for policy reform. During this period, donor agencies like the World Bank and International Monetary Fund made loans conditional upon the implementation of such reforms. The guiding premise was that more, and faster, reform would result in less (systemic) corruption.

This early wave of anticorruption soon led to disillusionment; success stories were few and far between, despite the superficial diffusion of reforms (or reform rhetoric). The idea of a universal, one-size-fits-all strategy came to be rejected in many circles. A new wave, starting around the turn of the millennium, recognized that differences in capacities, forms of corruption, and societal norms needed to be taken into consideration while designing anticorruption strategies. As a result, the focus has shifted from market reforms to capacity building, customization to local realities, and the promotion of good governance principles. Broadly speaking, anticorruption efforts today are focused on increasing transparency in public administration and enforcing international conventions on corruption control.

Transparency and Accountability

Transparency has been touted as an important deterrent to corruption and an essential enabler of meaningful government accountability. Increasing transparency in all spheres of public management, such that government officials can be better monitored and held accountable, has become the underlying principle behind a number of reform efforts:

- In the area of public procurement, Transparency International has championed the cause of integrity pacts among governments and bidders to ensure that information about every level of the public contracting process—from regulations on the bidding process to awarding of contracts—is made public.
- Increasing emphasis is being placed on promoting transparency in government budgets and revenues, and on allowing citizens to monitor fiscal policies and the usage of public funds.
- Citizen charters—documents stating rights, service standards, and stipulated fees for government services, avenues for grievance redress, and other information—have been adopted by many local governments and agencies.
- Transparency has been championed as tool for minimizing fraud and corruption in the electoral process.
- As a significant step toward promoting government transparency, some 85 countries have enacted freedom of information laws guaranteeing citizens access to most or all public records.

International Conventions

Anticorruption conventions have provided a framework for international cooperation as well as an impetus for domestic standard setting. Several conventions have been agreed upon by multiple governments in the past ten years.

Early conventions were signed at regional levels, noteworthy among them are the Inter-American Convention Against Corruption (1996), the OECD Convention on Combating Bribery of Foreign Public Officials in International Business Transactions (1997), and the African Union Convention on Preventing and Combating Corruption (2003). The most important to date has been the United Nations Convention against Corruption (UNCAC), adopted in 2003 with a total of 140 signatories as of this writing. It represents international consensus on states prevention of corruption, criminalization and law enforcement, asset recovery, and international cooperation. A country's status of UNCAC implementation is widely considered to be an important indicator of that country's anticorruption efforts.

Impact of Corruption

Several empirical studies have revealed that corruption has a negative effect on development, and that it has a disproportionate impact on the poor and vulnerable sectors of the population. Since the 1990s there has been a frenzy of research activity centered on corruption that has advanced our understanding of the different ways in which corruption affects development. According to Transparency International, the cost of widespread corruption in a country must be assessed in four categories: economic, political, social, and environmental.

Economic Costs

Cross-country analyses of the effects of corruption on the economy have shown that corruption has a negative effect on GDP per capita growth. Corruption can affect economic growth both directly and indirectly. Its direct impact can be felt through the leakage of revenue from public coffers.

The indirect costs imposed by corruption are equally significant. It reduces both domestic and foreign direct investment since it acts as a tax on business and increases the cost of transactions. It hinders competition and the development of market structures essential for growth. It also results in the distortion of government expenditure and lowering of the quality of public infrastructure, since public resources get allocated on the basis of corrupt gains rather than efficiency and effectiveness. Empirical studies also suggest that corruption increases the shadow economy and results in reduced spending on important determinants of growth like health and education.

Corruption also has distributional consequences. It results in reduced effectiveness of aid and thereby has implications for a wide range of poverty-reduction development projects. It further perpetuates inequalities in society by benefiting the elite and powerful and concentrating asset ownership in their hands. In addition, corruption increases the costs of, and reduces access to, vital public services. Survey evidence indicates that there is a direct correlation between incidents of bribery encountered and income levels.

Political and Social Costs

Corruption is particularly detrimental to political development and imposes very serious social costs.

Perhaps its biggest political cost is manifested in the erosion of public trust in political institutions. Lack of trust in public officials and institutions, and the accompanying sense of despair, can result in reduced political participation and a weakened civil society. It deters honest individuals from entering government service, ultimately allowing for the political system to be hijacked by dishonest, unscrupulous, and often authoritarian elements. Thus, democratic institutions can be seriously undermined by pervasive corruption. Further, denial of access to public services and continuous extortion can lead to the loss of regime legitimacy in the long run.

Corruption also weighs heavily on the social fabric of nations, and is found to strongly correlate with reduced levels of interpersonal trust. Distrust and a culture of suspicion have the potential to accentuate class-based, ethnic, and sectarian divisions, increasing the chances of conflict in society. The erosion of social safety nets for vulnerable populations and the general subversion of the rule of law that result from corruption can also lead to a higher incidence of other criminal activity. When corruption becomes entrenched in a society, it may in essence become a social norm in its own right, making it a much more difficult problem to resolve. Much like poverty, corruption can be considered a vicious cycle that perpetuates many other social evils.

Environmental and Other Costs

The effects of corruption on the natural environment are also increasingly being examined. Environmental resources are particularly prone to being captured by corrupt interests. Corruption in governing the environment can result in the unsustainable exploitation of natural resources, nonenforcement of critical environmental regulation, and approval of environmentally harmful projects.

Apart from threatening the environment, corruption is also considered a threat to national security. Corruption in the public organizations responsible for national security (e.g., defense, police, and national security agencies) can render a country vulnerable to internal and external security threats.

Given that these ramifications of corruption are most observable in developing countries with weak institutional structures, there is a general tendency to think that corruption is not a problem in the developed world. This view is problematic. In his landmark 2005 book *Syndromes of Corruption*, Michael Johnston finds that wealth is often used to seek political influence even in these countries. Lobbying and campaign contributions tend to be the main vehicles for such influence peddling. Though such corruption does not usually result in significant undermining of economic or political institutions, it can influence details of policies themselves, favoring some groups (usually the more powerful ones) over others, which in turn can render the system vulnerable to many of the political, economic, and environmental effects of corruption discussed above, over the long term.

Limited Progress

Much more is understood about corruption than was even understood two decades ago. Significant progress has been made in understanding the conditions that make an organization, sector, city, or country more vulnerable to corrupt practices, and there has been an explosion of creative practices from around the world that might effectively combat it. Yet significant gaps remain in both our knowledge and in the practice on the ground, even where policy intentions to fight corruption have been clearly announced. After two decades of at times frenzied anticorruption reforms, few if any countries have demonstrably moved from high levels of systemic corruption to relatively low levels. Whether this is because such efforts take long periods of time—perhaps even generations—to take root, or the strategies themselves have been ill-conceived, or political will to fight corruption has been lacking, is an open question and undoubtedly varies from case to case. One thing seems clear: citizen expectations for cleaner government are increasing around the world, and most likely at a pace that far exceeds the progress that most systems will make in fighting corruption. This fact sets the stage for continued ferment around the issue and study of corruption in the coming years.

Shreya Basu and Scott A. Fritzen

See also: Deficits and Sovereign Debt; Failed States and Nation-Building; Law, Rule of; Police Corruption and Brutality; Secrecy, Government.

Further Reading

Bardhan, Pranab. "Corruption and Development: A Review of Issues." *Journal of Economic Literature* 35:3 (1997): 1320–1346.
Dreher, Axel, Christos Kotsogiannis, and Steve McCorris-
ton. "Corruption Around the World: Evidence from a Structural Model." *Journal of Comparative Economics* 35:3 (2007) 443–466.
Florini, Ann, ed. *The Right to Know: Transparency for an Open World*. New York: Columbia University Press, 2007.
Johnston, Michael. *Syndromes of Corruption: Wealth, Power, and Democracy*. New York: Cambridge University Press, 2005.
Klitgaard, Robert. *Controlling Corruption*. Berkeley: University of California Press, 1988.
Lambsdorff, Johann. *The Institutional Economics of Corruption and Reform: Theory, Evidence, and Policy*. New York: Cambridge University Press, 2007.
Noonan, John. *Bribes*. Berkeley: University of California Press, 1984.
Rose-Ackerman, Susan. *Corruption and Government: Causes, Consequences and Reform*. New York: Cambridge University Press, 1999.

Web Sites

Anti-Corruption Research Network: http://corruptionresearchnetwork.org
Global Integrity: www.globalintegrity.org
Global Organization of Parliamentarians against Corruption: www.gopacnetwork.org
Internet Center for Corruption Research: www.icgg.org/corruption.research.html
OECD Anti-Bribery Convention: www.oecd.org/depart ment/0,2688,en_2649_34859_1_1_1_1_1,00.html
Transparency International: www.transparency.org
U4 Anti-Corruption Resource Centre: www.u4.no
United Nations Convention Against Corruption: www.unodc.org/unodc/en/treaties/CAC

Documents

Document 1: "The Forty Ways of Embezzlement," from Kautilya's *Artha-shastra*, Third Century B.C.E.

One of the greatest political and economic theoreticians of the ancient world, the Hindu scholar Kautilya is best known for his third-century B.C.E. work Artha-shastra (The Science of Material Gain). *A synthesis of earlier writings, the* Artha-shastra *provides a blueprint for governance, including how a state's economy should be organized, how it should conduct wars, and how a ruler can maintain control over state apparatus. Among the most famous sections of the work is Kautilya's description of official malfeasance or, as he put it, "the forty ways of embezzlement," one of the earliest extant descriptions of government corruption.*

There are about forty ways of embezzlement: what is realised earlier is entered later on; what is realised later is entered earlier; what ought to be realised is not realised; what is hard to realise is shown as realised; what is collected is shown as not collected; what has not been collected is shown as collected; what is collected in part is entered as collected in full; what is collected in full is entered as collected in part; what is collected is of one sort, while what is entered is of another sort; what is realised from one source is shown as realised from another; what is payable is not paid; what is not payable is paid; not paid in time; paid untimely; small gifts made large gifts; large gifts made small gifts; what is gifted is of one sort while what is entered is of another; the real donee is one while the person entered (in the register) as donee is another; what has been taken into (the treasury) is removed while what has not been credited to it is shown as credited; raw materials that are not paid for are entered, while those that are paid for are not entered; an aggregate is scattered in pieces; scattered items are converted into an aggregate; commodities of greater value are bartered for those of small value; what is of smaller value is bartered for one of greater value; price of commodities enhanced; price of commodities lowered; number of nights increased; number of nights decreased; the year not in harmony with its months; the month not in harmony with its days; inconsistency in the transactions carried on with personal supervision (*samágamavishánah*); misrepresentation of the source of income; inconsistency in giving charities; incongruity in representing the work turned out; inconsistency in dealing with fixed items; misrepresentation of test marks or the standard of fineness (of gold and silver); misrepresentation of prices of commodities; making use of false weight and measures; deception in counting articles; and making use of false cubic measures such as *bhájan*—these are the several ways of embezzlement.

Source: Kautilya, *Artha-shastra,* from the translation by Rudrapatna Shama Shastri, Mysore, India: Wesleyan Mission Press, 1923.

Document 2: UN Convention against Corruption (excerpts), 2004

Recognizing the need for an effective, all-encompassing international legal instrument against corruption, the United Nations General Assembly in 2000 established a committee to negotiate such a document. The text of the UN Convention against Corruption, written between January 21, 2002, and October 1, 2003, by the Ad Hoc Committee for the Negotiation of the Convention against Corruption, was approved by the General Assembly and went into force on December 14, 2005. The United Nations Convention against Corruption is the first globally agreed-upon framework for combatting corruption on both national and international levels. An extensive document of eight chapters and 71 articles, it covers a comprehensive range of issues associated with prevention, asset recovery, criminalization, law enforcement, and international cooperation.

Foreword

Corruption is an insidious plague that has a wide range of corrosive effects on societies. It undermines democracy and the rule of law, leads to violations of human rights, distorts markets, erodes the quality of life and allows organized crime, terrorism and other threats to human security to flourish.

This evil phenomenon is found in all countries—big and small, rich and poor—but it is in the developing world that its effects are most destructive. Corruption hurts the poor disproportionately by diverting funds intended for development, undermining a Government's ability to provide basic services, feeding inequality and injustice and discouraging foreign aid and investment. Corruption is a key element in economic underperformance and a major obstacle to poverty alleviation and development.

. . . The adoption of the United Nations Convention against Corruption will send a clear message that the international community is determined to prevent and control corruption. It will warn the corrupt that betrayal of the public trust will no longer be tolerated. And it will reaffirm the importance of core values such as honesty, respect for the rule of law, accountability and transparency in promoting development and making the world a better place for all.

Preamble

The States Parties to this Convention,
Concerned about the seriousness of problems and threats posed by corruption to the stability and security of societies, undermining the institutions and values of democracy, ethical values and justice and jeopardizing sustainable development and the rule of law . . .

Chapter I. General provisions

Article 1. Statement of purpose
The purposes of this Convention are:
   (a) To promote and strengthen measures to prevent and combat corruption more efficiently and effectively;
   (b) To promote, facilitate and support international cooperation and technical assistance in the prevention of and fight against corruption, including in asset recovery;
   (c) To promote integrity, accountability and proper management of public affairs and public property.

Chapter II. Preventive measures

Article 5. Preventive anti-corruption policies and practices

1. Each State Party shall, in accordance with the fundamental principles of its legal system, develop and implement or maintain effective, coordinated anti-corruption policies that promote the participation of society and reflect the principles of the rule of law, proper management of public affairs and public property, integrity, transparency and accountability.

2. Each State Party shall endeavour to establish and promote effective practices aimed at the prevention of corruption.

3. Each State Party shall endeavour to periodically evaluate relevant legal instruments and administrative measures with a view to determining their adequacy to prevent and fight corruption. . . .

Source: United Nations Convention against Corruption, United Nations Office on Drugs and Crime.

HEALTH CARE

The term "health care" refers to the provision of medical and public-health services and consists of various disciplines and levels of care. Although such medical services have been part of the human experience for thousands of years, the modern system of health care, based on scientific understanding and delivered by accredited professionals, emerged only with the Enlightenment of the eighteenth century. Schemes to pay for health care—whether private or public—began in the eighteenth and nineteenth centuries, but only became universal or near-universal in the second half of the twentieth century, and then largely in the developed world.

Two basic issues confront health-care systems today: access and costs. The former is largely associated with the inadequate health-care systems of the developing-world countries, though rationing or insufficient insurance coverage affects some developed-world countries. According to health-care experts, access will continue to be a problem in the developing world, though rapid economic growth in Asian and Latin American countries will likely alleviate this somewhat. Costs, however, are a major problem confronting developed-world systems. The developed world faces the problem of an aging population, which requires more health-care services, further driving up costs.

This chapter is devoted to the ways in which the health-care system is organized, the way it functions, and the way it is financed, rather than to medical treatment and care. (For fuller discussions of the science of medicine and medical treatments, the reader should turn to the many chapters in this collection devoted to specific ailments and conditions.)

Definition and Types

Health care refers to the prevention, diagnosis, and treatment of diseases, medical conditions, and injuries. Such services are provided in out-patient settings such as doctor's offices and clinics; in-patient facilities such as hospitals; and "in the field"—where people live, work, recreate, and are educated. Services are provided by professionals—medical doctors, pharmacists, nutritionists, dentists, and various categories of alternative medical practitioners. Health-care systems also include facilities and personnel dedicated to research and to the education of health-care professionals.

Although health care is divided into specialized fields corresponding to various medical conditions, bodily systems, procedures, and approaches, it is generally broken into four general categories of care: primary, secondary, tertiary, and quaternary.

Primary care is provided by nonspecialized medical doctors, nurses, and other basic health-care practitioners. This kind of care is typically dispensed in doctor's offices and clinics on an out-patient basis, or in the field, and is reserved for low-level illnesses, conditions, and injuries. The primary-care setting is sometimes the first contact with the medical system for a person suffering from more serious health problems, because it is more local and accessible, because it is less costly, or because seeing a primary care provider is a requirement of a health insurer before more specialized care can be provided.

More serious or unusual health problems are typically attended to at the secondary-care level. Such conditions are illnesses for which the diagnosis and treatment require the knowledge and skills of specialized professionals, such as cardiologist or pulmonologists. Secondary care can be administered on an out-patient basis at a specialist's office or on in-patient or out-patient basis in hospitals or specialized clinics.

Tertiary care, or the provision of advanced or complex diagnostics or treatment, such as major surgery, almost always occurs on an in-patient basis at a hospital. Such treatment can be provided by a secondary-care specialist or, in the case of a surgeon or diagnostician with specialized knowledge and skills, by a tertiary-care specialist.

Quaternary-care diagnostics and treatment are far

rarer, usually involving extremely specialized professionals at a handful of medical facilities around the world. Quaternary care typically includes procedures that are experimental in nature and performed by specialists who are both researchers and clinicians.

History

Medicine and doctors have existed throughout human history, while locations designated for medical care go back to the earliest civilizations, in Egypt and elsewhere. But given the limited understanding of human health and medicine before the modern age—along with the belief that so much of the natural world was controlled by deities and supernatural forces—many medical practitioners were actually priests and other religious figures, and their medical practice typically took place in temples and at other religious sites and buildings. In ancient Greece, for example, temples dedicated to the healing god Asclepius, whose snake-entwined staff is still the symbol for medicine today, doubled as doctor's offices, surgical rooms, and pharmacies while priests performed health consultations, treatments, and operations. Some scholars believe that the first civic hospitals—that is, hospitals organized and financed not by religious figures and tithes but via government officials and tax revenues were created in India at the end of the first millennium B.C.E.

Medieval Arab civilizations developed the most elaborate and sophisticated health-care systems before the modern age. Major hospitals—both publicly financed and affiliated with religious schools and mosques—were constructed in Baghdad, Damascus, and other urban centers. Some of these facilities were devoted to specific aspects of medicine, such as psychiatry or ophthalmology, and trained and employed specialized medical professionals.

The health-care system as it is known today, with its fully scientific and secular orientation, and its accredited ranks of professionals, emerged in early modern Europe. By the sixteenth and seventeenth centuries, the concept of Christian care—that is, of facilities operated by monastic and other religious institutions and treatment based on acts of faith, belief in miracles, and the performance of Christian duty to the ill—began to be superseded by scientifically informed medicine and professionals motivated by both professional duty and financial gain. The rise of modern hospitals in the eighteenth century was paid for either by the government or by philanthropic individuals and organizations, though some of the latter had religious affiliations. By the mid-nineteenth century, elaborate systems of publicly and privately financed and run hospitals—some of them devoted to primary care and others to specialized medicine—were common in most European countries, as well as in colonies and nations settled by Europeans in the Americas and elsewhere.

Whether they were seeing a doctor or being treated in a hospital, patients usually had to pay their own way, though costs were subsidized in the sense that the facilities received, as noted above, financial support from governments, philanthropists, and philanthropic organizations, both secular and religious. In the eighteenth century, however, mutual aid societies emerged as the forerunners to modern private health insurance companies. Self-organized, usually by members of similar professions, these societies provided funds to members to pay for medical treatment, though most of the money raised was disbursed for death and survivor benefits.

Germany, under the autocratic but modernizing Otto von Bismarck, developed the first national health insurance system. The Health Insurance Act of 1883—which at first largely covered low-income workers and government employees but was later expanded to the entire population—was compulsory, paid for by both employers and provided benefits-in-kind, or vouchers, to patients.

In the first half of the twentieth century, such schemes spread to other European countries, though they remained modest in scope. At the same time, a private health insurance industry also evolved, much of it organized on a nonprofit basis. For example, the Blue Cross and Blue Shield network of insurance providers—the former organized by hospitals and the latter to pay physicians—were founded in the United States in 1938 and 1939, respectively.

Not until the post–World War II era did public health-care programs in Europe and in other parts of the industrialized world develop, spurred on by new views of the role of government in providing for the welfare of citizens and by the revenues generated by booming postwar economies. Although the programs varied widely among countries—some were totally government-run and -financed, and others relied on private insurance providers—they shared some common traits, including government subsidization of health-care costs and the requirement of universal coverage. Among industrialized countries, the United States remained an outlier, by not developing a universal government program—Medicare and Medicaid—until 1965 and then only for seniors over age 65 and the indigent.

Outside the industrialized West, communist states established fully government-owned-and-operated health-care systems of varying quality. Many of these systems went into serious decline after the collapse of Eastern European communist regimes and then the Soviet Union in the late 1980s and early 1990s. Although some developing-world countries introduced public health-care coverage for government workers, the rest of the population was required to buy insurance from private providers, if they even existed, or pay for medical care out-of-pocket.

Meanwhile, after the conclusion of World War II, an unprecedented expansion occurred in medical knowledge, new medical treatments, new medical infrastructure, and new ranks of primary-care and specialized medical professionals. The end result was vastly improved health indicators, though some of this progress was achieved by public-health measures dating from the first half of the twentieth century. Especially in the developed world, life expectancy increased; infant, child, and maternal mortality rates steadily declined; and morbidity and mortality rates from communicable diseases dropped precipitously. Some of these benefits came to the developing world as well, but to a much more limited extent, usually among wealthier, urban residents.

Although all these advances led to dramatic quality-of-life gains for most people in the developed world, they came with problems, most notably, increasing costs. New treatments, facilities, equipment, and professionals were expensive. But few governments, for political reasons, were willing to ration care, and few individuals were willing to forgo treatments, at least until costs began spiraling upward at the end of the century. At the same time, as noted earlier, improved health care and medicine increased lifespans, which, in turn, led to other problems. First, a larger population of elderly meant that more people suffered from the chronic diseases of old age that are costly to treat. Second, a larger cohort of post-retirement elderly reduced the proportion of those in the workforce and thus of those paying the taxes that government contributes to cover health care costs.

Issues

As mentioned earlier, the two fundamental unresolved in issues health care are access and cost. They are related because people who cannot afford health care are, effectively, denied access to it, and a lack of health-care facilities and professionals is often related to an inability to finance their costs.

Access

The issue of access to health care has two basic aspects—one more associated with the developing world and the other with the developed world. First, basic health-care services are often in short supply in poorer countries for several reasons, though most come down to financing. Many developing-world governments have devoted a disproportionate share of their limited health-care budget to the building of sophisticated, Western-style hospitals in their capitals, shortchanging the kinds of rural and urban primary clinics that would provide far more access for the kinds of basic medical services needed by a country's impoverished working class and peasantry. These countries often suffer from an extremely unequal distribution of wealth, which means that few of their citizens have the financial resources to access medical facilities or professionals of any kind.

Corruption often starves government budgets generally and their health-care budgets specifically, through tax evasion or embezzlement. The phenomenon of "brain drain," in which a developing country's skilled and educated classes emigrate to the developed world for reasons of personal and financial security, often deprives poorer countries of many active and potential health-care professionals, even as most of the money invested in their education and training accrues to the developed countries where they settle. Most important is the matter of poverty; countries that lack adequate wealth are, in the vast majority of cases, the ones that are unable to afford a decent health-care system. An inadequate health-care system leads almost inevitably to poor health outcomes, as the table of basic health indicators reveals. (Other factors matter as well, such as diet and nutrition, alcohol and tobacco consumption, and environmental factors.)

Aside from the poorer quality of life enumerated by such health indicators and the untold suffering and sorrow a lack of adequate health care brings to the sick and the injured and their loved ones, the poor health that results from an inadequate health-care system limits economic growth. Simply put, sick people, and the loved ones who miss work to care for them, are less productive. The result is a vicious

Health-Care Spending per Capita and Selected Health Indices, by Country Income Level, 2008–2009

Country income level (annual, per capita)	Per capita health-care spending (2008)*	Neonatal mortality rate, per 1,000 live births (2009)	Life expectancy at birth (2009)
Low (under $1,000)	$74	36	57
Middle ($1,000–$4,000)	$197	26	68
Upper middle ($4,000–$12,000)	$830	11	71
High (over $12,000)	$4,246	4	80

* At purchasing power parity, which takes into account that many goods and services in poorer countries cost less than they do in richer countries.

Source: World Health Organization.

cycle of poverty and ill health, as lower productivity means less revenue and capital accumulation available to invest in health-care infrastructure.

Most experts agree that breaking this cycle requires a comprehensive approach, combining more appropriate spending priorities—such as a concentration on a health-care infrastructure that is locally based and emphasizes primary care—more aid from the developed-world governments and philanthropic organizations and a renewed promotion of public-health measures, particularly in the areas of preventive medicine (e.g., more vaccines), improved environmental factors (such as switching from wood-burning stoves, which cause many respiratory illnesses, to gas stoves), and education of the public in the basic hygiene measures they can take for themselves, such as regular hand washing.

For developed-world countries, the problem is somewhat different. Most high-income countries have sufficient primary-care facilities and professionals to ensure that all people have access to health care, barring financial obstacles, discussed below. But problems sometimes arise at the secondary and, particularly, the tertiary levels. In order to keep spending in check, many developed countries have set up policies that either limit the number of secondary- and tertiary-level professionals and facilities or provide incentives for medical providers to emphasize primary care, as this is the most cost-effective form of health care and the type that affects most people. But limiting secondary and tertiary care can result in rationing, in which patients with conditions that are not immediately life threatening are required to wait to receive treatment. Because diagnostic medicine is not always an exact science, those who ration the care are liable to commit errors in calculating when a treatment is immediately necessary, which can lead to further health complications and even death for the person forced to delay treatment.

Because it lacks guaranteed universal coverage, the United States has unique health-care access problems. Although the country has one of the most sophisticated and extensive health-care systems, roughly 50 million people—or one in six Americans—lack health insurance and so do not have regular access to it. This lack of access, or rather, lack of insurance to pay for it, causes many to forgo the preventive measures that could both alleviate future suffering and health complications and are more cost-effective than treatment.

Americans by and large obtain health insurance through their employer, which means that if they lose their jobs, change jobs, are self-employed, or work for an employer that does not provide it, they do not have coverage. Although many of these people, particularly those who are young and healthy, choose not to buy insurance, many others cannot afford the premiums. The problem becomes most acute for those with pre-existing conditions, who, by definition, are most in need of health insurance. Private insurers prefer not to insure such people and typically refuse to do so for those who seek it after they are diagnosed with a serious illness. Offering coverage to such people would upset the actuarial calculations that keep the insurers profitable. That is, insurance companies collect premiums from healthy people and make payments to sick ones. If their customer base starts tilting too heavily toward sick people, they might find that the economics of their payments make it difficult to stay in business.

To help solve this problem, the administration of President Barack Obama instituted major health-care reform in 2010 through the Patient Protection and Affordable Care Act. The complicated bill had many components. The two most important were a requirement that insurers provide coverage to individuals with pre-existing medical conditions and, to untie the Gordian knot of actuarial imbalance, a mandate that most uninsured Americans—sick and healthy alike—

buy health insurance, with subsidies for those who could least afford it. The mandate component of the law proved the most controversial politically, particularly with conservatives, who argued that requiring Americans to buy a product was an unprecedented expansion of government power and intrusion into the decision making of private citizens. They argued that lifting regulations on health care and health insurance, and allowing market forces more play, would make health insurance more affordable, thus allowing more people access to insurance and the health-care system. Many on the Left were critical of the law, too, saying that the government would be better served by eliminating private insurers altogether, and, thus, the actuarial problems outlined above, and simply expand the existing government-administered Medicare program for the aged to all Americans.

Costs

In developing-world countries, the problem is more about access than cost. Most care in such countries is already so minimal and low cost as to resist cost-cutting initiatives. The problem there is simply that the vast majority of people are poor and lack health insurance, thus putting even the most basic care out of their financial reach. Some steps have been taken to lower health-care costs. First among them have been initiatives to lift or modify the patent restrictions on critical drugs held by developed-world pharmaceutical companies so that those drugs, notably vaccines and treatments for AIDS, can be manufactured and sold less expensively as generics by companies based in developing countries.

In developed-world countries where the health-care infrastructure is extensive and where most, if not all, people are covered by some form of insurance—the United States being the sole exception—the cost problem is more acute. These countries, which guarantee universal or near-universal coverage, provide such coverage through various programs. In Britain, for example, the government not only pays for health care directly but hires most of the country's health-care professionals directly and owns most health-care facilities. In Canada, health care is provided by non-governmental organizations but is paid for directly by the government. In many continental European countries, such as the Netherlands, highly regulated and noncompetitive, nonprofit health insurance providers pay the bills, with the government dictating what they cover, whom they cover, and what the costs

of various procedures are. In most of these countries, more affluent people can buy special coverage for amenities, like access to private doctors or private rooms in hospitals.

Regardless of how it is paid for, health care in the developed world is inherently expensive for several reasons. It is labor intensive, requires costly equipment that is constantly being improved at great expense, is often resistant to economies of scale, and is subject to economically irrational human psychology. That is, when it comes to their own health care or that of their loved ones, many people are unwilling to consider cost, regardless of the likelihood that a particular treatment will have a successful outcome. This is especially true when the costs of elaborate and expensive treatment regimens are met or subsidized by private or government health-care insurers or providers.

Various health-care systems have developed different tactics and strategies to bring down such costs. An emphasis on preventive care, which is far more cost-effective than treatment, has become an increasing focus of most developed world health-care systems. Education about healthy lifestyle choices, as well as taxes on consumer goods that have a negative impact on health, such as cigarettes and even soda, can help alleviate some of the chronic conditions, such as obesity and those associated with smoking, that drive up health-care costs. Another means of saving on cost has been the development of new health-care facilities and classes of professionals who provide effective primary care at lower expense than traditional doctors and hospitals. New treatment regimens that emphasize in-home care rather than hospital care have offered more cost-effective provision of care, as have advances in relatively inexpensive pharmaceuticals that make more expensive and invasive procedures unnecessary. Technology has provided yet another path for bringing down health-care costs by allowing for better record keeping and communication among health-care professionals in order to avoid duplication of services.

All the above initiatives—except the privacy issues associated with advancements in record keeping and communication technology, and perhaps certain forms of taxation—have come with relatively little controversy. This is not the case with rationing, in which all health-care systems have to engage to some degree because no country has unlimited health-care resources. Rationing involves several critical and politically fraught questions: Where should health-

Health-Care Expenditure and Selected Health Outcomes of Four High-Income Countries, 2008–2009

Country	Health-care expenditures as percentage of GDP (2008)	Life expectancy at birth (2009)	Neonatal mortality rate, per 1,000 live births (2009)
Canada	9.8	81	4
Netherlands	9.9	81	3
United Kingdom	8.7	80	3
United States	15.2	79	4

Source: World Health Organization.

care money be spent? Who is entitled to particularly expensive procedures? Who gets priority in treatment when facilities and professionals are in short supply? And who makes these decisions? Such questions are particularly acute when it comes to the elderly. For many reasons, the elderly require more—and often more expensive—health care, which sometimes involves highly costly, in-patient, end-of-life care. Should such care be provided without regard to cost? Does such care starve the system of resources to treat other people? Who has the right to decide when end-of-life care is not warranted and thus should be limited? For Americans debating the future of their health insurance system, there is an additional question: Should rationing decisions be made by government or by health insurance staff?

Because it lacks universal coverage, and had looser regulation of the private health insurance market, the United States faces unique cost problems of its own, as shown by the fact that it spends far more on health care, with no better health outcomes, than other developed countries. As noted earlier, people who lack insurance often forgo more cost-effective preventive treatment only to require costly interventions later on. Moreover, as the law requires hospitals to provide emergency care, often the most expensive kind of care, individuals who have forgone preventive health measures and develop acute conditions show up in emergency rooms, driving up health-care costs.

The U.S. health insurance system has several major built-in cost-control problems of its own. The first is that care is typically paid for on a procedure-by-procedure basis—even in the government-run Medicare program—that gives health providers an incentive to order more treatments. A corollary problem is that many providers order procedures of questionable necessity in order to be sure that they are not later found liable for a patient's worsening condition or death and thus subject to expensive lawsuits. The second problem is that, with the existence of a

multitude of for-profit insurance providers, secondary costs such as advertising, marketing, profit, and administration take up a disproportionate amount of health-care spending. It is estimated, for example, that Medicare's secondary costs add 3 percent to health-care costs, while those of private insurers add up to as much as 10 times that, depending on how the calculations are made. Since the end of World War II, many efforts have been made to address both the accessibility and cost problems associated with the U.S. health-care system, the most recent being the 2010 Patient Protection and Affordable Care Act.

The Future

In coming years, say experts, health-care systems around the world will continue to face many of the same problems that confront them today. In the developing world, the problem will continue to be access—that is, insufficient health-care infrastructure as well as insufficient personnel and professionals to staff it. Some hopeful signs have emerged in that many governments and nongovernmental organizations have recognized the need for basic primary care as opposed to expensive and limited Western-style care, as well as the economic and social benefits that accrue to countries with a competent and comprehensive health-care system. In addition, rapid economic growth should provide the revenues that both governments and individual citizens need to pay for health care.

In the developed world, with sophisticated and comprehensive health-care systems already in place, the ongoing problem will remain costs, which continue to advance at a rate outpacing general inflation in many countries. Exacerbating this situation are the aging populations characteristic of these countries. An aging population means proportionately fewer people in the workforce to pay for universal health care. That is why most developed-world countries—with varying degrees of seriousness and success—are actively seeking ways to rein in health-care costs in the future.

James Ciment

See also: Mental Health; Pharmaceuticals: Availability, Cost, Efficacy, and Safety; Public Health; Vaccination.

Further Reading

Bennett, Sara, Lucy Gibson, and Anne Mills, eds. *Health, Economic Development and Household Poverty: From Understanding to Action.* New York: Routledge, 2008.

Blank, Robert H., and Viola Burau. *Comparative Health Policy.* New York: Palgrave Macmillan, 2010.

Burns, Lawton R., et al. *The Health Care Value Chain: Producers, Purchasers, and Providers.* San Francisco: Jossey-Bass, 2002.

Flessa, Steffen. *Costing of Health Care Services in Developing Countries: A Prerequisite for Affordability, Sustainability and Efficiency.* New York: Peter Lang, 2009.

Fogel, Robert William. *The Escape from Hunger and Premature Death, 1700–2100: Europe, America, and the Third World.* New York: Cambridge University Press, 2004.

Mackintosh, Maureen, and Meri Koivusalo, eds. *Commercialization of Health Care: Global and Local Dynamics and Policy Responses.* New York: Palgrave Macmillan, 2005.

McPake, Barbara, and Charles Normand. *Health Economics: An International Perspective.* New York: Routledge, 2008.

Musgrove, Philip, ed. *Health Economics in Development.* Washington, DC: World Bank, 2004.

Navarro, Vicente, ed. *The Political and Social Contexts of Health.* Amityville, NY: Baywood, 2004.

Webster, Charles, ed. *Caring for Health: History and Diversity.* 3d ed. Philadelphia: Open University, 2001.

Web Sites

Global Health Council: www.globalhealth.org
World Health Organization, Health Systems Financing: www.who.int/healthsystems/topics/financing/en

Documents

Document 1: Hippocratic Oath, Ancient Greece, Late Fifth Century B.C.E.

Believed to have been written by the fifth-century B.C.E. Greek physician Hippocrates, considered by many to be the father of Western medicine, the Hippocratic Oath is still recited, though in many variations, by physicians around the world to the present day. The oath commits healers to educating others, empathizing with their patients, and keeping the conditions of their patients in confidence. Its most famous passage, to "never do harm to anyone," commits the physician to take the utmost care in treating patients, still the hallmark of professional health-care providers.

I swear by Apollo, the healer, Asclepius, Hygieia, and Panacea, and I take to witness all the gods, all the goddesses, to keep according to my ability and my judgment, the following Oath and agreement:

To consider dear to me, as my parents, him who taught me this art; to live in common with him and, if necessary, to share my goods with him; To look upon his children as my own brothers, to teach them this art; and that by my teaching, I will impart a knowledge of this art to my own sons, and to my teacher's sons, and to disciples bound by an indenture and oath according to the medical laws, and no others.

I will prescribe regimens for the good of my patients according to my ability and my judgment and never do harm to anyone.

I will give no deadly medicine to any one if asked, nor suggest any such counsel; and similarly I will not give a woman a pessary to cause an abortion.

But I will preserve the purity of my life and my arts.

I will not cut for stone, even for patients in whom the disease is manifest; I will leave this operation to be performed by practitioners, specialists in this art.

In every house where I come I will enter only for the good of my patients, keeping myself far from all intentional ill-doing and all seduction and especially from the pleasures of love with women or with men, be they free or slaves.

All that may come to my knowledge in the exercise of my profession or in daily commerce with men, which ought not to be spread abroad, I will keep secret and will never reveal.

If I keep this oath faithfully, may I enjoy my life and practice my art, respected by all humanity and in all times; but if I transgress from it or violate it, may the reverse be my life.

Source: National Library of Medicine, National Institutes of Health.

Document 2: Proposals for a National Health Service, Minister of Health Aneurin Bevin, United Kingdom, 1945

On July 5, 1945, British voters ousted Winston Churchill and the Conservative Party from power, despite their success in leading the country to victory over the Nazis in World

War II. One of the reasons for the change in power was the Labour Party promise to build a comprehensive welfare state once peace returned. Like many European countries in the decades after World War II, Britain opted for universal, government-guaranteed and -subsidized health insurance. With the National Health Service, inaugurated in 1948, the British went even further, putting most of the nation's health-care system itself in government hands. The text linked below is a December 1945 memorandum by Health Minister Aneurin Bevin, the chief architect of the National Health Service, that outlines the proposed health-care system to the cabinet of Prime Minister Clement Attlee.

www.sochealth.co.uk/history/Bevan/nhsprop.htm

Source: Socialist Health Association.

HEPATITIS

Hepatitis is an inflammation of the liver that is generally caused by a virus, but can also be triggered by toxins within the body or by other medical conditions. The symptoms of hepatitis may include abdominal discomfort, dizziness, jaundice, loss of appetite, nausea, and weakness, though it is also possible for the condition to be entirely asymptomatic. Hepatitis can be acute (lasting less than six months) or chronic, and is potentially fatal, particularly if left untreated. It can cause cirrhosis, coma, kidney failure, and internal bleeding, and can also contribute to other medical conditions, including AIDS, cancer, and pneumonia.

The viruses responsible for most cases of hepatitis are highly contagious—some of them 50 to 100 times more so than the HIV virus that causes AIDS. The condition represents a serious global health threat; more than 2.5 billion people worldwide have some form of hepatitis, and more than 1 million of them die from it annually.

History

Hepatitis has been present in human populations for millennia. It is mentioned in texts from both Mesopotamia and ancient Egypt. The ancient Greeks wrote extensively about the condition; it was they—specifically the physician Hippocrates—who first postulated that hepatitis was contagious. The Bible also appears to reference the condition; the illness experienced by the entire nation of Israel after consuming contaminated quail eggs, recounted in Numbers 11:32–33, was likely viral hepatitis.

Despite the insights of the Greeks, physicians and scientists paid hepatitis little notice for thousands of years. It was understood as a symptom of other conditions, and not as a condition unto itself. As such, no more effort was given to understanding the causes of hepatitis than was paid to understanding the causes of broken arms, or runny noses, or dizziness. Individuals who succumbed to hepatitis might have their cause of death listed as "alcoholism," "cirrhosis," "liver trouble," or "obstruction of the bile duct."

Given the manner in which hepatitis was understood, and the fact that it was consistently misidentified, there are no data available for judging the extent of the disease in past centuries. Certainly it was commonplace, but documentation of widespread epidemics does not come until the seventeenth and eighteenth centuries, when Australia, China, France, Sweden, the United Kingdom, and the United States were all victimized at various times.

Despite these incidents, hepatitis continued to be regarded as a symptom of other diseases, and so progress toward the modern understanding of the condition did not occur until relatively late. In 1883, in Bremen, Germany, 15 percent of 1,289 shipyard workers who were inoculated with a smallpox vaccine fell ill and were stricken with jaundice. A German physician who identified himself only as A. Lurman speculated that their "serum hepatitis" must have been caused by something within the vaccine. He did not know what that might be, however.

In 1908, the Scottish physician Stuart McDonald built upon Lurman's work. He examined several patients suffering from jaundice, and concluded that their condition—which he called "acute yellow atrophy"—was produced "when some special virus acts on a previously damaged liver." Though McDonald was unable to identify this special virus, he became the first modern physician to hypothesize that hepatitis might be a distinct condition with its own root cause. In the next decade, most physicians fell in line behind McDonald as they witnessed frequent hepatitis epidemics among the soldiers of World War I.

From that point forward, scientists searched actively for the virus that caused hepatitis. And after 1947, when the British physician F.O. MacCallum persuasively argued that there were two different variants of hepatitis (which he called hepatitis A and hepatitis B), scientists searched for two viruses. Hepa-

Variants of Viral Hepatitis

	A	B	C	D	E
Primary mode of transmission	Unclean food/water	Infected bodily fluids, usually blood	Infected bodily fluids, usually blood	Infected bodily fluids, usually blood, coupled with infection by hepatitis B variant	Unclean food/water
Vaccine exists	Yes	Yes	No	No, but can be prevented with variant B vaccination	Yes, but not widely available
Pharmaceutical cure exists	No	No	Yes	No	No
Possibly chronic	No	Yes	Yes	Yes	Yes

Source: World Health Organization.

titis B was the first of these to be isolated, in 1963, while hepatitis A was identified a decade later.

By the time hepatitis A had been isolated, the consensus was that there were several additional variants of the virus that MacCallum had not recognized. Hepatitis D was subsequently identified in 1977, while the variant that was originally called "non-A non-B hepatitis" was isolated in 1988 and labeled hepatitis C. In between those discoveries, in 1983, hepatitis E joined the list. Currently, scientists are debating whether certain rare reported variants of the virus actually exist, and if they should be labeled as hepatitis F and hepatitis G.

Types

The vast majority of hepatitis cases are caused by one of the five viruses that scientists have identified. There are substantial differences between the different types of viral hepatitis, however.

Some types of hepatitis (A and E) are transmitted through contaminated water or food, while the others (B, C, and D) result from exposure to infected body fluids, usually blood. Most variants (A, B, D, and E) can be prevented with vaccines, but hepatitis C—one of the most harmful forms of the virus—cannot, at least at present. Hepatitis B and C are the most common variants, and the most likely to be chronic. Hepatitis A and E are much less common, while Hepatitis D infections are rarest of all, as they only occur in individuals who have already contracted hepatitis B.

Besides these viruses, there are several other ways in which a person may develop hepatitis. Excessive consumption of ethanol, which is present in alcoholic beverages, can inflame the liver and cause alcoholic hepatitis. This condition is distinct from cirrhosis (scarring of the liver), though alcoholic hepatitis often leads to cirrhosis, particularly when it is paired with a hepatitis C infection.

Drugs can also trigger nonviral hepatitis, particularly agomelatine and amitriptyline (antidepressants), isoniazid and pyrazinamide (antibiotics), methyldopa and nifedipine (antihypertensives) and, most commonly, the pain reliever acetaminophen, found in Tylenol (as Tylenol is the world's most widely used drug, it is among the most likely to be overused and so to become toxic in the liver). In addition, there are several toxins known to cause hepatitis, including carbon tetrachloride, chloroform, mushrooms that contain anatoxin, and white phosphorous.

Metabolic disorders are yet another cause of nonviral hepatitis. The most common of these is nonalcoholic steatohepatitis (NASH), wherein fat accumulates in the liver for reasons that are currently not well understood. Hemochromatosis and Wilson's Disease, which respectively cause iron and copper to build up in the liver, can also lead to hepatitis.

A Global Issue

In the world's most developed nations, relatively little attention is paid to hepatitis by itself. Vaccinations against the variants of the disease that respond to immunization are currently near-universal, and the most common causes of outbreaks in the developed world—unclean needles, unprotected sex—are linked to other, broader social ills. Hepatitis is not wholly ignored, of course, and the search for better vaccines and treatments is ongoing. There is also some

A Chinese student receives the hepatitis B vaccine. With an estimated one-third of the world's hepatitis B sufferers, China has been conducting a massive child immunization program in the poorer provinces. One problem has been the reuse of unsterilized needles. *(Imaginechina via AP Images)*

small risk of a hepatitis resurgence, as an increasing number of parents decline vaccines for political or philosophical reasons. At present, however, few developed nations would list hepatitis among their most grave public health concerns.

The same cannot be said of many less developed nations, where vaccination is less common and hepatitis is often epidemic. While all variants of hepatitis are a concern, hepatitis B, C, and E pose the biggest threats.

Hepatitis B is the most serious form of the virus. More than 2 billion people worldwide suffer from this variant, and in 350 million of those individuals the condition is chronic. An estimated 600,000 people die each year from hepatitis B.

The hepatitis B virus is most problematic in Asia; China alone has fully one-third of the world's hepatitis B sufferers, amounting to roughly 10 percent of the nation's population. The virus is also quite prevalent in the Amazon Basin and in Eastern Europe, affecting approximately 8 percent of the people there. By contrast, less than 1 percent of the population of Western Europe and North America is afflicted with hepatitis B.

Hepatitis C is less common than hepatitis B, but still epidemic in many parts of the world, particularly North Africa and Asia. Approximately 150 million people worldwide have chronic hepatitis C infections, and 350,000 of those will die annually.

Though there is no vaccine for hepatitis C, there are effective cures, most notably the drug ribavirin in combination with interferon. Unfortunately, the treatment is too expensive for many citizens of underdeveloped nations. Further, hepatitis C often does not manifest symptoms until it is quite advanced, by which time drugs can be ineffective. These two factors account for the majority of the hundreds of thousands of deaths that occur from a hepatitis variant that is considered to be highly treatable.

Of the three most troublesome hepatitis viruses, the E variant is the least understood. At least 80 million people are infected worldwide, with concentrations in Africa, Asia, and Mexico. More than 160,000 sufferers perish each year.

What makes hepatitis E particularly nefarious is that its symptoms are nearly identical to those of the far less dangerous hepatitis A. Sophisticated blood tests are generally required to distinguish between the two, which means that many cases of hepatitis E are misclassified as hepatitis A. Further, while vaccines for hepatitis E have been developed, they are quite new, very expensive, and not widely available.

Combating the Disease

The substantial differences between variants of hepatitis dictate that efforts to combat the condition must focus on several fronts. The best way to reduce the incidence of hepatitis A and B/D is through vaccination. With the World Health Organization (WHO) taking the lead, there has been considerable progress on this front. Only 31 countries vaccinated against hepatitis in 1992; today the number exceeds 170.

More than 1 billion doses of hepatitis vaccines have been administered worldwide. The nations that suffer most from hepatitis B are those that have not yet found the resources to vaccinate their populations. In China, for example, only 20 percent of children have received immunizations.

The primary strategies for fighting hepatitis C focus on reducing exposure to infected bodily fluids. This means establishing blood screening programs, making certain that needles and other medical equipment are either new or properly sterilized, and encouraging the use of condoms. Addressing hepatitis C therefore requires tackling some very broad and far-ranging social issues. Indeed, these strategies are much the same as those being used in the effort to reduce AIDS. This is unsurprising, since AIDS and hepatitis C have similar causes and tend to be present among the same populations. However, while AIDS is in decline worldwide, hepatitis C remains stable, and may possibly be growing more prevalent. Some virologists predict that hepatitis C cases will outpace AIDS cases by the year 2020.

Hepatitis E presently has no cure, nor is there a cost-effective vaccine. As such, activists must focus on its root causes. Since hepatitis E is—like hepatitis A—caused by contaminated food and water, reducing its prevalence requires hygiene campaigns, the adoption of strict standards for public water supplies, food safety inspections, and proper disposal of waste.

As with hepatitis C, confronting hepatitis E means engaging with some exceedingly large and complex problems that go far beyond a single disease or condition. Unsurprisingly, progress has been slow.

The Future

Today, much effort is being expended in order to find affordable vaccines and treatments for the various types of hepatitis. In May 2011, for example, two new drugs for the treatment of Hepatitis C—boceprevir and telaprevir—were introduced in the United States. At least six others, notably an experimental drug known as BMS-790052, were under development. Similarly, several trials of vaccines for hepatitis E were under way, as were trials of drug treatments for hepatitis B.

In May 2010, the World Health Assembly—the decision-making arm of WHO—adopted resolution WHA63.18, which calls for the prevention and control of hepatitis worldwide. At the same time, July 28 was designated as World Hepatitis Day, in hopes of propagating information about the condition worldwide. Undoubtedly, WHO will continue to take a leading role in combating hepatitis.

Christopher Bates

See also: Gastrointestinal Disease; Public Health; Sexually Transmitted Infections; Vaccination.

Further Reading

Blumberg, Baruch S. *Hepatitis B: The Hunt for a Killer Virus.* Princeton, NJ: Princeton University Press, 2003.

Chow, James H., and Cheryl Chow. *The Encyclopedia of Hepatitis and Other Liver Diseases.* New York: Facts On File, 2006.

Dolan, Matthew. *The Hepatitis C Handbook.* Berkeley, CA: North Atlantic Books, 1999.

Garrett, Laurie. *The Coming Plague: Newly Emerging Diseases in a World Out of Balance.* New York: Penguin, 1995.

Koff, Raymond S. *Hepatitis Essentials.* Boston: Jones & Bartlett Learning, 2011.

Plotkin, Stanley A. *Mass Vaccination: Global Aspects— Progress and Obstacles.* New York: Springer, 2010.

Thomas, Howard, Stanley Lemon, and Arie Zuckerman, eds. *Viral Hepatitis.* Malden, MA: Blackwell, 2005.

Worman, Howard. *The Liver Disorders and Hepatitis Sourcebook.* New York: McGraw-Hill, 2006.

Web Sites

Centers for Disease Control: www.cdc.gov/hepatitis

Hepatitis Central: www.hepatitis-central.com

Hepatitis Foundation International: www.hepfi.org

National Alliance of State and Territorial AIDS Directors: www.hepprograms.org

U.S. National Library of Medicine: www.ncbi.nlm.nih.gov

World Health Organization: www.who.int/topics/hepatitis/en

World Hepatitis Alliance: www.worldhepatitisalliance.org/Home.aspx

Documents

Document 1: "Observations on the Hepatic State of Fever," George Logan, 1802

George Logan was a professor of medicine at the University of Pennsylvania, home to one of the world's first medical schools. His 1801 essay on hepatitis, which was wholly in line with the medical thinking of the day, shows how poorly the condition was understood prior to the twentieth century.

The remote causes of hepatic fever, are precisely the same which produce yellow fever, dysentery, cholera, and other forms of bilious fever. The following are the most uniform.

1st. Excess of heat.

2nd. Marsh miasmata [humid air], the influence of these destructive agents (it is a well authenticated fact) are not confined to the human species alone. The appearance of diseased livers in cattle which are killed during the summer and autumn, is so frequent, that there are few butchers who cannot bear testimony of it; their baneful effects are also exerted on a genus of animals still more remotely allied to man; this is remarkably the case in the East Indies, and particularly excited the notice of Dr. Pennent, who observes, that "the English foolishly enough, import into Bengal at a vast expence [sic] packs of grey hounds, which are soon worn out by the climate: they are landed in good health, but in about a month die of the liver complaint."

3d. Intemperance in eating and drinking, especially the frequent and excessive potation of spirituous liquors; this is the common remote cause of gout, mania, hepatitis and innumerable evils. There are few persons who become attached to strong drink before the meridian of life; hence perhaps its more frequent occurrence at that period. While considering this destructive agent, I shall take the liberty of quoting the explanation of the Fable of Prometheus, which the celebrated and ingenious Dr. Darwin has offered! "Prometheus was represented as stealing fire from heaven, which might well represent the inflammable spirit produced by fermentation, which may be said to animate the man of clay, whence conquests of Bacchus as well as the temporary mirth and noise of his devotees; but the after punishment of those who steal this accused fire, is a vulture gnawing the liver, which well allegorizes the poor inebriate, lingering for years under painful hepatic disease."

4th. Vicissitudes of temperature.

5th. Passions of the mind.

6th. Violent exercise. Dr. Clark, in treating of the diseases on the coast of Coromandel [in New Zealand], observes that among the Europeans who undergo much fatigue, and particularly, amongst the military: hepatitis, obstructions and swelling of the liver, were the most common diseases.

7th. Repelled eruptions. [Boils or pimples on the skin]

8th. Bad water.

Source: U.S. National Library of Medicine.

Document 2: World Hepatitis Day Message, Samlee Plianbangchang, 2011

As part of its efforts to combat hepatitis worldwide, the World Health Organization (WHO) declared July 28, 2010, to be the first World Hepatitis Day. On that occasion, Samlee Plianbangchang—WHO Regional Director for Southeast Asia—issued this statement outlining the extent and nature of the threat.

Viral hepatitis kills more people than any other communicable disease in the South-East Asia Region. In the next 10 years, over five million people in the region [are] projected to die from this disease and its consequences.

Today, more than 130 million people in South-East Asia alone, carry the hepatitis B or C virus, even though they may appear healthy. It usually strikes people at their most productive age.

The hepatitis B virus is 50 to 100 times more infectious than HIV, and just as lethal. Hepatitis E results in 2,700 stillbirths every year. For such a major public health threat, hepatitis has a low profile, among policy-makers and the public.

Recognising hepatitis as a threat to public health, the World Health Assembly passed a resolution to prevent and control the disease last year. The World Health Organization has decided to observe July 28 this year as the world's first ever World Hepatitis Day.

It is thus an opportune time to ask if we are doing enough to protect ourselves from this disease? . . .

WHO is developing guidelines, strategies and tools for surveillance, prevention and control of this disease. Prevention and focussing on the source and mode of spread of the virus, is crucial to control this disease.

Chronic hepatitis B and C are among the leading causes of preventable deaths in 11 countries of the region. About 100 million hepatitis B carriers, and 30 million hepatitis C carriers, live in South-East Asia.

However, about 60 percent of the infected are unaware of their status until the disease manifests as cirrhosis or liver cancer—an aggressive cancer without a cure. Hepatitis C, in particular, has no vaccine or effective cure. Those who undergo blood transfusion, as well as injecting drug users, are at risk.

Due to lack of knowledge and resources among health-care workers, many providers in the region do not comply with WHO's and national guidelines and recommendations for hepatitis B and C screening, prevention, treatment and follow-up services. A patient requiring transfusion may receive blood that has been screened for HIV, but not for hepatitis B or C.

The hepatitis B vaccine can go a long way to prevent hepatitis B. It is more than 95 percent effective in preventing infections and their chronic consequences, and is the first vaccine that protects against a major human cancer. In WHO's South-Asia Region, more than 130 million infants have received the three required doses of hepatitis B vaccine.

Hepatitis infection is also linked to personal hygiene, sanitation and urban health—hepatitis A and E are both commonly spread through eating or drinking contaminated food or water. Pregnant women are at high risk of hepatitis E. Hepatitis E acquired during pregnancy is also associated with prematurity, low birth weight and an increased risk of perinatal mortality.

In countries of WHO's South-East Asia Region, more than 6.5 million people are infected with hepatitis E annually accounting for half the cases worldwide, leading to an estimated 160,000 deaths.

Hepatitis E outbreaks often occur in urban areas when leaky underground water pipes are contaminated with sewage. In developing countries, with increasing population pressure and rapid urbanisation leading to people living in close, unsanitary conditions, such diseases are likely to increase rapidly.

So what can be done to prevent and control hepatitis?

To begin with, all countries, especially those urbanising rapidly, need to make hepatitis a health priority. Lives could be saved through simple preventive measures such as hand washing, eating cooked food and boiled water, using condoms and not sharing needles.

Countries need to make screening of all blood and blood products for hepatitis B and C mandatory. Governments should ensure that children are adequately immunised against hepatitis B. Healthcare workers, and the public, need to be educated on the risks and the surveillance system for hepatitis needs to be strengthened.

Unless we act now to create greater awareness among policymakers, healthcare workers, and the public, viral hepatitis will remain a major public health threat.

Source: World Health Organization.

HOMELESSNESS

"Homelessness" refers to much more than the situation of individuals who find themselves without an adequate place of residence. The standard legal definitions of homelessness (such as those found in the United States Code, Title 42, Chapter 119) overlook the conditions of detachment or separation from mainstream society that characterize many homeless people around the world. Whether identified as "living rough" in the United Kingdom, "street people" in the United States, "floating people" or *furosha* in Japan, "beggar tramps" or *gepeng* in Indonesia, "without shade" or *sans-abri* in France, or "without a roof" or *sin techo* in Latin America, the homeless are typically people whom mainstream society would prefer not to see.

Although homeless people are often detached from the mainstream of society, they are far from antisocial. Homeless people everywhere have their own sets of skills, specialized knowledge, and codes of behavior, which help them survive and cope with the adverse conditions under which they live. Nevertheless, most members of mainstream society who encounter homeless men and women neither understand nor appreciate the root causes of homelessness, the intelligence and resourcefulness of the homeless community, and the daily struggles for survival on the street. It may be a cliché to say that homeless individuals are just like any one of us—perhaps just unluckier, or victims of forces beyond their control—but there is much truth to the cliché.

Due to varying definitions and methods of enumeration, it is difficult to determine even approximate numbers of homeless people worldwide. What constitutes homelessness in one country, based on assessments of housing inadequacy, might not be defined as homelessness in another country. For instance, millions of people in Mumbai and Calcutta sleep on the streets, often in crude shelters of bamboo and tarpaulin, but do not consider themselves "homeless," because they belong to street communities that have lived this way for decades. As a result, the population estimates of homeless people in the world today range between 100 million and 1 billion. Even in the United States, where organizations as diverse as the U.S. Bureau of the Census, National Law Center on Homelessness and Poverty, and National Coalition for the Homeless all seek to enumerate the homeless, there is no clear consensus. The current estimates of homeless people in the United States vary from 500,000 to 2.5 million.

Categories and Causes

There have been itinerant individuals without permanent fixed residences since the dawn of humanity, but the first historical references to homelessness come primarily from the sacred texts of the major religions—including Judaism, Hinduism, Buddhism, Christianity, and Islam—which mention wandering strangers, beggars, and seekers of alms. Texts from the Middle Ages, such as Geoffrey Chaucer's *Canterbury Tales* (ca. 1380–1400) or Martin Luther's *The Book of Vagabonds and Beggars, with a Vocabulary of their Language* (1528), describe different types of homeless wanderers and their varying strategies for survival, including those who were early examples of migrant laborers.

In all groups and societies, human beings are subject to forces beyond their control, especially natural disasters—such as earthquakes, hurricanes, and long-standing droughts—that render groups of people homeless. Moreover, modern societies that follow the principles of capitalism will inevitably have their economic ups and downs. The number of homeless individuals typically increases during times of economic recession and depression and conversely decreases when times are flush.

The principles of capitalism, along with the Industrial Revolution of the eighteenth and nineteenth centuries, made it easier for migrant laborers to work for a period of time in one place and then travel to another. During the interim periods

Wealthier nations are not immune to the problem of homelessness. Here, a group of people "sleep rough" on the streets of London. Economic hard times, cuts in social programs, and population growth have caused the number of homeless to rise almost everywhere. *(Press Association via AP Images)*

of not working—which could be days, weeks, or months—they were essentially homeless. As a result, an informal hierarchy of itinerancy and homelessness emerged. One category consisted of migrant workers, colloquially known as "hoboes," who chose to work in fields and factories when they felt it was convenient for them to do so. A second category consisted of migrant nonworkers, colloquially known as tramps, who traveled freely across the land, proud of the fact that they could get by without working for wages. A third category consisted of nonmigrant nonworkers, known pejoratively as bums, who generally did not work, but rather begged for sustenance. Although this hierarchy is frequently cited—with hoboes and tramps celebrated in popular and folk culture as dynamic "men on the move"—the fact is that the homeless population was always much more fluid than hierarchical. Certain individuals might be "on the bum" for a period on Skid Row, before later "riding the rails" in search of migrant labor.

Economic fluctuations were especially pronounced in Europe and North America during the late nineteenth and early twentieth centuries, causing the homeless population to increase noticeably. In response to these developments emerged an assortment of advocates for the homeless, which comprised social reformers such as Charles Booth (1840–1916) and Mary Higgs (1854–1937), investigative journalists such as Jacob Riis (1849–1914), and progressive

sociologists such as Robert E. Park (1864–1944) and Nels Anderson (1889–1986). Their methods included the surveying and study of homeless individuals, the establishment of lodging houses for the needy, and the publication of articles and books that called attention to the problem.

Even though the worldwide economic depression of the 1930s displaced many more people from their homes, most reformers and sociologists of the early twentieth century believed that individuals became homeless for primarily three reasons: (1) by choice, as thought to be the case with hoboes and tramps; (2) by temporary forces beyond their control, as in economic downturns and natural disasters; and (3) by some inherent flaw in their character or physical being—be it an addiction to drugs or alcohol, mental disability, or genetic inferiority. According to this view, homelessness was a phenomenon that affected only a distinct class of people who did not belong to mainstream society.

Homelessness Today

It was not until the late twentieth century that homelessness became recognized as a global issue. Large numbers of people who had been largely invisible by virtue of their presence on the margins of society gradually found themselves with far fewer options. Urban neighborhoods that had remained undesirable for many years were disappearing, transformed by gentrification or simply converted into housing for the newest migrants to the cities. As a result, more of these displaced persons found themselves sleeping on public sidewalks and in doorways, under bridges and highway overpasses, in automobiles and bus shelters, in alleyways and abandoned buildings—no longer invisible, but now deemed a blight that had to be remedied.

New types of reformers emerged at this time who used unorthodox methods to call attention to the problem. One of the best-known was Mitch Snyder (1946–1990), a political activist who lived among the homeless in Washington, D.C., and whose fifty-one-day hunger strike in 1984 helped create a shelter run by his organization, the Community for Creative Non-Violence. Snyder's efforts also influenced Congressman Stewart B. McKinney (1931–1987), whose Homeless Assistance Act of 1987 remains the only major federal piece of legislation in response to homelessness in the United States.

As both the numbers and visibility of homeless individuals increased around the world, it became clearer to policy makers and scholars that homelessness was not a case of individuals down on their luck, but rather the result of several overarching socioeconomic factors: rapidly growing populations but decreasing availability of low-cost housing; increasing numbers of home foreclosures, especially when real estate bubbles began bursting in 2007; the widening gap between rich and poor; declining wages and fewer job opportunities; and the reduced availability of public assistance, such as Aid to Families with Dependent Children in the United States.

The reduction of aid to families is partly responsible for one of the most noticeable and distressing trends today: increasing numbers of homeless children—sometimes with parents, but more often children who have been orphaned or abandoned and are struggling to survive on their own. This is hardly a new phenomenon; for instance, there were an estimated 5 million homeless children on the streets of the Soviet Union in the early 1920s. But the magnitude of the problem today and its potential effect on future generations has generated worldwide calls to action. It also confirms and reinforces the notion that homelessness can affect even the most innocent—such as the street gamins in Colombia, the street children who beg and sell cigarettes in Cairo, the ragpickers in Nepal, the *omo gutter* (gutter children) in Nigeria, the *malunde* (children living wild) in South Africa, and the child prostitutes in many other regions.

Although the issue of homeless children is one that everyone agrees must be resolved, advocates for the homeless are still combating misconceptions about the nature and causes of homelessness. The widening economic stratification between the rich and the poor means not only that the two groups have little direct contact with each other, but also that the former begin to regard the latter as a public nuisance from which the rich must be protected. As the world economic situation once again worsens in the early twenty-first century, members of the privileged classes seem inclined to argue that homeless people are inherently blighted because of their alleged personal deficiencies, which may include mental illness or substance abuse. From this perspective, homeless people are so depressing—both economically and psychologically—that they should be removed from sight.

Certainly, there are homeless individuals who suffer from mental illness or have become addicted to drugs and/or alcohol. Surveys in the United States suggest that about 20 percent of homeless people are mentally ill and that 30 percent are substance abusers; the majority is neither. More to the point are the societal costs of homelessness, which economists and social policy experts have attempted to calculate and measure. For instance, in cities and countries that provide generous benefits for health care and social services, homeless individuals receive a disproportionately high percentage of those benefits, especially for medical care in public hospitals and emergency rooms.

Possible Solutions and Future Directions

The solutions for reducing homelessness worldwide are as varied as the reasons contributing to the problem. Seven major efforts are currently paramount: (1) reduce world population growth, especially in the cities, where homeless people tend to congregate; (2) increase the availability of affordable housing that meets or exceeds the most basic human needs, including access to clean water and proper sanitary facilities; (3) improve medical care to treat the chronic illnesses affecting homeless people, including more extensive educational outreach about health and nutrition; (4) build better unity and coordination among representatives of the public and private sectors to address the problem of homelessness; (5) encourage governments to support legislation and constitutional frameworks that will ameliorate many of the root causes; (6) consider legal action to ensure that everyone receives basic human rights, including the right to adequate housing; and (7) place a human face on the homeless population, in order to strengthen the connections between those in need of help and those with the resources to help. Advancing the public's knowledge and understanding of the causes and culture of homelessness could not only ameliorate a significant social problem, but also bring greater human dignity to many members of the homeless community.

Because homelessness has existed for thousands of years for manifold reasons, it is unlikely to disappear within the next century. Moreover, if current trends in population growth, urbanization, and economic instability continue, a more likely scenario is that the incidence of homelessness will continue to increase in the years ahead, thereby worsening the quality of life for many of the world's inhabitants.

James I. Deutsch

See also: Housing Costs, Finance, and Affordability; Inequality, Income and Wealth; Mental Health; Refugees, Displaced Persons, and Asylum Seekers.

Further Reading

Allsop, Kenneth. *Hard Travellin': The Hobo and His History.* London: Hodder and Stoughton, 1967.

Anderson, Nels. *The Hobo: The Sociology of the Homeless Man.* Chicago: University of Chicago Press, 1923.

Beier, A.L., and Paul Ocobock, eds. *Cast Out: Vagrancy and Homelessness in Global and Historical Perspective.* Athens: Ohio University Press, 2008.

Glasser, Irene. *Homelessness in Global Perspective.* New York: G.K. Hall, 1994.

Hombs, Mary Ellen. *Modern Homelessness: A Reference Handbook.* Santa Barbara, CA: ABC-CLIO, 2011.

Hombs, Mary Ellen, and Mitch Snyder. *Homelessness in America: A Forced March to Nowhere.* Washington, DC: Community for Creative Non-Violence, 1982.

Levinson, David, ed. *Encyclopedia of Homelessness.* 2 vols. Thousand Oaks, CA: Sage Reference, 2004.

McNamara, Robert Hartmann, ed. *Homelessness in America.* 3 vols. Westport, CT: Praeger, 2008.

Polakow, Valerie, and Cindy Guillean, eds. *International Perspectives on Homelessness.* Westport, CT: Greenwood, 2001.

Ravenhill, Megan. *The Culture of Homelessness.* Burlington, VT: Ashgate, 2008.

Wasserman, Jason Adam, and Jeffrey Michael Clair. *At Home on the Street: People, Poverty, and a Hidden Culture of Homelessness.* Boulder, CO: Lynne Rienner, 2004.

Web Sites

European Federation of National Organisations Working with the Homeless: www.feantsa.org/code/en/hp.asp

Homeless World Cup Statistics: www.homelessworldcup .org/content/homelessness-statistics

International Network of Street Newspapers: www.streetnewsservice.org

National Coalition for the Homeless: www.nationalhomeless.org/factsheets

United Nations Human Settlements Programme (UN-HABITAT): www.unchs.org

U.S. Code, Title 42, Chapter 119, Homeless Assistance: www.gpoaccess.gov/uscode/browse.html

U.S. Conference of Mayors. Hunger and Homelessness Survey: http://usmayors.org/pressreleases/uploads/ USCMHungercompleteWEB2009.pdf

Documents

Document 1: "Labour and Life of the People in London," Charles Booth, 1891

Charles Booth (1840–1916) was a British shipowner and social reformer whose efforts to survey and analyze poverty in London were enormously influential. As a successful businessman, he coordinated extensive research—both quantitative and qualitative—to better understand the root causes of poverty. This excerpt, from a study that would eventually reach seventeen volumes in 1902–1903, provides a frank assessment of "the homeless class" at that time.

The homeless class, whether casual workers or vagrants, seem to have been the source of as much anxiety to our forefathers as to ourselves. There are in every generation those who, without any other special defect of character, have a roving disposition and a general distaste for a quiet regular life or regular employment, be it brain work or manual labour. Though, at the outset, not necessarily either lazy or at all worthless, such men are apt to drift into idle ways. The good intentions which may cause them to work, even vehemently, for a time, will not suffice to maintain that life of steady, unbroken, laborious routine which is demanded of those who would succeed. Failure is dubbed bad luck, habits of idleness follow in natural course, and at last these men become industrially, if not morally, worthless. In every generation, too, we find the race of "sturdy vagabonds and valiant beggars" ready to beg, borrow, and perhaps steal, rather than to work for their livelihood. These two classes, with the addition of those who from illness, infirmity, age, incompetence or misfortune, are thrown out of employment, are the sources whence homeless men are drawn.

These men, of whom there are always a large number in London, with some women and a few children, are closely associated with the dwellers in common lodging-houses and occasionally sojourn there, or elsewhere in the poorest quarters of the Metropolis, when their funds permit this escape from the cold comfort of the embankment or the parks, the shelter of an archway, or hospitality of some open staircase, or from the regulations of night refuge and casual ward. They are not hopeful subjects; not easy to raise out of this existence when they have once settled down to it.

Our ancestors took a severe view of vagrants of this description, and their presence doubtless at times threatened to become a serious social danger. In the reigns of the Tudors the desire to put an end to the vagrant difficulty is attested by the passing of Act after Act; the Tudor efforts culminating in the famous 43rd Elizabeth, reported to owe the outlines of its plan to the genius of Lord Bacon. But even his interference can hardly be said to have done much, and succeeding generations continued to legislate; planning, hoping and failing with depressing regularity.

Source: Internet Archive.

Document 2: Istanbul Declaration on Human Settlements (excerpts), 1996

More than 170 nations took part in the second United Nations Conference on Human Settlements (Habitat II) in Istanbul, Turkey, June 3–14, 1996. On the final day of the conference, the participants adopted a declaration that reaffirmed the right of every world citizen to adequate shelter. Its vision of solidarity, dignity, and sustainable housing in the twenty-first century offers hope for the future.

1. We, the Heads of State or Government and the official delegations of countries assembled at the United Nations Conference on Human Settlements (Habitat II) in Istanbul, Turkey from 3 to 14 June 1996, take this opportunity to endorse the universal goals of ensuring adequate shelter for all and making human settlements safer, healthier and more liveable, equitable, sustainable and productive. Our deliberations on the two major themes of the Conference—adequate shelter for all and sustainable human settlements development in an urbanizing world—have been inspired by the Charter of the United Nations and are aimed at reaffirming existing and forging new partnerships for action at the international, national and local levels to improve our living environment. We commit ourselves to the objectives, principles and recommendations contained in the Habitat Agenda and pledge our mutual support for its implementation.

2. We have considered, with a sense of urgency, the continuing deterioration of conditions of shelter and human settlements. At the same time, we recognize cities and towns as centres of civilization, generating economic development and social, cultural, spiritual and scientific advancement. We must take advantage of the opportunities presented by our settlements and preserve their diversity to promote solidarity among all our peoples. . . .

4. To improve the quality of life within human settlements, we must combat the deterioration of conditions that in most cases, particularly in developing countries, have reached crisis proportions. To this end, we must address comprehensively, inter alia, unsustainable consumption and production patterns, particularly in industrialized countries; unsustainable population changes, including changes in structure and distribution, giving priority consideration to the tendency towards excessive population concentration; homelessness; increasing poverty; unemployment; social exclusion; family instability; inadequate resources; lack of basic infrastructure and services; lack of adequate planning; growing insecurity and violence; environmental degradation; and increased vulnerability to disasters. . . .

15. This Conference in Istanbul marks a new era of cooperation, an era of a culture of solidarity. As we move into the twenty-first century, we offer a positive vision of sustainable human settlements, a sense of hope for our common future and an exhortation to join a truly worthwhile and engaging challenge, that of building together a world where everyone can live in a safe home with the promise of a decent life of dignity, good health, safety, happiness and hope.

Source: United Nations Human Settlements Programme.

HOUSING COSTS, FINANCE, AND AFFORDABILITY

While housing is a basic human need, it has, in the last century, been increasingly produced, consumed, and perceived as a market good. Furthermore, the intensification of housing commodification in recent decades has been part of the restructuring of global capitalism that sustained both the economic boom of the early 2000s and the more recent series of financial crises. More commodified housing consumption along with the restructuring of housing finance has, in most contexts, made buying a home increasingly expensive. Declining affordability has not only crowded out low- and middle-income buyers, but also enhanced pressures on social and private rental sectors. Even in the crisis era, despite price declines and an explosion in home foreclosures, tighter credit conditions and poor employment stability have meant buying a home remains difficult for most, especially younger people. Housing affordability has come to feature heavily in political debates, and governments have become increasingly active in the housing market.

Basis of Modern Housing Systems

In the early twentieth century, the vast majority of urban housing in Western societies was rented, with poorer households often living in cramped conditions and poor-quality dwellings. In the United Kingdom, as many as nine out of ten households were private sector renters at the onset of World War I, with home purchase limited to the more affluent. Meanwhile, in the United States, more than half of households rented. By 2006, however, homeownership rates in these two countries had peaked at almost 70 percent. In part, the almost century-long shift away from private rental housing systems was driven by the declining economic attractiveness of rental housing, both for

landlords and dwellers. Housing has also increasingly become a government concern, especially after 1918, with poor conditions and exploitative landlordism (and unaffordable rents) seen as a source of social discontent and political unrest.

In many contexts, conflicts over poor housing conditions initially led to greater government support for subsidized rental housing construction and management by either local municipalities or private philanthropic organizations. This drove the expansion of social rental housing sectors accommodating working families at submarket rents. While social, and in particular public (state-owned), housing would later become associated with very poor and marginalized tenants, early social housing often accommodated better-off working-class and even middle-income households. In Europe especially, housing associations (often serving particular trade and labor union associations), proliferated in the 1920s and 1930s, with the construction of subsidized rental housing driving urban expansion and even new architectural experiments in mass housing construction. Amsterdam and Vienna are particularly good examples, with social housing movements dominating their housing markets throughout most of the twentieth century.

In Britain, too, social rental housing become an object of government support in the 1920s, and by the mid-1930s had grown to almost 10 percent of the total housing stock. Funds also flowed into public projects focused on the construction and finance of owner-occupied housing. As the desirability and affordability of homeownership grew among middle-class families, the sector began to swell, with homeownership representing 32 percent by 1938. Local Building Societies, established as private housing finance institutions in the nineteenth century, began to expand their business in this period, providing housing loans to members who had built up good savings records.

In the United States, there was far less appetite for public housing interventions. Nonetheless, the government was a key supporter of increasing home-ownership, particularly in the boom years of the 1920s. Increasing investment in owner occupation was considered a "bulwark to bolshevism," as property owners were thought more likely to be thrifty, autonomous, and to support the interests of capital. The major stumbling block was the limited lending capacity of savings and loan companies as well as the underdevelopment of mortgage products. Large down payment requirements (usually more than 50 percent) were also an impediment, as only a limited sum could be borrowed, for 5–10 years, with the typical borrower paying only interest, rather than repaying the debt (i.e., short-term nonamortizing loans). At the same time, lending institutions were limited in how much they could loan by the size of the pool of deposits provided by savers.

The Great Depression undermined the housing finance system, with many homeowners becoming unemployed and therefore unable to repay their mortgage. Many lost their homes. Meanwhile, those who stayed at work found it increasingly difficult to refinance their short-term loans as financial institutions withdrew from the mortgage market. In the years following the Wall Street Crash, 250,000 mortgages were foreclosed annually. A radical intervention was called for and initially led by President Herbert Hoover and then followed through by the Franklin Roosevelt administration. The 1930s saw the establishment of the Federal Housing Administration (FHA), the Home Owners' Loan Corporation, the Federal Loan Insurance Corporation, and the Federal National Mortgage Association (Fannie Mae). An infrastructure was thus assembled in which the government backed long-term (25 to 30 years) amortizing housing loans (the debt repaid over the life of the loan) and established a richer, more stable flow of finance for home purchase.

Extending House Building and Finance

In the new system, the FHA guaranteed mortgages and regulated low, fixed-term interest rates. Meanwhile, Fannie Mae replenished finance for the primary loan market by issuing securities based on approved loans in a secondary mortgage market. With hous-ing finance more freely available (and provided on better terms) homeownership rates and home values boomed in the postwar years along with economic growth and intensified suburbanization. The lending system was enhanced further by the privatization of Fannie Mae in 1968 and the establishment of the Federal National Home Loan Mortgage Corporation (Freddie Mac) in 1970, which extended the capacity of mortgage securitization. Increasingly, lenders did not have to rely on savings pools in order to fund their loans. With an ostensibly regulated market for mortgage debt, lenders could sell mortgages to investors and thereby recoup their funds, facilitating more lending. A clear divide emerged between the "originators," or retailers of loans, and the owner of the debt. Mortgage-backed securities (MBS) became particularly popular as investments as they were supported by a framework of government-sponsored enterprises (GSEs) such as Fannie Mae and Freddie Mac, which, while independent, were implicitly backed by federal finances.

In post–World War II Northern Europe, government responses to shortages and insufficient investment in house building were remarkably different. With the exception of a few countries (such as Germany, where subsidized low-cost private rental housing became the solution), a census emerged among governments, banks, and house-builders that supported the expansion of pre-existing social rental housing sectors. This move massively increased housing supply as well as affordability for working households. Governments also boosted private construction of housing for sale, either through supply subsidies for housing producers or demand subsidies for users (such as tax relief for mortgaged home buyers), or a combination of both. Essentially, the postwar period was the heyday of housing production, with the achievement of massive supply based on state support. In France, for example, the housing stock increased by almost 50 percent (8 million units) between 1953 and 1975, of which 80 percent profited from government funding. In the United States as well, housing supply was supported by state subsidies for builders, although there was strong resistance to the direct provision of public rental housing, which has never surpassed a 2 to 3 percent share of the total housing stock. Some relief was extended to very low-income households nonetheless, especially after 1974, through housing voucher schemes.

Makings of a Housing Bubble

The 1980s mark a turning point in approaches to affordable housing. UK prime minister Margaret Thatcher's neoliberal reforms involved not only the sell-off of public rental housing, but also the deregulation of the finance sector after 1985. New credit providers were encouraged into the mortgage market, with competition between financiers becoming more intense and nontraditional lenders increasingly involved in providing housing finance for a broadening range of nontraditional borrowers. In the United States, the Ronald Reagan administration argued for a new system of housing finance with unrestricted access of all mortgage lenders and borrowers to money and capital markets. The outcome was a lax regulatory environment with savings and loan companies moving further away from traditional lending and toward high-risk, speculative commercial ventures. By the late 1980s, the savings and loan sector, which had been inadequately equipped for this move, had entered a full-blown crisis. Over 1,000 United States lenders eventually collapsed, leading to federal intervention in 1989 in order to safeguard depositors' accounts. Meanwhile, in the United Kingdom, the 1980s economic boom ended with a housing market crash generating record amounts of negative equity and repossessions among mortgage holders, challenging the wisdom of deregulated lending practices.

Nevertheless, in the 1990s and the first decade after 2000, increased homeownership and further deregulation of borrowing for housing was pursued by governments, not only in the United States and Britain, but also in many of the countries where social rental housing sectors were prominent. The greatest increases in national ratios of mortgage debt in Western Europe were in countries like the Netherlands and Denmark, with, arguably, most room to expand owner-occupied housing. In East European post-socialist economies, homeownership rates and mortgage debt were also driven up by the opening of credit and mortgage markets as well as policy measures to privatize large public housing stocks. In the developing world, too, improving lending conditions for homebuyers became a prescription for accelerated economic growth. Wholesale increases in lending inevitably drove up the prices of housing goods, feeding a frenzy of mortgage loans and lending.

The increase in the value of residential property seen between 2000 and 2005 has been estimated at $40 to $70 trillion across developed economies. Ballooning real estate values helped stimulate extra aggregate demand in the rest of the economy and, in many contexts—especially those like Spain and Ireland, where house building became a key driver of the economy—stimulated growth rates to rise well above the average. Nationally, differences in the house price boom and bust are illustrated in the accompanying table. Sustained housing price increases were made possible by enhanced flows of capital being made available for homebuyers, with growth in the MBS market playing a particular role. For potential buyers,

House Price Changes from Previous Year, Selected OECD Countries, 2003–2010 (percentages)

	2003	2004	2005	2006	2007	2008	2009	2010
Australia	18.2	6.5	1.5	7.8	11.3	4.4	3.4	12.1
Belgium	6.9	8.7	12.7	11.8	9.3	4.9	−0.4	5.4
Canada	9.5	9.4	9.9	11.4	10.8	−1.3	4.6	6.8
Denmark	3.2	8.9	17.6	21.6	4.6	−4.5	−12	2.8
Finland	6.3	8.2	8.1	6.4	5.5	0.6	−0.3	8.7
France	11.9	15.1	15.4	12	6.5	0.9	−7.1	5.2
Germany	−1.3	−1.4	−0.9	0.1	1.1	0.6	0.6	2.3
Ireland	14.2	11.2	8.1	14.5	8.5	−5.9	−18.3	−13.1
Italy	10.3	9.9	7.5	6.4	5.2	1.7	−3.7	−2
Japan	−5.4	−6.1	−4.8	−3	−1	−1.6	−3.8	−3.7
Korea	9.1	1.1	0.8	6.2	9	4	0.2	2.4
Netherlands	3.6	4.3	3.8	4.6	4.2	2.9	−3.3	−2
New Zealand	19.4	17.8	14.5	10.5	10.9	−4.4	−1.6	1.9
Norway	1.7	10.1	8.2	13.7	12.6	−1.1	2	8.2
Spain	20	18.3	14.6	10	5.5	0.2	−7.6	−3.6
Sweden	6.6	9.3	9	12.2	10.4	3.3	1.6	7.8
Switzerland	3	2.4	1.1	2.5	2.1	2.6	5.1	4.7
UK	15.7	11.9	5.5	6.3	10.9	−0.9	−7.8	7.2
United States	6.2	9.3	11.3	7.3	1.4	−4.3	−4.6	−3.6

Source: OECD (2011). House prices. *Economics: Key Tables from OECD.* No. 17.

pressures to get on the market became more intense as the speed of house value inflation pushed the price of market entry upward. New entrants thus had to borrow much more than their predecessors both in terms of total price and price to income. Lenders, nonetheless, were happy to lend on increasingly risky terms to increasingly risk-taking customers, spurred on by both house price augmentation, which appeared to offset the potential damage of mortgage defaults, and the growing capacity to sell mortgage debt (and therefore risk) in the securities market.

A growing phenomenon in the 1990s and 2000s was the sub- and near-prime mortgage sector, which made home loans available to individuals with poor or nonexistent credit histories. Such loans featured "teaser" interest rates, which inflated rapidly after the first few years of the loan. These also became attractive to many regular lenders who took advantage of them by refinancing their loans after teasers expired. As financial institutions became increasingly aggressive in pursuing higher returns, forms of predatory lending advanced, with an emphasis on more economically vulnerable households and riskier loans with potentially higher returns. Subprime, which had been a marginal sector in the early 1990s, was generating well over $2 billion in loans a year in the U.S. market by the turn of the century. In Europe too, especially the United Kingdom, subprime lending also began to advance in the 2000s, albeit much more slowly and usually under stricter regulation. In most cases, the practice was tolerated by governments as it represented a means to extend access to homeownership to marginal and lower-income households at a time when home price inflation appeared to be excluding growing numbers of people.

Without adequate regulation, the practice of packaging subprime loans up with regular mortgages and selling them in the securities market as low-risk rather than high-risk investments had become widespread by 2005. However, after house prices peaked in 2006 and interest rates began to go up, many borrowers, especially subprime ones, found themselves with mortgage debts greater than the value of their homes and unsustainable repayments costs. As borrowers could walk away from their homes leaving lenders with the problem of recouping the debt via foreclosure, increasing numbers did. This undermined not only the housing market but also the basis of securities backed by these loans.

Due to the global distribution of MBS and the interconnectedness of financial institutions, the U.S. mortgage crisis spread to the rest of the world economy. The entire U.S. housing system began to implode, with the Federal Housing Finance Authority stepping in to save Fannie Mae and Freddie Mac in late 2008 at an estimated total cost to the public purse of between $400 and $500 billion. The spread of subprime-contaminated securities instigated a collapse in economic confidence culminating in the credit crisis, driving a tidal wave of corporate collapses and bankruptcies across the global financial sector. By the end of 2009, global losses in subprime-related credit were estimated at over $1 trillion.

Ownership and Affordability After the Credit Crisis

From the beginning of 2009 to the end of 2011, as many as 3 million homes were foreclosed upon in the United States. This record was set in the context of sustained house price volatility and the continued inability of millions of households to refinance their mortgages. With the spread of unemployment and a tightening of lending conditions, the numbers of housing transactions across developed societies have dropped substantially. Similarly, the construction of new properties has also fallen to historic lows. Initial efforts to cope with the collapse of the housing market focused on sustaining the refinance of regular mortgages. This was followed in 2009, under the Barack Obama administration, by the announcement of a $75 billion plan to help keep defaulting owners in their homes.

Leading up to the crisis, the U.S. government had actively pursued higher homeownership rates, especially among nonwhite minorities, through tax relief programs for builders of "affordable" single-family housing. On the demand side, measures like the American Dream Downpayment Act had also been introduced to assist low-income first-time buyers. The George W. Bush administration also sought to reinforce local self-help schemes, where local organizations coordinate the exchange of information and sweat equity in order to help poorer families into homeownership. One of the biggest long-term initiatives in housing, however, has been the HOPE VI program, which began in 1992. This scheme supports the restructuring of poor urban neighborhoods and public housing estates. This has often resulted in the displacement of high-density residents in public tenancies by low-density owner-occupied housing for mixed-income households. By 2005, the program had distributed $5.8 billion through 446 federal block grants to cities for redevelopment. HOPE VI continued to support revitalization projects through the crisis, although annual funding diminished from as much as $450 million in 2003 to about $150 million in 2010.

In the post–credit crisis milieu, housing conditions and affordability issues have developed differently in each country. In Spain and Ireland especially, housing markets have been dominated by conditions of oversupply due to government support for intensive housing production during the bubble years, which provided a substantial boost to the economy. After the crisis, overcapacity has come to the fore and house prices have been in free fall, bringing construction to a standstill. Most European countries have experienced substantial house price volatility, destabilizing markets, and a declining flow of households into and through homeownership. Nonetheless, problems of foreclosure and in finance have not been so extreme. This is in part a result of more responsible lending before the crisis and the efforts of governments to sustain the flow of lending. Another factor has been the larger capacity of social rental housing sectors, which have protected many low-income households from the vicissitudes of the market. In contexts where low-income rental housing has been supported by the state as both cheap *and* attractive, fewer marginal households have exposed themselves to the risks of the property market and private mortgage finance.

Arguably, one lesson learned by British lenders from the previous (1989–1990) housing crash was that aggressive home possessions on defaulting mortgages undermine market values overall and thus the capacity of banks to recoup losses. The unfolding of the latest housing market crisis in the United Kingdom thus reflected a level of caution among banks, with relatively few foreclosures (36,000 in 2010 compared to 75,000 in 1991). House prices initially dropped around 16 percent, but then began to readjust, representing an average loss by the end of 2010 of less than 10 percent from three years earlier. Nonetheless, English housing conditions have begun to reinforce socioeconomic polarization both spatially and socially. While national house prices fell by 1.3 percent in 2011 and as much as 7.1 percent in the northeast, they actually rose in London by 2.8 percent. Value losses and the risk of mortgage default have increased most for lower-income households in unstable employment as historically recent rises

The commodification of housing and the restructuring of global financial markets have made buying a home more difficult in many locations. In Seoul, South Korea (*above*), and elsewhere in East Asia, the state has subsidized more affordable rental housing. *(Jean Chung/Bloomberg via Getty Images)*

in homeownership have been supported by growing numbers of more vulnerable homebuyers. Indeed, owner occupation has been the majority tenure among the poorest decile of households since the late 1990s, with these owner-occupants typically spending far more proportional income on housing than either low-income renters or better-off owner-occupiers.

Ongoing and Future Developments

The economically liberal, English-speaking "homeowner" societies have recently begun to experience declines in the size of owner-occupied housing sectors. In the United States, almost 70 percent of households were occupied by homeowners in 2004, compared to less than 66 percent in 2010. Although affordability has increased since 2007, with lower prices and interest rates falling, housing has become less accessible to new buyers as lending conditions have deteriorated. In England, for example, while mortgage payments constituted an average of 18.4 percent of income in 2009 (0.4 percent less than 2001 and 5.4 percent less than 2007), the deposit required represented 27.7 percent of buyers' income, up from 16.7 percent eight years earlier. Essentially, lending has become more cautious, less flexible, and required higher down payments.

Significant divides have begun to emerge between different cohorts of market entrants. While older people typically bought when prices were historically lower and built up considerable equity in their homes, younger adults are more likely to hold negative equity, especially if they bought at the top of the bubble, or are struggling to either save or borrow in order to now buy. British media discourse has named the latter group Generation Rent. Emerging conditions have resulted in considerable "re-familization," with growing levels of parental assistance for adult children in buying a home, on one hand, and increasing numbers of multigenerational families coming together under one roof, on the other. Governments in many countries have responded to new housing conditions and declining access—featuring high numbers of empty or foreclosed homes, falling new supply, and restricted financial access for new entrants—with schemes to help people buy their homes.

Essentially, the last few decades of intensified housing commodification have realigned perceptions of housing markets, with homeownership becoming the norm across Europe and North America. It has become difficult for policymakers to think beyond market-based forms of production and consumption as solutions to emerging housing inequalities. An interesting development in some economically advanced and advancing East Asian contexts however, has been, despite traditions of state-supported expansion of owner-occupied housing markets, a shift toward public-oriented social housing projects. In China, for example, house prices have been accelerating since the early 1990s and more than doubled between 2004 and 2008. Measures such as property tax increases and higher down-payment requirements, aimed at cooling the market and sustaining affordability for even middle-class households, have failed. Subsequently, the state has announced the world's largest-ever social housing program, involving the construction of 36 million new subsidized rental and "affordable" owner-occupied units between 2011 and 2015. Taiwan also has plans to establish a bigger social rental housing sector, while South Korea has been building as many as 80,000 public rental units a year since 2004.

Richard Ronald

See also: Consumer and Investor Rights and Protections; Credit and Debt, Personal and Business; Homelessness.

Further Reading

Dorling, Danny, Janet Ford, A.E. Holmans, and Sue Regan, eds. *The Great Divide: An Analysis of Housing Inequality.* London: Shelter, 2005.

Forrest, Ray, and N.M Yip, eds. *Housing Markets and the Global Financial Crisis: The Uneven Impact on Households.* Cheltenham, UK: Edwin Elgar, 2011.

Groves, Richard, Alan Murie, and Christopher Watson. *Housing and the New Welfare State: Perspectives from East Asia and Europe.* Hampshire, UK: Ashgate, 2007.

Immergluck, Daniel. *Foreclosed: High-Risk Lending, Deregulation, and the Undermining of America's Mortgage Market.* Ithaca, NY: Cornell University Press, 2009.

Kemeny, Jim. *The Myth of Home Ownership.* London: Routledge & Kegan Paul, 1981.

Kurz, Karin, and Hans-Peter Blossfeld. *Home Ownership and Social Inequality in Comparative Perspective.* Stanford, CA: Stanford University Press, 2004.

Ronald, Richard. *The Ideology of Home Ownership: Homeowner Societies and the Role of Housing.* Basingstoke, UK: Palgrave Macmillan, 2008.

Ronald, Richard, and Marja Elsinga. *Beyond Home Ownership: Housing, Welfare and Society.* New York: Routledge, 2012.

Schwartz, Herman. *Subprime Nation: American Power, Global Capital, and the Housing Bubble.* Ithaca, NY: Cornell University Press, 2009.

Shiller, Robert. *The Subprime Solution: How Today's Global Financial Crisis Happened and What to Do About It.* Princeton NJ: Princeton University Press, 2008.

Web Sites

European Federation of Public, Cooperative and Social Housing: www.housingeurope.eu

Harvard, Joint Centre for Housing Studies: www.jchs.harvard.edu

Housing Education and Research Association: http://housingeducators.org

Hypostat, 2011: www.hypo.org/Content/default.asp?PageID=420

UN Habitat: www.unhabitat .org/?gclid=CImw3v21_K0CFcxofAodhUrDsA

U.S. Department of Housing and Urban Development: http://portal.hud.gov/hudportal/HUD

Documents

Document 1: Statement Announcing White House Conference on Home Building and Home Ownership, Herbert Hoover, 1931

With the advent of the Great Depression came a collapse in the construction industry, record home foreclosures, and widespread homelessness. To address these multiple problems, President Herbert Hoover organized the White House Conference on Home Building and Home Ownership in September 1931. Although Hoover was unable to enact major legislation based on the recommendations of the conference before voters drove him from office the following year, the meeting helped spur thinking that led to the various policies and programs aimed at supplying low-cost housing and mortgages to millions of Americans.

I wish to announce that the President's Conference on Home Building and Home Ownership for which preparations have been in progress for something over a year will be held in Washington, Wednesday, December 2 to Saturday, December 5, inclusive. About 400 persons have assisted in the preparatory work and 1,000 representative citizens from the 48 States, associated with building and housing activities, are expected to participate in the Conference. The Conference has been organized under the chairmanship of Secretary Lamont, of the Department of Commerce. Dr. John M. Gries is the Executive Secretary.

I decided a year ago after a conference with interested leaders in various parts of the country to undertake the organization of an adequate investigation and study, on a nationwide scale, of the problems presented in homeownership and homebuilding, with the hope of developing the facts and a better understanding of the questions involved and inspiring better organization and the removal of influences which seriously limit the spread of homeownership, both town and country.

A Planning Committee, comprising representatives of some 20 voluntary associations, was created to make the study and set up a national conference for consideration of the data and recommendations of expert committees. The plan is somewhat similar to that of the White House Conference on Child Health and Protection, held in Washington in November 1930. Funds have been provided privately to cover research and other activities of the committees of the housing conference.

Among the associations represented in the Planning Committee were the following:

American Civic Association
American Farm Bureau Federation
American Federation of Labor
American Home Economics Association
American Institute of Architects
Associated General Contractors Association of Life Insurance Presidents
Better Homes in America
Chamber of Commerce of the United States
General Federation of Women's Clubs
National Association of Builders' Exchanges
National Association of Real Estate Boards

National Congress of Parents and Teachers
National Farmers Union
National Grange
National Housing Association
Russell Sage Foundation
Savings Bank Division of the American Bankers Association
United States League of Building and Loan Associations
Women's National Farm and Garden Association

The Conference in December will be the first of its kind on this scale in the United States. It will deal with the whole question of home construction and ownership, and of the home environment. It will embrace finance, design, equipment, city planning, household management, and many other aspects.

Twenty-five committees headed by men and women of authority and experience in various phases of the question, have been engaged for months in gathering and analyzing available information and in making additional studies and inquiries. Their work is being correlated so that, on the basis of the facts, a collective judgment may be formulated upon the best contemporary experience of leaders who have special knowledge of the subjects. It, obviously, is not our purpose to set up the Federal Government in the building of homes. But the Conference will, I believe, afford a basis for the development of a sound policy and inspire better voluntary organization to cope with the problem.

Adequate housing goes to the very roots of well-being of the family, and the family is the social unit of the Nation. The question involves important aspects of health, morals, education, and efficiency. Nothing contributes more to social stability and the happiness of our people than the surroundings of their homes. Although we have a larger proportion of adequate housing than any other country, we have not yet reached our ideal of homes for all our people. It should be possible in our country for any person of sound character and industrious habits to provide himself with adequate and suitable housing and preferably to own his own home.

This principle, I believe, to be sound and controlling at all times. It is unnecessary to point out the beneficial effect which a well-considered nationwide program directed to the extension of homebuilding and homeownership in the immediate future would have upon our current unemployment and economic situation. The forthcoming Conference, however, was initiated to deal with the question under a long-range plan. It will be doubly fortunate if it should result not only in a sounder permanent policy, but in some degree of relief of current unemployment and in stimulation of the industries upon which building depends.

The question touches many phases of both public and private activity. One of the important questions is finance. The present depression has given emphasis to the fact that the credit system in homebuilding is not as satisfactorily organized as other branches of credit. Commerce, industry, and to a large extent farm mortgages, all have more effective financial reservoirs. In order to enable the purchase of homes on what amounts to the installment plan, it is necessary to place first and, often enough, second mortgages. The building and loan associations have performed a great service in this field, but they cannot without assistance carry the burden. First mortgages, carried so largely by the savings banks and insurance companies, have been affected by competition with bonds and other forms of investment. Second mortgages are also necessary to many people. In the period of expansion preceding the current depression rates for second mortgages, including commissions, discounts, and other charges, rose in many cities to the equivalent of 20 or 25 percent per annum. This not only stifled homeownership, but led to the loss of many homes through foreclosure. The present depression has been marked by unemployment in the trades involved.

Since a principal object of home construction and homeownership is to provide the best possible environment for the growing child, it is obvious that the work of the women's committees on homemaking and related subjects is a most vital phase of the Conference.

Special attention is being devoted to the problems of farm and village housing.

A committee of representative civic leaders of the Negro race are devoting attention to the problems of Negro housing.

Twenty-five committees have been charged each with the study of a special field within the general problem covered by the Conference. Six correlating committees deal with questions of aim and method common to the 25 committees. These correlating committees concern themselves with standards and objectives, legislation and administration, education and service, organization programs, local and national and technological developments.

Source: American Presidency Project.

Document 2: British House of Commons Debate, Housing Act, 1980

On January 15, 1980, the British House of Commons debated a plan introduced by the newly elected conservative government of Margaret Thatcher to institute what it called a "right to buy" scheme, whereby residents of council (i.e., public) housing could purchase their properties. Calling it "one of the most important social revolutions of this century," Environment Minister Michael Heseltine argued that the measure would give residents a vital ownership stake in British society. Labour Party opponents argued that it would not increase the stock of low-cost housing, that many of the houses were of low quality, and that it made it less likely that those who could not afford the downpayment would be able to find decent low-cost housing to rent. A transcript of the debate can be found at:

http://hansard.millbanksystems.com/commons/1980/jan/15/housing-bill

Source: UK Parliament.

HUMAN RIGHTS

Human rights constitute a set of norms that govern the treatment of individuals and groups by states and nonstate actors on the basis of ethical principles regarding what society considers fundamental to a decent life. These norms are incorporated into national and international legal systems, which specify mechanisms and procedures to hold the duty-bearers accountable.

Theoretical Background

Numerous theoretical debates surround the origins, scope, and significance of human rights in political science, moral philosophy, and jurisprudence. Roughly speaking, invoking the term "human rights" (which is often referred to as "human rights discourse" or "human rights talk") is based on moral reasoning (ethical discourse), socially sanctioned norms (legal or political discourse), or social mobilization (advocacy discourse). These three types of discourse are by no means alternative or sequential but are all used in different contexts, depending on who is invoking human rights discourse, to whom they are addressing their claims, and what they expect to gain by doing so. They are interrelated in the sense that public reasoning based on ethical arguments and social mobilization based on advocacy agendas influence legal norms, processes, and institutions, and thus all three assist human rights in becoming part of social reality.

Human Rights as Ethical Concerns

Human rights share an ethical concern for just treatment, built on empathy or altruism in human behavior and concepts of justice in philosophy. The philosopher and economist Amartya Sen considered, in his "Elements of a Theory of Human Rights," that "Human rights can be seen as primarily ethical demands. . . . Like other ethical claims that demand acceptance, there is an implicit presumption in making pronouncements on human rights that the underlying ethical claims will survive open and informed scrutiny." In moral reasoning, the expression "human rights" is often conflated with the more general concept of "rights," though "rights" refer to any entitlement regardless of its validity or legitimacy. The moral basis of a right can draw on concepts such as natural law, social contract, justice as fairness, or consequentialism. All these traditions conceive of rights as entitlements of individuals, by virtue of their humanity or their membership in a political community (citizenship). In law, however, a right is any legally protected interest, whatever the social consequence of the enforcement of the right on the well-being of persons other than the right-holder (e.g., the property right of a landlord to evict a tenant). To avoid confusion, it is helpful to use the term "human right" or its equivalent ("fundamental right," "basic freedom," "constitutional right") to refer to a higher-order right, authoritatively defined, that prevails over other (ordinary) rights and reflects society's essential values.

Enlightenment philosophers derived the centrality of the individual from their theories of the state of nature. Those who believed in a social contract, especially Jean-Jacques Rousseau, predicated the authority of the state on its capacity for achieving the optimal enjoyment of natural rights, that is, of rights inherent in each individual irrespective of birth or status. He wrote in *Discourse on the Origin and Basis of Inequality Among Men* that "it is plainly contrary to the law of nature . . . that the privileged few should gorge themselves with superfluities, while the starving multitude are in want of the bare necessities of life." Equally important was the concept of the universalized individual ("the rights of Man"), reflected in the political thinking of Immanuel Kant, John Locke, Thomas Paine, and the authors of the American Declaration of Independence (1776) and the French Declaration of the Rights of Man and the Citizen (1789). The Enlightenment represented for the West both the affirmation of the scientific method, as a basis of human progress, and the formulation of human rights, as a basis for freedom and equality of citizens—criteria on which modern governments are judged. Meanwhile, Karl Marx and other socialist thinkers stressed community interests and egalitarian values, dismissing individual human rights as a "bourgeois" formulation.

The ethical basis of human rights has been defined using concepts such as human flourishing, dignity, duties to family and society, natural rights, individual freedom, and social justice against exploitation based on race, sex, class, or caste. Although they are all part of the ethical discourse, the tensions in these ethical arguments—between political liberalism and democratic egalitarianism, between Locke and Rousseau, between liberty and equality, between civil and political rights and economic, social and cultural rights—have been part of the philosophical and political ambiguity of human rights for centuries.

Today, ethical and religious precepts continue to determine what one is willing to accept as properly a human right. Such precepts are familiar in debates over abortion, same-sex marriage, and the death penalty, just as they were in historic arguments over slavery and inequality between the sexes. What has survived Sen's "open and informed scrutiny"? The answer often lies in our laws and treaties, although for him, "even though human rights can, and often do, inspire legislation, this is a further fact, rather than a constitutive characteristic of human rights." Legal positivists would disagree.

Human Rights as Legal Rights (Positive Law Tradition)

Alternatively, legal positivists regard human rights as resulting from a formal norm-creating process, an authoritative formulation of the rule by which a society (national or international) is governed. Although natural rights derive from the natural order or divine origin, which are inalienable, immutable, and absolute, positive law rights are recognized through a political and legal process that results in a normative instrument, such as a law or treaty. These instruments can vary over time and frequently contain derogations or limitations by which the right may be suspended or reduced in scope, in order to optimize practical respect for the right, rather than setting an absolute standard. From this perspective, rights are part of the social order after being proclaimed as such by an authoritative body, and their universality derives

from the participation of virtually every country in the norm-creating process, which often results in compromise language that balances various interests. The International Bill of Human Rights (consisting of the Universal Declaration of Human Rights [UDHR] of 1948, the International Covenant on Civil and Political Rights, and the International Covenant on Economic, Social and Cultural Rights, both legally binding treaties opened for signature in 1966), along with the other human rights treaties of the United Nations (UN) and of regional organizations, constitute the primary sources and reference points for what properly belongs in the category of (legal) human rights.

Human Rights as Social Claims

Before they are written into legal texts, human rights often emerge from claims of people who are suffering injustice and thus are based on moral sentiment derived from cultural experience or belief systems. For example, the injustices of the Dreyfus Affair (1894) led to the creation of the Ligue française des droits de l'homme (French Human Rights League) in 1897, later internationalized into the International Federation of Leagues for the Rights of Man (now the International Federation for Human Rights). Amnesty International (founded in 1961), the Moscow Human Rights Committee (founded in 1970), and Helsinki Watch (founded in 1978 and expanded into Human Rights Watch in 1988) were among the more effective non-governmental organizations (NGOs), in the global North, while many NGOs from the global South have arisen, especially since the end of the Cold War.

These NGOs often emerged as social movements out of outrage, for example, at the mistreatment of prisoners, at the exclusion of persons with disabilities, or as part of struggles against colonialism. Such movements for social change often invoke human rights as the basis of their advocacy. If prevailing mores or law do not address their concerns, they agitate for a change in the theory or law. NGOs not only contributed to the drafting of the UDHR but also in bringing down apartheid, transforming East-Central Europe and restoring democracy in Latin America and, more recently, to challenging dictatorships in the Middle East and North Africa and promoting nondiscrimination against sexual minorities.

The appeal to human rights in advocacy discourse is no less legitimate than the legal and philosophical modes of discourse and is often the inspiration for the latter. Quoting Sen again, "The invoking of hu-

By a vote of 48–0, with eight abstentions, the UN General Assembly, meeting at the Palais de Chaillot in Paris on December 10, 1948, passed the Universal Declaration of Human Rights—the first global codification of rights to which all people are entitled. *(STF/AFP/Getty Images)*

man rights tends to come mostly from those who are concerned with changing the world rather than interpreting it. . . . The colossal appeal of the idea of human rights [has provided comfort to those suffering] intense oppression or great misery, without having to wait for the theoretical air to clear." Historical experience bears out that assessment.

Historical Background

The historical context of human rights can be seen from a wide range of perspectives. At the risk of over-simplification, four approaches to human rights history may be identified. The first approach traces the deeper origins to ancient religious and philosophical concepts of compassion, charity, justice, individual worth, and respect for all life found in all major religions. Precursors of human rights declarations are found in numerous texts from early civilizations, including the Code of Hammurabi (Babylon) and the Charter of Cyrus the Great (Persia). In the second, modern human rights are traced to the emergence of natural law theories in ancient Greece and Rome and Christian theology of the Middle Ages, culminating with the Enlightenment—and its contemporaneous

rebellions—in Europe, combined with nineteenth-century movements for the abolition of slavery, worker's rights, and woman suffrage. A third approach is to trace human rights to their enthronement in the United Nations Charter of 1945 and the Universal Declaration of Human Rights of 1948, drafted in reaction to the Holocaust and drawing on President Franklin Roosevelt's Four Freedoms. Post–World War II national constitutions and international treaties built on that foundation. A fourth approach is the recent revisionist history argued by Professor Samuel Moyn, which considers human rights peripheral in the aftermath of World War II and significant only as a utopian ideal and movement beginning in the 1970s as an alternative to the prevailing ideological climate.

Much scholarship, especially in Europe and North America, dates modern human rights theory and practice to the Enlightenment and the revolutions it spawned in France and the United States, giving rise to later anti-slavery and anti-colonial movements. As Lynn Hunt, in "The Revolutionary Origins of Human Rights," states:

Most debates about rights originated in the eighteenth century, and nowhere were discussions of them more explicit, more divisive, or more influential than in revolutionary France in the 1790s. The answers given then to most fundamental questions about rights remained relevant throughout the nineteenth and twentieth centuries. The framers of the UN declaration of 1948 closely followed the model established by the French Declaration of the Rights of Man and Citizen of 1789, while substituting "human" for the more ambiguous "Man" throughout.

Meanwhile, the contemporary German philosopher Jürgen Habermas has written that in the French Revolution "revolutionary consciousness gave birth to a new mentality, which was shaped by a new time consciousness, a new concept of political practice, and a new notion of legitimization." Although it took a century for this mentality to include women and slaves, social actors of the time, such as Mary Wollstonecreaft in *A Vindication of the Rights of Woman* (1792) and the Society for the Abolition of the Slave Trade (founded in 1783) anticipated future progress. The equal worth of all based on natural rights represented a sharp break from previous determinations of rights on the basis of hierarchy and status and gave rise to subsequent social movements on behalf of the marginalized and the excluded throughout the modern era. Still, the reality of inequality and discrimination has persisted, posing an enduring challenge to the theory of equal human rights for all.

World War II was the defining event for the internationalization of human rights. Human rights were a major part of Allied wartime goals, and they became enshrined after the conclusion of the war by the UN Charter (1945), bedrock human rights texts, including the Genocide Convention and the Universal Declaration of Human Rights in 1948, the Geneva Conventions in 1949, followed in 1966 by the International Covenants on Human Rights. Procedures were also formed for intergovernmental investigation and criminal accountability building on the experience of the Nuremberg Trials (1945–1946), which, after the hiatus of the Cold War, led to the ad hoc tribunals regarding the former Yugoslavia and Rwanda and eventually to the creation of the International Criminal Court in 2002.

Human Rights in the Global Context

To understand how human rights are part of the global agenda, we need to ask why states even accept the idea of human rights obligations when they are supposed to be sovereign. Then we explore what is the current list of human rights generally accepted, before asking whether they correspond to the basic values of all societies or are imposed from the outside for ideological reasons. Finally, we examine how they are transformed from word to deed, from aspiration to practice.

Why Do Sovereign States Accept Human Rights Obligations?

The principle of state sovereignty means that neither other states nor international organizations can intervene in a state's internal affairs. In international law and relations, this principle of nonintervention is balanced by the pledge states make in joining the UN "to take joint and separate action in co-operation with the Organization for the achievement of . . . universal respect for, and observance of, human rights and fundamental freedoms for all without distinction as to race, sex, language or religion."

So state sovereignty is balanced with legitimate concern of the international community about human rights in all countries. How that balance is interpreted varies according to theories of international relations. For *realists* (a theory that focuses on governments as sovereign actors in international affairs, that pursue their national interests through the projection of power, without constraints by any superior authority), only weak countries are under any constraint to allow international scrutiny of their human rights performance. For the *liberal internationalist*, global institutions and values, like human rights, matter more, although the international system is still based on state sovereignty. Theories of *functionalism* attach importance to gradual political federation via regional organizations that slowly shift authority to international institutions. Human rights take on even greater importance for *constructivism*, the most cosmopolitan of international relations theories, which holds that ideas define international structure, which in turn defines the interests and identities of states. Thus, social norms, such as human rights, can shape foreign policy. In sum, as Richard Falk and others argue, absolute sovereignty has given way to the conception of "responsible sovereignty," according to which sovereignty is conditional upon the state's adherence to minimum human rights standards and capacity to protect its citizens.

In practice, states have accepted human rights obligations in many forums, with many possible motivations, with the result that human rights have gradually become part of the definition of acceptable state behavior. In order to understand this phenomenon, it is useful to examine the current set of human rights standards.

How Do We Know Which Rights Are Recognized as Human Rights?

Although it is legitimate to draw on philosophical arguments or activist agendas to claim any global social issue as a human right, it is also useful to identify which rights are legally recognized, the core source for which is the International Bill of Human Rights. This document enumerates approximately 50 normative propositions that have served as the basis for further human rights instruments, including five group rights, 24 civil and political rights (CPR), and 14 economic, social, and cultural rights (ESCR). It also sets out seven principles that explain how the rights should be applied and interpreted. The table at right enumerates the first 43 of these rights.

Finally, the seven *principles of application and interpretation* include the principles of progressive realization of ESCR (states must take meaningful measures toward full realization of these rights), of immediate implementation of CPR (states have duties to respect and ensure respect of these rights), of nondiscrimination applied to all rights, of an effective remedy for violation of CPR, and equality of rights between men and women. The International Bill also specifies that human rights may be subject to limitations and derogations and that the rights in the covenants may not be used as a pretext for lowering an existing standard if there is a higher one under national law.

These rights are traditionally grouped in two major *categories of human rights* (CPR and ESCR, with a third category of solidarity rights—development, clean environment, humanitarian assistance, etc.— sometimes added), but the reasons for separating them into these categories have been questioned. For example, it is often claimed that CPR are absolute and immutable, whereas ESCR are relative and responsive to changing conditions. However, in practice, the establishment and expansion of all rights have been driven by changing power relations, as in the case of torture and slavery—both of which were considered acceptable for centuries.

It is also argued that CPR are to be implemented immediately, may be enforced through judicial remedies, and are relatively cost-free because they merely require the state to leave people alone ("nega-

International Bill of Human Rights, List of Rights, United Nations, 1948 and 1966

Group Rights
1. Self-determination
2. Permanent sovereignty over natural resources
3. Right to enjoy one's culture
4. Right to practice one's religion
5. Right to speak one's language

Civil and Political Rights (CPR)
6. Right to life
7. Freedom from torture
8. Freedom from slavery
9. Freedom from arbitrary arrest/detention
10. Right to humane treatment in detention
11. Freedom of movement and resident
12. Prohibition of expulsion of aliens
13. Freedom of thought, conscience, and religious belief
14. Freedom of expression
15. Right to privacy
16. Non-imprisonment for debt
17. Fair trial (subdivided into 16 enumerated rights)
18. Right to personhood under the law
19. Equality before the law
20. Freedom of assembly
21. Freedom of association
22. Right to marry and found a family
23. Rights of children
24. Right to practice a religion
25. Prohibition of war propaganda and hate speech constituting incitement
26. Right to hold office
27. Right to vote in free elections
28. Right to be elected to office
29. Equal access to public service

Economic, Social, and Cultural Rights (ESCR)
30. Right to earn a living by work freely chosen and accepted
31. Right to just and favorable work conditions
32. Right to form and join trade unions
33. Right to strike
34. Social security
35. Assistance to the family, mothers, and children
36. Adequate standard of living (including food, clothing, and housing)
37. Right to the highest attainable standard of health (mental and physical)
38. Right to education toward the full development of human personality
39. Free and compulsory primary education
40. Availability of other levels of education
41. Participation in cultural life
42. Protection of moral and material rights of creators and transmitters of culture
43. Right to enjoy the benefits of scientific progress

Source: United Nations.

tive rights"), whereas ESCR should be implemented progressively, in accordance with available resources, because they require state expenditure ("positive rights") and are not suitable for lawsuits. While often true, many ESCR have been made "justiciable" (subject to lawsuit by people unsatisfied by the state's implementation), and many CPR require considerable resources (e.g., the funding required for police and judicial systems). Others argue that CPR are appropriate for denouncing violations by states, while ESCR should be subject only to a cooperative approach. Again, reality has shown this is not always the case. So these two categories—which the UN regards as interrelated and equally important—are not watertight and reasons for considering them different by nature may be challenged. In practice, the context dictates the most effective use of resources, institutions, and approaches more than such categorizations.

Are Human Rights the Same for Everyone?

The term "universal human rights" implies that they are the same for everyone. The UDHR refers to "the inherent dignity and . . . equal and inalienable rights of all members of the human family [as] the foundation of freedom, justice and peace in the world." The fact that all countries have endorsed the UDHR implies their universality, at least formally. Conversely, cultural relativists claim that human rights are based on values that vary from one society to another, rather than being universal. For example, the "Asian values" argument states that human rights are a Western idea at odds with Asian governance models. A related view holds that the concept of human rights is a tool of imperialism used to disguise Western ambitions with respect to the developing world. A third is the "clash of civilizations" argument, in which only the liberal West is capable of realizing human rights because the other civilizations lack a sufficient concept of the individual and the rule of law. Compatibility of human rights with diverse belief systems was also an issue in the Arab Spring of 2011, in which both specific Muslim values and universal human rights concerns—as well as economic grievances—motivated peoples across the Middle East and North Africa to overthrow deeply entrenched dictatorships.

The World Conference on Human Rights (Vienna, June 1993, paragraph 5) addressed the general question of balancing universal and cultural claims with this compromise language:

All human rights are universal, indivisible and interdependent and interrelated. The international community must treat human rights globally in a fair and equal manner, on the same footing, and with the same emphasis. While the significance of national and regional particularities and various historical, cultural and religious backgrounds must be borne in mind, it is the duty of States, regardless of their political, economic and cultural systems, to promote and protect all human rights and fundamental freedoms.

This statement captures an important feature of human rights today, namely, that they are universal but must be realized in the context of the prevailing values of each society. To understand this issue fully requires an understanding of how universally accepted human rights are put into practice.

How Are Human Rights Put into Practice?

Human rights are traditionally studied in a global context through the norm-creating processes, which result in global human rights standards, and the norm-enforcement processes, which seek to translate laudable goals into tangible practices. There are continuing and new challenges to the effectiveness of this normative regime.

The norm-creating process refers to authoritative decision-making that results in specific human rights and obligations in a given society and clarifies what is expected to realize the right in practice. The typical norm-creating process in international human rights follows these steps:

1. Expression of concern by a delegate to a political body
2. Lobbying for co-sponsors leading to adoption of a resolution
3. Commissioning of a study on the issue
4. Drafting of a declaration, followed by experience promoting its standards
5. Drafting of a convention, followed by ratification by states, giving it force of law
6. Adoption of an optional protocol for complaints procedures

All the major human rights issues have gone through these phases, which can last decades. Through this process, the International Bill of Human Rights has given rise to several hundred global and regional treaties. A similar process occurs in specialized organizations dealing with such issues as

Means of Implementation and Enforcement of Human Rights

Means of Implementation	Examples
Promotion	
1. Developing awareness	Circulation of publications, media coverage, human rights education.
2. Standard-setting and interpretation	Adoption of declarations and conventions by UN Human Rights Council, regional bodies; general comments by treaty bodies, interpretation by tribunals.
3. Institution building	Judiciary and law enforcement, national commissions and ombudsman offices.
Protection	
4. Monitoring compliance with international standards	Reporting procedures, complaints procedures, fact-finding and investigation, special procedures, periodic review (UPR).
5. Adjudication	Quasi-judicial procedures by treaty bodies, judgments by international and regional tribunals.
6. Political supervision	Resolutions judging state policy and practice, by international bodies; "naming and shaming" by Human Rights Council, UN General Assembly, demarches, public and private statements by states and senior officials.
7. Humanitarian action	Assistance to refugees and internationally displaced persons in humanitarian emergencies; repatriation and resettlement.
8. Coercive action	UN Security Council sanctions, creation of criminal tribunals, and use of force under the doctrine of "responsibility to protect" people from genocide, war crimes, ethnic cleansing, and crimes against humanity.

Source: Author.

victims of armed conflicts, refugees, workers, and environmental protection.

Defining human rights is not enough; measures must be taken to ensure that they are respected, promoted, and fulfilled. In the domestic legal system, law is binding, and the courts and the police are available to use force to compel compliance. In the international human rights regime, law is not treated in quite the same way. The term "enforcement," for example, refers to coerced compliance, which is rare, while most efforts focus on "implementation," that is, a wide range of supervision, monitoring, and general efforts to hold duty holders accountable. Implementation is further subdivided into promotion—preventive measures to ensure respect for human rights in the future—and protection—responses to violations that have occurred in the past. The eight means and methods of implementation may be summarized in three forms of promotion and five forms of protection, given in the table above.

The adoption of norms and the implementation of accountability procedures are not enough to eliminate the deeper causes of human rights deprivation. Reliance on state action in global politics and on profit maximization in global economics—not to mention cultural traditions based on patriarchy, class, and ethnicity—pose major barriers to human rights realization. Because of their relationship to these structural forces, human rights are inherently political. At the same time, human rights offer a normative framework for achieving sustainable change in the midst of these macro forces. Appeals to human rights are generally supported, at least rhetorically, by the community of nations as well as by networks of global solidarity. These networks have profoundly affected history, and they will continue to play a role in the battles of the current century, from environmental degradation and poverty to terrorism and sexual discrimination, which will continue to test the value of human rights as a normative and institutional guide to policy and practice.

The Future

In the coming decades, further expansion of institutional human rights machinery in Asia and the Middle East and progress in treating ESCR as equal in importance to CPR are likely, as is further clarification of emerging issues, such as the rights of sexual minorities, and further refinement of the means of human rights promotion and protection. However, the essential value of human rights thinking and action will remain as a gauge for a government's legitimacy, a guide for prioritizing human progress, and a basis of global social consensus on the values that we share across diverse ideologies and cultures.

Stephen P. Marks

See also: Affirmative Action; Children's Rights; Crimes Against Humanity; Environmental Justice; Gay, Lesbian, Bisexual, and Transgender Issues; Indigenous Peoples' Rights; Law, Rule of; Police Corruption and Brutality; Press, Freedom of; Prisoners and Prisoner Rights; Privacy; Religious Freedom; Unions and Workers' Rights; War Crimes; Women's Rights.

Further Reading

Baxi, Upendra. *The Future of Human Rights*. 2d ed. New York: Oxford University Press, 2006.

Carey, Sabine C. *The Politics of Human Rights: The Quest for Dignity*. New York: Cambridge University Press, 2010.

Clapham, Andrew. *Human Rights: A Very Short Introduction*. New York: Oxford University Press, 2007.

Donnelly, Jack. *Universal Human Rights in Theory and Practice*. 2d ed. Ithaca, NY: Cornell University Press, 2003.

Falk, Richard A. *Human Rights Horizons: The Pursuit of Justice in a Globalizing World*. New York: Routledge, 2001.

Griffin, James. *On Human Rights*. Oxford: Oxford University Press, 2009.

Hunt, Lynn. *Inventing Human Rights: A History*. New York: W.W. Norton, 2008.

Ishay, Micheline. *The History of Human Rights: From Ancient Times to the Globalization Era, With a New Preface*. New York: W.W. Norton, 2008.

Lauren, Paul Gordon. *The Evolution of International Human Rights: Visions Seen*. Philadelphia: University of Pennsylvania Press, 1998.

Lauterpacht, Hersch. *International Law and Human Rights*. New York: Garland, 1950 (reprint 1973).

Moeckli, Daniel, Sangeeta Shah, Sandesh Sivakumaran, and David Harris. *International Human Rights Law*. New York: Oxford University Press, 2010.

Moyn, Samuel. *The Last Utopia: Human Rights in History*. Cambridge, MA: Belknap Press of Harvard University Press, 2012.

Nickel, James W. *Making Sense of Human Rights*. Malden, MA: Blackwell, 2007.

Salomen, Margot E. *Global Responsibility for Human Rights*. Oxford: Oxford University Press, 2007.

Sen, Amartya. "Elements of a Theory of Human Rights." *Philosophy & Public Affairs* 32:4 (2004): 313–356.

Sikkink, Kathryn. *The Justice Cascade: How Human Rights Prosecutions Are Changing World Politics*. New York: W.W. Norton, 2011.

Simmons, Beth A. *Mobilizing for Human Rights: International Law in Domestic Politics*. New York: Cambridge University Press, 2009.

Web Sites

Amnesty International: www.amnesty.org

Business and Human Rights: www.business-humanrights.org

Center for Economic and Social Rights (CESR): www.cesr.org

Human Rights First: www.humanrightsfirst.org

Human Rights Internet (HRI): www.hri.ca

Human Rights Watch: www.hrw.org

International Commission of Jurists: www.icj.org

International Federation for Human Rights (FIDH): www.fidh.org

International Service for Human Rights: www.ishr.ch

New Tactics in Human Rights: www.newtactics.org

Office of the High Commissioner for Human Rights (UN): www.ohchr.org/english/

Peoples Movement for Human Rights Learning: www.pdhre.org

University of Minnesota Human Rights Library: www.umn.edu/hrts/

World Health Organization: www.who.int/hhr/en/

Documents

Document 1: Declaration of the Rights of Man and of the Citizen, 1789

The fundamental document of the French Revolution, the Declaration of the Rights of Man and of the Citizen was written by the Marquis de Lafayette for the revolutionary National Assembly, which approved it on August 26, 1789. The declaration was the first great expression of the Enlightenment idea of natural rights (or human rights in modern political nomenclature)—that is, rights that do not necessarily come from government but are inherent in being human and are valid for all men (women were not generally included in such ideas), in all places at all times.

The representatives of the French people, organized as a National Assembly, believing that the ignorance, neglect, or contempt of the rights of man are the sole cause of public calamities and of the corruption of governments, have determined to set forth in a solemn declaration the natural, unalienable, and sacred rights of man, in order that this declaration, being constantly before all the members of the Social body, shall remind them continually of their rights and duties; in order that the acts of the legislative power, as well as those of the executive power, may be compared at any moment with the objects and purposes of all political institutions and may thus be more respected, and, lastly, in order that the grievances of the citizens, based hereafter upon simple and incontestable principles, shall tend to the maintenance of the constitution and redound to the happiness of all. Therefore the National Assembly recognizes and proclaims, in the presence and under the auspices of the Supreme Being, the following rights of man and of the citizen:

Articles:

1. Men are born and remain free and equal in rights. Social distinctions may be founded only upon the general good.

2. The aim of all political association is the preservation of the natural and imprescriptible rights of man. These rights are liberty, property, security, and resistance to oppression.

3. The principle of all sovereignty resides essentially in the nation. No body nor individual may exercise any authority which does not proceed directly from the nation.

4. Liberty consists in the freedom to do everything which injures no one else; hence the exercise of the natural rights of each man has no limits except those which assure to the other members of the society the enjoyment of the same rights. These limits can only be determined by law.

5. Law can only prohibit such actions as are hurtful to society. Nothing may be prevented which is not forbidden by law, and no one may be forced to do anything not provided for by law.

6. Law is the expression of the general will. Every citizen has a right to participate personally, or through his representative, in its foundation. It must be the same for all, whether it protects or punishes. All citizens, being equal in the eyes of the law, are equally eligible to all dignities and to all public positions and occupations, according to their abilities, and without distinction except that of their virtues and talents.

7. No person shall be accused, arrested, or imprisoned except in the cases and according to the forms prescribed by law. Any one soliciting, transmitting, executing, or causing to be executed, any arbitrary order, shall be punished. But any citizen summoned or arrested in virtue of the law shall submit without delay, as resistance constitutes an offense.

8. The law shall provide for such punishments only as are strictly and obviously necessary, and no one shall suffer punishment except it be legally inflicted in virtue of a law passed and promulgated before the commission of the offense.

9. As all persons are held innocent until they shall have been declared guilty, if arrest shall be deemed indispensable, all harshness not essential to the securing of the prisoner's person shall be severely repressed by law.

10. No one shall be disquieted on account of his opinions, including his religious views, provided their manifestation does not disturb the public order established by law.

11. The free communication of ideas and opinions is one of the most precious of the rights of man. Every citizen may, accordingly, speak, write, and print with freedom,

but shall be responsible for such abuses of this freedom as shall be defined by law.

12. The security of the rights of man and of the citizen requires public military forces. These forces are, therefore, established for the good of all and not for the personal advantage of those to whom they shall be intrusted.

13. A common contribution is essential for the maintenance of the public forces and for the cost of administration. This should be equitably distributed among all the citizens in proportion to their means.

14. All the citizens have a right to decide, either personally or by their representatives, as to the necessity of the public contribution; to grant this freely; to know to what uses it is put; and to fix the proportion, the mode of assessment and of collection and the duration of the taxes.

15. Society has the right to require of every public agent an account of his administration.

16. A society in which the observance of the law is not assured, nor the separation of powers defined, has no constitution at all.

17. Since property is an inviolable and sacred right, no one shall be deprived thereof except where public necessity, legally determined, shall clearly demand it, and then only on condition that the owner shall have been previously and equitably indemnified.

Source: Avalon Project.

Document 2: Universal Declaration of Human Rights (1948)

On December 10, 1948, the General Assembly of the United Nations, meeting in Paris, adopted and proclaimed the Universal Declaration of Human Rights. The document defines the aspirations of the international community to be guided by its 30 articles in national and international policy. The declaration grew out of previous human rights documents, from the French Revolution's Declaration of the Rights of Man and the Citizen in 1789 to Franklin Roosevelt's Four Freedoms, which were adopted by the Allied governments as the principles for a post–World War II global order.

PREAMBLE

Whereas recognition of the inherent dignity and of the equal and inalienable rights of all members of the human family is the foundation of freedom, justice and peace in the world,

Whereas disregard and contempt for human rights have resulted in barbarous acts [that] have outraged the conscience of mankind, and the advent of a world in which human beings shall enjoy freedom of speech and belief and freedom from fear and want has been proclaimed as the highest aspiration of the common people,

Whereas it is essential, if man is not to be compelled to have recourse, as a last resort, to rebellion against tyranny and oppression, that human rights should be protected by the rule of law,

Whereas it is essential to promote the development of friendly relations between nations,

Whereas the peoples of the United Nations have in the Charter reaffirmed their faith in fundamental human rights, in the dignity and worth of the human person and in the equal rights of men and women and have determined to promote social progress and better standards of life in larger freedom,

Whereas Member States have pledged themselves to achieve, in cooperation with the United Nations, the promotion of universal respect for and observance of human rights and fundamental freedoms,

Whereas a common understanding of these rights and freedoms is of the greatest importance for the full realization of this pledge,

Now, Therefore THE GENERAL ASSEMBLY proclaims THIS UNIVERSAL DECLARATION OF HUMAN RIGHTS as a common standard of achievement for all peoples and all nations, to the end that every individual and every organ of society, keeping this Declaration constantly in mind, shall strive by teaching and education to promote respect for these rights and freedoms and by progressive measures, national and international, to secure their universal and effective recognition and observance, both among the peoples of Member States themselves and among the peoples of territories under their jurisdiction.

Article 1.
All human beings are born free and equal in dignity and rights. They are endowed with reason and conscience and should act toward one another in a spirit of brotherhood.

Article 2.
Everyone is entitled to all the rights and freedoms set forth in this Declaration, without distinction of any kind, such as race, colour, sex, language, religion, political or other opinion, national or social origin, property, birth or other status. Furthermore, no distinction shall be made on the basis of the political, jurisdictional or international status of the country or territory to which a person belongs, whether it be independent, trust, non-self-governing or under any other limitation of sovereignty.

Article 3.
Everyone has the right to life, liberty and security of person.

Article 4.
No one shall be held in slavery or servitude; slavery and the slave trade shall be prohibited in all their forms.

Article 5.
No one shall be subjected to torture or to cruel, inhuman or degrading treatment or punishment.

Article 6.
Everyone has the right to recognition everywhere as a person before the law.

Article 7.
All are equal before the law and are entitled without any discrimination to equal protection of the law. All are entitled to equal protection against any discrimination in violation of this Declaration and against any incitement to such discrimination.

Article 8.
Everyone has the right to an effective remedy by the competent national tribunals for acts violating the fundamental rights granted him by the constitution or by law.

Article 9.
No one shall be subjected to arbitrary arrest, detention or exile.

Article 10.
Everyone is entitled in full equality to a fair and public hearing by an independent and impartial tribunal, in the determination of his rights and obligations and of any criminal charge against him.

Article 11.
(1) Everyone charged with a penal offence has the right to be presumed innocent until proved guilty according to law in a public trial at which he has had all the guarantees necessary for his defence.

(2) No one shall be held guilty of any penal offence on account of any act or omission which did not constitute a penal offence, under national or international law, at the time when it was committed. Nor shall a heavier penalty be imposed than the one that was applicable at the time the penal offence was committed.

Article 12.

No one shall be subjected to arbitrary interference with his privacy, family, home or correspondence, nor to attacks upon his honour and reputation. Everyone has the right to the protection of the law against such interference or attacks.

Article 13.

(1) Everyone has the right to freedom of movement and residence within the borders of each state.

(2) Everyone has the right to leave any country, including his own, and to return to his country.

Article 14.

(1) Everyone has the right to seek and to enjoy in other countries asylum from persecution.

(2) This right may not be invoked in the case of prosecutions genuinely arising from nonpolitical crimes or from acts contrary to the purposes and principles of the United Nations.

Article 15.

(1) Everyone has the right to a nationality.

(2) No one shall be arbitrarily deprived of his nationality nor denied the right to change his nationality.

Article 16.

(1) Men and women of full age, without any limitation due to race, nationality or religion, have the right to marry and to found a family. They are entitled to equal rights as to marriage, during marriage and at its dissolution.

(2) Marriage shall be entered into only with the free and full consent of the intending spouses.

(3) The family is the natural and fundamental group unit of society and is entitled to protection by society and the State.

Article 17.

(1) Everyone has the right to own property alone as well as in association with others.

(2) No one shall be arbitrarily deprived of his property.

Article 18.

Everyone has the right to freedom of thought, conscience and religion; this right includes freedom to change his religion or belief, and freedom, either alone or in community with others and in public or private, to manifest his religion or belief in teaching, practice, worship and observance.

Article 19.

Everyone has the right to freedom of opinion and expression; this right includes freedom to hold opinions without interference and to seek, receive and impart information and ideas through any media and regardless of frontiers.

Article 20.

(1) Everyone has the right to freedom of peaceful assembly and association.

(2) No one may be compelled to belong to an association.

Article 21.

(1) Everyone has the right to take part in the government of his country, directly or through freely chosen representatives.

(2) Everyone has the right of equal access to public service in his country.

(3) The will of the people shall be the basis of the authority of government; this will shall be expressed in periodic and genuine elections, which shall be by universal and equal suffrage and shall be held by secret vote or by equivalent free voting procedures.

Article 22.

Everyone, as a member of society, has the right to social security and is entitled to realization, through national effort and international cooperation and in accordance with the organization and resources of each State, of the economic, social and cultural rights indispensable for his dignity and the free development of his personality.

Article 23.

(1) Everyone has the right to work, to free choice of employment, to just and favorable conditions of work and to protection against unemployment.

(2) Everyone, without any discrimination, has the right to equal pay for equal work.

(3) Everyone who works has the right to just and favourable remuneration ensuring for himself and his family an existence worthy of human dignity, and supplemented, if necessary, by other means of social protection.

(4) Everyone has the right to form and to join trade unions for the protection of his interests.

Article 24.

Everyone has the right to rest and leisure, including reasonable limitation of working hours and periodic holidays with pay.

Article 25.

(1) Everyone has the right to a standard of living adequate for the health and well-being of himself and of his family, including food, clothing, housing and medical care, and necessary social services, and the right to security in the event of unemployment, sickness, disability, widowhood, old age or other lack of livelihood in circumstances beyond his control.

(2) Motherhood and childhood are entitled to special care and assistance. All children, whether born in or out of wedlock, shall enjoy the same social protection.

Article 26.

(1) Everyone has the right to education. Education shall be free, at least in the elementary and fundamental stages. Elementary education shall be compulsory. Technical and professional education shall be made generally available and higher education shall be equally accessible to all on the basis of merit.

(2) Education shall be directed to the full development of the human personality and to the strengthening of respect for human rights and fundamental freedoms. It shall promote understanding, tolerance and friendship among all nations, racial or religious groups, and shall further the activities of the United Nations for the maintenance of peace.

(3) Parents have a prior right to choose the kind of education that shall be given to their children.

Article 27.

(1) Everyone has the right freely to participate in the cultural life of the community, to enjoy the arts and to share in scientific advancement and its benefits.

(2) Everyone has the right to the protection of the moral and material interests resulting from any scientific, literary or artistic production of which he is the author.

Article 28.

Everyone is entitled to a social and international order in which the rights and freedoms set forth in this Declaration can be fully realized.

Article 29.

(1) Everyone has duties to the community in which alone the free and full development of his personality is possible.

(2) In the exercise of his rights and freedoms, everyone shall be subject only to such limitations as are determined by law solely for the purpose of securing due recognition and respect for the rights and freedoms of others and of meeting the just requirements of morality, public order and the general welfare in a democratic society.

(3) These rights and freedoms may in no case be exercised contrary to the purposes and principles of the United Nations.

Article 30.

Nothing in this Declaration may be interpreted as implying for any State, group or person any right to engage in any activity or to perform any act aimed at the destruction of any of the rights and freedoms set forth herein.

Source: United Nations.

HUNGER AND MALNUTRITION

Hunger and malnutrition are distinct social conditions. "Hunger" is commonly used to refer to the stomach pains that accompany a lack of food. In a global context, however, the word is used to mean a scarcity of consumable food—not having as many calories available as are necessary to sustain a healthy body. Regardless of age, race, gender, or nationality, hunger affects every aspect of a person's life. This includes an individual's physical and psychological development and well-being, learning ability and perceptions, ability to interact socially, and capacity to react to other human beings with appropriate emotions. Profound, lasting hunger can be fatal; death by hunger is called starvation.

"Malnutrition" refers to a significant and ongoing lack of specific nutritional elements necessary for good health such as proteins, fats, vitamins, and minerals. There are two basic types of malnutrition. The more lethal form is protein-energy deficiency—a shortage of protein, which is essential as a source of energy and amino acids and a building block for bodily tissues. The other form of malnutrition is micronutrient (vitamin and mineral) deficiency—in which an individual does not consume or does not absorb enough of one or more of the nutrients that the body requires to function. Over a period of time, both protein and micronutrient deficiencies can lead to health problems, and even death. Malnutrition can affect people of all ages, though infants and children are particularly vulnerable.

Hunger and malnutrition can exist independently from one another; it is possible to have enough calories without enough nutrients, or to have enough nutrients without enough calories. However, more often than not, the two conditions coexist. Currently, there are 925 million people in the world who are malnourished, and the great majority of those—850 million—also live in a perpetual state of hunger. The issue is primarily one that poorer nations grapple with; a staggering 98 percent of the people who do not get an adequate diet live in developing countries.

Historical Background

Hunger is such a ubiquitous and common human problem that history rarely takes note of its role in daily life, documenting only extensive and devastating shortages of food (that is to say, famines). The first recorded account of a famine comes from ancient Egypt, more than 4,000 years ago. After a severe drought, the kingdom experienced widespread starvation, and scribes reported that, "All of Upper Egypt was dying of hunger and people were eating their children."

Such shortages have been commonplace across the world in subsequent centuries. Chinese records, for example, document a remarkable 1,828 instances of famine between 108 B.C.E. and 1911 C.E. Europe has suffered as well, most notably during the Great Famine of 1315–1317, which killed as much as 10 percent of the population of some countries, and during Ireland's Potato Famine of 1845–1849, which left 1 million people dead and compelled at least 2 million more to flee the country. In Mexico, the native population was victimized by a catastrophic famine in 850 and another in 1454. Japan had at least 21 famines that swept across the island between 1603 and 1868. India has been highly susceptible to food shortages as well, the worst being the 1702–1704 Deccan famine, which claimed more than 2 million lives.

The cause-and-effect relationship at work during periods of famine—a lack of food leads to hunger and starvation—is self-evident and easily understood. It took much longer for human beings to fully appreciate the importance and mechanics of proper nutrition. The basic idea that underlies the science of nutrition—that some foods are better for the body, or are essential to good health—is an old one. More than 4,000 years ago, the ancient Egyptians learned that eating liver cured night blindness (caused by a deficiency of vitamin A, a compound abundant in liver). Around 475 B.C.E., the Greek philosopher and scientist Anaxagoras argued that foods contained "generative components" necessary for human health. The Old Testament book of Daniel, which dates roughly to 165 B.C.E., describes a scene in which captured Jewish soldiers prove that their kosher, vegetable-heavy diet is healthier than the diet of their Babylonian captors.

In the modern era, the first important step forward in understanding nutrition was taken by British physician and naval officer Dr. James Lind, who in 1747 demonstrated that sailors who consumed limes were able to avoid scurvy (a deficiency of vitamin C that causes lethargy and bleeding). Thus the slang term "limeys" was born. A century later, the Japanese physician and naval officer Kanehiro Takaki built upon Lind's work, demonstrating that a diet rich in vegetables and meats would accomplish the same goal as consuming limes. Not long thereafter, the German chemist Eugen Baumann and the Dutch physician Christiaan Eijkman, working independently, discovered that beriberi (a condition that causes neurological and cardiovascular dysfunction) could be combated by eating unprocessed brown rice. Like Lind and Takaki before them, Baumann and Eijkman had no explanation for their discovery, unaware that beriberi is caused by a shortage of vitamin B1 (thiamine), found in abundance in the hulls of brown rice.

It was not until the twentieth century that physicians and scientists finally solved the puzzle. In 1898, British physician Frederick Hopkins argued persuasively that some foods contained "accessory factors" that are necessary to survival and that the body cannot manufacture on its own. In 1910, Japanese scientist Umetaro Suzuki became the first person to isolate one of these accessory factors (the aforementioned vitamin B1). Unaware of Suzuki's findings, the Polish chemist Casimir Funk isolated the same compound in 1912, and proposed that the substances be called *vital amines*, ultimately shortened to vitamins. Funk's work opened the floodgates, and by 1941 another dozen vitamins had been isolated. As a consequence of their efforts in laying the groundwork for our understanding of vitamins and their role in nutrition, Eijkman and Hopkins shared the 1929 Nobel Prize for medicine.

These insights came just as hunger and malnutrition were reaching their worst levels in human history, claiming more than 70 million lives over the course of the twentieth century. This includes the most devastating famine of all time, which took place in China between 1958 and 1961. During those years,

Most Important Vitamins and Year of Discovery

Year of discovery	Vitamin
1913	A (Retinol)
1910	B1 (Thiamine)
1920	C (Ascorbic acid)
1920	D (Calciferol)
1920	B2 (Riboflavin)
1922	E (Tocopherol)
1926	B12 (Cobalamin)
1929	K1 (Phylloquinone)
1931	B5 (Pantothenic acid)
1931	B7 (Biotin)
1934	B6 (Pyridoxine)
1936	B3 (Niacin)
1941	B9 (Folic acid)

Source: Author.

Chinese premier Mao Zedong tried to forcibly convert his nation from an agricultural to an industrial economy. The Great Leap Forward, as he dubbed it, was a failure, and caused between 35 and 45 million Chinese citizens to starve to death.

In response to the suffering witnessed during and after World War II, the latter half of the twentieth century saw the first international efforts toward combating hunger and malnutrition. In 1954, U.S. president Dwight D. Eisenhower signed a bill creating the Food for Peace Program, which sends excess food produced by American farms to needy countries. In 1960, the United Nations created the World Food Programme (WFP) to distribute foodstuffs in impoverished nations. This was followed by the establishment of the World Food Council (WFC) in 1974, a UN bureaucracy that works with national governments to combat hunger.

The postwar years also witnessed remarkable technical progress in the areas of crop production, fertilizer, and pest control. Most significant was the work of geneticist Norman Borlaug, whose experiments with wheat culminated in the development of a strain that yielded considerably more grain than any other existing variety and was also nearly impervious to insects. Borlaug arranged for the propagation of the new species throughout Mexico, India, and Pakistan; these efforts are credited with saving a billion lives from starvation. For his work, Borlaug was awarded the Nobel Peace Prize in 1970.

Causes

Hunger is no longer a necessary burden for people to bear—the world produces enough food to feed all of its citizens. Studies suggest that if the total global output of foodstuffs were divided evenly among the population, each person would have 2,720 calories per day to live on. This is more than enough for adult males (who require 2,500 calories per day) and is considerably more than the needs of an adult female (2,000 calories per day) or a child (1,000–1,400 calories per day). Similarly, the world has abundant supplies of all the minerals needed for human health. The problem, then, is one of access and distribution.

The single most important factor keeping people from getting the food they need is poverty. More than a quarter of the world's population lives on $1.25 or less each day, and in many nations that is not enough to afford both shelter and adequate nutrition. The problem is exacerbated in countries with regimes that hoard resources, sometimes including foreign aid. It is also a self-reinforcing cycle, as hungry and malnourished people lack the energy to labor productively, which leads to lower wages, which leads to less food, and so forth.

Other factors can also cause—or exacerbate—hunger and malnutrition. Armed conflict disrupts supply chains and damages farms, commonly leading to famine. Wars tend to displace people, many of whom end up in refugee camps, where they are at the mercy of government authorities and likely to suffer from a shortage of resources. Currently, the UN estimates that there are 36 million displaced people and 10 million refugees in the world.

Climate change plays a role in hunger as well. Both droughts and flooding have been linked to the rise in temperatures across the globe; both can be devastating to farms. Further, most crops grow only under very specific climactic conditions. If the mean temperature or amount of moisture in an area changes, the crops that once grew there will not grow well, and may not grow at all.

Global Impact

The most profound consequence of poor nutrition, of course, is premature death. Experts estimate that over 9 million people die worldwide each year because of poor nutrition, including 5 million children. Put another way, a child dies from hunger or malnutrition every six seconds.

Beyond the risk of mortality, hunger and malnutrition also interfere with child development, beginning in the womb. Poor diets among pregnant women in

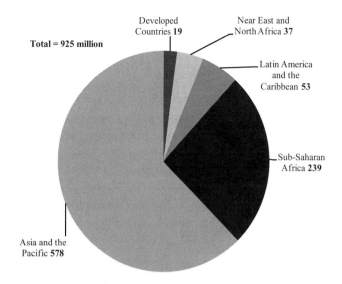

Global Undernourishment, by Region, 2010 (in millions)

Total = 925 million

Developed Countries **19**

Near East and North Africa **37**

Latin America and the Caribbean **53**

Sub-Saharan Africa **239**

Asia and the Pacific **578**

Note: All numbers are rounded.
Source: FAO.

developing countries result in 1 out of 6 infants being born with a low birth weight, which is a significant risk factor for neonatal death, as well as blindness, learning disabilities, mental retardation, and overall poor health. Following birth, a child that remains hungry or malnourished will not grow as rapidly as he or she should, a process called "stunting" or "failure to thrive." An estimated 171 million children worldwide are stunted, including 36 percent of children in Asia and 35 percent in Africa. As growth slows, brain development lags and children learn poorly.

In addition, hunger and malnutrition also trigger a host of health complications—again, especially in children. Poor diets magnify the effects of every disease, and undernourished children are ten times more likely to die from infections or illnesses than are children on a healthy diet. More specifically, hunger and malnutrition are contributing causes in the majority of cases in which a child dies of diarrhea (61 percent), malaria (57 percent), or pneumonia (52 percent).

Geographically, the burden of hunger and malnutrition weighs most heavily on Africa, Asia, and Latin America. In terms of deaths from hunger or malnutrition per 100,000 citizens, all but two of the 25 most vulnerable nations in the world are located in one of those three regions, a list led by Haiti (53.3 deaths per 100,000 people), Angola (36.2), Guatemala (33.2), Guinea-Bissau (32.3), Mali (30.1), and Laos (28.9). By way of comparison, the United States has a rate of 1.0 death from hunger or malnutrition per 100,000 people, Australia 0.5, and the United Kingdom 0.3.

The hunger and malnutrition crisis never recedes entirely, although its most serious manifestations are cyclical in nature. In times of global economic recession, food prices tend to rise while foreign aid is often reduced. This has a staggering impact on the poorest households, which slip from borderline subsistence to a wholly inadequate diet. Rates of death and disease skyrocket, taxing poor countries' medical systems and shrinking the pool of healthy laborers, thus aggravating an already weak national economy.

Food Insecurity and Protein-Energy Malnutrition

Much of the world's hunger is the product of "food insecurity," which is defined as the limited or uncertain availability of nutritionally adequate food. The term also encompasses circumstances in which food may technically be available, but acquisition or consumption of that food would violate cultural norms. If a Hindu could only have a balanced diet by eating beef, for example, or if a person could only be properly fed if they stole, they are still regarded as suffering from food insecurity.

A total lack of food leads to starvation. The more common type of food insecurity, however, is a diet with adequate or semi-adequate quantities of carbohydrates (rice and other grains) but short on fats and proteins (which tend to be the most resource-intensive foods to produce, and thus the most expensive foods to procure). Humans must ingest protein, which the body uses as a building block for muscles and as a source of amino acids.

A chronic lack of protein results in protein-energy malnutrition (PEM), in which the human body rapidly deteriorates, is depleted of strength, and becomes more susceptible to illness and chronic diarrhea. Children who suffer from PEM are susceptible to increased behavioral problems and low academic achievement.

In addition to these general health and development problems, there is a trio of syndromes specifically associated with PEM. Marasmus is a significant loss of body tissue (a symptom also known as "wasting"), particularly noticeable in the buttocks, chest, stomach, and thighs. Kwashiorkor is characterized by an enlarged liver, inflammation of the skin, loss of teeth and hair, and swelling (particularly in the feet and abdomen).

Marasmic KW is a combination of both conditions, with sufferers exhibiting the wasting typical of marasmus and the swelling typical of kwashiorkor. All three conditions are predominantly found among children, and afflict at least 10 million juveniles worldwide.

Micronutrient Malnutrition

Iron Deficiency: Iron, found in leafy green vegetables, red meat, and egg yolks, enables the blood to carry oxygen throughout the body, and helps the muscles to store and use that oxygen. Insufficient iron intake can result in iron-deficient anemia, the most common nutrition deficiency in the world.

In infants and small children, iron-deficient anemia leads to delayed motor and mental development. In older children, teenagers, and many adults, it can cause serious memory problems and confusion, and can result in severe muscle fatigue that affects their ability to work. Further, iron-deficient anemia can trigger unusual behaviors, most notably restless-leg syndrome (an uncontrollable urge to move one's body in response to uncomfortable sensations) or pica (an appetite for non-nutritious substances like dirt, glass, hair, or ice).

It is estimated that iron deficiency affects more than 2 billion people worldwide. It is particularly common in pregnant women (who are supplying blood to two, or more, bodies and thus need a greater amount of iron than most individuals). Roughly 42 percent of the world's pregnant women are afflicted with iron-deficient anemia, and the condition causes 20 percent of postpartum maternal deaths in Africa and Asia.

Iodine Deficiency: Iodine is acquired by consuming seafood, dairy products, plants, and fortified table salt. Iodine deficiency during fetal and child development is the most common cause of preventable brain damage in the world. A shortage can also lead to birth defects in infants and developmental delays in older children. Adult symptoms of iodine deficiency include goiters (swelling of the thyroid gland), skin and gastrointestinal problems, and fatigue.

It was not until the 1980s that physicians and scientists fully understood the significance of iodine deficiency. Today, we know it trails iron deficiency only slightly in terms of global prevalence, affecting 1.9 billion people across 54 countries.

Zinc Deficiency: Zinc is present in oysters, red meat, lobster and crab, beans, whole grains, oats, peas, nuts, and dairy products. Zinc deficiency (called

The World Food Programme makes an emergency delivery to North Korea, a nation beset by famine in the 1990s and chronic food shortages. Despite global food aid programs, one in seven people worldwide is undernourished, and the number is rising. *(Patrick Aventurier/Gamma-Rapho via Getty Images)*

hypozincemia) results in stunting, reduced immune function, loss of appetite, cognitive impairment, and diarrhea.

Hypozincemia affects about 1.7 billion people worldwide and is ranked by the United Nations as the fifth most important risk factor for disease in the developing world. In some nations—India and Turkey in particular—as much as 75 percent of the population lacks an adequate amount of zinc in their diets.

Vitamin A Deficiency: Vitamin A, found in meat, eggs, cheese, and many fruits and vegetables, is essential in the formation of healthy skin, teeth, skeletal and soft tissue, and mucus membranes. A deficiency can cause night blindness and reduce the body's resistance to infectious disease. A long-term deficiency can cause permanent loss of vision, stunting, and death.

Currently, it is estimated that between 100 and 140 million children throughout the world are vitamin A deficient, including one-third of children under the age of five. Each year, an estimated 250,000–500,000 of these vitamin A-deficient children become blind. Indeed, the United Nations regards vitamin A deficiency as the leading cause of preventable blindness in children.

Combating Hunger and Malnutrition

Hunger and malnutrition have been at the forefront of global activism for the past half-century and continue to receive a great deal of attention. There are dozens of prominent organizations working to solve the problem, among them the Bill & Melinda Gates Foundation, the Canadian International Development Agency, the Global Alliance for Improved Nutrition, UNICEF, the United States Agency for International Development, WFC, WFP, and the World Health Organization (WHO).

The most direct way to combat hunger, of course, is to provide food to undernourished people. Many organizations are active on this front, most notably WFP, which works with people who do not have adequate nutrition for themselves or their families. In an average year, WFP serves 90 million individuals, 58 million of them children.

For healthier babies, WHO and other organizations recommend exclusive breastfeeding for six months, followed by the introduction of age-appropriate foods at six months and continued breastfeeding for up to two years. Experts suggest that about 20 percent of deaths among children under five would be avoided by following these guidelines.

Dietary diversification is another means of combating hunger and malnutrition. In the short term, WFP and other programs distribute nutrient-rich foods like spinach and tuna. A more lasting solution is to help families—particularly in Asia and Africa—to plant and raise home gardens. In the spirit of Norman Borlaug, there has also been some experimentation with sustainable high-yield, protein-rich plants, notably the algae called spirulina. Though studies are ongoing, there is hope that it might be a potent weapon against protein-energy malnutrition.

High doses of deficient nutrients are another means of combating the ill effects of a poor diet. This approach works particularly well with vitamin A, which remains in the human body for a relatively long period of time. To this end, UNICEF partnered with the Canadian International Development Agency, the U.S. Agency for International Development, and the Micronutrient Initiative to launch the Vitamin A Global Initiative in 1988. The initiative pays the cost of vitamin A shots or pills for deficient children. It is estimated that the program has saved 1.25 million lives in 40 countries.

Similarly, ready-to-use therapeutic foods (RUTFs)—which are calorie-dense and high in nutrients—are being deployed in some places to help fight malnutrition in emergency cases. Among them is Plumpy'nut, a plastic-wrapped peanut-based paste manufactured in France. It has 500 calories per serving, plus a wide variety of vitamins and minerals. Further, in contrast to the treatments for severe malnutrition utilized in past decades, it does not require the supervision of a doctor nor does it need refrigeration. A two-month supply, which is enough to restore many individuals to full health, costs $60.

Fortified foods are a particularly promising tool in the fight against hunger and malnutrition. Iodized salt, for example, cures iodine deficiency and costs about five cents per person per year. In Guatemala, sugar has been fortified with vitamin A, with promising results. In India, scientists are experimenting with "golden rice," which has been manipulated at the genetic level to produce beta-carotene (used by the body to make vitamin A).

A final weapon in combating hunger is information. In 1986, WHO established the Integrated Nutrition Global Databases, which collect research on food and nutrition dating back to 1960. This was followed by the Global Database on National Nutrition Policies and Programmes in 1995, which tracks the progress being made in specific countries. WHO makes this information available to activists across the globe, while also using it as the basis for country-specific nutrition guidelines and policy statements like the 1992 World Declaration and Plan of Action for Nutrition.

The Future

Global hunger and malnutrition are unlikely to disappear anytime soon, given how very many people are still underfed. However, it cannot be denied that much progress has been made, and activists are particularly excited about their successes in addressing specific dimensions of the problem. For example, iodized salt is now available in 66 percent of the world's households, and by 2020 WHO and WFP hope that number will be in the 90s. Similarly, vitamin A deficiency is in steep decline worldwide thanks to the Vitamin A Global Initiative. In both cases, WHO has gone so far as to suggest that both problems might soon be eliminated. The signs are hopeful, but only time will tell if this is a realistic possibility.

Virginia Payne Dow

See also: Farm Policy; Obesity and Eating Disorders; Poverty; Public Health.

Further Reading

Barman, Dhiraj. *Child Undernutrition in India: Inter-state and Social Inequalities.* Saarbrücken, Germany: LAP Lambert, 2011.

Black, Robert E., et al. "Maternal and Child Undernutrition: Global and Regional Exposures and Health Consequences." *The Lancet* 371.9608 January 19, 2008: 243–260.

Fogel, Robert William. *The Escape from Hunger and Premature Death, 1700–2100: Europe, America, and the Third World.* New York: Cambridge University Press, 2004.

Fridell, Ron. *The War on Hunger: Dealing with Dictators, Deserts, and Debt.* Brookfield, CT: Millbrook, 2004.

Nardo, Don. *Malnutrition.* San Diego, CA: Lucent, 2007.

Schwartz-Nobel, Loretta. *Growing Up Empty: The Hunger Epidemic in America.* New York: HarperCollins, 2002.

Shepherd, Jack, and John R. Butterfly. *Hunger: The Biology and Politics of Starvation.* Lebanon, NH: University Press of New England, 2010.

Thurow, Roger, and Scott Kilman. *Enough: Why the World's Poorest Starve in an Age of Plenty.* New York: PublicAffairs, 2009.

Vesler, Lyman W., ed. *Malnutrition in the 21st Century.* Hauppauge, NY: Nova Science, 2007.

Von Grebmer, Klaus, et al. *2010 Global Hunger Index. The Challenge of Hunger: Focus on the Crisis of Child Undernutrition.* Washington, DC; Bonn; Dublin: International Food Policy Research Institute, 2010.

World Food Programme, United Nations. *Hunger and Markets: World Hunger Series.* London, UK: Routledge, 2009.

Web Sites

Alliance Against Hunger and Malnutrition: www.aahm.org

Children's Hunger Relief Fund: www.chrf.org

Global Malnutrition: www.actionagainsthunger.org

Hunger and Malnutrition, Africa: www.ncbi.nlm.nih.gov

Undernutrition: www.hunger-undernutrition.org

World Disasters Report: www.ifrc.org

World Food Programme: www.wfp.org

World Hunger and Poverty Facts and Statistics: www.worldhunger.org

World Hunger Relief Program: www.worldhungerrelief.org

Documents

Document 1: "The Irish Potato Famine," Article in the *Illustrated London News,* 1847

The Irish Potato Famine of the 1840s was one of the worst instances of mass starvation in human history. In 1847, the Illustrated London News *hired an Irish artist named James Mahoney to travel through the country and report on what he saw. The stories he filed, one of which is excerpted here, shocked the British public.*

I started from Cork, by the mail, for Skibbereen and saw little until we came to Clonakilty, where the coach stopped for breakfast; and here, for the first time, the horrors of the poverty became visible, in the vast number of famished poor, who flocked around the coach to beg alms: amongst them was a woman carrying in her arms the corpse of a fine child, and making the most distressing appeal to the passengers for aid to enable her to purchase a coffin and bury her dear little baby. This horrible spectacle induced me to make some inquiry about her, when I learned from the people of the hotel that each day brings dozens of such applicants into the town.

After leaving Clonakilty, each step that we took westward brought fresh evidence of the truth of the reports of the misery, as we either met a funeral or a coffin at every hundred yards, until we approached the country of the Shepperton Lakes. Here, the distress became more striking, from the decrease of numbers at the funerals, none having more than eight or ten attendants, and many only two or three.

We next reached Skibbereen . . . We first proceeded to Bridgetown . . . and there I saw the dying, the living, and the dead, lying indiscriminately upon the same floor, without anything between them and the cold earth, save a few miserable rags upon them. To point to any particular house as a proof of this would be a waste of time, as all were in the same state; and, not a single house out of 500 could boast of being free from death and fever, though several could be pointed out with the dead lying close to the living for the space of three or four, even six days, without any effort being made to remove the bodies to a last resting place.

After leaving this abode of death, we proceeded to High-street, or Old Chapel-lane and there found one house, without door or window, filled with destitute people lying on the bare floor; and one, fine, tall, stout country lad, who had entered some hours previously to find shelter from the piercing cold, lay here dead amongst others likely soon to follow him. The appeals to the feelings and professional skill of my kind attendants here became truly heart-rending; and so distressed Dr. Donovan, that he begged me not to go into the house, and to avoid coming into contact with the people surrounding the doorway . . .

Next morning . . . I started for Ballidichob, and learned upon the road that we should come to a hut or cabin in the parish of Aghadoe, on the property of Mr. Long, where four people had lain dead for six days; and, upon arriving at the hut, the abode of Tim Harrington, we found this to be true; for there lay the four bodies, and a fifth was passing to the same bourne. On hearing our voices, the sinking man made an effort to reach the door, and ask for drink or fire; he fell in the doorway; there, in all probability to die; as the living cannot be prevailed to assist in the interments, for fear of taking the fever.

We next got to Skull, where, by the attention of Dr. Traill, vicar of the parish (and whose humanity at the present moment is beyond all praise), we witnessed almost indescribable in-door horrors. In the street, however, we had the best opportunity of judging of the condition of the people; for here, from three to five hundred women, with money in their hands, were seeking to buy food; whilst a few of the Government officers doled out Indian meal to them in their turn. One of the women told me she had been standing there since daybreak, seeking to get food for her family at home.

This food, it appeared, was being doled out in miserable quantities, at 'famine prices,' to the neighbouring poor, from a stock lately arrived in a sloop, with a Government steamship to protect its cargo of 50 tons; whilst the population amounts to 27,000; so that you may calculate what were the feelings of the disappointed mass.

The Vicar sits while Mullins lies in the corner. Mullins died and 3 days later, so too did the Vicar. Again, all sympathy between the living and the dead seems completely out of the question . . . I certainly saw from 150 to 180 funerals of victims to the want of food, the whole number attended by not more than 50 persons; and so hardened are the men regularly employed in the removal of the dead from the workhouse, that I saw one of them, with four coffins in a car, driving to the churchyard, sitting upon one of the said coffins, and smoking with much apparent enjoyment. The people also say that whoever escapes the fever is sure of falling sick on the road (the Public Works), as they are, in many instances, compelled to walk from three to six miles, and sometimes a greater distance, to work, and back again in the evening, without partaking of a morsel of food. Added to this, they are, in a great number of instances, standing in bogs and wet places, which so affects them, that many of the poor fellows have been known to drop down at their work.

Source: James Mahony, *Sketches in the West of Ireland*, published in the *Illustrated London News* (1847).

Document 2: *Millennium Development Goals Report 2011,* on Hunger, United Nations

Following a special summit meeting at United Nations headquarters in New York City in September 2000, UN member states and a number of major international organizations agreed on a list of "millennium development goals," with specific targets, for improving human livability and the global environment by the year 2015. The first of the eight goals was to "eradicate extreme poverty and hunger." In its 2011 report, the Millennium Development Goals initiative stated encouraging progress in the fight against global poverty but that hunger and malnutrition remain more intractable, especially in the developing world.

Target. Halve, between 1990 and 2015, the proportion of people who suffer from hunger

The proportion of people going hungry has plateaued at 16 per cent, despite reductions in poverty

The proportion of people in the developing world who went hungry in 2005–2007 remained stable at 16 per cent, despite significant reductions in extreme poverty. Based on this trend, and in light of the economic crisis and rising food prices, it will be difficult to meet the hunger-reduction target in many regions of the developing world.

The disconnect between poverty reduction and the persistence of hunger has brought renewed attention to the mechanisms governing access to food in the developing world. This year, the Food and Agriculture Organization of the United Nations will undertake a comprehensive review of the causes behind this apparent discrepancy to better inform hunger-reduction policies in the future.

Disparities within and among regions are found in the fight against hunger

Trends observed in South-Eastern Asia, Eastern Asia and Latin America and the Caribbean suggest that they are likely to meet the hunger-reduction target by 2015. However, wide disparities are found among countries in these regions. For example, the strong gains recorded in Eastern Asia since 1990 are largely due to progress in China, while levels in South-Eastern Asia benefit from advances made in Indonesia and the Philippines. Based on current trends, sub-Saharan Africa will be unable to meet the hunger-reduction target by 2015.

Nearly a quarter of children under five in the developing world remain undernourished

In developing regions, the proportion of children under age five who are underweight declined from 30 per cent to 23 per cent between 1990 and 2009. Progress in reducing underweight prevalence was made in all regions where comparable trend data are available. Eastern Asia, Latin America and the Caribbean, and the Caucasus and Central Asia have reached or nearly reached the MDG target, and South-Eastern Asia and Northern Africa are on track.

However, progress in the developing regions overall is insufficient to reach the target by 2015. Children are underweight due to a combination of factors: lack of quality food, suboptimal feeding practices, repeated attacks of infectious diseases and pervasive undernutrition. In Southern Asia, for example, one finds not only a shortage of quality food and poor feeding practices, but a lack of flush toilets and other forms of improved sanitation. Nearly half the population practises open defecation, resulting in repeated bouts of diarrhoeal disease in children, which contribute to the high prevalence of undernutrition. Moreover, more than a quarter of infants in that region weigh less than 2,500 grams at birth. Many of these children are never able to catch up in terms of their nutritional status. All these factors conspire to make underweight prevalence in the region the highest in the world.

Nutrition must be given higher priority in national development if the MDGs are to be achieved. A number of simple, cost-effective measures delivered at key stages of the life cycle, particularly from conception to two years after birth, could greatly reduce undernutrition. These measures include improved maternal nutrition and care, breastfeeding within one hour of birth, exclusive breastfeeding for the first 6 months of life, and timely, adequate, safe, and appropriate complementary feeding and micronutrient intake between 6 and 24 months of age. Urgent, accelerated and concerted actions are needed to deliver and scale up such interventions to achieve MDG 1 and other health-related goals.

In Southern Asia, progress in combating child undernutrition is bypassing the poorest

Children from the poorest households are more likely to be underweight than their richer counterparts. Moreover, the poorest children are making the slowest progress in reducing underweight prevalence. In Southern Asia, for example, there was no meaningful improvement among children in the poorest households in the period between 1995 and 2009, while underweight prevalence among children from the richest 20 per cent of households decreased by almost a third.

Children in developing regions are twice as likely to be underweight if they live in rural rather than urban areas. Little difference was found in underweight prevalence between girls and boys.

Close to 43 million people worldwide are displaced because of conflict or persecution

Humanitarian crises and conflicts continue to uproot millions of people across the globe. They also hinder the return of refugees and those internally displaced. As of end 2010, close to 43 million people worldwide were displaced due to conflict and persecution, the highest number since the mid-1990s and about half a million more than the previous year. Of these, 15.4 million are refugees, including 10.5 million who fall under the responsibility of the United Nations High Commissioner for Refugees (UNHCR) and 4.8 million Palestinian refugees who are the responsibility of the United Nations Relief and Works Agency for Palestine Refugees in the Near East (UNRWA). In addition, 27.5 million people have been uprooted by violence and persecution but remain within the borders of their own countries. While often not displaced per se, UNHCR estimated that some 12 million people were stateless.

While millions of refugees have found a durable solution to their situation over the decades, others have been confined to camps and other settlements for many years without any solution in sight. Excluding refugees under UNRWA's mandate, UNHCR estimates that 7.2 million refugees spread across 24 countries are currently trapped in a protracted situation of this kind. This is the highest number since 2001 and clearly demonstrates the lack of permanent solutions for many of the world's refugees. The number of refugees who have returned to their homes has continuously decreased since 2004, with the 2010 figures (197,600 returns) being the lowest since 1990.

On average, four out of five refugees are hosted by developing countries. Afghans and Iraqis continue to be the largest refugee populations under the UNHCR mandate with 3 million and 1.7 million refugees, respectively, at the end of 2010. Together they account for nearly half of all refugees under UNHCR's mandate.

Source: United Nations, Millennium Development Goals.

IDENTITY FRAUD

As use of the Internet has become commonplace, the need for secure online transactions is growing increasingly more important. While there has always been the risk that the person one was dealing with face-to-face was not who they claimed to be, this problem becomes significantly worse in online interactions. Tasks that used to be relatively straightforward, such as opening a bank account or paying for items over the telephone are increasingly at risk for identity-related crimes. Is the person I am emailing really who they say they are? Am I about to buy this digital service from a reputable online merchant? If I give my name and address to this e-commerce site, can I be sure that the data won't be misused, possibly for criminal purposes?

In the extreme, individuals have been jailed because crimes were committed by someone else matching "their" identity. In other circumstances, identity crimes may become a security risk when terrorists are able to obtain identity documents in the names of other people or travel between countries using multiple identities. These crimes can become an immigration risk if illegal immigrants are able to assume the identity of a legitimate citizen, and, as noted above, a commercial risk exists if individuals and organizations do not have confidence in the identity of those with whom they are doing business.

Definition

Although these identity crimes are often referred to as identity "theft," it is more appropriate to use the term "identity fraud," as the offense of identity theft does not exist per se in many countries. Instead, identity crimes are typically associated with other offenses, such as concealing an existing identity, accruing a financial benefit, or avoiding a financial liability. In the United Kingdom, for example, identity fraud occurs "when a false identity or someone else's identity details are used illegally: for commercial or monetary gain; to obtain goods or information; or to get access to facilities or services (such as opening a bank account)." Similarly, recent legislation in the United States defines identity fraud or theft as taking place when someone "knowingly transfers or uses, without lawful authority, a means of identification of another person with the intent to commit, or to aid or abet, any unlawful activity that constitutes a violation of Federal law, or that constitutes a felony under any applicable State or local law."

A second point of clarification is that an identity may consist of various aspects, each of which, under normal circumstances, is linked to a particular person and each of which might be used fraudulently. Thus, part of an identity is attributed to a person, including their name, birth date, and place of birth. An individual's biographical history might include details of their education and employment as well as their address history as found on electoral rolls and credit records. And their biometric identity would include physical attributes associated with the individual such as facial image and fingerprints.

An attributed identity (name and birth information) is probably the easiest to assume and use fraudulently as it is often based on fabricated or stolen documents. Using a biographical identity fraudulently requires much more detailed knowledge of a person's life history and so this form of identity fraud would typically be the result of a targeted attack. In contrast, a biometric identity cannot be as readily assumed by an imposter, although there is always a risk that someone else's biometrics might be associated with a particular attributed or biographical identity.

When these various facets of identity are used online, the risks of identity related fraud increase because it is more difficult to evaluate various identity claims. That is, the relying party in the interaction must be able to assess the likelihood that the person they are interacting with is indeed who they claim to be, and that party might only be able to perform limited checks if the interaction solely takes place online.

Scale of the Problem

The growth of identity related-fraud shows that personal identities are becoming as valuable as material possessions. A case of identity-related fraud, perhaps resulting from the abuse of discarded utility bills and credit card statements, can result in large-scale financial loss, distress, and inconvenience for individuals. In addition, there is often a considerable temporal and emotional burden associated with resolving the issue. According to some estimates, individuals can spend an average of between 25 and 60 hours restoring their records. In addition, they must face coming to terms with being the victim of a crime.

Some of the best studies of the phenomenon emerge from the United States. One recent study reports that there were 8.4 million U.S. adult victims of identity theft in 2007, down from 10.3 million in 2003, at a cost to the economy of $49.3 billion in 2007. In response, the U.S. government has developed laws to prevent and investigate identity theft, and numerous individual states have also passed laws that provide assistance in recovery from identity theft.

In the United Kingdom, responsibility for identity-related fraud issues resides with the Home Office (equivalent to Interior or Justice departments in other countries). There have been a number of government assessments of the extent of identity crime in the United Kingdom. The first, produced in 2002, suggested that the minimum cost to the UK economy was £1.3 billion. Updated figures issued by the Home Office in 2006 suggested a new figure of £1.7 billion, although £400 million of this was attributed to items "not included in the 2002 study." In 2008, another set of figures was produced based on a new methodology that included operating costs of the Identity and Passport Service for "carrying out identity checks, investigating suspected identity fraud cases, implementing systems and processes to detect and prevent fraudulent applications of passports, including costs relating to the introduction of face-to-face interviews for all adult, first-time applicants for a UK passport." Using this new methodology the annual cost fell to £1.2 billion.

The discrepancy among the various UK figures, and the introduction of a new cost calculation methodology, highlights two key issues: first, as noted above, we still do not know how to define identity-related fraud, and second, we still do not know how to measure it.

There are considerable problems in measuring all kinds of fraud, with identity fraud being particularly difficult to pin down. For example, criminology experts Michael Levi and John Burrows do not even consider identity fraud as a distinct category of fraud because of the many problems associated with how it might be defined and calculated, including inconsistent definitions of fraud, poor response rates to surveys, and concerns about the unit of analysis used. Indeed, they note that many fraud studies, "particularly those conducted by professional consulting firms with marketing aims," lack the kind of detailed presentation of methodology found in academic research, resulting in findings based on loose methods with limited value for aggregation purposes.

Responsibility

At a time when risk of identity fraud is a feature of interacting in an online society, where should responsibility for dealing with identity fraud lie? A number of stakeholders have a role to play, including individual citizens, private corporations, and government.

Individual Citizens

Although identity fraud is frequently seen as a problem that arises when organizations mismanage the data they hold about individuals, consumers themselves are also key stakeholders in the effort to prevent identity fraud. For example, Donncha Marron argues that much of the legislation concerning identity fraud, particularly the Identity Theft and Assumption Deterrence Act (or ITADA) in the United States, is framed around the idea of the consumer. This, Marron suggests, arose in a context of neoliberalism, which makes consumers "responsible for their own condition," responsible for the "establishment and maintenance of an individualized sense of self or one's life as coherent narrative or biography." In particular, Marron suggests that this should be understood as part of a wider notion of consumption, meaning that identity fraud has the potential to affect an individual's ability to consume (for example, by denying them credit if their credit history has been abused), hence undermining their basic sense of security as well as their emotional and financial well-being.

From this perspective, therefore, it is hardly surprising that much of the onus for preventing and responding to identity fraud lies with the individual.

As Marron notes, the advice offered by organizations like the U.S. Federal Trade Commission encourages individuals to be "entrepreneurial." They must actively canvass credit reference agencies, creditors, and debtors if they discover their identity has been used fraudulently. Similar emphasis on the individual can be found on the United Kingdom's "Identity Theft" Web site, which has specific pages titled "Protecting yourself" and "What if it happens to you."

Private Corporations

Significant amounts of identity fraud are associated with commercial transactions. As a result, one might argue that much responsibility for preventing identity fraud lies with private sector companies. The ways in which they handle personal and identity data play a key role in preventing identity-related fraud, and they have particular responsibility for the management of personal data that might be used to perpetrate identity crimes. In addition, they normally have a statutory duty to properly identify individuals before undertaking high-value transactions.

In many countries, the handling of personal data by organizations is regulated by some form of data protection legislation (for example, in the European Union, national legislation such as the UK's Data Protection Act 1998 has been implemented following the Data Protection Directive 95/46/EC). Even in jurisdictions that do not have an explicit data protection regime, companies may be required to meet industry self-regulation standards (such as the Payment Card Industry [PCI] requirements on data security standards). Others may find themselves required to notify customers if they have suffered a data breach.

Public Sector

The third stakeholder in identity fraud is the public sector. Government systems typically handle large amounts of personal data and, as such, are vulnerable to the same risks of disclosing personal data as the private sector, although typically on a far larger scale. For example, in November 2007 it was revealed that the British government had misplaced two computer disks containing personal data on all families with a child under 16. In total, the personal details of 25 million people were lost. In the United States, the Veterans' Administration lost a laptop containing data on more than 26 million veterans.

The public sector, however, also plays another important role in relation to identity fraud in that it is frequently used to provide confirmation of various claims to identity. For example, most nation-states have various registers that contain details on most, if not all, residents and citizens. These might include population registers, tax and benefits records, passport databases, and so on. Thus, attempts to create or use an identity fraudulently might be prevented by checking the claimed identity against these records. For example, one might reasonably assume that the biographical identity of an individual would be recorded consistently across population registers, tax records, and such whereas a fraudulently created biographical identity would have no such "footprint." Similar records may also be held by private sector organizations, such as credit reference agencies, and these may also be used to detect fraudulent identity claims. Innovative antifraud measures might include automatic text message notifications whenever such claims are being made.

If these records are kept up to date and are available for checking by relying parties, then the risk of identity fraud can be mitigated. If, however, these conditions are not met, the public sector might actually be enabling fraud rather than preventing it. For example, the benefits of increasing the security measures on passports can be undermined if the process for issuing passports is vulnerable to fraud and error.

Addressing the Problem

The problems of identity fraud are complex and typically overflow from one part of life to another. For example, in response to concerns about the ways in which discarded bills might result in identity-related fraud, a utility company might begin encouraging customers to replace printed utility bills with online-only statements. While this practice might result in fewer paper statements being discarded by customers, it could also have unintended consequences. For example, it is known that individuals often end up using the same password or PIN for many, if not all, of their online accounts. If this password is compromised, the individual is potentially at increased risk of identity fraud as many parts of their biographical identity would be easily accessible by using the same compromised password.

However, despite the ever-present risk of unintended consequences, there are certain things that

FBI officials in Los Angeles announce the arrest of nearly 100 suspects in an identity theft ring operating in the United States and Egypt in 2009. Fake Web sites were used in "phishing" expeditions to acquire private account information. *(AP Photo/Nick Ut)*

individuals can do to minimize the risk of identity fraud. Perhaps the simplest and most effective is to treat personal data like anything else of value and look after it carefully. This means, for example, checking the identity of people with whom one interacts before providing identity data to them. For example, an unsolicited call claiming to come from a service provider such as your bank should be checked by asking for that person's internal telephone extension, calling the bank's main switchboard, and asking to be transferred to the extension. Shared secrets known only by the service provider and the individual can have the same effect.

Individuals should take all reasonable steps to ensure that their personal devices (computer, smartphone) are kept secure, for example by keeping appropriate security (e.g., antivirus programs) on and up-to-date. Paper documents that contain personal data should be destroyed (shredded) rather than just discarded, and governments might provide tax incentives to support the purchase of shredders.

Public and private sector organizations can also increase the security of the personal data they hold and should be encouraged to minimize the amount of data they hold. As the relying parties in many transac-

tions, organizations should move to an explicitly risk-based perspective. That is, rather than just accepting "self-asserted" claims ("I am Elizabeth Yap and I live at 1 Main Street"), *if* the risk associated with the transaction is sufficiently high, organizations should take reasonable steps to mitigate it, for example, by checking that 1 Main Street actually exists as a legitimate address and checking that Elizabeth Yap has a record of living there.

Indeed, such a risk-based perspective, if followed through logically, taking advantage of recent developments in computer science and cryptography, potentially removes the need to use identities for many transactions. Payments for an online purchase, for example, are currently based around the customer sending bank details and other personal data to the store as the relying party. However, all that should logically be required is for the online store to receive an assertion or guarantee that the customer's bank will cover the claimed payment. This guarantee could state that the customer does have a valid bank account and that a particular credit card can be used for this one purchase with this one online store and that this particular payment will be honored by the bank. If the customer makes another online transaction with a different store, a new one-off guarantee would be issued to this new store by the bank. Each online store would be able to process the payment securely without ever needing to know who the customer was and without the need to receive, and store securely, the customer's data.

In addition to these technological capabilities, any system that uses high-integrity identity claims (such as government-issued secure identity cards or passports) must include a suitable liability model that ensures their usage. That is, if a relying party uses such a credential as part of its identity checks (for example, for the "know your customer," or KYC, checks that exist to prevent money laundering), then checking the credential should absolve the organization of any associated liability should the credential turn out to be false. If the liability model is not present, relying parties will end up producing their own identity fraud measures that will almost certainly be less secure.

Identity fraud is a complex problem. If not tackled effectively, it may undermine our long-term usage of the Internet for commercial and social activities, and hence undermine trust in the online world.

Edgar A. Whitley

See also: Cybercrime; Digital Divide; Privacy; Social Networking.

Further Reading

Arata, Michael J. *Identity Theft for Dummies.* New York: John Wiley & Sons, 2010.

Barnard-Wills, David. *Surveillance and Identity: Discourse, Subjectivity and the State.* Burlington, VT: Ashgate, 2011.

Berghel, H. "Fungible Credentials and Next-Generation Fraud." *Communications of the ACM* 49:12 (2006): 15–19.

Hoffman, Sandra K., and Tracy G. McGinley. *Identity Theft: A Reference Handbook.* Santa Barbara, CA: ABC-Clio, 2010.

McNally, Megan. *Identity Theft in Today's World.* Santa Barbara, CA: Praeger, 2012.

Stickley, Jim. *The Truth About Identity Theft.* Upper Saddle River, NJ: FT Press, 2009.

Whitley E.A., and G. Hosein. "Global Identity Policies and Technology: Do We Understand the Question?" *Global Policy* 1:2 (2010): 209–215.

Web Sites

Fraudwatch International:
     http://fraudwatchinternational.com/identity-theft/
LSE Identity Policy Work: http://identitypolicy.lse.ac.uk/
Privacy Rights Clearinghouse:
     www.privacyrights.org/Identity-Theft-Data-Breaches
UK Fraud Prevention Service:
     www.cifas.org.uk/identity_fraud

Document

Document: Identity Fraud Study, United Kingdom Cabinet Office (excerpts), 2002

Issued by the United Kingdom's Cabinet Office, this study on identity fraud examined the various measures taken by the government to address identity fraud and found many of them misguided and even counterproductive. In part, this had to do with policymakers not understanding the technologies used by perpetrators of identity fraud.

Why this study?

1.1 The theft of an individual's identity is a harrowing experience for the victim and the theft and fabrication of identities is of increasing concern to the state.

1.2 For individuals, the experience of identity theft can touch centrally on the victim's relation to the world.

1.3 For the state, theft and fabrication of identity is linked to organised crime in a variety of ways.

1.4 Evidence from the private sector shows that identity fraud has grown significantly in recent years.

1.5 This study takes stock of the extent and nature of the problem and develops a range of solutions to counter identity fraud. . .

Conclusions

9.19 It is tempting to think that a simple solution can be found to prevent all misuse of identity documents after issue. That is not the case . . .

9.20 In this area, then, the best way forward lies in simple measures: continued vigilance, training and use of UV scanners to detect counterfeits and forgeries, and a central register to reduce the value of stolen documents.

9.21 Despite the best efforts of government and the private sector, however, identity theft and fraud will sometimes be committed . . .

Source: Cabinet Office, United Kingdom.

IMMIGRATION, ILLEGAL AND IRREGULAR

Illegal migrants, also known as undocumented, unauthorized, clandestine, or irregularly residing migrants, constitute an invisible part of most societies. Although some decades ago, illegal migration appeared to be a phenomenon that only affected the wealthier countries of the global North and West, it is now prevalent around the world. The existence of these migrants is largely hidden, but discussions of their impact on host societies rank high on national and international agendas and tend to polarize public opinion. Tragic individual cases provoke compassion, but illegal immigrants as a group are often blamed for a wide array of social ills in host countries, including crime, disorder, and joblessness among legal residents. Less attention is typically paid to the problems associated with illegal immigration in the countries of origin, which might face issues such as brain drain and concerns about the rights of their citizens abroad.

Definition

There is no separate, undocumented flow of transborder movers. Legal and illegal entry methods and flows of people are inextricably related. When facing restrictions, prospective immigrants employ an array of side doors and back doors to reach their destination. Illegal immigration is, in principle, a subcategory of international immigration that is unwanted by destination and transit societies, although in some cases it might be silently accepted for economic reasons. Even the very term is in dispute. Some scholars have strongly criticized the use of the term "illegal migrants" because of its connotations with criminality and call for replacing it with the less pejorative term "irregular" migrants. In the end, all terms used acquire similar connotations, so this chapter uses the term "illegal" because it is the most widely used and it is how the migrants themselves relate to what is legal and illegal.

Although the concept of illegal immigration is directly related to state control and state sovereignty, most immigration laws do not directly define who is an illegal immigrant. Moreover, there is no common definition accepted, for instance, by the European Union as an organization. The concept, then, is implicit, rather than explicitly described in law. The dimensions of illegality are: entry, stay, work, and, in more closed societies, such as China, exit. Although regulations differ across jurisdictions, the essential difference between the undocumented immigrants and legal residents is the fundamentally different position within national legal systems of the former—that is, they face the risk of expulsion and (temporary) imprisonment, or what one scholar calls "deportability."

Contrary to conventional views, not all illegal immigrants enter the country of destination by crossing a border without documents. Rather, many enter with legal permission (visas) and overstay or otherwise violate the terms of their admission. As for definitions, first, what states consider legitimate (legal) might not fully coincide with what individuals consider legal. Transnational movements of people are illegal because they defy the norms and formal authority, while in the participants' view they can be acceptable, even legal. Second, illegality is not a static condition. An illegal migrant can move in and out of illegality over time and space. Certain conditions might not be met over time, and what is legal in one country might be illegal in another. Third, there are different kinds of gray areas and shadowy forms of existence that lie somewhere between legality and illegality.

Pathways to Illegality

Pathways to illegality can be summarized as follows. First, there are geographic flows of people in breach of immigration laws over land and sea borders. These people usually avoid border controls (sometimes with the help of human traffickers) or use false documents or false identities. Some borders, for instance, the one between the United States and Mexico, are heavily fenced; others are much more open. Within the Schengen area comprising the 26 territories of the EU, those with valid residential status may travel freely between the member states, subject to no border inspection. Therefore an illegal border crossing occurs only when the person lacks the required documents, whether evidence of their residency in one of the member states or a proper travel visa.

Second, "status flows" occur when persons transition from legal status to illegal residence, or vice versa. People can enter a country legally with a temporary visa and overstay the allowed period of residence. Asylum applicants who do not leave after their application is rejected and appeals procedures are exhausted also add to the pool of illegal residents of a country.

Demographic flows refer to children who are born into illegality. In most countries, a child is considered to lack status if he or she is born to a mother who lacks status. In general, European countries do not grant citizenship to newborns based on where they are born. Citizenship is, instead, transmitted by virtue of having an ancestor who is a national of that particular state. This is a *jus sanguinis* policy, in contrast to the *jus solis* principle in citizenship law, according to which those born in a territory are immediately conferred with nationality regardless of the legal status of their parents, as is the case in Canada, Australia, and the United States. Some countries have changed their laws to impose additional requirements (such as a longer stay or legal permanent residency status for one parent).

The above-mentioned pathways contribute to the *stock* of illegal migrants in a given country. Pathways out of illegality include leaving a country (either voluntarily or not), obtaining legal status either during an amnesty or, for instance through marriage. And, of course, some illegal immigrants simply die in their host country.

Historical Overview

Much of the existing discussion of illegal immigration focuses on the ongoing problems and policies in Europe and North America. Relatively little attention has been paid to historical developments and to other

parts of the world. In Africa, for instance, scholars have demonstrated how contemporary trans-Saharan migration is rooted in the trans-Saharan trade migration of nomads, traders, and refugees to other African countries, such as Mauritania, Algeria, and Libya, since the 1970s. Moreover, common misconception exists that most migrants crossing the Sahara are "in transit" to Europe. In particular, Libya, until its recent revolution, was an important destination country in its own right.

In addition, there is a historical record of illegal immigration. Although the term "illegal immigrant" dates back to the 1930s, the concept of illegal residence is much older and is closely linked to the process of state formation and systems of local poverty relief. European regimes beginning in the mid-twentieth century, imposed various forms of "illegality." Poor migrants from the countryside often had to circumvent local restrictions and settle in towns without permission, until they were caught and deported.

Cities used to decide who were the wanted and who the unwanted. These decisions were often related to issues such as employment, poverty, and public disorder. In the mid-nineteenth century, the redefinition of aliens in national rather than local terms coincided with an international relaxation of migration controls, at least in the trans-Atlantic region. Passports were abolished and exit restrictions lifted, resulting in a spectacular increase in the volume of international migration. As long as states did not provide welfare or other social goods and services to their citizens, they welcomed cheap labor in the hope that this would boost their economy. This—as well as new modes of transportation—made the period between 1850 and 1914 the heyday of free migration, with some 50 million international migrants traveling across the Atlantic and an equal number moving within Europe.

Asia experienced similar developments, with large numbers of migrants flocking to centers of capital in North and Southeast Asia. At the same time, however, Asian migrants were excluded as much as possible from the Atlantic world and white settler colonies, creating a global, racially motivated migration regime that aimed to keep Asians in Asia, except for relatively small numbers of indentured migrant workers, mostly in the Caribbean. Over time, state attempts to control mobility increased with the states' interest in welfare and labor market regulation. This principle was more strongly enforced in industrialized post–World War II welfare states with highly protected labor markets. Despite some key differences, there is also a remarkable continuity across time and space. Migrants in general have been often perceived as poor and as likely to become a public charge. For men, this has often been framed in terms of taking local jobs or causing crimes and disorder; for women, issues of morality have often been an important argument in the call for restriction and control.

Illegal Migration Today

Perhaps the most important factor in illegal migration flows today is globalization. Improvements in communications and transportation have made once-secluded countries part of a global market and infrastructure. The availability of information and ties between individuals and communities also bring societies closer together, with networks of immigrants playing a crucial role in this respect.

Much of the current debate surrounding illegal migration revolves around numbers. According to some estimates, in the early twenty-first century between 10 percent and 15 percent of the world's migrants were living in an irregular situation, which is equivalent to between 20 million and 30 million people. The phenomenon is international in scope. In Malaysia, for example, one in four workers is believed to be an illegal worker. In Australia and Asia, illegal immigration appears to be on the rise. Recent EU estimates, by contrast, show that between 2000 and 2008, the number of irregular migrants living in European countries decreased because of increasingly strict immigration controls as well as because of the enlargement of the EU and its immigration regularization programs. A decrease has also been observed in Japan, and the number seems to have peaked in 2007 in the United States at 12 million and dropped steadily as the economy sank into recession, to around 11 million. These numbers will always be contested. In the media as well as in politics, "conventional numbers" (such as 100,000, 500,000 or 1 million for certain areas) are often cited in order to support the plea for more controls.

Growing empirical research on the living conditions of illegal immigrants shows that they are often men between 20 and 40 years old, although the share of women appears to be growing. Migrants typically travel from relatively poor areas to richer ones, but the poorest do not have the financial and social capital to move across borders. Illegal migrants are prepared to do the jobs that natives shun, often under poor conditions and for wages usually lower than those of the legal residents. This produces an economic push and pull for illegal immigration: The most important asset of undocumented migrants is their cheap, exploitable labor. Meanwhile, businesses need cheap labor while private homeowners welcome the domestic workers that they otherwise might not be able to afford. Studies have shown that in France, for instance, illegal workers have built one-third of the highways and automobiles in the post–World War II era.

Number of Undocumented Residents (Estimated), United States, 1969–2009

Year	Estimated number	Percentage of U.S. population	Source of estimate
1969	540,000	0.3	Robert Warren, former director of the Office of Immigration Statistics, and Jeffrey Passell, senior demographer, Pew Research Center
1974	1,116,000	0.5	Robert Warren
1980	3,000,000	1.3	Robert Warren
1983	2,093,000	0.9	U.S. Census Bureau
1992	3,400,000	1.3	Immigration and Naturalization Service
1996	5,000,000	1.9	Immigration and Naturalization Service
2000	8,460,000 to 10,242,000	3.0 to 3.6	Department of Homeland Security
2001	7,800,000	2.7	Pew Research Center
2004	9,300,000	3.2	Urban Institute
2005	10,500,000 to 11,100,000	3.5 to 3.7	Lower: Department of Homeland Security Higher: Pew Research Center
2006	11,550,000 to 11,750,000	3.9	Lower: Department of Homeland Security Higher: Pew Research Center
2007	11,780,000 to 12,400,00	3.9 to 4.1	Lower: Department of Homeland Security Higher: Pew Research Center
2009	10,750,000 to 11,100,000	3.5 to 3.6	Lower: Department of Homeland Security Higher: Pew Research Center

On the one hand, illegal immigrants are the victims of a number of social ills, including difficulty in areas such as locating and keeping jobs, housing, access to health care, and education for their children. On the other hand, many of these illegal immigrants remain active in their efforts to move beyond being victims. Illegal immigrants have divergent motivations and aspirations. Immigrant networks and communities have the functional role of mediating between the illegal migrant and the broader society. More important, these communities act as a bulwark against efforts by the state to deport illegal immigrants.

State Controls

Governments around the world invest in different methods and to different extents in trying to control unwanted immigration and illegal residence. Whereas in Asia control appears to be very lax, apart from large-scale deportations every now and then, Australia, the United States, and Europe devote much more energy to it. Yet even these countries and regions have different and sometimes highly ambiguous strategies and policies.

The regulation of illegal immigration is not a policy domain per se but, rather, an endeavor in areas such as asylum, trafficking, smuggling, security, and family reunification and formation to control unauthorized migration. This is why regulating illegal immigration is a multilevel effort, with measures taken in sending, transit, and receiving countries, and extending into an array of settings: border crossing, transport (e.g., carrier sanctions), welfare policies, employment, labor markets, security, external relations, and humanitarian and development aid. Moreover, the regulation of undocumented foreigners takes place both before their migration, through policies and laws aimed at deterring the illegal flows from entering a national territory, and after the fact, namely through discouragement policies aimed at illegal residents and those who employ them. Empirical studies in various countries demonstrate how the fight against illegal immigration pursued by governments is often cross-cut by an array of actors, both government (social workers, teachers) and nongovernment (members of the civil society, family, and friends of the illegal migrants). These agencies and individuals help immigrants integrate into the host society by providing them with information, various commodities and services, and jobs.

Efforts to control illegal immigration can also backfire. Some scholars have noted that the increasing digitization of control within Europe has made the cat-and-mouse game between states and illegal migrants harsher, threatening to their ability to function in society and pushing them further underground. Many countries are concerned that the criminalization of illegal immigration is becoming a fact of life. Organized crime appears to benefit, as increasingly illegal immigrants need the help of human traffickers to bring them to a country. The extent to which prospective immigrants rely on human traffickers and those traffickers are involved in organized crime or part of loosely coupled networks of acquaintances vary according to the countries of origin and motives for migration among the illegal immigrants.

Costs and Benefits

To fully assess the impact of illegal immigration on societies, one needs to look at both the winners and the losers in this process. The cost of illegal immigration for a host society includes the use of public services by illegal migrants, often without paying into the welfare system through taxes. Illegal migrants also compete with legal migrants and with natives, largely for unskilled jobs and cheap housing. As they usually work for less money and longer hours, they decrease the availability of certain types of jobs for legal residents. Arguably, illegal migrants increase crime in the host society. If they are out of work, they are more likely to commit "subsistence" crimes, as they have no other way to make a living.

On a more philosophical level, the presence of illegal migrants represents a challenge to the legitimacy of governments to enforce laws. At the same time, one could look at illegal migration as a response to costly market regulations and the lack of availability of local labor for certain type of jobs, usually the ones natives decline to take because they are considered dangerous, dirty, or demeaning. A logical implication, say some experts, is that it might be economically beneficial to use illegal migrants, because the *supply* of illegal workers would decline in the absence of a *demand* for such workers. In other words, some economists argue that the economically optimal level of illegal immigration for a state is greater than zero. Above a certain level, the costs of controlling illegal immigration are greater than the damage caused by the illegal migrants; therefore it is cheaper for a society to accept some illegal migrants in order to save on the costs of border and immigration control. In addition, consequences can also be less direct, but still significant. Illegal migration is often described as constituting a threat to state sovereignty, security, and the legitimacy of the state by undermining migration control.

In the majority of cases, the debate surrounding illegal immigration is about how it affects host societies and less about tensions faced by sending countries, which can include a loss of the most talented and educated workers, often in their prime working years after they have received an education, as well as the social disruption as families and communities are broken apart. On the benefit side, remittances can be critical to the economies of poor sending countries.

The Future

Long-term solutions to illegal migration, according to experts, would have to involve more opportunities for legal labor migration and narrower economic disparity between different parts of the world, which is not likely to come about soon. In the meantime, governments still have to deal with migration in many forms. In 1985, Tomas Hammar concluded his influential book on European migration policies—*European Immigration Policy: A Comparative Study*—by emphasizing that integration policies for former guest workers and other legal immigrants can be successful only when they go hand in hand with a strict stance toward illegal immigration. Yet time has shown that—for a number of reasons—restrictive policies in democratic societies do not effectively and fully curtail illegal immigration. Therefore, combating illegal migration will remain a challenging task.

The available literature suggests that states should take into account not only the desired effects (a decrease of illegal migration) but also the undesired side effects, including the criminalization of illegal migration and its facilitators. In the end, illegal migration does not exist in a vacuum. It arises not merely out of the will of individuals to better their lives but also out of the contradiction between increasingly restrictive admission and control policies in combination with persistent demands for cheap and flexible labor in receiving societies.

Joanne van der Leun

See also: Migrant Labor; Population Growth and Demographic Issues; Refugees, Displaced Persons, and Asylum Seekers; Slavery.

Further Reading

Bloch, A., and M. Chimientie. "Undocumented Migrants: Policy, Politics, Motives and Everyday Lives." *Ethnic and Racial Studies* (special issue) 34:2 (2011).

Bogusz, Barbara, Ryszard Cholewinski, Adam Cygan, and Erika Szyszcak, eds. *Irregular Migration and Human Rights: Theoretical, European and International Perspectives.* Leiden: Martinus Nijhoff, 2004.

Castles, Stephen, and Mark J. Miller. *The Age of Migration: International Population Movements in the Modern World.* 2d ed. Basingstoke, UK: Macmillan, 2009.

Cornelius, Wayne, Philip Martin, and James Hollifield, eds. *Controlling Immigration: A Global Perspective.* Palo Alto, CA: Stanford University Press, 2004.

De Haas, Hein. *The Myth of Invasion: Irregular Migration from West Africa to the Maghreb and the European Union.* Oxford: International Migration Institute, 2007.

Duvell, Franck. *Illegal Immigration in Europe: Beyond Control?* London: Palgrave Macmillan, 2006.

Hammar, Tomas, ed. *European Immigration Policy: A Comparative Study.* New York: Cambridge University Press, 1985.

Lucassen, L. "Migration and World History: Reaching a New Frontier." *International Review of Social History* 52:1 (2007): 89–96.

Mahler, Sarah J. *American Dreaming: Immigrant Life on the Margins.* Princeton, NJ: Princeton University Press, 1995.

Manning, Patrick. *Migration in World History.* New York: Routledge, 2005.

Portes, Alejandro, and Ruben G. Rumbaut. *Immigrant America: A Portrait.* Berkeley: University of California Press, 1990.

Schrover, M., J.-P. Van der Leun, L. Lucassen, and C. Quispel, eds. *Illegal Migration and Gender in a Global and Historical Perspective.* Amsterdam: Amsterdam University Press, 2008.

Van Schendel, William, and Itty Abraham, eds, *Illicit Flows and Criminal Things: States, Borders and the Other Side of Globalization.* Bloomington: Indiana University Press, 2005.

Web Sites

CLANDESTINO Database on Irregular Immigration: http://irregular-migration.net//Home.2560.0.html

International Labour Organization: www.ilo.org

International Organization for Migration: www.iom.int

United Nations, Department of Economic and Social Affairs: www.un.org/esa/population/migration/index.html

Documents

Document 1: Schengen Agreement (excerpts), European Economic Community, 1985

After enduring two world wars in the first half of the century, European leaders moved to create a single market throughout the western half of the continent from the 1950s on, both to foster economic growth and to cement continental peace. In 1985, five of the then ten members of the European Economic Community—the predecessor of the European Union—signed the Schengen Agreement (named for the town in Luxembourg where it was signed). In doing so, Belgium, France, Luxembourg, the Netherlands, and West Germany took the unprecedented step of opening their borders to the free movement of each other's citizens. Eventually the agreement would encompass all members of the European Union, now numbering 27 member states.

TITLE I
MEASURES APPLICABLE IN THE SHORT TERM
Article 1
As soon as this Agreement enters into force and until all checks are abolished completely, the formalities for nationals of the Member States of the European Communities at the common borders between the States of the Benelux Economic Union, the Federal Republic of Germany and the French Republic shall be carried out in accordance with the conditions laid down below.

Article 2
With regard to the movement of persons, from 15 June 1985 the police and customs authorities shall as a general rule carry out simple visual surveillance of private vehicles crossing the common border at reduced speed, without requiring such vehicles to stop.

However, they may carry out more thorough controls by means of spot checks. These shall be performed where possible off the main road, so as not to interrupt the flow of other vehicles crossing the border.

Article 6
Without prejudice to the application of more favourable arrangements between the Parties, the latter shall take the measures required to facilitate the movement of nationals of the Member States of the European Communities resident in the local administrative areas along their common borders with a view to allowing them to cross those borders at places other than authorised crossing points and outside checkpoint opening hours. . . .

Article 7
The Parties shall endeavour to approximate their visa policies as soon as possible in order to avoid the adverse consequences in the field of immigration and security that may result from easing checks at the common borders. They shall take, if possible by 1 January 1986, the necessary steps in order to apply their procedures for the issue of visas and admission to their territories, taking into account the need to ensure the protection of the entire territory of the five States against illegal immigration and activities which could jeopardise security.

Article 8
With a view to easing checks at their common borders and taking into account the significant differences in the laws of the States of the Benelux Economic Union, the Federal Republic of Germany and the French Republic, the Parties undertake to combat vigorously illicit drug trafficking on their territories and to coordinate their action effectively in this area.

Article 9
The Parties shall reinforce cooperation between their customs and police authorities, notably in combating crime, particularly illicit trafficking in narcotic drugs and arms, the unauthorised entry and residence of persons, customs and tax fraud and smuggling.

Article 10
With a view to ensuring the cooperation provided for in Articles 6 to 9, meetings between the Parties' competent authorities shall be held at regular intervals.

Article 13
The Parties shall endeavour to harmonise by 1 January 1986 the systems applying among them to the licensing of commercial road transport with regard to cross-border traffic. . . .

TITLE II
MEASURES APPLICABLE IN THE LONG TERM

Article 17
With regard to the movement of persons, the Parties shall endeavour to abolish checks at common borders and transfer them to their external borders. To that end they shall endeavour first to harmonise, where necessary, the laws, regulations and administrative provisions concerning the prohibitions and restrictions on which the checks are based and to take complementary measures to safeguard internal security and prevent illegal immigration by nationals of States that are not members of the European Communities. . . .

Article 20
The Parties shall endeavour to harmonise their visa policies and the conditions for entry to their territories . . .

Source: European Union.

Document 2: Immigration Reform and Control Act, United States, 1986

While the Immigration and Naturalization Act of 1965 opened U.S. borders to far greater numbers of legal immigrants from the developed world, larger economic and social forces—including improved transportation, connections between immigrants and their kin in sending countries, economic dislocations in sending countries, and demand for labor in the United States—sent the number of illegal immigrants soaring. By 1986, when the Immigration Reform and Control Act was passed, there were an estimated 5 million person in the United States illegally. IRCA granted them a path to legal status, so-called amnesty, while attempting to put in place tougher border restrictions and sanctions on employers who hired illegal immigrants.

An Act

To amend the Immigration and Nationality Act to revise and reform the immigration laws, and for other purposes.

Be it enacted by the Senate and House of Representatives of the United States of America in Congress assembled.
. . .

TITLE I-CONTROL OF ILLEGAL IMMIGRATION
PART A—EMPLOYMENT

"SEC. 274A. (a) MAKING EMPLOYMENT OF UNAUTHORIZED ALIENS UNLAWFUL.—

"(1) IN GENERAL.-It is unlawful for a person or other entity to hire, or to recruit or refer for a fee, for employment in the United States—

"(A) an alien knowing the alien is an unauthorized alien (as defined in subsection (h)(3)) with respect to such employment, or

"(B) an individual without complying with the requirements of subsection (b).

"(2) CONTINUING EMPLOYMENT.-It is unlawful for a person or other entity, after hiring an alien for employment in accordance with paragraph (1), to continue to employ the alien in the United States knowing the alien is (or has become) an unauthorized alien with respect to such employment.

"(3) DEFENSE.-A person or entity that establishes that it has complied in good faith with the requirements of subsection (b) with respect to the hiring, recruiting, or referral for employment of an alien in the United States has established an affirmative defense that the person or entity has not violated paragraph (1)(A) with respect to such hiring, recruiting, or referral.

"(4) USE OF LABOR THROUGH CONTRACT.—For purposes of this section, a person or other entity who uses a contract, subcontract, or exchange, entered into, renegotiated, or extended after the date of the enactment of this section, to obtain the labor of an alien in the United States knowing that the alien is an unauthorized alien (as defined in subsection (h)(3)) with respect to performing such labor, shall be considered to have hired the alien for employment in the United States in violation of paragraph (1)(A).

"(5) USE OF STATE EMPLOYMENT AGENCY DOCUMENTATION.—For purposes of paragraphs (1)(B) and (3), a person or entity shall be deemed to have complied with the requirements of subsection (b) with respect to the hiring of an individual who was referred for such employment by a State employment agency (as defined by the Attorney General), if the person or entity has and retains (for the period and in the manner described in subsection (b)(3)) appropriate documentation of such referral by that agency, which documentation certifies that the agency has complied with the procedures specified in subsection (b) with respect to the individual's referral.

"(b) EMPLOYMENT VERIFICATION SYSTEM.—
The requirements referred to in paragraphs (1)(B) and (3) of subsection (a) are, in the case of a person or other entity hiring, recruiting, or referring an individual for employment in the United States, the requirements specified in the following three paragraphs:

"(1) ATTESTATION AFTER EXAMINATION OF DOCUMENTATION.—

"(A) IN GENERAL.—The person or entity must attest, under penalty of perjury and on a form designated or established by the Attorney General by regulation, that it has verified that the individual is not an unauthorized alien by examining—

"(i) a document described in subparagraph (B), or

"(ii) a document described in subparagraph (C) and a document described in subparagraph (D).

A person or entity has complied with the requirement of this paragraph with respect to examination of a document if the document reasonably appears on its face to be genuine. If an individual provides a document or combination of documents that reasonably appears on its face to be genuine and that is sufficient to meet the requirements of such sentence, nothing in this paragraph shall be construed as requiring the person or entity to solicit the production of any other document or as requiring the individual to produce such a document.

"(B) DOCUMENTS ESTABLISHING BOTH EMPLOYMENT AUTHORIZATION AND IDENTITY.—A document described in this subparagraph is an individual's—

"(i)   United States passport;

"(ii) certificate of United States citizenship;

"(iii) certificate of naturalization;

"(iv) unexpired foreign passport, if the passport has an appropriate, unexpired endorsement of the Attorney General authorizing the individual's employment in the United States; or

"(v)   resident alien card or other alien registration card, if the card—

"(I)   contains a photograph of the individual or such other personal identifying information relating to the individual as the Attorney General finds, by regulation, sufficient for purposes of this subsection, and

"(II) is evidence of authorization of employment in the United States.

"(C) DOCUMENTS EVIDENCING EMPLOYMENT AUTHORIZATION.—A document described in this subparagraph is an individual's—

"(i)   social security account number card (other than such a card which specifies on the face that the issuance of the card does not authorize employment in the United States);

"(ii) certificate of birth in the United States or establishing United States nationality at birth, which certificate the Attorney General finds, by regulation, to be acceptable for purposes of this section; or

"(iii) other documentation evidencing authorization of employment in the United States which the Attorney General finds, by regulation, to be acceptable for purposes of this section.

"(D) DOCUMENTS ESTABLISHING IDENTITY OF INDIVIDUAL.—A document described in this subparagraph is an individual's—

"(i)   driver's license or similar document issued for the purpose of identification by a State, if it contains a photograph of the individual or such other personal identifying information relating to the individual as the Attorney General finds, by regulation, sufficient for purposes of this section; or

"(ii) in the case of individuals under 16 years of age or in a State which does not provide for issuance of an identification document (other than a driver's license) referred to in clause (ii), documentation of personal identity of such other type as the Attorney General finds, by regulation, provides a reliable means of identification. . . .

TITLE VII-FEDERAL RESPONSIBILITY FOR DEPORTABLE AND EXCLUDABLE ALIENS CONVICTED OF CRIMES

SEC. 701. EXPEDITIOUS DEPORTATION OF CONVICTED ALIENS.

Section 242 (8 U.S.C. 1254) is amended by adding at the end the following new subsection:

"(i) In the case of an alien who is convicted of an offense which makes the alien subject to deportation, the Attorney General shall begin any deportation proceeding as expeditiously as possible after the date of the conviction."

SEC. 702. IDENTIFICATION OF FACILITIES TO INCARCERATE DEPORTABLE OR EXCLUDABLE ALIENS.

The President shall require the Secretary of Defense, in cooperation with the Attorney General and by not later than 60 days after the date of the enactment of this Act, to provide to the Attorney General a list of facilities of the Department of Defense that could be made available to the Bureau of Prisons for use in incarcerating aliens who are subject to exclusion or deportation from the United States.

Source: U.S. Congress.

INDIGENOUS PEOPLES' RIGHTS

Though the term "indigenous peoples" is open to some interpretation, the definition crafted by Special Rapporteur of the United Nations (UN) José Martinez Cobo has achieved wide acceptance and is regarded as the most comprehensive available:

> Indigenous communities, peoples and nations are those which, having a historical continuity with pre-invasion and pre-colonial societies that developed on their territories, consider themselves distinct from other sectors of the societies now prevailing in those territories, or parts of them. They form at present non-dominant sectors of society and are determined to preserve, develop and transmit to future generations their ancestral territories, and their ethnic identity, as the basis of their continued existence as peoples, in accordance with their own cultural patterns, social institutions and legal systems.

Indigenous peoples are located in 85 countries in the Americas, Asia, the Middle East, Africa, Australia, Europe, and Oceania. Among them are more than 600 language groups and 5,000 ethnic groups.

Historical Background

Indigenous peoples' rights is an international human rights movement that attempts to protect indigenous peoples and build awareness of their history of oppression, subordination, and subjugation by dominant political and social groups. Indigenous peoples have had their lands taken away, have lost their cultures, and have had their basic human rights denied by national and international legal systems.

The history begins with the occupation and subjugation of indigenous peoples of South America by European colonial powers, mostly the Spanish, in the sixteenth century. The European colonial powers occupied indigenous lands, exterminated many indigenous peoples, and then claimed sovereignty over those lands, along with full internal sovereignty over the remaining indigenous peoples. However, theologian and scholar Francisco de Vitoria challenged Spanish claims to indigenous peoples' land based on his understanding of natural and divine law. His *On the American Indian*, published in 1537–1538, argued that the Indians were the true owners of their lands and affirmed that they were human and entitled to enjoy civil and political rights.

Several others followed in de Vitoria's footsteps. In 1542, historian and missionary Bartolomé de Las Casas defended indigenous rights against colonialist aggressions in *Twenty Reasons Against Encomienda.* In 1625, Hugo Grotius, the "father of modern international law," wrote *De Jure Belli et Pacis* opposing the subjugation of peoples and their lands and arguing that Portugal's claim to the East Indies was a violation of natural law. William Blackstone, a noted English jurist, wrote *Commentaries on the Laws of England* in 1765–1769, which only recognized colonizers' occupation of land that was empty or uncultivated. The issue of indigenous peoples' rights was even more widely discussed in international law and policy in the nineteenth century. During this time, activism against the slave trade brought awareness of indigenous rights, which caused the issue to be raised in international courts.

Despite the legal activism of Vitoria, Las Casas, Grotius, Blackstone, and others, dispossession of lands remained the general rule through the end of the nineteenth century. An extensive body of legal theory was developed to justify these actions. For example, "extinguishment" is a principle used by settlers and colonizers that allows the "sovereign" (essentially, any government body) to cancel aboriginal titles to land. The most important statement of this concept was U.S. Supreme Court chief justice John Marshall's 1823 opinion in *Johnson v. M'Intosh,* which declared that Native American tribes could not sell their land to individual citizens, as only the federal government could extinguish or assume the Indians' "right of occupancy."

The first attempt by indigenous people to have their rights recognized internationally occurred in 1923 when Cayuga (Iroquois) chief Deskaheh tried to speak to the League of Nations about the U.S.-Iroquois treaty and the need for Iroquois self-government. Although Chief Deskaheh's efforts were blocked by Great Britain, his attempt anticipated the long struggle for self-government and legal recognition by indigenous peoples around the globe that would take place with the United Nations as its primary forum.

The years after World War II witnessed an acceleration of the movement for indigenous peoples' rights. In 1945, the United Nations was formed with a mandate to "maintain international peace and security." The body took an immediate interest in indigenous peoples, though the initial focus was on how they might be assimilated into their broader society. The founding of the UN Working Group on Indigenous Populations in 1982 was a landmark, signaling a shift toward protecting indigenous cultures, rather than erasing them.

In 1992, the UN Conference on Environment and Development (UNCED) adopted three major UN conventions on climate, biodiversity, and desertification. During the UNCED, the indigenous lobby made major gains in having the rights, knowledge, resources, and identities of indigenous peoples recognized by the UN member states. In 1993, the UN gathered in Vienna, Austria, for the World Conference on Human Rights. Pressure to address indigenous peoples' rights was a central theme, with many diverse indigenous groups from around the world represented.

In the last decade, great strides have been made to address indigenous peoples' rights in international law. In 2007, the UN Declaration on the Rights of Indigenous People (UNDRIP) was signed, and the Organization of American States (OAS) issued the first draft of its Declaration on the Rights of Indigenous Peoples. Both documents call for broad protections for indigenous peoples' rights.

Indigenous Rights Today

Under international law, it has been firmly established that indigenous peoples' rights include the right to a reasonable environment, to economic development, to international peace and security, to the common heritage of mankind, and to communications and humanitarian assistance. This means that indigenous peoples' claims are closely related to land rights, self-government, control of natural resources, environmental protection, and development assistance.

North America

In the United States, the Supreme Court has consciously and steadily eviscerated tribal authority in traditional indigenous territories, with major legal opinions building upon one another to assert that an indigenous tribe's jurisdiction exists almost exclusively over its members and not over its land. This has led to the obliteration of tribal authority over indigenous land and resources.

Perhaps the longest struggle between indigenous peoples and the U.S. government involves the Western Shoshone. In 1863, the Western Bands of the Shoshone Nation of Indians signed the Treaty of Peace and Friendship in Ruby Valley, Nevada. By signing the treaty, the U.S. government and the Shoshone agreed to mutual use of the tribe's millions of acres of ancestral lands without transferring them to U.S. authority and ownership. Both the natives and the U.S. government also agreed to allow westward-bound settlers to cross through Western Shoshone territory.

The Shoshone argue that, despite the clear terms of the agreement, the U.S. Bureau of Land Management gradually assumed control over the land by redrawing the boundaries of reservation territories. In response to these claims, the U.S. government formed the Te-Moak Tribal Council in 1962, gathering tribes into one group and granting monetary compensation for lost land. The Dann Band of Shoshone rejected the settlement, claiming that it was never part of the small Western Shoshone reservation and therefore it was not bound by the Treaty of Peace and Friendship or any other agreement. The U.S. government in turn brought a trespass suit against the Dann Band, stating that the Western Shoshone title had been notionally "extinguished."

In 1985, the U.S. Supreme Court ruled against the Dann Band, stating that tribal rights to land had indeed been extinguished, including the right to hunt and fish. In 1994, the Dann Band filed a petition to the Organization of American States (OAS) Inter-American Court of Human Rights (IACHR). The IACHR ruled in favor of the Shoshone and overturned the Supreme Court's ruling that their land title was extinguished. It also declared the transfer of land title to be a violation of human rights. The U.S. rejected the ruling, and so the Dann Band has filed a new suit, thus continuing the fight.

A similar struggle is taking place in Hawaii. In 1976, the Native Hawaiian community sought to regain access to the island of Kaho'olawe. Initially, the group was forced to violate federal law in order to visit the island. After protests and calls for religious freedom, however, the government provided some access to the island for ceremonial practices. Since then, Ka Lahui Hawai'i, a Native Hawaiian initiative for sovereignty, has declared five stated goals in order to end U.S. sovereignty in Hawaii. These are (1) resolution of historic claims involving the overthrow and misuse of native trust lands, violation of human and civil rights, and the occupation of lands and resources; (2) U.S. recognition of Native Hawaiian sovereignty and recognition of Ka Lahui as a Hawaiian Nation; (3) Ka Lahui authority over national assets, lands, and natural resources; (4) decolonization of Hawaii via the United Nations process for non-self-governing territories; and (5) restoration of traditional lands, national resources, ocean, and energy resources to the Ka Lahui National Land Trust.

In Canada, indigenous tribes have won some important legal victories. For example, the landmark 1990 court case *Sparrow v. The Queen* confirmed aboriginal fishing rights in both the past and the foreseeable future. Such victories often prove hollow, however. In the case of *Sparrow v. The Queen*, a trio of 1996 court decisions undermined the ruling, producing a more narrow and precise definition of aboriginal rights. So, despite the 2004 court cases of *Taku River Tlingit First Nation v. British Columbia* and *Haida First Nation v. British Columbia*, all of which affirmed Canada's obligation to uphold indigenous nations' rights, court cases and opinions have gradually strengthened Canadian sovereignty, making it more difficult for Canada's indigenous peoples to assert their rights.

Mexico allows indigenous peoples the right to political and legal autonomy, though national unity is emphasized. Mexico also has collective rights, including the "preservation of their way of life and social, economic and political organization" and "preserving and enriching their languages." In addition, Mexico grants indigenous peoples "differentiated rights" to natural resources, according to the type of natural resource at issue. Also included in Mexico's

constitution is the right to a bilingual education for indigenous peoples. In fact, the country provides some of the broadest constitutional recognition of respect, promotion, guarantee, and cultural sensitivity toward indigenous peoples in the Americas.

Despite these constitutional provisions, there are several notable indigenous peoples' rights movements in Mexico. The most significant is the Zapatista resistance movement in southern Mexico, a recent development that is partly a result of the rise of maquiladoras (factories that import materials and equipment from another country and then export finished goods to that same country, a means of reducing labor costs for wealthy nations). The maquiladoras have had a decidedly negative effect on traditional indigenous communities. For example, the manufacturing plant situated in the village of Teziutlán introduced Western ideological and cultural practices and released toxic wastes into the soil. These developments, in turn, resulted in further poverty, crime, and drug abuse, despite the job opportunities that the plant ostensibly provided.

Latin America

There are 671 different indigenous peoples in the collective of nations referred to as Latin America. Nations that incorporated indigenous peoples' rights into their constitutions include Argentina, Brazil, Chile, Colombia, Costa Rica, Ecuador, El Salvador, Guatemala, Honduras, Mexico, Nicaragua, Panama, Paraguay, Peru, and Venezuela. The most extensive acknowledgement of indigenous peoples' rights in South and Central America occurs in Bolivia's constitution:

> Given the pre-colonial existence of nations and original indigenous peoples and their ancestral control over their territories, one guarantees their self-determination in the setting of State unity, that consists of their right to autonomy, to self-governance, to their culture, to the recognition of their institutions and the consolidation of their territorial identities, which conform to this Constitution and to the Law.

Most Latin American constitutions provide for indigenous rights to lands, territories, and natural resources. The constitutions of Brazil, Mexico, Ecuador, and Bolivia all contain language that establishes differentiated rights to indigenous peoples according to the type of resource, such as natural resources (land, lakes, rivers), hydraulic and mineral resources,

Bolivian president Evo Morales (*left*), an Aymara Indian and the nation's first indigenous head of state, is welcomed at a rally in La Paz in October 2011. Days later, Morales canceled plans to build a highway through protected native lands in the Amazon Basin. *(AP Photo/Dolores Ochoa)*

renewable resources, and nonrenewable resources.

Historically speaking, the use of indigenous languages has been prohibited due to each country's desire to assimilate indigenous peoples into the dominant culture. The majority of Latin American constitutions refer to the indigenous peoples' rights to an intercultural bilingual education, while a few other nations' constitutions use the terms "education" or "bilingual literacy." Bolivia is the country with the most advanced and progressive terms for indigenous peoples' rights to a bilingual education. It establishes "intercultural, intracultural, multilingual education in all of the educational systems" and at all levels.

As in the case of Mexico, however, well-defined legal rights have not shielded the tribes from damage by the modern world. To take one example, in Chile the demand for electricity has compromised the lives of the indigenous Pehuenche. Where once these indigenous peoples thrived in the Andes Mountains between the Bío Bío and Queco Rivers, their lives have now been drastically altered since the National Electric Company relocated them in order to build a dam. The Pehuenche have been forced to assimilate to foreign structures of family and community, where collective qualities are replaced with individuation. Urbanization of the Pehuenche has also resulted in greater accessibility to alcohol and thus dramatically higher rates of alcoholism and related diseases.

Africa

Given the fluidity of African cultures and the frequent and widespread migration of the region's natives historically, it is rather more difficult to identify distinct communities of indigenous peoples in Africa than in most other places. For this reason, at least in part, Africa was the last global region to take steps toward the recognition of indigenous peoples' rights.

The first important development in this regard was the creation of the Indigenous Peoples of Africa Coordinating Committee (IPACC) in 1997. The main goals of IPACC are indigenous peoples' equality and equity with independent states, and increased visibility and influence through use of international rights standards and instruments. The activities of this group created new alliances within Africa that spanned languages, borders, and ethnic identities and prompted dialogue on international law, rights, and good governance.

The efforts of IPACC paid dividends fairly rapidly. In 2003, a subcommittee of the African Commission on Human and Peoples' Rights tasked with examining indigenous peoples' issues released its *Report of the African Commission's Working Group on Indigenous Populations/Communities*. The report contained extensive recommendations for protecting the rights and improving the lives of indigenous Africans. This was followed by widespread African adoption of UN-DRIP in 2007 (only Kenya and Nigeria abstained).

Although much progress has been made, there are still significant areas of concern for indigenous rights advocates in Africa. There has been little participation in IPACC by indigenous Northeast Africans in Eritrea, Ethiopia, Somalia, and Sudan. The same is true of hunter-gatherers from Central African Republic, Mauritania, Senegal, and Republic of the Congo. The government of the latter nation took steps to rectify this problem in 2010, passing Africa's first law directed specifically toward the protection of indigenous peoples. It remains to be seen if other nations will follow suit.

Asia and the Middle East

As in other regions, the indigenous peoples of Asia have generally been treated as second-class citizens, or worse. In India, for example, the indigenous Adivasis have experienced thousands of years of subordination—first at the hands of the Mauryan, Gupta, and Vijayanagara Empires, then during English colonization, and today by the Republic of India. The Adivasis struggle to maintain forest rights, since they are a forest-dwelling people. Their territories contain timber and natural resources that India seeks to obtain; both the government and private industries in India have made consistent attempts to appropriate them.

An indigenous community in the Middle East—the Palestinians—has also struggled. The ancestral lands of the Palestinians were colonized by Western powers in the nineteenth century and then were used in 1947 to create a nation, Israel, for another displaced people. For those Palestinians who remain, their lands and culture have suffered serious damage, as Israel regards them as a threat to its security. More than 6 million have fled elsewhere, dispersing indigenous Palestinians across the Middle East, Europe, and the rest of the world. Nearly half of the people in the Palestinian Diaspora are refugees without citizenship or legal status in any nation.

Recent years have seen some limited efforts at indigenous rights advocacy in Asia. For example, the health of indigenous peoples is a paramount issue in the region for a number of reasons: (1) poor access to adequate and culturally appropriate health-care services due to the lack of health-care centers in indigenous territories; (2) discriminatory behavior of health personnel toward indigenous peoples and their practices; (3) pesticides, chemical fertilizers, mine tailings, and other substances that have left indigenous lands dangerously polluted; and (4) an increase in HIV/AIDS because of drug addiction and sex trafficking. In response to these problems, Indonesia staged the first Asia Indigenous Peoples Preparatory Meeting in 2006. The meeting developed Millennium Development Goals for health issues and has continued to meet annually since to continue work on the problem.

Europe

Although some of the 15 million Roma (sometimes called "gypsies," though they regard the term as derogatory) worldwide are scattered across the Americas, Australia, Africa, and some parts of Asia, Europe is the continent that contains by far the largest concentration of this indigenous group. About 70 percent of the nomads in Europe are Roma; others include the Yeniches in Belgium and France, the Woonwagenbewoners of the Netherlands, the Landfahrer in Germany, the Tattares in Sweden, and the Kalderash in Eastern Europe.

As with the Jewish Diaspora and the Irish Diaspora, the Roma have been victims of forced migrations (in their case, dating back to the tenth century C.E.). Like other diasporic peoples, the Roma have a history of persecution that continues to the present day. Currently, they tend to be targeted with legal charges centering on vagabondage. These charges often involve disputes over unauthorized camping, town planning, and trailer parks.

The primary questions affecting the Roma include illiteracy and the education of Roma children, official recognition of the Roma language, migration reforms that respect Roma cross-border travel, commercial support for nomadic trades, representation in domestic and European parliaments, and statehood (Romanestan). Thus far, Europe's national and regional institutions have done little to assist with these matters. Indeed, if anything, the trend has been in the opposite direction. For example, in 2008 the government of Italy declared the Roma a national security risk, blaming them for much of the crime in urban areas. Officials promised that steps would be taken to solve the *emergenza nomadi* (nomad emergency) and to eliminate the problem.

Oceania

Indigenous peoples in Australia and New Zealand are predominantly Torres Strait Islanders and Maori. In New Zealand, the Maori continue legal struggles over territorial rights to the foreshore (wetlands between the low and high tide marks) and the seabed. In Australia, the government has been supportive of indigenous peoples' rights, but was reluctant to support UNDRIP due to fears of secessionist movements that might arise following legal acceptance of indigenous rights. There has also been the concern that aboriginal law would supersede domestic law. The Department of Families, Housing, Community Services and Indigenous Affairs has been working with Australia's state and territory governments, indigenous groups, and external stakeholders such as the mining industry to address indigenous issues.

Ethnic Fijians and Fijians of Indian ethnicity have experienced recent conflicts. Fiji, which consists of 300 islands in the South Pacific, became an independent country in 1970. The Indian Fijians are descendants of large numbers of Indian laborers imported by the colonial British to work on sugar plantations between 1879 and 1916. For many years, land ownership was the privilege of indigenous Fijians. In 1987, a parliamentary election brought the Indian political party into power, and with it laws to change land ownership rules, which resulted in violence by ethnic Fijians against ethnic Indians. Indigenous peoples in several locations in Oceania have argued that because their ancestors have always inhabited the land, later immigrants cannot have the same rights to participate in political decisions regarding the land. However, this appears to be reverse discrimination, as the goals of human and indigenous rights activists are to have all peoples included in the political, social, economic, and cultural processes of a nation.

Judy M. Bertonazzi

See also: Environmental Justice; Ethnic and Religious Conflict; Human Rights.

Further Reading

Akhtar, Zia. "Human Rights and American Indian Land Claims." *International Journal of Human Rights* 11:4 (December 2007): 529–534.

"Asia Indigenous Peoples Caucus Statement: Millennium Development Goals and Indigenous Peoples: Redefining the Goals." *Asia-Pacific Journal of Human Rights and the Law* 8:1 (June 2007): 64–100.

Crawhall, Nigel. "Africa and the UN Declaration on the Rights of Indigenous Peoples." *International Journal of Human Rights* 15:1 (January 2011): 11–36.

Davis, Megan. "Indigenous Struggles in Standard Setting: The UN Declaration on the Rights of Indigenous Peoples." *Melbourne Journal of International Law* 9:2 (October 2008): 439–471.

Duncan, Ivison, Paul Patton, and Will Sanders, eds. *Political Theory and the Rights of Indigenous Peoples.* New York: Cambridge University Press, 2000.

Gilbert, Jérémie. *Indigenous Peoples' Land Rights Under International Law: From Victims to Actors.* Ardsley, NY: Transnational, 2006.

Iyall Smith, Keri E. "Comparing State and International Protections of Indigenous Peoples' Human Rights." *American Behavioral Scientist* 51 (2008): 1817–1835.

Manus, Peter. "Indigenous Peoples' Environmental Rights: Evolving Common Law Perspectives in Canada, Australia, and the United States." *Boston College Environmental Affairs Law Review* 33:1 (2006): 1–86.

Marsico, Katie. *Indigenous Peoples' Rights.* San Francisco: Essential Library, 2011.

Peang-Meth, Abdulgaffar. "The Rights of Indigenous Peoples and Their Fight for Self-Determination." *World Affairs* 164:3 (Winter 2002): 101–114.

Reisman, W. Michael. "Protecting Indigenous Rights in International Adjudication." *American Journal of International Law* 89:341 (1995): 350–362.

Sanders, Douglas. "The Re-Emergence of Indigenous Questions in International Law." *Canadian Human Rights Yearbook* 3:1 (1983): 12–30.

Thornberry, Patrick. *Indigenous Peoples and Human Rights.* Huntington, NY: Juris, 2002.

Westra, Laura. *Environmental Justice and the Rights of Indigenous Peoples.* London: Earthscan, 2008.

Web Sites

African Commission on Human and Peoples' Rights: www.achpr.org

Amnesty International: www.amnesty.org

Australians for Native Title and Reconciliation: www.antar.org.au

Cultural Survival Organization: www.culturalsurvival.org

Human Rights Watch: www.hrw.org

Indian Land Tenure Foundation: www.iltf.org

Indigenous Peoples in Nepal: www.iwgia.org/regions/asia/nepal

Indigenous Peoples of Africa Coordinating Committee: www.ipacc.org.za

Inter-American Commission on Human Rights: www.cidh.oas.org

International Working Group for Indigenous Affairs:
     www.iwgia.org
News on Indigenous Struggles:
     www.intercontinentalcry.org
Organization of American States: www.oas.org
Survival International: www.survivalinternational.org
Understanding Crown-Māori Relationships in New
     Zealand: www.posttreatysettlements.org.nz
United Nations Educational, Scientific and Cultural
     Organization: www.unesco.org
United Nations Permanent Forum on Indigenous Issues:
     www.un.org/esa/socdev/unpfii/

Documents

Document 1: "The Need to Turn Indians into U.S. Citizens," Chester A. Arthur, 1881

A common approach for dealing with indigenous peoples has been to try to assimilate them into the dominant culture. This impulse generally blends a charitable bent with an inherent and much less admirable assumption of indigenous inferiority. This excerpt from President Chester A. Arthur's 1881 State of the Union Address to the U.S. Congress provides an excellent example of this approach.

Prominent among the matters which challenge the attention of Congress at its present session is the management of our Indian affairs. While this question has been a cause of trouble and embarrassment from the infancy of the Government, it is but recently that any effort has been made for its solution at once serious, determined, consistent, and promising success.

It has been easier to resort to convenient makeshifts for tiding over temporary difficulties than to grapple with the great permanent problem, and accordingly the easier course has almost invariably been pursued.

It was natural, at a time when the national territory seemed almost illimitable and contained many millions of acres far outside the bounds of civilized settlements, that a policy should have been initiated which more than aught else has been the fruitful source of our Indian complications.

I refer, of course, to the policy of dealing with the various Indian tribes as separate nationalities, of relegating them by treaty stipulations to the occupancy of immense reservations in the West, and of encouraging them to live a savage life, undisturbed by any earnest and well-directed efforts to bring them under the influences of civilization.

The unsatisfactory results which have sprung from this policy are becoming apparent to all. As the white settlements have crowded the borders of the reservations, the Indians, sometimes contentedly and sometimes against their will, have been transferred to other hunting grounds, from which they have again been dislodged whenever their new-found homes have been desired by the adventurous settlers. These removals and the frontier collisions by which they have often been preceded have led to frequent and disastrous conflicts between the races.

It is profitless to discuss here which of them has been chiefly responsible for the disturbances whose recital occupies so large a space upon the pages of our history. We have to deal with the appalling fact that though thousands of lives have been sacrificed and hundreds of millions of dollars expended in the attempt to solve the Indian problem, it has until within the past few years seemed scarcely nearer a solution than it was half a century ago. But the Government has of late been cautiously but steadily feeling its way to the adoption of a policy which has already produced gratifying results, and which, in my judgment, is likely, if Congress and the Executive accord in its support, to relieve us ere long from the difficulties which have hitherto beset us.

For the success of the efforts now making to introduce among the Indians the customs and pursuits of civilized life and gradually to absorb them into the mass of our citizens, sharing their rights and holden to their responsibilities, there is imperative need for legislative action.

My suggestions in that regard will be chiefly such as have been already called to the attention of Congress and have received to some extent its consideration.

First. I recommend the passage of an act making the laws of the various States and Territories applicable to the Indian reservations within their borders and extending the laws of the State of Arkansas to the portion of the Indian Territory not occupied by the Five Civilized Tribes.

The Indian should receive the protection of the law. He should be allowed to maintain in court his rights of person and property. He has repeatedly begged for this privilege. Its exercise would be very valuable to him in his progress toward civilization.

Second. Of even greater importance is a measure which has been frequently recommended by my predecessors in office, and in furtherance of which several bills have been from time to time introduced in both Houses of Congress. The enactment of a general law permitting the allotment in severalty, to such Indians, at least, as desire it, of a reasonable quantity of land secured to them by patent, and for their own protection made inalienable for twenty or twenty-five years, is demanded for their present welfare and their permanent advancement.

In return for such considerate action on the part of the Government, there is reason to believe that the Indians in large numbers would be persuaded to sever their tribal relations and to engage at once in agricultural pursuits. Many of them realize the fact that their hunting days are over and that it is now for their best interests to conform their manner of life to the new order of things. By no greater inducement than the assurance of permanent title to the soil can they be led to engage in the occupation of tilling it.

The well-attested reports of their increasing interest in husbandry justify the hope and belief that the enactment of such a statute as I recommend would be at once attended with gratifying results. A resort to the allotment system would have a direct and powerful influence in dissolving the tribal bond, which is so prominent a feature of savage life, and which tends so strongly to perpetuate it.

Third. I advise a liberal appropriation for the support of Indian schools, because of my confident belief that such a course is consistent with the wisest economy.

Source: The Miller Center at the University of Virginia.

Document 2: UN Declaration on the Rights of Indigenous Peoples, Preamble, 2007

On September 13, 2007, indigenous peoples' rights groups reached a milestone regarding their efforts toward inclusion, equality, and understanding when the United Nations adopted the Declaration on the Rights of Indigenous Peoples. Approved by 144 member nations, the declaration was a global affirmation of indigenous peoples' rights to equality, intellectual and cultural pursuits, and land and legal rights previously unacknowledged by an international intergovernmental body. Several nations that initially rejected the document—notably Australia, Canada, Colombia, New Zealand, Samoa, and the United States—later signed. The text that follows is the preamble:

The General Assembly,

Guided by the purposes and principles of the Charter of the United Nations, and good faith in the fulfilment of the obligations assumed by States in accordance with the Charter,

Affirming that indigenous peoples are equal to all other peoples, while recognizing the right of all peoples to be different, to consider themselves different, and to be respected as such,

Affirming also that all peoples contribute to the diversity and richness of civilizations and cultures, which constitute the common heritage of humankind,

Affirming further that all doctrines, policies and practices based on or advocating superiority of peoples or individuals on the basis of national origin or racial, religious, ethnic or cultural differences are racist, scientifically false, legally invalid, morally condemnable and socially unjust,

Reaffirming that indigenous peoples, in the exercise of their rights, should be free from discrimination of any kind,

Concerned that indigenous peoples have suffered from historic injustices as a result of, inter alia, their colonization and dispossession of their lands, territories and resources, thus preventing them from exercising, in particular, their right to development in accordance with their own needs and interests,

Recognizing the urgent need to respect and promote the inherent rights of indigenous peoples which derive from their political, economic and social structures and from their cultures, spiritual traditions, histories and philosophies, especially their rights to their lands, territories and resources,

Recognizing also the urgent need to respect and promote the rights of indigenous peoples affirmed in treaties, agreements and other constructive arrangements with States,

Welcoming the fact that indigenous peoples are organizing themselves for political, economic, social and cultural enhancement and in order to bring to an end all forms of discrimination and oppression wherever they occur,

Convinced that control by indigenous peoples over developments affecting them and their lands, territories and resources will enable them to maintain and strengthen their institutions, cultures and traditions, and to promote their development in accordance with their aspirations and needs,

Recognizing that respect for indigenous knowledge, cultures and traditional practices contributes to sustainable and equitable development and proper management of the environment,

Emphasizing the contribution of the demilitarization of the lands and territories of indigenous peoples to peace, economic and social progress and development, understanding and friendly relations among nations and peoples of the world,

Recognizing in particular the right of indigenous families and communities to retain shared responsibility for the upbringing, training, education and well-being of their children, consistent with the rights of the child,

Considering that the rights affirmed in treaties, agreements and other constructive arrangements between States and indigenous peoples are, in some situations, matters of international concern, interest, responsibility and character,

Considering also that treaties, agreements and other constructive arrangements, and the relationship they represent, are the basis for a strengthened partnership between indigenous peoples and States,

Acknowledging that the Charter of the United Nations, the International Covenant on Economic, Social and Cultural Rights and the International Covenant on Civil and Political Rights, as well as the Vienna Declaration and Programme of Action, affirm the fundamental importance of the right to self-determination of all peoples, by virtue of which they freely determine their political status and freely pursue their economic, social and cultural development,

Bearing in mind that nothing in this Declaration may be used to deny any peoples their right to self-determination, exercised in conformity with international law,

Convinced that the recognition of the rights of indigenous peoples in this Declaration will enhance harmonious and cooperative relations between the State and indigenous peoples, based on principles of justice, democracy, respect for human rights, non-discrimination and good faith,

Encouraging States to comply with and effectively implement all their obligations as they apply to indigenous peoples under international instruments, in particular those related to human rights, in consultation and cooperation with the peoples concerned,

Emphasizing that the United Nations has an important and continuing role to play in promoting and protecting the rights of indigenous peoples,

Believing that this Declaration is a further important step forward for the recognition, promotion and protection of the rights and freedoms of indigenous peoples and in the development of relevant activities of the United Nations system in this field,

Recognizing and reaffirming that indigenous individuals are entitled without discrimination to all human rights recognized in international law, and that indigenous peoples possess collective rights which are indispensable for their existence, well-being and integral development as peoples,

Recognizing that the situation of indigenous peoples varies from region to region and from country to country and that the significance of national and regional particularities and various historical and cultural backgrounds should be taken into consideration,

Solemnly proclaims the following United Nations Declaration on the Rights of Indigenous Peoples as a standard of achievement to be pursued in a spirit of partnership and mutual respect.

Source: United Nations.

INEQUALITY, INCOME
AND WEALTH

Economists define income as the amount of money received over a period of time by an individual. Countries also have incomes, which consist of wages, interest payments, dividends, rents, capital gains, and profits. Wealth consists of the tangible and financial assets, less liabilities, of an individual, household, population cohort, or country at a given point in time.

Income and wealth are inevitably distributed unequally, among individuals, households, population cohorts, countries, and regions. This chapter examines two general aspects of this unequal distribution—within countries and between countries—with a focus on income, on which documentation tends to be more extensive than it is for wealth.

Historically, income and wealth tended to be more unequally distributed within countries and societies than between countries and societies. But after the Industrial Revolution, disparities increased greatly between countries, and the world came to be differentiated between what is now referred to as the developed and developing worlds. Meanwhile, income distribution within countries has varied widely, depending on a host of factors, including degree of industrialization and social welfare policies.

Inequalities of wealth between and within countries play an important role in economic growth and decline, stability in both national politics and geopolitics and human welfare. Addressing inequality, between and within countries, is a highly contentious issue for both theoreticians and policymakers. Similarly, those who study the topic disagree widely as to possible future trends in inequality within countries and between countries and regions.

Measuring Inequality

Income can be divided into a variety of types. For most people, it consists largely of wages and other forms of compensation for work performed. But income can also come in unearned forms, also known as capital gains, such as interest payments, dividends, and rents. Wealthier individuals tend to have a larger proportion of their income in these forms than do those who are less affluent. Income also comprises government compensation: Social Security, welfare, unemployment benefits, and so on. Although these are distributed to all sectors of society, they tend to represent a higher proportion of income among the poor and elderly. Wealth, as noted above, consists of two types of assets: tangible and financial. For individuals, the former consists of land, buildings, precious metals, and so on. For businesses, wealth can also include capital equipment. Financial assets include cash, bank deposits, and various forms of corporate and governmental securities. Like income, wealth can refer to the assets of an individual, a population cohort, or a country. For the latter, wealth consists of all tangible and financial assets owned, minus domestic and financial assets owed.

Distribution of income—and wealth—can be considered in global terms, that is, among countries and regions, or in national terms, among the citizens of a given country. Basically, income and wealth distribution can be considered in four ways. Intercountry distribution measures inequality between the average income or wealth holding of the citizens of one country compared with that of another and is not weighted for the population size of the country. International distribution measures countries against one another, but does factor in population size. Global distribution ignores nation-states and measures how income and wealth are distributed among the world's individuals while within-country distribution does the same for individual countries. In addition, it is possible to apply the principle of intercountry and international

Lorenz Curve, Concept of Income Distribution

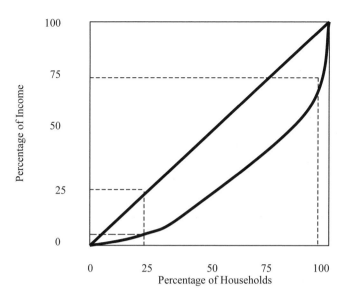

How Much Inequality and Why

Inequality of income and wealth among individuals has a number of different causes. Most important of these is the fortune—or misfortune—of where one is born and to whom. For example, to be born into a U.S. household with the median income of $49,909 in 2011 is to be born into the top 5 percent of households globally. Put another way, having the average income of the bottom 10 percent of the American population makes one richer than two-thirds of the world's people. Of course, there are vast disparities of income within countries as well. The top 20 percent of American households earn about 50 percent of all income, while the top 5 percent earn more than 20 percent of all income. With these statistics in mind, the United States has a Gini coefficient of about .45, one of the least equal of any large industrialized country. By comparison, Sweden, among the most equal of all countries in the world, has a Gini coefficient of .26, meaning that the richest 10 percent of the population make about 25 percent of the income. By comparison, South Africa, the least equal of all major world economies, has a Gini coefficient of .65, with the top 4 percent of the population earning about 40 percent of the income. Wealth distribution is even more skewed than income, because it represents the accumulation of income not spent on consumption over a person's lifetime, plus whatever that person inherited. The top 10 percent of households in Sweden, the United States, and South Africa controlled about 60, 70, and 85 percent of wealth, respectively. In general, more developed countries have a more equal distribution of income and, to a lesser extent, wealth than do developing countries. This is because developed countries have a larger, educated middle class, which can command more of the countries' resources in wages, which are, as noted, the primary source of income for most people.

distribution to a single country, when the goal is to ascertain income and wealth distribution among population cohorts, say by ethnicity, class, sex, and age. Both national and international measurements of inequality are tricky to calculate, as data might be sketchy in less developed countries, because governments there lack resources and because so much of the income generated in those countries comes from the informal economy, which often escapes government tabulators. And even where data are collected, comparing between countries may be difficult, as different measurement standards are used.

After data are collected, economists use two basic formulas for measuring income inequality. One is the Gini coefficient—a number between 0 and 1, in which 0 is perfect equality (a theoretical situation in which all persons have exactly the same income or wealth) and 1 is perfect inequality (in which one person has all the income and wealth). The second formula is the Lorenz curve, which measures how much of national income or wealth goes to each percentile of the population. A Lorenz curve is a graph with income percentage on the vertical axis and percentage of individuals or, often, households on the horizontal axis. Perfect distribution, in which all households have the same income, is the 45- degree curve that goes from the bottom left to the top right. Actual distribution is the sagging line beneath it. The gap between the two represents the degree and amount of inequality.

Numerous factors can explain why income and wealth is unequally distributed within countries. Again, birth circumstances are key. Not only do children from more affluent households inherit more wealth, but they are also more likely to be better educated and healthier, all of which leads to higher levels of productivity and, hence, income and wealth. In many countries, ethnic or racial background plays a role as well. A history of discrimination means people with certain backgrounds have not been able to accumulate wealth and the benefits that come with it. Thus, they do not inherit wealth and are unable to obtain the education necessary to command higher incomes and thus accumulate more wealth on their own. The skewed South African numbers are a case in point, reflecting more than a century of racial discrimination and legal apartheid by the minority white population over the majority black population. Sex is also important. For a variety of reasons, including lower levels of education, particularly in poorer countries, and discriminatory laws on inheritance, women tend to earn less than men and have less wealth. Less discriminatory factors play a role as well in income and wealth distribution. Among adults, the young and the elderly tend to have less income and wealth than the middle-aged; the young have not moved up the income ladder, and the elderly are not productive or are not earning anything at all and are therefore depleting their assets to survive.

Politics is an important factor as well in how income and wealth are distributed. Countries with more generous welfare systems—Sweden is a good example—tend to have more equally distributed income and wealth. This occurs because income is transferred from the rich to the poor, in terms of not only households but also school districts, which leads to a more equal educational outcome among rich and poor. Typically, as in Sweden, countries with generous welfare systems have highly progressive tax rates, reducing the top, post-tax income levels and mitigating the accumulation of great fortunes. In addition, countries with generous welfare and progressive tax systems usually have a more egalitarian culture, in which top executives and other highly skilled people do not expect their compensation to be orders of magnitude higher than that of ordinary workers.

Just as income and wealth disparities among individuals have numerous causes, so do wealth and income disparities among localities, countries, and regions. In general, though more acute in developing countries, incomes and wealth tend to be higher in urban than rural areas. Urban areas tend to have more economic options for all classes of people as well as higher populations of educated and skilled persons. Perhaps even more skewed is the distribution of income and wealth among countries. For example, Europe, which is home to less than 10 percent of the world's population, has more than 25 percent of the world's net worth, calculated according to purchasing power parity (PPP adjusts for the fact that the cost of living in poorer countries is usually lower than in richer countries, allowing incomes to go farther; not

Global Household Wealth Distribution, 2000

Region	Percent of world population	Percent net worth	Percent net worth by PPP*
Africa	10.66	0.54	1.52
America, North	5.17	34.39	27.10
America, Latin	8.52	4.34	6.51
Asia	52.18	25.61	29.40
Europe	9.62	29.19	26.42
Middle East	9.88	3.13	5.07
Other	3.14	2.56	3.70

* Purchasing power parity.
Sources: United Nations University; World Institute for Development Economics Research.

accounting for PPP, Europe's share of the world's net worth would be even higher). By comparison, sub-Saharan Africa, which has just over 10 percent of the world's population, has just 1.5 percent of the world's wealth.

Access to resources plays an important role here. The vast wealth of Persian Gulf states, for example, is due primarily to their location atop the world's most extensive hydrocarbon reserves. Although these countries have wide inequalities of wealth and income, they generate so much revenue that even the poorest citizens (as opposed to guest workers) share in the largesse. But resources alone do not guarantee a wealthy society, as resource-rich sub-Saharan Africa makes clear. Whereas that wealth is accumulated by a few elites, who spend it on consumption and not to fund the health and education initiatives that raise the productivity of ordinary citizens, wealth is squandered and its distribution remains grossly unequal.

Equally apparent is the fact that some resource-poor societies are collectively wealthy and have a relatively equal distribution of income and wealth. The successful Asian economies of Japan, Taiwan, and South Korea are prime examples. In these countries, experts cite a more controversial causation factor—culture. A Confucian tradition of valuing education, social harmony, order, and self-discipline, they say, goes a long way toward explaining both why these countries have high income and wealth levels and why they have comparably equal distributions of wealth and income. Politics and economics matter, too. South Korea and North Korea, for example, share the same Confucian culture, but the South, with its capitalist economy and freewheeling democracy, has a per capita income about 20 times that of the North, which has a highly authoritarian government and rigid state planning, though arguably wealth is more equally distributed in the North. But perhaps the most critical factor in explaining why some societies are richer than others is history.

History

Until the rise of centralized civilizations about 5,000 years ago, income, such as it was, and wealth were quite equally distributed, both within societies and among the various regions of the world. Hunter-gatherer cultures and even simple agricultural communities had little ability to generate surpluses that result in wealth accumulation. Moreover, most people performed the same work in agriculture and, hence, had the same income, if it can be called that, in the food they grew. Centralized civilizations, along with their differentiated workers and their ability to generate surpluses, changed that. It allowed for wealth accumulation, among a small political and religious elite, as well as higher incomes for those engaged in trade or able to hire others to work for them.

Still, for much of human history, the vast majority of people lived in roughly equal conditions within societies and between societies. As late as the early 1800s, say economic historians, people in the different regions of the world differed little in terms of wealth and income. According to one scholar, as late as 1820 most countries were less than 50 percent above or below the per capita income average for the world as a whole. (Today, by comparison, income in richer countries averages $25,000 per capita, while income in poorer countries averages about $1,200, a disparity factor of about 2,000 percent.) While more fertile and well-watered regions might produce more crops and, hence, wealth, they also led to larger populations among which that wealth was distributed. Thus, for most of human history, the great disparities of wealth were within societies—between the tiny elite at the top and the vast majority at the bottom—rather than between societies.

The advent of capitalism and the Industrial Revolution, as well as the conquest and colonization of much of the world by Europe and its settler offspring states, such as the United States, changed all that. While generating great wealth, it also produced far greater inequality of income and wealth within industrializing societies and between those societies and the rest of the world. As to the first phenomenon, capitalism and industrialization allowed those who controlled the means of pro-

duction to accumulate great fortunes even as they lowered the valued of skilled labor, creating an impoverished working class. In the countryside, new laws and new production methods resulted in the dispossession of the peasantry, who either flocked to industrial areas or became impoverished tenant farmers and agricultural laborers. Over the course of the nineteenth century, wealth and income in these industrializing countries became more unequally distributed, reaching the highest levels of inequality in the early twentieth century, before leveling off during World War II.

The first 30 years after the war ended saw reverses in inequality, for various reasons, including widespread education, progressive taxation, and social welfare policies unprecedented in world history. A

Gini Coefficient, Before Taxes and Transfers, Mid-1980s to Late 2000s, Selected OECD Countries

Country	Mid-1980s	Mid-1990s	Late 2000s
Canada	.395	.430	.441
France	.380	.473	.483
Germany	.439	.459	.504
Greece	.426	.446	.436
Israel	.472	.494	.498
Italy	.420	.508	.534
Japan	.345	.403	.462
Mexico	.453	.532	.494
Netherlands	.473	.484	.426
Sweden	.404	.438	.426
United Kingdom	.419	.453	.456
United States	.436	.477	.486

Note: The Gini coefficient is measured on a scale of 0 to 1, with higher numbers indicating higher levels of inequality.
Source: OECD.

Gini Coefficient, After Taxes and Transfers, Mid-1980s to Late 2000s, Selected OECD Countries

Country	Mid-1980s	Mid-1990s	Late 2000s
Canada	.293	.289	.324
France	.300	.277	.293
Germany	.251	.266	.295
Greece	.336	.336	.307
Israel	.326	.338	.371
Italy	.309	.348	.337
Japan	.304	.323	.329
Mexico	.452	.519	.476
Netherlands	.272	.297	.294
Sweden	.198	.211	.259
United Kingdom	.309	.336	.345
United States	.337	.361	.378

Note: The Gini coefficient is measured on a scale of 0 to 1, with higher numbers indicating higher levels of inequality.
Source: OECD.

variety of factors, however, led to a reversal of that equalizing trend in much of the developed world from the 1970s through the early 2000s. Between 1975 and 2010, for example, the aggregate income of the top 20 percent of earners went from less than 44 percent of total national income to more than 50 percent, while the bottom quintile saw aggregate income drop from 4.3 percent to 3.3 percent, a decline of nearly 25 percent.

Several factors explain this trend. The first is globalization. Because world markets were opening up, educated and skilled people in developed countries like the United States could command higher incomes because the value they added was much greater than when what they produced was destined solely for a domestic market. At the other end, globalization shifted manufacturing jobs—a source of relatively high wages for poorly educated, low-skilled workers—from high-wage countries to low-wage ones, undermining the income of those workers in developed countries. Technology played a role as well, making highly skilled people much more productive while often automating low-skilled jobs out of existence. Yet another factor was politics. In many developed countries, particularly the United Kingdom and the United States, a rising conservatism led to assaults on trade unions, which tend to keep wages up for low-skilled workers, cuts in income transfers (such as welfare payments), which hurt the poor most, and less-progressive tax systems, which allowed the better off, particularly those whose income depends on capital gains, to keep more of their income and pass on more of their wealth to their children. By the early 2010s, and partly as a result of the worst recession since the Great Depression, this trend had begun to inspire popular uprisings, for example, the Occupy Wall Street movement in the United States and demonstrations in various European countries.

Meanwhile, just as commercialization and industrialization led to higher levels of inequality in countries undergoing those processes, they also led to higher levels of inequality between countries, as most of the wealth they produced, even if unequally distributed, accrued to them. Equally important in terms of distribution of wealth and income among countries was the conquest by the more economically advanced countries' of much of the rest of the world, though the effects varied in different regions. In sub-Saharan Africa, it led to the slave trade, which decimated societies by draining them of their most productive members. In Latin America, it produced feudal agricultural systems that stunted economic growth. In virtually all parts of what is now the developing world, formal colonization led to distorted economic development, in which production was geared to the needs of the colonizing country, rather than the colonized.

The legacy lived on after the developing world achieved independence, in Latin America in the early nineteenth century and Asia, Africa, and the Caribbean in the mid-twentieth century. Not only were economies in this region underdeveloped or oriented in ways that largely benefited the developed world but their political systems were often stunted as well, leaving them prey to the political turmoil, corruption, and authoritarianism that undermined economic development or maintained gross inequalities in wealth and income, except that the elites were no longer colonialists but local elites.

The globalization phenomenon in the late twentieth and early twenty-first century, along with certain factors peculiar to individual countries, occasioned a reverse in inequality within societies and between societies. Globalization has allowed developing-world societies to sell more goods to the developed world, and to one another, allowing them to amass a higher percentage of the world's wealth and income. Moreover, technology transfers have allowed workers in developing countries to become more productive, allowing them to earn higher incomes, which generally should lead to better education and, hence, higher levels of productivity. As noted earlier, inequality can be measured in non-population-weighted intercountry terms or in population-weighted international terms. Using the former, wealth and income are only marginally better distributed, largely because the poorest countries, such as those in sub-Saharan Africa, have a birthrate that is far higher than that in developed countries. In international terms, the economic rise of China—and, to a lesser extent, India—which together comprise about one-third of world population means that inequality between the developed and developing world is diminishing at an ever-accelerating pace.

Impact and Policies

Most economists and social scientists agree that extremes of income and wealth equality and inequality are not particularly beneficial for societies. Too much inequality results in miserable living conditions for

Members of Occupy Rio set up their downtown encampment in October 2010. Inspired by the Occupy Wall Street and Spanish Indignants movements, young Brazilians protested global capitalism and economic and social inequality. *(Vanderlei Almeida/AFP/ Getty Images)*

the majority of people and requires an authoritarian political order to ensure social stability. The best examples of such societies were those of Latin America and much of Asia before the democratization era of the late twentieth century. Too much equality, especially if maintained by government diktat, can undermine economic innovation and incentives to work, because most of the income and wealth generated will be seized by the state and redistributed. The best examples of this were the Soviet Union and Eastern Europe before the fall of communism in the late twentieth century.

Thus most theoreticians and policymakers advocate more egalitarianism up to the point where it undermines economic motivation, but identifying this point is a matter of contention. Those toward the left end of the political spectrum argue that a more equal distribution of wealth ensures a higher level of aggregate demand for goods and services, because those with less wealth and income tend to spend, rather than save and invest, more of their money. Those toward the right argue that greater inequality creates more motivation to work and that accumulations of wealth and income at the top lead to more savings and investment, which improves productivity, benefiting the population as a whole.

Also contentious is the question of how best to achieve a more egalitarian economic and social order. Although all agree that better education and health care can lead to a more productive labor force and thus more wealth to be distributed, beyond that there is little consensus on how to achieve a wealthier and more egalitarian society, if that is even desired. Those on the right argue that this should be left largely to the private sector, which is best equipped to create steadier and more substantive growth in economic output, which, while perhaps benefitting the rich more, aids all members of society. From the left, the impetus is toward government programs, particularly in the realm of income transfers and social welfare programs, which equalize the distribution of wealth and income.

The Future

Looking into the future, the picture is complicated and somewhat cloudy. On the one hand, increased economic integration, technology transfer, and the rapid economic growth of large, medium-income countries—notably China, but also Brazil, Russia, and Indonesia—are likely to increase international income and wealth equality between the developing and developed worlds. Although they have the fastest population growth in the world, two of the most impoverished regions—sub-Saharan Africa and the Middle East, other than the oil-rich countries—could pull trends toward more equality in the other direction if they fail to grow economically. Meanwhile, within-country trends—including rapid economic growth, an expanding middle class, and urbanization—are likely to advance equality.

Yet other global trends point in the opposite direction. Rising debt levels are forcing developed countries to cut back on the income transfers and welfare programs that lead to more equality even as populations age, creating large cohorts of senior citizens living in poverty. In addition, political backlash could either lead to enhanced income transfers or to their curtailment. Long term, there is the matter of climate change. As experts note, climate change is most likely to have its greatest impact in the tropics, where the world's poorest citizens live. Moreover, climate change may create political instability in the developing world, leading to a slowdown in growth. Ultimately, the world is probably trending toward more equality but the process, as in centuries past, can be stubbornly slow.

James Ciment

See also: Credit and Debt, Personal and Business; Financial Crises; Poverty; Social Welfare; Taxation.

Further Reading

Bhalla, Surjit S. *Imagine There's No Country: Poverty, Inequality, and Growth in the Era of Globalization.* Washington, DC: Institute for International Economics, 2002.

Cooke, Lynn Prince. *Gender-Class Equality in Political Economies.* New York: Routledge, 2011.

de la Dehesa, Guillermo. *What Do We Know About Globalization? Issues of Poverty and Income Distribution.* Malden, MA: Blackwell, 2007.

Dowd, Douglas. *Inequality and the Global Economic Crisis.* New York: Pluto, 2009.

Firebaugh, Glenn. *The New Geography of Global Income Inequality.* Cambridge, MA: Harvard University Press, 2003.

Greig, Alastair, David Hulme, and Mark Turner. *Challenging Global Inequality: Development Theory and Practice in the Twenty-First Century.* New York: Palgrave Macmillan, 2007.

Levy, Ammon, and João Ricardo Faria, eds. *Economic Growth, Inequality and Migration.* Northampton, MA: E. Elgar, 2002.

Manza, Jeff, and Michael Sauder. *Inequality and Society: Social Science Perspectives on Social Stratification.* New York: Norton, 2009.

Milanovic, Branko. *Worlds Apart: Measuring International and Global Inequality.* Princeton, NJ: Princeton University Press, 2005.

Seligson, Mitchell A., and John T. Passé-Smith. *Development and Underdevelopment: The Political Economy of Global Inequality.* 4th ed. Boulder, CO: Lynne Rienner, 2008.

Wilkinson, Richard, and Kate Pickett. *The Spirit Level: Why Greater Equality Makes Societies Stronger.* New York: Bloomsbury, 2010.

Web Sites

Inequality.org: http://inequality.org

Institute for Economics and Peace: http://economicsandpeace.org

Share the World's Resources: www.stwr.org

United Nations, Department of Economic and Social Affairs: www.un.org/esa/

Vision of Humanity: www.visionofhumanity.org

World Bank: www.worldbank.org

Documents

Document 1: *Communist Manifesto,* Part I, Karl Marx and Friedrich Engels, 1848

The early Industrial Revolution in Britain and continental Europe produced vast accumulations of new wealth, even as it created growing disparities in income and wealth between those who labored (the proletariat) and those who owned the means of production (the bourgeoisie). In their Communist Manifesto, *Karl Marx and Friedrich Engels describe the process by which the bourgeoisie had usurped the commanding heights of the economy and how this had disrupted all previous economic and social relations. The manifesto became the founding document for a global movement aimed at redressing such inequalities by establishing what communists came to call a "dictatorship of the proletariat." In such a system, the means of production would be owned by those who worked, and all income and wealth would be exacted "from each according to his abilities" and distributed "to each according to his needs." This ideology eventually produced revolutions in Russia, China, Cuba, and elsewhere over the course of the twentieth century.*

www.gutenberg.org/catalog/world/readfile?fk_files=1441328

Source: Project Gutenberg.

Document 2: Remarks by President Barack Obama on the Economy (excerpt), Osawatomie, Kansas, December 6, 2011

In what many observers characterized as the opening salvo of his 2012 reelection campaign, President Barack Obama came to Osawatomie, Kansas, in December 2011, the site of a famous speech on economic inequality by President Theodore Roosevelt about a hundred years earlier. In his address, Obama explicitly evoked the progressive Republican in advocating government policies that would cre-

ate a more level economic playing field and address the growing inequality in the United States over the previous three decades. The subject was at the heart of the Occupy Wall Street movement that had spread across the country in 2011. Obama also set out to contrast himself with the Republican opposition, which, he said, advocated the same policies that had led to the growing levels of inequality, including deregulation and tax cuts for the wealthy.

[T]here's been a raging debate over the best way to restore growth and prosperity, restore balance, restore fairness. Throughout the country, it's sparked protests and political movements—from the Tea Party to the people who've been occupying the streets of New York and other cities. It's left Washington in a near-constant state of gridlock. It's been the topic of heated and sometimes colorful discussion among the men and women running for president.

But, Osawatomie, this is not just another political debate. This is the defining issue of our time. This is a make-or-break moment for the middle class and for all those who are fighting to get into the middle class. Because what's at stake is whether this will be a country where working people can earn enough to raise a family, build a modest savings, own a home, secure their retirement.

Now, in the midst of this debate, there are some who seem to be suffering from a kind of collective amnesia. After all that's happened, after the worst economic crisis, the worst financial crisis since the Great Depression, they want to return to the same practices that got us into this mess. In fact, they want to go back to the same policies that stacked the deck against middle-class Americans for way too many years. And their philosophy is simple: We are better off when everybody is left to fend for themselves and play by their own rules.

I am here to say they are wrong. I'm here in Kansas to reaffirm my deep conviction that we're greater together than we are on our own. I believe that this country succeeds when everyone gets a fair shot, when everyone does their fair share, when everyone plays by the same rules. These aren't Democratic values or Republican values. These aren't 1 percent values or 99 percent values. They're American values. And we have to reclaim them.

You see, this isn't the first time America has faced this choice. At the turn of the last century, when a nation of farmers was transitioning to become the world's industrial giant, we had to decide: Would we settle for a country where most of the new railroads and factories were being controlled by a few giant monopolies that kept prices high and wages low? Would we allow our citizens and even our children to work ungodly hours in conditions that were unsafe and unsanitary? Would we restrict education to the privileged few? Because there were people who thought massive inequality and exploitation of people was just the price you pay for progress.

Theodore Roosevelt disagreed. He was the Republican son of a wealthy family. He praised what the titans of industry had done to create jobs and grow the economy. He believed then what we know is true today, that the free market is the greatest force for economic progress in human history. It's led to a prosperity and a standard of living unmatched by the rest of the world.

But Roosevelt also knew that the free market has never been a free license to take whatever you can from whomever you can.

. . . Today, over 100 years later, our economy has gone through another transformation. Over the last few decades, huge advances in technology have allowed businesses to do more with less, and it's made it easier for them to set up shop and hire workers anywhere they want in the world. And many of you know firsthand the painful disruptions this has caused for a lot of Americans.

. . . Now, just as there was in Teddy Roosevelt's time, there is a certain crowd in Washington who, for the last few decades, have said, let's respond to this economic challenge with the same old tune. "The market will take care of everything," they tell us. If we just cut more regulations and cut more taxes—especially for the wealthy—our economy will grow stronger. Sure, they say, there will be winners and losers. But if the winners do really well, then jobs and prosperity will eventually trickle down to everybody else. And, they argue, even if prosperity doesn't trickle down, well, that's the price of liberty.

Now, it's a simple theory. And we have to admit, it's one that speaks to our rugged individualism and our healthy skepticism of too much government. That's in America's DNA. And that theory fits well on a bumper sticker. But here's the problem: It doesn't work. It has never worked. It didn't work when it was tried in the decade before the Great Depression. It's not what led to the incredible postwar booms of the '50s and '60s. And it didn't work when we tried it during the last decade. I mean, understand, it's not as if we haven't tried this theory.

Remember in those years, in 2001 and 2003, Congress passed two of the most expensive tax cuts for the wealthy in history. And what did it get us? The slowest job growth in half a century. Massive deficits that have made it much harder to pay for the investments that built this country and provided the basic security that helped millions of Americans reach and stay in the middle class—things like education and infrastructure, science and technology, Medicare and Social Security.

Remember that in those same years, thanks to some of the same folks who are now running Congress, we had weak regulation, we had little oversight, and what did it get us? Insurance companies that jacked up people's premiums with impunity and denied care to patients who were sick, mortgage lenders that tricked families into buying homes they couldn't afford, a financial sector where irresponsibility and lack of basic oversight nearly destroyed our entire economy.

We simply cannot return to this brand of "you're on your own" economics if we're serious about rebuilding the middle class in this country. We know that it doesn't result in a strong economy. It results in an economy that invests too little in its people and in its future. We know it doesn't result in a prosperity that trickles down. It results in a prosperity that's enjoyed by fewer and fewer of our citizens.

Look at the statistics. In the last few decades, the average income of the top 1 percent has gone up by more than 250 percent to $1.2 million per year. I'm not talking about millionaires, people who have a million dollars. I'm saying people who make a million dollars every single year. For the top one hundredth of 1 percent, the average income is now $27 million per year. The typical CEO who used to earn about 30 times more than his or her worker now earns 110 times more. And yet over the last decade the incomes of most Americans have actually fallen by about 6 percent.

Now, this kind of inequality—a level that we haven't seen since the Great Depression—hurts us all. When middle-class families can no longer afford to buy the goods and services that businesses are selling, when people are slipping out of the middle class, it drags down the entire economy from top to bottom. America was built on the idea of broad-based prosperity, of strong consumers all across the country. That's why a CEO like Henry Ford made it his mission to pay his workers enough so that they could buy the cars he made. It's also why a recent study showed that countries with less inequality tend to have stronger and steadier economic growth over the long run.

Inequality also distorts our democracy. It gives an outsized voice to the few who can afford high-priced lobbyists and unlimited campaign contributions, and it runs the risk of selling out our democracy to the highest bidder. It leaves everyone else rightly suspicious that the system in Washington is rigged against them, that our elected representatives aren't looking out for the interests of most Americans.

But there's an even more fundamental issue at stake. This kind of gaping inequality gives lie to the promise that's at the very heart of America: that this is a place where you can make it if you try. We tell people—we tell our kids—that in this country, even if you're born with nothing, work hard and you can get into the middle class. We tell them that your children will have a chance to do even better than you do. That's why immigrants from around the world historically have flocked to our shores.

And yet, over the last few decades, the rungs on the ladder of opportunity have grown farther and farther apart, and the middle class has shrunk. You know, a few years after World War II, a child who was born into poverty had a slightly better than 50–50 chance of becoming middle class as an adult. By 1980, that chance had fallen to around 40 percent. And if the trend of rising inequality over the last few decades continues, it's estimated that a child born today will only have a one-in-three chance of making it to the middle class—33 percent.

Source: White House.

INFANT MORTALITY

The term "infant mortality" is defined as the number of children per 1,000 live births who die before reaching the age of one. It is sometimes broken down into narrower categories: "perinatal mortality" refers to deaths that take place between fetal viability (no less than 22 weeks of age, more commonly 24–27 weeks) and the end of the seventh day after delivery; "neonatal mortality" refers to deaths in the first 28 days of life; and "postneonatal mortality" refers to deaths after 28 days but before one year.

Historically, infant mortality rates have been extremely high across the globe, regularly standing at 200–300 deaths per 1,000 live births, and occasionally reaching 500 or more deaths per 1,000 live births. These numbers did not show noticeable, permanent improvement until after 1900, with more developed countries making substantial progress in the first part of the century and less developed countries following suit in the latter part. Despite this, infant mortality remains a grave public health concern in many nations, particularly those in sub-Saharan Africa.

History

It is difficult to measure historical infant mortality rates with any sort of precision. The death of young children was so commonplace in past centuries that in many cultures babies were not given names or documented in any way until they were one year old. No nation kept records of infant deaths until the early 1800s, and even then the numbers were not terribly reliable, given the inability or disinclination of rural dwellers to report the passing of young children.

Working from the limited amount of available data, historians' best estimates are that between 200 and 400 of every 1,000 children born worldwide before 1750 died before reaching their first birthday. The numbers were certainly worst among marginalized populations such as slaves, the urban poor, peoples living under colonial rule, and post-Columbian Native Americans. The outbreak of epidemics—smallpox, malaria, yellow fever—led to temporary but dramatic increases in infant mortality rates, often pushing them above 50 percent.

In the eighteenth century, there was a perceptible improvement in infant survival in many Western nations. Swamps were filled, diminishing the mosquito population; food supplies increased in quality and quantity; and housing and sanitation both improved. These gains proved temporary, however, canceled out by industrialization. Crowded, filthy slums proved to be very efficient incubators for disease, and infant mortality rates again skyrocketed. "There is no more depressing feature about our American cities," observed one New Yorker, "than the annual slaughter of little children."

While people were saddened by the deaths of so many infants, the prevailing sentiment was that high mortality rates were simply a fact of life in cities and populous nations. As late as 1900, there were only three nations in the world (Sweden, Norway, and New Zealand) where the infant mortality rate was below 10 percent. In most nations, it remained between 15 percent and 30 percent.

In 1906, the British physician and reformer George Newman published *Infant Mortality: A Social Problem*. The book observed that no progress had been made in infant mortality rates in a century, suggested several possible causes of the problem, and identified areas where improvements might be made. The book led the British government, followed by dozens of other governments and organizations, to make infant mortality a priority. New therapies were developed, obstetricians became more skillful in coping with birth defects, and immunization was utilized aggressively. The result was a sharp decline in the number of infant deaths in the world's most developed nations by the middle of the twentieth century, first in older infants and then in newborns.

Less-developed countries did not have the same resources to cope with the problem and so did not see the same improvement during this time. As late as 1950, Latin American countries had a 12 percent average infant mortality rate, Asian countries were at 18 percent, and African countries over 20 percent.

As modern medicines and medical techniques were propagated more widely after World War II, however, the infant mortality rates in less-developed areas began to drop, albeit at different times and rates. Asian nations, particularly those in the Far East, were the first to see improvement, followed by those of Latin America. Africa was the last continent to have success in combating infant mortality, and the region still trails the rest of the world today, with sub-Saharan Africa the worst at more than 76 deaths per 1,000 live births. While that number is disconcerting, it still represents a 60 percent drop since the 1950s.

Causes

Physicians tend to organize the causes of infant mortality into two groups. Endogenous causes are internal to the mother and child and play a predominant role in perinatal and neonatal mortality. Exogenous causes are those that result from outside influences like germs and the environment. They are responsible for the majority of postneonatal deaths.

Foremost among endogenous causes of infant mortality is premature birth, which accounts for approximately 30 percent of perinatal and neonatal deaths. Preterm infants have an increased risk of cardiovascular complications, hypoglycemia, internal bleeding, neurological problems, pneumonia, and urinary tract infections, Especially common are respiratory conditions like infant respiratory distress syndrome (IRDS), wherein newborns are partially or wholly unable to breathe on their own. IRDS is the single most common cause of death in preterm infants.

Another significant endogenous cause of infant mortality is birth complications, which account for approximately 26 percent of perinatal and neonatal deaths. The most common is intrauterine hypoxia (IH, also known as birth asphyxia), in which a developing fetus does not have an adequate oxygen supply. This can cause death by itself and is also a contributing factor to many other life-threatening conditions, including brain damage and heart defects.

A third major endogenous cause of infant mortality is birth defects, which account for roughly 20 percent of perinatal and neonatal deaths. Heart defects are most common, followed by lung defects, chromosomal abnormalities (too many or too few), and defects of the brain and central nervous system.

Once an infant reaches 28 days of age—the postneonatal stage—the risk of death from endogenous causes decreases dramatically, while the threat posed by exogenous causes increases. Put more precisely, a postneonatal child is three times more likely to die of an exogenous cause rather than an endogenous condition. The most common exogenous danger is disease. Pneumonia poses the greatest risk to infants, followed by diseases that cause diarrhea, which can lead to a fatal case of dehydration in as little as 36 hours.

Nutrition is another endogenous factor that contributes significantly to infant mortality. Quantity of food is a major concern in underdeveloped nations, where, in some cases, half the infant population is underweight. Quality is a concern as well, as newborns need a balanced diet rich in calcium, iron, potassium, vitamin A, and vitamin C.

Environment also plays a role in infant mortality rates. The dangers posed by poor-quality air, unclean drinking water, or tainted foodstuffs are fairly evident. Somewhat less obvious are those environmental factors that threaten infants in an indirect fashion. For example, when a nation becomes involved in a war, mortality rates can rise by as much as 60 percent. This is not because of deaths resulting from bullets and bombs, although those certainly happen, but because wars disrupt communication and transportation networks, thus reducing access to food supplies and medical care.

Naturally, the divide between endogenous and exogenous causes of death is not absolute. Exogenous influences—air pollution, for example—can contribute substantially to endogenous problems like birth defects. And endogenous complications like premature birth can exacerbate the effects of exogenous factors like poor nutrition. Further, the root cause of some conditions—most notably sudden infant death syndrome (SIDS)—is unknown, and so such deaths cannot currently be classified as either endogenous or exogenous.

More-Developed Nations

UNICEF and the World Health Organization have taken the lead in combating infant mortality worldwide, providing antibiotics, education, food, and medical assistance. These efforts have been remarkably successful, as the worldwide rate of infant mortality has dropped 40 percent since the mid-1980s.

Worldwide Infant Mortality, 1970–2010 (deaths per 1,000 live births)

Region	1970	1975	1980	1985	1990	1995	2000	2005	2010
East Asia & Pacific	76.18	62.03	52.53	45.38	39.95	35.13	29.11	23.46	18.79
European Union	25.71	20.47	16.00	12.74	10.42	7.96	6.29	5.17	4.22
Latin America & Caribbean	86.40	75.24	63.13	51.44	42.99	35.75	28.48	22.44	18.09
Middle East & North Africa	127.12	105.42	84.60	65.72	53.49	44.04	36.69	30.45	25.57
North America	19.77	15.72	12.39	10.36	9.17	7.72	6.96	6.68	6.39
South Asia	131.81	119.48	107.17	96.25	85.86	75.35	65.66	57.98	51.64
Sub-Saharan Africa	136.63	123.77	115.70	109.14	105.16	101.92	94.26	85.53	76.36
Total, World	95.19	85.70	76.70	68.21	62.37	57.88	52.04	46.24	41.00

Source: The World Bank.

As remarkable as this improvement has been, however, there are still enormous disparities between nations, even among the wealthiest and most developed nations of the world. According to figures from the United Nations' Population Division, 18 different countries have been able to reduce infant mortality rates to less than 5 deaths per 1,000 live births, including Denmark (4.53), Germany (4.21), France (4.10), Japan (3.14), Iceland (2.89), and the world's leader, Singapore (2.60). Other developed countries, by contrast, have not fared nearly as well. For example, the United Kingdom (5.38) is 25th on the list, while New Zealand (5.59) is 29th. The U.S. mortality rate—7.07 deaths per 1,000 live births—is more than double that of Singapore or Japan, and lags behind several much poorer countries, including Slovenia (4.18), Croatia (6.66), and Cuba (6.95).

A close examination of the United States, as a case study, elucidates some of the difficulties entailed in measuring and reducing infant mortality. To start, the country's relatively poor showing is partly a product of inconsistencies in record keeping, as standards for tracking infant deaths vary from nation to nation. In Japan, for example, an infant must take a breath to be considered "alive." Those that do not are automatically classified as stillborn, regardless of their other vital signs. This has the effect of driving stillbirth rates up and infant mortality rates down.

In the United States, by contrast, an infant that shows any signs of life whatsoever—heartbeat, muscle contraction—is judged to have been born alive, even if he or she never takes a breath. As such, many infants that would be judged stillborn in Japan or Europe are included in U.S. infant mortality figures. This is not to suggest, however, that the difference between the United States and other nations is entirely illusory; American infants are unquestionably at higher risk than infants in most other developed nations. One major reason is that premature births are unusually common in the United States. Only 1 in 18 Icelandic infants is born premature, to take one example, but for American infants the number is 1 in 8.

Physicians have only partial explanations for this disparity. Women who smoke and/or drink are at much greater risk for premature births, and both habits are more common among pregnant Americans than they are among their counterparts in other developed nations. Further, fertility treatments increase premature births, and such treatments—which are expensive—are more common in the United States than elsewhere. Still, these and other known risk factors do not fully account for the 540,000 premature births that take place annually in the United States.

Another reason for the unusually high U.S. infant mortality is the fact that the survival rates for children of color lag well behind those of white children. Most notably, African American infants are 2.4 times more likely to die than white infants. The survival rates for other ethnic populations—Mexican Americans, Native Americans, Asian Americans—are also worse, albeit by a lesser degree.

Again, it is difficult to satisfactorily explain this disparity. Without question, the social and economic disadvantages faced by minority populations are partly to blame. However, most scholars are unconvinced that this alone accounts for the difference. They observe that the divide between white and ethnic infant mortality rates in other diverse countries—Great Britain, for example—is not nearly as stark as it is in the United States. They also note that SIDS, which only mildly correlates with socioeconomic status, is twice as common among African American infants as white infants. The presumption, then, is that there must be factors that contribute to the disparity that are currently unknown.

In short, reducing infant mortality rates—even in highly developed nations—is not only a matter of adjusting public policy or expending money. The problem is at least partly rooted in deeply ingrained social behaviors and historical inequities, and also has dimensions that have yet to be fully understood by scientists and physicians. Resolving these issues presents a daunting challenge.

Less-Developed Nations

Though there has been a dramatic decrease in global infant mortality in the past three decades, there are still many areas where the problem is epidemic. A total of 30 nations, most of them in Africa, have a rate higher than 80 deaths per 1,000 live births. At the very bottom of the list are Guinea-Bissau (126.15), Chad (131.94), Sierra Leone (134.57), and Afghanistan (144.01). Put simply, an infant in a developing country is 14 times more likely to die than one in a developed country.

Though there are some infant deaths whose cause remains unclear, the vast majority are due to factors—diarrhea, poor sanitation, pneumonia, malnutrition—that are well understood and can be addressed by modern medicine. As such, the focus of organizations like UNICEF and the World Health Organization is to make certain that the necessary knowledge and resources are available to mothers and infants worldwide.

There are four main strategies for reducing infant mortality. The first is to prevent illnesses through vaccination (particularly for polio and measles) and the provision of folate and vitamin supplements to both infants and mothers. The second is to properly treat conditions like pneumonia and chronic diarrhea. The former can be alleviated with antibiotics, the latter with electrolytes, zinc and other trace metals, and rehydration. The third means of combating infant mortality is to improve the health care available to mothers before, during, and after their deliveries. The fourth is to improve nutrition, both in terms of quality and quantity of food.

The nation of Nepal presents a useful example of these strategies in action. In 1990, Nepal had one of the worst infant mortality rates—98.9 deaths per 1,000 births—in both Asia and the world. This prompted the Nepalese government, aided by the United Nations, to move aggressively to combat the problem. Vaccinations and vitamin supplements were made widely available to mothers at no cost, and were promoted aggressively. A team of 48,000 women known as Female Community Health Volunteers (FCHV) was trained and deployed throughout the nation. The FCHV assist in deliveries and are able to treat many basic conditions, including pneumonia and diarrhea.

As a consequence of these efforts, several life-threatening conditions—measles, neonatal tetanus, and vitamin deficiencies—have nearly been eliminated in Nepal's infant population. Others, particularly pneumonia, have been substantially reduced. Consequently, the infant mortality rate in Nepal has declined precipitously. It had dropped below 40 deaths per 1,000 births by 2009, and is expected to drop by another 25 percent to 30 percent by 2015.

The nation of Angola is another instructive example of the ongoing fight against infant mortality in underdeveloped countries. The country was torn apart by a series of wars that began in the early 1960s and did not end until 2002. By the time a permanent peace was finally achieved, Angola had the worst infant mortality rate in the world, with more than 250 deaths per 1,000 births. Once the government of Angola had stabilized, the nation's Ministry of Health established the Municipal Health System (MHS), which is working to provide universal access to a broad variety of services—prenatal and postnatal care, immunizations, antibiotics, vitamin supplements, and insecticide-treated bed nets for pregnant women and children in order to prevent malaria. Thus far, aided by the growth of the nation's economy and by outside funding, the MHS has been able to institute these reforms in 16 municipalities, reaching approximately 40 percent of the Angolan population. The results have been encouraging, with a 30 percent drop in infant mortality in less than a decade. Still, Angola lags well behind most of the world, and the nation's leadership remains at work on the problem.

Though Nepal and Angola are at different points in the process, both illustrate that rapid progress can be made in combating infant mortality rates simply by utilizing resources and information that are already widely available.

The Future

In the long term, fully meeting the challenges of infant mortality will require extensive development in the areas of health care, infrastructure, food supplies, and air and water quality. It will require knowledge that

Melinda Gates, co-chair of the Bill & Melinda Gates Foundation, announces the 2011 launch of a partnership with the U.S. Agency for International Development, World Bank, and other groups to fight maternal and infant mortality in developing nations. *(Mark Wilson/Getty Images)*

does not currently exist and scientific discoveries that have not yet been made. It will require greater socio-economic equality within nations, and across national boundaries. These are not easy problems to solve, and so it may be many decades—or even centuries—before the entire world achieves the standard currently being set by Singapore, Iceland, and Japan.

In the short term, governments and activists—particularly in less developed nations—are focusing primarily on solutions that promise the greatest benefit per dollar spent. For example, the Indian physician Abhay Bang, a leading authority on infant mortality, founded the Society for Education, Action and Research in Community Health (SEARCH). Through SEARCH, Bang works directly with the leaders of underdeveloped nations to reduce infant mortality.

In the SEARCH program, which costs $2.64 per child, workers are trained to provide essential care and diagnose complications like pneumonia and IH. Each worker has a kit with baby sleeping bags, a bag and mask for resuscitation, and antibiotics. The program has already been deployed in parts of Bangladesh, Ethiopia, India, Kenya, Madagascar, Malawi, Mozambique, Uganda, and Zambia. The results are difficult to measure precisely, but Bang estimates that mortality rates have been cut by half in the communities he works with.

Thanks to organizations like SEARCH and UNICEF, as well as the efforts of activists and governments across the globe, worldwide infant mortality has been on the decline every year since 2006. There is every indication that this progress will continue, and the United Nations is hopeful that by the year 2015, mortality rates will be reduced by as much as two-thirds from their 1980s levels.

Christopher Bates

See also: Gastrointestinal Disease; Health Care; Hunger and Malnutrition; Population Growth and Demographic Issues; Vaccination; Water Supply and Access; Waterborne Disease.

Further Reading

Bideau, Alain, Bertrand Desjardins, and Hector Perez Brignoli, eds. *Infant and Child Mortality in the Past.* Oxford, UK: Clarendon, 1997.

Chandrasekhar, S. *Infant Mortality, Population Growth, and Family Planning in India.* Chapel Hill: University of North Carolina Press, 2011.

Colletta, Nat J., Jayshree Balachander, and Xiaoyan Liang. *The Condition of Young Children in Sub-Saharan Africa: The Convergence of Health, Nutrition, and Early Education.* Washington, DC: World Bank, 1996.

Corsini, Carlo A., and Pier Paolo Viazzo, eds. *The Decline of Infant and Child Mortality: The European Experience, 1970–1990.* The Hague: Martinus Nijhoff, 1997.

El-Khorazaty, M. Nabil. *Infant and Childhood Mortality in Western Asia.* Baghdad: United Nations Economic and Social Commission for Western Asia, 1989.

Gardarsdottir, Olof. *Saving the Child: Regional, Cultural and Social Aspects of the Infant Mortality Decline in Iceland, 1770–1920.* Reykjavik: University of Iceland Press, 2002.

Garrett, Eilidh, Chris Galley, Nicola Shelton, and Robert Woods, eds. *Infant Mortality: A Continuing Social Problem.* Burlington, VT: Ashgate, 2006.

Kaul, Chandrika. *Statistical Handbook on the World's Children.* Westport, CT: Oryx, 2002.

Meckel, Richard A. *Save the Babies: American Public Health Reform and the Prevention of Infant Mortality.* Baltimore: Johns Hopkins University Press, 1990.

Newland, Kathleen. *Infant Mortality and the Health of Societies.* Washington, DC: Worldwatch Institute, 1981.

Newman, George. *Infant Mortality, A Social Problem.* New York: E.P. Dutton, 1907.

Preston, Samuel, and Michael Haines. *Fatal Years: Child Mortality in Late Nineteenth-Century America.* Princeton, NJ: Princeton University Press, 1991.

United Nations Children's Fund. *The State of the World's Children 2009: Maternal and Newborn Health.* New York: UNICEF, 2008.

van der Veen, Willen Jan. *The Small Epidemiologic Transition: On Infant Survival and Childhood Handicap in Low Mortality Countries.* Amsterdam: Rozenberg, 2001.

Web Sites

Children's Rights Portal:
    http://childrensrightsportal.org/focus/infant-mortality
Global Health Council:
    www.globalhealth.org/childhealth
SEARCH: www.searchgadchiroli.org
UNICEF: www.unicef.org/childsurvival/index.html
U.S. National Institute of Child Health:
    www.nichd.nih.gov
World Health Organization:
    www.who.int/topics/infant_newborn/en

Documents

Document 1: "On Cutting the Tongue," 1811

Given the high infant mortality rates of past centuries, there was no shortage of advice—most of it questionable—for parents on how to improve their child's chances of survival. The following selection comes from one of many books on the topic, titled The Maternal Physician: A Treatise on the Nurture and Management of Infants, from the Birth Until Two Years Old: Being the Result of Sixteen Years' Experience in the Nursery. *Its author was identified only as "An American Matron."*

This is an operation so simple and so easily executed that no mother need to hesitate a moment about performing it herself, as I have done for several of my children with perfect safety and success; by taking a pair of very sharp scissors and holding them between her fingers very near the points, so as to preclude the possibility of cutting more than the very outward edge of the string that confines the tongue, and thus avoid all danger of cutting too far, or wounding any of the veins beneath the tongue; from which it is said infants have sometimes bled to death. Another danger arising from this operation is said to be suffocation, from the child's swallowing the point of its tongue and which is owing to cutting too much of the string or bridle; but I can truly say that although there may be danger of one or both these dreadful consequences, yet I verily believe any judicious mother may perform the operation without the least apprehension, provided she feels sufficient resolution: otherwise she had better employ some professional gentleman to do it. My babe, who is now in arms, had his tongue tied to the very end, so that whenever he cried or attempted to lift his tongue it was drawn into the form of a heart. As soon as I was able to attend to him, I seized an opportunity when he was asleep on my lap; and, gently placing the fingers of my left hand under the tongue, I took a pair of nice scissors, and in the manner above directed with ease severed so much of the string as allowed him to suck with freedom, and the babe never awoke or appeared to feel it in the least: but I soon found the operation was not complete enough to permit the tongue to move as it ought to do; and when he was two months old, fearful lest it might cause some impediment in his speech, I cut the string a little more, and although the child was then awake, he never showed the least uneasiness by which I could suppose it caused him any pain; but smiled the whole time. His tongue bled a very little and ever since has appeared perfectly free.

Source: U.S. National Library of Medicine.

Document 2: "Sevagram to Shodhgram," Address by SEARCH Co-founder Abhay Bang, (excerpt), 2001

The Indian physicians Abhay Bang and Rani Bang are the founders of SEARCH (Society for Education, Action and Research in Community Health) and rank among the world's foremost activists in the effort to reduce child mortality. Here, in an excerpt from an address he delivered in 2001, Abhay Bang describes a pivotal incident in his career and explains his practical approach to solving problems.

One evening in Shodhagram I returned home at around 7 p.m. It was raining heavily and was dark outside. Suddenly, two women rushed into my house through the door—a young mother accompanied by her mother. The young mother held a weak infant in her hands. The child's skin was wrinkled and it was all bones. It looked like a live "mummy" and was gasping.

I immediately got up and placed the child on my bed for examination. It was very seriously malnourished and ill. The stethoscope revealed bubbly sounds in the chest. He had pneumonia as well. And before I could do anything it stopped breathing. It died on my bed while I helplessly watched.

"What had happened to the child? Why didn't you come a little early?" I asked.

Between sobs they recounted their story. They came from a nearby village, Khursa. The young mother lost her first son so she was happy when she became pregnant again. The family was miserably poor. Her husband was a drunkard while she worked as a labourer. Food was scarce. On the top of it she suffered from malaria during pregnancy. Thus foetus didn't grow well and was born weak. It was not breast-fed for the first three days—this being the local custom. Later as the breast milk failed the child was bottle-fed on ordinary milk diluted with three parts of water. The child remained hungry and cried continuously which made its voice hoarse. The unclean, contaminated feeding bottle gave him diarrhoea. The mother tried magic cures and charms but that didn't help. Someone advised her to stop milk. Then on they fed the child on a dilute gruel made of sago [palm stems] which made the child weaker still. There was no local medical help available and they had no means to travel. The husband being a drunkard didn't care. The young mother herself suffered from malaria and the child from pneumonia. When the child became critically ill they went to the witch-doctor; who sacrificed a fowl but to no avail. Finally they walked and came to our hospital. Though their village was just four kilometres, travelling even this short distance during the monsoons was an ordeal. The river was in spate. The proposed bridge stood unfinished. They waited. With every passing moment the child's condition deteriorated but the river swelled. They could cross it only in the evening when the flood receded. By then, it was too late.

From a purely medical point of view it is easy to list [the causes of death]. The child was born low birth weight, contracted diarrhea, got malnourished, developed pneumonia and finally died. But the story is not so simple; it has many tragic layers and is intricately linked to an unjust social system. For instance, why was the child born weak? Because the mother did not have enough to eat so the child's malnourishment began in the womb itself. Pregnant mothers often ate less because of fear that a heavy child could create complications during delivery. So, the foetus is deliberately starved to ensure an easy delivery. According to local custom the baby was not breast-fed for three days after birth. A contaminated bottle gave him diarrhea. No local medical help was available. The family resorted to a witchdoctor due to superstitions. In the end the child was fed sago gruel, which increased malnourishment and made him vulnerable to pneumonia. Still no medical treatment was available. The distance from the village to the hospital,

the river in spate, the unfinished bridge—if we count them all, we can list eighteen causes for the child's death.

Eighteen causes for the death of a child is depressing. How and when will we eliminate them? When will our women become literate? When will they get enough to eat? When will we win the fight against malaria? When will malnutrition be banished? When will the bridges be completed and when will the corruption eradicated? All this may not be possible.

But perhaps we need not wait to solve all the eighteen problems. In this chain of the causes of death, if we can break just one single link, then the whole chain will automatically snap. If the woman was educated; if the husband abandoned the bottle; if superstitions were eradicated; if health services reached the home; if the bridge was constructed; if the pneumonia was treated in time—if any of these things had happened, the child might have survived.

This problem challenged us. We started research to reduce child mortality. The hundred odd villages in Gadchiroli became our laboratory. We carefully recorded every child birth and death in these villages. In the first year we estimated that out of 1000 infants born, 121 died with one year. Terrible! What caused the most [of the] 18 deaths? It turned out that pneumonia in children caused 40 percent of the infant deaths. The researchers from other countries also gradually found similar figures. The dreaded pneumonia was the number one killer of infants throughout the world.

What could be done? Pneumonia can be treated with antibiotics. However, to diagnose pneumonia expensive X-ray machines are needed. They are unlikely to reach villages, where even a stethoscope or a doctor is difficult to find. What could one possibly do? Children frequently develop ordinary cough, cold and phlegm. Was there a simple and sure way of diagnosing pneumonia in a child with cough? Was there an effective way of delivering the necessary antibiotics?

Dr. Frank Shan in Papua New Guinea found a simple and effective way to diagnose pneumonia. If the child's breath rate was over 50 per minute then it was most likely to be pneumonia. This diagnosis could be done without the help of a stethoscope or X-ray. It was a superb, low-cost technique and we decided to adopt it. There were still other issues to contend with. Will the parents of the sick child come to get medicines? Cough is a common malady. How will they distinguish between ordinary cough and pneumonia? Will the medicines reduce the death rate? A field trial was necessary.

We chose 104 villages for our field trial. It was a controlled experiment where we provided treatment in only half of the villages. In the remaining villages we just observed the results of the ongoing government health programmes and private practitioners. The net difference in two areas could be attributed to our treatment.

We started educating the parents. How do people suspect that their child has contracted pneumonia? Using locally prevalent words for describing pneumonia would certainly make communication more effective. The local words for breathlessness were 'lahak' and 'dhapa' and pneumonia was 'dabba.' So if a child with cough had 'lahak' and 'dhapa' he may have 'dabba' and should be immediately treated. This was easily understood by the village folks. We also printed all this information in posters to aid communication.

A fifth or eight class pass youth [elementary or junior high school graduate] in each village was selected as the Arogyadoot, or messenger of health from each village. He was trained to examine children suffering from cough and to count their breath rate. If an infant two months or less had a breath count of more than 60 per minute then he was likely to have pneumonia. Similarly, an older infant with a breath rate of more than 50 per minute was likely to be suffering from pneumonia. The educated boys could do this quite easily. The challenge was to teach the illiterate midwives to count breaths.

The midwives could not count up to 50 but they were adept at counting up to 12 because that made a dozen. For their benefit we designed a simple breath counting instrument which consisted of a one-minute sand timer along with two horizontal rows of beads. The upper row had 5 beads: four green and one red; while the lower had 6 beads: five green and one red.

The midwives had to sit in front of the child sick with cough and simply upturn the breath counter. This started the clock. For every ten breaths they had to shift one bead to the right. For an infant above two months, if they shifted all the five beads on the "upper" row to the right with the sand clock still running (i.e. less than a minute) then it meant the child had pneumonia. For diagnosing infants below two months the lower row with six beads had to be used. The traditional midwives did not know whether the breathing rate was 40 or 50 or 60. They only knew that if the last (red) bead was moved before the entire sand passed, it was pneumonia. So simple!

After training the midwives in this technique we tested their abilities. They had to test 50 infants with cough using the breath counter. Later I tested the same infants using a stethoscope. We independently diagnosed pneumonia. It was surprising to find that 82 percent of the results tallied! As if the midwives had become 82 percent doctors of pneumonia!

The low-cost breath counter proved a boon in diagnosing pneumonia. The Arogyadoots and midwives started treating the children with pneumonia by using antibiotics. We kept a meticulous record of treatments and of births/deaths and watched the results of the experiment with bated breath. Children receiving antibiotics had a mortality rate of just 0.8 percent as compared to 13 percent in children who got no treatment.

In the last 12 years the Arogyadoots have treated over 6,000 children for pneumonia. We have fed all this data in our computer. The death rate has plummeted to a mere 0.5 percent which means that 99.5 percent of children with pneumonia have been treated successfully. It proved that unschooled midwives and semiliterate village youth could be trained to successfully treat pneumonia. The Infant Mortality Rate (IMR) due to pneumonia was brought down by 74 percent leading to a decline in the overall IMR by 25 percent. In 1990, this research was published in the *Lancet*.

Did the research have any wider ramifications? According to the WHO, every year 4 million children die of pneumonia all over the world. India alone accounts for a million deaths. Can these deaths be prevented? By using simple techniques demonstrated by us mortality could certainly be brought down. A global conference on Acute Respiratory Infections held in Washington in 1991, passed the following resolution: 'Train millions of community health workers to diagnose and treat pneumonia in children, ensure antibiotic supply and educate mothers about pneumonia.' This resolution was based on the work done by SEARCH and other researchers. Today this method of pneumonia control is being used in over 77 countries.

Source: Society for Education, Action and Research in Community Health.

INFLUENZA

Influenza is a virus regarded by most people today as a nuisance, a disease that is contracted and gotten over rather quickly. But influenza, or the "flu," is actually much more complicated and dangerous than that. It was responsible for the most deadly disease outbreak of human history and more recently has caused grave economic turmoil for local economies. It is poised to remain a serious global public health concern into the foreseeable future.

History

There is no clear agreement as to when influenza first became a disease of humans. Evidence suggests that we have been sickened by the virus since at least the fifteenth century and perhaps far longer than that. Hippocrates penned a description of a flulike disease some 2,400 years ago, and many texts thereafter refer to similar conditions, often referring to them as the "grip" or "grippe." Because the flu manifests in a fashion very similar to other respiratory diseases, however, it is uncertain which of these authors was actually documenting cases of influenza.

The first instance of a verified influenza pandemic occurred in 1580, though earlier possible pandemics have been noted. We also know of pandemics in 1688, 1693, and 1699. There were as many as six pandemics during the eighteenth century and at least four in the nineteenth, including a particularly deadly one in 1847–1848. A pandemic of "Russian flu" swept parts of Europe and the United States in 1889–1890.

Flu virus comes in three different strains : A, B, and C. The C type is very rare in humans. B is found in humans and can cause sickness, but does not trigger epidemics. The A strain is the one that is most dangerous and is responsible for influenza epidemics and pandemics (epidemics that spread to larger geographic areas and generally have higher mortality rates than normal outbreaks).

Scientists believe that the flu virus originated in birds and that populations of aquatic migratory birds continue to be the primary repository and breeding ground for influenza A. Typically, the viruses are transmitted from birds to humans through an intermediary mammal population, like pigs. The virus affects different species differently; in birds, it generally attacks the gastrointestinal tract; while in humans, it targets the respiratory system.

The virus is spread between humans by airborne droplets from a cough or sneeze, even from talking. Less commonly, it can spread by contact with surfaces. The point of entry is the mouth, eyes, or nose. Infected persons can spread the flu as much as a week before they realize that they are sick, but generally they are most contagious one day before developing symptoms and for up to seven days after symptoms appear.

Common symptoms of flu include fever, chills, headache, body aches, and coldlike symptoms. Vomiting and diarrhea can also be present; however, if the only symptoms are gastrointestinal, most likely the person does not have a true case of influenza. Most of the time, those sickened by this virus face nothing more than a few days to a week in bed feeling miserable. Sometimes, however, flu can be deadly. Even when victims die from the disease (that is, flu is their proximate cause of death), the actual cause of death is often pneumonia, one of the most common complications of influenza.

Today, in most developed parts of the world, flu vaccines are widely available, reducing the impact of the disease. Vaccines, however, have only limited effectiveness. In contrast to diseases like measles or polio, influenza is continually evolving. Indeed, many virologists regard it as the most mutation-prone of all viruses. This tendency to mutate has thus far made the development of a consistent vaccine for influenza impossible. This rapid mutation also makes influenza extremely dangerous in epidemic or pandemic situations. The disease can become more virulent and deadly as it spreads, leaving medical professionals scrambling to create an effective, updated treatment for the quickly changing virus. Further, this constant mutation means that the immune system of a flu victim is not likely to be equipped to combat a new variant of influenza. As a result, there is no long-term immunity to flu for those who have had it already, unlike chicken pox or measles.

Pandemic of 1918–1919

By far the most deadly outbreak of disease in human history was the flu pandemic that began in 1918, as World War I was reaching its conclusion. It was a true pandemic, spreading rapidly across the world. Although the outbreak lasted approximately two years, as many as two-thirds of the deaths occurred in a six-month period (roughly September 1918 to February 1919). By any measure, this was the most lethal single disease outbreak in human history. Because of the general chaos attending a world war, the task of reliably determining how many actually died has been difficult, though it was undoubtedly in the tens of millions.

Although experts do not fully agree on this point, the most likely origin of this outbreak was somewhere in the United States, having spread from bird populations to swine to humans. In February 1918, soon after its appearance, the flu was apparently brought to Camp Funston, a military base at Fort Riley, Kansas, by conscripted civilians. At the camp, the huge population of potential carriers and victims allowed the virus to spread rapidly. Within three weeks, more than 1,000 men were hospitalized, sick with the flu.

As World War I raged on, the virus spread easily via troop transport ships. When it hit Spain in May 1918, it was erroneously called Spanish flu, a name that is still used despite current knowledge that it did not originate there. Apparently, the lack of wartime censorship permitted more widespread reporting of the outbreak in Spain—a noncombatant in World War I—thus giving the impression that the flu was at its worst there.

In early September, the pandemic returned to the United States, again via troop transports, striking Camp Devens outside Boston. This second outbreak was not like the one of the previous spring, however, as the virus had mutated into a much deadlier form during the intervening months. The flu rolled across the United States, from east to west, leaving devastation in its wake. In a normal influenza outbreak, 10 percent or less of deaths occur among those age 16 to 40. In the 1918 pandemic, by contrast, as many as half of those who died were in their twenties and thirties. The flu was also dangerous for children, the elderly, and pregnant women. Nearly half of all deaths in the United States in 1918 are attributed to influenza.

The worst of the fatal cases were truly horrific. The onset of illness was sudden and often completely unexpected. The victim could expect not just the usual mild fever and aches associated with flu, but extreme fever and chills and excruciating pain. His or her lips and skin might turn blue or nearly black. Some would experience hemorrhaging from the nose or mouth, or even the ears or eyes, losing vast quantities of blood. For better or worse, such suffering was often relatively brief. It was not unusual for a seemingly healthy person to become ill and succumb within a day or two.

Although the flu spread worldwide, it was experienced differently in different countries. It was actually made up of several waves of the virus, which continued around the world well into 1919, with sporadic flare-ups in 1920. Regions that escaped earlier waves could be hit hard by later ones. Australia, for example, had avoided the earlier outbreak but felt the full force of the pandemic in early 1919.

As noted, experts have only rough estimates of the death toll from the pandemic, but the figures that are available indicate its terrible impact. In Paris, 10 percent of those who contracted the flu died; for those who also developed complications such as pneumonia, the mortality rate jumped to 50 percent. The United States had a death toll of approximately 675,000 (by contrast, about 118,000 Americans were killed in World War I, and about 418,000 were killed in World War II—a total of 536,000 deaths). In some regions, the figures were particularly ghastly. Alaska and Samoa lost one-quarter of their population, and in the northern Canadian region of Labrador, one-third or more of the population died. In Iran, one nomadic tribe lost nearly one-third of its members to the disease.

Some estimates put the global death toll from the 1918 pandemic at 20 million, but others estimate the death toll in India alone at 21 million. Most who study the 1918 pandemic now agree that the total death toll was likely at least 50 million, perhaps as high as 100 million. Nothing else in human history—not plague, the Holocaust, atomic weapons, or any other form of warfare—has killed as many people in as short a time.

More recently, fears of pandemics have often outstripped the actual threat, though medical experts charged with preventing the next global outbreak have no way of knowing which particular varieties of flu will turn as deadly as that of 1918. Another, much less deadly, influenza pandemic broke out in 1957–1958. In 1976, fear of an epidemic of swine flu led to a massive vaccination effort in the United States, with unfortunate consequences. The feared epidemic did not occur, but more than 30 people died of complications from the vaccine. This incident left some people with a lasting distrust of the flu vaccine.

Influenza in the Modern World

Influenza is still with us today. Although nothing close to a repeat of the 1918 pandemic has occurred, there is an outbreak of seasonal flu every year, which causes more deaths than most people realize. A 2003 study by the *Journal of the American Medical Association* examined influenza mortality in the United States between 1990 and 1999, finding that it ranged between 17,000 and 52,000 deaths in a single year. This article is the source of the often-cited figure of 36,000 as the average number of U.S. fatalities due to influenza every year, though clearly there is tremendous annual variation.

As has been the case for centuries—with notable exceptions like the 1918 pandemic—most people who contract the flu today will have a short bout of illness from which they will fully recover within a week or so. The risk of serious complications or death is considerably higher among certain segments of the populace: children, the elderly, and pregnant women; people with chronic blood disease, liver or kidney disorders, or blood disorders; and people with a weakened immune system due to cancer or AIDS.

Flu vaccines, currently available by injection (the most common form) or nasal spray, represent the best available hope for avoiding future pandemics. The ongoing challenge is to stay ahead of the shifting varieties of the virus. As each flu season approaches—November through March, in the Northern Hemisphere—medical experts try to predict which particular flu types will be problematic for that year. If their predictions are incorrect, and a variant that is not targeted by the current year's flu vaccine begins to spread, even those who have been vaccinated will be left vulnerable.

In most years, this represents a small problem, but if a strain as virulent and deadly as the 1918 Spanish flu were to strike too close to the flu season for an effective vaccine to be made available, another devastating pandemic is certainly possible. The medical profession is well aware that the risk of a pandemic is small but that if one did occur, the consequences could be severe. For this reason, physicians are occasionally accused of overstating potential influenza threats and causing panic. It is more accurate, however, to say that that health experts must err on the side of caution or risk another global disaster.

The potential for just such a disaster raised concerns in 1997, as avian flu (H5N1) began to spread. Avian flu, or "bird flu," comes in many forms, most of which do not infect humans. Generally present in wild waterfowl, this type of flu can become a serious problem when it spreads to domesticated poultry, sometimes sickening and killing them quite rapidly. It can then occasionally spread further, to mammals or even humans. The 1997 outbreak most affected Hong Kong, where 18 people were infected and six died. Africa, too, has experienced several outbreaks of avian flu since 2006.

At present, avian flu does not present a major public health risk. The most common way it is contracted is by sustained contact with infected birds—for example, on a poultry farm. This is a circumstance that most humans do not encounter on a regular basis. There is no evidence that avian flu can be contracted by consuming properly cooked poultry or eggs, and it cannot be passed from human to human. The fear among experts, however, is that a mutation could someday appear that would be able to spread directly from one human to another, which could set the stage for another deadly pandemic.

More recently, the rapid spread of the H1N1 virus in 2009 raised alarm bells among medical professionals because H1N1 was the flu variety responsible for the 1918 influenza pandemic. The possibility of a repeat of that deadly scenario called for quick action. In April 2009, the director-general of the World Health Organization (WHO) issued a statement on the spread of H1N1, calling it "a public health emergency of international concern," but also noting that "the likelihood of a pandemic has increased, but . . . a pandemic is [not] inevitable." Although the virus seemed to be spreading fairly rapidly, cases were relatively mild, and the number of deaths was not high enough to cause great alarm. Still, experts feared that the virus could mutate and become much more dangerous, as it had in 1918, and therefore issued warnings and urged worldwide H1N1vaccination.

In response to H1N1, the United States collaborated with Australia, Brazil, France, Italy, New Zealand, Norway, Switzerland, and the United Kingdom to distribute vaccines widely. By early 2010, authorities declared that the danger had passed. Although vaccines were developed and distributed, this event demonstrated that preparedness for a potential flu pandemic is sometimes undercut by a virus proving to be more benign than originally feared. In July 2011, WHO issued its second Global Action Plan for Influenza Vaccines with the goal of ensuring that the world's health professionals would be as ready as they could be to meet the next possible pandemic threat.

The Future

The avian flu that began in 1997 was followed by another avian flu outbreak in 2003–2004. This time the virus was identified among poultry populations in Cambodia, China, Indonesia, Japan, Laos, Pakistan, South Korea, Thailand, and Vietnam. The situation forced authorities to choose between two unappealing options: destroy entire poultry flocks, and therefore economic livelihoods, or allow for the possibility that the virus might spread to the human population and perhaps mutate into a more deadly form. They chose the former; the resultant destruction of poultry stocks had a devastating effect on local economies. Agriculture in these areas was further ravaged when China imposed a ban on the importation of poultry from some affected countries.

In the years following this outbreak, avian flu spread beyond Asia. In summer 2006, it was identified in Kazakhstan, Mongolia, Russia, Turkey, western Europe, and several African nations. By August 2006 more than 220 million birds had been destroyed in an effort to halt the spread.

Such events pit the needs of local economies against the larger public health. Beyond the agricultural impact, a localized outbreak of avian flu (or swine flu or any other variant) can also deter tourism, causing a further detrimental effect on the local economy. Global trade can also be severely disrupted if there are fears of contaminated food, as happened with avian flu and poultry. If a nation completely outlawed the importation of products from a flu-infected region, the ripple effect on the global economy could be severe. In the event that a dangerous strain became capable of spreading from one human to another, further issues relating to human rights could arise, such as the need or desire to quarantine infected populations.

Good hygiene, vaccinations, and separating the living quarters of humans and livestock are the best ways to avoid being infected with the flu virus. Many populations, however, have poor access to vaccines. Moreover, even in economically developed nations, many people resist flu vaccines out of fear and misconceptions. Some, for example, incorrectly believe that the flu shot can actually give them the flu. This is not the case, as the injected vaccine uses an inactivated, or killed, virus. Others believe that the flu is a minor ailment, not worth worrying about. Repeated warnings of pandemics that never materialize only persuade some people that the virus is not a serious threat.

Regardless of this perception, influenza remains a threat. Because of its rapidly evolving nature, efforts to keep it in check with immunization face even more hurdles than do other disease-control programs. Some immunologists hold out hope for a universal influenza vaccine, but for the moment health professionals must continue to rely on trying to predict what the next big influenza threat will be, developing the vaccine ahead of outbreak, and hoping for the best.

Julie Turner

See also: Drug Resistance; Public Health; Vaccination.

Further Reading
Barry, John M. *The Great Influenza: The Epic Story of the Deadliest Plague in History.* New York: Viking, 2004.

Crosby, Alfred W. *America's Forgotten Pandemic: The Influenza of 1918.* Cambridge: Cambridge University Press, 1989.

Davies, Pete. *The Devil's Flu: The World's Deadliest Influenza Epidemic and the Scientific Hunt for the Virus That Caused It.* New York: Henry Holt, 2000.

Dehner, George. *Influenza: A Century of Science and Public Health Response.* Pittsburgh, PA: University of Pittsburgh Press, 2012.

Jenning, Roy, and Robert C. Read. *Influenza: Human and Avian in Practice.* 2d ed. London: Royal Society of Medicine, 2006.

Kawaoka, Yoshihiro, ed. *Influenza Virology: Current Topics.* Wymondham, UK: Caister Academic, 2006.

Kolata, Gina. *Flu: The Story of the Great Influenza Pandemic of 1918 and the Search for the Virus That Caused It.* New York: Touchstone, 1999.

Mitrasinovic, Petar M. *Global View of the Fight Against Influenza*. Hauppauge, NY: Nova Science, 2009.

Osterholm, Michael T. "Unprepared for a Pandemic." *Foreign Affairs* 86:2 (March–April 2007): 47–57.

Torrence, Paul F. *Combating the Threat of Pandemic Influenza: Drug Discovery Approaches*. Hoboken, NJ: John Wiley and Sons, 2007.

Van-Tam, Jonathan, and Chloe Sellwood, eds. *Introduction to Pandemic Influenza*. Cambridge, MA: CAB International, 2010.

Web Sites

Centers for Disease Control and Prevention: www.cdc.gov

National Library of Medicine, National Institutes of Health: www.nlm.nih.gov

World Health Organization: www.who.org

Documents

Document 1: "Dying by Hundreds: The Influenza Scourge in Cape Town" (excerpt), Published Letter, 1919

The text that follows is excerpted from a letter by a nun assigned to New Somerset Hospital in South Africa. The letter was printed in the leading British newspaper, The Times, *during the influenza pandemic of 1919 and details the terrible suffering that took place in Cape Town.*

We have had a most terrible time in Cape Town, and, in fact, all over South Africa with Spanish influenza. It has upset everything; the rush in Cape Town has been so dreadful that every one who was not ill has been worked to the limit. At first we laughed and joked about the "flu," but in a few days people began to be ill by the dozens; the sickness was very violent, very short, and very fatal. Before the first week was out they were dying as if with a plague, by the scores, and later by the hundreds. The deaths started at 20 at day, and before many days were over mounted up to 500 and even 600 a day. In two weeks 6,000 people died, and Cape Town was like a city of the dead. In the hospital here the servants took ill first; then all the laundry people, then porters and ward maids; last of all the doctors and nursing staff. The people died in the streets; at one point big covered wagons patrolled the streets to pick up the dead. A house-to-house visitation was started, and the most terrible state of affairs was discovered; whole families stricken, the dead and living in the same beds, no food in the house, no one able to crawl about to get it; hundreds of people starving because they could not go out to get food; all delivery carts stopped,

no one to drive them; shops shut, the people being ill; business houses shut up; trains and trams stopped running; theatres, bioscopes, and churches all empty and closed. It was like the Great Plague of London.

In the great cemetery 6 miles out of Cape Town, there were no people to dig the graves; people carried to their friends and relatives from a motor car to the plots and had to dig graves themselves; often they were so weak that they could only dig two or three feet deep, and as they turned to get the body they had brought, other people came and threw the bodies of their friends into the grave others had dug; fights ensued, and the scenes were terrible. No clergymen or priests to bury anyone. At the height of the plague there were no coffins, and the people, rich and poor, were buried in blankets. . . .

Source: The Times *(London), January 6, 1919, p. 7.*

Document 2: "Treatment and Cure of Influenza" (excerpt), *Good Housekeeping* 1890

The following excerpt, from an article that appeared in the American women's magazine Good Housekeeping *in February 1890, outlines the standard treatment advice for influenza that doctors prescribed during the Victorian era.*

Having gone to bed at once, the patient should be kept in a well-ventilated, not too warm room. If he can have a flannel nightdress, by all means let him do so. In any case, be sure to have the back and chest well protected by large squares of soft all-wool flannel.

Many people, while covering the chest, fail to remember that cold attacks the lungs at the back as well as the front. Round the loins and stomach similar flannel should be worn, then, if in the restlessness of a feverish attack, the clothes should be tossed off at any moment, the patient has the most vital parts guarded from exposure to cold. During the shivering fit he should be covered with plenty of warm but light bed-clothes, and hot bottles should be kept to the feet, as it is important to keep up the temperature of the body, and this is the best way of doing it. When the temperature rises much above the normal rate (98.4°), and there is profuse perspiration, the invalid is much safer in the blankets than in the sheets, particularly if the perspiration is sour smelling, as this indicates a rheumatic affection which comes from the presence of acid in the system.

On no account should such a patient ever be put into linen sheets. The strength must be kept up with milk, milk and soda, white wine, whey, beef-tea, gruel, eggs beaten up with milk, and all such light and nourishing foods. In some cases, where there is great debility and prostration, it is necessary to give stimulants—wine, brandy, or champagne; but such things are always better given according to the order of the medical attendant. All milk given should be previously well boiled, and the less acids, as lemonade, &c., the better. Barley-water, with as little lemon as possible, may be freely taken, and potash or soda water with the boiled milk. Everything had better be taken just warm, neither hot nor cold, unless it be a hot drink in the cold fit. Water also, if the source is known to be thoroughly pure, may be freely drunk. Quinine is a most useful drug in this malady for pulling up the strength; but it should be impressed on every one that no treatment or prescriptions can be laid down for all cases.

Source: Good Housekeeping, February 15, 1890, p. 191.

INFRASTRUCTURE

Infrastructure facilitates economic and social activities, and its constituent sectors include energy (electricity and natural gas); telecommunications (fixed phone lines, mobile phone service, and Internet connection); transportation (airports, railways, roads, and seaports); and water supply and sanitation (piped water, irrigation, and sewage collection and treatment). It is important to distinguish between infrastructure facilities (such as miles of road or installed generation capacity), about which discussions usually address investment and financing of new facilities, and infrastructure services (such as phone calls made or electricity used), about which discussions usually address the management, operation, and maintenance of infrastructure facilities. Facilities are long lived and costly, and funding them is often controversial in times of straitened budgets, but the services they produce are vital to national economies and thus demonstrate their indispensable importance.

Infrastructure has several features that make it different from normal economic goods. The networks used by many infrastructure services (e.g., rail lines, power grids, roadways) are often called natural monopolies because constructing competing parallel networks is usually economically unfeasible. In the past, many countries have managed these natural monopolies through government ownership, while others (notably the United States) have used private ownership with government regulation. Recently, more countries have been moving toward private provision. Infrastructure also often has spillovers in the form of costs, benefits, or interactions that affect various components of society. Providing sewers in urban areas, for example, reduces risks of disease for those who live in surrounding areas. Electricity and transport improve access to, and the quality of, schools, and improved transportation expands labor markets. Over time, infrastructure is shaped by and is a determinant of the form of human settlements. The costliness and long life of facilities, the natural monopolies inherent in networks, and spillovers all complicate the analysis of infrastructure.

Although infrastructure often seems to be a staid and settled topic, major changes have affected the way it is owned, financed, and regulated around the world. Its social and economic impacts are great; for example, the effects of the Internet are still evolving. In many countries, the public sector no longer provides infrastructure services but now regulates private suppliers. Foreign private investment in infrastructure in developing countries has mushroomed, and many countries are tapping domestic and international bond markets for financing. At the same time, insufficient maintenance, service deficits, and low-quality infrastructure services are long-standing and ongoing problems in many countries.

Historical Background

The history of infrastructure has been shaped largely by technology advances that have fostered new infrastructure sectors and services. Roads comprise the world's oldest infrastructure, dating from Roman times, along with facilities that serve water-borne transport. In the 1800s, new infrastructure technologies began to appear that lowered the costs and stimulated large increases in demand for infrastructure services. Paved and macadam surfaces improved road quality, allowing for heavier vehicles and higher speeds. In the United States, extensive networks of canals were constructed in the early nineteenth century, soon to be followed (and displaced) by the development and expansion of railways. Well into the 1800s, poor sanitation in cities created serious urban public health problems, including cholera epidemics, and life expectancy was much lower for urban than rural residents. The development of citywide sanitation and water systems improved the health of urbanites, and soon their life expectancy surpassed that in rural areas. The need for urban fire protection and the invention of the flush toilet in the 1830s

U.S. Infrastructure, Percent of Full Network Size or Maximum Potential Reached, by Year, United States

	Canals	Railways	Telegraphs	Roads	Gas pipelines	Phones	Internet
1800	1.5						
1810	3						
1820	10						
1830	36	1.2					
1840	69	2					
1850	87	4					
1860	96	9.5	2				
1870		17	5				
1880		33	10				
1890		55	30	1.5	1		
1900		65	45	3	2.5		
1910		85	62	6	6	9	
1920		91.5	75	10	8	20	
1930		95	93	14	11	38	
1940		96	94	36	14	32	
1950				62	16	46	
1960				70	44	71	
1970				81	65	85	
1980				87	75	95	
1990						92	
2000						94	14
2005						94	52

Source: Arnulf Grübler, *Technology and Global Change,* 2003; and Pippa Norris, *The Digital Divide,* 2002.

dramatically increased the demand for water in cities, and a central water supply was extended along with sewer lines. The development in the 1880s of alternating current and long-distance transmission allowed the use of larger generators that took advantage of scale economies in power generation at that time. Telecommunication expansion started with the invention of the telegraph in the 1840s, grew further with the telephone in 1876, and now features cell phones and the Internet, both initiated in the late twentieth century.

When new infrastructure technologies are introduced, their associated networks tend to be constructed relatively quickly. In the United States, the time it took to build the networks for railways, telegraphs, and surface roads was similar, and this build time has varied subsequently. For example, the expansion of telephone service, briefly reversed by the Great Depression, also took several decades. In some cases, new infrastructure services substitute for earlier services. For example, railways replaced canals, and telephones displaced the telegraph. The expansion of new technologies is often accompanied by dramatic cost reductions. As of 2012, the investment cost associated with mobile phone subscriptions had fallen from its 2000 level of $700 to around $100 per subscription.

Forms of finance and ownership have tended to migrate from private (nineteenth to early twentieth century) to public (mid-twentieth century) to public/private (1980s to the present). Shifts between nationalization and privatization of infrastructure finance have reflected contemporaneous ideas about the government's economic role. European countries have tended more toward public provision of power and telephone services, while U.S. telephone and power services have been largely private and regulated by government authorities that oversee and set rules for specific infrastructure services, originally to constrain monopoly firms. The first infrastructure regulatory agency in the United States—the Interstate Commerce Commission (ICC), established in 1887—addressed price discrimination in the railway industry. The United States subsequently implemented regulatory agencies to control monopoly power in other sectors and industries.

The advent of new infrastructure services and technologies can erode monopoly power. For example, the growth of motor trucking provided effective competition for railway freight, and the ICC was abolished in 1996. Changing technology has ended some network-based monopolies, for example, in telecommunications, in which microwave transmission and then the use of satellites made long-distance wire-based networks obsolete and enabled competition among local telephone service providers. Deregulation grew in the 1980s in the United States and United Kingdom, allowing market forces to function subject to only economy-wide regulations. Deregulation was notable in trucking and transformed the airline industry by fostering competitive pricing that made airfares more affordable. Developing countries, which often nationalized power and telecommunication in the mid-twentieth century, have recently followed similar trends from public ownership and operation to regulated private participation and ownership.

Current Issues

Debates about infrastructure now focus on how much infrastructure a country should have, how it will be financed, and how efficiently it performs and associated issues with political implications. Current data indicate that the total value of infrastructure facilities in a country varies roughly in proportion to that country's income. Countries that grow more rapidly need to invest a higher share of national income in infrastructure facilities to enable them to grow at a similar rate. However, sectors such as electrical power grow more rapidly with income than sectors such as water supply. As a result, the composition of infrastructure facilities differs across countries according to income level. Electricity generation is not very extensive in developing countries but grows rapidly, and its value eventually exceeds that of paved roads in newly industrialized and developed countries. Paved roads constitute a large proportion of infrastructure at all income levels. Water and sanitation grow less rapidly than income, and their share of total infrastructure decreases as income levels rise.

Infrastructure financing methods vary widely across sectors and countries; however, user charges, subsidies, and borrowing are the primary sources of funds to cover operating costs and support investment. User fees are common in many sectors: Phone service is often paid for monthly or by direct purchase of mobile minutes; transit fares are charged per subway or bus ride; and road construction and maintenance are financed through fuel taxes and tolls. In view of the long life of infrastructure, borrowing from both public and private lenders is a sensible source of investment funds. In industrialized countries, sovereign bond financing grew in the 1930s to fund large projects, such as hydroelectric dams and road systems. Municipal bonds issued by cities, counties, municipalities, and special districts are now widespread, funding roads, water and sanitation, and other related public projects, especially in the United States. Some cities in developing countries are following industrialized urban areas in the direct sale of municipal bonds on national and international markets.

Many countries use innovative strategies to raise funds for infrastructure. In Latin America, "value capture"—using land value increases associated with service provision to finance infrastructure—is a common practice. Colombia's capital, Bogotá, has used a form of value capture—betterment levies—since the 1930s to finance roads, water and sewer systems, and, more recently, sidewalks and public parks. In Hong Kong, transit companies used value capture to fund transit projects with revenues from the co-development of residential and commercial areas served by public transit. The selling of carbon credits—payments for activities that reduce carbon emissions—is a recent strategy for funding sustainable infrastructure development.

Infrastructure performance is key, yet service quality varies widely across sectors and within countries. Electricity losses range from 5 to 25 percent, faults per 100 phone lines range from 1 to 70, and unpaved roads range from zero to 80 percent of all roads across countries. Sector performance also varies within countries, irrespective of income levels, meaning that both developing and developed

---

Percentage Monetary Value Invested in Various Forms of Infrastructure by Income Level of Country,* 2011
(Data show percent of total value by sector)

	Electric generation	Paved roads	Phone lines	Mobile subscriptions	Water	Sanitation
Low	19.70473	41.28813	1.036006	4.132701	18.17444	15.66399
Lower-middle	35.58036	38.69596	2.016003	4.508388	8.201243	10.99805
Upper-middle	45.15473	39.71211	1.768258	3.459345	4.05814	5.847422
High	49.53173	43.70557	1.507961	1.633575	1.311063	2.310103

* Low = Under $1000 per capita income annually; middle = $1000–$4000; upper middle = $4000–$12000; high income = above $12,000.
Source: Author.

countries might have a well-run electric power sector yet, for example, poor phone service. Service quality depends on three factors: maintenance of existing infrastructure, effective pricing, and management. First, much inefficiency is rooted in inadequate maintenance, leading to sanitation system overflows, irrigation canal leakages, road deterioration, and power distribution loss. Second, offering services below cost promotes overuse, a particular problem with electrical power and water, and subsidized rates undermine end-user efficiency and increase demand for services and investment. Third, infrastructure operations benefit from modern business practices to improve service delivery.

Political Implications

The politics of infrastructure include debates over public or private provision, maintenance, consumer payments, and regulation. Current practices are moving toward more private involvement, but the situation varies by sector. Telecommunications typically are provided privately, and most investment in such facilities is now private. Private involvement is more common in electricity generation than in distribution. Roads are largely publicly provided with the exception of specific facilities—bridges, tunnels, and some toll roads—but many privately financed toll roads have faced financial difficulties because toll increases have been limited by political opposition. Water provision ranges from state-owned monopolies, through private management contracts and build-operate-transfer arrangements, to complete privatization, as in the United Kingdom.

In the past two decades, public-private partnerships have dramatically increased in developing countries. Private participation in infrastructure (PPI)—in which private and public entities work together to finance infrastructure in developing countries through direct investment, leases, and operating contracts—increased in the late 1980s and grew in the 1990s. In 2007, PPI-driven foreign private investment was nearly ten times larger than development assistance for infrastructure. The development assistance predominantly targets developing countries and finances the water, sanitation, transport, and energy sectors. The foreign private investment goes mainly to developing and newly industrialized countries, with the largest share going to telecommunications. Despite the large amounts, foreign private investment and development assistance provide less than half of

Foreign Private Investment Versus Development Assistance, Developing Countries, 1990–2008
(millions of U.S. dollars)

Year	Foreign private investment	Development assistance
1990	21,074	9,656
1992	29,436	9,258
1994	52,479	11,902
1996	92,210	13,715
1998	127,068	9,459
2000	109,534	8,711
2002	61,189	6,496
2004	77,584	13,662
2006	130,393	13,662
2008	154,413	20,881

Source: Author.

2010 annual developing country investment needs (US$450 billion) and do not cover maintenance needs (US$300 billion).

Maintenance is a major issue in many industrialized countries, particularly for publicly provided services such as roads and transit, in which funding is insufficient—especially in the United States. The American Society of Civil Engineers (ASCE) issues an annual *Report Card for America's Infrastructure* that grades infrastructure stocks and services. The most recent 2009 U.S. overall grade was a D, with delayed maintenance and underfunding in nearly every category. This situation implies shortsightedness, because appropriate maintenance has large economic returns in the form of reductions in longer-term investment requirements and in current consumer costs. A reduction in road maintenance increases private vehicle user costs by much more than the maintenance savings. Repairing neglected roads costs 2 to 3 times more than appropriate ongoing maintenance. Of course, technological improvements are reducing some maintenance costs. Trenchless technologies such as cured-in-place pipes allow robotic devices and cameras to repair water, sewer, gas, and chemical pipes with minimal excavation. Automated monitoring and global positioning system (GPS) use on subway and bus lines can signal potential maintenance problems.

Charges to consumers for services are often below cost and politically difficult to raise. Increasing user charges such as tolls, transit fares, and water fees meets political resistance. Underpricing stimulates overconsumption, a serious issue for electrical power in many developing countries. In Latin America, electricity tariffs are about 75 percent of tariff levels in

Children in the slums of Jakarta, Indonesia, fish on a river bank next to a public toilet. Inadequate urban infrastructure not only poses a threat to public health, but is a major obstacle to investment, growth, and reversing the cycle of despair in poor countries. *(Bay Ismoyo/AFP/Getty Images)*

member countries of the Organisation for Economic Cooperation and Development (OECD) and do not cover full costs, while in other regions power tariffs range from one-third to half of OECD levels, with the weakest cost recovery in Africa and South Asia. Revenues from users cover the smallest share (about one-third) of service costs in water supply and sanitation in developing countries. Fees for water usage are perhaps the most debated infrastructure charges as many argue it is inappropriate to charge for a basic need that is an accessible natural resource. Although subsidies that keep service charges low in developing countries are defended on social welfare grounds, the beneficiaries are predominantly the nonpoor who have access to regular services while the poor are left with higher-cost, nonregular suppliers. Poor urban households not served by city water systems pay 5 to 10 times more per liter when they buy water from tank trucks. Connection subsidies for services such as electricity and water (which favor the poor, as the rich are already connected) are a more effective approach to increasing access to services than are subsidized services.

Technology allows pricing for infrastructure ser-
vices where it was not previously possible. Congestion tolls that charge higher rates for road use during peak hours shift some vehicles to off-peak travel times and some passengers to public transit. Charges are currently based on the reading of electronic tags using overhead antennas, camera systems that record license plates, and variably priced lanes that charge single-occupancy users higher rates. GPS technology has obvious potential applications for congestion pricing systems. Electricity usage is being priced according to time of usage by special meters that charge higher rates at times of peak loads. Similarly, mobile phone companies typically offer reduced evening and weekend rates. These pricing approaches reduce congestion on transport facilities and peak loads on electrical power and telephone systems, also reducing the need for new facilities and lowering system costs.

The need for, and state of, regulation varies by infrastructure sector and country and has been an important element in the growth of PPI. In fact, effective regulation is essential for the efficient provision of services from a natural monopoly, whether public or private. As natural monopolies declined, private provision with competition was facilitated by deregulation, such as in the United States, Great Britain, and other countries during the 1980s—notably in airline, bus, and trucking services. When natural monopolies still exist, firms unbundle activities where competition is possible. For example, while a country's power grid may still be a natural monopoly, many utilities procure power from generating plants that compete with one another to provide electricity. In telecommunications, regulatory reform increased competition by removing barriers to entry, specifying standards for network interconnections, and rebalancing prices between local and long-distance service. Unbundling is also becoming common in rail, where some countries separate track provision from train services.

The economic impacts of infrastructure are highly debated. Although the causal linkage is unclear, a one-percentage-point increase in infrastructure is associated with a one-percentage-point increase in the gross domestic product. Research shows that transportation improvements increase the size of markets and that access to water, sanitation, and electricity positively affect human capital. Rates of return estimated for infrastructure vary widely in economic research, in which some experts find negative or zero returns and others find large positive impacts on economic growth. The preponderance of evidence indicates that infrastructure's impact is lower in more prosperous countries than in others. Some studies find that the social rate of return to infrastructure is particularly high in countries that have insufficient amounts of infrastructure facilities, particularly paved roads and electricity-generating capacity. This is an area that merits further work. Estimating infrastructure's economic impact is complicated because such estimates must take account of infrastructure's long-term impact on the location and scale of other activities, of the productivity of other investments, and of its own effective management, pricing, and maintenance practices.

Future Uncertainties

Recent decades have witnessed a profound change in the way infrastructure is organized and financed in both industrial and developing countries. Private participation and financing have increased dramatically in developing countries, and regulatory reform has improved services and reduced costs in industrial countries. While infrastructure facilitates economic growth, the benefits of overall investment in infrastructure are still uncertain because of its long-term

effects and its numerous spillovers and interactions with activities, such as the location decisions of firms and households in metropolitan areas.

Infrastructure providers must combine revenue from user charges and from public budgets to fund investments and particularly to provide adequate maintenance, an ongoing challenge in both industrial and developing countries. Countries with high growth rates need to invest larger shares of national income in infrastructure to support their growth. Although external assistance for infrastructure in developing countries increased dramatically beginning in the 1980s, recipient countries need to ensure that this development assistance and private foreign investment are well used. Developing countries such as China and India are beginning to make substantial infrastructure investments in other developing countries, and such flows are also likely to grow.

Innovations in green infrastructure will multiply in the coming years in both developed and developing countries. For example, storm water management through green roofs, rain gardens, and permeable pavements reduces the maintenance and investment needs for larger drainage systems. Wind and solar generation are proliferating in the power sector. The regulation of carbon emissions is creating an infrastructure financing market for developing countries, offering them an opportunity to build low-carbon infrastructure and sell credits to developed countries. The growth of renewable energy capacity will reduce the associated costs of its investment and services, as has happened when other infrastructure sectors expanded in the past. Renewable energy has the potential to produce impacts similar to those of the rail, road, and telecommunication waves witnessed in the past two centuries.

Gregory K. Ingram and Karin Brandt

See also: Digital Divide; Traffic and Mass Transit; Urbanization.

Further Reading

American Society of Civil Engineers (ASCE). *2009 Report Card for America's Infrastructure.* Washington, DC: ASCE, 2009.

Brenneman, Adam. "Infrastructure and Poverty Linkages: A Literature Review." Washington DC: World Bank, 2002.

Canning, David. "A Database of World Infrastructure Stocks 1950–1995." Policy Research Working Paper 1929. Washington, DC: World Bank, 1998.

Canning, David, and Ezra Bennathan. "The Social Rate of Return on Infrastructure Investment." Policy Research Working Paper 2390. Washington, DC: World Bank, 2000.

Estache, Antonio, and Marianne Fay. "Current Debates on Infrastructure Policy." Policy Research Working Paper 4410. Washington, DC: World Bank, 2007.

Gómez-Ibáñez, José A. *Regulating Infrastructure: Monopoly, Contracts, and Discretion.* Cambridge, MA: Harvard University Press, 2003.

Grübler, Arnulf. *Technology and Global Change.* Cambridge, UK: Cambridge University Press, 2003.

Hirschman, Albert O. *The Strategy of Economic Development.* New Haven, CT: Yale University Press, 1958.

Ingram, Gregory, and Marianne Fay. "Physical Infrastructure." In *International Handbook of Development Economics*, ed. A.K. Dutt and Jaime Ros, pp. 301–315. Northampton, MA: Edward Elgar, 2008.

Ingram, Gregory K., Zhi Liu, and Karin Brandt. "Metropolitan Infrastructure and Capital Finance." In *Metropolitan Government Finance in Developing Countries*, ed. Roy Bahl, Johannes Linn, and Deborah Wetzel. Cambridge, MA: Lincoln Institute of Land Policy, forthcoming.

Lewis, W. Arthur. *The Evolution of International Economic Order.* Princeton, NJ: Princeton University Press, 1977.

Norris, Pippa. *The Digital Divide: Civic Engagement, Information Poverty, and the Internet Worldwide.* Cambridge: Cambridge University Press, 2001.

Web Sites

Africa Infrastructure Knowledge Program: www.infrastructureafrica.org

American Society of Civil Engineers Report Card for America's Infrastructure: www.infrastructurereportcard.org

Infrastructure Consortium for Africa: www.icafrica.org/en/

Private Participation in Infrastructure Database: http://ppi.worldbank.org

Public-Private Infrastructure Advisory Facility: www.ppiaf.org/ppiaf/

World Bank DataBank: http://data.worldbank.org/topic/infrastructure/

INTELLECTUAL PROPERTY RIGHTS

"Intellectual property" is an umbrella term for a variety of different fields of law that all, in essence, protect creations of the mind. The most commonly known intellectual property rights (IPR) are copyrights, trademarks, and patents. Aside from these three, the following rights are also categorized as IPR: related rights, database rights, plant breeder's rights, geographical indications (for example, *champagne*, which can only be named as such when the bubbly drink originates from the Champagne region in France), industrial designs, computer circuits, and trade secrets.

IPR give the owner a temporary monopoly on the use of his or her creation. In some cases the term of protection can be extended without limit—for example, for trademarks—thereby in theory creating an infinite monopoly. An intellectual monopoly means that whenever a person creates a work, registers a trademark, or obtains a patent right, nobody but the owner of the right is allowed to use the work, trademark, or patented invention, except of course with consent of the IPR owner.

One may wonder why such a monopoly is provided by law. Indeed, the exclusiveness of IPR could give the owners an unbridgeable lead over their competitors. Their market power could drive up prices, force competitors to step out of the market, and ultimately slow down development. However, IPR are generally regarded as favoring competition. They can be seen as the engine of development, giving people an economic and moral incentive for further creativity. For example, if a corporation invests billions of dollars in developing a new medicine—and, let us say, these costs are integrated in the selling price—and after a week a competitor releases a medicine with the same effect, which costs only a fraction of the price of the original, the developing corporation will undoubtedly lose the economic incentive to further develop its products.

The legal basis for IPR has largely been laid down in international treaties and conventions. Among these are the Paris Convention for the Protection of Industrial Property of 1883, the Berne Convention for the Protection of Literary and Artistic Works of 1886, and the Agreement on Trade-Related Aspects of Intellectual Property Rights (TRIPS) of 1995. These three conventions together create a worldwide and (more or less) uniform IPR system.

For the sake of brevity, the following discussion will focus on the three most well-known IPR: copyrights, trademarks, and patents.

Brief History of Intellectual Property Rights

In the centuries before the eighteenth, kings and heads of the church offered "copyright" protection by granting privileges. Privileges provided book printers and publishers an exclusive right to print and publish a work for a certain period and in a certain region. These "copy" rights—hence the name—were aimed on the one hand at securing the economic interests of the printers and publishers and on the other at giving the king or church the opportunity to censor the published works. The second function proved especially convenient during the Reformation, the European Protestant uprising against the Catholic Church during the fifteenth century. Copy privileges thrived particularly in the centuries following the invention of the printing press by Johannes Gutenberg in or around the year 1450. In some countries during the following centuries, the economic notion of copyright evolved to a more personal concept of copyright: the personal right of authors to be able to freely and exclusively use their intellectual creations. As a result, countries with the civil law system speak of "author's right" rather than "copyright."

Patent rights—albeit in the form of privileges—were

already regulated by fifteenth-century Italian statutes. Although both copyright and patents were issued in the form of privileges, patent privileges were, and are, different in the way that they provide protection against economic risks for invented products rather than the risks of printing and publishing works. Patent privileges granted the inventor the exclusive right to use the invention for a limited period and usually in a certain region, much the same as copy privileges. Patents proved especially helpful during the Industrial Revolution. One can imagine the advantages of a monopoly on the steam engine or spinning machine.

IPR that did not originate from privileges, but rather from the industry itself, are trademark rights. Although branding was already known in the Roman Empire, mainly for cattle and weaponry, modern trademarks have been in use since the Middle Ages, when guilds would prevent others from using their reputation and product quality by affixing their mark to their goods—for example, the "hallmarks" on silver. In the eighteenth and nineteenth centuries, during the Industrial Revolution, businesses increasingly used trademarks to prevent deception about the origin of goods and services, thereby preventing economic devaluation of their reputation.

In more recent years, technological developments that have continued to change society have created the need to update IPR legislation. Various developments in the digital electronic and biological sciences realms have raised a host of problems for those seeking to regulate and order IPR. How does society deal with a worldwide exchange platform that enables free downloading of copyright-protected material with a single mouse click? However, not only copyright needs to adapt to recent developments. What is to be done about cloning and creating donor organs from stem cells? Is it ethically and legally allowed to patent a human body? And what should be done about mass counterfeiting of trademarks?

Copyright, Trademarks, and Patents

Many recent developments have led to the expansion in IPR legislation. Basically, the structure of these three rights is the same. When authors, owners of trademarks, or patentees satisfy a certain legal threshold, they receive exclusive legal protection and are thereby in principle allowed to exploit their right to gain personal and economic benefits (aside from possible restrictions and limitations).

It is important to take account of the aforementioned international treaties. The TRIPS agreement, in particular, plays a vital role, since this agreement is the most comprehensive international agreement on IPR. The TRIPS agreement also commits signatories to comply with most parts of the Paris Convention and the Berne Convention, thereby covering most areas of IPR.

Copyright

Copyright is the exclusive right of authors to disclose or reproduce their work. The author is the legal or natural person who creates a "work." According to Article 2 of the Berne Convention, a "work"' is "every production in the literary, scientific and artistic domain, whatever may be the mode or form of its expression." This definition comes down to practically anything from software, encyclopedias, paintings, and furnishings to architectural works. Because of the undesirable effect if copyright protection were to be extended in unlimited fashion to all creations, a threshold for protection was introduced: a work has to be original. On this point there is a disparity between civil and common law systems. While civil law countries generally require "creativity"—reflecting the author's personality—common law countries usually have a more economic notion of originality, requiring "sweat of the brow," indicating that the work shows skill, judgment, and labor. This dissimilarity is slowly converging toward the requirement of "a little creativity," which can be seen notably in the *Feist v. Rural* decision (1991) in the United States and the *Infopaq* decision at the Court of Justice of the European Union (2009).

Trademarks

Trademarks are registered signs that allow the owners thereof to exclude all other parties from using this sign in the course of trade.

According to Article 15 of the TRIPS agreement, a trademark has to be a sign, or a combination of signs, which is "capable of distinguishing the goods or services of one undertaking from those of other undertakings." The function to distinguish goods or services, also called the distinctiveness requirement, is the key element of a trademark. A simple color, a series of numbers, or a descriptive word—such as the sign "car" for cars or "cola" for soda—is not likely to be considered distinct.

The owner of a trademark has the right to prevent all other parties from using that registered trademark in the course of trade, either if there is a likelihood of confusion or if the signs are identical. The trademark right owner thereby acquires exclusive ownership of the sign. This rule also partly clarifies the reason why nondistinctive signs in principle cannot constitute a trademark. Indeed, if a party had the exclusive right to use a certain color, other parties could be excluded from *ever* using this same color in the course of trade, since trademarks usually can be renewed indefinitely. The restriction to register such general symbols and signs is based on the German concept of *freihaltebedürfnis*, the freedom to be able to use basic and descriptive signs in the course of trade.

Patents

Patents give the holder the exclusive right to prevent all others from using, making, offering, selling, or importing a certain invention, either a product or a production process, in the field of technology (Article 28 of the TRIPS agreement).

Inventions can only be patented when they are novel, involve an inventive step, and are susceptible to industrial application. Novelty means that the invention has to be new in the most absolute sense of the word. This is primarily a factual determination: the invention must not be found anywhere, in any way. The inventive step requirement is much more subjective. This requires that the invention should not be "obvious," or logically follow from prior art. In other words, the invention has to show technological progress. The third condition means that the invention must be capable of being created (a product) or of achieving a certain result (a production process).

Inventions need to be registered in order to be protected as patents. Because of the extensive research procedure, it can take a months, even years, before the patent is actually granted. Between the moment of application and the moment of granting, applicants often use the term "patent pending" when using their invention in the course of trade.

Contemporary Issues in IPR

The first issue in IPR is the relationship between copyright and technology, notably the Internet. On this file-sharing platform, copyright violations are common: a simple keyboard combination or a mouse click is sufficient to reproduce and disclose protected material. An additional problem is the anonymity of users, which makes it especially hard to enforce digital copyright.

The second issue is the relationship between IPR and developing countries. Most IPR, especially trademarks and patents, are owned and used by companies in highly developed countries such as Japan and the United States. In developing and upcoming industrial countries, mainly in Southeast Asia, the enforcement of IPR is often conducted passively, if at all. As a result, counterfeiting is an increasing practice in these regions.

The third and last issue is the relation between patents and ethics. Theoretically, embryos, fetuses, and even babies resulting from using cloning or fertilization processes are eligible for patent protection. Of course it is absurd that the birth of a human being could be called a "patent infringement" and thus it is not so considered.

Complications of File Sharing

Downloading music, videos, and software has become one of the most common online activities. Needless to say, songs, movies, and programs can all be considered copyright-protected works. Laws and regulations concerning the legitimacy of downloading copyright-protected material vary from country to country. In many countries, individuals have the right to download, or "reproduce," a work for personal use. Under those circumstances, downloading is legal. Uploading, or "disclosing," on the other hand, is usually allowed only under strict conditions.

There has been much recent discussion about the economic consequences of downloading and uploading copyright-protected material. File sharing is often seen as a reaction to the high price of recorded and live entertainment. As numerous studies make clear, illegal file sharing is costing the entertainment industry billions of dollars and jeopardizes thousands of jobs. This has led many, though not all, governments to crack down on those who illegally share files, particularly music and video files, with copyrighted material in them. However, numerous studies also show that the primary income of most music artists depends on live music performances, not the sales of CDs. Furthermore, the drop in CD and DVD sales caused by illegal file sharing has been accompanied by an increase in digital music sales by an increasing number of legal digital music providers, such as iTunes, Rhapsody, and Google Music. Net sales of Apple's iTunes increased by an average of 28 percent per year during the period 2005–2010, reaching $5 billion in the latter year. Similar mitigating arguments can be conceived for the movie and software industry.

Nevertheless, and for obvious reasons, these industries continue to pursue efforts to stop file-sharing. As of 2011, there were a number of pending lawsuits against organizations that infringe on, or assist the infringement on, copyright. Defendants in these legal filings include Napster, KaZaA, BitTorrent, and The Pirate Bay. The question for these plaintiffs, say many experts, is whether such suits are worth the enormous expense they incur. For instance, the Swedish Pirate Bay's Web site was ordered shut down by national authorities in 2006, but it remained freely accessible in most countries through 2011.

With regard to the enforcement of copyright on the Internet, one recent development needs mentioning, namely the 2010 Anti-Counterfeiting Trade Agreement (ACTA). This agreement is an initiative by several developed countries—notably the United States and Japan—and the European Union to tackle large-scale IPR infringement. With regard to file sharing, ACTA requires member states' enforcement of procedures to safeguard IPR in the digital environment, notably against "technologies that can be used to facilitate widespread infringement," such as file sharing and unlawful streaming.

Developing Countries and Counterfeiting

There has also been much discussion in recent years about counterfeiting of intellectual property and compliance with trademark legislation in a number of developing and newly developed countries, including China, South Korea, and Singapore. Some of these countries have become notorious for their mass counterfeiting of luxury brands and products, such as clothing, jewelry, perfumes, software, medicines, and electronics. Particularly in some East Asian countries, such as China, India, and Thailand, counterfeiting is a lucrative business. The table provides some rough estimates of the global economic effects of counterfeiting.

Counterfeiting, according to IPR experts, not only is detrimental economically to businesses that specialize in intellectual property and to nations where such production is an important component of their economies but can even pose potential threats to people's health. Recent examples of dangerous counterfeited products include fake brand-name baby formula made with health-impairing chemicals,

Estimated Impact of Counterfeit Products on Global Economy, 2008 and 2015

	2008	2015 (est.)
Value of internationally traded counterfeit products	$325 billion	$865 billion
Value of nationally produced and sold counterfeit products	$175 billion	$470 billion
Total	$500 billion	$1,335 billion

Source: Frontier Economics, 2011.

and the erectile-dysfunction drug Viagra made with pesticides, brick dust, and blue paint. Indeed, many medicines are becoming increasingly counterfeited, with huge consequences for human well-being. According to the World Health Organization, in some developing regions nearly 40 percent of all antimalarial drugs are fake, being either worthless or having deleterious effects on those who take them. Initiatives such as the 2006 Declaration of Rome and the International Medical Products Anti-Counterfeiting Taskforce, established in the same year, have not yet had a major impact on such illegal trade.

Counterfeiting is extremely difficult to combat. The organizations behind these activities are often run by sophisticated and well-educated professionals with the means to accurately fake the product and its presentation, sometimes even falsifying the holograms that are used to authenticate the product. Often the only way to tell the difference between an original and a counterfeit is the inferior quality of the latter, which can be determined only after the product is purchased or used.

Still, efforts to combat counterfeiting are being actively pursued around the world. For example, a number of developed world countries have signed the above-mentioned ACTA. This agreement aims to prevent counterfeiting through enhanced international cooperation. Among other things, signatories have to provide both civil and criminal enforcement procedures for trademark right owners. Despite such good intentions, critics believe that since many problem-causing countries, such as China, India, and Thailand, are not signatories of ACTA, the impact of the agreement will probably remain limited until they come aboard.

IPR and Ethics

According to Article 27(3) of the TRIPS agreement, members may exclude from patent protection in-

A shopkeeper hangs signs at an unauthorized Apple store in Kunming, China, in 2011. Despite a special antipiracy campaign by the Beijing regime, the sale of fake foreign goods and other infringements of intellectual property rights run rampant in China. *(AP Photo)*

ventions that violate public order or morality. In most countries, this includes cloning and, in others, includes genetically modified organisms. Ethicists generally do not oppose the breeding of animals and plants—which, after all, mankind has done for millennia—but rather the recombining of genes and DNA transplantation from one species to another.

On the one hand, allowing patents that involve genetic engineering with animals, plants, and humans provides incentives for the further development of technologies. And this could lead, among other things, to disease-resistant vegetables, new medicines, and new models for the examination of diseases and gene regulation.

On the other hand, one negative consequence of allowing medicine-related patents could be increasing prices for use of patented technology. These costs may in fact stymie further development, for instance when medical specialists are more or less obligated to use cheap, unpatented medicines and as a consequence will not be able to treat their patients as well as they could with the use of expensive, patented medicines. Furthermore, patentees may shelve their patents, thereby blocking access to these technologies for further development for at least twenty years. In this context, the Doha Development Round of the World Trade Organization (WTO) needs mentioning. One of the topics of this discussion round is the modification of the TRIPS agreement, whereby the least-developed members of the WTO will be granted access to patented medicines.

The Future

Most experts agree that it will be very difficult to put the genie unleashed by the Internet back into the bottle. That is to say, it will remain very difficult to stop file-sharing sites as long as there is an economic incentive and the technological means to maintain them. Moreover, treaties such as ACTA are likely to remain ineffective as long as developing world countries such as China continue to provide a haven for, or at least turn a blind eye to, such copyright-infringing activities, which provide a lucrative income for a significant portion of their populations. And as long as these file-sharing sites exist, there will be customers for them, since the product they offer is free. Educational efforts to dissuade consumers have proved and are likely to continue to prove ineffectual in overcoming such economic incentives.

More likely is international cooperation to prevent the counterfeiting of illegal medicines, since such activity has a deleterious effect on all parties—the pharmaceutical companies in the developed world that lose income and, more importantly, the inhabitants of developing world countries who suffer by such medicines.

Peter Ras

See also: Cybercrime; Education, Higher; Press, Freedom of; Protectionism and Free Trade.

Further Reading

Beer, Jeremy de, ed. *Implementing the World Intellectual Property Organization's Development Agenda*. Waterloo, Ontario: Wilfrid Laurier University Press, 2009.

Bin, Roberto, Sara Lorenzon, and Nicola Lucchi, eds. *Biotech Innovations and Fundamental Rights*. Berlin: Springer-Verlag, 2011.

Correa, Carlos M. *Intellectual Property Rights, the WTO and Developing Countries: The TRIPS Agreement and Policy Options*. London: Zed Books, 2000.

Correa, Carlos M., and Abdulqawi A. Yusuf, eds. *Intellectual Property and International Trade: The TRIPs Agreement*. Dordrecht, Netherlands: Kluwer Law International, 1998.

Gervais, Daniel. *The TRIPS Agreement: Drafting History and Analysis*. London: Sweet & Maxwell, 2008.

Greenhalgh, Christine, and Mark Rogers. *Innovation, Intellectual Property, and Economic Growth*. Princeton, NJ: Princeton University Press, 2010.

Maskus, Keith E. *Intellectual Property Rights in the Global Economy*. Washington, DC: Institute for International Economics, 2000.

Pires de Carvalho, Nuno. *The TRIPS Regime of Patent Rights*. The Hague, Netherlands: Kluwer Law International, 2005.

———. *The TRIPS Regime of Trademarks and Designs*. The Hague, Netherlands: Kluwer Law International, 2006.

Schmidt, Aernout, Wilfred Dolfsma, and Wim Keuvelaar. *Fighting the War on File Sharing*. The Hague, Netherlands: T.M.C. Asser, 2007.

Weinstock Netanel, Neil, ed. *The Development Agenda: Global Intellectual Property and Developing Countries*. New York: Oxford University Press, 2009.

Web Sites

United States Patent and Trademark Office: www.uspto.gov

World Health Organization: www.who.int/medicines/services/counterfeit/en/

World Intellectual Property Organization: www.wipo.int

World Trade Organization: www.wto.org

Documents

Document 1: *WIPO Intellectual Property Handbook: Policy, Law and Use,* 2004

The World Intellectual Property Organization (WIPO), located in Geneva, Switzerland, is a specialized agency of the United Nations that seeks to develop and harmonize the world's intellectual property system. Its Intellectual Property Handbook *offers a good general introduction in Chapter 2, outlines international enforcement in Chapter 4, and describes in detail the intellectual property conventions administered by WIPO in Chapter 5 (notably the Berne and Paris Conventions).*

www.wipo.int/about-ip/en/iprm

Source: World Intellectual Property Organization.

Document 2: World Trade Organization TRIPS Agreement, Overview

The World Trade Organization is an independent international organization established in 1995 to supervise and liberalize world trade. Annex 1C to the Agreement Establishing the World Trade Organization is the Agreement on Trade-Related Aspects of Intellectual Property Rights, one of the most important international documents in the field. In this overview, the authors of the TRIPS agreement give a short description of the agreement and summarize its different provisions in understandable language.

www.wto.org/english/tratop_e/trips_e/intel2_e.htm

Source: World Trade Organization.

KIDNAPPING AND HOSTAGE-TAKING

Kidnapping and hostage-taking are two related activities considered criminal in every nation and jurisdiction in the world. In both cases, persons are seized, or abducted, and held against their will. Kidnapping and hostage-taking are undertaken for one of three motives, though in some cases more than one motive may be at work: emotive satisfaction (as in the case of child abduction by an estranged parent), monetary gain, and/or political statement or gain. On occasion, hostage-taking is incidental, as when criminals seize hostages when the original criminal activity—such as a bank robbery—goes awry. The main difference between kidnapping and hostage-taking is that, in the former, the crime is often kept secret and the victims are sequestered in unknown locales, while in the latter, the action is public and authorities are aware of the location of the seized person or persons.

Both kidnapping and hostage-taking—particularly of the political kind—have well-documented ancient origins, when high-level personages were seized by enemies in wartime in order to extract ransoms or to gain the compliance or surrender of the people ruled over by the seized hostage. Kidnapping and hostage-taking for emotional or criminal ends also have long histories, though the historical record is less clear on the specifics. The modern era of political kidnapping and hostage-taking—usually of high-level or politically targeted personages—began with the abductions undertaken by left-wing revolutionaries in Latin America in the late 1960s and early 1970s. At the same time, Palestinian and other Middle Eastern [...] more indiscriminate forms of [...] seizing airliners filled with [...] rally of countries with which [...] political differences.

[...] tage-taking impose costs be- [...] damage done to victims and [...]s. If they become endemic,

they can cause political turmoil and social unease and even threaten economic activity. Over the years, governments, businesses, and individuals—particularly in jurisdictions prone to kidnapping and hostage-taking—have taken a number of measures for combating and responding to these crimes. These measures include changes in an individual's daily routines, the establishment of companies specializing in kidnapping victim recovery, police negotiation training, and the training and equipping of security force assault teams. These measures have had only mixed success; kidnapping and hostage-taking remain a perennial bane in many parts of the world.

History

While the origins of the word "kidnapping" date to seventeenth-century England—"napping" is an archaic word for stealing—its existence in ancient times is attested to by, among other things, its condemnation in the book of Deuteronomy (24:7), which states that any Israelite who kidnaps and enslaves a fellow Israelite should be condemned to death. The widespread existence of slavery in virtually all societies until the modern age provided the motivation and opportunity for kidnapping ordinary persons for criminal ends.

Hostage-taking, too, has occurred for as long as there have been warfare and conflict between peoples. In ancient and medieval times, hostages were usually of high status, as the lives of ordinary persons in these highly hierarchical societies were not considered important or valuable enough to warrant a ransom or political concession. Kings and other leaders were sometimes seized in warfare as a way to extract money or surrender by the group from whom the victim came. But sometimes hostage-taking was undertaken to prevent conflict, as in medieval

514

Europe, when nobles were seized when one side in a conflict was seen as preparing for war. The seizing group would then threaten the noble with death to get the other side to call off its plans for war. With the rise of the modern nation-state in the middle of the past millennium, such hostage-taking diminished, as nobles and kings became less critical to—and became less identified with—the existence and functioning of the jurisdiction over which they ruled.

The modern era of political kidnapping and hostage-taking dates to the left-wing urban guerrilla groups operating in a number of Latin American countries in the late 1960s, among them the October 8 Revolutionary Movement in Brazil and the Tupamaros of Uruguay. In 1969, the October 8 group briefly kidnapped the American ambassador, successfully forcing the right-wing military government in Brasilia, which they opposed, to release 15 left-wing prisoners it was holding. But it was the Tupamaros who most effectively utilized kidnapping as a political weapon, developing a revolutionary rationale for these acts. In the early 1970s, they kidnapped numerous Uruguayan businesspersons and government officials in order to protest both capitalism and the increasing government crackdown against left-wing and labor agitators. Indeed, they seized so many that they actually ran a clandestine prison to hold their victims. In 1970, the Tupamaros kidnapped an American embassy official and FBI agent named Dan Mitrone, who they claimed was training Uruguayan security forces in torture techniques. They put him on "trial" in a secret "revolutionary court," found him guilty, and executed him. The kidnappings were perpetrated for four ends—to obtain ransom money to conduct further operations, to win the release of compatriots held by the government, to highlight the Tupamaros' political grievances to the Uruguayan public and a larger world audience, and to foment a crackdown by the government, which would further alienate the citizenry and trigger broader revolutionary resistance.

A slightly different scenario was emerging around the same time in the Middle East, a result of the ongoing struggle of the Palestinian people against the state of Israel. In 1968, under the leadership of pan-Arabist and Marxist-Leninist revolutionary George Habash, the Popular Front for the Liberation of Palestine (PFLP) hijacked an Israeli commercial airliner, seizing dozens of passengers and crew members and holding 12 of them hostage in Algiers for 39 days. The hijackers seized the flight because they believed, mis-takenly, that Yitzhak Rabin, then Israel's ambassador to Washington, was on board, making this hijacking somewhat similar to the Latin American kidnappings, in that the primary target was a high-level personage. Similar, too, was the motivation. The PFLP hoped to win the release of Palestinian militants and, in this, they were successful.

Gradually, however, PFLP terrorists and others connected to the Palestinian cause began to target airliners in order to take ordinary persons—though usually citizens of target countries, such as Israel or Western allies—hostage. In such cases, the goals were similar to those of the Latin American revolutionaries, though extracting monetary ransoms was usually not on the agenda. Instead, the PFLP and other groups hoped to win the release of compatriots held by the Israeli government; highlight their cause—Palestinian liberation and the destruction of the state of Israel—to a world public through international media; inspire broader revolutionary acts, particularly in the Middle East; and put pressure on the Israeli government and people to make concessions by increasing their level of anxiety and insecurity. Through the 1970s and into the 1980s, hijackings of planes and even ships—usually by Palestinian militants and their sympathizers—grew in frequency. Ground-based kidnappings and hostage-taking were also adopted as a tactic by other Middle Eastern militants from the late 1970s onward. These included, most notably, the 1979 seizure of the American embassy in Tehran by Islamist revolutionary students and, in the mid-1980s, a series of kidnappings of Western officials by Hezbollah militants during the Lebanese Civil War.

Several factors—some conflict-specific and others more general—led to a diminishing of such hijackings, hostage-taking episodes, and kidnappings from the 1980s into the 1990s. The ending of the Lebanese war in 1990 and the easing of tensions between Palestinian militants and the Israeli government led to the Oslo Accords of 1993. More general reasons were heightened security precautions in airline travel and the decision by many governments to take a harder line against hostage-seizing terrorists. Israel and many Western governments announced that they were no longer going to negotiate with terrorists—though such blanket declarations were frequently ignored—and began to employ special forces to liberate hostages.

While such hostage-taking diminished in the Middle East, it was increasingly adopted by revolutionaries, terrorists, militants, and criminal syndicates in other

Ranking of Nations by Number of Kidnappings, 1999, 2006, 2008

Rank	1999	2006	2008
1	Colombia	Iraq	Mexico
2	Mexico	Mexico	Brazil
3	Brazil	India	Colombia
4	Philippines	South Africa	Venezuela
5	Venezuela	Brazil	Philippines
6	Ecuador	Pakistan	Nigeria
7	Russia	Ecuador	Russia
8	Nigeria	Venezuela	Afghanistan
9	India	Colombia	Iraq
10	South Africa	Bangladesh	Haiti

Source: Guild of Security Controllers; Castle Rock Global Corporation.

parts of the world after 1990. In the late 1990s, the left-wing Revolutionary Armed Forces of Colombia (its Spanish acronym, FARC) inaugurated a wave of kidnappings of prominent persons in both the private and public sector. At first, these acts were undertaken to highlight the group's cause and inspire other revolutionary actions by the Colombian people. Later, say experts, the kidnappings became a large-scale criminal enterprise, a means of extorting ransoms from increasingly wealthy and high-profile victims not only to pay for further FARC operations but also to line the pockets of its leadership. Another group to undertake high-profile political hostage-taking at that period was the Islamist group Abu Sayyaf, which sought an independent state for the Muslim areas of the southern Philippines. Usually seizing Western hostages, often tourists, the group sought publicity for its cause and demanded ransom money and the release of fellow militants held by the Filipino government. It gained notoriety for its unusual brutality after beheading several of its captives.

Types and Numbers

For all the attention paid to them, high-level political kidnappings and hostage-taking episodes are rare. In most countries, the vast majority of abductions are undertaken for emotive reasons and by persons who know their victims. In the United States, for example, roughly 900,000 persons are reported missing each year, about 90 percent of whom are juveniles. Of the 900,000, about 150,000 cases are deemed by law enforcement to be involuntary or constitute endangerment for the victim. Of this latter category, about 50 percent of victims are kidnapped by family

members—typically separated or divorced parents involved in custody disputes—and another 30 percent are perpetrated by acquaintances of the victim. In both cases, most of the kidnappings occur in the home. The vast majority of the latter cases are perpetrated by other juveniles; acquaintance kidnapping also represents the highest percentage of kidnapping cases where violence occurs. Kidnappings by strangers constitute the remaining 20 percent, most typically occur in public places, and are usually conducted in order to sexually abuse the juvenile victim.

Criminal kidnappings for monetary gain are far more rare, both in the United States and around the world. Experts estimate that there are about 8,000 such kidnappings globally each year, though some companies that specialize in insurance against kidnapping estimate the total as closer to 20,000. Of these 8,000, 75 percent occur in Latin America and the Caribbean and fully half of these latter cases occur in Mexico, usually undertaken by criminal syndicates often aligned with drug cartels. As high as these numbers are, they pale in comparison with the level experienced in Iraq at the height of its recent civil war. Between 2003 and 2009, it is estimated that approximately 30,000 Iraqis were kidnapped. Globally, roughly 90 percent of kidnap victims are locals and the other 10 percent are foreigners.

Finally, political kidnappings, sometimes with a criminal aspect, are the rarest of all, amounting to several hundred in a given year, though occasionally, as in the case of Colombia in the 1990s and Iraq in the first decade of this century, these figures rise dramatically because of war or societal chaos.

Responses

The different types of kidnappings and hostage-taking incidents require different responses from authorities and the family members of victims. In every country in the world, as well as in most subjurisdictions, kidnapping or hostage-taking of any kind is a criminal offense, while kidnapping for ransom or for political ends is considered among the most serious of felonies, accompanied by grievous penalties up to and including death. Until the past few decades, however, abductions by family members were either not criminalized or often ignored by law enforcement authorities, being seen as purely domestic concerns. That began to change in the 1980s, as nations passed tougher laws against such abductions and adopted new technologies, including national computerized databanks, and new media outreach campaigns to respond to them. In 1996, several U.S. states adopted the so-called Amber Alert system, named after a high-profile kidnap victim, which uses the mass media to alert the public about juvenile abductions perpetrated by family members or strangers.

In many developing-world nations—particularly in kidnap-prone Latin America—the primary victims of criminal kidnappings either belong to middle-income or wealthy families or work for large corporations. In such cases, potential victims undertake common-sense strategies for avoiding kidnapping, including altering daily routines and hiring security guards to protect their homes and themselves. In addition, because local law enforcement agencies have limited resources and training or may themselves be connected to the criminal syndicates undertaking the kidnappings, many companies and families purchase kidnapping and ransom (K&R) insurance from specialized insurance firms or specialized divisions of larger insurance companies, which will negotiate and pay the ransoms for their clients.

Because kidnapping involves the sequestration of victims in secret locales, it limits law enforcement's options. Raids are difficult to conduct, and time is usually on the kidnapper's side. This is because kidnappers are usually in more comfortable circumstances than hostage takers and because the anxiety level of the victims' loved ones often forces the hands of authorities. Indeed, worldwide, just 10 percent of kidnappings are even reported to police. Because so many kidnappings occur outside the purview of government authorities, statistics are hard to come by, but it is estimated that between 40 and 90 percent of kidnap victims are released unharmed after ransom is paid. For this reason, most experts agree that, in the case of criminal kidnappings, there is little to be gained from resisting kidnappers' demands, assuming the victims' families have the resources to pay the ransom.

Hostage-taking episodes require a very different approach from kidnappings. In the case of kidnappings for political ends, the calculus around meeting the kidnappers' demands becomes more complicated. First, the demands are not always for money or exclu-

Mexican army troops rescued a group of kidnap victims from a compound of drug traffickers not far from the Texas border in 2010. Mass kidnappings of migrants and traditional kidnappings for ransom have provided a steady stream of money for drug gangs. *(Dario Leon/AFP/Getty Images)*

sively for money but may include the release of the kidnapping group's members or others sympathetic to the kidnappers' cause. There may be large demands that are difficult or even politically impossible to meet. The Abu Sayyaf kidnappers, for example, demanded that the Filipino government surrender sovereignty over part of its territory. Whatever the demands, the government is also faced with a delicate balancing act, specifically, the fear that meeting the kidnappers' demands will demonstrate weakness and inspire other kidnappers to do the same versus the political backlash for refusing to negotiate and losing the lives of its own citizens. Such was the dilemma facing the Ronald Reagan administration when it offered weapons in Iran for that government's cooperation in getting its Hezbollah allies in Lebanon to release American hostages, and that facing the Israeli government of Benjamin Netanyahu when it agreed to free more than 1,000 Palestinian prisoners in 2011 in exchange for the release of a single Israeli soldier held by Hamas militants in Gaza for more than five years. In both cases, the governments in question paid a high political cost in lost support and public trust.

Less political are criminal hostage situations, most of which are of an incidental nature, occurring as a result of a botched robbery attempt. In such cases, police organizations have become increasingly sophisticated in their negotiating techniques, employing various psychological tactics to put the hostage-takers at ease, to win their trust, and to get them to release their hostages unharmed. Good police negotiators understand that the early hours of a hostage situation is the most fraught with danger, when the need for defusing tensions is most critical, and that time is on the side of the authorities, as the comfort level of the hostage takers goes down and their level of anxiety goes up.

Finally, in both criminal and political hostage-taking situations, there is always the option of forcibly overcoming the hostage takers. This situation presents the same dilemma, in reverse, of meeting the hostage takers' demands. That is, forcibly overcoming hostage takers shows a resolve that may deter future acts of hostage-taking and kidnapping, but it also puts the victims at a higher risk of harm. While successful rescues—such as the Israeli assault on a hijacked plane at Entebbe, Uganda, in 1976—are rightfully praised, the reality is that most such assaults result in the deaths of hostages.

Kidnapping and hostage-taking differ in terms of what happens to perpetrators after the victims are released or killed. Because hostage-taking occurs in public, most perpetrators are either killed in assaults or captured by authorities soon after. While this is not usually a desirable outcome for the perpetrators, it is sometimes expected and even sought, especially for those who undertake their actions for political purposes and who may seek martyrdom. Since most kidnappings are conducted for criminal ends, the kidnappers want to escape justice and usually have a better chance at this, since they operate, or try to operate, clandestinely. In such cases, the likelihood of punishment rises or falls with the competency of local security authorities and justice systems. In the United States, it is estimated that roughly 95 percent of kidnappers for ransom are convicted of their crimes, while the rate for Colombia at the height of the kidnapping wave of the 1990s was just 3 percent.

Consequences and Costs

Both kidnappings and hostage-taking incidents have very serious consequences for societies, particularly those where such incidents occur regularly. The most obvious consequences, of course, fall to the victims, who may be killed by the kidnappers or, more typically, in the assaults undertaken by authorities. Indeed, more hostages are killed by authorities than by hostage takers; in Latin America, the survival rate of kidnap victims in assaults by authorities is just one in five. Even for those who survive, there may be physical injuries or, more typically, lasting psychological ones, akin, say experts, to the post-traumatic stress disorders suffered by war veterans. Family members may bear psychological scars as well. Hostages may also demonstrate the less common reaction known as the Stockholm syndrome, whereby the hostage comes to psychologically identify with the hostage taker or kidnapper. The syndrome got its name from a 1973 incident in which a hostage in a bank robbery had consensual sex with the hostage taker during the crime and then visited him in prison after he was caught and convicted.

For the larger society, the costs are more indirect. Chronic kidnapping and hostage-taking, especially of the political sort, may lead to more authoritarian forms of government, a diminution of privacy rights and increased police surveillance, and a loss of civil liberties. Hostage-taking and kidnapping can also have international repercussions. The 1979 seizure of the U.S. embassy and seizing of more than 50 American hostages by Islamist militants—abetted by the new revolutionary government in Tehran—led to a cessation of diplomatic relations between the United States and Iran and contributed to the intense hostility that has marked relations between the two countries ever since.

Kidnapping and hostage-taking of all kinds also impose enormous economic costs on countries or localities that are prone to them. Some of these costs are direct ones. It is estimated that the total global ransom paid to kidnappers and hostage takers amounts to roughly half a billion dollars a year. Meanwhile, K&R insurance premiums come to several billion each year, and tens of billions more are spent on preventive measures, though these are also undertaken to avoid other crimes, such as robbery, and such related political acts as terrorist bombings. Indirect costs may be the largest of all, though also the hardest to quantify, and include the loss of economic activity when foreign corporations refuse to invest money in countries prone to kidnapping and hostage-taking and tourists refuse to visit such places.

In the future, the problem of kidnapping and hostage-taking may go in either one of two directions, though fluctuations are inevitable as conflict and social breakdown in various places—or the resolution of same—raise and lower the number of incidents. But in the long term, the trends are likely to be mixed. On the one hand, improved technology and policing, along with higher levels of the rule of law that accompany increased prosperity, particularly in emerging economies, may ease the problem around the world. Exacerbating factors for criminal kidnapping, however, include heightened levels of income and wealth inequality, while heightened levels of global communications connectivity may make the publicity rewards for political kidnapping and hostage-taking all the more attractive.

James Ciment

See also: Aviation Security; Crime, Organized; Piracy, Maritime; Slavery; Terrorism; War Crimes.

Further Reading

Auerbach, Ann Hagedorn. *Ransom: The Untold Story of International Kidnapping.* New York: Henry Holt, 1998.

Bruce, Victoria, and Karin Hayes, with Jorge Enrique Botero. *Hostage Nation: Colombia's Guerrilla Army and the Failed War on Drugs.* New York: Alfred A. Knopf, 2010.

Dabbagh, Maureen. *Parental Kidnapping in America: An Historical and Cultural Analysis.* Jefferson, NC: McFarland, 2012.

Gero, David. *Flights of Terror: Aerial Hijack and Sabotage Since 1930.* Newbury Park, CA: Haynes, 2009.

McGovern, Glenn P. *Targeted Violence: A Statistical and Tactical Analysis of Assassinations, Contract Killings, and Kidnappings.* Boca Raton, FL: CRC/Taylor & Francis, 2010.

Newton, Michael. *The Encyclopedia of Kidnappings.* New York: Facts On File, 2002.

Poland, James M., and Michael J. McCrystle. *Practical, Tactical, and Legal Perspectives on Terrorism and Hostage-Taking.* Lewiston, NY: Edwin Mellen, 1999.

Rogan, Randall G., and Frederick J. Lanceley, eds. *Contemporary Theory, Research, and Practice of Crisis and Hostage Negotiation.* Cresskill, NJ: Hampton, 2010.

Tyner, James. *The Business of War: Workers, Warriors and Hostages in Occupied Iraq.* Burlington, VT: Ashgate, 2006.

Wright, Richard P. *Kidnap for Ransom: Resolving the Unthinkable.* Boca Raton, FL: CRC, 2009.

Web Sites

Castle Rock Global Insurance: www.castlerockinternational.com

Federal Bureau of Investigation: www.fbi.gov

Hostage UK: www.hostageuk.org

United Nations Office on Drugs and Crime: www.unodc.org

Documents

Document 1: U.S. Federal Kidnapping Act (Lindbergh Law), 1932

On March 1, 1932, an ex-convict named Bruno Hauptmann kidnapped for ransom the 20-month-old son of famed aviator Charles Lindbergh. The crime shocked the nation, especially when the boy's body was found two months later virtually a stone's throw from the Lindbergh estate in Hopewell, New Jersey. Disputes between local and federal authorities over who was in charge of the investigation led to passage of the Federal Kidnapping Act in June of that year. The law stated that if kidnapping victims are not found within 24 hours, it would be the presumption that they had been transported across state lines or national borders, thus making the crime a federal issue.

TITLE 18, PART I, CHAPTER 55, § 1201
§ 1201. Kidnapping

(a)   Whoever unlawfully seizes, confines, inveigles, decoys, kidnaps, abducts, or carries away and holds for ransom or reward or otherwise any person, except in the case of a minor by the parent thereof, when—

   (1) the person is willfully transported in interstate or foreign commerce, regardless of whether the person was alive when transported across a State boundary, or the offender travels in interstate or foreign commerce or uses the mail or any means, facility, or instrumentality of interstate or foreign commerce in committing or in furtherance of the commission of the offense;

   (2) any such act against the person is done within the special maritime and territorial jurisdiction of the United States;

   (3) any such act against the person is done within the special aircraft jurisdiction of the United States as defined in section 46501 of title 49;

   (4) the person is a foreign official, an internationally protected person, or an official guest as those terms are defined in section 1116 (b) of this title; or

   (5) the person is among those officers and employees described in section 1114 of this title and any such act against the person is done while the person is engaged in, or on account of, the performance of official duties,

shall be punished by imprisonment for any term of years or for life and, if the death of any person results, shall be punished by death or life imprisonment.

(b)   With respect to subsection (a)(1), above, the failure to release the victim within twenty-four hours after he shall have been unlawfully seized, confined, inveigled, decoyed, kidnapped, abducted, or carried away shall create a rebuttable presumption that such person has been transported in interstate or foreign commerce. Notwithstanding the preceding sentence, the fact that the presumption under this section has not yet taken effect does not preclude a Federal investigation of a possible violation of this section before the 24-hour period has ended.

(c)   If two or more persons conspire to violate this section and one or more of such persons do any overt act to effect the object of the conspiracy, each shall be punished by imprisonment for any term of years or for life.

(d)   Whoever attempts to violate subsection (a) shall be punished by imprisonment for not more than twenty years.

(e)   If the victim of an offense under subsection (a) is an internationally protected person outside the United States, the United States may exercise jurisdiction over the offense if

   (1) the victim is a representative, officer, employee, or agent of the United States,

   (2) an offender is a national of the United States, or

   (3) an offender is afterwards found in the United States. As used in this subsection, the United States includes all areas under the jurisdiction of the United States including any of the places within the provisions of sections 5 and 7 of this title and section 46501 (2) of title 49. For purposes of this subsection, the term "national of the United States" has the meaning prescribed in section 101(a)(22) of the Immigration and Nationality Act (8 U.S.C. 1101 (a)(22)).

(f)   In the course of enforcement of subsection (a)(4) and any other sections prohibiting a conspiracy or attempt to violate subsection (a)(4), the Attorney General may request assistance from any Federal, State, or local agency, including the Army, Navy, and Air Force, any statute, rule, or regulation to the contrary notwithstanding.

(g)   Special Rule for Certain Offenses Involving Children.—
   (1) To whom applicable.—If—
      (A) the victim of an offense under this section has not attained the age of eighteen years; and
      (B) the offender—
         (i) has attained such age; and
         (ii) is not—
         (I)   a parent;
         (II)   a grandparent;
         (III) a brother;
         (IV)   a sister;
         (V)   an aunt;
         (VI)   an uncle; or
         (VII) an individual having legal custody of the victim; the sentence under this section for such offense shall include imprisonment for not less than 20 years.

   [(2) Repealed. Pub. L. 108–21, title I, § 104(b), Apr. 30, 2003, 117 Stat. 653.]

(h)   As used in this section, the term "parent" does not include a person whose parental rights with respect to the victim of an offense under this section have been terminated by a final court order.

Source: Legal Information Institute.

Document 2: International Convention Against the Taking of Hostages, 1979

Responding to the wave of hijackings and other hostage-taking incidents that hit the global community in the late 1960s, various nations negotiated the International Convention Against the Taking of Hostages, which was signed in 1979 and went into force in 1983. While virtually all nations had laws against hijackings, they faced the dilemma that hostage-takings were often international in nature, since perpetrators committed the crime in one country and then fled to another, often at political or ideological odds with the first. The convention of 1979 committed nations to cooperation in the prevention, apprehension, and prosecution of those who seized hostages.

www1.umn.edu/humanrts/instree/takinghostages.html

Source: United Nations.

LAND MINES

Land mines, defined as "area denial weapons," are justified on the grounds that they serve a primarily defensive purpose. The presence of a minefield is intended to prevent, to restrict, or to inhibit enemy access to particular locations. Minefields are confining devices, technology designed to channel mobility into specific destinations, redirecting movement into "killing zones." Buried beneath the ground, lying silently in wait, land mines are barriers without walls.

Historical Background

Although historians have traced the use of land mines and land mine–type weapons to both ancient China and Rome, it was not until the twentieth century that the "age of land mine warfare" arrived in full force. Since the Second World War, upward of half a billion landmines have been laid. While initially considered cowardly weapons by the military establishment, land mines have become an accepted component of many of the world's armies. Established military doctrine, as exemplified by the United States and other industrialized countries, defends the use of land mines as a crucial factor in shaping the contemporary battlefield. As "defensive weapons," land mines are utilized primarily to force enemy troops either to slow down their advance or to redirect their movement into sites of ambush.

Land mines are, conceptually, very simple devices. In general, they consist of a plastic or metal casing that houses a detonator, booster charge, and main explosive charge. There are two main "families" of land mines, based on the primary intended target: anti-personnel mines (APMs) and anti-vehicle mines (AVMs). Anti-personnel mines are designed to kill or to injure soldiers. In fact, many anti-personnel land mines are designed to inflict severe injuries as opposed to killing their victims. The military rationale is that other, noninjured soldiers will have to tend to and carry the wounded soldiers.

Anti-personnel mines are subdivided into three types, based on the type of explosion produced upon detonation: blast mines, bounding mines, and directional mines. Blast mines cause large, upward explosions and are designed to inflict serious injury (i.e., blowing apart of limbs from the torso). Bounding mines explode various fragments into the air upon detonation, usually to a height of about 3 feet (1 meter). The explosion diffuses outward and upward in an arc, with lethal fragments striking the head and torso of the victim or victims. Bounding mines are designed to kill large numbers of people. Lastly, directional mines explode in a predetermined direction and pattern. One of the most well known directional mines is the U.S.-produced M-18, or "Claymore" mine. The M-18 consists of a plastic, convex-shaped pack containing explosives and 700 steel balls, each weighing about 0.75 grams. Claymore mines are inserted into the ground and, when detonated, blast the metal balls outward in a 60-degree arc upward to a height of over 6 feet (1.83 meters) and a horizontal arc spanning 164 feet (50 meters). Directional mines are used to defend trails and roads and also to kill enemy troops in ambushes.

Anti-vehicle land mines, on the other hand, are designed to destroy or incapacitate vehicles such as armored trucks or tanks. This does not mean, however, that AVMs cannot be detonated by people walking on them. The pressure plates of many anti-vehicle mines, for example, can be detonated with pressures of less than 330 pounds per square inch (966 kilograms per square centimeter)—about the amount of pressure exerted by an adult running across the ground.

The military use of land mines has rapidly devolved from a purported defensive function to an offensive measure. Unlike the wars of earlier generations, which generally pitted two opposing armies against one another, today's conflicts, with a predominance of mercenaries and child soldiers, are less organized and more "irregular." Lightweight and easily portable, land mines have been used by both government and rebel groups haphazardly. In the numerous wars that have beset the African continent throughout the late twentieth and the early twenty-first century, for example, land mines have been used specifically to terrorize local civilian populations. Mines have been indiscriminately laid in and around schools and markets, bridges and roads, rivers and streams, forests and farms. Consequently, over the last few decades, an estimated 2 million children have been killed throughout Africa, with an additional 6 million disabled, 12 million made homeless, 1 million orphaned or separated from their families, and 10 million suffering from psychological trauma.

Impact on Civilian Populations

An estimated 60 to 70 million land mines remain in more than 90 countries and territories. In Afghanistan, there are an estimated 8 million; 4 to 6 million land mines remain in Cambodia; and 5 to 10 million land mines lie in wait in Angola. The world over, every year, between 15,000 and 20,000 people are victims of land mines—approximately one person killed or injured every 30 minutes. Indeed, land mines (and other explosive remnants of war) have killed and injured more people over the past hundred years than all other weapons of mass destruction—nuclear, chemical, and biological—combined.

Land mines disproportionately kill and injure the innocent—men, women, and children who are not soldiers. The victims are most often "ordinary" people who are simply engaged in everyday activities: farming, tending livestock, collecting food and water, walking to school. In 2006, for example, civilians accounted for approximately 75 percent of all recorded casualties, with children making up over one-third of all civilian casualties. Such sweeping statistics, however, mask even more disturbing trends at the local level. In Afghanistan and Nepal, for example, children under 15 years of age comprise 59 and 53 percent of casualties, respectively.

The effects of a land mine explosion are devastating to the families involved. Often, the victims are the primary wage earners for their households. Even if a victim survives, his or her potential for income generation is significantly reduced. Many mine victims are physically unable to work and, because of their incapacitation, become a financial "burden" on the family. The land mine crisis therefore cannot be defined solely by the number of people killed or maimed. Instead, the crisis must be viewed from the standpoint of people's everyday lives: entire families devastated, lands rendered inaccessible or unusable,

A legacy of the Khmer Rouge regime of the 1970s and the civil war that followed, an estimated 4–6 million live land mines remain buried in rural Cambodia. Every year, hundreds of Cambodians, many of them children, are killed or maimed by exploding ordnance. *(AP Photo/ Heng Sinith)*

and economies weakened. It is estimated that landmines have restricted agricultural production on a land area equivalent to 6 percent of the 3.6 billion acres (1.5 billion hectares) of land cultivated globally. In terms of economic loss, studies suggest that, were it not for land mines, agricultural productivity could have increased by 88 to 200 percent in Afghanistan, by 135 percent in Cambodia, 11 percent in Bosnia, and 4 percent in Mozambique.

When people are denied safe access to land, they are forced to use (or abuse) marginal lands—thereby exacerbating both famine and environmental degradation. In Angola, despite abundant fertile lands and adequate precipitation, famine is killing thousands of people, in part because of the presence of land mines. Decreases in the overall availability of land have also led to more intensive forms of agriculture; these practices may endanger the health of the soil, for example, by causing the rapid exhaustion of the soil's fertility.

Responses

Land mines are inexpensive and easy to manufacture. Depending on the type—between 340 and 360 different mines have been designed—land mines cost as little as $3 to produce; more sophisticated models might approach $30. And newer models are being developed every year. Not counting home-made or "improvised explosive devices" (IEDs, commonly used in the recent Iraq War, for example), land mines are manufactured in nearly 50 countries, with the majority of mines designed, produced, and exported by just a handful of states: the United States, Russia, and China.

In the mid-1990s a global movement to ban the production, export, and use of land mines developed. This grassroots effort culminated in the 1997 Ottawa Convention (also known as the Mine Ban Treaty). The treaty required that all signatories destroy stockpiles of land mines within four years; it also mandated the removal of all landmines in the ground within 10 years. Since 1997, the treaty has been ratified by more than 140 countries. Many governments, however—including the major producers—have not yet ratified the treaty. The United States, for example, refuses to abide by the Ottawa Convention. The land mine policy of the George W. Bush administration (2001–2009) was clear: the United States would continue to develop nonpersistent anti-personnel and anti-tank land mines. Aside from the design of traditional victim-activation mines, the United States invested millions of dollars into the development of so-called command-detonation mines; new models were also to include self-destruct features, theoretically rendering these devices inoperative (i.e., "nonpersistent") after a certain period of time. And, in a semantic twist, many of these products were no longer called "land mines," thus potentially offering a linguistic loophole to international conventions.

The policy under President Barack Obama is less clear. In November 2009, the State Department announced that President Obama would not sign the 10-year-old treaty banning land mines. Faced with immediate outrage, the Obama administration backpedaled on its position. In the years since, the U.S.

land mine policy has been "under review." In the interim, the United States continues to design, manufacture, and produce land mines. From the Minnesota-based Alliant Techsystems to the Massachusetts-based Textron Defense Systems, corporations continue to provide new weapons systems "for force protection consistent with twenty-first-century warfare," weapons that are theoretically "both safe and effective" and thus serve as "suitable humanitarian alternative force protection," as Textron Defense Systems describes its newly designed "Spider" land mine.

Current and Future Trends

As the recent experience of the United States illustrates, and despite the Ottawa Convention, land mines will continue to be designed, manufactured, exported, and used. Their presence, combined with the prevalence (and use) of "homemade" land mines, means that tens of millions of men, women, and children will continue to live with the reality that any step taken may be their last. However, there are some positive signs. Through the combined efforts of willing governments and dedicated nongovernmental organizations, millions of acres of land have been cleared and millions of land mines destroyed. Consequently, as reported by the International Campaign to Ban Landmines (ICBL), the number of civilian deaths and injuries has been decreasing globally. The future depends on both our willingness to render obsolete these weapons of mass destruction and our ability to seek peaceful rather than military solutions to our political conflicts.

James A. Tyner

See also: Arms Trade; War Crimes.

Further Reading

Albertyn, R., S.W. Bickler, A.B. van As, A.J. Millar, and H. Rode. "The Effects of War on Children in Africa." *Pediatric Surgeon International* 19 (2003): 227–232.

Berhe, A.A. "The Contributions of Landmines to Land Degradation." *Land Degradation and Development* 18 (2007): 1–15.

Bolton, Matthew. *Foreign Aid and Landmine Clearance: Governance, Politics and Security in Afghanistan, Bosnia and Sudan.* New York: I.B. Tauris, 2010.

Davies, Paul. *War of the Mines: Cambodia, Landmines and the Impoverishment of a Nation.* Boulder, CO: Pluto, 1994.

International Campaign to Ban Landmines (ICBL). *Land-*

mine *Monitor Report 2007: Toward a Mine-Free World.* Geneva, Switzerland.

Matthew, Richard A., Bryan McDonald, and Kenneth R. Rutherford, eds. *Landmines and Human Security: International Politics and War's Hidden Legacy.* Albany: State University of New York Press, 2004.

McNab, Chris, and Hunter Keeter. *Tools of Violence: Guns, Tanks and Dirty Bombs.* New York: Osprey, 2008.

Oppong, Joseph, and Ezekiel Kalipeni. "The Geography of Landmines and Implications for Health and Disease in Africa: A Political Ecology Approach." *Africa Today* 52 (2005): 3–25.

Roberts, Shawn, and Jody Williams. *After the Guns Fall Silent: The Enduring Legacy of Landmines.* Washington, DC: Vietnam Veterans of America Foundation, 1995.

Tyner, James A. *Military Legacies: A World Made by War.* New York: Routledge, 2010.

Webster, Donovan. *Aftermath: The Remnants of War.* New York: Vintage Books, 1998.

Web Sites

Electronic Mine Information Network: www.mineaction.org

International Campaign to Ban Landmines (ICBL): www.icbl.org

Stop Landmines.org: www.stoplandmines.org

Documents

Document 1: Convention on the Prohibition of the Use, Stockpiling, Production and Transfer of Anti-Personnel Mines and on Their Destruction, 1997

On December 3, 1997, representatives of more than 100 countries signed the Mine Ban Treaty in Ottawa, Canada. This occasion marked the culmination of years of grassroots mobilization to work toward the elimination of land mines. Since that date, 156 countries have become signatories to the convention, all pledging to render obsolete the production, exchange, and use of land mines. Excerpts from the convention follow.

The States Parties,

Determined to put an end to the suffering and casualties caused by anti-personnel mines, that kill or maim hundreds of people every week, mostly innocent and defenseless civilians and especially children, obstruct economic development and reconstruction, inhibit the repatriation of refugees and internally displaced persons, and have other severe consequences for years after emplacement,

Believing it necessary to do their utmost to contribute in an efficient and coordinated manner to face the challenge of removing anti-personnel mines placed throughout the world, and to assure their destruction,

Wishing to do their utmost in providing assistance for the care and rehabilitation, including the social and economic reintegration of mine victims, . . .

Welcoming furthermore the measures taken over the past years, both unilaterally and multilaterally, aiming at prohibiting, restricting or suspending the use, stockpiling, production and transfer of anti-personnel mines,

Stressing the role of public conscience in furthering the principles of humanity as evidenced by the call for a total ban of anti-personnel mines and recognizing the efforts to that end undertaken by the International Red Cross and Red Crescent Movement, the International Campaign to Ban Landmines and numerous other non-governmental organizations around the world, . . .

Basing themselves on the principle of international humanitarian law that the right of the parties to an armed conflict to choose methods or means of warfare is not unlimited, on the principle that prohibits the employment in armed conflicts of weapons, projectiles and materials and methods of warfare of a nature to cause superfluous injury or unnecessary suffering and on the principle that a distinction must be made between civilians and combatants,

Have agreed as follows:

Article 1

General Obligations

1. Each State Party undertakes never under any circumstances:
   a) To use anti-personnel mines;
   b) To develop, produce, otherwise acquire, stockpile, retain or transfer to anyone, directly or indirectly, anti-personnel mines;
   c) To assist, encourage or induce, in any way, anyone to engage in any activity prohibited to a State Party under this Convention.

2. Each State Party undertakes to destroy or ensure the destruction of all anti-personnel mines in accordance with the provisions of this Convention.

. . .

Source: United Nations Office at Geneva (UNOG).

Document 2: Letter to President Barack Obama Calling for the United States to Sign the Landmine Ban Treaty, 68 U.S. Senators, 2010

On May 18, 2010, Senator Patrick Leahy (D-Vermont), along with 67 other senators, sent a letter to President Barack Obama requesting that the United States join the

Convention on the Prohibition of the Use, Stockpiling, Production and Transfer of Anti-Personnel Mines and on Their Destruction. The "Leahy Letter" was occasioned by the thirteenth anniversary of the Ottawa Convention. The letter is informative in that it (1) connects the ban of mines to contemporary foreign relations; (2) highlights that the United States has in fact been following many of the recommendations of the Ottawa Convention; and (3) that ratification by the United States would be important symbolically for the country. The letter is somewhat misleading, however, in that the United States does continue to produce and export mines, but these devices are simply not called "mines."

Dear Mr. President,

We are writing to convey our strong support for the Administration's decision to conduct a comprehensive review of United States policy on landmines. The Second Review Conference of the Convention on the Prohibition of the Use, Stockpiling, Production and Transfer of Anti-Personnel Mines and on Their Destruction, held last December in Cartagena, Colombia, makes this review particularly timely. It is also consistent with your commitment to reaffirm U.S. leadership in solving global problems and with your remarks in Oslo when you accepted the Nobel Peace Prize: "I am convinced that adhering to standards, international standards, strengthens those who do, and isolates and weakens those who don't."

These indiscriminate weapons are triggered by the victim, and even those that are designed to self-destruct after a period of time (so-called "smart" mines) pose a risk of being triggered by U.S. forces or civilians, such as a farmer working in the fields or a young child. It is our understanding that the United States has not exported anti-personnel mines since 1992, has not produced anti-personnel mines since 1997, and has not used anti-personnel mines since

1991. We are also proud that the United States is the world's largest contributor to humanitarian demining and rehabilitation programs for landmine survivors.

In the ten years since the Convention came into force, 158 nations have signed including the United Kingdom and other ISAF partners, as well as Iraq and Afghanistan which, like Colombia, are parties to the Convention and have suffered thousands of mine casualties. The Convention has led to a dramatic decline in the use, production, and export of anti-personnel mines.

We note that our NATO allies have addressed their force protection needs in accordance with their obligations under the Convention. We are also mindful that anti-personnel mines pose grave dangers to civilians, and that avoiding civilian casualties and the anger and resentment that result has become a key priority in building public support for our mission in Afghanistan. Finally, we are aware that anti-personnel mines in the Korean DMZ are South Korean mines, and that the U.S. has alternative munitions that are not victim-activated.

We believe the Administration's review should include consultations with the Departments of Defense and State as well as retired senior U.S. military officers and diplomats, allies such as Canada and the United Kingdom that played a key role in the negotiations on the Convention, Members of Congress, the International Committee of the Red Cross, and other experts on landmines, humanitarian law and arms control.

We are confident that through a thorough, deliberative review the Administration can identify any obstacles to joining the Convention and develop a plan to overcome them as soon as possible. . . .

Source: United States Senate.

LAW, RULE OF

The rule of law is a concept that describes the supreme authority of the law over government action and individual behavior. It corresponds to a situation in which both the government and individuals are bound by the law and comply with it. It is the antithesis of tyrannical or arbitrary rule.

The rule of law, the product of historical developments over centuries, is linked to the rise of the liberal democratic form of government in the West. For some, the concept has a purely formal meaning. Under this concept of the rule of law, the state must act in accordance with the laws that it has promulgated and these laws must meet a certain number of minimum characteristics. For others, the concept has a wider, more substantive meaning that incorporates ideals of justice and fairness.

Although it is generally accepted that the extent to which a government adheres to the rule of law is indicative of the degree of legitimacy of its actions, the divergent use of the term illustrates that the concept is far from having achieved a universally accepted meaning. Indeed, while some declare the concept to have attained the status of a new universally accepted political ideal after the end of the Cold War, others on the contrary have gone so far as to assert that the term has been misused and abused to such an extent that it has become a meaningless phrase, devoid of any real meaning.

Historical Evolution

The rule of law has evolved over centuries and is inextricably linked to historical developments that have led to the gradual emergence of liberal democracies and their underlying modes of governance and legal systems.

The role that law plays in society was the subject of philosophical discussions in Greek and Roman antiquity, debated by Plato, Aristotle, Cicero, and others. The general conclusion was that the law must be for the good of the community as a whole,

thereby subjecting law to ideals of justice. The fall of the Roman Republic at the hands of emperors gave way to autocratic rule. During the reign of Emperor Justinian I, Roman law was codified. The resulting *Corpus Juris Civilis* (529–534 C.E.) constituted a setback for the rule of law insofar as it provided that the emperor was above the law and not subject to it, thereby sanctioning the rule of man.

Although these philosophical works discussed various modes of government and the role played by the law in those systems, it is in medieval Europe that the rule of law truly began to take shape. Popes and kings vied for control and authority over both religious and secular affairs. Conflict arose as a result of monarchs seeking to reserve to themselves the power to appoint religious leaders within their realms. The Catholic Church retaliated in kind by claiming the authority of the Roman pontiff over all emperors and princes on the theological basis that the religious realm took precedence over the physical. While initially resisted, over the course of time, the coronation of monarchs came to incorporate the taking of an oath affirming the Church's supreme authority and a commitment to uphold the law.

The disappearance of Greek and Roman texts and the loss of codified legal texts meant that law in the Middle Ages in former Roman possessions reverted to customary law in unwritten form, though in time many rulers oversaw the codification of their customs. Customs enjoyed legitimacy by virtue of being reflective of norms and traditions accepted by the community. In the Germanic lands that had not been conquered by the Romans, the customary law also applied to the monarch, who came to be seen as the guardian of the law. This legal principle came to influence much of Central and Western Europe.

In England, the principle that the king was bound by the law was a prominent feature of the Magna Carta, signed by King John in 1215. It was the product of a revolt by the nobility against the king following his attempts to extract more resources from them to fund war with France. The agreement sought to place constraints on the king's powers and protect the nobles' privileges. Although King John repudiated the document soon after it was signed, the Magna Carta came to be confirmed and modified by successive monarchs and parliaments on numerous occasions. Among its many provisions, the Magna Carta declared that no person should be deprived of liberty or property "except by the lawful judgment of his equals or by the law of the land." This historically significant document is seen by many not only as protecting individuals from the arbitrary will of the monarch but also as the source of the fundamental right to a fair trial (the right to "due process of law" in U.S. legal terminology). It is also seen as the source of constitutionalism, the legal organization of the fundamental relationship between a government and the people it oversees.

Later in the medieval period, the rediscovery of classical texts, including those of Aristotle, meant that they became available again to European scholars. The Catholic priest Thomas Aquinas developed a theory of natural law in *Summa Theologicae* (1265–1274), in which he affirmed Aristotle's views that law is based on human reason and must be promulgated for the common good. Although Aquinas acknowledged that the sovereign was exempt from the law because no other person was competent to pass sentence on him, he reasoned that it was proper for kings to submit to the law because whatever law a sovereign makes, he should also respect it himself.

As a result of these developments, one of the major medieval contributions to legal theory was to displace the idea that the monarch was above the law, which had been inherited from Roman law, by giving way to the convention that the sovereign was bound by law and marking a return to the position advocated by classical philosophers.

As a legal concept, the convention did not go unchallenged. The doctrine of the divine right of kings, according to which kings were appointed directly by God, was elaborated by French jurist Jean Bodin in the sixteenth century in response to the Wars of Religion occasioned by the Protestant Reformation and the split with the Catholic Church. However, the convention that monarchs were bound by the law survived these challenges because not only was it often in the monarch's interests to abide by the law, but it had also become a firmly entrenched principle that was jealously protected by the legal profession.

Demographic changes also played a part in shap-ing these legal developments. Over the centuries, towns grew, populations increased, and commerce began to thrive. The artisan and merchant classes, the bourgeoisie, had no part to play in land-based feudal systems and sought greater latitude to engage in their crafts and trades and accumulate wealth. Over time, the source of wealth gradually shifted from the holding of land to trade in goods and services. The bourgeoisie sought protection of its interests against oppressive feudal lords and monarchs and forged alliances with those who could provide it. The bourgeoisie sought greater political influence and legal recognition of its interests, such as the freedom of contract, the provisions of the means to enforce contracts, and the protection of property rights.

The Renaissance and its renewed interest in the arts, science, and learning; the gradual separation of church and state; and the bourgeoisie's desire for greater protections set the stage for the emergence of liberalism as a political theory during the Enlightenment. Although liberalism comes in many variations, at its core the political theory of liberalism places emphasis on individual liberty and its protection through the conferral of individual rights.

For the English philosopher John Locke, who is considered the "father" of liberalism, liberty means to be free from restraint and violence, with the law playing a role in preserving and enlarging this freedom. In *Two Treaties of Government* (1690), Locke formulated his idea of the "social contract," under which individuals voluntarily agree to be governed in exchange for the government's agreeing to protect their personal freedoms and property. Under this arrangement, the government derives its legitimacy from popular consent and individuals delegate to the government the power to make, execute, and enforce laws in the common good. These laws should be enacted in the interests of the majority by a legislature that is separate from the executive and promulgated so that individuals are able to determine the extent of their duties. However, the existence of a separate judiciary was absent from Locke's discussion.

This theory set the stage for further evolution of the rule of law. In *L'esprit des lois* (1748), Montesquieu formulated a theory for the separation of powers as a means of preventing government abuse and preserving liberty, which he defined as "the right of doing whatever the laws permit." In his view, "power should be a check to power," and so the legislative, executive, and judicial functions of government should all be held in separate hands. Compared with previous writers, he devoted significant attention to the central role of the judiciary. In his view, the judiciary should be independent from the other two branches of government, although he advocated that it be composed exclusively of juries rather than a professional corps of judges.

The theories of Locke and Montesquieu profoundly influenced the framers of the U.S. Constitution. In the *Federalist Papers* (1787–1788), Alexander Hamilton, James Madison, and John Jay argued for a representative democratic form of government with multiple layers of divisions incorporating the vertical separation of powers between the federal and state levels and the horizontal separation of legislative, executive, and judicial functions at the federal level, with the legislature further divided between upper and lower houses. Further safeguards against the concentration of power were provided by giving the courts the power to control the constitutionality of enacted legislation through judicial review.

The phrase "rule of law" entered common parlance only in the nineteenth century, thanks to the writings of British constitutionalist Albert V. Dicey. His *Introduction to Study of the Laws of the Constitution* (1885) provides the first major explanation of what the rule of law entails in a liberal democracy. According to Dicey, the rule of law consisted of three interconnected elements. First, the rule of law demands that no person be subject to punishment except for a breach of a preestablished law and it is the ordinary courts that are the proper venue for determining whether such a breach of law has occurred. The rule of law is therefore incompatible with the "exercise of wide, arbitrary, or discretionary powers of constraint" by government officials. Second, under the rule of law, everyone is equal in the eyes of the law. This implies that government officials enjoy no special immunities (save for the monarch) and be held accountable for their actions before the ordinary courts. Third, at least in the United Kingdom, where there is no comprehensive written constitution, the rule of law flows from the judicial recognition of individuals' rights. This aspect of the rule of law consists in the array of legal safeguards that protect individuals from arbitrary action taken by government, with the courts empowered to act as the custodians of those safeguards.

Dicey's third component has been the subject of different interpretations. Despite the legal safeguards that may be adopted to provide a comprehensive system of checks and balances on government abuse, a state's constitutional framework should not be seen to operate in a cultural or societal void, even in cases like the United Kingdom, where there was, and is, no written constitution. The rule of law can therefore thrive in the absence of specific legal mechanisms contained in a written constitution. This suggests that for the rule of law to exist, there must be a cultural tradition of respect for the law. Indeed, the existence of a strong and independent legal profession plays a significant role in the rule of law.

Sixty years after Dicey first gave us an explanation of what the rule of law should entail, Austrian economist and philosopher Friedrich Hayek echoed many of Dicey's prescriptions in *The Road to Serfdom* (1944). For Hayek, the rule of law requires that laws be general, equal, and certain and that the law must provide for recourse to judicial review. Laws must be general in that they must be set out in advance in abstract terms and govern everyone's conduct. Implicit in the need for law to be general is that laws must be adopted by a legislature that is separate from the judiciary. Laws must be equal in that they apply to everyone equally without providing for arbitrary differences in treatment; however, where differences do occur, these must be the subject of a law that is approved by the majority of those included and those excluded by the law. Laws must be certain so that individuals are able to foresee in principle the legal consequences of their behavior and that of the others with whom they interact. Finally, the rule of law requires that judicial review by independent courts be available in all situations where the government interferes with an individual's person or property.

In countries that follow the civil code tradition, the rule of law was influenced by Austrian legal theorist Hans Kelsen, who helped draft the Austrian Constitution of 1920. In his view, the rule of law (*Rechsstaat*) requires a hierarchy of norms within the legal order with the constitution at its apex. All laws are subject to compliance with the constitution, and government action is constrained by this legal framework. Kelsen's formulation is also the inspiration for the French legal concept of *état de droit*.

After the end of World War II, the rule of law as a global ideal was given expression by the adoption in 1948 of the Universal Declaration of Human Rights, in which the General Assembly of the United Nations proclaimed that "it is essential if man is not to have recourse as a last resort, to rebellion against tyranny and oppression, that human rights should be protected by the Rule of Law."

Rule of Law Today

The rule of law is a phrase that we hear with increasing regularity from diverse quarters, including world leaders such as U.S. president Barack Obama and UN secretary-general Ban Ki Moon and from dissidents such as the Myanmar pro-democracy advocate Aung San Suu Kyi. We sometimes also hear it from unlikely quarters, such as Chinese president Hu Jintao, who declared following his appointment that the People's Republic of China "must build a system based on the rule of law and should not pin our hopes on any particular leader." It is clear from these examples that the concept can be the subject of disparate, even contradictory, usage. One of the reasons is that the rule of law today remains the subject of competing theories. Moreover, these do not always coincide with popular perceptions of what the rule of law comprises.

Competing Theories

For some, the concept has a purely formal meaning, in which the rule of law requires the state to act in accordance with the laws that it has promulgated, and these laws must have some minimum characteristics. However, for others, the concept has a wider, more substantive meaning that incorporates ideals of justice and fairness and respect for fundamental rights.

Under formalistic theories—termed by some as the "thin rule of law" or "rule by law"—the government must operate within the confines of the law, whatever that law might be. Contemporary formalistic theories tend to share the liberal view of the rule of law as equivalent to formal legality. From this perspective, the rule of law is therefore concerned not with the content of the laws but, rather, the optimal functioning of the legal system with a view toward providing individuals with a certain degree of predictability as regards the legal consequences of their actions. Formal theories of the rule of law tend to be the most widely accepted and are embraced by international development agencies because they have universal appeal regardless of whether certain countries recognize fundamental rights or democratic values.

In *The Morality That Makes Law Possible* (1964), Lon Fuller explained that, in order to act as a proper guide to behavior, the law must be characterized by the existence of a system of rules with certain characteristics. Although Fuller acknowledged that the occasional and partial absence of any of these criteria was unavoidable because a balance has to be achieved between legal certainty and society's ability to change laws, he also stressed that the complete absence of one or more criteria would result in complete failure of the law. Although these criteria were not directed at providing a definition of the rule of law but, rather, of law itself, Fuller's list of characteristics has been incorporated one way or another in contemporary definitions of the rule of law.

Formalistic theories have been developed by several leading contemporary legal scholars. One classic definition has been formulated by Professor Joseph Raz in his essay "The Rule of Law and Its Virtue," in *The Authority of Law* (1979). For Raz, the rule of law consists of a number of principles, and he went on to enumerate the most important: (i) all laws should be prospective, adequately publicized and contain clear, unambiguous rules; (ii) all laws should be relatively stable and not be changed too often; (iii) the making of the laws themselves should be guided by public, stable, clear, and general rules; (iv) the independence of the judiciary must be guaranteed to ensure that the courts correctly apply the law; (v) the principles of natural justice must be observed, so that court hearings are both fair and open and decisions taken without bias; (vi) the courts should have the power of judicial review over both legislation and administrative action to ensure their compliance with the law; (vii) the courts should be easily accessible and minimize long delays and excessive costs; and finally, (viii) the discretion of the law enforcement agencies should not be allowed to circumvent the law.

Like Fuller, Raz recognizes that the rule of law requires compliance with these principles to a certain degree but that total compliance with the rule of law should not be the ultimate aim of society; rather, the rule of law should serve as a means of achieving other social goals. However, he disagreed with Fuller that the rule of law is necessarily a moral good. Instead, he takes the view that the rule of law is a morally neutral concept, which although necessary to achieve good ends can also be placed in the service of immoral ends citing as an example the existence of the rule of law in the United States when slavery was still legal. For Raz, the abuse of power is wider than the rule of law. As a result, violations of the rule of law will necessarily amount to violations of human dignity, but violations of human dignity do not necessarily comprise violations of the rule of law. Formalists consider that the rule of law is not concerned about the content of laws: for them, it is immaterial whether the rule of law works for the common good. Like Hayek, Raz considers that the rule of law in its formalistic guise is nonetheless a useful concept because it enables individuals to plan their behavior by knowing in advance what the legal consequences of their actions will be. As Raz himself acknowledged, observance of the thin rule of law does not guarantee that a government will refrain from enacting repressive and discriminatory laws. From this perspective, the enactment of the Nuremburg laws in Nazi-era Germany or apartheid laws in South Africa would appear to have been enacted in accordance with the rule of law, which most would agree is an abhorrent proposition.

In opposition to formal theorists, proponents of the substantive rule of law—also called "thick" rule of law—consider that the rule of law should also encompass ideals of justice and fairness. Ronald Dworkin is one of the leading protagonists of the substantive rule of law, which he calls "rights conception" of the rule of law, as opposed to the "rule book" conception advocated by formal theorists. In his view, the rule of law not only requires compliance with formal legality but also requires laws to recognize moral and political rights and permit individuals to enforce those rights through the courts or some other mechanism. One of the problems with such an approach is that the nature of "moral rights" tends to be nebulous and can polarize opinions, such as diverse public attitudes regarding same-sex marriage or the death penalty.

Other substantive theorists, such as Professors Richard Bellamy and T.R.S. Allan, go even further, suggesting that democracy is an inherent part of the rule of law. However, this approach minimizes the uses to which the rule of law can be put as a legal concept. It is also criticized as conflating two interrelated but nonetheless distinct concepts: the rule of law and democracy. While it is true that the rule of law is an essential component of democracy because it provides safeguards against government excesses, democracy is not a prerequisite for the rule of law.

Role in International Development

After the end of the Cold War, many countries abandoned communist forms of government and embraced liberal democracy and capitalism. In the transitional period, many of those countries sought to reform their legal systems, and international development agencies began to fund projects to build "the rule of law" in those countries. In the 1990s many development banks imposed rule of law benchmarks as a condition of providing financial assistance.

As a result, the rule of law has become a significant component of international development, with billions of dollars spent since the 1990s or so on reforming legal systems. Donor agencies, including the European Commission, the United States Agency for International Development, the Japan International Cooperation Agency, and the World Bank, all fund rule of law projects in countries around the world, such as China, Ecuador, Liberia, and Papua New Guinea. Technical assistance is often provided to donor recipients by specialized nongovernment organizations including Avocats sans Frontières (Lawyers Without Borders), the American Bar Association Rule of Law Initiative, and the International Legal Assistance Consortium, but private companies are also used on larger projects.

Such initiatives are not without criticism. As with other international development activities, many commentators denounce the lack of empirical evidence as to the effects and impact of such programs, a lack of proper coordination between donors, and the unsustainable nature of many programs. More damning is the charge that rule of law assistance programs have led to very limited long-term improvements on the ground, that programs are too narrow in focus because they address only judicial or legal institutions without, at the same time, addressing the police or prisons, that they lack clearly articulated objectives directly linked to improving the various constitutive elements of the rule of law, and that, in some instances, such efforts have been counterproductive. Aspects of these criticisms can be attributed to the absence of a universally accepted definition of the rule of law. In any event, most observers agree that much more needs to be done to develop a more consistent approach to rule of law assistance and to take meaningful steps to measure the impact of rule of law programs.

Further Criticisms

It is undeniable that the rule of law forms an integral part of the liberal form of democratic government worldwide. It goes without saying that "freedom under the rule of law" is an oft-repeated mantra of Western liberal democracies. In this sense, adherence to the rule of law therefore appears to carry with it a number of connotations of a social and political nature. Seen in this light, the rule of law is not necessarily a politically neutral concept.

For instance, some argue that a model of government based on the welfare state is incompatible with the rule of law. In a later edition of *Introduction to Study of the Laws of the Constitution*, Dicey deplored what he saw as the decline in the rule of law that owed in part to the emergence of the welfare state and the adoption of legislation giving regulatory and adjudicatory powers to administrative entities without recourse to judicial review by the courts. Nonetheless, it could be argued that these concerns have been tempered by the rise of administrative law as a distinct area of law in common law countries, where the ordinary courts have developed an elaborate body of case law that has placed limits on administrative discretion, some of which has been codified into legislation. However, it is now recognized that the establishment of administrative courts that are distinct from the civil and criminal courts in countries that follow the civil code tradition has ensured to a large extent that discretionary actions taken by the government do not go unchecked. Moreover, it is undeniable that certain countries that follow the civil law tradition—for example, Belgium and Sweden, which pride themselves on having a political system that embraces social welfare—are also widely accepted as adhering to the rule of law.

The rule of law is criticized as serving a convenient justification for the capitalist system of economic governance and the social inequities that may flow from it. Locke's view that the government should serve to secure the property rights of individuals was shared by Adam Smith, the pioneer of political economy. In *Lectures on Jurisprudence* (1763), he declared: "Laws and government may be considered . . . as a combination of the rich to oppress the poor, and to preserve to themselves the inequality of the goods which would otherwise be soon destroyed by the attacks of the poor." Hayek wrote, "It cannot be denied that the Rule of Law produces economic inequality—all that can be claimed for it is that this inequality is not designed to effect particular people in a particular way." Given the unapologetic stance of liberal theorists, it is no wonder that these views have fed the arguments of their ideological opponents. In the communist theory of class struggle elaborated by Karl Marx and supported by Friedrich Engels, the law is one of the means by which the capitalist class maintains its exploitation of the proletariat. Supporters of the rule of law argue that the concept is not inherently ideological in nature and that the rule of law is essentially concerned with ensuring respect for the law, whatever that law may be. Proponents of the substantive rule of law also contend that the rule of law incorporates ideals of fairness and justice that can be used to address economic inequality.

The rule of law also falls victim to accusations of Western cultural imperialism or neocolonialism. Law does not necessarily play a prominent role in the organization of Eastern societies. For example, in Confucian theory, a far greater emphasis is placed upon the observance of rites (*li*) or rules of conduct to achieve civilized behavior and social harmony in society and limits the application of the tools of law (*fa*) and punishment (*xing*) to those who fail to abide by the *Liji* (Record of Rites). In Confucian and the other distinctive cultural traditions of Asia and beyond, the modes of social governance that these traditions advocate often place an emphasis on the community rather than the individual. As a result, some see in the promotion of rule of law a way for the West to impose its values on the rest of the world. However, supporters of the rule of law point out that the majority of countries are members of the United Nations and as such agree to abide by the Universal Declaration of Human Rights, which calls for the respect of human rights based on the rule of law. Many developing countries are also signatories to a large array of international and regional treaties and declarations that commit them to upholding standards such as those relating to the functioning of their legal systems and the independence of the judiciary. Finally, and perhaps most important, many developing countries have adopted their own constitutions that encapsulate many elements of the rule of law. In recent years, the leaders of many developing countries have made public pronouncements that declare their commitment to upholding the rule of law.

General Prospects

In its present meaning, the rule of law is often used as shorthand for the existence of good governance in a particular country. In the West and other countries that have adopted a liberal democratic mode of governance, the rule of law is seen as essential for economic and social development and as a necessary prerequisite for the existence of democratic mode of government.

Although the concept of the rule of law is the subject of competing theories, the existence of a divergence of views as to its precise meaning does not invalidate the rule of law as a concept in law. Most theorists tend to agree that, at the very minimum, it does include a requirement that the government observe a country's laws and the existence of institutions and mechanisms that allow individuals to enforce the laws against officials. In time it is hoped that the rule of law will not just gain universal acceptance as to its desirability but also further agreement as to its precise meaning.

Anthony Valcke

Further Reading

Bingham, Tom. *The Rule of Law*. New York: Allen Lane, 2010.

Carrothers, Thomas. *Promoting the Rule of Law Abroad: In Search of Knowledge*. Washington, DC: Carnegie Endowment of International Peace, 2006.

Kleinfeld, Rachel. *Advancing the Law Abroad: Next Generation Reform*. Washington, DC: Carnegie Endowment for International Peace, 2012.

Rubin, Edward L. *Beyond Camelot: Rethinking Politics and Law for the Modern State*. Princeton, NJ: Princeton University Press, 2005.

Shapiro, Ian, ed. *The Rule of Law*. New York: New York University Press, 1995.

Tamanaha, Brian Z. *On the Rule of Law: History, Politics, Theory*. New York: Cambridge University Press, 2004.

Zoller, Elisabeth. *Introduction to Public Law: A Comparative Study*. Leiden: Martinus Nijhoff, 2008.

Web Sites

American Bar Association Rule of Law Initiative: http://apps.americanbar.org/rol

Avocats sans Frontières: www.asf.be

International Development Law Organisation: www.idlo.org

International Legal Assistance Consortium: www.ilac.se

International Network to Promote the Rule of Law: http://inprol.org

United Nations Rule of Law: www.unrol.org

World Justice Project: http://worldjusticeproject.org

Documents

Document 1. Ancient Philosophers on the Rule of Law, 360–51 B.C.E.

The fourth-century B.C.E. Greek philosophers Plato and Aristotle were among the first in the Western tradition to emphasize the importance of the rule of law. Both argued that the rule of law is based on reason, while the rule of men is dictated by passions. The first-century B.C.E. Roman statesman and political theorist Cicero expanded on these concepts by arguing that the law should serve the people, thereby upholding the basic concept of legal justice. The ideas of these three classical thinkers, in modified and modernized form, remain at the core of the rule of law concept within the Western tradition and, increasingly, within the international community as a whole.

Plato, *The Laws* (ca. 360 B.C.E.)

[W]e must not entrust the government in your state to any one because he is rich, or because he possesses any other advantage, such as strength, or stature, or again birth: but he who is most obedient to the laws of the state, he shall win the palm. . . . [N]or are laws right which are passed for the good of particular classes and not for the good of the whole state. States which have such laws are not polities but parties, and their notions of justice are simply unmeaning. . . . And when I call the rulers servants or ministers of the law, I give them this name not for the sake of novelty, but because I certainly believe that upon such service or ministry depends the well- or ill-being of the state. For that state in which the law is subject and has no authority, I perceive to be on the highway to ruin; but I see that the state in which the law is above the rulers, and the rulers are the inferiors of the law, has salvation, and every blessing which the Gods can confer.

Source: Plato, *The Laws* (trans. Benjamin Jowett), 1871.

Aristotle, *Politics* (ca. 350 B.C.E.)

[L]aws, when good, should be supreme; and that the magistrate or magistrates should regulate those matters only on which the laws are unable to speak with precision owing to the difficulty of any general principle embracing all particulars. But what are good laws has not yet been clearly explained; the old difficulty remains. The goodness or badness, justice or injustice, of laws varies of necessity with the constitutions of states. This, however, is clear, that the laws must be adapted to the constitutions. But if so, true forms of government will of necessity have just laws, and perverted forms of government will have unjust laws . . .

Now, absolute monarchy, or the arbitrary rule of a sovereign over all citizens, in a city which consists of equals, is thought by some to be quite contrary to nature; . . . That is why it is thought to be just that among equals everyone be ruled as well as rule, and therefore that all should have their turn. . . . And the rule of law, it is argued, is preferable to that of any individual. On the same principle, even if it be better for certain individuals to govern, they should be made only guardians and ministers of the law. . . . Therefore he who bids the law rule may be deemed to bid God and Reason alone rule, but he who bids man rule adds an element of the beast; for desire is a wild beast, and passion perverts the minds of rulers, even when they are the best of men. The law is reason unaffected by desire.

Source: Aristotle, *Politics* (trans. Benjamin Jowett), 1885.

Cicero, *De Legibus* (ca. 54–51 B.C.E.)

For men prove by some such arguments as the following, that every law which deserves the name of a law ought to be morally good and laudable. It is clear, say they, that laws were originally made for the security of the people, for the preservation of states, for the peace and happiness of society; and that they who first framed enactments of that kind persuaded the people that they would write and publish such laws only as should conduce to the general morality and happiness, if they would receive and obey them. And then such regulations, being thus settled and sanctioned, they justly entitled Laws. From which we may reasonably conclude that those who made unjustifiable and pernicious enactments for the people acted in a manner contrary to their own promises and professions and established anything rather than laws, properly so called, since it is evident that the very signification of the word "law" comprehends the whole essence and energy of justice and equity.

Source: Oliver J. Thatcher, ed., *The Library of Original Sources* (Milwaukee: University Research Extension Co., 1907), vol. 3, *The Roman World,* 216–241.

Document 2: UN General Assembly Resolution 64/116: The Rule of Law at the National and International Levels, 2010

Since 1948, when it declared in the Declaration of Human Rights that if "man is not to be compelled to have recourse, as a last resort, to rebellion against tyranny and oppression, that human rights should be protected by the rule of law," the United Nations has reiterated time and again its commitment to the rule of law at the national and international levels. Many criticize the world body for its failure to live up to this ideal, but its commitment underlines the concept that the rule of law is not necessarily a construct of the West but a concept applicable to all the world's peoples. Periodically, as in the following General Assembly resolution, the United Nations reconfirms its commitment to the pursuit of the rule of law.

Resolution adopted by the General Assembly . . .

64/116. The rule of law at the national and international levels

The General Assembly,

Recalling its resolution 63/128 of 11 December 2008,

Reaffirming its commitment to the purposes and principles of the Charter of the United Nations and international law, which are indispensable foundations of a more peaceful, prosperous and just world, and reiterating its determination to foster strict respect for them and to establish a just and lasting peace all over the world,

Reaffirming that human rights, the rule of law and democracy are interlinked and mutually reinforcing and that they belong to the universal and indivisible core values and principles of the United Nations,

Reaffirming also the need for universal adherence to and implementation of the rule of law at both the national and international levels and its solemn commitment to an international order based on the rule of law and international law, which, together with the principles of justice, is essential for peaceful coexistence and cooperation among States,

Convinced that the advancement of the rule of law at the national and international levels is essential for the realization of sustained economic growth, sustainable development, the eradication of poverty and hunger and the protection of all human rights and fundamental freedoms, and acknowledging that collective security depends on effective cooperation, in accordance with the Charter and international law, against transnational threats,

Reaffirming the duty of all States to refrain in their international relations from the threat or use of force in any manner inconsistent with the purposes and principles of the United Nations and to settle their international disputes by peaceful means in such a manner that international peace and security, and justice are not endangered, in accordance with Chapter VI of the Charter, and calling upon States that have not yet done so to consider accepting the jurisdiction of the International Court of Justice in accordance with its Statute,

Convinced that the promotion of and respect for the rule of law at the national and international levels, as well as justice and good governance, should guide the activities of the United Nations and of its Member States,

Recalling paragraph 134(*e*) of the 2005 World Summit Outcome,

1. *Takes note* of the annual report of the Secretary-General on strengthening and coordinating United Nations rule of law activities;

2. *Reaffirms* the role of the General Assembly in encouraging the progressive development of international law and its codification, and reaffirms further that States shall abide by all their obligations under international law;

3. *Stresses* the importance of adherence to the rule of law at the national level, and the need to strengthen support to Member States, upon their request, in the domestic implementation of their respective international obligations through enhanced technical assistance and capacity-building, based on greater coordination and coherence within the United Nations system and among donors, and calls for greater evaluation of the effectiveness of such activities;

4. *Calls upon* the United Nations system to systematically address, as appropriate, aspects of the rule of law in relevant activities, recognizing the importance of the rule of law to virtually all areas of United Nations engagement;

5. *Expresses full support* for the overall coordination and coherence role of the Rule of Law Coordination and Resource Group within the United Nations system within existing mandates, supported by the Rule of Law Unit in the Executive Office of the Secretary-General, under the leadership of the Deputy Secretary-General;

6. *Requests* the Secretary-General to submit his next annual report on United Nations rule of law activities, in accordance with paragraph 5 of resolution 63/128, taking note of paragraph 97 of the report;

7. *Welcomes* the dialogue initiated by the Rule of Law Coordination and Resource Group and the Rule of Law Unit with Member States on the topic "Promoting the rule of law at the international level," and calls for the continuation of this dialogue with a view to fostering the rule of law at the international level;

8. *Encourages* the Secretary-General and the United Nations system to accord high priority to rule of law activities;

9. *Invites* the International Court of Justice, the United Nations Commission on International Trade Law and the International Law Commission to continue to comment, in their respective reports to the General Assembly, on their current roles in promoting the rule of law;

10. *Invites* the Rule of Law Coordination and Resource Group and the Rule of Law Unit to continue to interact with Member States on a regular basis, in particular in informal briefings;

11. *Stresses* the need to provide the Rule of Law Unit with the necessary funding and staff in order to enable it to carry out its tasks in an effective and sustainable manner and urges the Secretary-General and Member States to continue to support the functioning of the Unit. . . .

Source: United Nations Rule of Law.

LITERACY

It is difficult to assign one universal definition to the term "literacy." As recently as the 1950s, the term primarily referred to the ability to read and write. As the world rapidly shifted into the multifaceted, highly industrialized entity we know today, however, the term has been expanded to include proficiency in the skills needed to function in modern society—"politically literate," for example, and "computer literate" are two examples of the contemporary understanding of the concept.

For much of human history, literacy—however it was defined—was the province of the elite. Political leaders, priests, and scribes recognized that maintaining control over information helped them to retain their grip on power, and they worked actively to keep the masses from becoming literate. In the past two centuries, however, the ability to access, read, and process information has increasingly been understood as a necessity and even a basic human right. The result has been a dramatic rise in worldwide literacy rates, although the populations of less developed nations lag behind those of more developed nations, sometimes by a considerable margin.

Theoretical Background

In the past several generations, scholars have taken great interest in the function and impact of different types of literacy. At the forefront of this development was classicist Eric Havelock, with his 1963 work *A Preface to Plato*. As the title suggests, the book postulates that the beginnings of the shift to literacy, which occurred some 6,000 years ago, set in motion the future global shift of language and consciousness.

Havelock's work shaped the thinking of Walter Ong, perhaps the most influential theorist to write about literacy in the past century. His seminal text, *Orality and Literacy: The Technologizing of the World* (1982), sought to define characteristics of oral cultures—that is, cultures that do not have writing or print—and to detail how they differ from literate cultures. He noted, for example, that at the time of the publication of *Orality and Literacy*, of the more than 3,000 languages spoken in the world, only 78 had a literature. Ong described how the shift from orality to literacy—or, in simpler terms, from strictly oral cultures to cultures that developed a written language—not only changed the method of communication but also restructured consciousness itself.

According to Ong, consciousness was restructured because expressing oneself through writing distances the person who expresses a thought from the person who receives it. In Ong's own words, this discourse "cannot be directly questioned or contested as oral speech can be because written discourse is detached from the writer." Furthermore, literacy restructures consciousness because the dominant method of receiving information shifts from oral to visual, forcing the informational world to be structured by sight; because the visual representation of words insists that "words [like the ideas they represent] are things"; and because, whereas ideas in oral cultures are usually always in flux, changing in subtle ways from their telling to retelling, the printing of words on a page grants them a sort of authority or finality that is not generally found in oral cultures.

Another critical scholar of literacy is Marshall McLuhan, who contributed much to early media theory studies and is credited with coining the phrase "the medium is the message." His 1961 text *The Gutenberg Galaxy: The Making of the Typographic Man* described how the technologies used to communicate—such as the alphabet, the printing press, and, jumping forward a few steps, the Internet—eventually grow to shape cognitive organization. McLuhan posited that, with electronic media overtaking traditional printed communication, we are moving into a "global community" devoid of any true individualism. Rather, a "tribal base" will serve to replace individual communities, and the global community will function as just that—one worldwide "city."

Historical Background

Although pictographic writing is known to have existed as early as 3500 B.C.E., the earliest known books are dated around the end of the Roman Republic, or about 23 B.C.E. However, until Johannes Gutenberg's invention of the printing press in the mid-fifteenth century, books were extremely expensive and thus difficult for the average citizen to afford. The enormous availability of books that we know today was largely a product of the Industrial Revolution of the mid-nineteenth century. It was only as the prices of paper and binding fell that printed manuscripts began to become as common as they are today. As books became more popular and more easily obtained, the literacy rate began to climb.

Social historian Harvey J. Graff suggests in his text *Literacy Myth* (1991) that the rise of public schooling in the nineteenth and twentieth centuries also contributed to increased literacy rates. According to Graff, public schooling provided a venue for the teaching of literacy that was beneficial in two ways: it provided children with access to literature, and it also offered a way to control what types of literature would be available to read. Public schooling was thus an attempt to control literacy as much as to promote it. The traditional elite's fears of an educated working class were dissipating and, through public schooling, the production of social stability and uniformly functioning citizens was regarded as increasingly more possible and desirable than ever before.

Literacy Today

In the modern world, literacy is widespread, though certainly not universal. Overall, 84 percent of the world's adult population (age 15 and older) was considered literate by the UNESCO Institute for Statistics (UIS) in a 2005–2009 survey. Moving from lowest rate to highest, sub-Saharan Africa and western Asia both had a 62 percent literacy rate, while Arab states were 73 percent literate. A considerable jump in percentages can be seen between these and the Latin American and Caribbean regions, which boasted a 91 percent literacy rate, while eastern Asia and the Pacific were 94 percent literate. Central Europe was even higher, at about 98 percent, while North America, Western Europe, and Central Asia all had a rate of 99 percent. As for the world's illiterate population, 36 percent of the 793 million illiterate adults lived in India, and 8 percent were found in China.

The UIS report also addressed literacy rates among those aged 15 to 24. Eighty-nine percent of the world's population that falls into this age group is considered literate by the UIS, and the ranked world regions are generally consistent with the adult statistics. The UIS reported that 71 percent of sub-Saharan Africa's youth was literate, compared with 80 percent in southern and less developed parts of eastern Asia and 88 percent in the Arab states. Children in Latin America and the Caribbean were 97 percent literate, while children in the more developed countries of eastern Asia, the Pacific, and Central and Eastern Europe were reported as being 99 percent literate. Even more encouraging, the children of North America, Western Europe, and Central Asia were 100 percent literate. Females composed 61 percent of the world's illiterate youth population, and, consistent with the adult statistics, the majority of illiterate youths can be found in India, which is reported as being 32 percent illiterate.

Interestingly, the regions listed in these UNESCO literacy surveys generally appear in the same order, although it is important to note that each region boasts higher literacy rates in the youth survey. This is indicative of the growing trend of literacy throughout the world, even in less developed countries: each successive generation is more literate than the last. For example, while UNESCO reports that only 73 percent of the adult population of the Arab states was literate through 2009, 88 percent—a full 15 percent increase—of the youth population was literate at the same time. In short, more youths than adults are literate in the Arab states, a trend that should only increase with each new generation as literacy becomes more accessible and more possible to attain.

The spread of literacy is a cause that has inspired a great deal of activism around the world. Literacy Bridge, for example, is currently at work promoting and furthering literacy in the African country of Ghana, most of which is still without electricity. Literacy Bridge's solution is the "Talking Book," an inexpensive piece of technology that allows users to read actively and interactively, listen and repeat, and adjust the speed of audio recordings during playback. In addition, users can add to the information stored in the device by recording their own voices and passing it along to someone else. According to the organization's Web site, the Talking Book is especially beneficial to communities struggling to disseminate information due to isolation and lack of electricity; in some of these communities, classrooms hold up to 100 students

India still has the world's highest illiterate population, but remedial programs have helped. The literacy rate for people over age seven rose from 65 percent in 2001 to 74 percent in 2011. Here, children in a New Delhi slum take part in a mobile literacy program. *(AP Photo/Kevin Frayer)*

each, making it nearly impossible to pay attention to students with special needs.

UNESCO has also implemented a program called the UNIVA Functional Literacy Programme (UFLP). Co-implemented by the University Village Association (UNIVA), UFLP is currently dedicated to improving literacy in the African country of Nigeria, whose overall poverty is so extensive that a full 70 percent of its population lives on less than one U.S. dollar per day. According to UFLP leadership, previous Nigerian efforts to improve literacy fell short of effecting any long-term benefits because basic literacy was usually the declared goal, leaving participants in the programs literate but not to a point where they were able to enter the job market or create better living conditions. UFLP, by contrast, endeavors to promote the development of community, to teach participants how to improve their living conditions, to get citizens active in political activities, and to improve income-generating activities.

BuildOn is an organization dedicated to creating schools in some of the poorest countries in the world. Its "Global School Construction" program accepts donations and volunteers in order to reach the goal of educating those who need it most. Its slogan—"Empowering youth to change the world"— encompasses some of the most encouraging outcomes of educating impoverished communities in literacy.

Literacy Bridge, UFLP, and BuildOn are just representative examples of the worldwide effort to promote literacy. Several dozen (perhaps as many as a 100 or more) similar programs exist, some focused on a single community, state, or nation (such as Literacy Bridge and UFLP), others with a much broader reach (e.g., BuildOn).

Ramifications

The consequences of illiteracy on societies are profound, especially in today's global, postindustrial political climate. A few examples will serve to illustrate this point, though it should be noted that the effects of illiteracy can vary widely across cultures and nations.

In India, for example, the substantially lower literacy rate of females has led to problems in population stabilization. According to Arunachalam Dharmalingam and S. Philip Morgan's 1996 essay "Women's Work, Autonomy, and Birth Control," a strong correlation exists between women's literacy and the use of contraception during sex. Further, illiterate women are not just more likely to get pregnant; they are also more likely to be poor. When a family cannot afford to live on a day-to-day basis, the probability is slim that its children will go to school regularly—as late as 1999, poverty kept between 35 million and 60 million children between the ages of 6 and 14 from being enrolled in school. Thus, the children born to illiterate women are themselves likely to be illiterate, perpetuating the cycle.

India also has the specific issue of a caste system. In a society where one's social standing is determined by birth, it is not surprising that the majority of youths born into the lower castes have high dropout figures. Again, however, if poverty is linked to overpopulation, and overpopulation is linked to literacy, it quickly becomes necessary to somehow implement education and literacy in such a way that their effect will be widespread.

The disparity of literacy rates between genders bears consequences beyond population stabilization, however. The Summer Institute of Linguistics (SIL) reports that fully two-thirds of the 1 billion illiterate people in the world are women. In addition to having fewer, but healthier, children, literate women are more likely to avoid the trauma of infant deaths, will be better sheltered and stay healthier, and live in wealthier households than those who are illiterate. Literate women are much better equipped to aid their families in staying healthy, and these improved living conditions in turn often lead to better opportunities for sustainable living and meaningful jobs.

It is also important to understand that an illiterate population, unfortunately, is also less able to express itself or strive for advocacy or activism. The resources available to more literate countries simply are not there. As a result, it is difficult to prevent corruption in politics or to exert any real agency over life at a very basic, personal level. This is another reason why the quality of life decreases so dramatically for the illiterate population in developing countries.

In developed countries—for example, the United States, which was reported by UIS in 2009 to be 100 percent literate, although it can safely be assumed that this is a rounded figure—illiteracy also poses serious challenges. To begin with, the possibilities of finding a job that will allow for a sustained and adequate lifestyle lessens exponentially when one is not literate. With higher education becoming commonplace and more citizens holding multiple degrees, the desired levels of qualification for a given job are also increased. A growing number of college graduates also means that more and more jobs have become more technical, thus weeding out those who do not hold a degree. Competition becomes more pronounced, and as a result, nontechnical jobs are more sought after by illiterate citizens, which increases competition at lower levels as well.

Also problematic for illiterate citizens of developed countries are the inability to vote properly (if nothing else, it becomes dramatically more difficult to make an informed decision) and the social disdain of the elite. Too often, it is reported that the cycle of poverty is extremely difficult to break, a fact due in large part to the lack of availability and the high cost of education. If citizens cannot afford to educate themselves to stay competitive with their peers, the resulting inequality can very quickly become crippling.

The Future

Literacy is a global issue and one that is ignored only to the detriment of developing and industrialized civilizations. Countries with high literacy rates generally boast higher standards of living than other countries, less poverty, better health knowledge and awareness, and greater worldwide political security. Efforts to increase global literacy over the past several decades have met with both challenges and success, and organizations such as UNESCO, BuildOn, and SIL will no doubt continue to labor tirelessly to improve literacy—and, by extension, standards of living—in impoverished countries around the world.

As Walter Ong notes in *Orality and Literacy*, the shift from oral to literate cultures restructured our very consciousness. In the postindustrial world of the twenty-first century, it is impossible to ignore the fact that literacy has become a necessary standard if societies are to succeed and thrive. Much like the differing exchange rates of currency around the world—currency that is required for the importing and exporting of goods and services—literacy is now a requirement for countries to effectively enter and participate in the global market. Humanitarian organizations show no signs of slowing or decreasing their efforts to bring literacy to every impoverished area, and it is just this cooperative spirit that will effect change in illiterate countries.

Nicholas Beishline

See also: Children's Rights; Digital Divide; Education, Primary and Secondary.

Further Reading

Ahmad, Kamal, David E. Bloom, Kenneth Prewitt, Mamphela Ramphele, and Henry Rosovsky, eds. "The Importance of General Education." *Higher Education in Developing Countries: Peril and Promise* (2000): 83–90.

Edmonson, Monro E. *Lore.* New York: Holt, Rinehart & Winston, 1971.

Freire, Paulo. *Pedagogy of the Oppressed.* New York: Continuum, 2006.

Freire, Paulo, and Donald Macedo. *Literacy: Reading the Word and the World.* New York: Routledge, 1987.

Graff, Harvey. *The Literacy Myth: Cultural Integration and Social Structure in the Nineteenth Century.* Piscataway, NJ: Transaction, 1991.

Hawisher, Gail E., and Cynthia L. Selfe. *Global Literacies and the World Wide Web.* New York: Routledge, 1999.

Sandlin, Jennifer A., and Corrine M. Wickens. "Literacy for What? Literacy for Whom? The Politics of Literacy Education and Neocolonialism in UNESCO and World Bank–Sponsored Literacy Programs." *Adult Education Quarterly* 57:4 (August 2007): 275–292.

Web Sites

BuildOn: www.buildon.org

Literacy Bridge: www.literacybridge.org

National Institute for Literacy (Statistics): www.caliteracy.org/nil

ProLiteracy: www.proliteracy.org

Route 66 Literacy: www.route66literacy.org

UNESCO Program Descriptions: www.unesco.org/uil/litbase/?menu=4

UNIVA Functional Literacy Programme: www.unesco.org/uil/litbase/?menu=4&programme=17

Documents

Document 1: *Democracy and Education: An Introduction to the Philosophy of Education* (excerpt), John Dewey, 1916

The following excerpt from Chapter 1 ("Education as a Necessity of Life") of John Dewey's classic work illustrates a prevailing attitude toward education and literacy in the early twentieth century. The book's subtitle reflects Dewey's belief that education is indeed a form of philosophy and as such should not be left to stagnate. His prolific writing earned him a position of considerable influence in such fields as psychology, philosophy, and education.

So obvious, indeed, is the necessity of teaching and learning for the continued existence of a society that we may seem to be dwelling unduly on a truism. But justification is found in the fact that such emphasis is a means of getting us away from an unduly scholastic and formal notion of education. Schools are, indeed, one important method of the transmission which forms the dispositions of the immature; but it is only one means, and, compared with other agencies, a relatively superficial means. Only as we have grasped the necessity of more fundamental and persistent modes of tuition can we make sure of placing the scholastic methods in their true context.

Society not only continues to exist by transmission, by communication, but it may fairly be said to exist in transmission, in communication. There is more than a verbal tie between the words common, community, and communication. Men live in a community in virtue of the things which they have in common; and communication is the way in which they come to possess things in common. What they must have in common in order to form a community or society are aims, beliefs, aspirations, knowledge—a common understanding—like-mindedness as the sociologists say. Such things cannot be passed physically from one to another, like bricks; they cannot be shared as persons would share a pie by dividing it into physical pieces. The communication which insures participation in a common understanding is one which secures similar emotional and intellectual dispositions—like ways of responding to expectations and requirements.

Persons do not become a society by living in physical proximity, any more than a man ceases to be socially influenced by being so many feet or miles removed from others. A book or a letter may institute a more intimate association between human beings separated thousands of miles from each other than exists between dwellers under the same roof. Individuals do not even compose a social group because they all work for a common end. The parts of a machine work with a maximum of cooperativeness for a common result, but they do not form a community. If, however, they were all cognizant of the common end and all interested in it so that they regulated their specific activity in view of it, then they would form a community. But this would involve communication. Each would have to know what the other was about and would have to have some way of keeping the other informed as to his own purpose and progress. Consensus demands communication.

We are thus compelled to recognize that within even the most social group there are many relations which are not as yet social. A large number of human relationships in any social group are still upon the machine-like plane. Individuals use one another so as to get desired results, without reference to the emotional and intellectual disposition and consent of those used. Such uses express physical superiority, or superiority of position, skill, technical ability, and command of tools, mechanical or fiscal. So far as the relations of parent and child, teacher and pupil, employer and employee, governor and governed, remain upon this level, they form no true social group, no matter how closely their respective activities touch one another. Giving and taking of orders modifies action and results, but does not of itself effect a sharing of purposes, a communication of interests.

Not only is social life identical with communication, but all communication (and hence all genuine social life) is educative. To be a recipient of a communication is to have an enlarged and changed experience. One shares in what another has thought and felt and in so far, meagerly or amply, has his own attitude modified. Nor is the one who communicates left unaffected. Try the experiment of communicating, with fullness and accuracy, some experience to another, especially if it be somewhat complicated, and you will find your own attitude toward your experience changing; otherwise you resort to expletives and ejaculations. The experience has to be formulated in order to be communicated. To formulate requires getting outside of it, seeing it as another would see it, considering what points of contact it has with the life of another so that it may be got into such form that he can appreciate its meaning. Except in dealing with commonplaces and catch phrases one has to assimilate, imaginatively, something of another's experience in order to tell him intelligently of one's own experience. All communication is like art. It may fairly be said, therefore, that any social arrangement that remains vitally social, or vitally shared, is educative to those who participate in it. Only when it becomes cast in a mold and runs in a routine way does it lose its educative power.

In final account, then, not only does social life demand teaching and learning for its own permanence, but the very process of living together educates. It enlarges and enlightens experience; it stimulates and enriches imagination; it creates responsibility for accuracy and vividness of statement and thought. A man really living alone (alone mentally as well as physically) would have little or no occasion to reflect upon his past experience to extract its net meaning. The inequality of achievement between the mature and the immature not only necessitates teaching the young, but the necessity of this teaching gives an immense stimulus to reducing experience to that order and form which will render it most easily communicable and hence most usable.

Source: Electronic Text Center, University of Virginia Library.

Document 2: "Literacy and Education in a 21st-Century Economy" (excerpt), Speech by U.S. Senator Barack Obama, 2005

In a speech before the American Library Association's annual convention on June 25, 2005, U.S. senator and future president Barack Obama expressed the American ideal of literacy and the global importance of literacy in the twenty-first century.

I believe that if we want to give our children the best possible chance in life; if we want to open doors of opportunity while they're young and teach them the skills they'll need to succeed later on, then one of our greatest responsibilities as citizens, as educators, and as parents is to ensure that every American child can read and read well.

This isn't just another education debate where the answer lies somewhere between more money and less

bureaucracy. It's a responsibility that begins at home—one that we need to take on before our kids ever step foot in a classroom; one that we need to carry through well into their teenage years.

That's because literacy is the most basic currency of the knowledge economy we're living in today. Only a few generations ago, it was okay to enter the workforce as a high school dropout who could only read at a third-grade level. Whether it was on a farm or in a factory, you could still hope to find a job that would allow you to pay the bills and raise your family.

But that economy is long gone. As revolutions in technology and communication began breaking down barriers between countries and connecting people all over the world, new jobs and industries that require more skill and knowledge have come to dominate the economy. Whether it's software design or computer engineering or financial analysis, corporations can locate these jobs anywhere there's an Internet connection. And so as countries like China and India continue to modernize their economies and educate their children longer and better, the competition American workers face will grow more intense; the necessary skills more demanding.

These new jobs are about what you know and how fast you can learn what you don't know. They require innovative thinking, detailed comprehension, and superior communication.

But before our children can even walk into an interview for one of these jobs; before they can ever fill out an application or earn the required college degree; they have to be able to pick up a book, read it, and understand it. Nothing is more basic; no ability more fundamental.

Reading is the gateway skill that makes all other learning possible, from complex word problems and the meaning of our history to scientific discovery and technological proficiency. In a knowledge economy where this kind of learning is necessary for survival, how can we send our kids out into the world if they're only reading at a fourth-grade level?

I don't know, but we do. Day after day, year after year.

Right now, one out of every five adults in the United States can't read a simple story to their child. During the last twenty years or so, over ten million Americans reached the 12th grade without having learned to read at a basic level.

But these literacy problems start far before high school. In 2000, only 32% of all fourth graders tested as reading proficient. And the story gets worse when you take race and income into consideration. Children from low-income families score 27 points below the average reading level, while students from wealthy families score fifteen points above the average. And while only one in twelve white seventeen-year-olds has the ability to pick up the newspaper and understand the science section, for Hispanics the number jumps to one in fifty; for African Americans it's one in one hundred.

In this new economy, teaching our kids just enough so that they can get through Dick and Jane isn't going to cut it. Over the last ten years, the average literacy required for all American occupations is projected to rise by 14%. It's not enough just to recognize the words on the page anymore—the kind of literacy necessary for 21st-century employment requires detailed understanding and complex comprehension. But too many kids simply aren't learning at that level.

And yet, every year we pass more of these kids through school or watch as more drop out. These kids who will pore through the Help Wanted section and cross off job after job that requires skills they just don't have. And others who will have to take that Help Wanted section, walk it over to someone else, and find the courage to ask, "Will you read this for me?"

We have to change our whole mindset in this country. We're living in a 21st-century knowledge economy, but our schools, our homes, and our culture are still based around 20th-century expectations. It might seem like we're doing kids a favor by teaching them just enough to count change and read a food label, but in this economy, it's doing them a huge disservice. Instead, we need to start setting high standards and inspirational examples for our children to follow. While there's plenty that can be done to improve our schools and reform education in America, this isn't just an issue where we can turn to the government and ask for help. Reading has to begin at home.

We know that children who start kindergarten with an awareness of letters and basic language sounds become better readers and face fewer challenges in the years ahead. We also know that the more reading material kids are exposed to at home, the better they score on reading tests throughout their lives. So we need to make investments in family literacy programs and early childhood education so that kids aren't left behind before they even go to school. And we need to get books in our kids' hands early and often.

Source: obamaspeeches.com.

MARRIAGE AND DIVORCE

Marriage is a protean concept, defined differently by various cultures and in different eras. In its broadest definition, it is social bond or legal contract between persons that establishes kinship, usually sanctified by religious authorities or the state. Divorce is the undoing of a marriage either as a social bond or a legal contract, again conducted under the purview of religious authorities or the state.

Predating written history itself, marriage has typically been an institution linking two adult persons of opposite sex. But exceptions to this rule are plentiful, as has been evident throughout history and is still across the globe today. The exceptions include marriage between children, between children and adults, between more than two persons, and, most recently, between persons of the same sex.

While love and personal affinity have always been factors in why people marry, through much of history—and in many cultures today—marriage has also been motivated by financial and larger social and familial concerns. Indeed, these are often the primary considerations, especially in cases in which the marriage is arranged by families rather than the marrying individuals themselves. Divorce, too, seems to predate the written record and has been part of the human experience in nearly all cultures since ancient times.

Marriage and divorce rates vary widely around the world. In recent decades the former have generally tended to be higher in the developing world; marriage rates have declined in many developed world countries. Meanwhile, divorce rates tend to be higher in the developed world, a result of liberalized laws and evolving social norms, although there is much concern about the impact divorce has on social cohesion, the experiences of children of divorced parents, and socioeconomic indices.

Across the globe in the early twenty-first century, a number of critical issues relating to marriage are being debated, although these tend to differ in various cultures. In many developing-world countries, the issues are related to the ongoing transition from traditional-style marriages to more modern ones. In the developed world, there is the ongoing decline of marriage as an institution as well as a new struggle about the definition of the institution and whether it can include persons of the same sex.

Looking toward the future, marriage and divorce are likely to remain at the center of what has come to be called the "values" debate, which includes questions about the role of women in society, the centrality of marriage to social cohesion, and how marriage itself should be defined.

History: Marriage

Anthropologists contend that marriage originated in human society to serve two basic ends. One was to ensure that males would know who their progeny were; the second was to prevent socially corrosive competition among males over the most desirable women.

With the development of centralized and hierarchical civilizations, marriage evolved into a more formal institution. In the Babylonian Code of Hammurabi of the late third millennium B.C.E., one of the oldest extant legal codes, much attention was paid to marriage, which was essentially a financial arrangement. The husband would pay a bride price to the woman's father, who would then provide his daughter with a dowry. Once that was effectively negotiated, a legal contract was drawn up. Within a marriage, a woman was expected to be loyal—adultery was a capital crime—and the husband had complete control over the household, even to the point of being allowed to sell his wife or children to settle a debt. Nevertheless, the woman did not surrender her property rights, and she retained control over her dowry. Either party could initiate divorce, but there were stiff penalties to be paid by the person initiating it. Through the early modern era, with some variants, marriages secured by financial exchanges of goods and in which the wife remained subservient to the husband remained the norm throughout the Western world.

Another aspect of marriage in the ancient world—polygamy, or one man having multiple wives—did not survive in the West, however. The Code of Hammurabi allowed men to marry multiple wives, including their first wife's own maids, and very young girls, although the latter often could remain in their father's household until they reached maturity. This arrangement, in which a girl was betrothed without having any say in the decision, highlights another aspect of marriage in the ancient world: its role in establishing political alliances and strategic economic business partnerships among families. Much the same kind of arrangements existed in other, non-Western ancient civilizations, including those of India and China.

By the early Christian era in the West, marriage had taken on some aspects of its modern form; that is, it had increasingly become a bond between one man and one woman. Most theologians agree that the New Testament is largely devoid of personages with multiple wives, which may be a reflection of the Roman practices of the time. Such practices carried forward through the Middle Ages and into the early modern era.

Medieval Islamic marriage practices were much like contemporaneous practices of Christian Europe and of Confucian China. Marriage was considered too important a decision to be made by the young partners themselves, who might let emotion dictate their choices. In addition, to assure the virginity of the bride and a long period of fertility within marriage, girls as young as 12 or 13 were expected both to marry and to consummate the marriage. Islam's sanctioning of multiple wives—up to four, according to the Koran—remains open to some controversy. Islam's holy book speaks of multiple marriages being justified only where the husband can provide for perfect equality and justice among his various wives, an impossible task for imperfect humans. Still, the practice became widespread in early Islam, and it remains legal in virtually all majority-Muslim countries to this day, although it has increasingly gone out of favor in modern times.

Marriage along modern Western lines—that is, with partners courting and choosing one another and basing their relationship primarily on emotional affinity as opposed to financial and political considerations determined by family—is largely a product of the nineteenth century. The transition was the result of several parallel historical phenomena. The

first was the rise of romantic love as an ideal. While love for another is, of course, a human instinct, and certainly was a part of many marriage equations even in ancient times, it increasingly became the primary consideration in Western societies over the course of the nineteenth century and was idealized in popular culture. Obviously, this emphasis on love and compatibility shifted the primary decision making about whom one married from the family to the individual. Even when family and financial considerations still played a role, especially among the upper class, increasingly such considerations had to accommodate the romantic desires of the potential future newlyweds. With this change in priorities came shifts in the rituals of marriage as well. Negotiations between families gave way to courtship, and wedding-related activities became more personal, as indicated by the development of a new ritual, the honeymoon.

Meanwhile, urbanization and industrialization played their roles in this new type of marriage arrangement. With increased geographic mobility and the atomistic anonymity of city life, it became more and more difficult for families to exert control over the decision making of offspring. Moreover, success in this new world depended less on physical property—a key factor in arranged marriages—and more on intangible assets, such as education and skills. At first this new ideal of partner-determined marriage based on romantic love was largely a phenomenon of the urban middle classes of Europe, the United States, and other Western countries. By the twentieth century, however, it had become the norm among all classes.

Outside the West, however, more traditional ideals of marriage still held sway, at least through the latter part of the twentieth century. But cultural globalization spread Western values even as increased industrialization and urbanization in the developing world produced the same forces that had transformed marriage in the West a hundred years before. Again, the shift to partner-determined, romantically based marriage in the more rapidly modernizing parts of the developing world remains, even in the early twenty-first century, most prevalent among the urban middle classes. In rural areas and among more traditional sectors of the urban populace, arranged marriages based on family alliances remain the norm, particularly in Asian countries. Indeed, in many cultures, such as India's, such practices continue to be the norm even among the educated urban middle class—and, in fact, even among diaspora Indians living in Western countries. Nevertheless, in many cases, the two forms of marriage decision making live on simultaneously, with families playing a major role in the choice of marriage partners but also taking into consideration their offspring's desires.

History: Divorce

Divorce, meanwhile, has undergone a transformation over the past century or so, beginning in the West, although the most significant changes have largely been a product of the post–World War II era.

All cultures allow for some means by which persons can sever the bonds of matrimony, usually for a very specific and often legally determined causation—infertility, adultery, and abandonment being the primary considerations. In most ancient cultures, divorcing a partner was a relatively easy thing to achieve, particularly for men. But in the West, with the rise of Christianity, which reconceptualized marriage as an institution sanctioned by God, the barriers to breaking up a marriage became higher, making divorce increasingly socially unacceptable and rare. Islam and the faiths of Asia were more forgiving of divorce, although all insisted on specific causation and all made it easier for the husband than for the wife to break up a marriage.

In the West, at least, until the nineteenth century, divorce was kept relatively rare because it required a special dispensation from either ecclesiastical or civil authorities. That made it a complicated and expensive process, reserved only for those with money or power. Of course, lower-class persons who sought ways out of marriage could find them, through flight or simply by gaining the consensus of the community. It was only with the development of standardized procedures that formal divorce became a possibility for people of more modest economic backgrounds. The rise of romantic marriage played a role in this transformation: if a marriage was about emotional affinity, then one partner's disaffection undermined the validity of the marriage. In addition, changing attitudes about women—seeing a wife more as the partner rather than the property of her husband, contributed to the easing of divorce law. Between 1857 and 1937, for example, the United Kingdom passed laws regularizing divorce procedures and then allowing more and more causes for divorce—first adultery and eventually matters such as insanity and drunkenness.

The women's liberation movement and increased sexual permissiveness of the late 1960s, especially in the West, brought perhaps the most significant shifts in attitudes about divorce, leading to substantial changes in the law. More and more, various countries began to allow for what was called no-fault divorce, which allowed a single partner to choose to dissolve the marriage, without the consent of the other, and for such nonspecific reasons as—in the phrasing of a pioneering 1969 California law—"irreconcilable differences." Unsurprisingly, this liberalization of the law, along with changing social attitudes and the increasing economic independence of women, led to rapidly rising divorce rates. In the United Kingdom, which passed a law similar to California's in the same year, the rate climbed from one divorce for every 1,000 inhabitants in 1970 to 2.7 in 1990, a near-tripling. In France the rate climbed from 0.8 to 1.9 over the same period. Indeed, the increases might have been greater had it not been for another phenomenon of the period—the rise of persons living together out of wedlock, to be discussed below.

Statistical Summary

In the early twenty-first century, marriage and divorce rates vary widely around the world. As regards marriage, as observed above, the rates tend to be higher in developing-world countries than in developed-world countries. There are two primary reasons for this. The first is related to countries' demographics. Where there are more young persons in the population, as is the case in most developing-world countries, there is naturally going to be a higher rate of marriage. Thus, marriage rates in the Indian Ocean nation of Mauritius and the Islamic Republic of Iran are about twice those of many European countries. The second reason has to do with the fact that increasing numbers of persons in developed countries are choosing to live together, and even to have children, outside of formal wedlock, especially as laws are passed allowing such couples to enjoy many of the same legal rights and government benefits provided for married couples.

Divorce rates around the world vary far more widely than do marriage rates, because they tend to be more affected by country-specific legal and cultural factors. That is to say, marriage is a universally accepted institution, while divorce is not. In general, divorce rates tend to run in the two to three per 1,000 population range, or about half the rate of marriages, in most developed democracies, where

Marriage Rates per 1,000 Population, Selected Countries, 2006–2010

Country	2006	2007	2008	2009	2010
Argentina	3.5	3.5	3.3	3.1	n/a
Australia	5.5	5.5	5.5	5.5	n/a
Cuba	5.0	5.1	5.5	4.9	5.2
France	4.3	4.3	4.2	3.9	3.9
Germany	4.5	4.5	4.6	4.6	4.7
Iran	11.0	11.8	12.2	12.2	n/a
Italy	4.2	4.2	4.1	3.8	3.6
Japan	5.8	5.7	5.8	5.5	n/a
Kazakhstan	9.0	9.5	8.6	n/a	n/a
Korea, South	6.8	7.0	6.6	6.2	n/a
Mauritius	9.2	9.2	8.8	8.3	8.2
Poland	5.9	6.5	6.8	6.6	6.0
Russia	7.8	8.9	8.3	8.5	8.5
Turkey	9.2	9.1	9.0	8.2	7.9
United States	7.3	7.3	7.1	6.8	6.8

Source: UNdata.org.

Divorce Rates per 1,000 Population, Selected Countries, 2006–2010

Country	2006	2007	2008	2009	2010
Australia	2.5	2.3	2.2	2.3	n/a
Chile	0.2	0.1	0.1	n/a	n/a
Cuba	3.2	3.1	3.2	3.1	n/a
France	2.2	2.2	2.1	n/a	n/a
Germany	2.3	2.3	2.3	2.3	2.3
Iran	1.3	1.4	1.5	1.7	n/a
Italy	0.8	0.9	0.9	0.9	n/a
Japan	2.0	2.0	2.0	2.0	n/a
Kazakhstan	2.3	2.3	2.3	n/a	n/a
Korea, South	2.5	2.5	2.4	2.5	n/a
Mauritius	1.1	1.0	1.2	1.7	n/a
Poland	1.9	1.7	1.7	1.7	1.6
Russia	4.5	4.8	5.0	4.9	4.5
Turkey	1.3	1.3	1.4	1.6	1.6
United States	3.6	3.6	3.5	3.4	3.4

Source: UNdata.org.

laws and customs concerning divorce have become liberalized. There are exceptions to this. Strongly Catholic countries, such as Poland, Italy, and Chile, have lower rates, due to lingering cultural taboos and tougher laws about divorce. Muslim countries, such as Iran and Turkey, also have rates about half those of most developed countries. Even more striking is that while about half of all marriages in many Western countries end in divorce, just one in seven marriages in Iran and just one in five in Turkey end in divorce. This much lower rate is explained not just by lower divorce rates but also by the context of much higher marriage rates.

Critical Issues

As with all social institutions, marriage evolves over time, creating tensions between older and newer norms and practices. These, of course, differ among cultures. In more traditional societies, the evolution away from older ideas about marriage—that they should be arranged by families—is the source of such tensions. In modern societies the issues are twofold. One is the decline in formal marriage as people seek other "kinship" relationships. The other concerns the definition of marriage itself and whether it can include same-sex couples.

Arranged marriages are not particularly controversial in and of themselves in most countries or among groups that have it as the cultural norm. At the same time, human rights advocates, both local and international, have raised concerns when those arranged marriages involve minors, particularly girls and particularly those under the age of 15. The issue here is that such early marriages not only deprive the female partner of choice in a lifelong mate but also deprive her of a proper education. While declining around the world, such arranged marriages of girls remain prevalent in sub-Saharan Africa and South Asia. The rates are particularly high in the Sahel region of sub-Saharan Africa, where roughly one-third of all girls under the age of 15 are already in a marital union and another third are married by age 18, many of them to men much older than themselves. In Bangladesh the figures are much the same, while those for India are approximately 20 percent for those under 15 and another 25 percent for those between 15 and 17 years of age.

In the developed world, the institution of marriage is undergoing fundamental change. First, it is becoming less common. The divorce rates cited above are one factor, but so is the fact that people are tending to get married later in life. In the United States, a not-atypical example for the developed world, the average age for marriage is currently about 26 for women and about 28 for men, for both sexes up by about five years from the average age at marriage in 1960. Economics is critical here, since the need for education and other career considerations cause many to postpone marriage and children. In addition, it is becoming more costly to set up a household, another reason to delay marriage. Yet another factor contributing to lower rates of marriage is that another option—cohabitation—has gained more cultural acceptance throughout the developed world in recent decades. That trend is particularly noticeable in Scandinavia. In Norway, for example, people aged 20 to 34 are just as likely to be cohabiting as to be married, with the percentage of each at about 25 percent. Moreover, these couples are also having children at roughly the same rate, about 6 out of 10.

Even as marriage has been declining among heterosexuals in much of the developed world, it has been gaining acceptance as an institution open to same-sex couples. As of early 2012, 13 countries permitted same-sex marriage, either completely or in some jurisdictions, with all but three of these—Argentina, Mexico (where it is permitted in the Federal District only), and South Africa—in either Europe or North America. A dozen years earlier, there were no countries that allowed for same-sex marriage.

The Future

The institution of marriage will, most sociologists agree, continue to evolve over time. Modernization and economic growth in the developing world, as well as a growing consensus about the rights of women, is likely to continue to shift marriage decisions away from families and toward the partners themselves. Similarly, attitudes about women's subservience to their husbands within families are likely to evolve toward more equal relationships, especially as current trends favoring more women being educated accelerate in coming decades.

In the developed world, the trends toward later marriages, higher divorce rates, and higher rates of cohabitation—all factors leading to fewer marriages —appear to have peaked in the 1990s and have even experienced some minor reverses in some countries. Still, these countries are unlikely to revert to the high marriage rates that characterized the early post–World War II period. It also seems likely that gay marriage will become more accepted and widespread.

Changes in such a fundamental institution have produced a backlash, particularly from more traditionalist sectors of society, in both the developed and developing worlds, as the resistance to gay marriage in the United States, among other countries, reveals. But as polls around the world consistently show, young people are far more accepting of new ideas of marriage, divorce, cohabitation, and same-sex marriage than are their more elderly compatriots, promising that while the changes in the institution of marriage outlined above may meet resistance and proceed in a halting manner, they are unlikely to be reversed to any significant extent.

James Ciment

See also: Domestic Violence; Gay, Lesbian, Bisexual, and Transgender Issues; Population Growth and Demographic Issues; Women's Rights.

Further Reading

Abbott, Elizabeth. *A History of Marriage: From Same Sex Unions to Private Vows and Common Law, the Surprising Diversity of a Tradition.* New York: Seven Stories, 2011.

Andress, Hans-Jürgen, and Dina Hummelsheim, eds. *When Marriage Ends: Economic and Social Consequences of Partnership Dissolution.* Northampton, MA: Edward Elgar, 2009.

Blankenhorn, David. *The Future of Marriage.* New York: Encounter, 2009.

Coontz, Stephanie. *Marriage, a History: From Obedience to Intimacy or How Love Conquered Marriage.* New York: Viking, 2005.

Corvino, John, and Maggie Gallagher. *Debating Same-Sex Marriage.* New York: Oxford University Press, 2012.

Crouse, Janice Shaw. *Marriage Matters: Perspectives on the Private and Public Importance of Marriage.* New Brunswick, NJ: Transaction, 2012.

Phillips, Roderick. *Untying the Knot: A Short History of Divorce.* New York: Cambridge University Press, 1991.

Simon, Rita J., and Howard Altstein. *Global Perspectives on Social Issues: Marriage and Divorce.* Lanham, MD: Lexington Books, 2003.

Web Sites

Alliance for Marriage: www.allianceformarriage.org

Human Rights Campaign: www.hrc.org

United Nations Population Division: www.un.org/esa/population

Documents

Document 1: *Book of Common Prayer*, The Celebration and Blessing of a Marriage (excerpt), 1549

The Book of Common Prayer, *actually a series of prayer books, was first promulgated in 1549 by the Church of England shortly after its break with the Catholic Church of Rome. The work provided instructions for various liturgies and sacraments, including that of Holy Matrimony. The following excerpt is The Celebration and Blessing of a Marriage, with instructions on what participants must say (in regular script) and do (in italics). In altered form, it remains the standard for church weddings throughout the English-speaking world to the present day.*

At the time appointed, the persons to be married, with their witnesses, assemble in the church or some other appropriate place.

During their entrance, a hymn, psalm, or anthem may be sung, or instrumental music may be played.

Then the Celebrant, facing the people and the persons to be married, with the woman to the right and the man to the left, addresses the congregation and says

Dearly beloved: We have come together in the presence of God to witness and bless the joining together of this man and this woman in Holy Matrimony. The bond and covenant of marriage was established by God in creation, and our Lord Jesus Christ adorned this manner of life by his presence and first miracle at a wedding in Cana of Galilee. It signifies to us the mystery of the union between Christ and his Church, and Holy Scripture commends it to be honored among all people.

The union of husband and wife in heart, body, and mind is intended by God for their mutual joy; for the help and comfort given one another in prosperity and adversity; and, when it is God's will, for the procreation of children and their nurture in the knowledge and love of the Lord. Therefore marriage is not to be entered into unadvisedly or lightly, but reverently, deliberately, and in accordance with the purposes for which it was instituted by God.

Into this holy union N.N.. and N.N.. now come to be joined. If any of you can show just cause why they may not lawfully be married, speak now; or else for ever hold your peace.

Then the Celebrant says to the persons to be married

I require and charge you both, here in the presence of God, that if either of you know any reason why you may not be united in marriage lawfully, and in accordance with God's Word, you do now confess it.

The Declaration of Consent

The Celebrant says to the woman

N., will you have this man to be your husband; to live together in the covenant of marriage? Will you love him, comfort him, honor and keep him, in sickness and in health; and, forsaking all others, be faithful to him as long as you both shall live?

The Woman answers
    I will.

The Celebrant says to the man

N., will you have this woman to be your wife; to live together in the covenant of marriage? Will you love her, comfort her, honor and keep her, in sickness and in health; and, forsaking all others, be faithful to her as long as you both shall live?

The Man answers
    I will.

The Celebrant then addresses the congregation, saying

Will all of you witnessing these promises do all in your power to uphold these two persons in their marriage?

People   We will.

Source: The (Online) Book of Common Prayer.

Document 2: Defense of Marriage Act, United States, 1996

While marriage has been an evolving institution for thousands of years, marriage between persons of the same sex is a relatively new phenomenon, dating back to the gay rights movement of the late twentieth century. More than any other change to the institution of marriage, including the easing of divorce laws, gay marriage has sparked controversy, particularly among conservatives and those professing strong religious beliefs. In the United States, the prospect of states legalizing gay marriage prompted Congress in 1996 to pass the Defense of Marriage Act, or DOMA, which stated that no state should be bound to recognize a same-sex marriage performed in any other jurisdiction within the United States.

Public Law 104–199
104th Congress

An Act
To define and protect the institution of marriage.

SECTION 1. SHORT TITLE.
This Act may be cited as the "Defense of Marriage Act'.'

SEC. 2. POWERS RESERVED TO THE STATES.
    (a) IN GENERAL.—Chapter 115 of title 28, United States Code, is amended by adding after section 1738B the following:

"**§ 1738C. Certain acts, records, and proceedings and the effect thereof**

"No State, territory, or possession of the United States, or Indian tribe, shall be required to give effect to any public act, record, or judicial proceeding of any other State, territory, possession, or tribe respecting a relationship between persons of the same sex that is treated as a marriage under the laws of such other State, territory, possession, or tribe, or a right or claim arising from such relationship.'

(b) CLERICAL AMENDMENT.—The table of sections at the beginning of chapter 115 of title 28, United States Code, is amended by inserting after the item relating to section 1738B the following new item:

"1738C. Certain acts, records, and proceedings and the effect thereof.'.'

SEC. 3. DEFINITION OF MARRIAGE.

(a) IN GENERAL.—Chapter 1 of title 1, United States Code, is amended by adding at the end the following:

"**§ 7. Definition of 'marriage' and 'spouse'**

"In determining the meaning of any Act of Congress, or of any ruling, regulation, or interpretation of the various administrative bureaus and agencies of the United States, the word 'marriage' means only a legal union between one man and one woman as husband and wife, and the word 'spouse' refers only to a person of the opposite sex who is a husband or a wife.'.'

(b) CLERICAL AMENDMENT.—The table of sections at the beginning of chapter 1 of title 1, United States Code, is amended by inserting after the item relating to section 6 the following new item:

"7. Definition of 'marriage' and 'spouse.".'

Approved September 21, 1996.

Source: U.S. Government Printing Office.

MENTAL HEALTH

Although in the past, mental health was defined as the absence of mental illness or behavioral problems, most mental-health professionals today define it in more positive terms, as the psychological state of a person who is at a satisfactory level of emotional function and behavioral adjustment.

Scholars and doctors have noted the phenomenon of mental illness—and have suggested causes and possible cures—since at least the second millennium B.C.E. Over the centuries, and particularly since the nineteenth century, the diagnosis and treatment of mental disorders have become scientifically based and have resulted in a variety of therapies, including talk therapy and pharmaceuticals.

Today, many biological and environmental causes are acknowledged to play a role in both mental health and mental illness. Various cultures have different attitudes about mental illness, and so treatment regimens, or the lack thereof, vary from society to society. Attitudes and treatment have also varied over time. In addition, such pragmatic factors as accessibility and cost also play a role in determining the kind of treatment a sufferer receives, or if he or she receives any treatment at all.

People with mental illness suffer from a wide range of problems, from depression to social isolation to imprisonment for bad behavior. Societies also suffer a cost from mental illness, paid in lost productivity, crime, and familial dysfunction, among others. Looking toward the future, most experts believe that mental-health issues are likely to play an even more important role in society and policy-making circles than they have in the past.

Definition, Causes, and Extent

A consensus has emerged among mental health-care professionals that the definition of mental health as the absence of mental illness no longer suffices. The World Health Organization (WHO) takes such an approach. Its constitution defines health in general as "a state of complete physical, mental, and social well-being and not merely the absence of disease or infirmity." The organization goes on to define mental health for policy-making purposes "as a state of well-being in which every individual realizes his or her own potential, can cope with the normal stresses of life, can work productively and fruitfully, and is able to make a contribution to her or his community."

Most mental illnesses fall into six general categories: addiction or impulse control disorders, anxiety disorders, eating disorders, mood disorders, psychotic disorders, and personality disorders. Arguably, the most serious of these are psychotic disorders, such as schizophrenia, in which the sufferer experiences hallucinations and delusions. Perhaps the most serious with respect to physical health are eating disorders, such as bulimia and anorexia nervosa, in which sufferers refuse to eat food or voluntarily regurgitate, out of mistaken perceptions of body weight. Anxiety disorders range in seriousness and include panic disorders, social anxiety disorders, some forms of obsessive-compulsive disorders, and post-traumatic stress disorders (PTSDs). Impulse control and addiction disorders are typically associated with the excessive use of alcohol and drugs but can also refer to pathological or antisocial behaviors, such as stealing (kleptomania), setting fires (pyromania), and even excessive gambling. Personality disorders are characterized by extreme and inflexible personality traits, such as certain forms of obsessive-compulsive disorders, milder forms of paranoia, and a general inability to cope with changing social situations. Mood, or affective, disorders are marked by periods of extreme sadness not specifically associated with tragedies in life (depression) and mood swings from extreme depression and low energy to states of euphoria and high energy (mania). Less-common disorders include dissociative disorders, marked by loss of memory and even multiple or split personalities, tic disorders, sexual or gender disorders, and

As in other developing nations, care and facilities at Nicaragua's National Psychiatric Hospital in Managua deteriorated during the global financial crisis of the 2000s. Often stigmatized or abused, the mentally ill in poorer countries tend to receive little or no care. *(AP Photo/Esteban Felix)*

adjustment disorders, or the inability to cope with tragedy or trauma.

Mental-health problems occur in all societies, cultures, and countries. But determining how common they are in various parts of the world is rendered nearly impossible by the simple fact that measuring mental illness occurrence is a matter of measuring the number of people seeking treatment. Because most people in the world live in societies where such facilities are in short supply, if they exist at all, it is difficult to ascertain how many people might make use of them if they were available. Moreover, in most cultures, mental-health problems still carry serious stigmas that would prevent people from seeking help. That said, most countries of the developed world do have extensive mental-health facilities and, especially in recent decades, lower levels of stigma attached to those who seek them out. Thus, one can get a very rough sense of how often mental illness occurs by examining these numbers. About 1,800 out of 100,000 population in high-income countries seek outpatient care for mental-health problems annually, while about 175 are admitted to inpatient hospital beds reserved for psychiatric patients.

Mental-health disorders have both biological and environmental causes; sometimes they are triggered by a combination of the two. Biological factors include genetic predispositions to mental illness, pathogens that trigger mental illness, age-related issues, such as puberty or menopause, and chemical changes caused by substance abuse. Environmental factors are almost too numerous to count but fall into two general categories: those involving major social disruptions, such as war, natural disaster, and economic depression, and those involving personal stressors, such as being the victim of rape or assault, familial troubles, such as divorce, stress on the job, financial worries, and the loss of a loved one. In some cases, stressful and traumatic situations trigger latent organic factors, such as genetic predispositions, which helps to explain why some people experience more profound mental disorders in the wake of major social disruptions or personal stressors than others experiencing the same thing.

History

As animal behaviorists have noted, many higher-order animals, including primates, experience mental-health problems. Not surprisingly, then, mental health and mental illness have likely been part of human experience since the origin of the species.

Thinkers and writers in many ancient cultures catalogued various mental disorders and tried to explain their causes. The ancient Greek physician Hippocrates of the fifth and fourth centuries B.C.E. suggested three basic mental disorders: melancholia (what today would be described as affective disorders), mania (a variety of behavioral disorders), and phrenitis, which was really more physical than mental, as its main symptoms were the delirium and headaches associated with high fevers. Hippocrates also listed a number of phobias. Hindu scriptures from as early as the seventh century B.C.E. speak of depression and anxiety, while Chinese texts going back to the first millennium B.C.E. list a host of ailments now considered mental in nature. Various traditions ascribed various causes to these illnesses, some physical and some metaphysical. For Hippocrates, mental illness, like its physical counterpart, was associated with imbalances in the four humors of the body—blood, yellow bile, black bile, and phlegm. Chinese conceptions of the bodily energies of yin and yang also led to conclusions that an imbalance of these led to illness, both mental and physical. But supernatural causes were also associated with mental illness—spirits, magic, the wrath of the gods, and so on. Similarly, treatments often included efforts to alleviate physical symptoms, such as the ingestion of potions or the application of ointments, though these were sometimes also meant to address the more metaphysical causes of the disease.

Greek ideas focusing on the physical causes of mental illness pervaded thinking in the medieval Arabic world, a leader in medical understanding at the time, and that of Christian Europe, though, especially in the latter, supernatural causes, such as satanic possession, were also seen as the cause of particularly severe disorders, including schizophrenia. By the time of the Enlightenment in seventeenth- and eighteenth-century Europe, the prevailing view tended toward physical causation. But this did not necessarily lead to enlightened treatment, as most thinkers associated mental illness with uncontrolled animal passions. Thus, those who had a mental illness were sent to asylums, where beatings and other measures to control such passions were applied liberally. Industrialization and urbanization were accompanied by more bureaucratization in the classification and treatment of mental illness, with various laws and procedures put in place to confine people for serious mental disorders, though under somewhat more humane conditions following the work of reformers, such as America's Dorothea Dix. Those who suffered from lesser mental disorders—a common one in nineteenth-century Europe and America was hysteria, especially among women—were often treated with medications aimed at the symptoms rather than the cause of the disorder, such as laudanum, a mix of alcohol and opium, that sedated the patient.

In the late nineteenth and early twentieth centuries, the first major breakthroughs were made in the diagnosis of mental illness since the ancient Greeks. Of these breakthroughs, arguably the most important were made by Sigmund Freud, the Austrian father of modern psychotherapy, who argued that mental illness was primarily a problem associated with the ego,

which communicated impulses from the id, or source of basic drives, such as sex, and the conscious superego. Treatment advanced as well, though the asylum model continued to be used for the most seriously disturbed. In 1938, psychiatrists introduced electroshock therapy (now known as electro-convulsive therapy, or ECT), in which jolts of electricity were applied to the brain. For lesser disorders, such as depression, the Freud-inspired talk therapy model became the standard for treatment, as it brought up the causes of the depression, which allowed patients to change their thinking and behavior to better cope with the illness. But there were also less positive developments, such as the movement to reduce the presence of the mentally ill through sterilization and euthanasia programs.

As was the case with physical illness, in the post–World War II era, great advances were made in the treatment of mental illness, even though the diagnoses remained anchored in the work of earlier theorists and clinicians, such as Freud, the Swiss psychiatrist Carl Jung, and the American Clifford Beers, founder of the so-called mental hygiene movement. Growing recognition of the importance of mental health and its treatment are evinced in the establishment of various laws and institutions, both governmental and non-governmental, to regulate treatment, including the World Federation for Mental Health in Europe (1946) and the National Institute of Mental Health in the United States (1949). Perhaps more far-reaching were the development in the 1950s of the first antipsychotic and mood-altering drugs, such as Thorazine for schizophrenia and Librium and valium for anxiety disorders; lithium could be used for the treatment of mood disorders, but it was not approved for use in the United States until 1970.

Since the 1960s, several trends have emerged in the diagnosis and treatment of mental illness. The first is the development of various forms of emotional, or talk, therapy treatments, some of which (e.g., cognitive therapy for minor disorders) rely less on retrieving hidden traumas and memories (as in Freudian therapy) than on identifying coping mechanisms for day-to-day life. The second is the development of a panoply of drugs for both serious mental disorders and less severe mood disorders. The most notable of the drugs for minor disorders is fluoxetine, better known by the brand name Prozac, a treatment for depression, which received regulatory approval in many countries in the 1980s. The introduction of new and more effective drugs, particularly antipsychotics, along with more enlightened attitudes about mental illness and the rights of those who suffer from it, and concerns about the costs associated with large-scale psychiatric hospitals led to yet another major development in the postwar period: the wholesale de-institutionalization of the residents of those hospitals. These patients, including those suffering from schizophrenia, were released from their institutional confinement to rejoin society, with effective medications but not the services to support them in living independently. Third, certain forms of behavior formerly listed as mental disorders, most notably, homosexuality, were reclassified, first by the psychiatric profession and then by much of the public, as, variously, non-disorders, within the realm of normal behavior, or simple lifestyle choices.

Impact and Treatment

People who have a mental disorder often suffer several types of ill effects. First are the symptoms and effects of the disease itself, in terms of a lower quality of life because of a diminished or altered mental capacity and negative physical effects, ranging from a lack of energy associated with depression to the serious physical repercussions of eating and addictive disorders to the self-inflicted injuries that often accompany manic and psychotic disorders.

The mentally ill also experience indirect effects. Although the social stigma attached to mental illness has diminished somewhat, particularly in the developed world, discrimination and social isolation are still hallmarks of society's reaction to mental disorders, particularly those that are more severe. Such discrimination can contribute to problems, as when people are denied housing or employment. So prevalent are these stigmas and discrimination that the World Health Organization has made addressing and eliminating such attitudes a key part of the mental health-care model programs that it offers to member countries.

Meanwhile, the impact of mental illness is felt not only by those who experience it but also those with whom they have relationships or even just encounters. Families in which one member has mental illness experience higher rates of divorce, abandonment, and domestic violence, especially when alcohol and drugs are involved.

Society suffers as well, both in direct and indirect ways. Impulse, addictive, anxiety, and psychotic disorders can lead to crimes ranging from shoplifting

Mental Health Expenditures per Capita, Countries by Income Level, 2011

Income level	Median spending on mental health per capita	Percentage of health budget spent on mental health
Low (less than $1,000 per capita)	$0.20	0.53
Middle ($1,000–$4,000)	$0.59	1.90
Upper-middle ($4,000–$12,000)	$3.76	2.38
High (more than $12,000)	$44.84	5.10

Source: World Health Organization.

Expenditures on Mental Health Medication, Countries by Income Level, 2011

Income level	Spending on mental health medication*
Low (less than $1,000 per capita)	$1,700
Middle ($1,000–$4,000)	$17,200
Upper-middle ($4,000–$12,000)	$82,700
High (more than $12,000)	$2,630,500

* Median per 100,000 population.
Source: World Health Organization.

(kleptomania) to armed robbery (associated with those suffering addiction to narcotics) to suicide and homicide in the case of PTSD and schizophrenia, along with rarer forms of extreme psychotic and sociopathic behavior. Moreover, sizable financial resources are committed annually to mental-health treatment, particularly in the developed world. It has been estimated that in the United States, spending on mental health accounts for about 6.2 percent of the $2.5 trillion spent on health care annually, or about $155 billion; indirect costs include lost productivity and earnings. One study from 2008 has estimated that earnings for a person with a serious mental disorder are reduced by about $16,000. Other studies estimate that about 22 percent of prisoners in the country suffer from mental-health problems, adding to direct and indirect costs there. The study found that mental-health problems cost the U.S. economy about $320 billion in direct and indirect costs, or about $1,000 per person.

As noted earlier, mental-health disorders have both biological and environmental causes, such as trauma associated with natural disasters and war. Although such trauma can occur anywhere—as inhabitants of the Tohoku coast of Japan suffered from widespread PTSD after the devastating earthquake and tsunami of 2011—wartime trauma typically affects

Mental-Health Facilities and Patients, per 100,000 Population, Countries by Income Level, 2011

Income level	Outpatient facilities (median)	Annual number of outpatients	Psychiatric beds in hospitals (median)	Annual admission rates to psychiatric beds
Low (less than $1,000 per capita)	0.04	48	0.60	6.0
Middle ($1,000–$4000)	0.29	271	0.40	5.7
Upper-middle ($4,000–$12,000)	1.05	861	2.70	36.6
High (more than $12,000)	2.32	1,829	13.6	175.4

Source: World Health Organization.

Mental-Health Professionals, per 100,000 Population, Countries by Income Level, 2011

Income level	Psychiatrists	Other mental-health doctors	Mental-health nurses	Psychologists	Social workers	Occupational therapists
Low (less than $1,000 per capita)	0.01	0.47	1.34	0.02	0.01	0.00*
Middle ($1,000–$4,000)	0.04	2.47	4.88	0.03	0.00*	0.00*
Upper middle ($4,000–$12,000)	0.08	5.33	5.53	0.15	0.00*	0.00*
High (more than $12,000)	0.30	8.67	19.35	2.15	4.10	0.75
World	0.04	3.34	5.15	0.09	0.01	0.00*

*rounded down
Source: World Health Organization.

poor countries. Civil wars, in particular, often lead to horrendous acts of brutality inflicted on a civilian population, which can suffer PTSD. Combatants suffer as well, as evidenced by the many U.S. and NATO veterans of the Iraqi and Afghanistan conflicts experiencing PTSD and, even more tragically, by the traumas suffered by the thousands of child soldiers recruited for a number of African conflicts in recent decades. Reintegrating them into the societies they often terrorized requires addressing their mental-health issues.

Moreover, funding, facilities, and professionals for mental-health treatment are often in short supply in the low- and middle-income countries that experienced some of the worst conflicts in the late twentieth and early twenty-first centuries. On average, low-income countries spend about 220 times less on mental health than high-income countries while middle-income countries spend about 70 times less. Low-income countries have less than 5 percent of the psychiatric beds in hospitals that high-income countries do and more than 60 times fewer outpatient clinics. Meanwhile, low-income countries have 300 times fewer psychiatrists and more than 100 times fewer psychologists. And, as most in the field note, the facilities and the training of these mental-health professionals are usually of poorer quality in low- and middle-income countries.

The Future

As is the case with so much else in health care, the future presents a mixed picture for those with mental illness and their prospects for receiving effective treatment. On the positive side, continued economic growth, particularly in middle- and upper-middle-income countries, will provide some of the resources necessary to address the problem. In addition, better education, also a result of economic growth, can help dispel some of the existing prejudice and stigma attached to mental illness and ease the isolation and discrimination experienced by those who suffer from mental disorders. Less-expensive pharmaceuticals, including generics and illegal counterfeits produced in developing-world countries, such as India and Brazil, will allow more of the mentally ill to receive cost-effective treatment. On the downside, continuing fiscal difficulties are leading to cuts in mental-health treatment in many developed-world countries, which has caused many insurers to switch patients from the more expensive talk therapy to less expensive drug regimes, even as rapid population growth in some parts of the developing world places an increasing burden on the health-care system generally and mental health-care facilities specifically.

James Ciment

See also: Alcohol Use and Abuse; Disability Rights; Drug Abuse; Neurological Disease; Public Health; Suicide.

Further Reading

Avison, William R., Jane D. McLeod, and Bernice A. Pescosolido, eds. *Mental Health, Social Mirror*. New York: Springer, 2007.

Bährer-Kohler, Sabine, ed. *Social Determinants and Mental Health*. Hauppauge, NY: Nova Science, 2011.

Cohen, Alex, Arthur Kleinman, and Benedetto Saraceno, eds. *World Mental Health Casebook: Social and Mental Health Programs in Low-Income Countries*. New York: Kluwer Academic/Plenum, 2002.

Kahn, Ada P., and Jan Fawcett. *The Encyclopedia of Mental Health*. New York: Facts On File, 2008.

McKenzie, Kwame, and Trudy Harpham, eds. *Social Capital and Mental Health*. Philadelphia: Jessica Kingsley, 2006.

Pilgrim, David, Anne Rogers, and Bernice Pescosolido, eds. *The SAGE Handbook of Mental Health and Illness*. Los Angeles: Sage, 2011.

Porter, Roy, and David Wright, eds. *The Confinement of the Insane: International Perspectives, 1800–1965*. New York: Cambridge University Press, 2003.

Tew, Jerry. *Social Approaches to Mental Distress*. Basingstoke, Hampshire, UK: Palgrave Macmillan, 2011.

World Health Organization. *Mental Health Atlas 2011*. Geneva: World Health Organization, 2011.

Web Sites

National Institute of Mental Health: www.nimh.nih.gov

World Federation for Mental Health: www.wfmh.org

World Health Organization, Mental Health: www.who.int/mental_health/en/

Documents

Document 1: Report of the Metropolitan Commissioners in Lunacy to the Lord Chancellor (excerpt), United Kingdom, 1844

Mental illness, or lunacy as it was once called, was once a topic largely banished from polite conversation in the West. By the mid-nineteenth century, however, reformers had raised public awareness of the cause of mental illness sufferers and the conditions of the asylums in which they were placed. As noted in this report from the British Metropolitan Commissioners in Lunacy, such asylums presented a varying degree of humanity and professionalism. However, asylums established by various government entities for the poor were almost uniformly awful, as this description of the facility at Haverfordwest indicates.

The Asylum at Haverfordwest was first visited by the Commissioners on the 13th of September, 1842. Their Report states that this Asylum was formerly a small gaol [jail], for the criminals of the town, but was (in 1822), by virtue of an Act of Parliament, appropriated to the reception of Lunatics. It did not appear that any addition or alteration whatever had been made, so as to adapt it to the accommodation of patients. On the contrary, all the cells and rooms were apparently in their original condition, not even windows having been added, except in the part which faces the public street.

The Asylum, at that time, (1842,) contained eighteen Patients, nine being Males and nine Females; and the Corporation of Haverfordwest contracted with a person to supply the Patients with food and other necessaries. The Commissioners felt it their duty to report that the Asylum was deficient in every comfort, and almost in every convenience; the rooms being small and ill ventilated, some of the lower rooms (originally cells for Prisoners), being almost dark, and the interior of the Asylum altogether out of repair. The two day rooms, in which the less violent Patients were confined, (one having seven Males and the other five Females), each measured about twelve feet by nine feet: the floors were of soft stone, but parts of it (in the Female ward considerable parts), had been torn up and destroyed. There was no seat, or table, or any article of furniture in the Women's Room, and nothing, except a table, in the Men's Room. The Men were standing; the Women standing or sitting on the floor. On the circumstance being noticed by the Commissioners, a long board or seat was brought into the Men's Room from the airing-ground, and fixed against the wall. It was not sufficient for the seven Male Patients who were in the room to sit on. Four of the Men, however, sat down on it; the others remained standing. In the airing-ground belonging to the Women, there was a bench, which apparently belonged to their Room. There were large holes in some of the walls and ceilings. The airing-courts were very small and cheerless, particularly that belonging to the Men, and they were both strewn with large stones, which had fallen or been forced from the Building. There were two mischievous Patients, unrestrained, amongst the Men, (in whose hands these stones might be formidable weapons,) and another fastened in a chair, in a separate room or cell.

The dress of the Patients was, in almost every Bad state of instance, dirty, ragged, and insufficient. One of the Female Patients pulled off her shoes and stockings, which were nothing more than rags, such as are occasionally seen on heaps of rubbish. The Commissioners were informed that there was not a single change of linen (either for the beds or for the person), throughout the Asylum. This fact was complained of by the Matron. Indeed, the Commissioners could not discover any linen whatever, except upon the persons of some of the Patients, and the dirty cases of the straw beds, throughout the House. There were only sixteen single beds for the eighteen Patients confined in the Asylum. One Patient (a Boy of nineteen) slept on loose straw, on the stone floor, in a small dark cell; and one other Patient (a Girl), who was convalescent, slept in the same room with the Keeper and his Wife, on a bed belonging to them. She must otherwise have slept upon the floor, and apparently without Restraint.

The Commissioners caused many of the beds to be uncovered, and found that there were no sheets or blankets, and little more than a single rug to cover the Patients. In more than one instance, the scrap of blanket (allowed in addition to the rug) was insufficient to cover half the person. The beds were of straw, and almost all of them were inclosed in coarse linen cases; but although there were several dirty Patients, there was not more than one case for each bed. Some of the cases were soiled, and all of them appeared dark, as if from long use. The Matron stated that she had applied repeatedly for more bed-clothes and for linen, but without effect; the Contractor would not send them. She complained to the Commissioners, that the state of the Asylum (in reference to its want of repair, comfort, and accommodation, and the destitute condition of the Patients) was dreadful; and she expressed her earnest hope that some person would speedily interfere on behalf of "the poor creatures confined there."

In regard to restraint, the Commissioners found that no belts, hand-locks, or strait-jackets were allowed, but the refractory Patients were confined in strong chairs, their arms being also fastened to the chair. Two were thus confined, separately, in small rooms, into which scarcely any light entered through the gratings. One was the Boy before mentioned, who slept at night on the floor of the same room; the other was a Woman who was entirely naked, on both the days on which the Commissioners visited the Asylum, and without doubt during the whole of the intermediate night. Both these were dirty Patients. In the Woman's room, the stench was so offensive, that it was scarcely possible to remain there.

During wet weather, there was no place whatever for exercise; and at other times there was not sufficient space for the purpose. No attempt was made to employ any of the Patients, and no books or other amusements were provided. Prayers were never read, and no Clergyman ever visited the Asylum, although one of the Female Patients, who was occasionally depressed, and imagined that she had not done her duty to a child who had died, appeared especially to require such consolation as a Clergyman might afford.

The Keeper and his Wife (the Matron) appeared well-disposed towards the Patients, but they were themselves scarcely above the rank of Paupers. They were allowed the same rations as the Pauper Patients, and a salary of 201 [pounds] a year, between them. They had no assistant or servant, for the purpose of keeping the Asylum or the Patients clean, for cooking the food, for baking the bread, or for any other purpose connected with the Establishment. At our first visit, the Keeper was absent. The Commissioners were informed that he was at work for some person in the neighbourhood.

The Patients were allowed water only for their drink; culm and clay for firing; straw (chopped and whole) for the beds—of the clean as well as of the dirty. The bread was dark and heavy, and was made of barley-meal and wheaten flour. The Matron said that the yeast allowed was insufficient, and that the oven was out of repair, and that consequently she could not make the bread good or wholesome. She had repeatedly complained of these things without effect.

As evidence of the spirit in which this establishment was upheld, the Commissioners were informed that a few years ago a person was directed by Government to examine the buildings constituting the Asylum, and that, some notice being had of his expected arrival, work- men were employed during the whole of the preceding night upon the repairs, so that when the Governmen[t] Agent visited the building in the morning, he found it Undergoing repair. These repairs, however, were discontinued immediately after the Agent left the Asylum . . .

Source: Internet Archive.

Document 2: *Mental Health Atlas 2011,* World Health Organization, 2011

*Mental-health issues are a global problem; no country or society is immune. But as detailed in the World Health Organization's most recent assessment of mental health care around the world—*Mental Health Atlas 2011—*the difference in resources devoted to the problem between low- and high-income countries is immense. Even beyond the allocation of resources, according to the report, there are major shortcomings in countries that have mental health-care plans in place—let alone those that do not. Indeed, the number of countries without a mental health-care policy actually declined in the six years since the previous report—from 64 percent of countries in 2005 to 62 percent in 2011.*

http://whqlibdoc.who.int/publications/2011/9799241564359_eng.pdf

Source: World Health Organization.

MIGRANT LABOR

Migrant labor can be defined in several ways. The term may refer to persons working in a country other than their own, persons who travels to another country for work but do not become citizens of that country for various reasons, or persons who travel from place to place in search of work, usually in the agricultural sector, inside one country.

Migrant labor has a long history but became an important component of the global economy in the nineteenth century. Today, most migrant workers travel from developing countries or regions to work in more developed regions or countries, or in countries with resource wealth. Migrant laborers are critical to the economies of the countries where they work and, in the form of remittances and other benefits, the countries that they have left.

Migrant laborers, however, face a number of legal, political, economic, and social problems. They are often paid poorly, have few rights, exist in a legal limbo that makes them vulnerable to exploitation, and suffer from any number of social ills, including poor access to health care and education, among others.

With populations of the developing world expanding; economic gaps between rich and poor nations remaining high; and globalization and technology knitting the world closer together, migrant labor is only likely to become more significant in coming decades, forcing sending and receiving countries, as well as the international community, to come up with strategies to make the existence of these workers more tolerable.

History

People have left their homelands to find work for millennia. For most of human history, this was done by force, with workers becoming slaves in their new environs. Such was the case as far back as the ancient civilizations before the Common Era and as recently as the nineteenth-century trans-Atlantic world.

With the conquest of the Americas, the near decimation of its indigenous population, and the development of commercial agriculture in the New World from the sixteenth century onward, came the need for large numbers of migrant workers, usually in the form of slaves but also as indentured servants, who were required to work for a period of years to pay for their passage and other costs.

But only with the development of modern transportation systems and a fully integrated globalized economy in the nineteenth century did the large-scale migration of workers come into being, especially in the wake of slavery's demise in the Americas and other parts of the European colonial world during the middle and latter years of the century.

While emancipation ended the forced recruitment of labor, migration of nonslave workers was not entirely voluntary. Many European regimes imposed various forms of taxes, requiring payment in cash. The only way to get such cash was to go to work on commercial plantations and other labor-intensive enterprises, such as mines. Other migrants, however, were drawn into the commercial economy by the lure of imported goods available only to those with money. Both forces led to the mass migration of African laborers to the mines of South Africa from the late nineteenth century, for example.

The immediate post-emancipation period in Africa also saw the imposition of economic regimes that barely differed from slavery. In the Congo Free State, actually a virtual personal fiefdom of Belgium's King Leopold II, millions of central Africans were forced from their villages to tap rubber trees in the rainforest around the turn of the twentieth century. French colonial administrators and others imposed corvées labor, the temporary recruitment of labor gangs to work on public projects, usually as an alternative to paying taxes.

In other regions, economic modernization—typically in the form of land reforms that displaced peasants—created the push that led people into migrant labor. Such was the case in Latin America, where hundreds of thousands of workers were lured to the plantations and ranches of Brazil and Argentina in the late nineteenth century or, in the case of Mexicans, to the United States. Much of the latter came under the auspices of the Bracero Program, a federal program that allowed the importation of Mexican farmworkers into the American Southwest on temporary permits during the early and middle years of the twentieth century.

From Asia came the so-called coolie trade, or migration of Indian, Chinese, and other Asian laborers under set contracts to the far-flung corners of the British and other empires. The term "coolie" is believed to have derived from the Kul people of northwest India, among the first to be recruited under such labor regimes. Coolie labor was put to work on the plantations, mines, and railroad work sites of the Caribbean, Latin America, the American West, South and East Africa, the Pacific, and Southeast Asia. Displaced European peasants, particularly from Italy, were also brought to the United States and Latin America in the late nineteenth and early twentieth century by labor contractors to work in factories and on railroad construction sites.

Internal migration of workers was also a hallmark of the nineteenth and twentieth centuries. Many southern Italians migrated to north Italy to work in agriculture and industry. Impoverished and landless peasants in northern Brazil were brought to the mines and plantations of the more prosperous southern regions of the country. And, with the extensive drought and deep economic depression of the 1930s, tens of thousands of "Okies," or displaced farmers from Oklahoma and other parts of the lower Great Plains, migrated to California in search of agricultural work for wages.

Where and How Many

Since the end of World War II, international migrant laborers have largely come from Latin America, South and Southeast Asia, southern Africa, and southern Europe. For the most part, Latin American migrant workers—primarily from Mexico and Central America—have headed north to the American Southwest and, more recently, the South and Midwest. There they have gone to work in the agricultural sector, typically moving from place to place as they follow the harvests of various crops.

The recruitment of southern Africans to the mines of South Africa and plantations of Zimbabwe (formerly Rhodesia) has continued from the prewar era, though the collapse of the Zimbabwean economy since the 1990s has halted the flow there. The reconstruction of western and northern European economies after World War II created a huge demand for laborers, largely fed by poorer southern European countries such as Portugal, Spain, Greece, and Italy, as well as Turkey and various former British and French colonies in North and sub-Saharan Africa, South Asia, and the Caribbean. Many of these people were brought in under various forms of "guest worker" programs, which allowed for temporary residence but no path to citizenship. With the fall of communism after 1990, an increasing number of workers migrated from Eastern Europe to Western Europe.

Measuring how many migrant laborers currently work around the world is a tricky business. The line between ordinary migrants and immigrants, who seek permanent residence and even citizenship, is often difficult to discern. In the United States, there are an estimated 10–15 million persons without documentation, of whom about 2–3 million work on farms or in farm-related activities, such as food processing. In 2010, about 4 percent of the European Union population consisted of citizens of countries outside the union, or about 20 million people overall, many of them originally temporary workers. To take the largest pairing of sending and destination countries for guest workers in the postwar Europe, it is estimated that there are about 4 million persons of Turkish descent living in Germany today.

Yet another lure for migrant workers has been the Middle East, especially the oil-rich countries of the Persian Gulf, where the dramatic rise in oil prices in the early 1970s, combined with small native-born populations and ambitious modernization plans of governments, created a huge demand for migrant laborers. There are an estimated 12 million foreign workers in the region today, of which 5 million reside in Saudi Arabia alone, along with 3.8 million in the United Arab Emirates, 2.3 million in Kuwait, and 1.1 million in Qatar, the latter making up no less than 90 percent of the working population. Most of these laborers came from South Asian, Southeast Asian, and non-oil-rich Arab countries and territories, such as Bangladesh, Egypt, India, Pakistan, the Palestinian Territories, and the Philippines.

Altogether, estimates put the number of foreign workers worldwide at about 50 million. Large as it is, this figure pales in comparison to the internal move-

Inflow of Foreign Workers into Select OECD Countries and Russia, 2000–2009 (in thousands)

Country	2000	2001	2002	2003	2004	2005	2006	2007	2008	2009
Australia	71.5	71.6	69.5	74.3	81.0	81.7	130.6	148.1	176.0	170.8
Canada	116.6	119.7	110.9	103.2	112.6	122.7	139.1	164.9	192.5	178.5
France	14.4	19.4	18.3	17.5	17.6	19.8	21.6	27.5	33.7	28.0
Germany	333.8	373.8	374.0	372.2	380.3	n/a	30.1	29.2	30.7	26.2
Israel	n/a	78.2	33.2	31.1	47.9	29.4	32.7	36.5	30.3	26.6
Italy	58.0	92.4	139.1	n/a	n/a	75.3	69.0	150.1	145.1	n/a
Japan	129.9	142.0	145.1	155.8	158.9	125.4	81.4	77.9	72.1	53.5
Russia	n/a	n/a	n/a	n/a	n/a	n/a	n/a	1,189.0	1,343.6	1,052.3
United Kingdom	64.6	85.1	88.6	85.8	89.5	86.2	96.7	88.0	77.7	52.7
United States	461.7	592.3	531.7	433.8	552.0	635.2	603.5	666.1	616.4	492.9

Source: Organisation for Economic Co-operation and Development (OECD).

ment of people within China—indeed, the largest mass movement of people in human history—which, since the 1980s, is estimated to be between 100 and 300 million, depending on how the term "migrant labor" is defined. Chinese peasants have moved from the rural regions of the country to the industrial cities in the north and east of the country, particularly along the coast. This has been especially the case since the rapid modernization and opening up of the Chinese economy to global trading networks since the 1980s.

Problems and Benefits

Migrant laborers bring benefits and problems to both origin and destination countries. For the origin countries, the problem largely arises out of the fact that migrant workers are often the youngest and healthiest workers. This deprives sending economies of their most productive workers and also shifts the benefits of the education they received, which the sending country largely paid for, to the destination country. Migrant workers are usually required by law or circumstance to leave spouses and families behind, leading to social problems in the sending community. At the same time, sending countries benefit from the remittances those migrant laborers send home, especially because it does not entail those countries having to provide the worker with any costly services. The top four remittance-receiving countries in the world—India, China, Mexico, and the Philippines—receive collectively about $100 billion annually. At home, these workers might not have been able to find employment, and if they did, it probably would not have paid as much as the person was able to remit, especially considering that the remittances often come in much-needed hard currencies, such as the U.S. dollar and the euro.

Migrant workers also present a mixed picture for the receiving country. They often provide much-needed labor, particularly in low-wage and undesirable fields such as agriculture, which do not attract citizens and permanent residents. In the Persian Gulf countries, many migrant laborers are actually high-skilled technicians in the business of oil extraction, providing expertise unavailable in sufficient amounts among the local population. At the same, migrant laborers may take jobs away from citizens and can add to governmental expenditures, in the form of social services such as health care, crime control, and education. Extensive studies of illegal labor in the United States point to differing conclusions, though most concur that the costs and benefits do not tilt too strongly one way or another.

For migrant workers themselves, the benefits are obvious—employment and higher wages than they could have earned in their home country. Indeed, that is the primary reason why they migrated in the first place. But those jobs and wages come at a cost. The most significant is separation from family and community at home. Unlike legal immigrants and those intending to ultimately settle in their new country, many migrants do not establish families in their destination countries. Instead, they live on the margins, sometimes by choice but usually by necessity. Many are barred from participating in civic life or taking advantage of government services. When illegal, they are forced to live in the shadows, avoiding contact with government officials and police. This is even the case with internal Chinese migrants, who may not possess the documents that permit them to live in their destination cities.

Because migrant laborers' status may be illegal, or because they may only be allowed to remain in the destination country as long as they hold a job, they are easily subject to exploitation by employers. Many migrant domestic workers in the Persian Gulf

A Malaysian security guard checks detainees at an overcrowded immigrant holding facility near Kuala Lumpur. With up to one in every four of the nation's workers believed to be illegal, the government has cracked down on human trafficking. *(AP Photo/Mark Baker)*

countries, for example, complain of actual physical abuse by their employers, while migrants in other countries have been known to be locked up at night in dormitories, often on factory sites. Often of a different ethnic group than the majority of native citizens, they are frequently discriminated against, not just officially but by the population at large.

The Future

Various forces are likely to perpetuate migrant labor patterns into the foreseeable future. One is globalization. The integration of developing world countries into the international economy is likely to create wealth and opportunity disparities between urban industrial and rural areas, leading to large-scale internal migration, as is the case in China. Moreover, as some countries in the developing world develop faster than others, they may attract more migrant laborers, as is currently the case with Cambodian and Laotian workers flocking to Thailand and Malaysia.

Demography is another such force. With their re-

cent high birth rates, many developing countries have an excess of working-age youth. More developed economies, such as those of Europe and Japan, have aging populations that require either an increase in their immigration quotas—a politically contentious policy—or the importing of more migrant laborers to fill labor needs and pay for the social welfare programs of growing numbers of seniors.

Other trends, however, could lead to a leveling off and even a downturn in the number of migrants. As countries in the developing world become more prosperous and productive, they will be able to retain more of their own workers. Moreover, China, where most of the world's labor migration occurs, is rapidly undergoing two processes that could lead to less internal migration—improved living standards in the countryside and the shift of industry from the coastal or destination regions of most current internal migrants, where labor costs are rising, to the interior or sending provinces, where labor costs remain low.

James Ciment

See also: Brain Drain and Talent Mobility; Child Labor; Farm Policy; Immigration, Illegal and Irregular; Slavery; Working Conditions.

Further Reading

Berger, John, and Jean Mohr. *A Seventh Man: A Book of Images and Words About the Experience of Migrant Workers in Europe.* New York: Verso, 2010.

Kamrava, Mehran, and Zahra Babar, eds. *Migrant Labor in the Persian Gulf.* New York: Columbia University Press, 2012.

Lutz, Helma. *The New Maids: Transnational Women and the Care Economy.* Trans. Deborah Shannon. New York: Zed Books, 2011.

Murphy, Rachel, ed. *Labour Migration and Social Development in Contemporary China.* New York: Routledge, 2008.

Overmyer-Velázquez, Mark. *Beyond La Frontera: The History of Mexico–U.S. Migration.* New York: Oxford University Press, 2011.

Özden, Caglar, and Maurice Schiff, eds. *International Migration, Remittances, and Brain Drain.* New York: Palgrave Macmillan, 2006.

Rodriguez, Robyn Magalit. *Migrants for Export: How the Philippines State Brokers Labor to the World.* Minneapolis: University of Minnesota Press, 2010.

Shelley, Toby. *Exploited: Migrant Labour in the New Global Economy.* New York: Zed Books, 2007.

Stark, Oded. *The Migration of Labor.* Cambridge, MA: Basil Blackwell, 1991.

Zimmermann, Klaus F., ed. *European Migration: What Do We Know?* New York: Oxford University Press, 2005.

Web Sites

Global Workers Justice Alliance: www.globalworkers.org
International Labour Organization: www.ilo.org
International Organization for Migration: www.iom.int
Migration Information Source: www.migrationinformation.org

Documents

Document 1: Agricultural Labor Relations Act (excerpts), California, 1975

Since at least the Great Depression of the 1930s, migrant labor has been a key component of California's massive agricultural industry. By the 1960s, migrants from Oklahoma and the Great Plains had been replaced by those from Mexico and the Philippines, though the harsh conditions and lack of labor rights remained the same. Extended strikes, political organizing, and boycotts by the National Farm Workers Association and Agricultural Workers Organizing Committee (later the United Farm Workers) had forced the major growers to accept collective bargaining by farmworkers. The Agricultural Labor Relations Act of 1975 was a piece of state legislation, among the first in the world, aimed at legalizing and institutionalizing those rights for migrant laborers, many of whom were non-U.S. citizens. Among the provisions of the law were the creation of an Agricultural Labor Relations Board to arbitrate labor disputes and the right of workers to organize unions and seek collective bargaining agreements without interference and harassment from employers.

1141. (a) There is hereby created in the Labor and Workforce Development Agency the Agricultural Labor Relations Board, which shall consist of five members . . .

(b) The members of the board shall be appointed by the Governor with the advice and consent of the Senate . . .

(b) Whenever a petition for an election has been filed in a bargaining unit in which a majority of the employees are engaged in a strike, the necessary and appropriate services of the board in the region in which the election will be held shall be available to the parties involved 24 hours a day until the election is held . . .

1151. For the purpose of all hearings and investigations, which, in the opinion of the board, are necessary and proper for the exercise of the powers vested in it by Chapters 5 (commencing with Section 1156) and 6 (commencing with Section 1160) of this part:

(a) The board, or its duly authorized agents or agencies, shall at all reasonable times have access to, for the purpose of examination, and the right to copy, any evidence of any person being investigated or proceeded against that relates to any matter under investigation or in question. The members of the board or their designees or their duly authorized agents shall have the right of free access to all places of labor. The board, or any member thereof, shall upon application of any party to such proceedings, forthwith issue to such party subpoenas requiring the attendance and testimony of witnesses or the production of any evidence in such proceeding or investigation requested in such application. . . .

1152. Employees shall have the right to self-organization, to form, join, or assist labor organizations, to bargain collectively through representatives of their own choosing, and to engage in other concerted activities for the purpose of collective bargaining or other mutual aid or protection, and shall also have the right to refrain from any or all of such activities except to the extent that such right may be affected by an agreement requiring membership in a labor organization as a condition of continued employment as authorized in subdivision (c) of Section 1153.

1153. It shall be an unfair labor practice for an agricultural employer to do any of the following:

(a) To interfere with, restrain, or coerce agricultural employees in the exercise of the rights guaranteed in Section 1152.

(b) To dominate or interfere with the formation or administration of any labor organization or contribute financial or other support to it. However, subject to such rules and regulations as may be made and published by the board pursuant to Section 1144, an agricultural employer shall not be prohibited from permitting agricultural employees to confer with him during working hours without loss of time or pay.

(c) By discrimination in regard to the hiring or tenure of employment, or any term or condition of employment, to encourage or discourage membership in any labor organization.

Source: California Agricultural Labor Relations Board.

Document 2: UN Convention on the Protection of the Rights of All Migrant Workers and Members of Their Families, 1990

Recognizing the various problems facing migrant laborers and their families around the world, the United Nations General Assembly adopted the Convention on the Protection of the Rights of All Migrant Workers and Members of Their Families on December 18, 1990. Among the rights the convention says all countries should honor are freedom from arbitrary abuse by officials, rule of law, the guarantee of basic human rights and dignity, freedom from discrimination, and certain economic rights. The convention also calls for a ban on all forms of coercion in international labor markets.

www2.ohchr.org/english/law/cmw.htm

Source: Office of the United Nations High Commissioner for Human Rights.

MINING ISSUES

Mining is a major business in many countries of both the developed and developing worlds. Although mining produces substantial economic benefits—particularly for the latter group of countries, but also in developed-world economies such as Australia—it nevertheless causes significant problems, among them environmental degradation. Also, mining operations often bring little financial reward to the communities that they disrupt.

In response, since the early 1980s mining legislation has been revised in more than 50 developing countries, many under the watchful eye of international donors. With few exceptions, these revisions have had two objectives: to resuscitate large, industrial-scale mining activity and to formalize artisanal and small-scale mining (ASM) activities. Most host governments have heavily prioritized the large-scale activity, offering a series of generous tax breaks in the hope of attracting foreign investment to bolster mineral exploration activity and develop viable mining projects. By waiving import duties on mining equipment, offering low royalty payments, and providing extended tax holidays, numerous countries in Asia, Latin America, and sub-Saharan Africa have succeeded in convincing scores of companies to participate in this industry. Backed by billions of dollars, including, in many cases, contributions from the International Finance Corporation (IFC), the financial arm of the World Bank, these companies have changed the economic profile of the developing-world countries considerably since the early 1990s. Efforts have concentrated mainly on the extraction and processing of gold—whose value has experienced an unprecedented upsurge since the onset of the 2008 financial crisis—as well as the mining of gemstones and industrial minerals (copper, iron, nickel, and bauxite).

Efforts to reform mechanized large-scale mining in developing countries, however, have typically overshadowed those to formalize ASM. Specifically, in many cases—as most recently illustrated in Ghana, Mali, Mozambique, and other countries in sub-Saharan Africa—governments have struggled to provide

titling and support to prospective ASM licensees in areas now under concession to foreign multinationals. This is proving problematic because the blueprint of large-scale mine development championed by the World Bank and the International Monetary Fund (IMF) has failed to yield the developmental impact anticipated. Instead of giving rise to an industry that is fully integrated economically, the reforms have spawned industrial-scale enclave-type mining operations that have failed to stimulate downstream industries and generate much employment.

The ASM industry, however, is the very antithesis of this development, and a potential tonic to the burgeoning poverty that now engulfs many corners of the developing world. Impelled by domestic investment, ASM provides direct employment to millions of people worldwide and has spawned the many related service industries that large-scale extraction has had difficulty creating. But the sector, which accomplished this with minimal support from host governments and donors, is under serious threat from a perpetually expanding large-scale mining economy.

Growth of Large-Scale Mining: Issues and Impacts

In March 2012, the government of Indonesia passed new legislation that required all foreign companies developing mines in the country to sell at least 51 percent of shares to Indonesians after the mines have been in operation for ten years. The government also announced plans to ban the exportation of unprocessed ore by 2014, which would undoubtedly bolster the added-value activity of domestic smelting. Concerns were voiced in private sector circles, however, that these changes will discourage significant mining investment in Indonesia, which is currently the world's top exporter of thermal coal and tin.

Indonesia is by no means alone in its efforts to overhaul national mining legislation and codes. In 2011–2012 alone, at least 25 countries increased mine taxes or royalties. Notable on this list was Ghana, which boosted its royalty payment from 3 to 5 percent and taxes from 25 to 35 percent. Peru, Zambia, and Tanzania followed this example, and countries such as the Democratic Republic of Congo and Sierra Leone undertook comprehensive reviews of national mining contracts, many of which were signed while transitional governments were in power. These sweeping changes have sparked concerns over resource nationalism, forcing many mining companies to venture into more politically risky countries such as Mauritania, Laos, and Burkina Faso.

Although the specific motivation for this sudden wave of legislative amendment is unclear, in most cases, the change was initiated at least in part by mounting public pressure over government failure to derive sufficient revenue from mineral resources. The reforms have bolstered large-scale mineral exploration and mining across the developing world, but this pattern of development, outlined in documents such as the World Bank's landmark report *A Strategy for African Mining*, has given rise to an enclave-type economy that, with few exceptions, has failed to fully integrate into local societies.

The formula of a liberalized large-scale mining sector has repeatedly failed to deliver on promises of employment and local economic development, largely because of the capital-intensiveness and highly mechanized nature of the activity being developed. In Mali and Ghana, for example, research has shown that, for every $250,000–$500,000 invested, large-scale gold-mining projects generate, on average, only one job for the locals. In the face of mounting pressure to disclose details of financial transactions in the sector, impoverished local communities and the nongovernmental organizations (NGOs) lobbying on their behalf are becoming increasingly aware of the massive difference between the level of profits and earnings of large-scale mining companies, on the one hand, and the mine royalties and taxes being received by host government, on the other. This disparity is reflected by the small contribution that booming mining industries make to the gross domestic product (GDP) of a number of countries (e.g., Ghana, 5 percent; Chile, 6.8 percent; and Indonesia, 11 percent) in relation to other economic sectors, such as agriculture and manufacturing, many of which are deteriorating.

The concern for local communities and NGOs is the policy context in which large-scale mine development often takes place: an atmosphere of regulatory laissez faire. Not only have vibrant operations gener-

ated, proportionally, very little economically for host countries, but perhaps of greater concern, the laws and contracts in place have often given free rein to the multinationals driving the sector. Numerous complications have arisen because of the paucity of requirements to address environmental and social concerns proactively. Environmentally, a lack of monitoring and enforcement has, not surprisingly, culminated in problems, in particular chemical spills and contamination from drainage, which have had a devastating impact on local ecosystems and indigenous communities. Because they have no real means of regulating and coping with the influx of mining activity that has taken place over the past three decades, a growing number of developing-world governments have rather naively relied on the companies themselves to ensure compliance with legal requirements.

The evidence, however, indicates that many mining companies are relocating to developing-world countries in a "race to the bottom," seeking opportunities in regions with lax regulation and enforcement. The results have been disastrous, particularly with respect to the environment. At the Mt. Tapian mining complex in the Philippines, for example, an estimated 84 million tons of mine tailings were dumped into Calancan Bay between 1975 and 1988. A tailings spill in 1990 at the Freeport mine in neighboring Indonesia had a similar impact, affecting an estimated 7,400 acres (3,000 hectares), and on May 4, 2000, a period of excessive rainfall resulted in the slippage of a mine waste stockpile in the Wanagon Basin into the Wanagon Valley. At Newmont Gold Mining's Minahasa Raya site, also in Indonesia, it has been estimated that more than 2.8 million tons (2.5 million metric tons) of toxic mine waste have been deposited into the waters of Buyat Bay since 1996. The company had long employed a waste disposal method, dumping in waterways, that was banned in the United States because of the potential impacts it has on the oceanic ecosystem. These are but a few selected examples from Asia; the list of accidents and incidents is extensive and affects all the areas with intensive mining.

Arrival of new mining operations also has serious implications for local communities, which are often displaced to make way for such ventures. The case of Ghana clearly illustrates the magnitude of this impact. In Tarkwa, one of the country's mining localities, an estimated 30,000 people were displaced between 1990 and 1998. The inadequate compensatory packages typically awarded to dislocated groups compound the problem. Following largely outdated

The October 2010 rescue of 33 Chilean miners who had been trapped underground for 69 days was cause for international celebration. But the collapse of the mine spotlighted the unsafe working conditions and the government's failure to enforce safety regulations. *(Hugo Infante/AFP/ Getty Images)*

compensation templates produced by national land valuation boards, companies rapidly encounter problems as soon as negotiations with communities begin, the latter believing that compensation is inadequate. Negative consequences can ensue even in cases in which companies award compensation beyond scheduled amounts, as shown in the case of the Asutifi District of the Brong-Ahafo region of Ghana, where Newmont Gold Mining awarded a sum to displaced individuals for each teak and cocoa tree lost. Significantly, compensation for these and other trees is generally a one-time payment for items that could have generated consistent revenue for the local population over a 25-to-30-year period.

Worker Safety Issues

Large-scale mining operations also create worker safety issues, as shown by high-profile disasters that occurred in 2010 in Chile and the United States. In Chile, 33 miners were trapped in a cave-in at a copper and gold

operation in Copiapó for more than two months, before eventually being rescued in a multinational effort. Not so fortunate were the coal miners at the Upper Big Branch Mine in West Virginia, where 29 of the miners were killed in an explosion. In both cases, but particularly in West Virginia, the mining companies were faulted for taking safety shortcuts. In addition, many blamed the West Virginia disaster on inadequate government oversight, caused, say some, by an excessively close relationship between regulators and company officials and, according to others, by a federal Mine Safety and Health Administration hit by budget cuts.

Although these two accidents captured the world's attention, particularly the dramatic rescue of the Chilean miners, the most acute ongoing safety problems take place in China, which has by far the highest death rates for miners. Around the same time as the West Virginia accident, more than 50 miners were killed in five separate coal mine explosions in various parts of China, contributing to a total of 1,261 deaths overall for the year, or 80 percent of all mining fatalities in the world. Some of the Chinese coal mines were operating illegally, according to the government, but others were fully licensed and a few were operated by state-owned businesses. Outside experts say that this indicates a lack of effective oversight. The Chinese government has made efforts to improve mine safety and points to the fact that the number of deaths in 2010 was only about one-fourth of the total just five years earlier and half the figure in 2009. As China continues its breakneck pace of development, much of it fueled by coal-fired power plants, the country is likely to continue to be the world's epicenter of coal-mining disasters and deaths.

Rapid Rise of Small-Scale Mining

Only in the past decade have policymakers and donors come to recognize that the majority of people engaged in ASM are not rugged entrepreneurs but, rather, genuine job seekers. In many developing countries, ASM is now well integrated into the rural economy, interconnected with a host of cottage industries such as agriculture, equipment repair services, and transport. At the beginning of the 1980s, when the World Bank and the IMF began to provide structural adjustment loans to a host of developing-world governments, donors seemed to share the view that they could best support those engaged in ASM by mechanizing their operations and providing them with more efficient equipment. This thinking led to a series of efforts aimed at improving the efficiency of ASM operations. More important, it contributed to the sector's long-standing peripheral position on the mine development agenda.

Less than two decades ago, experts began to concede that ASM was not an industry populated exclusively by ambitious entrepreneurs. Influential donors and NGOs, among others, began to recognize that many people who had turned to this sector to supplement their income had done so to support their family economically. The experts convened the International Roundtable on Artisanal Mining in May 1995 at the World Bank's headquarters in Washington, DC, at which a near-consensus was reached among delegates that ASM was largely a poverty-driven activity, engaged in by individuals with few employment alternatives. Hardships had been caused by the structural adjustments imposed by the international lending institutions, including mass redundancies in the public sector and exposure

of small-holder farmers to liberalized agricultural markets. In this environment, they concluded, ASM was paradoxically flourishing.

By this time, however, a significant share of land in developing-world countries was in the hands of foreign multinational mining companies. Moreover, superimposed regulatory structures and licensing systems were already in place for ASM in a host of countries. Significantly, the designs of most of these frameworks had been heavily informed by perceptions that the sector's operators were mobile entrepreneurs with access to finance, *not* subsistence, marginalized groups who are largely disconnected from the wage economy. The establishment of a legalized and formalized ASM sector has complicated matters because of the difficulties people have had with securing licenses. Its establishment has also been very much an afterthought, as countries, under the direction of donors, have been guided to prioritize the overhaul of mineral investment policies with the aim of developing a vibrant, export-based large-scale mining economy. Only after the reestablishment of large-scale mining has attention turned to formalizing ASM.

The problem facing regulators and donors is that illegal ASM is growing rapidly in all corners of the developing world. Failure to address the deficiencies of these regulatory frameworks and assist unlicensed operators has given rise to an industry with unique attributes. The media, NGOs, donors, and host governments have been quick to highlight many of these characteristics and, in the process, paint an extremely negative picture of the industry.

Estimates of the number of people directly engaged in ASM worldwide are wide-ranging. In the mid-1990s, the United Nations estimated that 6 million people were employed directly in the sector, a number that the International Labour Organization revised to 13 million in the late 1990s. It was also indicated at the time that an additional 80 million to 100 million people worldwide depended on the sector indirectly for their livelihoods. The number employed in large-scale mining is a small fraction of even these conservative estimates. Notable among these individuals are dependent family members and the individuals working in downstream industries, including those who provide transportation and equipment repair services. The most recent estimates place the global ASM workforce at 20 million to 25 million.

But because most ASM activities take place illegally, often in remote locations such as deserts and the interior of forests and on concessions awarded to large companies, it is almost impossible to arrive at an exact employment figure. Some scholars have claimed that the latest figure of 20 million to 25 million is an accurate estimate of the small-scale coal-mining workforce in China alone. What *is* certain is that, because ASM is predominantly poverty driven and occurs in countries that are struggling to develop economically, it is safe to assume that the number of people employed in the industry is continuing to rise. Selected country-level estimates of the ASM workforce underscore the economic importance of the industry and provide an idea of its size. For example, Africa alone has at least 1 million artisanal diamond diggers and even more small-scale gold miners: at least 1 million in Ghana, more than 750,000 in Tanzania, 500,000 in Mozambique, and an indeterminate number in the Democratic Republic of Congo. In the Guianas (Suriname, Guyana, and French Guiana) in South America, a region with a combined population of approximately 1.3 million, some estimates point to more than 600,000 working in the small-scale gold-mining communities in the forested interior.

Based on the few countries that provide fairly detailed reporting on production from ASM, the sector appears to have a significant economic impact. Their production output, if captured, could make an important contribution to foreign exchange: The minerals and stones being mined—colored gems, diamonds, and gold—are the most widely traded commodities in the world and can therefore be considered a kind of universal currency. In Ghana, for example, nearly 20 percent of the country's gold originates from mainly illegal ASM operations. The Ghanaian government has in place a comprehensive gold-purchasing network made up of over 700 buyers who purchase from both illegal and licensed operators of gold mining establishments. In Guyana, at present, the gold-mining economy is made up entirely of small-scale operators, whose annual production is $300 million.

If properly formalized, the ASM sector has the potential to make an even greater contribution to national coffers and development than it does in its present form.

Giving Small-Scale Mining Greater Priority

Although it receives negative press, ASM's environmental impact is negligible compared to that of large-scale mining. Moreover, its social impacts are very much a product of its existence as an informal sector of industry operating illegally. Policymakers, donors, and host governments regard unlicensed ASM operators as "criminals," while failing to recognize that the decision to operate illegally is often a response to the legislation and policies they themselves have instituted. Specifically, most regulatory frameworks provide foreign large-scale operations with a host of incentives, which has resulted in an acute shortage of land. This has made it difficult for prospective small-scale operators to secure a license to operate legally.

Thousands of small-scale miners have struggled to secure licenses to operate legally. For many of these individuals, in addition to the acute shortage of available land, exorbitant licensing fees and lengthy delays on application decisions have inhibited formalization. Continued operation in the informal economy has had its share of consequences: Those who operate without a license cannot access educational and technical support services financed by donors and host governments, who cannot be seen to be endorsing illegal activity in their programs. Supported by informal networks and backed by middlemen, many of these miners end up clashing with the management of large-scale operations over land. In many instances, sections of concessions awarded to the larger concerns are not being worked. The ASMs, therefore, encroach on these parcels of land because the deposits within them can be worked by artisanal means. The complaint voiced by encroaching artisanal miners is that they are being prevented from accessing these areas because concessions have been awarded to companies for lengthy periods, 20 to 30 years in many cases.

Working informally also has significant implications for environmental health. Because the priority of its predominantly poverty-driven workforce is to accumulate sufficient income to cover daily needs, it is not surprising that environmental and health-related issues are neglected. One of the most serious problems is pollution from mercury, which is used by panners in over 50 countries to amalgamate gold. Workers typically administer inorganic mercury without any protective clothing, applying it to gold particles. The mercury forms a paste, after which it is burned and additional impurities are removed. After it is in the natural environment, however, this inorganic mercury is transformed by microorganisms into toxic methylmercury. Over time, it accumulates in soil, water, and plant matter as well as in the tissues of fish. When ingested, this methylmercury poses a serious health threat to humans, leading to ailments including convulsions, headaches, nausea, deterioration of motor functions, and respiratory problems. Every year, approximately 440 tons (400 metric tons) of mercury are released by small-scale gold-mining activity into the natural environment. The sector today accounts for 33 percent of global anthropogenic mercury emissions.

A second significant environmental concern is excessive land degradation, largely a result of the hit-or-miss nature of the sector's activities. Without appropriate assistance and guidance, artisanal miners prospect and excavate rather anarchically, removing vast tracts of vegetation, digging numerous pits and trenches, and felling countless trees. As operators are itinerant and frequently on the move, defaced landscapes are rarely reclaimed and are left exposed to the agents of erosion. Some of the most significant degradation has taken place in the interior of the Amazon—Brazil, Suriname, Guyana, and Ecuador—where miners, in many cases outside the reach of authorities, have ruined vast sections of pristine tropical forest.

In addition to causing significant environmental impact, many of the world's ASM communities are now prey to social ills. Many ASM communities in impoverished developing countries such as Guyana, Suriname, Zimbabwe, Ghana, Sierra Leone, and Papua New Guinea have become epicenters of prostitution and excessive consumption of narcotics. Host governments and donors blame the working conditions: miners live in remote, makeshift settlements and often spend their income as quickly as they earn it on alcohol, drugs, and unnecessary luxury items. Expenditures on medicine can also be significant, as their unhygienic working conditions often give rise to diseases such as typhoid and tuberculosis that require costly medical treatment. But often the workers must choose between spending on these work-related medical needs and on their dependents, for household expenses, family farms, and children's school fees.

An additional concern with several of the commodities being mined on a small scale is that they have at times fueled civil violence. This is especially true with alluvial gemstones, many of which have vertical supply chains and are found only in certain parts of the world. Key examples include Myanmar (Burma), the largest producer of rubies; Sierra Leone and Angola, both of which have rich reserves of alluvial diamonds; and the Democratic Republic of Congo, which has the world's largest reserve of coltan (tantalite), used to produce electronic chips and SIM cards for mobile phones. In each case, the minerals of interest have been readily accessible, their extraction has been very difficult to regulate, and they have spawned criminal networks or provided a source of finance for insurgencies.

Why do people continue to engage in arduous ASM activity at the expense of their health? There is growing consensus that, once immersed in the activity, people find themselves trapped in a vicious cycle of poverty, in debt to unscrupulous middlemen. In order to break this cycle, it is argued, miners must accumulate earnings but find it impossible to do so. Having borrowed funds to cover their expenses, many have unknowingly made commitments to middlemen and are forced to sell mined product at below-market prices to their sponsors. These lost earnings, in turn, exacerbate their hardships.

Continuing Challenges

After reforms, many developing countries have attempted to bolster large-scale mining activity through foreign investment and formalized ASM. Evidence indicates that large-scale mining has not spurred overall development. ASM, by contrast, plays a key economic role in some of the poorest countries, offering a rare source of stability for many rural families in Latin America, sub-Saharan Africa, and Asia. It not only employs millions of people directly but also contributes significantly to mineral output, supplying host governments with supplies of tradable precious minerals and stones. For the most part, this has been achieved with very little support from governments and donors. The global ASM workforce is likely to continue to increase in the years to come. The challenge facing policymakers and donors, therefore, is how to bring operators—who have been marginalized by the legislation and reforms governments have endorsed—into the realm of legal activities, where they can be educated and have recourse to legal remedies. As long as ASM continues to flourish illegally, a situation brought about largely through catering to the needs of foreign mining companies, it will continue to be overlooked in the context of economic development.

Gavin M. Hilson

See also: Child Labor; Pollution, Water; Toxic Waste; Working Conditions.

Further Reading

Bebbington, Anthony, ed. *Social Conflict, Economic Development and the Extractive Industry: Evidence from South America*. New York: Routledge, 2011.

Bell, FredericG., and Laurance J. Donnelly. *Mining and Its Impact on the Environment*. New York: Taylor & Francis, 2006.

Craddock, Paul, and Janet Lang, eds. *Mining and Metal Production Through the Ages*. London: British Museum, 2003.

Hilson, Gavin M. *Small-Scale Mining, Rural Subsistence and Poverty in West Africa*. Rugby, Warwickshire, UK: Practical Action, 2003.

International Labour Organization. *Social and Labour Issues in Small-Scale Mines: Report for Discussion at the Tripartite Meeting on Social and Labour Issues in Small-Scale Mines*. Geneva: International Labour Organization, 1999.

Lynch, Martin. *Mining in World History*. London: Reaktion, 2003.

Moody, Roger. *Rocks and Hard Places: The Globalization of Mining*. New York: Zed Books, 2007.

O'Faircheallaigh, Ciaran, and Saleem Ali, eds. *Earth Matters: Indigenous Peoples, the Extractive Industries and Corporate Social Responsibility*. Sheffield, UK: Greenleaf, 2008.

Richards, Jeremy P., ed. *Mining, Society, and a Sustainable World*. New York: Springer, 2009.

Yakovleva, Natalia. *Corporate Social Responsibility in the Mining Industries*. Burlington, VT: Ashgate, 2005.

Web Sites

Communities and Small-Scale Mining: www.casm.org: www.artisanalmining.org/casm

International Council on Mining & Metals: www.icmm.com

International Labour Organization, Mining and Quarrying: www.ilo.org/ipec/areas/Miningandquarrying/lang—en/index.htm

Documents

Document 1: "Finance, Mining and Sustainability" (excerpt), UN Environment Programme and World Bank, 2001–2002

In the wake of a series of catastrophic environmental disasters related to large-scale mining, the United Nations Environment Programme and the World Bank examined the role that financial institutions and lenders could play in ensuring better safety and reducing environmental repercussions in this highly capital-intensive industry. The text that follows is the introduction to a report on the subject by the two organizations, highlighting the dangers financial institutions face should they fail to improve mining safety and environmental impact.

Mining by its very nature is financially expensive, environmentally invasive and socially intrusive, yet many countries have successfully managed to convert their mineral endowment into national wealth providing the country with the economic means to address its environmental problems and social aspirations.

Recently, the mining industry as been experiencing a spate of accidents, intense social conflicts and political debate, in both developed and developing countries which have focussed attention not only on the mining industry but on its financiers, investors, lenders and insurers as the costs of mitigating the environmental and social damage can be enormous.

Financing

The financing of mining and minerals projects is not only important, but is increasingly under scrutiny regardless whether it be debt or equity financing. All financial involvement carries risk and it is the financial institution's skill in identifying and quantifying the different levels of risk that separates good decisions from bad ones.

Environmental, social and increasingly reputational risks are just a few of the many risks to be assessed each time a financial institution gets involved in a business. From this point of view, risks can be characterized in three ways:

Direct Risk

As countries tighten their environmental regulations and public concern about the mining industry grows, pressures increase on companies to minimize their environmental impacts and pay greater heed to local social issues. This may increase companies' capital and operating costs in order to comply with increased environmental regulations and social expectations. This can have an impact on cash-flow and profitability, a borrower's ability to meet loan repayments and the value of the entire operation. It is therefore, important to thoroughly assess environmental performance as part of the normal credit appraisal process.

Indirect Risk

Legislation differs from country to country but many adopt the 'polluter pays' principle to pollution incidents. Financiers are increasingly concerned to avoid being placed in positions where they might be considered directly responsible for the polluting actions of their clients, in this case mining companies. Otherwise, in the case of a pollution incident, financial entities may find that not only have they lost the value of their original involvement in a particular project, but they may find themselves being forced to meet what may prove to be substantial clean-up costs or even further liabilities.

Reputational Risk

Financial institutions are under increasing scrutiny concerning their involvement in a number of sectors, from governments, regulators, NGOs, the public and the media. Failure to give careful consideration to environmental impacts from projects financed, invested in or insured can result in negative publicity for both the respective company and the financial institution.

Source: United Nations Environment Programme, Mining Department; World Bank Group Mining Minerals and Sustainable Development Project.

Document 2: Girls in Mining: Research Findings from Ghana, Niger, Peru, and the United Republic of Tanzania (excerpts), 2007

Artisanal or small-scale mining is widespread throughout the developing world where significant mineral deposits are found. In many developing countries, children are often employed in mining activities both above and below ground, with significant negative consequences for their health and educational opportunities. As this report from the International Labour Organization's International Programme on the Elimination of Child Labour makes clear, the problem is particularly acute in Africa.

1. Underground—Out of sight

Research carried out by the International Labour Organization's International Programme on the Elimination of Child Labour (ILO–IPEC) between April and December 2006 has produced evidence that girls as well as boys are involved in hazardous work in the small-scale mining industry.

Due to the fact that boys are statistically more likely to be involved in hazardous child labour than girls, the appalling work of girls is often overlooked. In the small-scale mining industry especially, little is understood about the roles and activities of girls and the effect that this has on their lives and livelihoods . . . The issue of girl child labour in mining is largely unknown, it is often not fully recognized by the law, and missed by the intervention services and the media.

New evidence presented in this paper challenges the general understanding of gender roles in small-scale mining communities. It forces us to acknowledge a more intricate reality for boys and girls as the evidence shows that the involvement of girl child labour in mining is much more frequent and far-reaching than was previously recognized . . . girls are involved in tasks related to the extraction, transportation and processing stages of mining as well as in other mining-related jobs such as selling food and supplies to the miners . . .

2. The role of women and girls

It is important to note that child labour in mining, in this paper, refers to informal, small-scale mining; there is no known child labour in the formal sector. Small-scale mining is defined as the low output, non-mechanized, highly labour intensive extraction of minerals for economic gain. It refers specifically to "family-based mining" using small pits or artisanal methods . . .

Although still excluded from underground extraction, women are involved in tasks deeper and deeper into the interior of the mine, transporting materials, removing rubble and rocks from the mines, sorting mineralized rocks, breaking stones and processing the minerals . . .

5. Conclusion

This research proves that a substantial number of girls, under the legal working age, are involved in hazardous mining activities in different areas of the world. This is child labour at its worst, putting girls at serious risk of lifelong and life-threatening injury and illness, impeding their attendance and performance at school, and locking them into a life of poverty and few options other than continued work in the small-scale mining industry . . .

The studies demonstrated that girls are working longer hours, carrying out more activities and in some cases entering into even riskier underground work than in times past. . . .

Source: International Labour Organization.

MONEY LAUNDERING AND ILLEGAL TRANSFERS

"Money laundering" is the term used to describe disguising the illicit origin of the criminal proceeds of drug sales, fraud, corruption, and other crimes by bringing them back into the financial circuit of the legal economy. It owes its name to Chicago gangster Al Capone, who used the cash-intense business of laundries to hide his illegal alcohol proceeds during the Prohibition era of the 1920s and early 1930s.

An estimated $1.5 trillion to $3 trillion circulates around the world as illegal money transfers. These transfers take place using the banking sector as well as in the form of bogus invoices for exports and imports, unusually priced real estate transactions, or new electronic payment methods, like digital cash or e-gold. Although money laundering took place in ancient Chinese trading, it became criminalized only in the late 1980s. Since the inclusion of terrorism financing in laws to combat money laundering after the September 11 attacks, money laundering has developed into a matter of international safety and security. Fighting it turned from targeting Al Capone to targeting al-Qaeda.

Historical Background

After several decades of an unsuccessful U.S. war on drugs, the administration of Ronald Reagan chose a new method of "combat": If drug dealers and other criminals could not be pursued directly, then at least they should be discouraged by not being able to reap the monetary benefits of their acts. Thus, in 1986, money laundering became criminalized in the United States with penalties of up to 20 years' imprisonment and $500,000 in fines. Further legal arrangements were made that permitted seizing, freezing, and confiscation of assets by the authorities.

Because money laundering is a crime that respects no borders, Washington made strenuous efforts to convince the international community of its impor-

tance. At a global level, policy aimed at addressing money laundering started with the UN Convention on Drugs and Narcotics of 1988. In 1989, the Financial Action Task Force (FATF), an intergovernmental body tasked with combating money laundering, was established by the member countries of the G-7. Since then, international efforts to combat money laundering have proceeded apace. The FATF now comprises 34 member jurisdictions and two regional organizations, representing most major financial centers in the world. The fight against money laundering accelerated after the terrorist attacks of September 11, 2001. Thwarting terrorists by targeting their financing became part of the policies to combat money laundering generally. The FATF publishes no fewer than 40 recommendations to fight money laundering and nine recommendations to combat terrorist financing, with which countries that are suspected of permitting money laundering or failing to combat it adequately have to comply.

Member governments face regular scrutiny and, in the event of noncompliance with the recommendations, are subject to blacklisting for noncooperation. This can be economically harmful, because these countries risk the possibility that important international banks will refuse to do business with them. In this way the FATF sets the international standards. Countries have to convert these standards into national law, adapting their administration and law enforcement to combat laundering and terrorism. Lawyers in ministries, police officers, public prosecutors, and judges are all involved in the fight against money laundering, and special agencies, often known as Financial Intelligence Units (FIUs), must be established to fight laundering in each country. Countries have to introduce plans to implement ongoing customer due diligence (CDD), to identify nondomestic politically exposed persons (PEPs), and ascertain beneficial ownership of offshore accounts. Banks, real estate agents, notaries public, and traders in expensive goods are all obliged to screen their clients and to identify persons, activities, or transactions suspected of laundering money or financing terrorism. The FIUs collect suspicious transaction reports. Supervisory authorities are involved in controlling the compliance of banks and other sectors with the regulations aimed at combating money laundering. Some countries, like the United States, have high sanctions for not reporting suspect transactions, including a fine of up to $250,000 or five years' imprisonment.

Launderers and Their Techniques

The definition of money laundering relates to predicate offenses, activities that generate the proceeds that make laundering necessary. Hiding or disguising the source of certain proceeds does not amount to money laundering unless these proceeds were obtained through criminal activity. The United States has developed a list of over 130 predicate crimes for money laundering. Because more and more predicate offenses have been added to the definition over the years (today financing for terrorism and tax crimes are included), the amount of laundering is assumed to have increased.

Because money laundering takes place in secret, estimates of how much is being laundered vary considerably, from several hundred billion dollars to about US$3 trillion. The first rough estimate of the International Monetary Fund in 1998 said that laundering and illegal transfers totaled 5 percent of world GDP, then about $1.5 trillion (about $2 trillion in 2011 dollars). This amount still seems reasonable in light of the findings of the sophisticated economic and econometric models that followed. A much higher estimate was given by analyst Raymond Baker in 2005; he calculated that for every dollar of development aid given to the third world, $10 flows back into rich countries through capital flight. But his definition includes all sorts of (legal) capital flight in addition to money laundering; nevertheless, his results are discouraging to those trying to fight laundering and illegal transfers.

When it comes to deciding which countries are most attractive for launderers, small countries and offshore islands are often found atop FATF blacklists. Indeed, some small islands openly compete for criminal money and might have more incentives to attract laundered money without having to deal with the underlying predicate crime. However, the world's largest launderer in volume has been and still is the United States, which accounts for about half of global laundering. This explains the great interest on the part of the United States in a global fight against laundering, say experts. Launderers prefer rich countries, which have well-developed financial markets and large trade volume, enabling them to hide their illegal activities. Small islands, where each inhabitant becomes the legal but non-active head of hundreds of companies, are not a good disguise in the long run.

Launderers have many ways of hiding their illicit proceeds. A launderer first collects the small bills of cash from drug sales on the street and tries to deposit them in a bank (this is the placement phase). A cash courier then deposits the money into another country's bank if the domestic banks are very strictly controlled. After the money is in a bank account, it can be sent around the globe, using fake companies and fake bills and loans to disguise the original transaction (the layering phase). In this way, the criminal money is diluted, like a drop of ink falling into water. After the money is no longer identifiable as deriving from criminal activity, it can be invested in legal businesses (integration phase).

Because policy to combat money laundering originally focused mainly on regulating the banking sector, criminals have discovered new methods of laundering their ill-gotten gains. One technique consists of trade-based money laundering. Individual "A" uses drug money to buy a very expensive watch he exports for, say, US$100,000 to individual "B" in another country, but lists only $50 on the invoice. "B" receives the expensive watch, sells it and puts the $99,050 in a bank account in his home country for the exporter. Scholar John Zdanowicz has calculated that almost $200 billion flow from and to the United States through unusually high or low product prices.

In addition, Brigitte Unger and Joras Ferwerda have shown that the real estate sector is also used by criminals who launder money by buying houses and other property. Speculation is typical in this market, the economic and legal owners can differ, and real estate properties can be used for engaging in criminal activities or for generating legal rent income.

The development of new payment technologies has given criminals new ways to launder money. For example, they can buy legitimate prepaid automated teller machine (ATM) cards or smartcards, use dirty money to add value to the card, and then withdraw the newly cleaned funds from an ATM anywhere in the world. Mobile phone payments are an especially popular method for making transactions in the Middle East. In addition, electronic payment transfers such as Eurobonds, eCash or digital cash can conceal the money's origins and keep owners anonymous.

Combating Money Laundering

The hope is that efforts to combat money laundering will make drug dealing a less profitable business and will therefore deter drug dealers or other criminals from engaging in such activities. But not all money launderers are drug dealers. They can rely on a large group of facilitators, such as bank employees, notaries, lawyers, real estate agents, and accountants. For example, a bank employee might overlook a suspicious client; a notary or lawyer might accept cash for signing off on the buying of a business; a real estate agent might overlook a large increase in a house's price because a buyer wants to launder a large amount of money; and an accountant might overlook strange export and import activities at his company. Money laundering is a white-collar crime. In addition, the more people it involves, the larger the share of the community that gets drawn into the underworld.

Unger and others have identified some 25 negative effects that money laundering and illegal money transfers can have on the economy. Laundering infiltrates society and politics with criminals; it can crowd out entire branches of honest business; it can destabilize financial markets; and it can lead to less growth, more corruption, and more crime, among other effects. However, it should not be overlooked that criminally obtained money has all the same positive features of liquidity as legitimately obtained money. The UN has noted that international organized crime injected several hundred billion U.S. dollars into the world economy during the financial crisis. Out of a concern that disrupting any positive flow of liquidity and additional opportunities for profit in the banking sector, even if it derives from criminal sources, some countries hesitate to fully comply with international agreements on deterrence.

The Future

Even after decades of efforts aimed at combating money laundering, no decline has occurred in the revenue of crime and money laundering. In part, this is due to a broadening of the definition of money laundering. But it also shows that criminals have found new ways to launder money. Less controlled parts of financial markets (such as over-the-counter derivatives trading), electronic money, trade-based money laundering, and the real estate sector have offered new opportunities for launderers. At the same time, policies to combat money laundering has become fiercer, involving more and more sectors. Dealers in large sums of money, like buyers and sellers of diamonds or cars, are under increasing legal obligations in much of the world to report suspicious transactions, as are notaries and lawyers. However, the latter group is especially concerned about maintaining attorney–client privilege, which guarantees confidentiality of such interactions by law.

European countries with legal systems that are less adversarial than that in the United States face the problem of having to transform and adjust their systems more in the direction of control and punishment rather than of educating and finding common solutions with the private sector. At the moment, the inclusion of tax evasion in the definition of money laundering is an issue likely to face some resistance in Europe. It means that money launderers, whether they are drug dealers, tax evaders, or facilitators, will all be treated in the same way as terrorists, namely as threats to national security. Some European critics—particularly in countries where tax evasion is often seen as sport rather than a major crime—fear this will allow government to gain additional power to spy on people's economic activities. But the confiscation of criminally obtained money and its use for social purposes has also met with great success in some European countries, such as Italy, with widespread support among the public.

The speed with which this new policy field has developed around the world in recent years is, say experts, nothing short of astonishing and means that money laundering will remain high on the policy agenda of many governments in the future. It also means that it will be the subject of further academic inquiry, alongside tax evasion, tax compliance, and underground economic activities generally.

Brigitte Unger

See also: Corporate Social Responsibility; Crime, Organized; Government Corruption and Transparency; Regulation, Business and Financial; Terrorism.

Further Reading

Baker, Raymond. *Capitalism's Achilles' Heel—Dirty Money and How to Renew the Free-Market System.* New York: John Wiley & Sons, 2005.

Cox, Dennis W. *Introduction to Money Laundering Deterrence.* Hoboken, NJ: Wiley, 2010.

Gnutzmann, Hinerk, Killian J. McCarthy, and Brigitte Unger. "Dancing with the Devil: Country Size and the Incentive to Tolerate Money Laundering." *International Review of Law and Economics* 30 (2010): 244–252.

Masciandaro, Donato, Elod Takats, and Brigitte Unger. *Black Finance: The Economics of Money Laundering.* Cheltenham, UK: Edward Elgar, 2007.

Naylor, R.T. *Wages of Crime: Black Markets, Illegal Finance, and the Underworld Economy.* Ithaca, NY: Cornell University Press, 2004.

Rawlings, Gregory, and Brigitte Unger. "Competing for Criminal Money." *Global Business and Economics Review* 10:3 (2008): 331–352.

Schneider, Friedrich, and Ursula Windischbauer. "Money Laundering: Some Facts." *European Journal of Law and Economics* 26:3 (December 2009): 387–404.

Truman, Edwin, and Peter Reuter. *Chasing Dirty Money: The Fight Against Money Laundering.* Washington, DC: Institute for International Economics, 2004.

Unger, Brigitte. "From Al Capone to Al Qaeda: Regulating Money Laundering." In *Handbook of Regulation*, ed. David Levy. Cheltenham, UK: Edward Elgar, 2011.

———. *The Scale and Impact of Money Laundering.* Cheltenham, UK: Edward Elgar, 2007.

Unger, Brigitte, and Joras Ferwerda. *Money Laundering in the Real Estate Sector.* Cheltenham, UK: Edward Elgar, 2011.

Zdanowicz, John S. "Trade-Based Money Laundering." *Review of Law and Economics* 15 (December 2009): 855–878.

Web Sites

Financial Action Task Force: www.fatf-gafi.org
United Nations Office on Drugs and Crime (UNODC): www.unodc.org

Documents

Document 1: Money Laundering Control Act (United States), 1986

One of the first statutes of its kind anywhere in the world, the U.S. Money Laundering Control Act of 1986 defined and criminalized a host of activities associated with converting illegitimate financial gains into assets that appeared to be unassociated with criminal activity. Originally aimed at money obtained through drug dealing, the act has since been expanded—most notably, through the 2001 USA PATRIOT Act—to disrupting the financing of terrorists and terrorist organizations.

www.ffiec.gov/bsa_aml_infobase/documents/regulations/ML_Control_1986.pdf

Source: Federal Financial Institutions Examination Council.

Document 2: UN Convention Against Illicit Traffic in Narcotic Drugs and Psychotropic Substances (excerpts), 1988

In response to the growing problem of illicit narcotics production, trade, and use, the United Nations convened a meeting in 1988 to draw up a convention setting out the rules for multinational cooperation in combating the drug trade and drug abuse. Building on the pioneering work of the United States, the convention included a number of provisions aimed at dismantling the global financial underpinning—including money laundering and illegal money transfers—of the illegal trade. The following are the relevant excerpts of the 1988 UN convention on the illicit traffic in narcotics.

The Parties to this Convention . . .

Aware that illicit traffic generates large financial profits and wealth enabling transnational criminal organizations to penetrate, contaminate and corrupt the structures of government, legitimate commercial and financial business, and society at all its levels . . .

Article 5 Confiscation

3. In order to carry out the measures referred to in this article, each Party shall empower its courts or other competent authorities to order that bank, financial or commercial records be made available or be seized. A Party shall not decline to act under the provisions of this paragraph on the ground of bank secrecy . . .

Article 7 Mutual Legal Assistance

1. The Parties shall afford one another, pursuant to this article, the widest measure of mutual legal assistance in investigations, prosecutions and judicial proceedings in relation to criminal offences established in accordance with article 3, paragraph 1.

2. Mutual legal assistance to be afforded in accordance with this article may be requested for any of the following purposes: . . .

f) Providing originals or certified copies of relevant documents and records, including bank, financial, corporate or business records;

g) Identifying or tracing proceeds, property, instrumentalities or other things for evidentiary purposes.

Source: United Nations Office on Drugs and Crime.

MOSQUITO-BORNE DISEASE

Mosquito-borne diseases are viral or parasitic illnesses transmitted to humans through bites from infected mosquitoes. The most common mosquito-borne diseases that affect humans include malaria, dengue fever, rift valley fever, yellow fever, and arboviral encephalitides (viral diseases that cause brain inflammation, or encephalitis; they include Eastern equine encephalitis, Japanese encephalitis, La Crosse encephalitis, St. Louis encephalitis, West Nile virus, and Western equine encephalitis).

Presently, mosquito-borne illnesses are responsible for millions of deaths annually, along with a substantial portion of the global burden of disease. Far from being controlled, mosquito-borne diseases are actually burgeoning in many parts of the world, disproportionately affecting children and the poor. Mosquitoes, particularly those that infect humans, are ubiquitous in their geographical distribution, from the tropics to the arctic. Mosquito-borne diseases have been a source of concern since ancient times, and are likely to persist as a global public health issue well into the future.

Malaria

Malaria is a parasitic disease that is currently the fifth leading cause of death from infectious disease worldwide, and is the most common mosquito-borne disease globally. It has been documented in human populations for millennia; Chinese medical writings from 2700 B.C.E. describe malaria symptoms, and malaria was well known to the ancient Greeks by the fourth century B.C.E. Charles Louis Alphonse Laveran, a French army surgeon working in Algeria, discovered the parasite that causes malaria in 1880, and by 1886 it was established that there are different species of the parasite. It was not until 1897, however, that physicians understood that mosquitoes transmit malaria parasites.

The development of the insecticide DDT (dichlorodiphenyltrichloroethane) after World War II and the discovery of the antimalarial drug chloroquine prompted the first international campaigns aimed at eliminating malaria. The most aggressive of these was the Global Malaria Eradication Program, launched by the World Health Organization (WHO) in 1955. Some nations with temperate climates and seasonal transmission patterns have had successes in malaria control, including the elimination of malaria from the United States by the end of the 1950s, but the emergence of drug resistance in humans and insecticide resistance in mosquitoes has halted progress in many other parts of the world.

The increased mobility of both people and pathogens in today's modern, globalized world has made malaria eradication even more challenging. This development, coupled with a global failure to implement adequate measures in resource-limited settings, means that malaria remains a major cause of death and disease in developing nations. Today, WHO estimates the global burden of malaria to include approximately 216 million cases and 655,000 deaths annually; this means that a child dies from malaria every minute of every day.

Mosquitoes of the genus *Anopheles* transmit malaria parasites, which in turn are protozoa of the genus *Plasmodium*. Of the more than 120 species of *Plasmodium*, only five infect humans: *Plasmodium falciparum*, *P. vivax*, *P. ovale*, *P. malariae*, and *P. knowlesi*. Each of these five Plasmodium species differs in geographical distribution, epidemiology, clinical features, and patterns of drug resistance. *P. falciparum* is the cause of most severe cases of the disease.

Malaria tends to manifest in one of three ways. The first is asymptomatic or uncomplicated malaria, in which the infected person does not display any visible physical symptoms of being infected. This may result from partial immunity from living in malaria-endemic areas. People with asymptomatic infections can still spread the disease, however, posing a challenge for transmission control. Second, an infected person may have symptomatic, mild malaria, with periodic high temperatures, headaches, shivering, muscle pains, and/or diarrhea, among other influenza-like symptoms. The majority of malaria cases worldwide fall into this category. Last, severe malaria is a life-threatening condition that must be medically treated. It can result in severe anemia, swelling of the brain, or kidney failure, all of which have a high mortality rate.

Active malaria infections may be acute (one time) or chronic (ongoing). The determinants of malaria transmission vary broadly depending on the specific parasite, but include mosquito, climatic, and human factors. Currently, there is no effective malaria vaccine, and drug resistance is widespread. Antimalarial drugs are used for both prevention and curative therapy, though only with partial success.

Yellow Fever

Yellow fever, so named because yellowing of the skin from jaundice is among its symptoms, is relatively new. It is thought to have emerged in East Africa sometime in the sixteenth century and to have been transported by ship to South America. The first recorded outbreak of yellow fever was in Mexico in 1648, and the disease had a profound influence in the Americas thereafter, with at least 25 major outbreaks claiming hundreds of thousands of lives. Fear of the "Yellow Jack," as it became known, made the European colonies of the New World—particularly the Caribbean—unpopular postings for soldiers, occasionally to the point of encouraging mutiny and open rebellion. The disease was responsible for devastating French losses in Haiti in 1802, prompting Napoleon Bonaparte to all but abandon the Western Hemisphere and to sell Louisiana to the United States.

Yellow fever was the first mosquito-borne disease to be linked to mosquitoes; the idea was first proposed by Cuban physician Carlos Finlay in 1881 and was confirmed by a team of military doctors under the command of Major Walter Reed in 1900. In 1927, the specific virus that causes yellow fever was isolated in West Africa, laying the groundwork for the development of a pair of vaccines in the 1930s—17D (which won its developer, microbiologist Max Theiler, the Nobel Prize) and French neurotropic vaccine (FNV). FNV has been proven to be dangerous, and was abandoned in the 1960s, but 17D is still in use today, with over 400 million doses having been administered.

Because 17D was highly effective, the number of yellow fever cases dropped precipitously in the first 50 years after it was introduced, which in turn encouraged complacency on the part of many governments. In the Americas, vaccination programs were often underfunded or suspended entirely, while in Africa and other parts of the world, resources were invested in combating diseases that seemed more pressing. Meanwhile, little attention was paid to research—either to finding treatments or cures for yellow fever, or to finding a new vaccine to replace what is now 70-year-old technology.

Consequently, yellow fever is now a reemerging disease, with the number of cases growing steadily each year since the 1980s. Today, there are an estimated 200,000 cases of yellow fever and 30,000 deaths annually. Further, after the world went decades without a widespread outbreak, Paraguay suffered a yellow fever epidemic in 2008. There is some concern that the Paraguayan incident could be the first in a new wave of outbreaks, and that the tools currently available for fighting yellow fever will be inadequate to the task at hand.

Aedes aegypti mosquitoes are the primary transmitters of yellow fever, though some other species in the genus *Aedes* can also carry the disease. It is caused by a single-strand RNA virus, and is currently found only in Africa (90 percent of cases) and South America.

Transmission of yellow fever generally follows one of three patterns. In a sylvatic (or jungle) yellow fever outbreak, monkeys pass the disease to mosquitoes, which in turn bite humans (primarily young men at work in the forest). In intermediate yellow fever outbreaks, which comprise the vast majority of incidents, the disease is introduced into one or more rural villages by "domestic" mosquitoes. With urban yellow fever outbreaks, the disease reaches densely populated areas where immunity is rare and *Aedes* mosquitoes are common. This is the rarest transmission pattern, but also the most deadly.

Once a person is infected with yellow fever, symptoms—chills, fever, headache, loss of appetite, nausea, and vomiting—will emerge within three to six days, and will usually last for less than a week. In the most dangerous cases of yellow fever—about 15 percent—the disease enters a second phase characterized by abdominal pain, severe fever, jaundice, and vomiting of blood. One in five people who reach this stage will not survive.

There is, as noted, an effective vaccination for yel-

A municipal health worker in Santa Cruz, Bolivia, fumigates the street against mosquitos during a national outbreak of dengue fever in 2009. Up to 100 million people annually are infected with the disease worldwide, predominantly in equatorial regions. *(STR/AFP/Getty Images)*

low fever, and individuals who are not inoculated and contract the disease also become immune. Beyond this, however, there is no treatment or cure for yellow fever. Physicians can mitigate specific symptoms, but otherwise have no option but to stand by and let the disease run its course.

Dengue Fever

Dengue fever is an old disease, the first recorded case appearing in a Chinese medical encyclopedia published in 992 C.E. However, as with malaria, it was not until the turn of the twentieth century that physicians recognized that the disease was transmitted by mosquitoes. Dengue hemorrhagic fever, the most severe and potentially fatal form of the disease, was first documented in the 1950s during outbreaks in Thailand and the Philippines.

In the latter portion of the twentieth century, dengue fever underwent extensive geographic expansion, partially attributable to globalization, ineffective control efforts, and rapid unplanned urbanization, making it one of the most important urban tropical infectious diseases today. More than 100 countries in Asia, the Pacific, the Americas, Africa, and the Caribbean have endemic dengue (the infection is consistently active among the population), and over 40 percent of the world's citizens live in areas at risk for dengue transmission. There are approximately 50 to 100 million dengue infections and 25,000 deaths per year, primarily in children.

Mosquitoes of the genus *Aedes,* which are globally distributed, transmit dengue fever. The disease primarily affects urban areas in tropical and subtropical regions, as *Aedes* mosquitoes are well adapted to urban environments. Water storage containers and other sources of standing water serve as breeding sites for the mosquitoes.

Dengue is caused by any of four related viruses (DENV1, DENV2, DENV3, DENV4), and can have a range of clinical manifestations, from asymptomatic to high fever and severe joint pain to severe hemorrhaging and death. Infection from one dengue virus does not confer immunity against any of the others, and sequential infections result in greater risk of the severe form of disease, dengue hemorrhagic fever. Typically, symptoms begin 4 to 7 days after being bit by an infected mosquito and last for 3 to 10 days. No vaccines or effective antiviral drugs currently exist, and prevention efforts are primarily focused on mosquito control.

West Nile Virus

West Nile virus is endemic to Africa, Asia, Europe, and Australia. It was first identified in Uganda in 1937, and has since spread to temperate regions of the world, including North America and Europe. It was identified as a cause of severe human encephalitis during an outbreak in Israel in 1957; in the summer of 1999 West Nile virus was discovered in New York. It is currently found throughout most of the United States. Outbreaks of West Nile virus encephalitis have also been documented in Algeria (1994), the Czech Republic (1997), the Democratic Republic of Congo (1998), and Russia (1999). There are no reliable estimates for the worldwide incidence of the disease, but in the United States the Centers for Disease Control and Prevention reported 690 cases and 43 deaths for the year 2011. This makes West Nile virus a deadlier threat in the U.S. than either dengue fever or malaria.

West Nile virus is a single-stranded RNA virus transmitted by mosquitoes of the species *Culex,* with most human infections occurring in the summer or early fall in temperate and subtropical areas, and during the rainy season in tropical zones. Risk factors for contracting West Nile virus include exposure to infected mosquitoes via outdoor activity,

Prominent Mosquito-borne Diseases

Disease	Pathogen	Type	Primary vector
Yellow fever	Flavivirus	Virus	*Aedes aegypti, A. africanus*
Dengue fever	Flavivirus	Virus	*Aedes aegypti*
Malaria	*Plasmodium* spp.	Protozoan	*Anopheles* spp.
Filariasis	*Wucheria bancrofti*	Nematode	*Anopheles* spp., *Culex spp.*
Rift Valley fever	Phlebovirus	Virus	*Culex* spp.
West Nile virus	Flavivirus	Virus	*Culex pipiens. C. quinquefasciatus*
St. Louis encephalitis	Flavivirus	Virus	*Culex pipiens. C. quinquefasciatus*
Eastern Equine encephalitis	Alphavirus	Virus	*Culiseta melanura*
LaCrosse encephalitis	Bunyavirus	Virus	*Aedes triseriatus*
Western Equine encephalitis	Alphavirus	Virus	*Aedes* spp., *Culex* spp.
Chikungunya	Alphavirus	Virus	*Aedes aegypti, Aedes albopictus*
Japanese encephalitis	Flavivirus	Virus	*Culex tritaeniorhynchus*

Source: Adapted from Jerome Goddard, *Infectious Diseases and Arthropods,* 2d ed. (New York: Humana, 2008).

failure to use mosquito repellents, and proximity to standing water sources that serve as mosquito breeding sites. West Nile virus is zoonotic (caused by infectious agents that can be transmitted between animals and humans). It primarily circulates among birds and *Culex* mosquitoes, with humans serving as incidental hosts. Although rare, West Nile virus may also spread through blood transfusions, organ transplants, breastfeeding, or from mother to child during pregnancy.

The risk of encephalitis and death, once an individual is infected with West Nile virus, increases with age, with people over age 50 most at risk for severe disease. As with malaria, the disease may manifest in any of three different clinical outcomes, including asymptomatic, mild, or severe. About 80 percent of infections are asymptomatic, while the remaining 20 percent of cases are mostly mild, with sufferers experiencing fever, headache, body aches, nausea, vomiting, and occasionally skin rashes or swollen lymph glands for a few days to several weeks. Severe disease is rare, affecting approximately one in 150 infected people, with symptoms including high fever, headache, neck stiffness, stupor, disorientation, coma, tremors, convulsions, muscle weakness, vision loss, numbness, and paralysis for up to several weeks with potentially permanent neurologic damage. West Nile virus symptoms generally manifest within 3 to 14 days of being bit by an infected mosquito. There is currently no vaccine or specific treatment for West Nile virus.

Global Impact

Mosquito-borne diseases not only have clinical ramifications for individuals, but also have significant population health and economic impacts. At the individual level, these diseases can cause symptoms that are debilitating for the infected person, and can lead to death. Additionally, mosquito-borne illnesses may result in having to miss school or work, which can be highly detrimental to low-income individuals, particularly in developing countries. In today's integrated, global economy, the flow of mosquitoes, pathogens, and hosts can also result in rapid movement of disease across political and geographic boundaries, making this a truly global issue.

On a societal level, mosquito-borne disease treatment, control, and prevention have huge economic costs. Maintaining human resources for health, financing the procurement of drugs and insecticides, and supply-chain management all require substantial investments and political will. There are also indirect economic costs to mosquito-borne diseases, including the cost of lost productive labor time. This is particularly challenging for the resource-limited countries that also suffer from the highest burden of disease. Mosquito-borne diseases that affect livestock, such as Rift Valley fever, may also have considerable economic impact due to limited trade and depletion of resources.

Combating Mosquito-borne Diseases

Currently, effective treatments are only available for some mosquito-borne diseases. There are ten known antimalarial drugs; all but primaquine (therapeutic against *P. vivax, P. ovale,* gametocytes), clindamycin (used in combination with chloroquine), and tetracycline (used against multi-drug-resistant malaria) have documented cases of drug resistance. There is no malaria vaccine currently on the market, although clinical trials are under way and there is much promise for a viable vaccine in the near future. For dengue fever and West Nile virus, there are currently no specific antiviral therapies available; however, there is much ongoing research into potential drugs and vaccines. Yellow fever can only be controlled with vaccines, though it too is now the subject of much research.

Mosquito-borne diseases can also be prevented or lessened by efforts to control mosquito populations. This includes the use of insecticides as well as eliminating standing water and other mosquito-breeding sites wherever possible. At the same time, it is important to minimize human exposure to infected mosquitoes. The use of bed nets, particularly insecticide-treated long-lasting nets, is helpful, as is individual use of mosquito repellents during the day. Surveillance is important as well; data on incidents of mosquito-borne diseases can help to identify problem areas and forestall epidemics.

In short, while there is no single solution for combating mosquito-borne diseases on a global scale, strategic, community-specific, and integrated control and prevention measures can effectively reduce the magnitude of this global health problem.

The Future

Mosquito-borne diseases are likely to remain a significant global challenge in the coming decades. The expected consequences of global environmental change, demographic change, and urbanization add an additional level of complexity to the issue. Changing climates and landscape ecologies will likely have an impact on the dynamics of mosquito-borne diseases, and control programs will need to adapt accordingly in the future. Urbanization and growing populations, especially in regions most vulnerable to mosquito-borne diseases, pose interesting questions regarding the future of urban mosquito-borne diseases, such as dengue. The continuing problem of drug resistance also calls for further investment in researching improved vaccines, drugs, and diagnostics. Political will to support the scale-up of existing tools and investment in exploration of novel instruments will be essential for reducing the global burden of mosquito-borne diseases.

Jennifer Ward

See also: Drug Resistance; Infant Mortality; Parasitic Disease; Public Health; Vaccination; Waterborne Disease.

Further Reading

Cook, Gordon C. *Manson's Tropical Diseases.* 20th ed. Philadelphia: W.B. Saunders, 2003.

Cox, F.E.G. *Illustrated History of Tropical Diseases.* London: The Welcome Trust, 1996.

Goddard, Jerome. *Infectious Diseases and Arthropods.* 2d ed. New York: Humana, 2008.

Gubler, D.J. "Dengue/Dengue Haemorrhagic Fever: History and Current Status." *Novartis Foundation Symposium* 277 (2006): 3–16.

———. "Resurgent Vector-borne Diseases as a Global Health Problem." *Emerging Infectious Diseases* 4:3 (July–September 1998): 442–450.

Gubler, Duane, and Clark, Gary. "Dengue/Dengue Hemorrhagic Fever: The Emergence of a Global Health Problem." *Emerging Infectious Diseases* 1:2 (April–June 1995): 55–57.

Guerrant, Richard L., David H. Walker, and Peter F. Weller. *Tropical Infectious Diseases: Principles, Pathogens, and Practice.* Philadelphia: Churchill Livingstone, 1999.

Kaplan, Colin. *Infection and Environment.* Woburn, MA: Butterworth-Heinemann, 1997.

Krause, Richard M. *Emerging Infections.* San Diego, CA: Academic, 1998.

Reiter, P. "Climate Change and Mosquito-borne Disease." *Environmental Health Perspectives* 109:1 (2001): 141–161.

Tolle, M.A. "Mosquito-borne Diseases." *Current Problems in Pediatric and Adolescent Health Care* 39:4 (2009): 97–140.

Web Sites

American Mosquito Control Association: www.mosquito.org/mosquito-borne-diseases

Centers for Disease Control and Prevention: www.cdc.gov/ncidod/diseases/list_mosquitoborne.htm

World Health Organization, Dengue Fever: www.who.int/topics/dengue/en

World Health Organization, Malaria: www.who.int/topics/malaria/en

World Health Organization, West Nile Virus: www.who.int/csr/don/archive/disease/west_nile_fever/en

World Health Organization, Yellow Fever: www.who.int/topics/yellow_fever/en

Documents

Document 1: Nobel Lecture (excerpt), Alphonse Laveran, 1907

In 1880, Charles Louis Alphonse Laveran, a French physician working at a military hospital in Algeria, was the first to realize that malaria was caused by a protozoan parasite living in people's red blood cells. Prior to Laveran's discovery, scientists suspected that the disease was caused by bacteria living in the soil or water. While Laveran was greeted with skepticism at first, new methods of detection confirmed his discovery and eventually he was awarded the Nobel Prize in Physiology or Medicine for his work on the role of protozoan parasites in disease. The following is an excerpt from his Nobel lecture, discussing how he came to his discovery.

Protozoa as Causes of Diseases

My scientific colleagues of the Caroline Institute having done me the very great honour of awarding me the Nobel Prize in Medicine this year for my work on diseases due to Protozoa, the regulations of the Nobel Foundation oblige me to give a summary of my main researches on this question.

I must however go back a little in order to explain how I was led to concern myself with the pathogenic protozoa.

In 1878 after having finished my course of instruction at the School of Military Medicine of Val-de-Grâce, I was sent to Algeria and put in charge of a department of the hospital at Bone. A large number of my patients had malarial fevers and I was naturally led to study these fevers of which I had only seen rare and benign forms in France.

Malaria which is almost unknown in the north of Europe is however of great importance in the south of the Continent particularly in Greece and Italy; these fevers in many of the localities become the dominant disease and the forms become more grave; alongside the intermittent forms, both the continuous forms and those called malignant appear. In the tropical and subtropical regions, endemic malaria takes first place almost everywhere among the causes of morbidity and mortality and it constitutes the principal obstacle to the acclimatization of Europeans in these regions. Algeria has become much less unhealthy than it was at the commencement of the French occupation but one still comes across regions such as the banks of Lake Fezzara, not far from Bone, in which endemic-epidemic malaria rages every year.

I had the opportunity of making necropsies on patients dead from malignant fever and of studying the melanaemia, i.e. the formation of black pigment in the blood of patients affected by malaria. This melanaemia had been described by many observers, but people were still in doubt about the constancy of the alteration in malaria, and about the causes of the production of this pigment.

I was struck by the special characters which these pigment grains presented especially in the capillaries of the liver and the cerebrospinal centres, and I tried to pursue the study of its formation in the blood of persons affected by malarial fever. I found in the blood, leucocytes more or less loaded with pigment, but in addition to these melaniferous leucocytes, pigmented spherical bodies of variable size possessing amoeboid movement, free or adherent to the red cells; non-pigmented corpuscles forming clear spots in the red cells; finally pigmented elements, crescentic in shape attracted my attention, and from then on I supposed they were parasites.

In 1880 at the Military Hospital at Constantine, I discovered on the edges of the pigmented spherical bodies in the blood of a patient suffering from malaria, filiform elements resembling flagellae which were moving very rapidly, displacing the neighbouring red cells. From then on I had no more doubts of the parasitic nature of the elements which I had found; I described the principal appearances of the malarial haematozoon in memoranda sent to the Academy of Medicine, the Academy of Sciences (1880–1882) and in a monograph entitled: *Nature parasitaire des accidents de l'impaludisme, description d'un nouveau parasite trouvé dans le sang des malades atteints de fièvre palustre*, Paris, 1881.

These first results of my researches were received with much scepticism.

In 1879, Klebs and Tommasi Crudeli had described under the name of *Bacillus malariae*, a bacillus found in the soil and water in malarial localities and a large number of Italian observers had published papers confirming the work of these authors.

The haematozoon which I gave as the agent of malaria did not resemble bacteria, and was present in strange forms, and in short it was completely outside the circle of the known pathogenic microbes, and many observers not knowing how to classify it found it simpler to doubt its existence.

In 1880, the technique of examination of the blood was unfortunately very imperfect, which contributed to the prolongation of the discussion relative to the new haematozoon and it was necessary to perfect this technique and invent new staining procedures to demonstrate its structure.

Confirmatory investigations at first rare, became more and more numerous; at the same time endoglobular parasites were discovered in different animals which closely resembled the haematozoon of malaria. In 1889, my haematozoon had been found in the majority of malarial regions and it was not possible to doubt any more either its existence or its pathogenic role.

Many observers before me had sought without success to discover the cause of malaria and I should also have failed if I had been content merely to examine the air, water, or the soil in malarial localities as had been done up till then, but I had taken as the basis of my investigations the pathological anatomy and the study in vivo of malarial blood and this is how I was able to reach my goal.

The malarial haematozoon is a protozoon, a very small protozoon since it lives and develops in the red blood cells which in man have a diameter of only 7 microns. . . .

After the discovery of the malarial parasite in the blood of the patients an important question still remained to be solved: in what state does the haematozoon exist outside the body and how does infection occur? The solution of this problem required long and laborious researches.

After having vainly attempted to detect the parasite in the air, the water, or the soil of malarial areas and trying to cultivate it in the most varied media, I became convinced that the microbe was already present outside the human body in a parasitic state and very probably as a parasite of mosquitoes . . .

To summarize: for twenty-seven years, I have not ceased to busy myself with the study of the parasitic Protozoa of man and animals and I can say, I believe without exaggeration, that I have taken an important part in the progress which has been made in this field.

Before the discovery of the malarial haemotozoon no pathogenic endoglobular haematozoon was known; today the *Haemocytozoa* constitute a family, important for the number of genera and species and also for the role some of these Protozoa play in human or veterinary pathology.

By directing the attention of doctors and veterinary surgeons to examination of the blood, study of the endoglobular haematozoa prepared the way for the discovery of the diseases due to trypanosomes which themselves also constitute a new and very important chapter in pathology.

The knowledge of these new pathogenic agents has thrown a strong light on a large number of formerly obscure questions. The progress attained shows once more how just is the celebrated axiom formulated by Bacon: "Bene est scire, per causas scire."

Source: www.nobelprize.org.

Document 2: "The Global Malaria Action Plan for a Malaria-Free World," Roll Back Malaria Partnership, 2008

Launched by the World Health Organization, the United Nations Development Programme, UNICEF, and the World Bank in 1998, the Roll Back Malaria Partnership was set up to coordinate the antimalarial activities of hundreds of nongovernmental organizations and government entities around the world. A decade later, the Partnership announced its Global Malaria Action Plan, the two main goals of which were to scale up the development and distribution of preventive and therapeutic interventions, and to sustain the control of malaria over time. The plan set ambitious targets, including a reduction in the number of malarial cases by 50 percent from 2000 levels by 2010 and by 75 percent by 2015. As of early 2012, the initiative had mixed success, meeting goals in some countries but failing to meet them in others.

www.rbm.who.int/gmap/gmap.pdf

Source: World Health Organization.

NATURAL DISASTERS, PREPAREDNESS AND RESPONSE

Natural disasters are events of nature that have a significant and negative impact on human life and civilization, resulting in large-scale loss of life, injury, and property damage. Natural disasters are caused either directly or indirectly by climatic or tectonic events.

Natural disasters have always been part of human existence and have even altered history. For most of that history, humans ascribed supernatural causes to natural disasters and had little capacity to prepare for them. Although these events are still called "acts of God," advances in science have allowed people to understand that natural disasters are caused by natural forces, some of which can be predicted and their effects mitigated through better preparedness, advanced construction standards, and other measures.

As human society has become wealthier and better governed, it has also developed policies, technologies, and protocol to respond to natural disasters in ways that help to minimize long-term losses to life and property. At the same time, other historical trends—most notably, population growth and shifts in settlement and farming patterns—have exposed far more people to the effects of natural disasters. Looking toward the future, anthropogenic climate change is likely to aggravate climate-based natural disasters.

Types and Impact

Earth is a dynamic planet. Its climate is shaped by a variety of natural forces, including solar energy, planetary rotation, ocean currents, and topography. Its surface is also in motion, though much more slowly, driven by plate tectonics, whereby large pieces of the surface are moved about by heat and motion within the earth's molten and semi-molten interior.

For the most part, climatic events remain within certain parameters of temperature and precipitation; humans have developed their societies to function within these parameters. However, climatic events frequently exceed the bounds of these parameters. When they do, and when those events have an impact on human life and property, the results are natural disasters. Climate-based natural disasters come in three basic forms. The more publicized ones are of the catastrophic type, caused by immediate weather events such as hurricanes (known as typhoons in the Pacific Ocean and cyclones in the Indian Ocean), tornadoes, electrical storms or thunderstorms, wind shear, blizzards, hail and ice storms, and unexpected frosts. More indirectly, immediate weather events may trigger other disasters—typically flooding, wildfires, insect infestations, and even epidemics.

Weather events can also interact with topography to produce landslides, snow avalanches, and certain forms of flooding, or with man-made structures to produce secondary disasters, as was the case when flooding caused by Hurricane Katrina breached levies in New Orleans. Chronic climate events include periods of excessive cold or heat as well as drought, which is arguably the most catastrophic of all natural disasters, even if the least spectacular in its impact, as it often leads to famine and mass loss of life. Tectonic events include volcanic eruptions and earthquakes. When these events occur under the sea, they are capable of generating tsunamis.

The impact of natural disasters varies widely by type of disaster, intensity of the disaster, and where and when it occurs. Most disasters result in both loss of life and limb and property damage, while others—such as hail or unexpected frosts—largely result in property damage, usually to agriculture.

It is extremely difficult to assess aggregate loss of life due to natural disasters, as they may have long-term consequences such as disruptions to agriculture, health care, and economic activity that lead to deaths long after the event is over. Among the generally agreed-upon figures, annual figures vary widely depending on how many natural disasters have occurred in a given year and how severe they were. Between 2000 and 2010, it has been estimated that approximately 28,000 people, about 3 persons per million, died annually as a direct result of extreme weather events globally. Of these, about 50 percent died from wind-related events of various kinds, 25 percent from floods, 20 percent from extreme temperatures, and the remaining 5 percent from all other events.

Altogether, extreme weather events are responsible for approximately 0.03 percent of all deaths annually. This is compared to about 59 percent, or 34 million, from noncommunicable health conditions; 31 percent, or 18 million, from communicable diseases; 9 percent, or about 5 million, from injuries; and about 1 percent from famine and nutritional deficiencies, or just over half a million people. In the United States, a study of deaths due to weather-related events between 1979 and 2002 found just over half, or about 16,000, were due to extreme cold, with just under 30 percent due to extreme heat, about 8 percent to flood, about 5 percent to lightning and tornadoes each, and the remainder to hurricanes.

Tectonic events, largely earthquakes and the tsunamis they occasionally trigger, were responsible for approximately 80,000 deaths annually between 2000 and 2010, though this was somewhat high as compared to other decades, a result of the catastrophic Indian Ocean tsunami of 2004 and the devastating Haitian earthquake of 2010. In short, then, natural disasters are directly responsible for about 120,000 deaths annually, or about 0.1 percent of all deaths. However, most experts agree that a substantial number of the deaths from nutritional deficiencies, and a smaller percentage of those from communicable diseases, can be traced to such natural disasters as drought, flooding, and, to a lesser extent, earthquakes.

Even more difficult to analyze and measure than death rates is property damage, which often goes unmeasured in those places or cases where there is no insurance that requires such accounting. Best estimates come from more developed countries, where there

are the resources and motivation to assess property damage more thoroughly in the form of collecting on insurance and for the purposes of government aid to victims. According to figures compiled by the National Climatic Data Center for 2011, a not atypical year in which no truly catastrophic events occurred in the United States, the total for property damage was an estimated $50 billion. Of this, the largest figures came from the summer and fall drought and heat wave of the Southern Plains, at $10 billion; the tornado outbreak in the Midwest and Southeast in late April, at $10 billion; and August's Hurricane Irene along the Eastern seaboard, at about $7 billion. By comparison, it is estimated that Hurricane Katrina—the worst weather-related disaster in U.S. history—caused more than $100 billion in damage. In contrast, the most recent large tectonic event in a major urban U.S. area—the Northridge, California, earthquake of 1994—caused about $20 billion dollars in damage. Worldwide, it was estimated that about $366 billion was lost to natural disasters in 2011.

In general, property damage is often higher in developed countries, simply because there is more valuable property to be damaged and more costly infrastructure to be replaced. On the other hand, loss of life tends to be far higher in developing countries, for a variety of reasons: people live in more hazard-prone areas; poorer building standards and less preparedness; inadequate response capacity; and the presence of a more vulnerable population due to poor nutrition and health. While each disaster is unique—earthquakes of the same magnitude, for example, can be far more destructive if they happen to the earth's surface or near urban areas—some comparisons between the developed and developing worlds make a point. The Kobe, Japan, earthquake of 1994 was of similar magnitude and proximity to an urban area as the Haitian earthquake of 2010; the former resulted in some 6,400 lives lost and $100 billion in property damage while the latter resulted in 300,000 deaths and about $10 billion in property damage.

Tectonic and weather-related disaster events occur globally, though some regions are more prone to them than others. The vast majority of deaths from drought, for example, occur in sub-Saharan Africa, while flooding causes the most amount of damage and loss of life in South and East Asia. Wind events are more frequent in eastern North America and the Caribbean Basin, the islands and mainland of Southeast Asia, and the lands bordering the Bay of Bengal in South Asia. As for earthquakes, the greatest

Ten Deadliest Natural Disasters in Human History

Type of Disaster	Year	Location	Estimated loss of life
River flooding	1931	Central China	1,000,000–2,500,000
River flooding	1887	Yellow River Basin, China	900,000–2,000,000
Earthquake	1556	Shaanxi Province, China	830,000
Cyclone	1879	East Pakistan (now Bangladesh)	500,000
Earthquake	2010	Haiti	316,000
Cyclone	1839	Andhra Pradesh, India	300,000
Earthquake	526	Antioch, Byzantine Empire (now Turkey)	250,000–300,000
Earthquake and tsunami	2004	Sumatra and Indian Ocean basin	230,000–310,000
Earthquake	1976	Hebei, China	242,000
Earthquake	1920	Ningxia-Gansu, China	234,000

Source: Author.

number typically occur along the major fault lines that outline the world's tectonic plates—the Pacific Rim and a band of territory between 25 degrees and 45 degrees north latitude stretching from East Asia to the Mediterranean Basin.

History

Natural disasters have been part of human experience from the time our species evolved from its pre-hominid ancestors. Indeed, it is likely that such disasters played a role in humanity's evolution—adapting to long-term climate change and the shorter-term weather events it triggered—and its migration in pre-historic times out of the African homeland and across the rest of globe.

In the historical era, both weather-related and tectonic natural disasters have changed the course of civilizations. Some archaeologists have argued that a massive eruption on the Mediterranean island of Thera (now Santorini) caused the destruction of the Minoan civilization around 2600 B.C.E., one of the proto-civilizations that predated ancient Greece. Long-term drought is the explanation scholars have posited for the demise of the Anasazi of the American Southwest in the early centuries of the last millennium, a contributing factor in the rise of Navajo and Hopi cultures. In more recent times, the great Lisbon earthquake of 1755, arguably the greatest tectonic disaster in recorded European history, undermined faith in a benevolent Christian God for many thinkers, contributing to the Enlightenment and a turn toward more scientific understanding of the natural world and its events. The eruption of the volcano on the island of Tambora in the Dutch East Indies (now Indonesia) in 1815 spewed so much ash into the air that it diminished the amount of solar energy reaching Earth, affecting global climate patterns and resulting in what contemporaries referred to in 1816 as "the year without a summer."

And in our own era, drought conditions in the African Sahel have resulted not just in massive loss of life but have contributed to the political instability that has plagued that region. In addition, the massive famines produced by these recurrent droughts have had a profound effect on international politics and philanthropy, helping to spur media-based popular relief efforts and the global infrastructure of nongovernmental famine-relief organizations.

In general, lives lost to natural disasters have climbed as population rose throughout human history, until the early twentieth century, when various scientific measures in prediction, preparedness, and response have lowered the cost in lives. Since these developments, the number of lives lost to natural disasters has steadily fallen, though specific catastrophes can cause the numbers to spike from time to time.

Even as human civilization has been affected by catastrophic and chronic natural disasters, so human thought has evolved in its explanation for the causes of these phenomena. The history of thinking about earthquakes—perhaps the most capricious of frequently experienced natural disasters—illustrates how human thinking has evolved over the millennia of human existence. Most ancient cultures viewed the earth as an object manipulated by mythic creatures and gods. Monotheistic theologies have ultimately placed causation in the hands of an omnipotent deity whose motives and actions, such as earthquakes that kill the good and innocent along with the evil and guilty, were ultimately unknowable to mortal humans. The great flood described in the Book of Genesis, for example, was attributed to God's wrath at a humanity steeped in sin.

The ancient Greeks were perhaps the first that we know of to attribute the direct causation of earthquakes to natural forces. Anaxamines, a philosopher of the sixth century B.C.E., said earthquakes were the result of interactions between water and land. Aristotle, two centuries later, attributed the shakings to compressed gases within the earth, an explanation he offered for extreme meteorological phenomena as well. In the late medieval world of Europe, God and science often intermingled, as in the view of thirteenth-century Italian philosopher Thomas Aquinas that God causes earthquakes but uses natural forces, such as vapors and winds, to bring them about. Early Enlightenment scientists of the seventeenth and eighteenth century, including those much affected by the Lisbon earthquake, also ascribed earthquakes to the weather. Only in the late nineteenth century were the foundations of modern thinking on earthquake causation first laid, and it was not until the theory of plate tectonics and continental drift came about in the twentieth century that our fundamental understanding of earthquake causation was fully formed.

Prediction, Preparation, Response

Our understanding of natural disasters is a critical component in how humanity has coped with them in trying to mitigate the loss of life and property that they cause and to relieve the suffering and damage they wreak. Understanding their underlying causes has led to improvements in prediction. Better knowledge of their dynamics has allowed for improvements in preparedness and a deeper awareness of how they cause damage has led to improved response systems.

Prediction

The key to effective prediction of natural disasters is increasing what is known as lead time, that is, the time between a reasonably certain prediction of a given event and the event itself. Different kinds of weather disasters allow for varying lead times. Large-scale events such as hurricanes and typhoons take days and even weeks to form, while tornadoes and hail can be spawned from thunderstorm cells in a matter of minutes. Nevertheless, while the existence of hurricanes, typhoons, and other large-scale weather events over their ocean breeding grounds is apparent days before they affect human populations

and become natural disasters, their intensity and their course remain unpredictable.

Data collection, data interpretation, and communications are critical not only in making predictions but in forwarding those predictions to populations and appropriate emergency and security personnel, thereby allowing the predictions to limit loss of life and limb and property damage. The more data available and the better it is distributed and interpreted, the more accurate the predictions can be. As early as the late nineteenth century, weather stations in the Caribbean and continental North America were collecting data on hurricanes and passing them on by means of telegraphs and undersea cables. By the early twentieth century, wireless technology was allowing data collected by ships to be forwarded to weather stations.

Various forms of remote detection, beginning with radar, allowed for the collection of data far from Earth-bound, traditional weather monitoring devices and closer to the higher altitudes of atmosphere where weather events are formed and shaped. Perhaps the most important of these new technologies has been Doppler radar, an augmented form of traditional radar that beams microwave signals at a weather system and then measures how the return signal is affected by the motion of the system. First theorized by Austrian physicist Christian Doppler in the mid-nineteenth century, but not made operational until after World War II, Doppler radar provides the most accurate picture of the internal dynamics of weather events, particularly as they take shape. Over time, comparisons of Doppler information on the formation of weather systems and the mature events that formative period led to has allowed scientists to make ever more accurate predictions. While not exclusively meteorological, two other technologies have been crucial in the field of weather prediction—high-speed computers, which allow for large amounts of data to be analyzed quickly, and satellites, particularly the geo-synchronous ones found in fixed positions above the earth since the early 1960s, which provide hemisphere-wide picture of the atmosphere.

Earthquake prediction is a far more rudimentary science than weather prediction. No technology has yet been developed to reliably predict earthquakes even minutes before they occur, although Japanese scientists have recently developed methods for interpreting certain kinds of long waves produced by tectonics that arrive seconds before the shorter, damage-producing waves arrive. While useless for notifying the public, a few seconds of advanced warning can allow technicians running transportation systems or electrical grids to shut down operations in preparation for a quake. As for the tsunamis triggered by undersea earthquakes, a system of ocean buoys capable of detecting wave patterns that signal a tsunami and linked to warning stations has been in operation in the Pacific since the late 1940s and was augmented for the Indian Ocean in the wake of the disastrous tsunami of 2004.

Preparedness and Prevention

Preparing for natural disasters can either be long-term, for those in disaster-prone areas, or short-term, in advance of a disaster for which there is reliable forewarning. Long-term preparedness consists of bolstering the defense of the two components of natural disaster costs—human beings and property. Drills designed to alert the public in how to respond to a natural disaster—such as knowing the location of the nearest storm shelter in tornado country or finding a sturdy object to take shelter under during an earthquake—have been proven to dramatically reduce the number of injuries and deaths caused by natural disasters.

Reinforcing buildings and infrastructure against predictable disasters is, say experts, by far the most effective means both for preparing for disasters and even, as in the case of flood, preventing them. At least since the great San Francisco and Tokyo earthquakes of 1906 and 1923, respectively, scientists and engineers have begun to develop and implement a variety of technologies to minimize damage due to tectonic activity. Perhaps the most important developments have been the reinforcement of masonry and, for taller buildings, new foundations built on rollers, which allow buildings to flex and adjust to tectonic movement, and base isolation, which allows the superstructure of a building to move independently of its foundation, allowing for greater flexibility. Building codes are important in this regard, but even more so is the political will to enforce them. Some earthquake-prone countries, such as Turkey and Iran, have very effective codes, but because of corruption and a lack of resources they are haphazardly enforced, undermining their effectiveness.

Mitigating damage from major weather events is often much harder to achieve than it is for tectonic events. For tornadoes, whose wind velocities can reach in excess of 300 miles per hour, very little can be done to mitigate damage at all. For hurricanes and other less powerful tropical storms, simple measures, such as boarding up windows, are often sufficient to protect against the wind, although in a large-scale storm, the vast majority of damage and loss of life results from flooding not wind. Here, basic measures can be employed, such as effective dikes and levees, though this creates problems of its own. By narrowing river flows, dikes and levees often deepen channels and increase flow speed, creating the potential for more damage in future flooding events. Officials can sometimes open certain levees to shift where the flooding occurs, as happened during the great flooding of the Mississippi Valley in 2010. Here, the decision was made to protect certain high-value urban areas by diverting floodwaters to less valuable agricultural land.

Perhaps the most important antiflood measures involve stopping people from building and living in areas prone to flooding or storms, such as flood plains and low-lying sea islands, or in forested or chaparral areas where wildfires are likely to occur. This can be quite expensive and politically contentious, as people may not want to move and the law requires adequate compensation be paid. Still, some experts argue that such measures are far cheaper and less politically perilous than allowing the damage or loss of life to occur.

Response

There is very little human beings can do to stop most natural disasters once they have started. One exception is wildfire, and countries prone to these disasters spend large sums and make Herculean efforts to put them out. While no policymaker or politician would argue against saving property and lives immediately threatened by wildfire, many experts and scientists say that a policy of stamping out all wildfires is counterproductive as it only allows more fuel to build up for the next fire, which could in turn be even more catastrophic. The scientific view is that fires are a natural part of many ecosystems, and putting them out disrupts natural burn-and-recovery cycles, potentially leading to environmental harm.

Most responses to natural disasters are aimed at rescuing trapped individuals, mitigating suffering, providing medical care for the injured, providing long-term aid for victims, and preventing or mitigating calamities associated with the disasters, such as famine and epidemics. As with preparing for

Indonesian soldiers and volunteers unload relief aid for victims of the 2004 Indian Ocean earthquake and tsunami—one of the deadliest natural disasters in history. Inefficiencies, lack of transportation, and the remoteness of many victims made distribution slow. *(Dimas Ardian/Getty Images)*

earthquakes, the richer the country the more likely it is to have effective response plans and protocols along with the economic resources to put them into effect. Generally, when there are small-scale disasters, local authorities take charge, backed by national governments. In the case of major disasters, however, particularly in poorer and less effectively governed countries, the international community is required to provide an effective response, as has been the case with the recurrent droughts and famines plaguing the Sahel region of Africa or with other massive catastrophes, such as the Indian Ocean tsunami of 2004 and the Haitian earthquake of 2010. Even wealthier countries may find their response systems taxed by a massive disaster, as was seen with Hurricane Katrina on the U.S. Gulf Coast in 2005 and the Japanese earthquake and tsunami of 2011. In such instances, these countries also turn to the well-developed, internationally coordinated system of emergency responders.

The Future

Natural disasters will always be a part of human existence. But looking to the future, three important trends may be noted. The first is the degree to which climate change will increase the frequency and severity of weather-related natural disasters. There is virtual scientific consensus on this, as rising temperatures increase climatic volatility, producing more frequent and intense storms. Warmer global temperatures also lead to rising sea levels, both because warmer water takes up more space than colder water and because of the melting of land-based ice caps; rising seas lead in turn to coastal flooding. Thus, one could argue that efforts to prevent climate change are, in effect, efforts at mitigating natural disasters.

Most scientists agree that it is too late to stop anthropogenic climate change altogether. Indeed, carbon levels in the atmosphere have already increased dramatically while average global temperatures have also gone up. While no serious thinker disputes these facts, there is much debate about how to lessen the effects, whether it makes more sense to devote scarce resources to fighting the causes of climate change or toward preventing or mitigating their effects, for example, via coastal flooding infrastructure.

Aggravating the situation are demographics. As Earth's human population increases, more people will be forced to live in disaster-prone areas due to overcrowding, making it likely that the human and property costs of natural disasters in the future will be that much higher. In fact, with much of the developing world becoming richer, the costs to property are likely to rise faster still.

But rising world wealth also portends improvements in disaster preparedness and response. Not only does it allow for more resources to be devoted to such measures, but there is much evidence that increased wealth—and its effective distribution among larger sectors of the population—creates the conditions for more effective and responsive governance, along with less corruption. In disaster-prone areas, what people may demand of their governments is that they take measures to enforce building codes and prevent contractors from bribing inspectors to get around them.

Technology also offers the opportunity for improved methods of disaster prediction and preparedness. There is great economic motivation for lessening the effects of natural disasters, and hence large amounts of resources are devoted to developing technologies to improve prediction, preparedness, and response. More generally, the spread of the Internet and mobile telephony allows authorities to more effectively warn people in the path of disaster, and, in the wake of disaster, to better help them cope with the pain and loss that result.

James Ciment

See also: Refugees, Displaced Persons, and Asylum Seekers; Water Supply and Access.

Further Reading

Aldrich, Daniel P. *Building Resilience: Social Capital in Post-Disaster Recovery.* Chicago: University of Chicago Press, 2012.

Benson, Charlotte, and Edward Clay. *Understanding the Economic and Financial Impacts of Natural Disasters.* Washington, DC: World Bank, 2004.

Dowty, Rachel, and Barbara Allen. *Dynamics of Disaster: Lessons on Risk, Response, and Recovery.* Washington, DC: Earthscan, 2010.

Farmbry, Kyle. *Crisis, Disaster, and Risk: Institutional Response and Emergence.* Armonk, NY: M.E. Sharpe, 2012.

Few, Roger, and Franziska Matthies, eds. *Flood Hazards and Health: Responding to Present and Future Risks.* Sterling, VA: Earthscan, 2006.

Larson, Erik. *Issac's Storm: A Man, a Time, and the Deadliest Hurricane in History.* New York: Crown, 1999.

Mauch, Christof, and Christian Pfister, eds. *Natural Disasters, Cultural Responses: Case Studies Toward a Global Environmental History.* Lanham, MD: Lexington Books, 2009.

Miller, DeMond Shondell, and Jason David Rivera, eds. *Community Disaster Recovery and Resiliency: Exploring Global Opportunities and Challenges.* Boca Raton, FL: CRC, 2011.

Pampel, Fred C. *Disaster Response.* New York: Facts On File, 2008.

Ride, Anouk, and Diane Bretherton. *Community Resilience in Natural Disasters.* New York: Palgrave Macmillan, 2011.

Web Sites

Global Disaster Watch: http://globaldisasterwatch.blogspot.com

Iflood: www.iflood.com

National Climatic Data Center: www.ncdc.noaa.gov

National Geographic Magazine, Natural Disasters: http://environment.nationalgeographic.com/environment/natural-disasters

Oxfam: www.oxfam.org

United Nations International Strategy for Disaster Reduction: www.unisdr.org

Documents

Document 1: On the Lisbon Earthquake, from *Candide* (excerpt), Voltaire, 1759

In his 1759 satiric novella Candide *and in his "Poem on the Lisbon Disaster," penned in the year of the great quake, 1755, the French Enlightenment philosopher Voltaire mused on the worst disaster in modern European history. The Lisbon earthquake, which destroyed up to three-quarters of the city and took tens of thousands of lives, led Voltaire, like many other thinkers of his day, to question traditional Christian faith in a benevolent God. At least in part, scholars attribute the shift to more scientific thinking about natural disasters to this great cataclysm. In the following passage from* Candide, *Voltaire continues the sarcastic assault on faith and optimism and the disillusionment of the title character that provide the core theme and plot line of his classic novella.*

As soon as they recovered themselves a little they walked toward Lisbon. They had some money left, with which they hoped to save themselves from starving, after they had escaped drowning. Scarcely had they reached the city, lamenting the death of their benefactor, when they felt the earth tremble under their feet. The sea swelled and foamed in the harbour, and beat to pieces the vessels riding at anchor. Whirlwinds of fire and ashes covered the streets and public places; houses fell, roofs were flung upon the pavements, and the pavements were scattered. Thirty thousand inhabitants of all ages and sexes were crushed under the ruins. The sailor, whistling and swearing, said there was booty to be gained here.

"What can be the *sufficient reason* of this phenomenon?" said Pangloss.

"This is the Last Day!" cried Candide.

The sailor ran among the ruins, facing death to find money; finding it, he took it, got drunk, and having slept himself sober, purchased the favours of the first good-natured wench whom he met on the ruins of the destroyed houses, and in the midst of the dying and the dead. Pangloss pulled him by the sleeve.

"My friend," said he, "this is not right. You sin against the *universal reason*; you choose your time badly."

"S'blood and fury!" answered the other; "I am a sailor and born at Batavia. Four times have I trampled upon the crucifix in four voyages to Japan; a fig for thy universal reason."

Some falling stones had wounded Candide. He lay stretched in the street covered with rubbish.

"Alas!" said he to Pangloss, "get me a little wine and oil; I am dying."

"This concussion of the earth is no new thing," answered Pangloss. "The city of Lima, in America, experienced the same convulsions last year; the same cause, the same effects; there is certainly a train of sulphur underground from Lima to Lisbon."

"Nothing more probable," said Candide; "but for the love of God a little oil and wine."

"How, probable?" replied the philosopher. "I maintain that the point is capable of being demonstrated."

Candide fainted away, and Pangloss fetched him some water from a neighbouring fountain. The following day they rummaged among the ruins and found provisions, with which they repaired their exhausted strength. After this they joined with others in relieving those inhabitants who had escaped death. Some, whom they had succoured, gave them as good a dinner as they could in such disastrous circumstances; true, the repast was mournful, and the company moistened their bread with tears; but Pangloss consoled them, assuring them that things could not be otherwise.

"For," said he, "all that is is for the best. If there is a volcano at Lisbon it cannot be elsewhere. It is impossible that things should be other than they are; for everything is right."

A little man dressed in black, Familiar of the Inquisition, who sat by him, politely took up his word and said:

"Apparently, then, sir, you do not believe in original sin; for if all is for the best there has then been neither Fall nor punishment."

"I humbly ask your Excellency's pardon," answered Pangloss, still more politely; "for the Fall and curse of man necessarily entered into the system of the best of worlds."

"Sir," said the Familiar, "you do not then believe in liberty?"

"Your Excellency will excuse me," said Pangloss; "liberty is consistent with absolute necessity, for it was necessary we should be free; for, in short, the determinate will—"

Pangloss was in the middle of his sentence, when the Familiar beckoned to his footman, who gave him a glass of wine from Porto or Opporto. . . .

After the earthquake had destroyed three-fourths of Lisbon, the sages of that country could think of no means more effectual to prevent utter ruin than to give the people a beautiful *auto-da-fé*; for it had been decided by the University of Coimbra, that the burning of a few people alive by a slow fire, and with great ceremony, is an infallible secret to hinder the earth from quaking.

In consequence hereof, they had seized on a Biscayner, convicted of having married his godmother, and on two Portuguese, for rejecting the bacon which larded a chicken they were eating; after dinner, they came and secured Dr. Pangloss, and his disciple Candide, the one for speaking his mind, the other for having listened with an air of approbation. They were conducted to separate apartments, extremely cold, as they were never incommoded by the sun. Eight days after they were dressed in *san-benito* and their heads ornamented with paper mitres. The mitre and *san-benito* belonging to Candide were painted with reversed flames and with devils that had neither tails nor claws; but Pangloss's devils had claws and tails and the flames were upright. They marched in procession thus habited and heard a very pathetic sermon, followed by fine church music. Candide was whipped in cadence while they were singing; the Biscayner, and the two men who had refused to eat bacon, were burnt; and Pangloss was hanged, though that was not the custom. The same day the earth sustained a most violent concussion.

Candide, terrified, amazed, desperate, all bloody, all palpitating, said to himself:

"If this is the best of possible worlds, what then are the others? Well, if I had been only whipped I could put up with it, for I experienced that among the Bulgarians; but oh, my dear Pangloss! thou greatest of philosophers, that I should have seen you hanged, without knowing for what! Oh, my dear Anabaptist, thou best of men, that thou should'st have been drowned in the very harbour! Oh, Miss Cunegonde, thou pearl of girls! that thou should'st have had thy belly ripped open!"

Thus he was musing, scarce able to stand, preached at, whipped, absolved, and blessed, when an old woman accosted him saying:

"My son, take courage and follow me."

Source: Candide by Voltaire, translated by Philip Littell, 1918.

Document 2: "A Failure of Initiative: Final Report of the Select Bipartisan Committee to Investigate the Preparation for and Response to Hurricane Katrina," Executive Summary of Findings, U.S. Congress, 2006

In late August of 2005, Hurricane Katrina made landfall near New Orleans, Louisiana, causing extensive damage to the city and the surrounding Gulf Coast. Far more destructive than the gale-force winds were the high floodwaters and levee breaches, which resulted in the flooding of much of the city, the loss of more than 1,000 lives, and more than $100 billion in property damage. Virtually all levels of government came under much criticism for their failure to prevent the disaster and, especially, for their inadequate response to it. After the disaster, the U.S. Congress commissioned a special bipartisan committee to examine what went wrong and the measures needed to prevent a recurrence. The following document is the executive summary of the committee's findings, with plenty of blame—and some praise—to go around.

www.gpoaccess.gov/serialset/creports/katrina.html

Source: U.S. Government Printing Office.

NEUROLOGICAL DISEASE

Neurology is the branch of medicine devoted to the nervous system, including both the central nervous system (brain and spinal cord) and the peripheral nervous system (cranial, somatic, visceral, and motor nerves). Some diseases of muscle are also considered neurological diseases. Physicians who practice neurology, called neurologists, treat a wide variety of movement, sensation, coordination, thought, and behavior disorders.

Some of the most common, well-known, and feared diseases fall under the purview of neurology, including Alzheimer's, Parkinson's, and Huntington's diseases; multiple sclerosis; amyotrophic lateral sclerosis (ALS, commonly known as Lou Gehrig's disease); dementia; and autism. Stroke and other cerebrovascular diseases are the second-leading cause of death worldwide, according to the World Health Organization (WHO). Nonfatal neurological disorders are also widespread. For example, headaches account for almost 10 million doctor visits in the United States every year, as one in six Americans suffers from chronic headache. Between 3 and 5 percent of people worldwide will have a seizure at some point in their life; about 1 percent of the world's population suffers from epilepsy (defined as having multiple seizures not caused by trauma, anoxia, infection, or other secondary factor).

Neurological diseases can be found across the globe and affect people of all ages and ethnicities. In children, increasing recognition and growing rates of the autism spectrum disorders have caused a flurry of research into causes of and treatments for the condition. In children and adults, the rising frequency of metabolic syndrome (obesity, Type II diabetes, high cholesterol, and high blood pressure) is leading to increasing rates of neurological diseases such as stroke, retinopathy (eye damage), and neuropathy (nerve damage). Similarly, the aging of the world's population is contributing to an increase in neurological diseases of the elderly, particularly Alzheimer's disease and other forms of dementia.

The availability of the tools needed to diagnose and treat these conditions is strikingly disparate in low-, middle-, and high-income countries. In highly developed nations—the United States, Canada, Japan, and most of Western Europe, in particular—patients often have financial means and access to academic medical centers. Proper diagnosis of neurological conditions is therefore commonplace, and many therapies and medicines are deployed to cure those who are afflicted (or, at very least, to mitigate or manage their symptoms).

In middle- and low-income countries, by contrast, neurological problems often go undiagnosed or untreated. A neurological workup is quite expensive, as it relies heavily on complex modern equipment like magnetic resonance imaging machines and pricy genetic tests. Neurological treatments are similarly high in cost, in part because many are experimental and unproven. Indeed, the ability to treat neurological conditions is so far beyond the health-care systems of many nations, and the prevalence of other conditions (AIDS, malaria, malnutrition, and tuberculosis, among others) is so pronounced that this area of medicine has received relatively scant attention in poorer countries. Consequently, there is very little statistical data available for measuring accurately the prevalence and severity of neurological disease in Africa, Eastern Europe, South America, and much of Asia.

Historical Background

Neurology is considered distinct from neuroradiology, neurosurgery, neuropathology, neuro-ophthalmology, and neuro-oncology, which are considered branches of radiology, surgery, pathology, ophthalmology, and oncology, respectively. Specialists in these disciplines work together to treat neurological disease. For example, a patient with a headache goes to see a neurologist, who prescribes a pain reliever for the headache and orders a magnetic resonance image.

The image is interpreted by a neuroradiologist, who identifies a brain tumor and informs the neurologist. The patient is then referred to a neurosurgeon, who performs a biopsy, and a neuro-oncologist, who orders chemotherapy or radiation therapy. The biopsy is interpreted by a neuropathologist, who informs the other physicians about the type of tumor. The neuro-oncologist may then select different chemotherapy or radiation therapy approaches. The neurosurgeon may then perform a resection of the tumor. If the patient begins having seizures, the neurologist prescribes antiseizure medications.

For reasons that are largely historical, neurology is also considered distinct from psychiatry. Today it is taken for granted that behavior arises from electrical and chemical processes that occur in the brain; however, this view did not begin to take hold until the last half of the nineteenth century. Before that time, human behavior was thought to arise from more mystical sources. Philosophers such as Plato and René Descartes championed the notion that the soul, and thus personality and complex human behavior, were separate from the human body. Ancient societies, including the Greek and Roman, ascribed behavior to organs other than the brain and to bodily fluids, and believed that disease arose when these elements or "humors" were out of balance. For example, a patient who suffered from melancholia (depression) might be said to have an excess of the "black bile" humor, which was attributed to an overactive spleen. Treatments such as bloodletting and enemas were used to relieve the body of these humors and cure the patient's condition. Although it was known by the 1600s that the human body was made up of cells, it was not until Rudolf Virchow and the "cellular pathology" school took hold in the mid-1800s that physicians and scientists began to conceive of the body as a complex, multicellular machine. Even so, it would be some time before the medical and scientific communities accepted that the cells of the brain could give rise to complex behaviors.

There remains no separation a priori between the diseases that are treated by neurologists and psychiatrists. The history of Parkinson's disease is particularly illustrative of the artificial separation between the disciplines. It was originally recognized as the "shaking palsy" by the famous Greek physician Galen around 175 C.E.; English physician James Parkinson penned the first article consistent with our current understanding of the disease in 1817. French neurologist Jean Martin Charcot wrote extensively on the condition and named the collection of symptoms as Parkinson's disease in the late 1800s. Without effective treatment for the underlying disease, however, symptoms such as depression, bradykinesia (slow walking), and the characteristic lack of emotion on the faces of the patients (masked facies) were treated primarily by psychiatrists until the discovery of the drug levodopa in the 1960s. Today, Parkinson's disease is managed largely by neurologists. For similar reasons owing more to historical accident than scientific taxonomy, neurologists tend to treat diseases with known central nervous system pathophysiology (e.g., ALS, stroke, multiple sclerosis) while psychiatrists tend to treat diseases for which the neuroanatomical basis is unclear (e.g., depression, bipolar disorder, schizophrenia, anxiety disorders, personality disorders). In the United States, certification to practice either discipline is issued by the same organization (the American Board of Psychiatry and Neurology).

The story of Phineas Gage has come to illustrate the interplay between brain structure (long the interest of neurologists and neuroanatomists) and complex human behavior (long the interest of psychiatrists and philosophers). In the mid-1800s, Gage was a pleasant, soft-spoken foreman working on the railroads of New England. During work one afternoon an explosion propelled a tamping rod 1.25 inches in diameter through the left side of his brain and skull. Remarkably, Gage was not killed; indeed, he was still able to walk and talk, and his memory and other complex behaviors were intact. When he recovered from his wounds, however, those who knew him detected changes in his personality (for example, he was more impulsive and profane than he was before the accident), and his friends declared that he was "no longer Gage." It was fairly novel at that time to think that a change to a person's fundamental character could occur due to a structural, electrical, or chemical manipulation of the brain. It should be noted that at the time (and even to this day), scholars continue to debate how much of Gage's personality change was due to his brain injury and how much to the sudden celebrity he gained when his condition became a public spectacle.

In the late 1800s, French neurologist Pierre Paul Broca made a more rigorous argument that the neurons of the brain were responsible for complex human behaviors. Just one year after the death of Phineas Gage, Broca examined the brain of a patient known as Tan who suffered from syphilis and developed a condition called aphasia, which is the inability to produce language; uniquely, this patient could only produce the word "tan," hence the moniker. Examining Tan's brain after he died, Broca observed damage to a region of the frontal lobe known today as Broca's area, which is responsible for generating language (both oral and written). After confirming his findings in a second patient, Broca presented his discovery in 1868. This started a neurological golden age of structure-function correlation in which individual abilities and behaviors were found to be critically dependent on specific areas of the brain (for example, in modern terms, Phineas Gage probably suffered damage to the dorsolateral prefrontal cortex, which often produces a syndrome of disinhibition and inappropriate social behavior).

This work was greatly advanced in the early 1900s when neuroanatomists, led by German neurologist Korbinian Brodmann, studied the underlying architecture of the cerebral cortex and found subtly different patterns of cellular arrangement that somewhat correlated with the specific functions of different brain regions (for example, Broca's area has a distinct pattern of neuronal arrangement that has been classified as Brodmann areas 44 and 45). It should be noted that these functional and anatomic distinctions are not reflected by overlying skull features, as proposed by practitioners of the pseudoscientific discipline of phrenology.

The nervous system is responsible for controlling movements, relaying sensations from the body to the brain, regulating body functions like temperature and circadian rhythms, producing complex behaviors like thought and memory, and governing how we interact with the world. It should be no surprise, then, that forces in the external world also have a profound affect on the nervous system and that neurological disease is substantially affected (or even produced) by the world's ever-changing social, economic, and political environment.

The Obesity Epidemic

Rising rates of metabolic syndrome (obesity, Type II diabetes, high cholesterol, and/or high blood pressure) are of growing concern to neurologists. According to the World Health Organization, obesity rates have doubled worldwide since 1980 such that, in 2002, 1.5 billion adults were overweight (body mass index > 25) and 500 million were obese (body mass index > 30). This means that more than 10 percent of

adults on Earth are obese. Further, 43 million children under the age of five were overweight, according to a 2010 study. WHO has found that obesity is especially prevalent among low-income, urban populations worldwide and can coexist in countries with high rates of starvation and malnutrition. This is due, in part, to the availability of inexpensive, energy-dense, nutrient-poor, packaged snack foods high in fat and sugar; by contrast, fresh fruits and vegetables are expensive, are difficult to transport, and spoil easily. Children in low- and middle-income countries are especially susceptible to obesity caused by access to inappropriate nutrition sources.

Similar patterns were found when researchers examined rates of diabetes and high cholesterol. According to the Centers for Disease Control and Prevention (CDC), about 26 million Americans suffer from diabetes (about 8 percent of the population) while a remarkable 35 percent of Americans qualify for a diagnosis of prediabetes by laboratory testing criteria. Worldwide, it is estimated that 346 million people suffer from diabetes. In perhaps the clearest example of the disparity in health outcomes between wealthy and poorer nations, more than 80 percent of deaths from this easily managed disease occur in low- and-middle income countries.

It is widely agreed that high cholesterol is a problem worldwide, but efforts to collect data have been difficult as many countries do not keep systematic data on cholesterol levels. One WHO study from 2011 found broad discrepancy between diagnosis and treatment rates for high cholesterol in different countries; for example, in that study 78 percent of adults in Thailand with high cholesterol had never been diagnosed, whereas only 18 percent of adults in the United States with high cholesterol had never been diagnosed (although, unfortunately, 40 percent of those diagnosed were not adequately treated).

The metabolic syndrome is highly correlated with neurological disease. Diabetes, high cholesterol, and high blood pressure are some of the strongest risk factors correlated with cerebrovascular disease. Diabetic retinopathy, a disease commonly diagnosed and treated by neuro-ophthalmologists, affects almost 4 million Americans and is the leading cause of blindness in people aged 20 to 74. Peripheral diabetic polyneuropathy, which damages the myelin coating surrounding axons in nerve cells, is a painful, limb-threatening condition affecting 50 to 70 percent of people with long-standing diabetes. In fact, according to the National Institutes of Health, 60 percent of nontraumatic limb amputations in the United States (about 66,000 amputations in 2006) were related to diabetic neuropathy.

As the prevalence of the metabolic syndrome rises worldwide, the rates of neurological disease related to metabolic syndrome will rise as well. The best therapy for metabolic syndrome is lifestyle management, including weight loss and increased physical activity. It is no surprise that the rates of metabolic syndrome are highest in low-income, urban areas where unhealthy convenience food is abundant but open space for exercise is at a minimum. Some municipalities are experimenting with public policy solutions, such as discouraging fast-food restaurants from marketing unhealthy food choices to children or offering incentives to commuters who bike or jog to work rather than drive. Aggressive public education campaigns to encourage healthy food choices and more exercise are under way at many levels of government.

Medical therapies play a role as well. Lowering blood pressure, reducing cholesterol, losing weight, restoring proper heart rhythm if necessary, and providing proper anticoagulation via blood thinning medications all significantly lower the rate of stroke. Tight control of blood sugar levels (with medication as well as lifestyle modification) can prevent progression of diabetic polyneuropathy and diabetic retinopathy and prevent the need for amputation, although this does not generally lead to restoration of sensation or cessation of pain. Several medications including gabapentin and some antiseizure medications can decrease the pain of diabetic polyneuropathy.

The worldwide epidemic of the metabolic syndrome will require new and creative solutions. On a government level, recognition of the problem, funding for research into effective treatment strategies, and novel public policy campaigns are under way but need to be expanded. The medical community must educate the public about the problem and form collaborations across specialties to provide patients with comprehensive care. For example, primary care physicians are often responsible for cholesterol control, neurologists handle the patient's anticoagulation, and endocrinologists treat diabetes; some medical centers and health plans are working to form collaborative clinics to better coordinate care for patients. Finally, all the efforts of government and the medical community will be for naught if individuals do not start making better food and exercise decisions.

Global Aging

A study by the United Nations in 2002 called the aging of the global population "unprecedented, without parallel in human history" and noted that "the twenty-first century will witness even more rapid aging than did the century just past." The reasons for this are manifold, including declining fertility, a global trend toward smaller families, longer life expectancy, and advanced medical treatments that allow a sicker, older population to survive.

The aging of the global population has profound implications for governments, economies, and social policy. For example, pension and retirement programs, both public and private, will be paying out benefits to retirees for longer periods of time than may have been anticipated when the programs were conceived. From a medical standpoint, old people (even healthy ones) have more expensive medical needs than younger people. Neurologically, many diseases are much more common in the elderly than in the young and it is unclear whether current global health systems are prepared to deal with dramatically higher rates of diseases of the elderly.

Alzheimer's disease is the best-studied example of a disease with increasing incidence (new cases) and prevalence (total number of cases) as a result of aging. About 5 percent of people with Alzheimer's disease are 30 years old or less, most or all with rare genetic conditions. According to the U.S. Alzheimer's Association, one in eight people age 65 or older have Alzheimer's disease. The incidence of Alzheimer's disease doubles every five years after age 65, with the result that fully one half of Americans over 85 years old have a diagnosis of Alzheimer's disease. Estimates put the total number of cases of Alzheimer's disease in the United States between 5 and 10 million. In 2010, direct costs from Alzheimer's disease (including Medicare, private insurance, and out-of-pocket health expenditures) were estimated at $173 billion; by 2050, that number is expected to rise to $1.078 trillion. This figure does not include, for example, wages lost when a healthy adult chooses to quit a job and stay home to care for an elderly parent with Alzheimer's disease. No clear estimate exists to quantify the total economic effects of Alzheimer's disease.

Many other neurological diseases will also become more prevalent, and thus have a larger economic and social impact, as the population ages. About 75 percent of all cases of Parkinson's disease start after the age of 60, and incidence roughly doubles every decade up to 80 years. Somewhat similarly, nearly 75 percent of strokes occur in people over 65 years old. The risk of stroke doubles every decade of life after 55 years of age. With new and better treatments for acute stroke (such as tissue plasminogen activator) and improved management of stroke risk factors like high blood pressure and high cholesterol, more and more people are surviving many years after they have a stroke. This increases the rate of recurrent stroke; currently, about 30 percent of strokes are recurrent strokes, but this number could rise dramatically in the future. Further, people who survive stroke often require physical, occupational, and speech therapy to help them recover; some require expensive long-term hospitalization or long-term nursing home care.

It is unlikely that advances in medical technology will solve this problem; in fact, advances in medical care are likely to raise costs even as they prolong survival. New diagnostic techniques such as magnetic resonance imaging may help doctors diagnose Alzheimer's disease earlier, but performing more MRIs on elderly patients will further increase medical costs. Any treatment that prolongs survival or improves quality of life in patients with these neurological conditions would be welcome, but these treatments would come with their own costs and probably increase costs in the long run as older and sicker patients survive longer and develop other, expensive-to-treat medical conditions.

No clear policy answers to this dilemma exist at this time. In most developed countries, the idea of rationing care away from the elderly toward younger patients is anathema, not to mention politically difficult or impossible. The United Kingdom, which has a national health service, is instructive in this regard. British officials developed a "quality-adjusted life years" measure; under this system, health insurance will not pay more than about $45,000 for treatments that will not extend to the recipient a year of quality life. Thus, if elderly patients required care in a nursing home, MRIs to evaluate the progression of their Alzheimer's disease, and an expensive new medication with no proven ability to reverse their condition, it is possible that payment for some or all of these treatments would be denied. Opponents of this controversial system assert that it is devastating for elderly patients and their families; proponents of the system argue that by denying these expensive, futile therapies, more money would be available for the treatment of patients more likely to benefit from

care. Thus far, few other nations have been willing to follow the lead of the British.

Autism Spectrum Disorder and Developmental Delay

Just as care for the world's increasing aged population causes challenges for neurologists, so too does care for the world's youngest citizens. One branch of neurology (pediatric neurology) deals with neurological disease in children from birth to maturity (alternately defined as 18, 21, and 25 years). Like their counterparts who treat adults, pediatric neurologists treat patients with seizures, strokes, movement disorders, muscle weakness, and other disorders of the central and peripheral nervous system. Pediatric neurologists also treat a few categories of neurological disease that are quite rare in adult populations, among them congenital neurological disease (as might occur when, for example, the brain does not develop correctly) and developmental delay.

Developmental delay occurs when children do not demonstrate age-appropriate motor skills (either gross motor skills such as walking or jumping, or fine motor skills such as using eating utensils or stacking blocks), language abilities (receptive and expressive), or social interactions. Normative tables have been developed that define the ages at which children should meet certain milestones; these include the Denver Developmental Screen Test (now in its second edition) and the Bayley Scales of Infant Development. Children who do not demonstrate age-appropriate developmental skills are often referred to pediatric neurologists for evaluation, as a variety of neurological diseases have developmental delay as a common feature. Pediatric neurologists may order neuroimaging (to determine whether the child has a brain malformation or has suffered brain damage), an electroencephalogram (to determine whether the child has predisposition toward epilepsy), or genetic tests (to determine whether the child has a genetic syndrome that causes developmental delay).

Often parents and pediatricians are worried that the child's developmental delay is a symptom of autism (or, more accurately in the current classification system, an autism spectrum disorder). The *Diagnostic and Statistical Manual* (DSM-IV) defines autism as impairment of social interaction and communication coexistent with restricted, repetitive, and/or stereotyped patterns of behavior with onset before the age of three years. Practically, children are suspected of being autistic when they fail to engage socially (e.g., failing to make eye contact, to look where people point, or to seek play with others), have difficulty with language (e.g., failing to speak by 15 to 18 months, tending to repeat verbatim what is said by others), and engage in repetitive and self-stimulatory behavior such as hand flapping, body rocking, or head banging. Often children will seem to be developing normally, meeting developmental milestones for six months or an entire year before failing to progress further or sometimes losing skills they previously had (for example, a child who previously said a few words may stop talking entirely).

The cause of autism is unknown. Some autism may be genetic, since parents with one autistic child are more likely than the rest of the population to have a second autistic child. However, autism is clearly not a case of simple genetics; for example, an autistic child can have a nonautistic identical twin. Nevertheless, extensive work by neuroscientists and geneticists has identified hundreds of genetic mutations that occur more commonly in autistic children than in the general population. Other work has attempted to find environmental factors that are linked with autism, including mercury and aluminum exposure, nutritional deficiencies in pregnant women, childhood vaccines, and cell phone–related radiation. One popular theory hypothesizes that autism is caused by a "double hit"; that is, children with a genetic predisposition come in contact with an environmental factor, and this combination produces autism.

Autism is one of the most active fields of research in all of medicine, in part because there has been a dramatic increase in the number of children diagnosed in the last 30 years. It is unclear exactly when autism was first described, but by 1940 the modern definition was in use throughout the neurological community. However, autism was not formally included in the DSM until the third edition in 1980. Early studies suggested the rate of autism in the United States was between 3 and 5 per 10,000 children. By 1996, a CDC study found that 36 of 10,000 met criteria for a diagnosis of autism. Two studies by the federal government reported in 2007 revised that to about 67 per 10,000; this was similar to prevalence reported by England, Japan, Sweden, and Canada around the same time. A landmark study released in 2009 officially revised the U.S. estimate to between 90 and 100 per 10,000 children.

Almost certainly, some of this increase in incidence is due to a broadening of the diagnostic criteria for autism. The condition could not be formally diagnosed until 1980 and then could be diagnosed only by the narrow diagnostic category of "infantile autism." Today's DSM-IV allows diagnoses of multiple types and severities of autism spectrum, encompassing Asperger syndrome and pervasive developmental delay not otherwise specified. Widespread awareness of autism has also taught physicians and parents to look for the symptoms of the disorder, thereby allowing the diagnosis to be made when previously it may have been missed. Previously stigmatized, parents are more willing to have their children diagnosed now than in the past when children may have been simply labeled by pejorative terms like "retarded." Indeed, carrying a diagnosis may allow children to receive physical, occupational, speech, and behavioral therapies, qualify for placement in special classes or special schools, or receive special consideration such as extra time to take tests; thus, some parents actively seek the diagnosis for their children.

Despite the proliferation of research, no treatment for autism exists. Studies show that children who receive physical, occupational, speech, and adaptive behavioral therapy before the age of three have better outcomes than those who do not. Some children with the disorder improve over time and can obtain jobs and live alone, while others live at home their entire lives or need to be institutionalized due to a tendency to hurt themselves or others. Expensive, unproven, and often dangerous therapies (such as chelation therapy, in which compounds that are claimed to bind toxins are injected into the body) are marketed to desperate parents as cures. The world's scientific community is racing to find causes and treatments for autism, but more time is needed. Until then, governments, physicians, and family members are struggling to deal with the complex needs of an ever-expanding population of autistic children with no answers in sight.

Future Directions

Neurological disease can be found in people of all ages and races in every part of the world. Headaches, strokes, brain tumors, epilepsy, dementia, and other neurological disorders are major sources of morbidity and mortality across the globe. As the world's population ages, neurological diseases of the elderly are becoming more prevalent (even if we cannot say precisely how much more). Similarly, as the obesity epidemic expands, rates of neurological diseases associated with the metabolic syndrome continue to rise. For unknown reasons, estimates of the proportion of children with autism spectrum disorders have also increased dramatically in the last 30 years. Neurologists and neuroscientists are working on new diagnostic and treatment strategies to address these problems, but need help from governments and individual patients to maximize outcomes.

There are grounds for optimism. When U.S. president George H.W. Bush declared 1990–2000 "The Decade of the Brain," research in the neurosciences and neurology increased exponentially. Scientists and doctors understand more about the nervous system today than at any time in human history. Conditions like Parkinson's disease and multiple sclerosis, long thought to be death sentences, are now commonly treated with well-tolerated, easily managed medications and have promising medical and surgical treatment options on the horizon. Biotechnology and pharmaceutical companies are actively pursuing promising therapies for stroke, headache, dementia and other neurological conditions. It will be up to the physicians and government agencies that make up the global community to see these therapies through to fruition and put toward the common goal of the amelioration of neurological disease.

Jeffrey Gold

See also: Mental Health; Polio.

Further Reading

Greenberg, David, Michael J. Aminoff, and Roger P. Simon. *Clinical Neurology.* 5th ed. New York: McGraw-Hill/ Appleton & Lange, 2002.

Hare, Edward. "The History of 'Nervous Disorders' from 1600 to 1840, and a Comparison with Modern Views." *British Journal of Psychiatry* 159 (1991): 37–45.

Hirschmuller, Albrecht. "The Development of Psychiatry and Neurology in the Nineteenth Century." *History of Psychiatry* 10:40 (1999): 395–423.

Riese, Werner. "History and Principles of Classification of Nervous Disorders," *Bulletin of the History of Medicine* 18:5 (1945): 465–512.

———. "An Outline of a History of Ideas in Neurology." *Bulletin of the History of Medicine* 23:2 (1949): 111–136.

Ropper, Allan, and Martin Samuels. *Adams and Victor's Principles of Neurology.* 9th ed. New York: McGraw-Hill Professional, 2009.

Squire, Larry R., Floyd E. Bloom, Nicholas C. Spitzer, Sascha du Lac, Anirvan Ghosh, and Darwin Berg. *Fundamental Neuroscience.* 3d ed. Burlington, MA: Academic, 2008.

Viets, Henry R. "The History of Neurology in the Last 100 Years." *Bulletin of the New York Academy of Medicine* 24:12 (1948): 772–783.

Web Sites

American Academy of Neurology: www.aan.com

American Academy of Pediatrics: Health Topics: www.aap.org/topics.html

Autism Speaks: www.autismspeaks.org

Centers for Disease Control and Prevention (CDC): Autism Spectrum Disorders: www.cdc.gov/ncbddd/autism/index.html

Centers for Disease Control and Prevention (CDC): Stroke: www.cdc.gov/stroke

International Headache Society: www.i-h-s.org/frame_non_members.asp

International League Against Epilepsy: www.ilae-epilepsy.org

Movement Disorder Society: www.movementdisorders.org

National Institute of Neurologic Disease and Stroke (NINDS): www.ninds.nih.go

National Stroke Association (NSA): www.stroke.org/site/PageNavigator/HOME

Society for Neurosciences: www.sfn.org

World Health Organization (WHO) Health Topics: www.who.int/topics

Document

Document: "An Essay on the Shaking Palsy" (excerpt), James Parkinson, 1817

James Parkinson's 1817 monograph on what he called the "shaking palsy" summarized the symptoms of the condition and discussed in depth six case studies. The essay, which includes the first published description of what is now known as Parkinson's disease, is considered one of the foundational documents of the field of neurology.

So slight and nearly imperceptible are the first inroads of this malady, and so extremely slow is its progress, that it rarely happens, that the patient can form any recollection of the precise period of its commencement. The first symptoms perceived are, a slight sense of weakness, with a proneness to trembling in some particular part; sometimes in the head, but most commonly in one of the hands and arms. These symptoms gradually increase in the part first affected; and at an uncertain period, but seldom in less than twelvemonths or more, the morbid influence is felt in some other part. Thus assuming one of the hands and arms to be first attacked, the other, at this period becomes similarly affected. After a few more months the patient is found to be less strict than usual in preserving an upright posture: this being most observable whilst walking, but sometimes whilst sitting or standing. Sometime after the appearance of this symptom, and during its slow increase, one of the legs is discovered slightly to tremble, and is also found to suffer fatigue sooner than the leg of the other side: and in a few months this limb becomes agitated by similar tremblings, and suffers a similar loss of power.

Hitherto the patient will have experienced but little inconvenience; and befriended by the strong influence of habitual endurance, would perhaps seldom think of his being the subject of disease, except when reminded of it by the unsteadiness of his hand, whilst writing or employing himself in any nicer kind of manipulation. But as the disease proceeds, similar employments are accomplished with considerable difficulty, the hand failing to answer with exactness to the dictates of the will. Walking becomes a task which cannot be performed without considerable attention. The legs are not raised to that height, or with that promptitude which the will directs, so that the utmost care is necessary to prevent frequent falls.

At this period the patient experiences much inconvenience, which unhappily is found daily to increase. The submission of the limbs to the directions of the will can hardly ever be obtained in the performance of the most ordinary offices of life. The fingers cannot be disposed of in the proposed directions, and applied with certainty to any proposed point. As time and the disease proceed, difficulties increase: writing can now be hardly at all accomplished; and reading, from the tremulous motion, is accomplished with some difficulty. Whilst at meals the fork not being duly directed frequently fails to raise the morsel from the plate: which, when seized, is with much difficulty conveyed to the mouth. At this period the patient seldom experiences a suspension of the agitation of his limbs. Commencing, for instance in one arm, the wearisome agitation is borne until beyond sufferance, when by suddenly changing the posture it is for a time stopped in that limb, to commence, generally, in less than a minute in one of the legs, or in the arm of the other side. Harassed by this tormenting round, the patient has recourse to walking, a mode of exercise to which the sufferers from this malady are in general partial; owing to their attention being thereby somewhat diverted from their unpleasant feelings, by the care and exertion required to ensure its safe performance.

But as the malady proceeds, even this temporary mitigation of suffering from the agitation of the limbs is denied. The propensity to lean forward becomes invincible, and the patient is thereby forced to step on the toes and fore part of the feet, whilst the upper part of the body is thrown so far forward as to render it difficult to avoid falling on the face. In some cases, when this state of the malady is attained, the patient can no longer exercise himself by walking in his usual manner, but is thrown on the toes and forepart of the feet; being, at the same time, irresistibly impelled to take much quicker and shorter steps, and thereby to adopt unwillingly a running pace. In some cases it is found necessary entirely to substitute running for walking; since otherwise the patient, on proceeding only a very few paces, would inevitably fall.

In this stage, the sleep becomes much disturbed. The tremulous motions of the limbs occur during sleep, and augment until they awaken the patient, and frequently with much agitation and alarm. The power of conveying the food to the mouth is at length so much impeded that he is obliged to consent to be fed by others. The bowels, which had been all along torpid, now, in most cases, demand stimulating medicines of very considerable power: the expulsion of the feces from the rectum sometimes requiring mechanical aid. As the disease proceeds towards its last stage, the trunk is almost permanently bowed, the muscular power is more decidedly diminished, and the tremulous agitation becomes violent. The patient walks now with great difficulty, and unable any longer to support himself with his stick, he dares not venture on this exercise, unless assisted by an attendant, who walking backwards before him, prevents his falling forwards, by the pressure of his hands against the fore part of his shoulders. His words are now scarcely intelligible; and he is not only no longer able to feed himself, but when the food is conveyed to the mouth, so much are the actions of the muscles of the tongue, pharynx, &c. impeded by impaired action and perpetual agitation, that the food is with difficulty retained in the mouth until masticated; and then as difficultly swallowed. Now also, from the same cause, another very unpleasant circumstance occurs: the saliva fails of being directed to the back part of the fauces, and hence is continually draining from the mouth, mixed with the particles of food, which he is no longer able to clear from the inside of the mouth.

As the debility increases and the influence of the will over the muscles fades away, the tremulous agitation becomes more vehement. It now seldom leaves him for a moment; but even when exhausted nature seizes a small portion of sleep, the motion becomes so violent as not only to shake the bed-hangings, but even the floor and sashes of the room. The chin is now almost immoveably bent down upon the sternum. The slops with which he is attempted to be fed, with the saliva, are continually trickling from the mouth. The power of articulation is lost. The urine and feces are passed involuntarily; and at the last, constant sleepiness, with slight delirium, and other marks of extreme exhaustion, announce the wished-for release.

Source: Gutenberg.org

NUCLEAR ENERGY

Nuclear energy has long been a controversial issue. Those who support the development of nuclear power see it as a reliable, sustainable, and virtually carbon-free alternative to fossil fuels, the world's current primary source of energy. Arguments against nuclear energy point out the risks, cost, and complexity of building and maintaining nuclear power plants. Since its development in the 1950s, nuclear energy has been seen by some as the answer to the world's energy problems and by others as one of the greatest dangers of the modern age. Underlying the politics and lobbying, the debate over nuclear energy revolves around shifting perceptions of risks and costs.

History

The use of nuclear fission for energy was preceded by the development of the atomic bomb. In the early 1900s, experiments with neutrons—particles without electrical charge found in the atom's center (known as the nucleus)—revealed the possibility of nuclear fission. Nuclear fission is a process by which the nucleus splits into smaller parts and releases large amounts of energy and several neutrons. This can occur spontaneously or as a result of being bombarded by another neutron. When the atom breaks apart, there is a chance the neutrons will split another atom and release additional neutrons. If one of these neutrons then finds another atom, it could split in turn, and a chain reaction would ensue. In a reactor, a fissile isotope like uranium-235 or plutonium-239 is hit with a neutron, and as the atom splits it ejects a few more neutrons, which hit other atoms, thereby sustaining the reaction. The whole process emits large amounts of energy, which can then be converted to electricity. In a reactor, the chain reaction is moderated with the aid of materials (such as graphite) that slow neutrons to keep the process going.

The first use of nuclear fission was in the Manhattan Project, a U.S. program that developed atomic weapons for use in World War II. After the war it was clear that the massive amounts of energy produced through nuclear fission had peaceful applications if the energy could be converted to electricity to power factories, homes, and businesses. The first reactor to deliver electricity to the power grid was located at Obninsk, in the USSR, and had an output of 5 megawatt electrical (MWe). Very small compared to the 1,000 MWe reactors that would come later, it was connected to the Mosenegro grid in 1954. In 1957, the first commercial nuclear power plant went into operation in Shippingport, Pennsylvania. By 1960, 15 nuclear power reactors with a combined capacity of 1,087 MWe were operational in four countries: France, the USSR, the United Kingdom, and the United States. Another six countries had started their nuclear power programs by this time as well.

The years between 1965 and 1975 saw large numbers of orders for nuclear power plants. The increased popularity was due not only to the appeal of new reactor designs that permitted substantially higher outputs in electricity, but also to the instability of the oil markets, which pushed countries to look at other forms of energy production. By 1970 there were 90 operating reactors in 15 countries, with a total capacity of 16,500 MWe. Orders for power plants reached their peak in the early 1970s, as the world reacted to shocks from increased oil prices. After that, the enthusiasm for nuclear power in the United States came to a halt. All 41 reactors ordered in the United States after 1973 were canceled. The reasons for this initial drop were largely economic. Inflation and rising energy costs led to decreased growth in global electricity demand (hence, profit) while utility costs continued to rise. Furthermore, new regulations and licensing structures being implemented in the United States as a response to the environmental movement increased costs. When the United States began deregulating its energy markets beginning with the natural gas market in 1978, nuclear power plant operators faced the prospect of being unable to recover their initial startup costs.

Number of Nuclear Reactors in Operation Worldwide, 1955–2010

Year	Number of reactors in operation
1955	1
1960	15
1965	48
1970	84
1975	169
1980	245
1985	363
1990	416
1995	434
2000	435
2005	441
2010	441

Source: International Atomic Energy Agency.

From a global perspective, the 1970s and 1980s saw the continued expansion of nuclear energy production. Germany, France, and Japan built extensively during this time period. In Western Europe, nuclear energy production increased from 8.4 gigawatt electrical (GWe) per year in 1973 to 84 GWe, while Japan alone increased from 1.1 GWe per year to 22 GWe in the same time frame. France especially became heavily dependent on nuclear power; by 1990, approximately 75 percent of its electricity supply came from its nuclear power plants. The Soviet Union also invested in nuclear power, and by the end of 1980 it had 29 reactors operating at 13 nuclear power stations. Until the 1990s, growth would be seen primarily in Western Europe and Asia.

High-profile disasters at nuclear power plants in the late 1970s and the 1980s helped turn public opinion in some countries against new nuclear power construction. On March 28, 1979, the Three Mile Island 2 reactor in Pennsylvania experienced a malfunction in the secondary cooling circuit, which caused the reactor to automatically shut down. At the same time, a relief valve (emergency valve that opens to relieve high pressures within the reactor) did not properly close, which allowed much of the primary coolant to drain away. This left the reactor core exposed with little cooling. While the accident released only a small amount of radiation, there was a large public outcry that was increased by the strength of the environmental movement, and the Three Mile Island accident led the United States to strengthen its regulations and oversight.

The explosion at the Chernobyl 4 reactor in Ukraine on April 26, 1986, caused a global response. Operators had shut off some of the reactor's safety systems to run a series of tests. When the reactor overheated, a series of steam explosions resulted, exposing the core and propagating radioactive debris over great distances. The resulting radioactive plume drifted across Europe. As details emerged about the accident, populations were outraged that they had been unknowingly exposed to radioactivity, which can have serious health effects. Countries responded with a series of conventions to strengthen the global standards for safety and responsibility of countries to share information in case of a disaster. The Chernobyl accident influenced a wide range of political issues, from fueling the environmental movement to putting internal and external pressure on the USSR to become more transparent.

As public opinion turned against nuclear power, global construction of new nuclear plants slowed, particularly in democratic countries. During the 1990s, there was a slow but continuing growth of global capacity, but virtually no new construction in Western countries.

Why Nuclear Energy?

One of the most attractive qualities of nuclear power is the large amount of energy nuclear power plants can reliably produce. Since a nuclear power plant can operate at a predictable, sustained level, it is ideal for providing "base load" power, the consistent amount of power that is needed no matter the time of day or seasonal fluctuations. By contrast, the amount of power produced by alternative energy sources fluctuates, depending on the availability of wind, sun, and water. Furthermore, while nuclear energy does create hazardous radioactive by-products, many proponents point out that nuclear power plants do not emit greenhouse gases.

Countries are also attracted to nuclear energy because of the low cost of fuel relative to the large output of energy. The primary cost of nuclear power plants comes from building the plant (including related financing costs); once it is in operation, the price of nuclear fuel is low compared to fossil fuels. The large initial costs of building a nuclear power plant could be offset by the plant's long lifespan of 40 to 60 years. Moreover, the global supply of uranium is unlikely to be disrupted or experience large price shocks because of the political stability of some of its largest producers, such as Canada and Australia.

Nonetheless, the large financial and technical resources required for nuclear energy mean that until recently, nuclear power has largely been limited to industrialized countries like France, Russia, Japan, and the United States. Building and maintaining a nuclear power plant requires large amounts of capital, a developed infrastructure, highly educated personnel, an ability to manage advanced technology, and an effective way to regulate the industry. Today, however, some developing countries and rising powers, such as China, are beginning to see nuclear energy as an efficient, reliable source of energy for their growing economies.

The primary arguments against nuclear power center on the cost of the entire process, the impacts of nuclear processes on the environment, and the proliferation risks associated with the nuclear fuel cycle. The high cost of building a nuclear power plant and the potential liabilities in case of an accident have deterred many countries from pursuing nuclear power, or make it difficult for countries to convince firms to build new plants. A common argument is that the total cost of nuclear power, including constructing the plant, maintenance, and long-term storage of nuclear waste, outweighs the benefits or profits, making it uneconomical.

High-profile accidents at the Three Mile Island (U.S.), Chernobyl (Ukraine), and Fukushima Dai-ichi (Japan) reactors have mobilized public opinion against the development of nuclear power. When radioactive by-products escape containment structures (whether deliberately or by accident), they can contaminate the air, water, and ground, making the nearby land unsafe for human habitation. There is also the problem of what to do with the spent fuel once it has been used up inside the reactor. Because of the long half-lives of the radioactive by-products, which can extend to millions of years, scientists and industry have struggled to find ways to safely and securely store the material. No matter the method of storage or permanent disposal, some communities have taken the "Not in My Backyard" (NIMBY) stance; they do not want to have highly toxic waste stored near their homes.

There is also concern that countries possessing nuclear energy technology could create secret nuclear weapons programs or fail to prevent terrorists from gaining access to dangerous material. Much of the technology for nuclear power is "dual-use": the same processes used to produce nuclear power are employed to create weapons. The beginning and end processes of the nuclear fuel cycle merit particularly heavy scrutiny. On the "front end" of the fuel cycle,

uranium is enriched to different concentrations depending on whether it is being used for a reactor or a bomb. Since the same process is used for both, attempts have been made to restrict the spread of enrichment technology to prevent new countries from being able to build weapons. This has not stopped some countries from gaining the technology. Iran has continued to develop enrichment capabilities despite opposition from other countries and in violation of UN sanctions. It initially obtained the technology through an international black market operated by Pakistani scientist A.Q. Khan. Though Iran says it is enriching uranium to produce medical isotopes and eventually to provide fuel for its reactors, other countries suspect the uranium will be used for military purposes. On the "back end" of the fuel cycle, recycling spent fuel is controversial because the process separates out plutonium, a material that can fuel bombs such as the one used against Nagasaki in World War II and that has been used more recently by North Korea for the same purpose.

Production Levels and Industry Structure

Despite the slowdown in plant construction at the end of the twentieth century, nuclear energy remains an important part of the current global landscape. In 2010, the International Atomic Energy Agency (IAEA, the United Nations' nuclear agency) reported that nuclear energy contributed to slightly less than 14 percent of all electricity produced globally and constituted 5.7 percent of the total primary energy generated globally. These percentages translated into 441 plants operating in 29 countries, with a combined capacity of 375 GWe. Western Europe has been a leader in nuclear energy production; in 2008, 27 percent of its generated electricity came from nuclear power. France remains a leader in the region, with about 75 percent of its electricity production coming from nuclear energy since the early 1990s. Eastern Europe and North America were slightly behind Western Europe, with about 18 percent of electricity coming from nuclear reactors in each region. In the Far East, nuclear energy contributed to approximately 10 percent of overall electricity production. In 2008, South Korea utilized 20 nuclear power reactors, which generated 144.3 terrawatt-hours of electricity in 2008, a little more than one-third of the country's total electricity production. South Korea, which has since build an additional reactor and plans to produce nearly two-thirds of its electricity from nuclear power in two decades, only slightly trails Russia in nuclear energy production, although its output still falls considerably behind that of world leaders France, the United States, and Japan. By contrast, Latin America and Africa produced 2 percent of their electricity from nuclear power. Nuclear energy production is out of the reach of many poor countries, who operate electricity grids that would be unable to accommodate the large output of many of today's massive nuclear plants, and for whom constructing and managing a power plant would be too expensive.

The structure of the industry varies by country. Some of the largest firms that build and maintain plants are from France, Japan, Russia, and the United States. The industry is worth billions of dollars; for example, the French nuclear giant Areva declared €9.104 billion in revenue in 2010 alone. In France, Russia, and South Korea, nuclear technology companies are state-owned, which has made it easier for the companies to secure funding to build new plants and export reactors to other countries. The United States, by comparison, provides minimal support for its industry, contributing to a situation in which no new plants have been constructed since the 1970s.

Common Reactor Types

In 2010, the two most common designs of nuclear reactor were the pressurized water reactor (PWR) and the boiling water reactor (BWR). They are both based on the principle of using "light" (regular) water to moderate and cool the fuel rods. In a BWR, the water turns to steam as it cools the rods, which then powers a turbine to produce electricity. The PWR has a more complex design than the BWR, using the supply of water that pushes past the fuel rods to heat a separate supply of water that will drive the turbine. There were 269 PWRs and 92 BWRS operating in 26 countries in 2010.

Another type of reactor in use is the pressurized heavy water reactor (PHWR). It was first marketed as the CANada Deuterium-Uranium reactor, also known as CANDU. This type of reactor uses "heavy water"—water molecules with an extra neutron in the hydrogen atoms—as a moderator and coolant. Since heavy water absorbs fewer neutrons, PHWR reactors have a wider variety of fuel options, including unenriched uranium. The reactor design uses a large collection of pressurized tubes instead of one large pressure vessel, which means one ruptured pressure tube in a PHWR theoretically does not pose the same safety risk as a ruptured pressure vessel in a light water reactor. The way the fuel is distributed—small pellets loaded into small elements, which are then packaged in bundles called fuel assemblies—means that the reactor does not need to be shut down in order to be refueled. Most PHWR reactors are found in Canada and India. In 2010, the 46 PHWR reactors operating globally had a total capacity of 22,840 MWe.

However, CANDU reactors have faced declining interest both in Canada and around the world. The proliferation risk of CANDU reactors became a concern after India used Canadian nuclear technology to build its weapons program. In the 1980s and 1990s, CANDU reactors gained a reputation in Canada for being expensive and accident prone, in part due to the high level of expertise required to operate them. Lacking domestic political consensus for further building, the CANDU reactor has fallen out of favor as promoting its export has become more difficult. Reflecting its declining support for nuclear energy, in 2011 the Canadian government moved to privatize the CANDU vendor, Atomic Energy of Canada Ltd., by selling its share to SNC-Lavalin.

Regulation

Each country has its own regulatory structure to oversee its nuclear industries. These agencies, such as the U.S. Nuclear Regulatory Commission, French CEA (Commissariat à l'énergie atomique), and Russian Federal Environmental, Industrial and Nuclear Supervision Service of the Russian Federation (Rostekhnadzor), have a broad range of responsibilities, from licensing reactors, setting national safety and security standards, to determining how to store spent fuel. Countries also set regulations for what technology their firms are allowed to export; and because peaceful nuclear technology can have military applications, countries often want control over where their nuclear technology is sold.

Since nuclear activities have international ramifications, however, there is also substantial coordination among countries. The IAEA provides support to UN member states in developing peaceful nuclear applications as well as ensuring that nuclear material under its supervision is not diverted for military purposes. Created in 1957, the IAEA also provides technical support to developing countries to create the necessary regulatory structures for a nuclear program and helps countries gain access to relevant nuclear technology in medicine and global health. An international group consisting of 46 countries also exists to negotiate on export controls. The Nuclear Suppliers Group meets annually to set standards on what criteria should determine the export of nuclear technology.

Effects

The most controversial aspects of nuclear energy include its impact on the environment and human health, whether it is economically sound, and how to determine whether the technology is being used for peaceful purposes. The risks posed by nuclear energy are not well understood, but have long drawn the attention of the environmental movement. Radioactive materials can cause serious health problems and be fatal in large doses. If radioactive materials escape containment, they enter the environment in ways that make them difficult to extract. Especially since accidents like Chernobyl, some populations around the world have demonstrated a strong opposition to nuclear power. Often, experts perceive the risk posed by nuclear power as the probability of an accident occurring, while the public tends to think of the risk as the seriousness of an accident if it were to occur. Added to this, in the minds of many people, radiation is an unseen (and therefore difficult to quantify) danger, leading to a fear beyond what is scientifically known. As a result, the decision about whether to build a nuclear power plant is affected by the level of risk the population perceives.

Another problem posed by nuclear energy production is what to do with the spent fuel, both in the short and long term. In the short term, the by-products of nuclear energy are both hot and radioactive; after the spent fuel is removed from a reactor, it is placed in a pool of water (known as wet storage) for anywhere from a few years to decades to allow its heat and radiation levels to decrease. After this period of cooling, it can be moved to an air-cooled dry cask for storage. In some countries, such as France and Japan, the spent fuel is sent to a plant for reprocessing, where the fuel is dissolved and the uranium and plutonium produced during reactor operations are separated out for re-use. The separated plutonium is intended for re-use in reactor fuel. However, reprocessing creates an opportunity for the plutonium to be diverted to weapons use. The issue of reprocessing is therefore highly politicized because of proliferation risks. Originally, countries pursued this technology because it was thought that uranium sources were scarce, though 2011 studies by the Massachusetts Institute for Technology and a U.S. government Blue Ribbon Commission both indicated that this should not be a concern for the next few decades.

In the long term, countries are faced with the problem of what to do with the high-level waste, whether it is retained in the spent fuel or separated from the plutonium and depleted uranium. The most common solution is to send the waste to a geological repository, where it is placed underground in a way that minimizes risks to local populations. While Sweden and Finland have successfully won public support for creating geological repositories by encouraging broad public participation in the site selection process, other countries have met with resistance when communities are not given sufficient choice. Winning such support means overcoming the opposition inherent to such a complicated and potentially risky technology, particularly one that aims to safely store waste for tens of thousands of years. The growth potential for the nuclear energy industry will be significantly affected by whether countries can find politically and technologically acceptable sites to store nuclear waste.

A new question facing some countries is the cost and political feasibility of replacing existing nuclear power production, either with new reactors or a different type of energy. In countries such as the United States, upgrades and expansions to aging reactors have so far allowed the country to postpone finding a long-term answer to the question. For Germany, the question is more immediate since it decided to phase out nuclear energy production by 2022. Before this point, nuclear energy constituted almost 23 percent of Germany's overall electricity production. To replace this, Germany will be required to import energy and make major investments in renewable energy if it is still committed to reducing carbon emissions. Even ramping up production in renewable energy, however, is unlikely to immediately cover the gap that nuclear energy has filled.

The industry's continued growth will also depend on global sensitivities to proliferation. As more developing countries become interested in nuclear power, nuclear supplier countries are faced with the dilemma of whether to export technology to certain countries that have indicated a willingness to pursue a nuclear weapons program if threatened. Building

Two of four damaged reactors at the Fukushima Daiichi Nuclear Power Station in northern Japan lie smoldering after the disastrous tsunami and earthquake of March 11, 2011. The accident led to a reassessment of energy policies throughout the developed world. *(Kyodo via AP Images)*

a nuclear energy program gives a country some of the technology and expertise required to produce a nuclear weapon. While exporters can put export control laws in place to help avoid the technology being diverted for military purposes, these rules are an imperfect means of control over countries that are intent on obtaining nuclear technology. Moreover, after the attacks of September 11, countries became concerned about ensuring the security of nuclear materials, which extremists could use in an explosive device. There was also increased fear that extremists would attack nuclear facilities, causing the release of radiation similar to a nuclear accident.

The Future

Beginning in the early 2000s, many countries expressed a new or renewed interest in nuclear energy. The reasons for the resurgence were growing energy demands among developing countries, concerns about climate change, and unstable fossil fuel prices. Many developing countries approached the IAEA and other countries with existing nuclear energy programs to determine if nuclear power was an economically

viable alternative to fossil fuels or other renewable resources. In terms of building new plants, Asia has led the way. Of the 65 reactors under construction in 2011, 27 were located in China, 11 in Russia, 6 in India, and 5 in South Korea. There has also been increased interest in the Middle East, where in 2009 the United Arab Emirates signed a contract for South Korea to build four nuclear power plants, which would be the first nuclear power plants in the Arab world as well as the first exports of South Korean power reactors. Experts and industry watchers began to speculate that more countries would introduce nuclear power within the coming decade, predicting a "nuclear renaissance."

In March 2011, however, three reactors at the Fukushima Daiichi plant in Japan experienced a loss-of-coolant accident after an earthquake and a tsunami disabled emergency generators needed to cool the reactors. The ensuing release of radiation required the evacuation of the surrounding area and prompted fears of a contaminated food supply. Initially, the Japanese government recommended that a 12-mile (19 kilometer) radius around the plant be evacuated, though this was widened to 19 miles (31 kilometers) two weeks after the tsunami as the crisis progressed. The U.S. government evaluated the situation differently, and recommended to its citizens in the area that everyone within a 50-mile (80 kilometer) radius of the plant be evacuated. The disaster brought the issue of nuclear safety into the international spotlight, with the European Union beginning an inspection of safety features of all nuclear power plants located within its member states. There was an immediate chilling effect on the "nuclear renaissance"—Germany, for example, decided to move away from nuclear power entirely only six months after having agreed to extend the lifespan of its aging nuclear power plants. In Japan, there was a large public backlash against nuclear energy, and the government halted its plans to expand its nuclear energy industry, an abrupt change that left uncertainty about the future of nuclear power in the country.

Nuclear energy will likely be a part of the global energy landscape for years to come. As described above, nuclear power plays a significant role in existing energy supplies for many countries, and despite accidents, developing countries and rising powers remain interested in building new plants. However, the debate remains whether it is truly a cost-effective form of energy, and whether the risks of an accident, extremist attack, or diversion to a weapons program outweigh the benefits. Ensuring that nuclear energy remains safe, secure, and peaceful is essential if it is to contribute to slowing global warming.

Miles A. Pomper and Michelle E. Dover

See also: Energy, Alternative; Environmental Illnesses; Nuclear Proliferation; Toxic Waste.

Further Reading

Bodansky, David. *Nuclear Energy: Principles, Practices, and Prospects.* New York: Springer, 2004.

Fanchi, John, and Christopher Fanchi. *Energy in the 21st Century.* Hackensack, NJ: World Scientific Publishing, 2011.

Feiveson, Harold, Zia Mian, M.V. Ramana, and Frank Von Hippel, eds. "Spent Fuel from Nuclear Power Reactors." Princeton, NJ: International Panel on Fissile Materials, 2011.

Ferguson, Charles. *Nuclear Energy: What Everyone Needs to Know.* New York: Oxford University Press, 2011.

Goldemberg, José. "Nuclear Energy in Developing Countries." *Daedalus* 138:4 (2009): 71–80.

Interdisciplinary MIT Study Group. *The Future of the Nuclear Fuel Cycle.* Cambridge: Massachusetts Institute of Technology, 2011.

———. *The Future of Nuclear Power.* Cambridge: Massachusetts Institute of Technology, 2003.

Levi, Daniel J., and Elaine E. Holder. "Psychological Factors in the Nuclear Power Controversy." *Political Psychology* 9:3 (September 1988): 445–457.

Tabak, John. *Nuclear Energy.* New York: Facts On File, 2009.

Walker, J. Samuel. *Three Mile Island: A Nuclear Crisis in Historical Perspective.* Berkeley: University of California Press, 2004.

Web Sites

Blue Ribbon Commission on America's Nuclear Future: www.brc.gov

Canadian Centre for Treaty Compliance, Carleton University: www2.carleton.ca/cctc

Environmental Protection Agency: www.epa.gov

Greenpeace International: www.greenpeace.org

International Atomic Energy Agency: www.iaea.org

International Panel on Fissile Materials: www.fissilematerials.org

Nuclear and Radiation Studies Board: dels.nas.edu/nrsb

Nuclear Regulatory Commission: www.nrc.gov

Nuclear Suppliers Group: www.nuclearsuppliersgroup.org

OECD Nuclear Energy Agency (NEA): www.oecd-nea.org

World Nuclear Association: www.world-nuclear.org

Documents

Document 1: Address by U.S. President Dwight D. Eisenhower to the 470th Plenary Meeting of the UN General Assembly, 1953

In the early 1950s, nuclear technology for both military and peaceful uses was quickly developing, along with an arms race between the Soviet Union and the United States. On December 8, 1953, U.S. president Dwight D. Eisenhower gave an address at the United Nations General Assembly titled "Atoms for Peace," which highlighted the threat of nuclear weapons and proposed that an international agency should oversee the development of nuclear energy on a global scale, ensuring its peaceful use. This address was a catalyst for the creation of the International Atomic Energy Agency, whose mandate includes ensuring that nuclear material is not diverted to military purposes and promoting the peaceful use of nuclear technology.

www.iaea.org/About/history_speech.html

Source: International Atomic Energy Agency.

Document 2: Declaration by the IAEA Ministerial Conference on Nuclear Safety in Vienna on 20 June 2011, INFCIRC 821 (excerpt), 2011

Following the disaster at the Fukushima Daiichi Power Plant in Japan, there was public pressure to increase safety standards at nuclear facilities. In June 2011, the International Atomic Energy Agency (IAEA) director general, Yukiya Amano, held a ministry-level conference on nuclear safety. The following document is the declaration agreed upon by the ministers underscoring the dangerous effects of a nuclear accident and calling for an increased role for the IAEA in nuclear safety. The ministers also stress the need for transparency in responding to a nuclear disaster.

We, the Ministers of the Member States of the International Atomic Energy Agency (IAEA) . . .

1. Express sympathy for and solidarity with Japan in connection with the unprecedented earthquake and tsunami of 11 March 2011, which caused much loss of life and severe damage, and the accident at the Fukushima Daiichi Nuclear Power Station . . .

2. Recognize the efforts of the international community to enhance knowledge in nuclear safety and radiation protection and strengthen international standards in nuclear safety, emergency preparedness and response and radiation protection of people and the environment and the need to draw the lessons from the accident at the Fukushima Daiichi Nuclear Power Station;

3. Recognize that some States consider nuclear power as a viable option in meeting their energy needs, while other States have decided not to use or to phase out nuclear energy;

4. Recognize that nuclear accidents may have transboundary effects and raise the concerns of the public about the safety of nuclear energy and the radiological effects on people and the environment; and emphasize the importance of adequate responses based on scientific knowledge and full transparency, should a nuclear accident occur;

5. Underline that States with nuclear power programmes have a central role in ensuring the application of the highest standards of nuclear safety; and emphasize the responsibility of these States for providing a timely, transparent and adequate response to nuclear accidents in order to minimize their consequences;

6. Emphasize the importance of implementing enhanced national and international measures to ensure that the highest and most robust levels of nuclear safety are in place, based on IAEA safety standards, which should be continuously reviewed, strengthened and implemented as broadly and effectively as possible and commit to increase bilateral, regional and international cooperation to that effect;

7. Commit to strengthening the central role of the IAEA in promoting international cooperation and in coordinating international efforts to strengthen global nuclear safety, in providing expertise and advice in this field and in promoting nuclear safety culture worldwide;

8. Encourage the close cooperation and coordination among the relevant intergovernmental and nongovernmental organizations on nuclear safety related matters;

9. Stress the importance that the IAEA should be further enabled to meet the high level of public expectation to provide timely, factually correct and objective information and assessments of nuclear accidents and their radiological consequences . . .

10. Welcome the reports submitted by Japan and the IAEA International Fact-Finding Mission to Japan, which include preliminary assessments of the accident at the Fukushima Daiichi Nuclear Power Station;

11. Stress the need to receive from Japan and the IAEA a comprehensive and fully transparent assessment of the Fukushima Daiichi Nuclear Power Station accident in order for the international community to be able to draw and act upon the lessons learned, including a review of IAEA safety standards that are relevant to the accident, in particular those pertaining to multiple severe hazards;

12. Underline the benefits of strengthened and high quality independent international safety expert assessments, in particular within the established IAEA framework, through periodic reviews and evaluation missions assessing national regulatory frameworks, emergency preparedness and response and nuclear power plant operation in order to ensure continuous improvement of the safety of nuclear installations on the basis of internationally agreed rules and procedures . . .

Source: International Atomic Energy Agency.

NUCLEAR PROLIFERATION

The term "nuclear proliferation" refers to the spread of nuclear weapons, weapons-grade nuclear materials, and expertise and technologies for the processing of nuclear-grade materials or their fabrications to states or nonstate actors that previously did not possess them.

Technically speaking, nuclear proliferation began with the U.S. development of the atom bomb during World War II. Generally, however, the term applies to the acquisition of nuclear materials, know-how, and weapons by states or nonstate actors outside the original so-called nuclear club of nations—the United States, the Soviet Union, Great Britain, France, and the People's Republic of China—that possessed such weapons by the mid-1960s.

The history of the period since America's deployment of nuclear weapons against Japan in 1945 is one of slow but steady acquisition of nuclear weapons by several nations, as well as the abandonment of nuclear programs by several others. For much of this period, the main fear associated with nuclear weapons was not so much proliferation as possible use, either accidentally or intentionally, by the two superpowers—the United States and the Soviet Union—locked in a Cold War and nuclear arms race from 1945 through the late 1980s.

While such fears persisted through the 1980s and, arguably, persist today, new concerns about proliferation arose in the late 1970s, as new nations, including several in volatile regions, acquired weapons. The rise of transnational terrorism from the 1970s through the September 11, 2001, attacks on the United States, and a shift in the tactics of some terrorist organizations from hostage taking to mass killing, has raised concerns about nonstate actors acquiring and using nuclear weapons or nuclear materials against civilian populations. The collapse of the Soviet Union in 1991 has compounded this fear, for while the event helped to ease Cold War tensions with the United States, it also put at jeopardy the vast stores of nuclear materials, expertise, and weapons that were once part of the Soviet Union's arsenal.

History

Five nations had acquired nuclear weapons by 1964, the last being China. These five nations were divided between the "free" and communist worlds, as the divisions of the global community of nations were once described. The former group included the United States, Great Britain, and France; the latter included the Soviet Union and China.

Between 1945 and 1980, these five nations—but especially the United States and the Soviet Union—expanded their nuclear arsenals exponentially. From just six at the end of 1945, the number of nuclear weapons in the world grew to nearly 400 in 1950, more than 20,000 in 1960, nearly 40,000 by 1970, and more than 50,000 by 1980. Even during this period of nuclear expansion, the leading nuclear powers were agreeing to treaties to constrain testing (a ban on atmospheric testing was signed in 1963), deployment (a ban on their use in outer space was signed in 1967), and counter-systems (an anti–ballistic missile treaty in 1972). In addition, two weapons limitation treaties were signed in 1972 and 1979. In 1996, a comprehensive test ban treaty—banning all nuclear explosions in all environments—was adopted by the United Nations General Assembly but has yet to be ratified by a sufficient number of states, including

Number of Nuclear Weapons Worldwide, 1945–2011

Year	Number
1945	6
1950	374
1960	22,069
1970	38,153
1980	54,706
1990	55,863
2000	21,851
2011	20,500*

* Estimate.

Sources: Natural Resources Defense Council; Federation of American Scientists.

such existing and potential nuclear powers as China, India, Israel, North Korea, Pakistan, and the United States, although China, Israel, and the United States did sign the treaty.

Despite increasing Cold War tensions in the 1980s, the number of nuclear weapons leveled off through the early 1990s. This occurred for several reasons: the sheer number of weapons already in existence obviated the need for many more; popular resistance, particularly in the West, made it less politically possible; the growing accuracy of delivery systems made existing stockpiles more effective; arms control and limitation treaties came into force, setting limits and even imposing reductions on the stockpiles of U.S. and Soviet weapons; economic stress within the Soviet Union that constricted resources devoted to defense; and, finally, Cold War tensions eased following the collapse of the Soviet Union.

Even before that event, there was a growing political impetus within both the United States and the Soviet Union not just to limit arsenals but to reduce them, especially after the coming to power of Soviet reformer Mikhail Gorbachev in 1985. In 1987, the two powers signed a treaty banning intermediate range missiles. Then, in 1991 and 1993 (by 1993, the Soviet Union had been replaced by Russia), the two powers signed agreements calling for dramatic reductions in nuclear weapons.

But even as the two superpowers expanded and then contracted their arsenals, the problem of nuclear proliferation steadily grew as various other nations pursued nuclear weapons and as the technology and expertise for developing them became more widespread. In response to this growing concern, the United States, the Soviet Union, and the United Kingdom formulated and signed the Nuclear Non-Proliferation Treaty of 1968, committing themselves not to transfer weapons to nonnuclear states or assist those states in developing their own weapons. By the time the treaty went into effect in 1970, some 130 nations had signed on, agreeing not to attempt to acquire by transfer or research nuclear weapons of their own. The treaty allowed signatory nations to pursue nuclear power for peaceful means and committed the nuclear powers to helping countries develop peaceful uses for nuclear power. It also called on the nuclear powers to pursue disarmament policies and treaties of their own, though this was the portion of the treaty that nuclear powers did the least to implement.

Underpinning the Non-Proliferation Treaty idea were two basic premises. The first and most obvious

Nations Possessing Nuclear Weapons, 1945–Present

Nation	Dates
United States	1945– present
Soviet Union/Russia	1949–present
United Kingdom	1952–present
France	1960–present
China	1964–present
India	1974–present
Israel*	1979–present*
South Africa	1979–early 1990s**
Belarus***	1991–1996
Kazakhstan	1991–1995
Ukraine	1991–1996
Pakistan	1998–present
North Korea	2006–present

　* Believed to have nuclear weapons; estimated date of acquisition.
　** Dates are estimates.
　*** Following independence from Soviet Union until turning them over to Russia or disposing of them under international observation.
　Source: Author.

was that the world would be a more dangerous place if more nations acquired nuclear weapons. But there was also the notion that the five states that already had nuclear weapons were essentially rational enough to recognize that their own self-interest dictated against their use, as the offending countries risked massive destruction of themselves, their armed forces, or their allies. The fear was that less rational leaders in more volatile states might not be as reticent.

But the flaw in the Non-Proliferation Treaty was that it only applied to signatory states; any other nation with an ambition to acquire such weapons simply did not sign the accord and was therefore not bound by it. From the time the treaty was signed until the end of the Cold War in the early 1990s, a disparate collection of nations around the world pursued nuclear weapons, technology, expertise, and materials, either through purchase, transfer, or independent development. These included Argentina, Brazil, Israel, Libya, North Korea, South Africa, India, and Pakistan. Of these, India (in 1974), Israel (believed to have done so in 1979), and South Africa (also believed to have done so in 1979) succeeded. (In fact, South Africa and Israel have never admitted to having weapons, though the former gave up whatever arsenal it had in the early 1990s.) Each of these countries pursued a nuclear arsenal for different reasons: India to counter rival China; Israel as a defense against the numerically superior forces of a hostile Arab world; and South Africa in defense of apartheid.

Later, Pakistan would acquire nuclear weapons in 1998, to counter rival India, and North Korea would do so in 2006. For the latter, the reasons for pursuing nuclear arms are obscured by the secrecy and opacity of the regime, though most observers say the reasons include prestige, to counter perceived threats from the United States, and as a bargaining chip in negotiations with the outside world over food and other aid. As of 2012, no nonstate organization has been able to develop or acquire nuclear weapons, while three states have given them up. These are Belarus, Kazakhstan, and Ukraine, all of which came into possession of nuclear weapons stationed on their soil with the collapse of the Soviet Union in 1991 and all of which voluntarily destroyed the weapons or turned them over to Russia, as per agreements reached between these states, and under the watch of international observers.

Developing Nuclear Weapons

Nuclear weapons come in a variety of types. They can vary in terms of yield, usually measured by the explosive force of kilotons or megatons of TNT; delivery systems, most commonly bombs and missiles; and how they achieve their destructive power. The latter can occur through fission, or the splitting of atoms (of the elements uranium or plutonium), or the exponentially more powerful fusion process, whereby two atomic nuclei of the element hydrogen are fused together to produce one heavier nucleus. As fusion devices require fission devices as ignitions, most experts say it is likely that only the most advanced nuclear nations are capable of producing them.

The technology and expertise needed to design a fission weapon is not particularly hard to come by or develop. Indeed, there are a number of sophisticated plans available on the Internet. The trick is obtaining enough fissionable material, such as the element plutonium or the isotope uranium-235, and the material must be of weapons grade. Uranium naturally occurs with less than 1 percent of the isotope U-235, while reactor grade uranium usually contains 3 to 4 percent U-235. To produce the type of runaway nuclear chain reaction necessary to unleash the explosive power of fission, the fissionable material must contain at least 20 percent U-235, though such a percentage will produce a very low explosive yield. Even the relatively primitive device dropped on Hiroshima in 1945 contained upward of 85 percent U-235.

There are, as noted, two ways to obtain such fissionable material—purchase from an existing nuclear power or independent development. The former requires a willing seller, and thus far there appears to be no verifiable evidence that any nuclear state has engaged in the sale of fissionable material to a nonnuclear state or entity, though there have been cases of materials showing up on the black market, probably from sources within the former Soviet Union's nuclear weapons establishment. Developing fissionable material requires the use of a large number of sophisticated centrifuges, capable of producing U-235 in quantities sufficient to make a nuclear weapon. At 85 percent purity, it would take a minimum of about 30 to 50 pounds (14 to 23 kilograms). By comparison, the bomb dropped on Hiroshima, with a yield of 20 kilotons of TNT, had about 140 pounds (64 kilograms) of 85 percent U-235 uranium in it.

Far simpler to construct—and thus most feared by many who study nuclear proliferation—is a radiological weapon, whereby radioactive material is wrapped around a conventional explosive. Here, there is no minimum enrichment requirement since a chain reaction is not necessary. Instead, the conventional explosive delivers the radioactive payload. While there is less physical destruction, since conventional explosives are exponentially less powerful than nuclear ones, these devices can cause widespread radioactive contamination.

Threats of Proliferation Today

While the overall number of nuclear weapons has dropped dramatically over the past two decades, experts on nonproliferation cite a number of concerns—many of them interconnected and associated with various world hot spots—about the status of nuclear weapons in the world and the possibility that they might be used in hostile action.

Former Soviet Union

Although the collapse of the Soviet Union in 1991 eased Cold War tensions with the United States, and thus the possibility of nuclear conflict between the superpowers, that collapse created new threats. First, Russia, which ultimately came into possession of all of the working weapons in the former Soviet arsenal, went into rapid economic decline and political turmoil. Many in the West feared that the various systems put into place to control nuclear missiles might deteriorate, leading to an accidental firing. A second concern was that the vast arsenal of weapons and radioactive materials might fall into the wrong hands. To counter this threat, the United States and the various affected states of the former Soviet Union developed the Cooperative Threat Reduction Program, also known as the Nunn-Lugar Program, after its U.S. Senate sponsors, in 1992. The program was largely successful in decommissioning weapons or moving weapons and radioactive materials to safe locations in Russia and the United States. Still, a number of cases arose in the 1990s of radioactive materials going missing or showing up on the black market. Equally worrisome was the possibility that Soviet nuclear scientists—unemployed and impoverished because of their nation's economic turmoil—might sell their expertise to nuclear aspirant nations and terrorist organizations. As with weapons and materials, several programs were set up between the United States and former states of the Soviet Union to identify key scientists and find them employment so that they would not be tempted to sell their expertise. These programs were largely successful, although at least one scientist, Vyacheslav Danilenko, is believed to have gone to work for the Iranians in the 1990s.

India–Pakistan Conflict

With the departure of the British in 1947, the Indian subcontinent was divided into several states, the most important of which are Hindu-dominated India and Muslim-dominated Pakistan. At the time of the division, the northern region of Kashmir was also divided, with the lion's share going to India despite the fact that the population was largely Muslim. Between 1947 and 1999, the two nations have fought four wars, three of them primarily over Kashmir.

Even during peacetime, tensions between the two countries have remained taut. In 1974, India conducted its first nuclear weapons test. Though it abjured from further testing or deployment, India's action sparked a regional nuclear arms race, as Pakistan immediately moved to develop nuclear weapons of its own. In response, India renewed its program, testing no fewer than five nuclear devices on May 11, 1998. By the end of that month, Pakistan had responded with six nuclear tests of its own.

This nuclear arms race has raised three different sets of concerns. The first is that the tensions between the two countries that have sparked previous conflicts may yet trigger another, this time resulting

in the use of nuclear weapons. This concern has diminished as tensions between the two countries have eased, despite provocations such as the 2008 attack on Mumbai, conducted by terrorists based in Pakistan and, according to Indian officials, with the aid of some elements within Pakistan's military and security agencies.

A second concern is that people within Pakistan's nuclear program, most notably nuclear scientist A.Q. Khan, have aided other nuclear aspirants, including North Korea, Iran, and Libya, in their efforts—successful in the case of North Korea—to develop the technology necessary to produce fissionable material and nuclear weapons. Khan has admitted to such charges and claims he did so with the cooperation of top civilian and military leaders, though all of these deny the allegations.

The third concern is Pakistani politics. The country is highly volatile, with a fractious polity, various civil conflicts, ongoing tensions with India, a weak economy, and a powerful minority determined to install a radical Islamist regime. Should any or all of these forces lead to the collapse of the state or its takeover by forces sympathetic to al-Qaeda or other anti-Western groups, the potential for a transfer of radioactive or fissionable material, or worse, nuclear weapons, into terrorist hands would be great.

Iran

One of the states to which A.Q. Khan and others in Pakistan's security and military establishments have been accused of selling nuclear technology and expertise is Iran. Ruled by an Islamic regime since its 1979 revolution, Iran has become increasingly anti-Western under the leadership of President Mahmoud Ahmadinejad, in office since 2005. This Islamist regime inherited an ongoing nuclear energy program, established by strongly pro-Western shah. In the 1990s and early 2000s, Iran forged an alliance with Russia in which the latter would provide expertise and technology to finish the reactors started by the shah at Bushehr. By the latter period, however, Iranian dissidents were warning the international community that Iran was setting up facilities to enrich uranium as well. The question then became to what degree was Iran enriching the uranium—to the level needed for nuclear power generation or that required for nuclear weapons? Iran has insisted on the former while many experts and policymakers in the West claimed that it is the latter.

In 2006, Ahmadinejad announced that Iran had, in fact, achieved enrichment to 3.5 percent U-235, necessary for nuclear power. The UN Security Council then demanded that Iran halt its enrichment program, which the country refused to do. By 2007, the International Atomic Energy Agency estimated that Iran could develop a nuclear weapon within three to eight years. Such a possibility worried a number of other countries, both in the region and in the West. Islamist Iran has long had testy relations with its more conservative Arab neighbors in the Persian Gulf, with the latter fearing that a nuclear-armed Iran would become more belligerent. This has also sparked concern in the West, as much of its oil comes from the Persian Gulf region. Western policymakers also feared that if Iran developed a nuclear weapon, it might trigger a nuclear arms race in the region. But the nation most concerned about Iran's developing a nuclear weapon—and the missiles to deliver it—was Israel, especially since the rise to power of Ahmadinejad, who has called for the Jewish state's destruction. While Israel is believed to possess a significant nuclear arsenal—perhaps as many as 200 warheads, easily capable of destroying much of Iran—its leaders feared that Iran's leadership was ideologically so radical that it would not be deterred by the threat of an Israeli counterattack.

In response to all of these fears and developments, the United States and various other countries began to ratchet up the pressure on Iran, imposing sanctions aimed at crippling the economy and undermining internal support for the regime. But such efforts have been stymied by Iran's vast oil wealth, which prevents sanctions from having a major economic impact, and by allies China and Russia, who refuse to go along with the most stringent sanctions. Efforts by the West in late 2011 to impose even tighter sanctions, including the shutting down of Iran's banking system from the outside world, have prompted threats from Iran to close the strategic Strait of Hormuz, through which about 25 percent of the world's oil is shipped.

In the meantime, Iran has come under another kind of assault, as the computer systems used to operate its nuclear program have been cyber-attacked and several of its nuclear scientists assassinated. No nation has claimed responsibility for these actions but it is generally believed the United States or Israel, or the two working together, are involved.

Korean Peninsula

The most recent nation to obtain nuclear weapons is North Korea, a highly secretive nation, which, technically speaking, is still in a state of war dating to the 1950s with its counterpart, South Korea, and South

North Korea fired a battery of short-range missiles on May 25, 2009, the same day it carried out its second underground detonation of a nuclear weapon. North Korea joined the ranks of nuclear nations with its first test in October 2006. *(AFP/Getty Images)*

Korea's chief ally, the United States. Tensions between the two Koreas, as well as between North Korea and the West, remain high, as North Korea has engaged in a number of belligerent acts, including the firing of missiles over Japan, the sinking of a South Korean warship in 2010, and two underground nuclear tests in 2006 and 2009.

North Korea's ruling regime is not just belligerent and secretive, say experts, but paranoid as well, convinced that it is targeted for destruction by the United States. Thus, it has not only developed nuclear weapons but a military establishment far in excess of its actual defense needs and what its economy can reasonably support. For this reason, as well as general mismanagement, North Korea remains one of the most impoverished countries in Asia, unable at times even to feed its own people. This has forced it to rely on aid from much richer South Korea, China—its only significant ally—and the West. According to those who study the country, the North Korean regime—which underwent a change in leadership in December 2011 with the death of Kim Jong-Il and his replacement by his young and politically inexperienced son Kim Jong-un—has used its nuclear weapons program to exact aid concessions from the outside world.

The Future

Nuclear proliferation and its threats to global security are likely to intensify in coming years, according to most security analysts. The various trouble spots noted above remain tense, and the technology needed to enrich uranium and construct nuclear weapons is only going to become more available. The world is awash in scientists, particularly from the former Soviet Union, with expertise in these fields.

Meanwhile, terrorist groups—most notably, the al-Qaeda network—have made it clear that their number-one tactical aim is to obtain a nuclear weapon and use it to exact concessions from the West. Pakistan, Iran, and even North Korea are all potential sources, especially Pakistan, if it should undergo a political collapse or takeover by Islamist extremists, which many experts say is within the realm of possibility. Even easier to obtain by terrorists would be radioactive materials that could be used to construct a radiological weapon. Such a device—even if set off in a highly populated urban area such as Manhattan—would be unlikely to cause immediate large-scale casualties but could nevertheless have a devastating impact, exposing thousands to long-term cancer risks

and forcing the decontamination or even long-term closure of very valuable real estate, with an economic impact likely to dwarf even that produced by the attacks of September 11.

James Ciment

See also: Arms Trade; Defense Spending; Nuclear Energy.

Further Reading

Albright, David. *Peddling Peril: How the Secret Nuclear Trade Arms America's Enemies.* New York: Free Press, 2010.

Ganguly, Sumit, and S. Paul Kapur. *India, Pakistan, and the Bomb: Debating Nuclear Stability in South Asia.* New York: Columbia University Press, 2010.

Hymans, Jacques E.C. *The Psychology of Nuclear Proliferation: Identity, Emotions, and Foreign Policy.* New York: Cambridge University Press, 2006.

Karpin, Michael. *The Bomb in the Basement: How Israel Went Nuclear and What That Means for the World.* New York: Simon & Schuster, 2006.

Levy, Adrian, and Catherine Scott-Clark. *Deception: Pakistan, the United States and the Secret Trade in Nuclear Weapons.* London: Atlantic, 2007.

Medeiros, Evan S. *Reluctant Restraint: The Evolution of China's Nonproliferation Policies and Practices, 1980–2004.* Palo Alto, CA: Stanford University Press, 2007.

Pollack, Jonathan. *No Exit: North Korea, Nuclear Weapons, and International Security.* Oxford, UK: Routledge, 2011.

Rhodes, Richard. *The Making of the Atomic Bomb.* New York: Simon & Schuster, 1987.

West, Joshua A. *Activities in Nuclear Security.* New York: Nova Science, 2011.

Web Sites

Federation of American Scientists: www.fas.org/programs/ssp/nukes/index.html

Natural Resources Defense Council: www.nrdc.org/nuclear

Nuclear Threat Initiative: www.nti.org/db/nisprofs/russia/forasst/nunn_lug/overview.htm

United Nations Office for Disarmament Affairs: www.un.org/disarmament/WMD/Nuclear

Documents

Document 1: Treaty on the Non-Proliferation of Nuclear Weapons, 1968

Written and opened for signature in 1968 and going into force in 1970, the Nuclear Non-Proliferation Treaty had

been signed by 190 states and other parties as of 2011, including all five nuclear-armed permanent members of the UN Security Council. Developed as a means of deterring the spread of nuclear weapons, the treaty represented a grand bargain between then-current nuclear and non-nuclear states. The latter agreed to forgo developing or acquiring such weapons, while the former agreed to share peaceful nuclear technology with them and to shrink, eventually to zero, their own nuclear arsenals. The treaty has been regarded as a relative success, preventing some states from acquiring nuclear weapons but failing to block others—India, Pakistan, Israel, and North Korea were all non-signatories when they developed their weapons—and failing to get nuclear powers to reduce or eliminate their arsenals.

The States concluding this Treaty, hereinafter referred to as the Parties to the Treaty,

Considering the devastation that would be visited upon all mankind by a nuclear war and the consequent need to make every effort to avert the danger of such a war and to take measures to safeguard the security of peoples,

Believing that the proliferation of nuclear weapons would seriously enhance the danger of nuclear war,

In conformity with resolutions of the United Nations General Assembly calling for the conclusion of an agreement on the prevention of wider dissemination of nuclear weapons,

Undertaking to co-operate in facilitating the application of International Atomic Energy Agency safeguards on peaceful nuclear activities,

Expressing their support for research, development and other efforts to further the application, within the framework of the International Atomic Energy Agency safeguards system, of the principle of safeguarding effectively the flow of source and special fissionable materials by use of instruments and other techniques at certain strategic points,

Affirming the principle that the benefits of peaceful applications of nuclear technology, including any technological by-products which may be derived by nuclear-weapon States from the development of nuclear explosive devices, should be available for peaceful purposes to all Parties to the Treaty, whether nuclear-weapon or non-nuclear-weapon States,

Convinced that, in furtherance of this principle, all Parties to the Treaty are entitled to participate in the fullest possible exchange of scientific information for, and to contribute alone or in co-operation with other States to, the further development of the applications of atomic energy for peaceful purposes,

Declaring their intention to achieve at the earliest possible date the cessation of the nuclear arms race and to undertake effective measures in the direction of nuclear disarmament,

Urging the co-operation of all States in the attainment of this objective,

Recalling the determination expressed by the Parties to the 1963 Treaty banning nuclear weapons tests in the atmosphere, in outer space and under water in its Preamble to seek to achieve the discontinuance of all test explosions of nuclear weapons for all time and to continue negotiations to this end,

Desiring to further the easing of international tension and the strengthening of trust between States in order to facilitate the cessation of the manufacture of nuclear weapons, the liquidation of all their existing stockpiles, and the elimination from national arsenals of nuclear weapons and the means of their delivery pursuant to a Treaty on general and complete disarmament under strict and effective international control,

Recalling that, in accordance with the Charter of the United Nations, States must refrain in their international relations from the threat or use of force against the territorial integrity or political independence of any State, or in any other manner inconsistent with the Purposes of the United Nations, and that the establishment and maintenance of international peace and security are to be promoted with the least diversion for armaments of the world's human and economic resources,

Have agreed as follows:

Article I
Each nuclear-weapon State Party to the Treaty undertakes not to transfer to any recipient whatsoever nuclear weapons or other nuclear explosive devices or control over such weapons or explosive devices directly, or indirectly; and not in any way to assist, encourage, or induce any non-nuclear-weapon State to manufacture or otherwise acquire nuclear weapons or other nuclear explosive devices, or control over such weapons or explosive devices.

Article II
Each non-nuclear-weapon State Party to the Treaty undertakes not to receive the transfer from any transferor whatsoever of nuclear weapons or other nuclear explosive devices or of control over such weapons or explosive devices directly, or indirectly; not to manufacture or otherwise acquire nuclear weapons or other nuclear explosive devices; and not to seek or receive any assistance in the manufacture of nuclear weapons or other nuclear explosive devices.

Article III
1. Each non-nuclear-weapon State Party to the Treaty undertakes to accept safeguards, as set forth in an agreement to be negotiated and concluded with the International Atomic Energy Agency in accordance with the Statute of the International Atomic Energy Agency and the Agency's safeguards system, for the exclusive purpose of verification of the fulfilment of its obligations assumed under this Treaty with a view to preventing diversion of nuclear

energy from peaceful uses to nuclear weapons or other nuclear explosive devices. Procedures for the safeguards required by this Article shall be followed with respect to source or special fissionable material whether it is being produced, processed or used in any principal nuclear facility or is outside any such facility. The safeguards required by this Article shall be applied on all source or special fissionable material in all peaceful nuclear activities within the territory of such State, under its jurisdiction, or carried out under its control anywhere.

2. Each State Party to the Treaty undertakes not to provide: (a) source or special fissionable material, or (b) equipment or material especially designed or prepared for the processing, use or production of special fissionable material, to any non-nuclear-weapon State for peaceful purposes, unless the source or special fissionable material shall be subject to the safeguards required by this Article.

3. The safeguards required by this Article shall be implemented in a manner designed to comply with Article IV of this Treaty, and to avoid hampering the economic or technological development of the Parties or international co-operation in the field of peaceful nuclear activities, including the international exchange of nuclear material and equipment for the processing, use or production of nuclear material for peaceful purposes in accordance with the provisions of this Article and the principle of safeguarding set forth in the Preamble of the Treaty.

4. Non-nuclear-weapon States Party to the Treaty shall conclude agreements with the International Atomic Energy Agency to meet the requirements of this Article either individually or together with other States in accordance with the Statute of the International Atomic Energy Agency. Negotiation of such agreements shall commence within 180 days from the original entry into force of this Treaty. For States depositing their instruments of ratification or accession after the 180-day period, negotiation of such agreements shall commence not later than the date of such deposit. Such agreements shall enter into force not later than eighteen months after the date of initiation of negotiations.

Article IV

1. Nothing in this Treaty shall be interpreted as affecting the inalienable right of all the Parties to the Treaty to develop research, production and use of nuclear energy for peaceful purposes without discrimination and in conformity with Articles I and II of this Treaty.

2. All the Parties to the Treaty undertake to facilitate, and have the right to participate in, the fullest possible exchange of equipment, materials and scientific and technological information for the peaceful uses of nuclear energy. Parties to the Treaty in a position to do so shall also co-operate in contributing alone or together with other States or international organizations to the further development of the applications of nuclear energy for peaceful purposes, especially in the territories of non-nuclear-weapon States

Party to the Treaty, with due consideration for the needs of the developing areas of the world.

Article V

Each Party to the Treaty undertakes to take appropriate measures to ensure that, in accordance with this Treaty, under appropriate international observation and through appropriate international procedures, potential benefits from any peaceful applications of nuclear explosions will be made available to non-nuclear-weapon States Party to the Treaty on a non-discriminatory basis and that the charge to such Parties for the explosive devices used will be as low as possible and exclude any charge for research and development. Non-nuclear-weapon States Party to the Treaty shall be able to obtain such benefits, pursuant to a special international agreement or agreements, through an appropriate international body with adequate representation of non-nuclear-weapon States. Negotiations on this subject shall commence as soon as possible after the Treaty enters into force. Non-nuclear-weapon States Party to the Treaty so desiring may also obtain such benefits pursuant to bilateral agreements.

Article VI

Each of the Parties to the Treaty undertakes to pursue negotiations in good faith on effective measures relating to cessation of the nuclear arms race at an early date and to nuclear disarmament, and on a treaty on general and complete disarmament under strict and effective international control.

Article VII

Nothing in this Treaty affects the right of any group of States to conclude regional treaties in order to assure the total absence of nuclear weapons in their respective territories.

Article VIII

1. Any Party to the Treaty may propose amendments to this Treaty. The text of any proposed amendment shall be submitted to the Depositary Governments which shall circulate it to all Parties to the Treaty. Thereupon, if requested to do so by one-third or more of the Parties to the Treaty, the Depositary Governments shall convene a conference, to which they shall invite all the Parties to the Treaty, to consider such an amendment.

2. Any amendment to this Treaty must be approved by a majority of the votes of all the Parties to the Treaty, including the votes of all nuclear-weapon States Party to the Treaty and all other Parties which, on the date the amendment is circulated, are members of the Board of Governors of the International Atomic Energy Agency. The amendment shall enter into force for each Party that deposits its instrument of ratification of the amendment upon the deposit of such instruments of ratification by a

majority of all the Parties, including the instruments of ratification of all nuclear-weapon States Party to the Treaty and all other Parties which, on the date the amendment is circulated, are members of the Board of Governors of the International Atomic Energy Agency. Thereafter, it shall enter into force for any other Party upon the deposit of its instrument of ratification of the amendment.

3. Five years after the entry into force of this Treaty, a conference of Parties to the Treaty shall be held in Geneva, Switzerland, in order to review the operation of this Treaty with a view to assuring that the purposes of the Preamble and the provisions of the Treaty are being realised. At intervals of five years thereafter, a majority of the Parties to the Treaty may obtain, by submitting a proposal to this effect to the Depositary Governments, the convening of further conferences with the same objective of reviewing the operation of the Treaty.

Article IX

1. This Treaty shall be open to all States for signature. Any State which does not sign the Treaty before its entry into force in accordance with paragraph 3 of this Article may accede to it at any time.

2. This Treaty shall be subject to ratification by signatory States. Instruments of ratification and instruments of accession shall be deposited with the Governments of the United Kingdom of Great Britain and Northern Ireland, the Union of Soviet Socialist Republics and the United States of America, which are hereby designated the Depositary Governments.

3. This Treaty shall enter into force after its ratification by the States, the Governments of which are designated Depositaries of the Treaty, and forty other States signatory to this Treaty and the deposit of their instruments of ratification. For the purposes of this Treaty, a nuclear-weapon State is one which has manufactured and exploded a nuclear weapon or other nuclear explosive device prior to 1 January 1967.

4. For States whose instruments of ratification or accession are deposited subsequent to the entry into force of this Treaty, it shall enter into force on the date of the deposit of their instruments of ratification or accession.

5. The Depositary Governments shall promptly inform all signatory and acceding States of the date of each signature, the date of deposit of each instrument of ratification or of accession, the date of the entry into force of this Treaty, and the date of receipt of any requests for convening a conference or other notices.

6. This Treaty shall be registered by the Depositary Governments pursuant to Article 102 of the Charter of the United Nations.

Article X

1. Each Party shall in exercising its national sovereignty have the right to withdraw from the Treaty if it decides that extraordinary events, related to the subject matter of this Treaty, have jeopardized the supreme interests of its country. It shall give notice of such withdrawal to all other Parties to the Treaty and to the United Nations Security Council three months in advance. Such notice shall include a statement of the extraordinary events it regards as having jeopardized its supreme interests.

2. Twenty-five years after the entry into force of the Treaty, a conference shall be convened to decide whether the Treaty shall continue in force indefinitely, or shall be extended for an additional fixed period or periods. This decision shall be taken by a majority of the Parties to the Treaty.

Article XI

This Treaty, the English, Russian, French, Spanish and Chinese texts of which are equally authentic, shall be deposited in the archives of the Depositary Governments. Duly certified copies of this Treaty shall be transmitted by the Depositary Governments to the Governments of the signatory and acceding States.

IN WITNESS WHEREOF the undersigned, duly authorized, have signed this Treaty.

Source: United Nations.

Document 2: Cooperative Threat Reduction with States of Former Soviet Union, U.S. Code, 1992

When the Soviet Union collapsed in 1991, fears about its vast nuclear arsenal spread around the world. There were three basic concerns: (1) that the nuclear weapons, or their component radioactive materials, might fall into the hands of terrorists or criminal organizations, either through theft or purchase; (2) that weapons themselves might not be maintained properly, leading to accidents; and (3) that technicians and scientists connected with the program, who were now unemployed or underpaid, might sell their expertise in building such weapons to terrorists and hostile or unstable non-nuclear states. In 1992, the U.S. Congress created the Cooperative Threat Reduction Program (CTRP), as part of the Defense Threat Reduction Agency, to move nuclear, biological, and chemical weapon stockpiles from former states of the Soviet Union back to Russia under the observation of U.S. subcontractors. The CTRP is popularly known as the Nunn-Lugar Program, after its two U.S. Senate sponsors, Sam Nunn (D-GA) and Richard Lugar (R-IN).

www.law.cornell.edu/uscode/22/usc_sup_01_22_10_68A p.html

Source: U.S. Code, Chapter 68A.

OBESITY AND EATING DISORDERS

Obesity is a health condition marked by excess body weight caused by too much fat. Eating disorders are psychological disorders that produce unhealthful eating habits, the two most prominent of which are anorexia nervosa (excessive restriction of food intake) and bulimia nervosa (binge-eating episodes followed by purging).

All of these conditions have serious health consequences, but obesity affects far more people, particularly in wealthier countries but increasingly in developing nations as well. Eating disorders are primarily a problem in high-income countries and among the upper classes in some developing countries, and they largely afflict girls and women.

Obesity was relatively rare prior to the modern age of agricultural abundance, largely affecting only those of high status. In the post–World War II era, and particularly in the past half century or so, obesity has reached epidemic proportions in a number of high-income countries. Researchers and clinicians say that obesity often has genetic and biological causes but that propensities toward the retention of fat are exacerbated by lifestyle choices and social factors.

Evidence of people suffering from eating disorders goes back to ancient times, but eating disorders, too, seem to have become more common in the post–World War II era.

Like obesity, eating disorders, may have underlying genetic or hormonal causes, but they are widely understood as primarily psychological disorders, often triggered by social factors.

The health consequences of obesity and eating disorders are severe. Not only is the sufferer's long-term health put in jeopardy, but he or she may also face social prejudice. Sufferers certainly experience restrictions on the kinds of activities they can engage in. For societies, obesity has consequences as well, most notably in the high health-care costs it incurs.

Over the past few decades, governments, nonprofit organizations, and, increasingly, private enterprise have come to recognize the dangers and costs of obesity and have developed programs to deal with them. Similarly, schools and other institutions with large numbers of girls and young women have begun in recent decades to implement programs to address the psychological issues behind eating disorders. Still, say experts, social factors contributing to obesity and eating disorders—including the prevalence of unhealthful fast foods and prepared foods, the sedentary lifestyles of both children and adults, and the media- and peer-generated pressures to lose weight that may prompt eating disorders—will continue to complicate the task of addressing these health and social problems into the foreseeable future.

Definition and Measurement

As clinically defined, obesity is not just being overweight or even grossly overweight, although being overweight and being obese overlap. Obesity means having too much fat in the body. Doctors and scientists measure obesity in two ways. One is the body mass index (BMI), a crude ratio of the subject's weight divided by the square of his or her height. Those with a BMI of 25 and above are considered overweight, those with a BMI of 30 or above are considered obese, and those with a BMI of 40 or above are considered morbidly obese. For example, a person whose height is 5 feet, 10 inches (1.8 meters) and who weighs more than 175 pounds (79 kilograms) but less than 210 pounds (95 kilograms) would be considered overweight, while such a person with a weight of 210 or more would be considered obese. At the other end of the spectrum, a person of the same height who weighs less than 130 pounds (59 kilograms) would be considered underweight, although not necessarily because of an eating disorder.

While it is simple to understand and allows ordinary people to determine with simple measurements whether they are overweight or obese, the BMI has its limitations. Specifically, it does not differentiate between the amount of fat versus muscle in a person's overall weight. Since muscle tissue is heavier than fat, it can skew results, making a person with above-average muscle content appear to be overweight (although not obese). To counter such problems with the BMI, doctors and researchers have devised other means for determining obesity, including both those that ordinary individuals can perform—such as providing a series of measurements of different parts of the body— and methods that require clinical testing.

Anorexia nervosa and bulimia nervosa, the two most common types of eating disorder, are a matter of behavior, not merely of extremely low body weight, although this is the most obvious symptom. Persons with anorexia nervosa effectively starve themselves through extreme restriction of their food intake or by excessive exercise, or both. Those with bulimia nervosa typically will have binge-eating episodes, during which they consume large quantities of usually fatty or carbohydrate-rich foods in a short period of time, followed by food purges, through either induced vomiting or laxative abuse.

History

Both obesity and eating disorders, particularly anorexia nervosa, have shown up in the historical record since ancient times, though the latter was not recognized as a specific medical condition until the nineteenth century.

Obesity has been with humankind since the beginning of recorded history—and perhaps even earlier, as seems to be indicated by prehistoric artifacts depicting obese persons, such as the so-called the Venus of Willendorf figurine, dating from around 23,000 B.C.E. and found in Central Europe. But to fully understand the significance of obesity in historical times, it is necessary to divide the topic into its health and social components.

Going back to Shustruta, of sixth-century B.C.E. India, and Hippocrates, of fifth- and fourth-century B.C.E. Greece, physicians recognized that obesity had serious health implications. Shustruta accurately noted that the condition contributed to heart disorders and diabetes. And, of course, those who have suffered from obesity—and those who have observed them—surely have been aware, at all times in human history, that it affects basic biological functions, from breathing to mobility.

The modern understanding of obesity begins with eighteenth-century scientific studies that laid out possible causes of the condition, both biological and behavioral. It was Adolphe Quételet, a Belgian statistician of the early nineteenth century, who first developed the BMI to measure the amount of fat in a person's body. An understanding of the role of metabolism in body weight resulted from the work of a number of scientists, beginning with eighteenth-century France's Antoine Lavoisier and his discovery of oxygen and its interaction with other elements. This breakthrough led to others in the understanding of how the human body utilizes matter to produce energy, that is, how it metabolizes food. By the late nineteenth century, researchers had developed ways to measure the caloric content of food. The twentieth century saw the greatest breakthroughs, however, in the understanding of fat within the body and the mechanisms for breaking it down into energy, or failure to do so. By the later years of the century, the role of genes in creating the propensity for obesity had been uncovered. Perhaps the greatest advance came in 1994: scientists discovered leptin, a protein hormone that regulates appetite and metabolism. Some people, it has been found, have a genetically determined resistance to the effects of leptin, a factor that contributes to their obesity.

Even with all of these breakthroughs in the understanding of obesity as a biological phenomenon, there is also the matter of obesity as a social phenomenon. For much of human history, obesity—or corpulence, as it was traditionally called—was a sign of wealth and status, since only those with money and power could afford the quantities of rich food, as well as the sedentary lifestyle, that led to being overweight. With industrialization and commercialization, and the abundance they produced, such distinctions began to fade, since even working people, particularly in wealthier countries, could afford adequate diets, often marked by a high content of animal fat and of sugar and other carbohydrates.

By the early post–World War II period, people in Europe and North America and in developed countries elsewhere, having reached their full genetic potential for height as a result of richer diets, began to become heavier. There were a number of reasons for this, both in the consumption of food energy and in the body's burning of that energy. While the biological factors creating the propensity for obesity remained the same, the lifestyles and behavior that might trigger them evolved.

On the energy-expenditure side of the obesity equation, there were changes in work patterns. The agricultural and manufacturing work that marked much of the history of human endeavor gave way to service and clerical, or "white collar," employment, both of which are generally more sedentary in nature. At the same time, television, and later, computers offered all matter of sedentary entertainment, leading people away from more active pursuits in their leisure time.

On the intake side of the equation was the rise of fast- and prepared foods, usually heavy in sugar and other carbohydrates and in animal fat, all contributors to weight gain. Adding to this development in the late twentieth century was corporate consolidation in the food industry, which often resulted in traditional restaurants being replaced by fast-food outlets and in lengthier food supply chains, a development that worked against the inclusion of more highly perishable vegetables and fruits. In many countries government farm subsidies, aimed at providing inexpensive food for the masses, encouraged the production of meat and foods heavy in carbohydrates. Furthermore, increasing numbers of women in the workforce meant that there were fewer persons available at home to prepare healthier and more balanced meals, leading many families to rely on fast-food outlets and high-fat-content prepared foods from supermarkets.

Paradoxically, or perhaps predictably, as food abundance and sedentary lifestyles became more widespread over the course of the late nineteenth and early twentieth century, the social definition of what constituted the ideal body weight—as well as the clinical one—began to shift from corpulence to leanness. While obesity had long been viewed as a moral failing—as evidenced in the inclusion of gluttony among the seven deadly sins of Christendom—from the late nineteenth century, it increasingly came to be viewed as physically unattractive and undesirable as well—particularly for women but, in the post–World War II period, for men as well. In psychologically vulnerable people, fear of weight gain and consequent social rejection could lead to eating disorders.

As with obesity, anorexia nervosa, or extreme restriction of food intake, has been evident since ancient times, particularly as an element of religious fervor. The rise of Christianity in the West, with its appeals to asceticism and renunciation of the body, led many women, in particular, to undergo extreme fasting as a form of ritualistic purification.

As Christianity began to shed its asceticism, self-induced food deprivation for religious ends gave way to that pursued toward aesthetic ends, particularly in the nineteenth century as the ideal body type for women came to include unnaturally cinched waists, evidenced by the rise of the use of corsets. In 1873 William Gull, one of Queen Victoria's personal physicians, published his seminal article "Anorexia Nervosa (Apepsia Hysterica, Anorexia Hysterica)," thus coining the term for the disease, from the Greek words for "without appetite" and "neurosis."

Hitherto rarely discussed outside of medical circles, anorexia nervosa entered the public conversation with two critical events of the post–World War II period. One was the 1978 publication of the international best-selling book *The Golden Cage: The Enigma of Anorexia Nervosa*, by American psychoanalyst Hilde Bruch, followed five years later by the high-profile death of internationally known American pop singer Karen Carpenter from complications aris-

Eating Disorder Deaths, Top 20 Countries, 2004

Country	Number of deaths from eating disorders*
United States	218
Japan	186
Germany	40
Brazil	28
Canada	19
Korea, South	14
Sweden	13
Australia	8
Netherlands	8
Mexico	7
South Africa	7
Austria	5
Denmark	5
Argentina	4
Norway	3
Chile	3
Spain	3
Finland	2
El Salvador	2
Slovenia	2

* Anorexia nervosa, atypical anorexia nervosa, bulimia nervosa, atypical bulimia nervosa, and overeating associated with other psychological disorders.

Source: Organisation for Economic Co-operation and Development.

ing out of anorexia nervosa. These events helped to reveal the extent of anorexia nervosa—which afflicts an estimated 70 million people around the world, 95 percent of them girls and women between the ages of 12 and 25, largely in the developed world—and put a spotlight on some of its causes. Increasingly coming under scrutiny were media images and messages, particularly from the world of fashion, about "ideal" body weights that were both too thin for good health and achievable only through extreme and unhealthful eating and exercise behavior.

The same messages contribute to the other major eating disorder, bulimia nervosa. Much more recently diagnosed than anorexia nervosa—the first study dates only to 1979—bulimia nervosa is nevertheless a more common condition among women in many developed-world countries. In the United States, for example, it is estimated that 1 percent of women suffer from anorexia nervosa, while 2 percent to 3 percent suffer from bulimia nervosa. Psychologists offer a host of reasons for both conditions, ranging from the genetic to the psychological to the cultural, although most agree that multiple factors probably play a role and that these factors differ among sufferers.

Incidence of Obesity

Obesity is a worldwide phenomenon, but it is one of the rare public-health problems that are more acute in the developed than in the developing world, for the obvious reasons that wealth allows for higher food intake and more people in the developed world than in the developing world pursue relatively sedentary occupations and lifestyles. Indeed, aside from the tiny island nations of Nauru, Tonga, and Seychelles, with their sedentary lifestyles and limited, high carbohydrate diet, virtually all of the countries with the highest rates of obesity are the wealthy regions of Europe, North America, and the Persian Gulf.

As reflected in the high obesity numbers for Mexico and Brazil, among others, the obesity epidemic is spreading to the more economically advanced and richer countries of the developing world. According to the World Health Organization (WHO), there is virtually no major country in the developing world where obesity rates are not climbing rapidly. Indeed, forecasts WHO, obesity is set to replace infectious disease and malnutrition as the leading cause of poor health globally in coming decades. At the same time, with a few noticeable exceptions, including the Unit-

Obesity Rate, Selected Countries, 2007

Country	Percentage obese*
Nauru	78.5
Tonga	56.0
Saudi Arabia	35.6
United Arab Emirates	33.7
United States	32.2
Bahrain	28.9
Kuwait	28.8
Seychelles	25.1
Mexico	24.2
United Kingdom	23.0
Slovakia	22.4
Greece	21.9
Australia	21.7
New Zealand	20.9
Hungary	18.8
Luxembourg	18.4
Estonia	18.0
Russia	17.0
Czech Republic	14.8
Canada	14.3
Brazil**	14.0
Spain	13.1
Ireland	13.0
Germany	12.9
Portugal	12.8
Finland	12.8
Iceland	12.4
Turkey	12.0
Korea, South***	4.0
Japan***	3.0
China**	2.0
India**	1.0
Indonesia**	1.0

   * Percentage of national population having a Body Mass Index of 30 or above.
    ** Figure for 2005.
   *** Figure for 2008.
   Source: Organisation for Economic Co-operation and Development.

ed States, it appears that obesity rates are leveling off and even declining in many developed countries—a trend, say experts, attributable to various anti-obesity efforts by governments, nongovernmental organizations, and even private enterprise—as well as to lifestyle choices by individuals, which are outlined in the section "Responses," below.

Despite such declines, obesity continues to be a growing problem among children and adolescents. For example, in the United States, the rate of obesity among children and adolescents between 2 and 19 years old rose from 5 percent in the early 1970s to nearly 17 percent by the late 2000s. While this is an extreme example, the growth in numbers in the United States represents a trend seen throughout the developed world and in increasing parts of the developing world.

Percentage of Overweight, Obese, and Extremely Obese* Persons, Aged 20–74, United States, 1960–2008**

Weight level	1960–1962	1971–1974	1976–1980	1988–1994	1999–2000	2001–2002	2003–2004	2005–2006	2007–2008
Sample size	6,126	12,911	11,765	14,468	3,603	3,916	3,756	3,835	4,881
% Overweight	31.5	32.3	32.1	32.7	33.6	34.4	33.4	32.2	33.6
% Obese	13.4	14.5	15.0	23.2	30.9	31.3	32.9	35.1	34.3
% Extremely obese	0.9	1.3	1.4	3.0	5.0	5.4	5.1	6.2	6.0

* Overweight = BMI of 25–29.9; Obese = BMI of 30–40; Extreme Obesity = BMI above 40.

** Based on National Health Examination Survey for 1960–1962; based on National Health and Nutrition Examination Survey for all other years.

Source: Centers for Disease Control and Prevention.

Percentage of Obese* Children and Adolescents, by Age, United States, 1963–2008**

Age group	1963–1970	1971–1974	1976–1980	1988–1994	1999–2000	2001–2002	2003–2004	2005–2006	2007–2008
2–5	n/a	5.0	5.5	7.2	10.3	10.6	13.9	11.0	10.4
6–11	4.2	4.0	6.5	11.3	15.1	16.3	18.8	15.1	19.6
12–19	4.6	6.1	5.0	10.5	14.8	16.7	17.4	17.8	18.1
Total	n/a	5.0	5.5	10.0	13.9	15.4	17.1	15.5	16.9

* Obese = BMI of 30 or above.

** Based on National Health and Nutrition Examination Survey.

Source: Centers for Disease Control and Prevention.

Impact and Costs

Obesity leads to a host of medical problems in those who suffer from it. Indeed, aside from smoking—which it may soon replace, since many countries continue to see tobacco use decline—it is cited by health experts as the leading preventable cause of illness. Obesity affects virtually every part of the body but is particularly hard on the cardiovascular system, leading to heart disease and strokes. But obesity is also a leading cause of metabolic disorders, skeletal issues, and respiratory problems, including diabetes, osteoarthritis, and sleep apnea. Also, much clinical evidence exists to show that obesity contributes to certain cancers, including uterine and breast cancer in women and prostate and colon cancer in men.

Anorexia nervosa and bulimia nervosa also have major health implications for sufferers and contribute to a small but not insignificant number of deaths in several countries, including the United States and Japan. Short of death, anorexia nervosa can cause bone weakening, arrhythmia in the heart, thyroid gland problems, and tooth decay. Bulimia nervosa can lead to digestive disorders, including constipation, tears in the esophagus, pancreatitis, and tooth decay.

Beyond the health impact on those afflicted with obesity, the condition affects society at large, primarily in terms of costs. While the United States is an outlier for obesity in the developed world—with about a 50 percent higher rate than its nearest competitor, the United Kingdom—the costs it incurs because of obesity can be extrapolated downward for many other developed countries. Recent studies have estimated that obesity in the United States is responsible for some $215 billion in direct and indirect costs each year. Experts estimate that obese persons incur twice the healthcare costs of nonobese persons, adding between $90 billion and $150 billion to the nation's healthcare bill annually, and that this cost has roughly doubled since 2000. There are also indirect costs, from lost productivity to the expense of redesigning facilities and infrastructure to accommodate obese persons.

Responses

The rising levels of obesity have prompted a number of responses from various institutions, including governments, nonprofits, and private businesses, as well as by individuals. Most of the institutional responses have come in the form of educational efforts, both to alert the public to the health dangers of obesity and to inform them about the various measures individuals can take to avoid or reverse obesity, including developing better eating habits and getting more exercise.

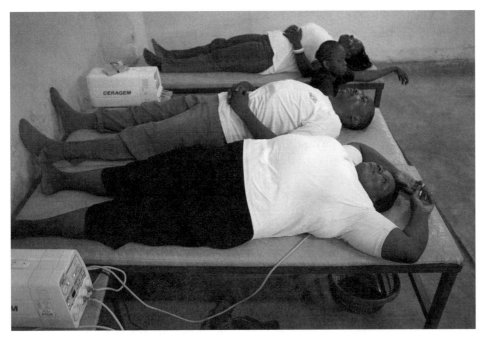

Overweight people get help at a weight-loss center in Kenya. Obesity is a global epidemic. Although rates are highest in the United States, the problem is not limited to wealthy industrialized nations. In many cultures, being heavy is a symbol of wealth and prestige. *(Sipa via AP Images)*

But more activist measures have also been taken. In the United States, for example, a number of communities have placed restrictions on the number of fast-food outlets that can operate in a given neighborhood. This measure is primarily intended for low-income areas, where other dietary options, such as markets with produce sections and more health-oriented restaurants, are not available. At the same time, tax and other incentives have been introduced to encourage businesses to provide such alternatives. To deal with the particularly alarming rise in child and adolescent obesity, school districts have revamped lunch menus and removed soft-drink machines from their premises.

Meanwhile, from private enterprise have come measures such as providing more exercise-at-work programs and rewarding employees—whose health-care costs are typically borne in large part by employers—for weight reduction, with lower health insurance premiums and other monetary incentives. The food industry, too, has begun to respond with smaller portions in supermarket offerings and more healthful options on restaurant menus.

More-radical activists have pushed for an entire revamping of the food industry, calling for more locally grown, less-processed foods. In Europe, in particular, there has been the growth of the so-called Slow Food movement emphasizing taste and local food traditions, an attempt to persuade people to avoid fast food and become more involved in food preparation.

Individuals suffering from obesity have taken measures themselves to fight the condition, including dieting, exercising, and exploring more extreme measures, such as taking prescription and over-the-counter weight-loss drugs and undergoing surgical procedures. Health-care advocates insist, however, that such measures should be undertaken only for the most extreme forms of obesity and only when other weight reduction options have been tried and proved futile.

Despite such rising levels of awareness and an increase in efforts to reduce weight problems, the struggle against obesity, say experts, is likely to be a long one. Humans are hardwired toward the intake of fats, given our evolutionary background in which foods high in fat—which, in limited amounts, are critical to good health—were hard to come by.

As for eating disorders, there are signs that even the fashion industry has become aware of the messages that media images of overly thin models send young girls and women, and there has been some effort to avoid portraying extreme thinness as an aesthetic ideal. In 2012 Israel became the first country in the world to set weight requirements for fashion models featured in runway shows and advertising. Nevertheless, such measures will have to overcome decades of promotion that have instilled the ideal of unnatural thinness into our popular culture and psyche.

James Ciment

See also: Cardiovascular Disease; Diabetes; Hunger and Malnutrition; Mental Health; Public Health.

Further Reading

Boskind-White, Marlene, and William C. White, Jr. *Bulimia/Anorexia: The Binge/Purge Cycle and Self-Starvation*. New York: W.W. Norton, 2000.

Brewis, Alexandra A. *Obesity: Cultural and Biocultural Perspectives*. New Brunswick, NJ: Rutgers University Press, 2011.

Brumberg, Joan Jacobs. *Fasting Girls: The History of Anorexia Nervosa*. New York: Vintage, 2000.

Burniat, Walter, ed. *Child and Adolescent Obesity: Causes and Consequences, Prevention and Management*. New York: Cambridge University Press, 2006.

Cawley, John, ed. *The Oxford Handbook of the Social Science of Obesity*. New York: Oxford University Press, 2011.

Cooper, Myra. *The Psychology of Bulimia Nervosa: A Cognitive Perspective*. New York: Oxford University Press, 2003.

Flamenbaum, Richard K., ed. *Global Dimensions of Childhood Obesity*. New York: Nova Science, 2007.

Gilman, Sander L. *Obesity: A Biography*. New York: Oxford University Press, 2010.

Hill, Susan E. *Eating to Excess: The Meaning of Gluttony and the Fat Body in the Ancient World*. Santa Barbara, CA: Praeger, 2011.

Wright, Jan, and Valerie Harwood, eds. *Biopolitics and the 'Obesity Epidemic': Governing Bodies*. New York: Routledge, 2009.

Web Sites

Centers for Disease Control and Prevention: www.cdc.gov/obesity

European Commission, Research and Innovation: http://ec.europa.eu/research/leaflets/combating_obesity/index_en.html

National Eating Disorders Association: www.nationaleatingdisorders.org

World Health Organization, Health Topics: www.who.int/topics/obesity/en

Documents

Document 1: On Anorexia Nervosa and Bulimia Nervosa, *Diagnostic Statistical Manual of Mental Disorders-IV,* 1994

Published by the American Psychiatric Association (APA), the Diagnostic Statistical Manual of Mental Disorders *(DSM) has come out in four editions since 1952; the latest, number 4, was published in 1994. Psychiatrists and other mental health professionals in the United States and other countries use the DSM to diagnose psychiatric disorders of various kinds. It is also the official classification system utilized by insurance companies and governments to determine eligibility for benefits. The following passages are excerpts from the DSM on the two official eating disorders of the APA, anorexia nervosa and bulimia nervosa.*

Anorexia Nervosa

Category
Eating Disorders

Etiology
Much research has been completed on this disorder, and results indicate a strong familial undercurrent. Many individuals with Anorexia come from over controlling families where nurturance is lacking. Studies suggest that sexual abuse survivors are more prone to the disorder, as are fraternal twins and first degree relatives of those who have anorexia, the latter suggesting a biological component as well.

Symptoms
Most often diagnosed in females (up to 90%), Anorexia is characterized by failure to maintain body weight of at least 85% of what is expected, fear of losing control over your weight or of becoming 'fat.' There is typically a distorted body image, where the individual sees themselves as overweight despite overwhelming evidence to the contrary.

Treatment
Treatment involves, initially, focusing on improving the individual's health. Once this is obtained, therapy can be useful in helping the individual maintain normal eating habits and explore faulty thinking which resulted in the distorted body image and excessive needs for control.

Prognosis
If caught in time, Anorexia is very treatable, but can easily lead to severe physical problems and death if it is allowed to continue. In many cases, an individual with anorexia is very reluctant to get treatment as this would mean giving up control. Inpatient or other hospitalization is often needed when health is at risk.

Bulimia Nervosa

Category
Eating Disorders

Etiology
Many individuals with Bulimia come from over controlling families where nurturance is lacking. Studies suggest that sexual abuse survivors are more prone to the disorder, as are fraternal twins and first degree relatives of those who have anorexia, the latter suggesting a biological component as well.

Symptoms

The key characteristics of this disorder include bingeing (the intake of large quantities of food) and purging (elimination of the food through artificial means such as forced vomiting, excessive use of laxatives, periods of fasting, or excessive exercise).

Treatment

Treatment is similar to Anorexia in that the primary focus is on restoring health and then focusing on normal eating patterns and exploring underlying issues.

Prognosis

Individuals with bulimia are less reluctant to get treatment due to the more obvious symptoms and self recognition of such. Prognosis is therefore improved.

Source: All Psych Online.

Document 2: "Global Strategy on Diet, Physical Activity and Health," World Health Organization, 2004

As the World Health Organization noted in its "Global Strategy on Diet, Physical Activity and Health," the "profound shift" from communicable to noncommunicable diseases that has long characterized the developed world has begun to occur in many parts of the developing world. As the report further noted, these noncommunicable diseases can often be attributed to lifestyle causes, including overeating, lack of exercise, and sedentary habits, all contributing to obesity. And, in turn, obesity contributes to heart disease, diabetes, and other rising killers in the developing world.

www.who.int/dietphysicalactivity/strategy/eb11344/strategy_english_web.pdf

Source: World Health Organization.

OIL, ECONOMIC AND POLITICAL ASPECTS

No commodity, aside from food and water, is more important in people's lives, the world economy, and indeed the very existence of modern civilization than hydrocarbons, primarily oil, but also natural gas and coal. For virtually everything that we need to survive and in nearly every activity that we engage in, oil plays a part.

Although oil's existence was known for centuries, it was not commercially exploited until the mid-nineteenth century, did not become the world's most prominent form of fuel until the first half of the twentieth century, and did not become the chief component of myriad petrochemical products—from plastics to pharmaceuticals—until the second half of the twentieth century.

Because of its importance and ubiquity in modern life, what happens in oil exploration and development and in oil markets has major repercussions for the economy, politics, and even social order of the countries that produce oil for the world market and those that consume it.

Nonetheless, however important oil is in the contemporary world, it is a finite commodity, which eventually will run out, though when that will occur is subject to debate. In the meantime, the problems that oil fosters—from political instability at the national and international levels to economic volatility related to price to environmental concerns both local and global—have led many to conclude that the world should wean itself from oil long before it runs out.

History

The history of oil begins before the advent of human beings, as it was biological and geological processes dating back hundreds of millions of years that led plant material, particularly algae and microscopic plankton, to become trapped beneath the Earth's sur-face, where compression, heat, and time transformed it into oil and pooled it in pockets.

That is where virtually all this oil remained until its commercial exploitation in modern times. A small amount, however, has always seeped to the surface, and it was this surface oil that was first used by human beings. The ancient peoples of Mesopotamia, going back 5,000 years, used asphalt, a viscous form of hydrocarbons, tapping such seeps for waterproofing, while surface oil was an ingredient in medications and embalming. Such usages were not confined to this region alone. Indeed, almost wherever such seepages occurred, local inhabitants found uses for the various hydrocarbons that they produced.

When such seeps were depleted, or when they failed to provide enough hydrocarbons, people began to pursue more, usually by digging but also using primitive forms of drilling. In China, people began to use hollow bamboo trunks, some going down hundreds of feet, to bring oil to the surface as early as the fourth century C.E. Oil was so well known that, in the mid-sixteenth century, the German geologist Georg Bauer coined a term for it—petroleum, Latin for "rock" or "mineral oil."

Two developments in the mid-nineteenth century transformed petroleum from a niche product into a widely used one. Until that time, coal was the primary hydrocarbon fuel for heating and transport while whale oil and tallow were used mainly for artificial light. The first development was Canadian geologist Abraham Gesner's 1849 discovery of a process for distilling oil into kerosene, the first clean, safe, and commercially viable form of petroleum-based oil. The second was the first commercial oil strike ten years later, by Edwin Drake, a railroad worker hired by the Pennsylvania Rock Oil Company, at Titusville, Pennsylvania.

The oil industry fostered by these two developments began as a free-for-all, with multiple entrepreneurs competing for access to reserves and markets. While drilling for oil remained a competitive business, the more lucrative refining and marketing of kerosene in America had, by the late 1870s, come under the near-total control of John D. Rockefeller and his Standard Oil, who also began to aggressively market his products overseas. There, he faced more competition, as new oil discoveries were made in Russia, Venezuela, and in the Dutch East Indies (now Indonesia) by the end of the century.

At the turn of the twentieth century, oil and kerosene production was an important business but not a dominant one. With the invention of electric incandescence in 1879, this business seemed to have a limited future. Then came the development of the internal combustion engine and the various vehicles that employed it, most notably, automobiles—all products of the nineteenth century that became commercially viable for the masses only after Henry Ford's development of the assembly line in the early twentieth century. Meanwhile, the various navies of the world gave an additional impetus to the burgeoning industry by converting their ships from coal-fired steam engines to more efficient and better performing diesel engines. Technologies at the production end played a role, too. The development of the thermal "cracking" process in 1913 made it cheaper and faster to turn crude oil into refined petroleum products.

The new demand and new technology spurred new exploration, which unearthed massive reserves in Texas, Oklahoma, and the biggest of them all—and the most important one for the long-term geopolitical impact of oil—the Middle East, beginning with those in Persia (modern-day Iran) by the British company Anglo-Persian (the predecessor to BP) in 1908.

Such finds contributed to two oil trends that marked the first decades of mass oil use—cheap crude and volatile prices. Indeed, the glut was so great that even during the boom years of the late 1920s the major oil companies were forced to agree on production quotas to keep the price from falling too low. This largely worked, maintaining relatively stable prices through the depression, two world wars, and the postwar booms.

Although World War II, the first fully mechanized conflict, had many causes, a key one—as well as a factor in where the battlefields were located—was oil reserves, as the Japanese and Germans sought to secure supplies by invading the Dutch East Indies and Russia, respectively. On the allied side, both Britain

Oil Prices, Barrel of Crude Oil in Nominal and Inflation-Adjusted U.S. Dollars, 1861–2011

Year	Nominal price	Price in 2011 U.S. dollars
1861	$0.49	$12.35
1870	3.86	69.13
1880	.95	22.29
1890	.67	21.93
1900	1.19	32.39
1910	.61	14.83
1920	3.07	34.83
1930	1.19	16.20
1940	1.02	16.53
1950	1.71	16.14
1960	1.90	14.58
1970	1.80	10.53
1975	11.53	48.74
1980	36.83	101.64
1985	27.56	58.25
1990	23.73	41.28
1995	17.02	25.39
2000	28.50	37.63
2005	54.52	63.48
2006	65.14	73.48
2007	72.39	79.39
2008	97.26	102.72
2009	61.67	65.37
2010	78.86	81.35
2011	98.83	98.83

Note: Figures for all years through 2009 are averages; for 2010 and 2011, price is of December 30.
Source: BP Statistical Review of World Energy; New York Stock Exchange.

and the United States made great efforts to secure steady supplies of inexpensive oil by creating alliances in the Middle East. The United States, in particular, was successful in establishing a cooperative relationship with Saudi Arabia, recognized even then for its grossly outsized reserves, that long outlasted the war, in which the United States provided security and a steady market in exchange for Saudi crude.

Despite the postwar economic boom in the West and, with it, a rapidly increasing demand for oil, the sheer volume of reserves and expansion of refining capacity kept oil prices low through the end of the 1960s. Adjusted for inflation, oil cost less in 1968 than it did in 1928. Indeed, the postwar boom itself was attributable in part to cheap energy. But cheap energy would also soon prove to have a downside, in that it encouraged wasteful consumption.

While the West—and, for that matter, the rest of the oil-consuming world—lapped up the cheap oil, producers were not so happy, especially because they had little bargaining power with the major Western oil companies that actually drilled for and refined the crude. In 1960, five of the biggest producers—Iran,

Average Daily Oil Production, by Region, in Thousands of Barrels/Percentage of Total, 1965–2008

Year	Africa N	Africa %	Asia/Pacific N	Asia/Pacific %	Europe and (Former) Soviet Union N	Europe and (Former) Soviet Union %	Middle East N	Middle East %	North America N	North America %	South and Central America N	South and Central America %	Total N
1965	2,240	7.0	898	2.8	5,652	17.8	8,387	26.3	10,296	32.4	4,334	13.6	31,807
1970	6,112	12.7	1,979	4.1	7,982	16.6	13,904	28.9	13,257	27.6	4,829	10.0	48,063
1975	5,047	9.0	3,806	6.8	10,994	19.7	19,733	35.3	12,549	22.5	3,698	6.6	55,827
1980	6,225	9.7	4,943	7.7	15,088	23.5	18,882	29.4	14,063	21.9	4,943	7.7	64,202
1985	5,433	9.5	5,928	10.3	16,442	28.6	10,645	18.5	15,304	26.6	3,720	6.5	57,472
1990	6,725	10.3	6,726	10.3	16,106	24.6	17,540	26.8	13,856	21.2	4,507	6.9	65,460
1995	7,111	10.4	7,350	10.8	13,830	20.3	20,239	29.7	13,789	20.2	5,782	8.5	68,101
2000	7,804	10.4	7,874	10.5	14,950	20.0	23,516	31.4	13,904	18.6	6,813	9.1	74,861
2005	9,846	12.1	7,845	9.7	17,541	21.6	25,262	31.2	13,696	16.9	6,899	8.5	81,089
2008	10,285	12.6	7,928	9.7	17,591	21.5	26,200	32.0	13,131	16.0	6,685	8.2	81,820

Source: BP Statistical Review of World Energy.

Iraq, Kuwait, Saudi Arabia, and Venezuela—formed the Organization of Petroleum Exporting Countries (OPEC) in order to gain a better negotiating position with which to fight for higher prices than those the major oil companies—popularly known as the "majors"—were paying them.

At first, OPEC was unsuccessful, undercut by producers outside the cartel and by the fact that oil production continued to outstrip demand. By the early 1970s, however, heightened demand had largely caught up with supply, leaving the international oil market particularly vulnerable to any exogenous shock. Just such a shock came with the Arab-Israeli War of 1973. To punish the United States and other Western countries for their support of Israel, Saudi Arabia and other major Middle East producers that were OPEC members—whose share of world oil supply had jumped from 38 percent in 1960 to 56 percent in 1973—imposed a boycott. A second shock came with the Iranian Revolution in 1979 and the outbreak of war between Iran and Iraq—the second- and third-largest exporters in the world, after Saudi Arabia—the following year. These two events sent oil prices skyrocketing from $4 to $40 a barrel in non-inflation-adjusted dollars (or from $22 to $110 in 2011 dollars). Even after the immediate crises were over, OPEC tried to sustain higher oil prices by establishing price quotas for its members.

The rapid rise in oil prices had, predictably enough, mirror effects in oil-importing and oil-exporting states. In the former, the result was the first major economic downturn of the post–World War II era, which produced a combination of slow, or negative, growth and high inflation that befuddled both economists and economic policymakers. Non–oil-producing developing countries were also hard hit as demand for some of their raw materials fell with the slump in Western economies. Meanwhile, for oil exporters, the price rise was like winning the lottery; it led to a flood of hundreds of billions in petrodollars. Some of these countries, such as Saudi Arabia, used the money to help buy equity in the majors while others simply used their new political clout to nationalize the oil industry in their countries. In either case, control of world supply and, to a lesser extent, prices shifted from the majors to the oil-producing countries themselves.

Such a dramatic rise in prices produced two reactions. The first was a rush to explore and drill in places—such as the North Sea between Britain and Norway, and the North Slope of Alaska—that were not economically viable before the price increase. These new oil supplies had two effects: They increased the available supply on the market, and that supply was not controlled by OPEC. (Western oil company deals with the Soviet Union—the world's second-largest producer after Saudi Arabia—also contributed to more non-OPEC supply.) The second main response was conservation. Because of new technologies, more efficient products, and changing consumer behavior, combined with a general shift from energy-intensive manufacturing to less energy-intensive service industries, oil usage for a given unit of economic output fell significantly, particularly in the developed countries in the West, which consumed the majority of the oil in the 1970s and 1980s.

By the 1980s, oil prices had collapsed, driven down not just by falling demand and new non-OPEC

Average Daily Oil Consumption, by Region, in Thousands of Barrels/Percentage of Total, 1965–2008

Year	Africa		Asia/Pacific		Europe and (Former) Soviet Union		Middle East		North America		South and Central America		Total
	N	%	N	%	N	%	N	%	N	%	N	%	N
1965	580.9	1.7	3,657.7	10.9	12,884.8	38.4	991.9	3.0	13,591.8	40.5	1,834.1	5.5	33,541.2
1971	762.8	1.6	7,253.9	15.0	19,603.9	40.5	1,217.1	2.5	17,188.9	35.5	2,338.9	4.8	48,365.5
1975	947.5	1.7	8,845.5	16.2	22,060.1	40.3	1,437.2	2.6	18,706.6	34.2	2,763.2	5.0	54,760.1
1980	1,360.7	2.2	10,152.4	16.7	23,506.9	38.8	2,222.0	3.7	20,011.5	33.0	3,397.1	5.6	60,650.6
1985	1,689.4	2.8	10,904.6	17.9	22,969.8	37.6	2,927.2	4.8	19,085.1	31.3	3,476.4	5.7	61,062.5
1991	1,961.9	2.9	14,464.3	21.7	23,021.0	34.5	3,427.2	5.1	19,908.1	29.9	3,849.7	5.8	66,632.2
1995	2,187.6	3.1	18,149.9	26.1	19,705.8	28.3	4,034.2	5.8	21,150.4	30.4	4,382.1	6.3	69,610.0
2000	2,451.9	3.2	21,225.3	27.7	19,746.6	25.8	4,601.9	6.0	23,548.3	30.7	5,009.2	6.5	76,583.2
2005	2,696.1	3.2	24,619.8	29.4	20,464.8	24.4	5,817.3	6.9	24,903.7	29.7	5,297.1	6.3	83,798.8
2008	2,880.9	3.4	25,338.8	30.0	20,158.4	23.9	6,423.5	7.6	23,752.9	28.2	5,901.0	7.0	84,355.1

Source: BP Statistical Review of World Energy.

sources but by OPEC members violating production quotas in a desperate attempt to keep revenues—which were needed to pay for infrastructure projects launched by that sudden influx in oil revenue—coming in. Saudi Arabia, as swing producer—that is, the country whose production capacity exceeded its output, allowing it to suddenly increase output when it needed to—attempted to enforce production quotas by flooding the market with oil, thereby punishing quota violators with even lower prices. The tactic worked, and OPEC became an effective cartel again by the early 1990s, though without the clout it had possessed two decades earlier.

Still, despite occasional spikes prompted by external events, such as the Persian Gulf War in 1991, oil prices remained relatively low through the end of the century. By then, however, several other forces began to increase prices again. The first was a period of relatively sustained economic growth in the West, except for brief recessions, from the early 1980s through the mid-2000s. The second was the depletion of older oil fields, such as those in the United States. Another was the development of new markets and financial products with which to trade in oil, attracting speculators and investors to the market. These could not in isolation trigger spikes in prices in the absence of real market forces, but they could drive price hikes to exceed the level determined by the forces of supply and demand alone. But most critical was rapidly rising demand in developing countries, particularly in China. Together these forces produced dramatic increases in prices in the late 2000s and early 2010s. Indeed, in June 2008, although developed Western economies were slumping in general, crude oil prices

reached their all-time peak, in inflation-adjusted 2011 dollars, at just above $130, compared with $110, the previous all-time peak, in December 1979.

Economic Impact

Oil is the essential industry of the modern industrial age in two ways. First, it is a massive industry by itself, employing tens of millions of people worldwide and earning revenues in the hundreds of billions annually. Indeed, eight of the 12 largest corporations in the world by revenue in 2011 were oil companies. Second, and more important, oil is a critical ingredient in virtually every other form of enterprise engaged in by human beings—to power those industries, ship their goods, and, in the case of plastics, petrochemicals, and other businesses, as a key ingredient. Oil production sustains the economy of numerous producing and exporting countries, generating vast revenues for governments. Oil also plays a role in financing governments in oil-consuming countries, who often earn large amounts of revenue by taxing fuel.

As noted earlier, however, oil and, more specifically, its price on global markets has different effects on those who import it and those who export it. For the former, whether a developing or developed world economy, the price of oil can be the critical factor in whether its economy grows or shrinks. Oil prices have an impact on the economy in three basic ways. A spike in oil prices can cause inflation, as occurred in the 1970s, because its cost is factored into every product and service that relies on it—that is, in virtually every product and service in a modern economy. It can also lead to massive transfers of wealth from oil importers to oil exporters, producing trade deficits that can, under some circumstances, drive up interest rates in the oil-consuming countries and thereby undermine investment. Finally, oil price increases can suppress demand, as consumers are forced to cut back on other purchases in order to fill up their car's gas tank, heat their homes, and pay their utility bills.

For oil exporters, price and production levels are, if anything, even more critical to the economy. For many producer countries, earnings from oil are essential in maintaining positive or neutral current account balances, are a chief source of hard currency earning, and provide the revenue needed by governments to provide services and to build necessary infrastructure. Used wisely, oil revenue can allow a country to modernize rapidly, as seen in some Persian Gulf countries, by allowing them to invest in infrastructure and, through better education and health care, the labor force. In view of all these things, high prices for oil would seem to be a good thing. But, in fact, high prices can have a deleterious economic effect. First, for the biggest exporters, such as Saudi Arabia, high oil prices bring in massive flows of funds that need to be invested; because the country's domestic markets are limited, these funds are invested overseas, sometimes through sovereign wealth funds, in all kinds of securities. But if oil prices rise too high, they can produce a general economic decline that undermines the values of those securities. Second, oil revenues often create artificially high currency values, undermining the international competitiveness of other industries in an oil-exporting country. Conversely, high oil prices can bring in so much money that they fuel overall inflation.

Falling oil prices can be even more catastrophic, as producer countries lose revenues and experience current account imbalances and even capital flight, which wreaks havoc on economies. Mexico offers an example. Because its projected earnings from oil exports gave investors confidence in the country's finances, international financial institutions lent heavily to Mexico in the 1970s and early 1980s. But after revenue began to fall in the mid-1980s, the Mexican government faced unsustainable debt servicing costs that led it to default on its foreign loans. The country was able to stabilize its currency and finances only by taking out new loans and receiving loan guarantees from the United States, Mexico's biggest trading partner, and various multilateral financial institutions, such as the International Monetary Fund.

Political Impact

The political impact of oil is generally, though not always, a by-product of the economic effect. (The exception is when environmental and health concerns produce a political backlash, in either producing or consuming countries.) For consuming countries, high oil prices or, worse, shortages, such as those experienced in the early and late 1970s, can cause a political backlash against those in power, one of the reasons that British prime minister James Callaghan and U.S. president Jimmy Carter were ousted convincingly by voters in 1979 and 1980. In countries where democratic rule is less firmly rooted, they can lead to the kinds of political unrest that triggers coups or crackdowns by authoritarian governments.

The critical revenue generated by taxes on fuel can also be politically contentious. In the United States, gas taxes are low compared with other advanced industrial countries, and no politician in a country so dependent on the automobile dares to raise them. Some critics argue that these low taxes, which result in relatively low gas prices, keep the country dependent on oil. Furthermore, they price oil below its true cost, if the health and environmental costs of oil-related pollution and global warming—as well as the defense costs in defending foreign supplies—are factored in. In some poorer countries—both oil producers and consumers—governments subsidize fuel prices. This is not only economically inefficient because it subsidizes the well off—who use more oil per capita—more than the poor but politically dangerous as it locks a government into commitments that might be financially unsustainable, and eliminating subsidies often leads to political unrest that might bring down that government.

The political impact of oil is far more complicated and nuanced for producer countries than it is for consuming countries. Oil money is often corrupting, as people seek government office in order to siphon off oil revenue. And, as social scientists have long demonstrated, corruption at the top can spread to all levels of government and to society at large, producing a culture of bribery and extortion. Frequently near the top of most corruption indexes is Nigeria, a country where vast oil reserves have produced a corrupt oligopoly that, when not engaging in conspicuous consumption, funnels it into foreign bank accounts, leaving little revenue to develop the country or educate and provide services to the vast majority, which remains mired in poverty. Oil money also allows those in power to hold on to it against the expressed wishes of the people, by using it to pay for internal security forces and crowd control apparatus, to buy off opposition figures, or to purchase elections by bribing voters.

At its worst, oil can fuel conflict. Two countries in Africa—Angola and Sudan—offer different examples of how this can occur. In Angola from the mid-1970s to the early 1990s, a rebel force backed first by the United States and then South Africa fought a government backed by the Soviet Union. For a while, the only thing keeping the government in power were the weapons that it was able to purchase with the revenue that it earned from offshore oil wells. In Sudan, a long ethnic and religious conflict between north and south—in which the latter sought and ultimately won the right to secede—was prolonged by disputes over oil fields that were, unfortunately, located on the border between the two halves of the country, causing both sides to seek advantage through military means to gain the revenue those oil fields would generate after the conflict was over and the border determined.

Twenty-First Century

Most experts agree that oil is likely to play a critical role in the world economy for the foreseeable future, despite efforts to wean industry, governments, and consumers off it by developing new technologies and exploiting alternative resources. Conservation efforts are the least expensive and disruptive way to lower oil usage, but they are only likely to slow the growth in demand, not reverse it. The reason for this is simple. Many countries that were part of what was once called the third world are rapidly developing, which increases demand as new energy-intensive industries are developed and as expanding middle classes purchase automobiles and electrical appliances and shift to diets that have a higher proportion of meat, which is more energy intensive to produce than their traditional diet.

For those on the conservative end of the political spectrum, the answer to the dilemma of rising demand and limited supplies—with all the potential economic and political problems that might follow—is to put more emphasis on oil exploration and development. There is still plenty of oil out there, especially in the tar sands of Canada, along with coal and natural gas, they say, to fuel the world's economy for the foreseeable future, especially due to new technologies, such as "fracking." Fracking, or the use of high-pressure steam, allows industry to access the vast reserves of oil and natural gas in underground shale deposits. Its use remains highly controversial, however, as there is evidence that it might pollute groundwater and even cause seismic activity. Those on the left argue that even if there is plenty of untapped hydrocarbon energy available, exploiting it will intensify the problems already associated with oil production use—namely, climate change, negative health effects, and geopolitical instability. They argue that the switch to alternative and renewable forms of energy must be pursued far more vigorously in the short term.

Those who study oil reserves are equally divided. Some believe that the world has already—or will soon reach—what is known as "peak oil," the point at which all the economically viable reserves have been tapped and production of this finite resource begins its inevitable decline. Such a decline is expected to lead to a sustained hike in oil prices and shortages, and all its attendant economic and political instability. Others, however, argue that new fields and new technologies for extracting oil will delay the moment of "peak oil" to the distant future.

Even if new alternatives to oil are pursued vigorously, it is unlikely that they will wean the world from oil any time soon. It also seems possible that increases in demand will outpace increases in supply, if not immediately, then in the not-too-distant future. What this means for the global economy and geopolitics remains to be seen.

James Ciment

See also: Defense Spending; Energy, Alternative; Government Corruption and Transparency; Oil, Environmental and Health Aspects.

Further Reading

Bower, Tom. *The Squeeze: Oil, Money and Greed in the Twenty-first Century.* London: HarperPress, 2009.

Hiro, Dilip. *Blood of the Earth: The Battle for the World's Vanishing Oil Resources.* New York: Nation Books, 2009.

Kaldor, Mary, Terry Lynn Karl, and Yahia Said, eds. *Oil Wars.* London: Pluto, 2007.

Looney, Robert E., ed. *Handbook of Oil Politics.* New York: Routledge, 2012.

Nersesian, Roy. *Energy for the 21st Century.* Armonk, NY: M.E. Sharpe, 2010.

Noreng, Oystein. *Crude Power: Politics and the Oil Market.* New York: I.B. Tauris, 2002.

Parra, Francisco. *Oil Politics: A Modern History of Petroleum.* New York: I.B. Tauris, 2004.

Roberts, Paul. *The End of Oil: On the Edge of a Perilous New World.* Boston: Houghton Mifflin, 2005.

Rubin, Jeff. *Why Your World Is About to Get a Whole Lot Smaller: Oil and the End of Globalization.* New York: Random House, 2009.

Shelley, Toby. *Oil: Politics and the Planet.* New York: Zed Books, 2005.

Yergin, Daniel. *The Prize: The Epic Quest for Oil, Money & Power.* New York: Free Press, 2008.

Web Sites

American Petroleum Institute: www.api.org

Natural Resources Defense Council:
    www.nrdc.org/energy

Oil & Gas Journal: www.ogj.com

Organization of Petroleum Exporting Countries:
    www.opec.org

Peak Oil: http://peakoil.com

United Nations Statistics Division, Energy Statistics:
    http://unstats.un.org/unsd/energy

U.S. Energy Information Agency: www.eia.gov

Documents

Document 1: Organization of Petroleum Exporting Countries (OPEC) Statute, 1961

The Organization of Petroleum Exporting Countries was founded in Baghdad in 1960 by Iran, Iraq, Kuwait, Saudi Arabia, and Venezuela (membership has since grown to 12 countries). As declared in the organization's founding statute—approved in January 1961 in Caracas, Venezuela—the main purposes of the organization were to coordinate policies to safeguard member-country interests, "devise ways and means" to ensure stable oil prices, and to secure a "steady income" from oil revenues for member countries. OPEC proved largely toothless until the Arab oil boycott of the West during the Arab-Israeli War of 1973 and the dramatic increase in oil prices that the conflict precipitated.

www.opec.org/opec_web/en/publications/345.htm

Source: Organization of Petroleum Exporting Countries.

Document 2: Crisis of Confidence Speech (excerpts), President Jimmy Carter, July 15, 1979

Upon coming to office in 1977, President Jimmy Carter was determined to wean the United States from its dependence on foreign oil. Two years later, in the midst of the Iranian Revolution, oil prices were approaching a new high, undermining the U.S. economy. In July 1979, Carter planned to deliver an address about energy independence, but before laying out his plans, he spoke about what he felt was a crisis of confidence. The "malaise" speech, as it was quickly dubbed, demonstrated both the impact that high oil prices could have on the nation's economy and spirit, as well as its apparent unwillingness to confront its energy dependency. Many experts ascribe the realistic but dour tone of the speech as one of the causes of Carter's landslide election loss to Ronald Reagan in the presidential election the following year.

Ten days ago I had planned to speak to you again about a very important subject—energy. For the fifth time I would have described the urgency of the problem and laid out a series of legislative recommendations to the Congress. But as I was preparing to speak, I began to ask myself the same question that I now know has been troubling many of you. Why have we not been able to get together as a nation to resolve our serious energy problem?

It's clear that the true problems of our Nation are much deeper—deeper than gasoline lines or energy shortages, deeper even than inflation or recession.

Our people are losing that faith, not only in government itself but in the ability as citizens to serve as the ultimate rulers and shapers of our democracy. . . .

The symptoms of this crisis of the American spirit are all around us. For the first time in the history of our country, a majority of our people believe that the next five years will be worse than the past five years. Two-thirds of our people do not even vote. The productivity of American workers is actually dropping, and the willingness of Americans to save for the future has fallen below that of all other people in the Western world.

As you know, there is a growing disrespect for government and for churches and for schools, the news media, and other institutions. This is not a message of happiness or reassurance, but it is the truth and it is a warning. . . .

Energy will be the immediate test of our ability to unite this nation, and it can also be the standard around which we rally. On the battlefield of energy we can win for our nation a new confidence, and we can seize control again of our common destiny.

In little more than two decades we've gone from a position of energy independence to one in which almost half the oil we use comes from foreign countries, at prices that are going through the roof. Our excessive dependence on OPEC has already taken a tremendous toll on our economy and our people. This is the direct cause of the long lines which have made millions of you spend aggravating hours waiting for gasoline. It's a cause of the increased inflation and unemployment that we now face. This intolerable dependence on foreign oil threatens our economic independence and the very security of our nation. The energy crisis is real. It is worldwide. It is a clear and present danger to our nation. These are facts and we simply must face them.

What I have to say to you now about energy is simple and vitally important.

Point one: I am tonight setting a clear goal for the energy policy of the United States. Beginning this moment, this nation will never use more foreign oil than we did in 1977—never. From now on, every new addition to our demand for energy will be met from our own production and our own conservation. The generation-long growth in our dependence on foreign oil will be stopped dead in its tracks right now and then reversed as we move through the 1980s, for I am tonight setting the further goal of cutting our dependence on foreign oil by one-half by the end of the next decade—a saving of over 4-1/2 million barrels of imported oil per day.

Point two: To ensure that we meet these targets, I will use my presidential authority to set import quotas. I'm announcing tonight that for 1979 and 1980, I will forbid the entry into this country of one drop of foreign oil more than these goals allow. These quotas will ensure a reduction in imports even below the ambitious levels we set at the recent Tokyo summit.

Point three: To give us energy security, I am asking for the most massive peacetime commitment of funds and resources in our nation's history to develop America's own alternative sources of fuel—from coal, from oil shale, from plant products for gasohol, from unconventional gas, from the sun.

I propose the creation of an energy security corporation to lead this effort to replace 2-1/2 million barrels of imported oil per day by 1990. The corporation will issue up to $5 billion in energy bonds, and I especially want them to be in small denominations so that average Americans can invest directly in America's energy security.

Just as a similar synthetic rubber corporation helped us win World War II, so will we mobilize American determination and ability to win the energy war. Moreover, I will soon submit legislation to Congress calling for the creation of this nation's first solar bank, which will help us achieve the crucial goal of 20 percent of our energy coming from solar power by the year 2000.

These efforts will cost money, a lot of money, and that is why Congress must enact the windfall profits tax without delay. It will be money well spent. Unlike the billions of dollars that we ship to foreign countries to pay for foreign oil, these funds will be paid by Americans to Americans. These funds will go to fight, not to increase, inflation and unemployment.

Point four: I'm asking Congress to mandate, to require as a matter of law, that our nation's utility companies cut their massive use of oil by 50 percent within the next decade and switch to other fuels, especially coal, our most abundant energy source.

Point five: To make absolutely certain that nothing stands in the way of achieving these goals, I will urge Congress to create an energy mobilization board which, like the War Production Board in World War II, will have the responsibility and authority to cut through the red tape, the delays, and the endless roadblocks to completing key energy projects.

We will protect our environment. But when this nation critically needs a refinery or a pipeline, we will build it.

Point six: I'm proposing a bold conservation program to involve every state, county, and city and every average American in our energy battle. This effort will permit you to build conservation into your homes and your lives at a cost you can afford.

I ask Congress to give me authority for mandatory conservation and for standby gasoline rationing. To further conserve energy, I'm proposing tonight an extra $10 billion over the next decade to strengthen our public transportation systems. And I'm asking you for your good and for your nation's security to take no unnecessary trips, to use carpools or public transportation whenever you can, to park your car one extra day per week, to obey the speed limit, and to set your thermostats to save fuel. Every act of energy conservation like this is more than just common sense—I tell you it is an act of patriotism.

Our nation must be fair to the poorest among us, so we will increase aid to needy Americans to cope with rising energy prices. We often think of conservation only in terms of sacrifice. In fact, it is the most painless and immediate way of rebuilding our nation's strength. Every gallon of oil each one of us saves is a new form of production. It gives us more freedom, more confidence, that much more control over our own lives.

So, the solution of our energy crisis can also help us to conquer the crisis of the spirit in our country. It can rekindle our sense of unity, our confidence in the future, and give our nation and all of us individually a new sense of purpose.

You know we can do it. We have the natural resources. We have more oil in our shale alone than several Saudi Arabias. We have more coal than any nation on Earth. We have the world's highest level of technology. We have the most skilled work force, with innovative genius, and I firmly believe that we have the national will to win this war.

I do not promise you that this struggle for freedom will be easy. I do not promise a quick way out of our nation's problems, when the truth is that the only way out is an all-out effort. What I do promise you is that I will lead our fight, and I will enforce fairness in our struggle, and I will ensure honesty. And above all, I will act. We can manage the short-term shortages more effectively and we will, but there are no short-term solutions to our long-range problems. There is simply no way to avoid sacrifice. . . .

Source: Jimmy Carter Library.

OIL, ENVIRONMENTAL AND HEALTH ASPECTS

The use of oil is ubiquitous in modern life. Beyond its role as the principal transportation fuel—transportation uses up about 84 percent of consumed oil—oil has applications in a host of products ranging from plastics to pharmaceuticals to perfumes. Without oil, modern civilization would grind to a halt.

Perhaps more than anything else, it is the energy content of oil and the diverse uses to which it has been put that has fueled unprecedented increases in human population, income, and life expectancy over the past hundred years. But more people living longer and more affluent lifestyles have come at a price. The quadrupling of global agricultural yields, for instance, has been accompanied by an 80-fold increase in the energy required to produce those yields.

While oil shapes much of the world people live in today, it also produces significant environmental and health impacts at every stage of its life cycle. From air and water pollution to acid rain and climate change, the ecological and human health effects of modern civilization's oil addiction are vast and indeed threaten the very living standards and quality of life oil itself has helped people to achieve. Moreover, as the world's most populous countries continue to develop their economies at a rapid pace, the ecological and health impacts of increased demand for oil, as well as the need for alternatives, will intensify. If the twentieth century was the century of oil, the twenty-first century will be profoundly shaped by humanity's ability to treat the symptoms of its oil addiction and transition to a low-carbon future.

Brief History

While humans and oil have a long history together, the modern oil industry begins in 1848 in Baku, then part of the Russian Empire of Czar Nicholas I and now part of the Azerbaijan Republic. The initial demand in the modern oil industry was for kerosene, distilled from oil for illumination. Baku would dominate the oil industry for the next two decades, but oil would not assume its revolutionary role until its center of gravity moved to the United States, where the age of oil was truly born in Titusville, Pennsylvania, in 1859. Spurred by the internal combustion engine, oil consumption soared after 1903 when Henry Ford invented the modern assembly line and began to mass produce his famous Model-T Ford, of which over 15 million units would be sold in the next 20 years. The oil industry was given another boost with the introduction of cracking, or conversion, whereby chemical by-products could be recovered and turned into petrochemicals. Standard Oil opened the first petrochemical plant in1920 and the industry grew rapidly, driven by two world wars and the shift from natural to synthetic products.

The postwar period saw the surge of oil production and consumption on a global scale, as discoveries across the Middle East were combined with rapid and sustained demand not only in the developed but also the developing world. World oil consumption rose from under 5 billion barrels per year in 1950 to over 20 billion barrels by 1980, and then to over 30 billion by 2010. The global rise of oil consumption, however, soon brought questions about its environmental and human health impacts to the forefront, driven by high-profile oil spills—such as the *Torrey Canyon* oil tanker spill off the United Kingdom in 1967 and the oil rig blowout off Santa Barbara, California, two years later—and concern about the more widespread effects of leaded gasoline. As scientists directed their attention toward the environmental and health effects of the oil industry, they began to discover the significant environmental and health impacts of oil at every stage of its life cycle.

During the Gulf War of 1991, Iraqi troops retreating from Kuwait set fire to more than 700 oil wells, which burned over a billion barrels during the course of the year. The environmental damage was devastating, and the Kuwaiti people suffered lasting health effects. (AP Photo)

Life Cycle of Oil: Environmental and Health Effects

The life cycle of oil has significant environmental effects at all of its stages, from exploration and extraction to the final consumption of fuel and petrochemicals. Because the exploration stage of oil recovery requires heavy equipment and infrastructure such as roads and landing strips, it can contribute to deforestation and reductions in biodiversity, particularly in countries like Ecuador and Nigeria, where oil reserves are located in the ecologically sensitive regions. Drilling and extraction likewise impose high environmental and health costs, of which chemical pollution is perhaps the most pervasive. In the United States, the oil industry produces more solid and liquid waste than all other industrial, mining, agricultural, and municipal sources combined, most of which consists of "produced water," or water contaminated during the extraction process by an array of toxic compounds linked to serious developmental and reproductive impacts. Fires also emit sulphur and carbon dioxide, thus contributing to acid rain and climate change. The Kuwaiti oil fires of 1991, for instance, saw more than 650 oil wells set on fire by the retreating Iraqi army during the First Gulf War.

The health repercussions of oil exploration and extraction are similarly significant. During the exploration stage, the arrival of foreign workers facilitates the spread of infectious diseases. Hazardous waste can contaminate adjacent water supplies, while mercury from offshore drilling can find its way into human foods systems and is suspected of links to birth defects and neurological disorders. In Ecuador, for instance, where more than 600 toxic waste pits were built to store the by-products from oil production and separation between 1972 and 1990, samples of drinking water have tested as high as 2,793 nanograms per liter of polycyclic aromatic hydrocarbons (PAHs), a probable carcinogen associated with a host of birth defects and abnormalities, well beyond the 28 nanograms per liter limit set by the U.S. Environmental Protection Agency (EPA). Worker safety is also an important health issue in the industry. Beyond the most tragic case of occupation-related fatalities, such as the 1988 explosion at the North Sea Alpha Piper platform that killed 167 people, oil field workers run nearly a 50 percent greater risk for occupational injury in the United States than the private sector average, and are exposed to a host of hard metals and chemicals.

The globalization of the oil industry has produced important effects at the transportation and distribution stages as well. Since 1960, it is estimated that spills of at least 10,000 gallons (45,500 liters) have occurred in the waters of 112 countries. The Deepwater Horizon oil spill of 2010, which flooded the Gulf of Mexico with more than 200 million gallons (900 million liters) of oil, was the largest offshore spill in history. In Nigeria, on the other hand, 300 spills contaminate the Niger River Delta annually,

Worst Oil Spills in History, by Amount

Name of Spill	Location	Year	Cause	Amount Spilled (millions of gallons*)
Lakeview Gusher	California/Kern County	1910	Oil well blowout	400 (est.)
Persian Gulf War	Kuwait/Persian Gulf	1991	Deliberate destruction by Iraqi troops during First Gulf War	380–520
Deepwater Horizon	United States/Gulf of Mexico	2010	Offshore rig blowout	206
Ixtoc 1	Mexico/Bay of Campeche	1979	Offshore rig blowout	140
Atlantic Empress	Trinidad and Tobago/Caribbean Sea	1979	Tanker collision	90
Kolva River	Russia/Kolva River	1983	Pipeline rupture	84
Nowruz Oil Field	Iran/Persian Gulf	1983	Tanker collision	80
Castillo de Bellver	South Africa/ Saldanha Bay	1983	Tanker fire	79
Amoco Cadiz	France/Portsall	1978	Tanker sinking	69
ABT Summer	Angola/South Atlantic Ocean	1991	Tanker fire	51–81
M/T Haven	Italy/Mediterranean Sea	1991	Tanker fire	45
Odyssey	Canada/North Atlantic Ocean	1988	Tanker fire	40.7

* One gallon is equal to 3.79 liters.
Source: Editor.

with unofficial estimates ranging as much as ten times higher. Aquatic spills can cause dramatic ecological disruptions. The toxicity of oil kills many animals upon ingestion. Oil hydrocarbons are also carcinogenic to fish, mammals, and birds, and oil exposure has been linked to declines in the reproductive capacity of seals. In the Persian Gulf, more than one million barrels of oil are spilled every year, and studies have concluded the gulf ecosystem is under significant stress, with high levels of heavy metals and other contaminants that pose risks not only to aquatic species but also to humans.

The process of refining crude oil into petroleum products such as gasoline, diesel fuel, and kerosene causes significant chemical, thermal, and noise pollution. While 99.7 percent of the weight of crude oil is refined, and only 0.3 percent is released into the environment, an average refinery processes nearly 4 million gallons (18 million liters) of crude oil per day, meaning that each refinery releases about 11,000 gallons (50,000 liters) of oil into the environment daily. In 2009 there were an estimated 700 oil refineries in the world, meaning that approximately 7.7 million gallons (35 million liters) of oil find their way into the air, water, and soil every single day. Not surprisingly, communities adjacent to oil refineries have displayed greater incidence of leukemia. Oil refineries also affect human health through workplace accidents and chronic illnesses, such as lung cancer, associated with petroleum by-products like benzene, as well as exposing the population to other hazardous materials,

such as arsenic, carbon monoxide, and even lead and asbestos in developing nations.

The principal environmental and health effects of oil during the consumption stage are caused by the combustion of fuel. The burning of fuel contributes to the formation of smog, the most visible form of air pollution, which causes health impacts such as emphysema, bronchitis, and asthma. Other forms of chemical and particulate air pollution resulting from the combustion of fuel can cause heart and lung disease as well as lung cancer, and there is a positive correlation between air pollution and mortality. Fuel combustion likewise releases sulfur oxides and contributes to acid rain, which acidifies and degrades soil, stunts tree growth, and causes eutrophication, whereby algal blooms prevent sunlight from penetrating the water surface, resulting in biologically unproductive "dead zones" in aquatic ecosystems. The most significant environmental and health impact of fuel combustion, however, is climate change. While there are greenhouse gas (GHG) emissions at every stage in the oil lifecycle, models suggest that about 80 percent of GHG emissions take place during the combustion stage. The impact of climate change ranges from rising temperatures and sea levels to changing and unstable weather patterns, with dramatic consequences.

Finally, the thousands of products derived from the petrochemical industry have many important environmental and health repercussions. Pesticides manufactured from petroleum can damage agricultural land, fisheries, and flora and fauna, affecting the health of farmers and agricultural laborers, particularly where proper safety precautions are not taken. Fertilizers manufactured with petroleum feedstock likewise have significant environmental impacts. Nitrogen-based fertilizers, for instance, can find their way into streams and result in algal blooms and dead zones, much like acid rain. The health effects of plastics made from petrochemicals, including their relationship to cancer, are now being widely investigated. Most prominently, bisphenol-A (BPA), a petrochemical used to make polycarbonate plastic, was potentially linked to breast cancer in 2006, and was declared a toxic substance by the Canadian government in 2010. BPA has also been banned in infant products in China, France, and Belgium, among other countries, as well as some states in the United States.

Ramifications and Mitigation Efforts

The economic and political ramifications of oil pollution are particularly severe in developing nations, which often lack the regulatory capacity to ensure that environmental and health standards are respected. In the Niger Delta, for example, oil pollution has rendered much of the land infertile and has contaminated air and drinking water supplies, in turn fueling violence and destabilizing the political system. The United Nations Environment Programme (UNEP) recently suggested it would take 25 to 30 years to clean up pollution from a half-century of oil operations in the delta. The initial price tag for the cleanup was $1 billion for the first five years alone, with billions more in future restoration and monitoring costs. Studies of the environmental and health impacts of the oil industry in the Middle East likewise suggest the enormity of the problem. The annual cost of water and air pollution in Iran to health, infrastructure, and other aspects of society, for example, is estimated to be 4.4 percent of gross domestic product (GDP). When one adds land and coastal contamination, as well as industrial waste, that figure rises to nearly 8 percent of GDP.

This is not to say that the impact of oil pollution in the developed world is negligible. The International Center for Technology Assessment has quantified the externalized costs of using internal combustion engines with gasoline. According to their calculations, the environmental, health, and social costs of gasoline

usage in the United States total between $231.7 and $942.9 billion per year. At a more concrete level, the costs of oil pollution are significant at all stages of the oil life cycle. The 2010 oil spill in the Gulf of Mexico carried an estimated cleanup cost of $42 billion. As far as impact on human health, the Ontario Medical Association (OMA) estimated in 2008 the number of deaths in the province from long-term and acute exposure to air pollution to be 23,682. The economic costs of air pollution to the province, moreover, were estimated at $8 billion (Canadian dollars) that same year, with projected accumulated costs of $250 billion (Canadian dollars) by 2031.

The environmental and health repercussions of the oil industry are also global in scale, the best example of which is climate change. Petroleum is the single largest fossil-fuel contributor to GHG emissions. Indeed, the emissions intensity of the oil industry is evidenced by the per capita carbon dioxide emissions of the oil-producing countries of the Persian Gulf. In 2008, the per capita emissions of the entire planet were 5,000 tons (4,537 metric tons), a figure dwarfed by the per capita emissions of the United States, which stood at 21,000 tons (19,164 metric tons). The figures for Qatar, Bahrain, and the United Arab Emirates, however, averaged out to 50,000 tons (45,850 metric tons). While significant debate exists around how to measure the costs of climate change, most agree these costs will be extraordinary. The Stern Review on the Economics of Climate Change, commissioned by the British Chancellor of the Exchequer, projected the cost of inactivity ranged from 5 to 20 percent of global GDP. Likewise, a report for the European Commission's Environment Directorate-General estimated that the cost of inaction will rise to €74 trillion by 2200.

In response to increased concern about the environmental and health effects of oil, companies have invested in technological and organizational advances to mitigate negative outcomes. At the exploration and drilling stage, for instance, the use of 3-D and 4-D time-lapse visualization and remote sensing has greatly reduced the number of drilling sites for finding potential petroleum sources. Moreover, the use of slim-hole drilling can reduce the area cleared for drilling by as much as 75 percent, while directional drilling allows companies to minimize the disruption in more ecologically sensitive environments. At the extraction phase, the freeze-thaw evaporation (FTE) process separates produced water into freshwater, concentrated brine, and solids. The freshwater output can then be used in agriculture and other activities, significantly reducing the volume of waste. In addition, drill cuttings, which display low levels of toxicity, are being used by companies in numerous ways to reduce environmental impact, from recycling into bricks for housing in Colombia to experiments using processed cuttings to restore wetlands.

At the refining stage, carbon capture and storage (CCS) technology, whereby carbon dioxide is separated from other emissions, converted into liquid, and pumped into underground rock formations, is being explored in numerous countries as a means of reducing greenhouse gas emissions. Millions of public and private dollars are presently being invested in Alberta, Canada, to explore the possibility of using CCS technology in oil sands facilities, which have come under heavy international fire for their contribution to global GHG emissions. Finally, at the consumption stage, government regulations have induced significant improvements in fuel efficiency and vehicles that run on alternative energies. Between 1975 and 2010, the average miles per gallon (mpg) of automobiles sold in the United States more than doubled, from less than 15 mpg to more than 30 mpg. The manufacture and sale of hybrid and electric vehicles has also grown steadily over the past years. By 2012, Honda had sold over 800,000 hybrid vehicles, while Toyota surpassed the 3 million mark. Newer hybrid models can get up to 50 mpg and produce fewer emissions than conventional internal combustion engines.

In addition to supporting technological advances, governments have responded to the environmental and health repercussions of the oil industry. Following oil price shocks of the 1970s, Europe began to lead the shift away from oil and fossil fuel dependency. For example, in 1976, Denmark began to pass a series of energy bills to reduce oil consumption, improve efficiency, promote conservation, and set carbon dioxide emissions limits, culminating in the approval of Europe's most successful carbon tax in 1992, revenues from which were used to subsidize renewable energy sources. As a result Denmark's foresight and planning, its economy grew by 78 percent between 1980 and 2009, yet its overall energy consumption remained stable. Carbon emissions per capita, therefore, fell by more than 12 percent from 1990 to 2008. Denmark is also a world leader in clean energy technologies; by 2008, clean energy technology represented 11 percent of Danish commodity exports, for a total value of €8.6 billion.

Other European nations have likewise pursued measures to mitigate the impacts of oil consumption. Not to be outdone by its Danish neighbor, Sweden commissioned a landmark report tabled in 2006 that laid out a blueprint for becoming the world's first oil-free economy; the Scandinavian country presently leads Europe in the share of total energy supply coming from renewable sources, at over 40 percent. Gasoline taxation is used by many European nations to deter oil consumption. In France, 60 percent of the consumer price of gasoline is accounted for by taxes, as compared to 21 percent in California. The European Union has been aggressive in its environmental policy targeting the oil and fossil fuel sectors. Perhaps the most ambitious initiative is the European Union Emissions Trading Scheme, which is the largest multinational emissions cap and trade system in the world. It is no surprise that total carbon dioxide emissions from the consumption of energy have fallen in Europe since 1990, as opposed to North America, where emissions have continued to rise.

It is not only the developed world that is moving to address the environmental and health impacts of oil production and consumption. In Mexico City, for instance, where internal combustion engines account for 80 percent of air pollution, the government implemented a rapid bus system in 2005 called MetroBus that by 2009 had reduced carbon dioxide emissions in the city by an estimated 88,000 tons (80,000 metric tons) per year. In China, moreover, while carbon dioxide emissions have risen dramatically as the Chinese economy expands, the government has positioned the country at the forefront of the renewable energy revolution. After passing its Renewable Energy Law in 2005, China had within five years become the world's largest single investor in renewable energy, and in 2010 it introduced subsidies for the purchase of hybrid and electric vehicles. The oil-producing states of the Middle East, moreover, long laggards in addressing the environmental and health effects of the oil industry, have begun to step up. In 2009, Syria established the country's first environment ministry, while oil-rich countries such as Iran and the United Arab Emirates were moving aggressively into the generation of solar and wind energy.

The environmental and health impacts of the oil industry are global in scope, and as a result numerous international initiatives have emerged to coordinate government and private sector efforts across borders. Because many developing countries lack the regulatory capacity to ensure that oil production and transportation is carried out according to best international practices, a variety of voluntary initiatives have sprung up around the principle of corporate social responsibility (CSR). Perhaps the best known of these is the International Standards Organization (ISO), a global standards body that brings together over 100 countries and includes standards for environmental management systems. ISO guidelines have been adopted by the International Association of Oil and Gas Producers and the American Petroleum Institute in the areas of environmental management, environmental auditing, and environmental reporting. Another key voluntary international code is the United Nations Global Compact, which is organized around 10 principles related to human rights, labor, environment, and anticorruption, and which has 8,700 corporate and other participants from over 130 countries.

The World Bank Group (WBG) has proven particularly influential in the push toward CSR in the oil industry. Recommendations of the Extractive Industry Review of the WBG resulted in the Equator Principles for the financing of extractive industries, launched in 2003 to ensure investment is channeled toward socially and environmentally responsible projects and signed by over 60 financial institutions. Another similar initiative is the Extractive Industry Transparency Initiative, spearheaded by Norway and the International Financial Corporation of the World Bank Group, which imposes performance standards in the areas of working conditions, the monitoring, mitigation, and restoration of environmental damage, and the health impacts on affected communities, among other areas, and receives the support of over 50 of the world's largest oil, gas, and mining companies. Some CSR initiatives have even been codified into law, such as in Article 26 of Angola's Petroleum Activities Law.

Finally, the most famous and ambitious international attempt to address the main environmental and health repercussion of the oil industry—climate change—is the Kyoto Protocol, adopted in December 1997 and ratified by 191 countries as of 2011. Notable exceptions are the United States, which signed the treaty in 1998 but has yet to ratify, and Canada, which ratified the protocol in 2002 but formally withdrew in December 2011. The objective of the protocol was to constrain and reduce greenhouse gas emissions from 1990 levels, focusing primarily on the developed countries that emit the vast majority of GHGs. The protocol also committed developed nations to establish a climate change fund to help developing countries adjust. Under the auspices of the UN Framework Convention on Climate Change, participant countries have met regularly at conferences and meetings of the parties to review progress and deepen the agreement.

The Future

The rise of the oil industry in the twentieth century facilitated an unprecedented growth in human population, higher incomes, and improved living standards, but it left the twenty-first century with a hefty bill to pay. In spite of our attempts to develop alternative energy sources, oil continues to account for the largest share of global energy consumption, ranging from 53 percent in the Middle East to 32 percent in Europe. Technological advances have made important improvements, but hybrid and electric cars still represent a small fraction of the automobile industry and technologies such as carbon capture and storage remain largely speculative. Technology is part of the solution, but alone it is inadequate. Domestic and international regulations must play a critical role, but here success is mixed. While many European countries have made important legislative advances to address the environmental and health impacts of the oil industry, North America has lagged behind, and many developing countries lack the means to enact and enforce more stringent regulations. Voluntary international initiatives to improve oil industry practices have provided few significant improvements, while the Kyoto Protocol successes are confined largely to Europe. In spite of all the aforementioned efforts, it is therefore no surprise that carbon dioxide emissions from the global consumption of petroleum rose by over 20 percent between 1990 and 2008.

What is more, the recent discovery of unconventional oil reserves, such as oil shale and oil sands in developing countries like Brazil, and the advance of unconventional production in developed countries like Canada, threaten to swallow up the gains made to date. This is because unconventional reserves, which cannot be extracted by conventional recovery methods, impose significantly higher environmental costs, owing to the much greater amounts of energy and water required for their extraction. In order to address the challenges of the future, governments in the developed world will have to continue to devise measures to mitigate the negative impact of the oil industry and encourage the shift toward alternative sources of energy, as well as supporting developing nations to construct regulatory mechanisms aimed at improving the social and environmental sustainability of oil and offsetting the costs of the transition. Finally, much greater leadership will be required from the most powerful developed and developing nations, particularly the United States and China, upon whose shoulders the possibility of a global and binding agreement on climate change will fall. The design and implementation of a truly global compact to reduce GHG emissions to sustainable levels will be required to avoid the most catastrophic climate-change scenarios.

Timothy David Clark

See also: Cancer; Environmental Illnesses; Oil, Economic and Political Aspects; Pollution, Air; Pollution, Water; Water Supply and Access.

Further Reading

Amao, Olufemi, ed. *Corporate Social Responsibility, Human Rights and the Law: Multinational Corporations in Developing Countries.* New York: Routledge, 2011.

Baumuller, Heike, et al. *The Effects of Oil Companies' Activities on the Environment, Health and Development of Sub-Saharan Africa.* Brussels, Belgium: European Parliament, 2011.

Beck, Marshall, Eduardo Canel, Uwakiokun Idemudia, Liisa L. North, David Szablowski, and Anna Zalik, eds. "Rethinking Extractive Industry." Special Issue, *Canadian Journal of Development Studies* 30:1–2 (2010).

Croitoru, Lelia, and Maria Sarraf, eds. *The Cost of Environmental Degradation: Case Studies from the Middle East and North Africa.* Washington, DC: World Bank, 2010.

Epstein, Paul R., and Jesse Selber. *Oil: A Lifecycle Analysis of Its Health and Environmental Impacts.* Boston: Center for Health and the Global Environment, 2002.

Gosselin, Pierre, et al. *The Royal Society of Canada Expert Panel: Environmental and Health Impacts of Canada's Oil Sands Industry.* Ottawa: Royal Society of Canada, 2010.

Homer-Dixon, Thomas, and Nick Garrison, eds. *Carbon Shift: How the Twin Crises of Oil Depletion and Climate Change Will Define the Future.* Toronto: Random House, 2009.

International Energy Agency. *World Energy Outlook 2011.* Paris: IEA, 2011.

Nakaya, Andrea C., ed. *Oil: Opposing Viewpoints.* New York: Thomson Gale, 2006.

Neiva de Figueiredo, João, and Mauro F. Guillén, eds. *Green Products: Perspectives on Innovation and Adoption.* Boca Raton: CRC, 2011.

North, Liisa L., Timothy David Clark, and Viviana Patroni, eds. *Community Rights and Corporate Responsibility: Canadian Mining and Oil Companies in Latin America.* Toronto: Between the Lines, 2006.

O'Rourke, Dara, and Sarah Connolly. "Just Oil? The Distribution of Environmental and Social Impacts of Oil Production and Consumption." *Annual Review of Environment and Resources* 28 (2003): 587–617.

Shah, Sonia. *Crude: The Story of Oil.* New York: Seven Stories, 2004.

U.S. Department of Energy. *Environmental Benefits of Advanced Oil and Gas Exploration and Production Technology.* Washington, DC: Department of Energy, 1999.

Watkiss, Paul, Tom Downing, Claire Handley, and Ruth Butterfield. *The Impacts and Costs of Climate Change.* Brussels: European Commission DG Environment, 2005.

Web Sites

American Petroleum Institute: www.api.org

Enerdata: Global Energy Statistical Yearbook: http://yearbook.enerdata.net

International Energy Agency: www.iea.org

International Labour Organization: www.ilo.org

The Oil Drum: www.theoildrum.com

Petrostrategies: www.petrostrategies.org/home.htm

United Nations Environment Programme: www.unep.org

U.S. Energy Information Administration: www.eia.gov

World of Oil: www.worldoil.com

Documents

Document 1: Oil Pollution Act, United States, Overview and Key Provisions, 1990

The U.S. Congress passed the Oil Protection Act in 1990 in response to the 1989 Exxon Valdez oil tanker accident in Prince William Sound, Alaska—which released between 10 million and 30 million gallons of oil into the sea, making it the worst offshore oil disaster in U.S. history to that time. As the disaster made clear, responsible parties, including Exxon, did not have adequate safety measures or cleanup plans in place. Thus, among the key provisions of the act were the establishment of greater legal liability for offending parties, better avoidance mechanisms for future spills, and more stringent accident preparedness on the part of oil companies and others responsible for the shipment of oil in U.S. waters. The following excerpt is the official overview of the act and its key provisions by the U.S. Environmental Protection Agency.

The Oil Pollution Act (OPA) was signed into law in August 1990, largely in response to rising public concern following the *Exxon Valdez* incident. The OPA improved the nation's ability to prevent and respond to oil spills by establishing provisions that expand the federal government's ability, and provide the money and resources necessary, to respond to oil spills. The OPA also created the national Oil Spill Liability Trust Fund, which is available to provide up to one billion dollars per spill incident.

In addition, the OPA provided new requirements for contingency planning both by government and industry. The National Oil and Hazardous Substances Pollution Contingency Plan (NCP) has been expanded in a three-tiered approach: the Federal government is required to direct all public and private response efforts for certain types of spill events; Area Committees—composed of federal, state, and local government officials—must develop detailed, location-specific Area Contingency Plans; and owners or operators of vessels and certain facilities that pose a serious threat to the environment must p epare their own Facility Response Plans.

Finally, the OPA increased penalties for regulatory noncompliance, broadened the response and enforcement authorities of the Federal government, and preserved State authority to establish law governing oil spill prevention and response.

Key Provisions of the Oil Pollution Act

§1002(a) Provides that the responsible party for a vessel or facility from which oil is discharged, or which poses a substantial threat of a discharge, is liable for: (1) certain specified damages resulting from the discharged oil; and (2) removal costs incurred in a manner consistent with the National Contingency Plan (NCP).

§1002(c) Exceptions to the Clean Water Act (CWA) liability provisions include: (1) discharges of oil authorized by a permit under Federal, State, or local law; (2) discharges of oil from a public vessel; or (3) discharges of oil from onshore facilities covered by the liability provisions of the Trans-Alaska Pipeline Authorization Act.

§1002(d) Provides that if a responsible party can establish that the removal costs and damages resulting from an incident were caused solely by an act or omission by a third party, the third party will be held liable for such costs and damages.

§1004 The liability for tank vessels larger than 3,000 gross tons is increased to $1,200 per gross ton or $10 million, whichever is greater. Responsible parties at onshore facilities and deepwater ports are liable for up to $350 million per spill; holders of leases or permits for offshore facilities, except deepwater ports, are liable for up to $75 million per spill, plus removal costs. The Federal government has the authority to adjust, by regulation, the $350 million liability limit established for onshore facilities.

§1016 Offshore facilities are required to maintain evidence of financial responsibility of $150 million and vessels and deepwater ports must provide evidence of financial responsibility up to the maximum applicable liability amount. Claims for removal costs and damages may be asserted directly against the guarantor providing evidence of financial responsibility.

§1018(a) The Clean Water Act does not preempt State Law. States may impose additional liability (including unlimited liability), funding mechanisms, requirements for removal actions, and fines and penalties for responsible parties.

§1019 States have the authority to enforce, on the navigable waters of the State, OPA requirements for evidence of financial responsibility. States are also given access to Federal funds (up to $250,000 per incident) for immediate removal, mitigation, or prevention of a discharge, and may be reimbursed by the Trust fund for removal and monitoring costs incurred during oil spill response and cleanup efforts that are consistent with the National Contingency Plan (NCP).

§4202 Strengthens planning and prevention activities by: (1) providing for the establishment of spill contingency plans for all areas of the U.S. (2) mandating the development of response plans for individual tank vessels and certain facilities for responding to a worst case discharge or a substantial threat of such a discharge; and (3) providing requirements for spill removal equipment and periodic inspections.

§4301(a) and (c) The fine for failing to notify the appropriate Federal agency of a discharge is increased from a maximum of $10,000 to a maximum of $250,000 for an individual or $500,000 for an organization. The maximum prison term is also increased from one year to five years. The penalties for violations have a maximum of $250,000 and 15 years in prison.

§4301(b) Civil penalties are authorized at $25,000 for each day of violation or $1,000 per barrel of oil discharged. Failure to comply with a Federal removal order can result in civil penalties of up to $25,000 for each day of violation.

§9001(a) Amends the Internal Revenue Act of 1986 to consolidate funds established under other statutes and to increase permitted levels of expenditures. Penalties and funds established under several laws are consolidated, and the Trust Fund borrowing limit is increased from $500 million to $1 billion.

Source: Environmental Protection Agency.

Document 2: *Making Sweden an Oil-Free Society,* Commission on Oil Independence, 2006

In response to growing concerns about the impact of oil on health and the national and international environments, as well as concerns about dependence on foreign oil and its impact on the economy, the Swedish government commissioned a landmark study exploring how to make that country the world's first oil-free economy. The commission report, published in 2006, represents one of the most ambitious attempts by a government to envision not only a world without dependence on oil but how that goal could be achieved.

www.sweden.gov.se/content/1/c6/06/70/96/7f04f437.pdf

Source: Government of Sweden.

ORGAN AND TISSUE TRADE

There is a worldwide shortage of human organs and tissues available for transplant into those who need them. Many different attempts have been made to address this shortage, ranging from efforts to encourage more altruistic donation, to the institution of more aggressive organ procurement strategies, such as instituting a system of mandated choice, or a system of presumed consent. To compound the difficulties faced by the medical establishment, the demand for organs is steadily increasing, in part a result of the increasing prevalence (especially in the West) of type II diabetes and obesity, which may require pancreatic transplants. This situation has led both to the emergence of black markets in human organs and tissues, as well as to increasing calls to legalize and regulate them.

Although there has long been a trade in human body parts, especially hair and teeth, it is only since the invention of medical technology (such as effective immunosuppressive drugs) making the transplantation of human organs and tissues from one person to another likely to be successful, that any significant trade in these objects has developed.

Legal Status

As of 2011, trade in human organs and tissues is illegal in most countries. In the United States, for example, the trade in human organs at the state level is prohibited under the standard interpretation of the Uniform Anatomical Gift Act, while at the federal level it is prohibited by the National Organ Transplant Act (NOTA) of 1984. Under the latter legislation, the purchase of human organs for transplantation carries upon conviction a fine of up to $50,000, or up to five years in jail, or both. Similarly, in the United Kingdom, making an offer to buy, or receiving payment for, either a live or cadaveric organ is illegal under the 1989 Human Organs Transplant Act.

These legal prohibitions on the trade in human organs and tissues reflect a widely held view that this trade is immoral. In the United Kingdom, for example, the Human Organs Transplant Act was passed as a result of the outrage that followed the revelation that a British citizen, Colin Benton, had purchased a kidney from a Turkish citizen who had traveled to Britain to sell it. Similarly, the legal prohibition of the trade in human organs in the United States was spurred by the moral condemnation of the testimony of Barry Jacobs, a physician from Virginia who had founded the International Kidney Exchange with the aim of matching poor persons in developing countries with Americans who needed to receive a kidney, for which service he would charge a brokerage fee of between $2,000 and $5,000 at 1983 prices. In addition to legal prohibitions on the trade in human organs and tissues, the trade is also widely condemned by professional associations. It has been denounced by the British Medical Association, the American Medical Association, UNESCO, the Transplantation Society, the World Health Organization, the Nuffield Council on Bioethics, and the U.S. Task Force on Organ Transplantation.

Although the trade in human organs and tissues is illegal in most countries around the world, the trade is not universally legally prohibited. In 1988, for example, a system of payment for kidneys from nonrelated "donors" (vendors) was instituted in Iran. Under the Iranian system, potential kidney recipients are counseled that it is in their best interests to secure an organ from a living related donor. If no such donor can be found who is willing to donate, and if the potential recipient does not receive an organ from a deceased donor within six months, he or she is referred to the Dialysis and Transplant Patients Association (DATPA), which will identify a compatible kidney vendor for the potential recipient. Vendors are compensated in two ways. They receive $1,200 from the Iranian government, plus limited health insurance coverage. They also receive remuneration from the recipient, or, if the recipient is impoverished, from one of a series of designated charities; this amount is usually between $2,300 and $4,500.

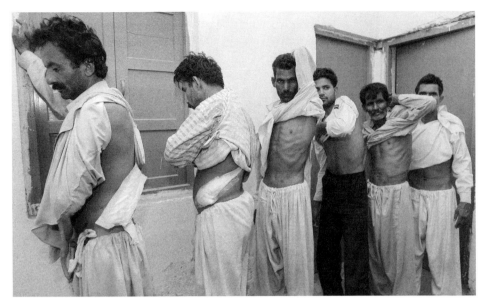

Pakistani men reveal their bandages and scars after having their kidneys removed in Lahore. Police there raided a clandestine clinic that paid poor people for their kidneys. South Asia is a hub of the international market in human organs. *(Arif Ali/AFP/Getty Images)*

Illegal Markets

While the Iranian trade in human kidneys is legal and heavily regulated, much of the current trade in human organs is illegal and consequently unregulated. The international trade in human organs is stimulated by the fact that every country in the world that prohibits it suffers from a shortage of transplant organs, with far fewer being available for transplant than are needed to meet the medical demand for them. This shortage has stimulated the black market in human organs, with persons who are in need of an organ, but who are both unlikely to receive one through licit means and can afford to buy one illegally, seeking out persons (typically from impoverished nations) who are both medically compatible and who would be willing to sell an organ.

While this international market for human organs is often described as "organ trafficking" by its detractors, this is a misnomer. The term "trafficking" carries with it connotations of involuntariness; "human trafficking," for example, involves the involuntary movement of persons from one location to another. The illegal market for human organs, however, is typically entered into voluntarily by both buyers and sellers. Rather than being trafficked, then, the organs are simply traded, even if economic circumstances lead people to sell their organs.

The trade is international in scope. One of main hubs of the illegal market for human organs is South Asia, with black markets in human organs flourishing in both India and Pakistan. In December 2003, police in both South Africa and Brazil broke up organ

markets, while that same year the Philippines passed the Implementing Rules and Regulations of Republic Act, which threatened fines of up to 2 million pesos (about $100,000) or twenty years in jail, or both, for buying or selling human organs. Organ trading is also widely reported in Kosovo and China.

Despite the widespread nature of the illegal trade in human organs and the claim that those who participate in it typically do so voluntarily, there are still grave risks associated with becoming involved in this trade, for both buyers and sellers. The sellers, for example, face the possibility that they will be defrauded by the brokers that they deal with, and will fail to receive the amount promised for their organ, or any promised medical care, or else the retrieval of the organ will be performed under conditions that are less sanitary than advertised. Meanwhile, the buyers face the possibility that the organ that they receive will be infected (with, for example, fungus, hepatitis, or HIV), or be a poor match—and, like the sellers, they too face the danger that the transplant will be performed in less than sanitary conditions.

Ethical Issues

The prevalence of fraud in black markets for human organs has led many to condemn the trade in human organs and tissues on moral grounds. To condemn the trade on the grounds that the black market is rife with abuse might, however, be overly hasty, say some experts. This is because this objection, they note, is not one that should be aimed at the trade in human organs and tissues itself, but at the illegal trade in these objects. And this is not only because the legalization of the organ and tissue trade would lead to its regulation and the elimination or curtailment of abuses, but because, were the trade to be legal, victims of fraud could seek restitution through civil litigation.

The dangers associated with the black markets in human organs and tissues have not been the only grounds that some have objected to regarding the trade in human organs and tissues from an ethical standpoint. These markets have been criticized on the grounds that they fail to respect the autonomy of those who participate in them as vendors. The advocates of this objection note that subjecting a person to coercion will compromise his autonomy with respect to his actions. They then argue that the typical vendor in a market for human tissues and organs sells as a result of economic desperation; he may, then, be coerced into selling by his poverty. Thus, since coercion serves to compromise the autonomy of those subject to it, were a market for human organs and tissues to be legal, persons might be coerced into participating in it as vendors by their poverty (and hence suffer from a diminution in their autonomy with respect to their vending actions). Concern for the autonomy of would-be vendors, say critics of such an approach, would thus militate against legalizing markets in human organs and tissues.

While this objection is prima facie plausible, it does not stand up to close scrutiny, say advocates of legalization. A person is coerced into performing a certain action when her coercer restricts her range of options so that she is motivated to perform the action that he wants her to perform. To legalize the trade in human organs and tissues would not, however, restrict the options that a would-be vendor was faced with, says some experts; rather, it would expand them. (She would now have the legal option to sell an organ or some tissue.) As such, then, persons cannot be coerced into selling in a market for human organs and tissues. Indeed, say some experts, if one is really concerned with protecting the autonomy of would-be vendors one should recognize that the prohibition of the trade in human organs and tissues is less respectful of persons' autonomy than its legalization, since the prohibition would serve to coerce some people into refraining from entering this trade when they otherwise would have done.

A further objection to the trade in human organs and tissues is that the removal of many human body parts from a human being carries with it significant risks. As such, it is argued, this trade should be prohibited to protect the would-be vendors from the risks of sale that they would otherwise choose to incur. It is certainly true that the removal of many human body parts carries with it significant risks. The removal of a kidney, for example, carries with it roughly a 0.06 percent risk of death and roughly a 0.23 percent chance of serious complications arising from the procedure. But the presence of these risks alone cannot justify banning the trade in human organs and tissues, say advocates of legalizing the trade. This is because other commercial activities that carry similar or greater risks are still legal. Commercial fishermen in Britain, for example, have a 0.103 percent risk of death while engaged in their professional activities, while there is a 0.399 percent risk of sustaining a major injury while quarrying in the United States. Thus, if the trade in human organs and tissues is prohibited on the grounds that it is too dangerous for persons to engage in, many other currently legal forms of employment will have to be prohibited, also.

The Future

Given the continuing shortage of human body parts that are available for transplantation, combined with the continued failure of nonmarket methods of organ procurement to secure enough needed organs and tissues, it is unlikely that the debate over whether or not to legalize the trade in human body parts will disappear soon. Instead, it is more likely that the chronic and increasing shortage of body parts will put additional pressure on countries to legalize this trade. It is unlikely, however, that a legal trade in human organs and tissues will be organized along the lines of a laissez-faire market. Instead, it is likely to be highly regulated (as is the Iranian system), possibly with nonfinancial incentives (such as health insurance or tax credits) being offered to persons who might be willing to give up their organs and tissue to secure them.

James Stacey Taylor

See also: Cardiovascular Disease; Gastrointestinal Disease; Health Care; Respiratory Disease.

Further Reading

Cherry, Mark J. *Kidney for Sale by Owner.* Washington, DC: Georgetown University Press, 2005.

Goyal, Madhav, R.L. Mehta, L.J. Schneiderman, and A.R. Sehgal. "The Economic and Health Consequences of

Selling a Kidney in India." *Journal of the American Medical Association* 288 (2002): 1589–1593.

Price, David. *Legal and Ethical Aspects of Organ Transplantation.* New York: Cambridge University Press, 2001.

Radcliffe-Richards, A.S. Daar, R.D. Guttmann, R. Hoffenberg, I. Kennedy, M. Lock, R.A. Sells, and N. Tilney. "The Case for Allowing Kidney Sales." *The Lancet* 351:9120 (1998): 1950–1952.

Taylor, James Stacey. *Stakes and Kidneys: Why Markets in Human Body Parts Are Morally Imperative.* Farnham, Surrey, UK: Ashgate, 2005.

Wilkinson, S. *Bodies for Sale: Ethics and Exploitation in the Human Body Trade.* New York: Routledge, 2003.

Web Sites

Human Trafficking Project: www.traffickingproject.org
World Health Organization: www.who.org

Documents

Document 1: National Organ Transplantation Act (United States), 1984

The National Organ Transplantation Act was passed by Congress in 1984 to address the shortage of organs available for transplant in the United States, as well as to improve the organ matching and placement process by establishing a national register for organ matching, termed the Organ Procurement and Transplantation network, which was to be run privately under federal contract. This act also prohibited the exchange of organs and other human body parts for "valuable consideration."

http://optn.transplant.hrsa.gov/policiesAndBylaws/nota.asp

Source: Health Resources and Services Administration.

Document 2: Declaration of Istanbul Abstract, 2008

The Declaration of Istanbul was developed at the International Summit on Transplant Tourism and Organ Trafficking, convened by the Transplantation Society and International Society of Nephrology in Istanbul, Turkey, from April 30 to May 2, 2008. The summit and declaration were spurred by the World Health Assembly in 2004, when it adopted resolution WHA57.18 urging member states "to take measures to protect the poorest and vulnerable groups from transplant tourism and the sale of tissues and organs, including attention to the wider problem of international trafficking in human tissues and organs." While the declaration is often seen as representing a remarkable consensus among transplant professionals, it is sometimes claimed that dissenting voices were not represented at the summit, and that the alleged consensus is illusory.

Organ commercialism, which targets vulnerable populations (such as illiterate and impoverished persons, undocumented immigrants, prisoners, and political or economic refugees) in resource-poor countries, has been condemned by international bodies such as the World Health Organization for decades. Yet in recent years, as a consequence of the increasing ease of Internet communication and the willingness of patients in rich countries to travel and purchase organs, organ trafficking and transplant tourism have grown into global problems. For example, as of 2006, foreigners received two-thirds of the 2000 kidney transplants performed annually in Pakistan.

The *Istanbul Declaration* proclaims that the poor who sell their organs are being exploited, whether by richer people within their own countries or by transplant tourists from abroad. Moreover, transplant tourists risk physical harm by unregulated and illegal transplantation. Participants in the Istanbul Summit concluded that transplant commercialism, which targets the vulnerable, transplant tourism, and organ trafficking should be prohibited. And they also urged their fellow transplant professionals, individually and through their organizations, to put an end to these unethical activities and foster safe, accountable practices that meet the needs of transplant recipients while protecting donors.

Countries from which transplant tourists originate, as well as those to which they travel to obtain transplants, are just beginning to address their respective responsibilities to protect their people from exploitation and to develop national self-sufficiency in organ donation. The Declaration should reinforce the resolve of governments and international organizations to develop laws and guidelines to bring an end to wrongful practices. "The legacy of transplantation is threatened by organ trafficking and transplant tourism. The *Declaration of Istanbul* aims to combat these activities and to preserve the nobility of organ donation. The success of transplantation as a life-saving treatment does not require—nor justify—victimizing the world's poor as the source of organs for the rich" (Steering Committee of the Istanbul Summit).

Source: www.declarationofistanbul.org

PARASITIC DISEASE

Technically, all disease-causing organisms are parasitic, in that they exploit their hosts for their own gain. However, epidemiologists generally use the term "parasitic diseases" to refer specifically to conditions caused by the approximately 300 helminths (worms) and 100 protozoa that can invade the body, leading to any of about 250 diseases.

The World Health Organization (WHO) estimates that one person in four worldwide is infected with some form of parasite. Though no population is immune, parasitic diseases are overwhelmingly found in developing countries. The burden weighs most heavily on children, for whom parasites can stunt growth, impair cognitive development, and cause permanent disfiguration.

History

Archaeological evidence—specifically the presence of helminth eggs and protozoan cysts in preserved bodies—confirms that human beings have contended with parasitic diseases for at least 8,000 years and almost certainly longer. The first known written account of a parasitic infection comes from an Egyptian text called the Ebers Papyrus. Dating to 1500 B.C.E., the document describes several different afflictions that are clearly recognizable as being caused by roundworms, threadworms, and Guinea worms. Guinea worms, in fact, are widely present in ancient texts, perhaps more than any other parasite. They appear to be the "fiery serpents" that afflicted the Israelites around 1250 B.C.E., according to the Book of Exodus. The Assyrians, Babylonians, Chinese, Greeks, Persians, and Romans also lamented the ill-effects of Guinea worm infections.

Likewise, schistosomiasis—which is particularly common among the peoples who live near the Nile River—is addressed with regularity in ancient medical texts. The Egyptians, not surprisingly, commented on the disease in many different documents, though they do not appear to have had a specific name for it,

suggesting that schistosomiasis was so common that a name was not needed. A number of other African and Middle Eastern cultures, as well as the Greeks and Romans, also recorded incidences of the disease, which is characterized by a range of symptoms. Similarly, scholars have discovered references to elephantiasis, malaria, and amoebiasis in the documentary records of various ancient civilizations. It should be noted, however, that while these civilizations were aware of the existence of these diseases, they rarely, if ever, understood their underlying cause.

The struggle to understand parasitic diseases continued for millennia and was slowed by all manner of incorrect interpretations. At various times, these afflictions were attributed to the cycles of the moon, divine will, earthquakes, and poisonous vapors (called miasma) from swamps. Achieving particularly widespread and lasting currency was the theory of "spontaneous generation"—that whatever it was that caused diseases like malaria and schistosomiasis grew spontaneously out of rotting animal or human flesh. This explanation predominated through the end of the medieval era.

The Age of Exploration, which began in the 1500s, helped lay the groundwork for modern understanding of parasitic diseases. New conditions, like Chagas disease and African sleeping sickness, were documented and became subjects of much study and discussion. At the same time, it was evident that several well-known diseases—like elephantiasis and malaria—were prevalent in some populations, but not others. This observation led several theorists to speculate that some element of the local environment must be to blame. In the 1590s, the Dutch navigator Jan Huygen van Linschoten correctly identified unclean drinking water as the culprit behind some conditions, particularly Guinea worm infections. In 1768, the English naval officer and physician James Lind demonstrated that such infections could be prevented if drinking water is boiled. These insights marked the first time that a parasitic disease, a cause, and an effective solution had all been linked. Still, Lind and his contemporaries remained unaware of which organism caused the infections and were not even certain that an organism caused the disease at all.

It was in the nineteenth century that scientists and physicians, aided by more powerful microscopes, as well as emerging new ideas about the spread of disease (e.g., the germ theory), unlocked most of the mysteries surrounding parasitic infections. The most important figure of the era was Scottish physician and pathologist Patrick Manson, the "father of tropical medicine," who helped to identify the parasites that cause elephantiasis and malaria and to explain how they are transmitted to humans. Dozens of Manson's contemporaries made additional contributions, either identifying the parasites behind various diseases or making clear how those parasites are able to infect human bodies.

Compared with the nineteenth century, which has been called the "golden age of parasitology," new insights about parasitic diseases were relatively rare in the twentieth century. A handful of remaining questions—about the root cause of Chagas disease, for example—were answered, and a small number of new conditions were identified and described (for example, cryptosporidiosis, which primarily affects AIDS sufferers and other immune-compromised patients). Primarily, however, the dominant focus of parasitologists since around 1900 has been the development of medicines and strategies for combating diseases that already have long histories and are well understood.

Parasitic Disease Today

Generally speaking, the hundreds of parasitic diseases are grouped by their vectors—that is, the primary manner in which they are propagated to human populations: blood and insects, food and animals, and water. It should be noted that these categorizations are not always absolute; while some conditions (malaria, for example) can be transmitted in only one way, others (amoebiasis, for example) are most commonly transmitted in one manner (water, in the case of amoebiasis) but can also be transmitted in other ways as well.

Blood and Insects

Blood-borne parasites can be acquired in a number of ways—through dirty needles, an infected transfu-sion, or contact with an open wound. However, the most common way in which blood-borne parasites are passed from one person to another is through insect bites. In fact, some blood-borne diseases—notably malaria—require an insect to serve as an intermediary. As such, blood-borne and insect-borne parasitic infections tend to be grouped together, even though insects are not always the culprit.

The most serious disease in this group is malaria. Mosquitoes of the genus *Anopheles* transmit malaria parasites, which are protozoa of the genus *Plasmodium*. In less severe cases, the disease causes flulike symptoms: aches, chills, fever, and so forth. More serious infections can cause kidney failure, severe anemia, and swelling of the brain, and can be fatal. It is estimated that there are 216 million cases of malaria each year, and 655,000 deaths, with 91 percent of these occurring in Africa.

Elephantiasis, also called lymphatic filiarisis, is usually caused by worms of the family Filarioidea, which are spread by mosquitoes. The parasites infect the host's lymph nodes, blocking the flow of lymph through the body, and resulting in the grotesque swelling associated with the disease. Currently, 120 million people suffer from elephantiasis, most of them in Africa and Southeast Asia. Forty million of these individuals are permanently disfigured.

Onchocerciasis, known commonly as river blindness, is an infection of the roundworm *Onchocerca volvulus*, passed to humans by black flies of the genus *Simulium*. The parasite interferes with the proper function of body organs, leading to swelling, compromised immune function, and loss of eyesight. Though not fatal, the disease can cause permanent blindness. There are approximately 18 million onchocerciasis-infected people worldwide—99 percent of them in Africa—and 300,000 of those have lost their sight.

Chagas disease is caused by the protozoa *Trypanosoma cruzi*, and is generally transmitted by bugs in the Reduviidae family, known popularly as "kissing bugs" or "assassin bugs." There are two phases of the disease. The acute stage lasts for weeks or months, and includes swelling and sometimes mild respiratory problems; this phase is very treatable. In the chronic stage, which takes years to unfold, victims are less likely to respond to treatment. The disease can be, and often is, asymptomatic in this phase, but in 20 to 40 percent of cases it produces life-threatening heart and digestive system disorders. Chagas disease is primarily found in poor, rural areas in the Americas, with about 8 to 10 million sufferers in Latin American countries and an additional 300,000 to

400,000 in the United States, Spain, and other nations that have frequent movement of people to and from Latin America. About 20,000 people succumb to the disease each year.

Leishmaniasis, caused by *Leishmania* protozoa and spread by sand flies of the genus *Phlebotomus*, produces severe lesions on the skin as well as anemia and swelling of the spleen and liver. The disease is found in all regions of the world except Oceania, though it is most common in Africa, South America, and southern Asia, particularly Bangladesh, Brazil, India, Nepal, and Sudan. There are 500,000 new cases of leishmaniasis and 60,000 deaths from the disease each year.

African sleeping sickness, properly known as African trypanosomiasis, is an infection of *Trypanosoma brucei* protozoa that are circulated by tsetse flies. Like Chagas disease, it affects victims in two phases—in the first, it causes flulike symptoms and swelling in the lymph nodes; in the second, it substantially affects neurological function, leading to confusion, reduced coordination, fatigue, and disrupted sleep cycles (hence the name). African sleeping sickness is fatal if untreated, but also relatively rare, with the number of reported cases dropping below 10,000 in 2009. It is prone to epidemic outbreaks, however, particularly in Kenya and Uganda.

Food and Animals

Parasitic diseases that are transmitted via animals other than insects are called zoonotic diseases. They can be acquired by living with, consuming, or being bitten by infected animals. This means that livestock—primarily, cows, pigs, and sheep—present a risk of infection, as do wild animals like raccoons and opossums, along with cats and dogs and other pets.

Toxoplasmosis is caused by a protozoa (*Toxoplasma gondii*) that thrives in the system of most warm-blooded animals but is particularly common in cats. It is generally acquired by humans through contact with feces from an infected cat, though it can also result from eating the meat of an infected animal (especially lamb, pork, and venison). Normally the symptoms of the disease are fairly mild—fever, respiratory problems, soreness—but it can be more serious (and even fatal) when it infects bodily organs and the central nervous system, particularly in immune-compromised patients and newborn infants. The disease is found worldwide; it is estimated that

more than one-third of the world's population has *T. gondii* in their system. The number of deaths from the disease is not well documented but is likely fewer than 10,000 each year.

Trichinosis is an infection of the roundworm *Trichinella spiralis*, generally due to the consumption of infected pork or the most of other game animals. In its more mild form, it causes nausea, diarrhea, and other digestive problems. It sometimes enters a second phase in which it invades tissues beyond the digestive tract, causing edema (swelling), fatigue, and muscle pain. If the parasite reaches the nervous system, it can trigger paralysis and stroke; if it reaches the lungs, it can cause pneumonia. Both of the latter circumstances can be fatal. There are 11 million trichinosis sufferers in the world, primarily in Eastern Europe and Asia. As with toxoplasmosis, fatalities are not well documented globally but number no more than a few thousand a year.

Water

Water-borne parasites typically thrive in freshwater and enter the body when that water is used for drinking, cooking, or bathing. In total, they are responsible for nearly 2 million deaths each year worldwide.

The most damaging water-borne illness globally is schistosomiasis (also known as bilharzia). Caused by a worm of the genus *Schistosoma*, the disease is not usually fatal, but it does interfere with children's growth and cognitive development, and it generates a host of chronic and debilitating symptoms, including cough, diarrhea, fatigue, organ damage, and sores on the skin. Schistosomiasis can also be a precursor to other diseases; for example, it can inflame the urinary tract, which in turn can lead to bladder cancer, or it can trigger hypertension, which can contribute to heart disease. The parasite is often found in water-dwelling snails and is most common in places where those snails are native—Africa (especially Egypt), the Caribbean, the Middle East, South America, and Southeast Asia. It is estimated that 200 million people worldwide have schistosomiasis; 20,000 of them succumb to it each year.

Cryptosporidiosis, known popularly as "crypto," is caused by the protozoan *Cryptosporidium*. It resides in the intestines, generally causing mild discomfort and diarrhea. However, in individuals with compromised immune systems, particularly AIDS patients, it can be debilitating and even fatal. The disease is common worldwide and is responsible for more than half of all water-borne disease caused by parasites. Because its symptoms are more mild than schistosomiasis and other parasitic infections, cryptosporidiosis often goes unreported, but there are at least 500 million cases a year.

Amoebiasis results from infection by the protozoan *Entamoeba histolytica*. The parasite invades the gastrointestinal tract via drinking water and generally either is asymptomatic or causes diarrhea, dysentery, and bloody stools. If the disease reaches the liver, it can result in abscesses, which is the most common manner in which amoebiasis becomes fatal. Roughly 50 million people worldwide suffer from the disease, primarily in Mexico, Central America, South Asia, sub-Saharan Africa, and the western half of South America. There are 70,000 amoebiasis fatalities annually.

Guinea worm disease, also known as dracunculiasis, occurs when larvae of the worm *Dracunculus medinensis*, which reside inside a water flea, are ingested by a person during bathing, swimming, or drinking. It is rarely fatal but does cause a great deal of pain, along with nausea and vomiting, as the larvae hatch and the adult worms eventually migrate toward the lower extremities and exit the body through the skin. So unpleasant and unremitting are these symptoms that the disease was widely feared in past centuries. However, it is now fairly rare. There are only about 80,000 sufferers in the world, and nearly all of those are in just five countries: Chad, Ethiopia, Ghana, Mali, and South Sudan. Prevention efforts have been so successful, and the decline of the disease has been so precipitous, that epidemiologists believe it will soon become the first parasite to be eradicated.

Other Vectors

Some parasitic infections can be acquired via one or more of the means listed above but are most typically passed through some other vector. Most notable in this group are hookworms. Hookworm larvae exit an infected host through its feces and contaminate soil. They generally enter a new host through the feet when the individual walks barefoot over infested ground. Once the larvae (primarily *Necator americanus* and *Anylostoma duodenale*) have entered the bloodstream, they pierce the walls of the intestines and feed off their host. An individual can have more than 100 worms at a time, which consume vital nutrients and interfere with the absorption of food. Between 700 and 900 million people worldwide, primarily in poor rural areas in China, Latin America, Southeast Asia, and sub-Saharan Africa, are confirmed to have hookworm. The majority of these are children, and only about 9 percent of those are being treated for it.

Combating Parasitic Disease

On an individual level, the single most important thing that can be done to avoid parasitic infections is to adopt rigorous hygienic practices. These include washing hands after using the bathroom and before handling food, avoiding tainted rivers or lakes, boiling of drinking water that may be infected, and wearing shoes to guard against hookworms and other parasites that can enter the body through the feet. Beyond that, mosquito nets and insect repellant sprays have both been proven to be very effective in battling parasites.

For individuals who develop a parasitic infection, there are a host of antiparasitic medications in use. The oldest are antimalarials like chloroquine, but there are also pills for sleeping sickness (melarsoprol and eflornithine), onchocerciasis (ivermectin), and elephantiasis (diethylcarbamazine), among others. Beyond pharmaceuticals, there are a handful of other treatment options. It is common to remove infected lesions or nodules from the skin of people who have those symptoms due to parasites. Similarly, parasites that live near the surface of the skin—or on the outside—often succumb to cryotherapy (freezing, usually with liquid nitrogen). Surgery is also utilized for some conditions, such as elephantiasis.

Combating parasitic disease is a complex matter. Clean drinking water, drug availability, and insect control are public health issues that require the attention of governments and international organizations. UNICEF, WHO, and scores of other organizations have responded aggressively to these challenges in recent years.

Many drugs are most effective when deployed as part of a community-wide effort. Some infections can thrive only in human hosts, so if all humans in an area are treated at once, the organisms have no viable means of survival. The African Programme for Onchocerciasis Control (APOC) takes this approach and has been able to eradicate river blindness in many communities. Similarly, there has been much success in combating hookworm by enlisting schools in the fight. School officials have access to, and the trust of, young children and can be trained fairly quickly to administer deworming drugs (primarily albendazole and mebendazole), which cost only fifty cents per student. The Clinton Global Initiative has pledged $10 million toward deworming efforts, and the Bill & Melinda Gates Foundation has likewise provided several million dollars in support.

Water treatment is another manner of combating parasites. The most established technique for doing so is with chlorination, but a great many protozoa have developed resistance to chlorine and other chemicals. The Water Research Foundation, among others, works on developing and implementing alternative strategies for making water potable. They have had success with various filtration techniques, as well as flocculation (the use of chemicals that cause organisms and other impurities to bind together, which facilitates removal). Recently, the use of low levels of ultraviolet radiation has produced encouraging results. At the same time, tests and tools are being developed that warn when water has become contaminated. For example, some countries have deployed highly accurate, real-time cryptosporidium detection systems that alert officials whenever that parasite is present.

Insect control is another effective tactic for reducing the prevalence of parasitic disease. For example, the Onchocerciasis Control Programme (OCP) was launched in 11 at-risk countries in 1974. Through the sustained deployment of pesticides, black fly populations were brought substantially under control and the incidence of onchocerciasis dropped dramatically. Similar initiatives have targeted malarial mosquitoes, sand flies, tsetse flies, and the snails that cause schistosomiasis, often with great success.

Careful management of blood supplies also helps to reduce parasitic infections. For example, in Latin America, Spain, and the United States, blood donors are now queried about their risk factors for Chagas disease, and most of the blood collected is tested for the parasite that causes Chagas. Since these measures were implemented, the disease appears to have gone into decline and pathologists are hopeful that it is on the road to elimination.

The Future

Many of the medications and other efforts described above have had highly encouraging results, raising hope that a great number of parasitic infections that have afflicted humanity for centuries or millennia—Guinea worm disease, Chagas disease, onchocerciasis—may well be eradicated in the next several decades.

For those infections that have proven more resilient, or are developing drug resistance, researchers are currently very optimistic about the potential for the creation of antiparasitic vaccines. Historically, much research has been done on this subject, particularly in the search for a malaria vaccine. These efforts have not yielded much results because helminths and protozoa are much more anatomically similar to human beings than bacteria, therefore it is difficult to find treatments that are lethal to parasites but do not harm their hosts. But in the last decade, the genomes of several of the most damaging parasites have been fully mapped, suggesting a great many potential directions for epidemiologists to explore. Already, work is in progress on new amoebiasis, hookworm, malaria, and schistosomiasis vaccines, with some studies having advanced to the stage of clinical trials. Nothing concrete has come from these efforts as yet, but WHO predicts that humankind may be on the verge of a revolution in fighting parasitic disease.

Christopher Bates and Jeffrey Gold

See also: Drug Resistance; Gastrointestinal Disease; Mosquito-borne Disease; Public Health; Vaccination; Waterborne Disease.

Further Reading

Bogitsh, Burton J. *Human Parasitology.* 4th ed. Boston: Academic, 2013.

Buckman, Robert. *Human Wildlife That Lives on Us.* Baltimore: Johns Hopkins University Press, 2003.

Crawford, Dorothy H. *Deadly Companions: How Microbes Shaped Our History.* New York: Oxford University Press, 2007.

De Bruyn, Olivier, and Stephane Peeters, eds. *Parasitology Research Trends.* New York: Nova Science, 2010.

Gardenour, Brenda, and Misha Tadd, eds. *Parasites, Worms, and the Human Body in Religion and Culture.* New York: Peter Lang, 2010.

Hamer, Davidson H., ed. *Public Health and Infectious Diseases.* San Diego, CA: Academic, 2010.

Hotez, Peter J. *Forgotten People, Forgotten Diseases: The Neglected Tropical Diseases and Their Impact on Global Health and Development.* Washington, DC: ASM, 2008.

McGuire, Robert A., and Philip R.P. Coelho. *Parasites, Pathogens, and Progress: Diseases and Economic Development.* Cambridge, MA: MIT Press, 2011.

World Health Organization. *Working to Overcome the Global Impact of Neglected Tropical Diseases: First WHO Report on Neglected Tropical Diseases.* Geneva: World Health Organization, 2010.

Web Sites

Centers for Disease Control and Prevention, Parasites:
www.cdc.gov/parasites
Medline Plus, Parasitic Diseases:
www.nlm.nih.gov/medlineplus/parasiticdiseases.html
World Health Organization, Neglected Tropical
Diseases: www.who.int/neglected_diseases/en

Documents

Document 1: *Tropical Diseases: A Manual of the Diseases of Warm Climates* (excerpt), Patrick Manson, 1898

European colonization and settlement of Africa in the late nineteenth century led to heightened urgency about understanding the causes of tropical diseases among scientists and others in European countries with imperial holdings on the African continent. Arguably the most influential of the scientists examining such diseases was the Scottish physician Patrick Manson. Building on the recently developed germ theory of disease, Manson provided new insights into the life cycles of parasitic organisms that led to such crippling and fatal tropical diseases as elephantiasis, "fly disease" (trypanosomiasis, or sleeping sickness), and malaria. The following explanation is from Manson's breakthrough 1898 text on tropical diseases.

In the majority of instances disease germs are true parasites, and therefore, to keep in existence as species, require to pass from host to host. If, during this passage from host to host, the temperature of the transmitting medium—be it air, water, or food—be too high or too low for the special requirements of the germ in question, that germ dies and ceases to be infective. In this way may be explained the absence from the tropics of a class of directly infectious diseases represented by scarlet fever, and the absence from temperate climates of a similar class of diseases represented by dengue. In the one case, during the short passage from one human being to another, tropical temperature is fatal to the air-borne germ; in the other the lower temperature of higher latitudes has the same effect.

In another type of disease, of which tropical scaly ringworm (Tinea imbricata) is an excellent example, the germ vegetates on the surface of the body, and is thus exposed to the vicissitudes of climate. One of the requirements of the germ referred to is a high atmospheric temperature and a certain degree of moisture. Given these it flourishes; remove these and it dies out, just as a palm tree or a bird of paradise would die on being transferred to a cold climate.

Many diseases require for their transmission from one individual to another the services of a third and wholly different animal. The propagation and continued existence of a disease of this description will depend, therefore, on the presence of the third animal. If the latter be a tropical species, the disease for whose transmission it is necessary must necessarily be confined to the tropics. The third or transmitting animal operates in one of several ways. Thus in "fly disease," the protozoal organism which is the direct cause of the disease is carried from one animal to another on the mandibles of the tsetse fly. Consequently, the passive role of the tsetse fly is intentionally imitated by man, the disease is not found outside what is known as "the fly belt," the geographical limits of which are very circumscribed, depending, among other things, on tropical conditions. Similarly, although on a somewhat different principle, the geographical range of malaria and of filariasis is determined by that of special species of mosquito which ingest and act as intermediate hosts to the respective germs, and, so to speak, prepare them for entrance into their human host. The distribution of a large number of animal parasitic diseases depends in this way on the distribution of the living inoculating agency, as in "fly disease," or of the intermediate hosts, as in malaria and filariasis. When this third animal happens to be a tropical species, the disease it subtends, so to speak, is, in natural conditions, necessarily tropical also.

Certain diseases are common to man and the lower animals. If these latter happen to be tropical species the opportunities for man to contract the common disease are most frequent, or are only found, in the tropics. Such, most probably, are some of the tropical ringworms.

Certain parasites are so organised that before re-entering man they must pass a part of their lives as free organisms in the outer world, where they require a relatively high temperature for their development. Such parasites, therefore, and the diseases they give rise to, must necessarily be tropical or sub-tropical. The Anhyloatomuni duodenale and ankylostomiasis is an instance in point.

There is a class of intoxication diseases which depend on toxins generated by germs whose habitat is the soil, water, or other external media, and whose germs do not enter the human body as a necessary feature in their life-histories, although their toxins may. The yeast plant and its toxin, alcohol, and the disease it causes, alcoholism, is the most familiar example of this. Such, too, are ergotism, pellagra, and, perhaps, lathyrism. The beriberi germ, its toxin and beriberi, is probably another. These germs require certain temperatures and certain media; consequently the diseases they produce have a corresponding geographical range. If one of these conditions be a high temperature, the disease, as in the case of beri-beri, is a tropical one.

Lastly, I can conceive, and believe, that there is another and less directly-acting set of conditions influencing the distribution of disease, conditions which as yet have been ignored by epidemiologists, but which, it seems to me, must have an important bearing on this subject. Disease germs, their transmitting agencies, or their intermediate hosts, being living organisms, are, during their extracorporeal phases, necessarily competing organisms, and therefore liable to be preyed upon, or otherwise crushed out, by other organisms in the struggle for existence. The malaria parasite is absent in many places in which, apparently, all the conditions favourable for its existence are to be found in perfection. Why is it not found there, seeing that it must certainly have been frequently introduced? I would suggest that in some instances this, and other disease germs, or the organisms subtending them, are kept under by natural enemies which prey on them, just as fishes prey on and keep down water-haunting insects, or as mice do bumble-bees. The geographical range of such germs, therefore, will depend, not only on the presence of favourable conditions but, also, on the absence of unfavourable ones. Herein lies a vast field for study, and one which, as yet, has not been touched by epidemiologists.

In these and similar ways the peculiar distribution of tropical diseases is regulated. The more we learn about these diseases the less important its bearing on their geographical distribution as a direct pathogenic agency, becomes the role of temperature *per se*, and the more important the influence of tropical fauna.

Source: Internet Archive.

Document 2: "Final Report of the Conference on the Eradicability of Onchocerciasis," World Health Organization, 2002

Launched in 1974 by the World Health Organization and other United Nations agencies, the African Programme for Onchocerciasis Control (APOC) has been one of the great success stories in global disease reduction. Prior to the program's launch, parasitic ochocerciasis, or river blindness, affected tens of thousands of people in 11 West African countries. By 2002, when APOC was discontinued, the disease had effectively been eliminated in 10 of those countries. Only war-torn Sierra Leone remained affected, but even there, cases loads were a fraction of what they had once been. The Executive Summary and Introduction of the conference's final report are presented below.

Executive Summary

Sixty-four experts from a variety of disciplines attended a Conference on the Eradicability of Onchocerciasis at The Carter Center, in Atlanta GA, held January 22–24, 2002....

The presentations underlined epidemiological and ento-mological differences between onchocerciasis in Africa and the Americas. Whilst onchocerciasis in Africa covers extensive areas and is associated with striking human and fly population migrations and remarkably efficient black fly vectors, in the Americas onchocerciasis is found in limited foci. Human and fly population migration are not major problems in the Americas, where most black fly species are inefficient, though some efficient black flies are also found there. Vector control has been effectively applied in the Onchocerciasis Control Program in West Africa (OCP) with remarkable results, interrupting transmission in most parts of the original Program area. The use of ivermectin has given variable results: while ivermectin treatment has been effective in all endemic areas in controlling onchocerciasis as a public health problem, its potential for interrupting transmission is more promising in hypo- and mesoendemic areas. The African Program for Onchocerciasis Control (APOC), which supports onchocerciasis control in endemic African countries outside the OCP, applies ivermectin—its principal control tool—to communities in high-risk areas as determined by rapid epidemiological mapping of onchocerciasis (REMO) and Geographic Information Systems (GIS). In the Americas, through support of the Onchocerciasis Elimination Program in the Americas (OEPA), a strategy of bi-annual ivermectin treatment of at least 85% of the eligible populations in all endemic communities is showing very good results and promises to be effective in eliminating onchocerciasis in the region.

The Conference concluded that onchocerciasis is not eradicable using current tools due to the major barriers to eradication in Africa. However, the Conference also concluded that in most if not all the Americas, and possibly Yemen and some sites in Africa, transmission of onchocerciasis can be eliminated using current tools.

The Conference recommended that where interruption of transmission is feasible and cost-effective, programs should aim for that goal using all appropriate and available interventions so that the *Onchocerca volvulus* can eventually be eliminated and interventions halted. Although interruption of transmission of onchocerciasis cannot currently be achieved in most of Africa, the Conference recommended that efforts be made to preserve areas in West Africa made free of onchocerciasis transmission through the Onchocerciasis Control Program over the past 25 years. In the remaining hyper and mesoendemic foci in Africa, continued annual distribution of ivermectin will keep onchocerciasis controlled to a point where it is no longer a public health problem or constraint to economic development.

Although not yet identified to exist, the specter of the emergence of resistance to ivermectin in *O. volvulus* was considered a future potential threat to the great progress and considerable investment made so far in research and control against this disease. In particular, there is need for additional research in developing macrofilaricides (drugs which could kill or permanently sterilize the adult *O. volvulus* parasite), tools for ivermectin resistance monitoring, and improved diagnostics.

Introduction

Onchocerciasis, or river blindness, is caused by the filarial parasite *Onchocerca volvulus*. It is transmitted by the black flies of the genus *Simulium* that breed in fast-flowing water. Manifestations of onchocerciasis include eye lesions that can cause visual loss culminating in blindness, and skin lesions (severe itching, disfiguring skin changes, and subcutaneous nodules). A WHO Expert Committee in 1995 estimated that over 120 million persons are at risk with some 17.6 million infected, 99% of whom live in Africa with the rest found in six countries of the Americas, and Yemen in the Arabian Peninsula. Onchocerciasis is a disease of remote, rural, poor populations. In Africa, onchocerciasis has been found to cause serious socio-economic problems; populations have in the past abandoned fertile land along the rivers that harbor the breeding sites of the *Simulium*, for fear of going blind, whilst persons with unsightly skin lesions have been socially marginalized.

Progress made in the last quarter century in the control of onchocerciasis, both in Africa and the Americas, has generated much interest and also raised questions about the feasibility of eradicating onchocerciasis using available tools. The Atlanta Conference on the Eradicability of Onchocerciasis was convened with the following purposes: 1) to review previous discussions and judgments on the eradication of onchocerciasis, 2) to discuss and evaluate the current knowledge base regarding the ability of existing interventions to interrupt parasite transmission, 3) to assess the status and prospects of new tools for treating, preventing, tracking, and diagnosing the infection, 4) to discuss evidence related to potential for emergence of resistance in *O. volvulus* to ivermectin, 5) to consider the scientific, operational, economic and political/social feasibility of eradicating onchocerciasis, using currently available tools; and 6) to propose future research needs and their implementation.

The feasibility of eradication of onchocerciasis was first examined during the meeting of the International Task Force for Disease Eradication (ITFDE) in 1992, which concluded that onchocerciasis could not be eradicated, but could be controlled to a point at which it would no longer be a public health problem. An international meeting on Global Disease Elimination and Eradication as Public Health Strategies, held in Atlanta in 1998, concluded that "reconsideration" of the perceived barriers to onchocerciasis eradication "is now appropriate, given the considerable progress" in morbidity control in West Africa and the Americas. The subject of eradication was again reviewed during a WHO meeting in September 2000, where the prevailing opinion emerged that eradication of onchocerciasis in Africa was not possible with the existing tools, but evidence suggested that onchocerciasis could be eliminated in the Americas.

A second ITFDE meeting on the subject of OEPA concluded in 2001 that eliminating ocular morbidity and interrupting onchocerciasis transmission in the Americas, using currently available tools, was scientifically feasible.

The deliberations of the Atlanta Conference on the Eradicability of Onchocerciasis ('the Conference') reported herein used the definitions of terms recommended by the ITFDE and endorsed by the Dahlem Workshop on the Eradication of Infectious Diseases in 1997. Thus:

Eradication is a permanent reduction to zero of the worldwide incidence of infection caused by a specific agent as a result of deliberate efforts; intervention measures thereafter are not needed.

Elimination is reduction to zero of the incidence of infection caused by a specific agent in a defined geographic area as a result of deliberate intervention efforts; continued measures to prevent reestablishment of transmission are required.

Control is the reduction of incidence or disease manifestations to a predefined point at which public health authorities declare the condition to no longer be a public health problem. Continued measures are needed to keep transmission or morbidity at or below this point.

It was noted that another meeting held in Atlanta in 1998 on Global Disease Elimination and Eradication as Public Health Strategies recommended use of the term "regional eradication" in lieu of "elimination."

Source: The Carter Center.

PESTICIDES AND ARTIFICIAL FERTILIZERS

Pesticides are agents used to reduce or eradicate plants and animals seen as harmful to agricultural crops, domesticated animals, and human beings. Artificial fertilizers are synthetic substances added to soil to increase its productive capacity.

Pesticides fall into a number of categories. Some are naturally occurring, and others are entirely synthetic. There are organic (carbon-based) and nonorganic (non-carbon-based) pesticides, as well as biopesticides, which are organisms, such as viruses, bacteria, and fungi, that cause disease in plants and animals considered to be pests. Pesticides can also be classified by the pests they are employed to fight, including insecticides, herbicides, fungicides, acaricides (which kill mites), nematicides (nematodes, or various microscopic worms), molluscicides (snails and other mollusks), and rodenticides. There are also plant growth regulators, used not to kill unwanted plants but to control the growth of desirable plants, such as grass on a golf course or tomatoes, the latter to ensure that they do not become too soft on the vine.

Artificial fertilizers are basically divided into four categories, though these are sometimes combined, depending on which critical, plant production–increasing chemicals they provide for the soil: nitrogen, phosphorous, potassium, and trace elements.

Naturally occurring pesticides and fertilizers have been used since the beginning of agriculture and animal domestication in Neolithic times. The twentieth century and particularly the post–World War II era have seen the development and widespread adoption of synthetic fertilizers and pesticides. While the use of these agents and substances has allowed for great advances in the production of food and control of disease, it has not come without its costs, in terms of human health, wild animal and plant populations, and the wider environment. These costs have led to popular concern and action in recent decades, as well as efforts to find alternative and natural ways to eliminate pests, control disease, and boost soil productivity. Most recently, breakthroughs in genetic engineering have allowed for the development of crops that have higher resistance to pests or can more effectively utilize nutrients in the soil, allowing reductions or the more targeted use of pesticides and artificial fertilizer applications.

Why They Are Used, How They Work

Pesticides are used to do one of two things. Herbicides are widely used to eliminate unwanted plants that compete with desirable plants for nutrients, water, sunlight, space, or any of the other things plants need to survive and thrive. All other forms of pesticides—insecticides, fungicides, and so forth—are designed to destroy those disease agents or parasitic life forms that threaten the health or survival of desirable plants and animals. Artificial fertilizers are used when naturally occurring fertilizers, such as animal manure and bird guano, are unavailable in sufficient amounts.

Naturally occurring pesticides can be derived from organic sources, such as pyrethrum from chrysanthemums or sassafras, or inorganic sources, such as arsenic or mercury. Synthetic pesticides, as well as artificial fertilizers, are derived from hydrocarbon sources, such as petroleum or coal. While use of natural and artificial fertilizers is widespread in modern agriculture, most pesticides used today are synthetic. Pesticides are used in the following areas of human activity: agriculture and crop storage; animal husbandry; horticulture and landscaping; forestry; disease control; the protection of materials such as wood and fiber; and warfare, to eliminate the vegetative covering used by enemy troops for hiding.

While some inorganic compounds are still used as herbicides, they have largely been replaced by organic compounds. This is because inorganic compounds are more difficult to manipulate chemically, meaning that they are toxic to a wide spectrum of plant—and, incidentally, animal—life and are very long lasting, making them dangerous to human health and the environment. Synthetic herbicides, some of which can kill all types of plants, can also be chemically manipulated to target specific pests, though many are also known as broad-spectrum herbicides. Such herbicides fall into two basic categories: pre-emergent and post-emergent, the former applied to soils before the crop is sowed or emerges and the latter to plants that have emerged. Herbicides are also classified as contact or systemic. As its name implies, the former kills undesirable plants on contact. These forms of herbicide are fast acting and work best on annuals. Systemic herbicides are taken in by the plant, which is poisoned as a result, usually by means of inhibiting the necessary biological functioning of proteins, amino acids, and hormones in the plant. Contact herbicides, by definition, must be applied at the post-emergent phase of the plant needing protection, while systemic herbicides can be applied before planting or at any stage in the growth cycle of the plant. Contact herbicides are usually applied by mixing with water and spraying, either by air or ground. Systemic herbicides may be applied in that fashion or by injections into the soil or mixing with fertilizer. Meanwhile, plant regulators substitute for or mimic the various hormones that regulate the growth of the plant.

As with herbicides, insecticides, nematicides, acaricides, and molluscicides work in different ways. They can be applied at any stage of the pest's life cycle or the life cycle of the plant or animal that is being protected. Some are contact and others are systemic, the latter being taken up by the animal as it eats a crop, or another form of food in the vicinity of the crop, or preys upon a domesticated animal. All insecticides and other substances used to reduce or eradicate animal pests work by interfering with the biological functions of the pest organism. Thiocyanate agents and carbamites, for example, disrupt enzyme systems, while organochlorines affect the transmission of nerve impulses.

As for artificial fertilizers, they perform the same function as natural fertilizers, in that they provide supplementary nutrition to the soil, which is required for healthy plant growth.

History

With the rise of agriculture at the beginning of the Neolithic era, some 10,000–12,000 years ago, came the need to supplement the soil and eliminate pests of various types. This is because agriculture involves the intense utilization of a given area of land, often taxing the soil's capacity to provide nutrients. And because farming concentrates certain forms of plants in a given area, it heightens the propensity for infestation by pests that prey upon such plants.

Pre-Synthetic Era

The earliest forms of fertilization were passive ones; that is, early farmers recognized that if they left certain fields fallow, allowing plants to repopulate such land, the soil would be replenished. More active to the process was the burning of such natural vegetation as part of this cycle, which often provided necessary nutrients in the form of ash. With the beginnings of the domestication of large animals, such as cattle and horses, came the recognition that manure increased crop yields and lessened the time required to leave fields fallow. Human feces were also used for the same purpose but were in much more limited supply, as most animal-raising societies have far more animals than people and because large domesticated animals produce larger quantities of manure.

But most manure has two related drawbacks as fertilizer. First, it mostly consists of water, making it very heavy. Second, much of the nitrogen in manure, particularly in mammals, comes in the form of ammonia, a volatile substance that evaporates within hours. Both of these factors limited the ability to transport fertilizer from where it was produced to where it was needed. Global exploration from the sixteenth century onward revealed vast and unexploited sources of guano, largely the excrement of seabirds, which is lower in water content and particularly rich in phosphorous and nitrogen. With the development of more effective forms of sea transport in the nineteenth century came the capacity to exploit these far-flung sources, and a huge industry sprang up to extract guano and transport it to agricultural regions in the industrializing countries and their colonial possessions.

While manure-based fertilizers have been widely used throughout history, pesticides were in limited use until the development of a modern chemical industry allowed the synthesis of compounds capable of

Consumption of Pesticides, Selected Countries

	Year (latest data available)	Consumption (thousands of metric tons)	Grams per inhabitant
High-income countries			
Belgium	2003	179.2	17
Czech Republic	2008	19.5	2
Germany	2008	162.5	2
Korea, South	2008	97.2	20
Spain	2008	137.3	3
Middle-income countries			
Brazil	2003	938.6	5
Chile	2008	18.7	1
China	2008	657.8	0.4
Iran	2008	21.9	0.3
Mexico	2008	62.0	0.6
Low-income countries			
Bangladesh	2003	3.8	negligible
Kenya	2008	0.52	negligible
Mozambique	2005	0.05	negligible
Tanzania	2008	1.7	negligible
Vietnam	2007	71.3	0.8

Source: United Nations.

acting as pesticides. For the most part, pesticide use took the form of allelopathy, the planting of certain organisms, such as black walnuts, sagebrush, and sunflowers, in close proximity to crops, so that the biochemicals produced by the former, and which were harmful or distasteful to pests that infested the latter, could operate effectively. Early on there also came the recognition that certain inorganic substances, such as arsenic, lead, and copper, could be used to poison weeds, although for the most part, the elimination of undesirable plants was largely a manual or mechanical activity. The first derived organic insecticides, such as rotenone from the derris plant, were developed in the nineteenth century. The nineteenth century also saw a dramatically increased understanding of chemistry and the beginnings of a major chemical industry, particularly in Germany and the United States.

Rise of Synthetic Pesticides and Fertilizers

The rise of modern pesticides and artificial fertilizers, however, dates from the first half of the twentieth century and particularly from World War II. With so many agriculturalists and agricultural regions sidelined by the conflict, the need arose to vastly increase agricultural production. In addition, the war, particularly in the tropical Pacific, created the need to control pathogen-transporting insects, such as mosquitoes. After the war, the various fertilizers and pesticides developed by industry, under contract with the government, were quickly adapted for civilian use.

Uses of both increased dramatically in the decades following the war. From virtually zero at the beginning of World War II, pesticide use has grown to more than 5 billion pounds (2 billion kilograms) annually by the late 2000s. The single heaviest national user of pesticides during this entire period has been the United States, the world's largest commercial agricultural nation and its largest exporter of agricultural crops. In 2008, the United States consumed just over 20 percent of the world's pesticides. Globally, herbicides are the most widely used pesticide, composing 40 percent of the market, with insecticides making up an additional 20 percent and fungicides 10 percent. Meanwhile, artificial fertilizer use boomed as well. From virtually zero right after World War II, consumption reached over 110 million tons (100 million metric tons) annually by the late 1970s; in 2008, the world consumed over 176 million tons (160 million metric tons), or more than 50 pounds (25 kilograms) per human on Earth.

The use of these synthetic substances had a number of benefits. The widespread use of insecticides, for example, essentially eliminated mosquito-borne

World Consumption of Major Fertilizer Types,*
1980–2009

Year	Consumption (metric tons)
1980	116,719,610
1990	137,829,315
2000	135,198,144
2005	158,717,716
2008	161,829,194

* Nitrogen, phosphates, potassium.
Source: UN Food and Agriculture Organization.

diseases, such as malaria, in much of the developed and parts of the developing worlds. But the most important gains were made in agriculture, in both the developed and developing worlds, the latter a result of the so-called Green Revolution from the 1960s onward, in which new farming technologies and more highly productive varieties of crop were specifically created to meet the demands of agriculture in the poorer nations of the tropics. Many of the new varieties could achieve their enormous productivity only through the application of large quantities of artificial fertilizer and pesticides, the latter especially necessary because many of these new crop varieties sacrificed natural defense mechanisms against infestation for higher yields.

Globally, and especially in the developing world, food production skyrocketed as a result, which, along with improved transportation to get crops to the people who consumed them, effectively eliminated the age-old scourge of famine by the end of the twentieth century, outside of certain regions of Africa. To take one key crop, world rice production roughly tripled from just over 243 million tons (220 million metric tons) in 1960 to just over 728 million tons (660 million metric tons) in 2008, or from 156 pounds (71 kilograms) per person to 210 pounds (95 kilograms), most of the growth coming in the developing world.

Negative Effects

It did not take long for people to realize that the widespread use of pesticides also had negative repercussions. (Similar realizations about the dangers of artificial fertilizers came more belatedly.) Among the most successful of the new chemical pesticide classes developed during the 1930s and 1940s were the diphenyl aliphatics, a form of organochlorine insecticide, the best known of which was dichlorodi-

phenyltrichloroethane, usually referred to as DDT. Inexpensive to manufacture and highly stable chemically, it was widely used in agriculture and in the control of mosquitoes and other disease-carrying insects from 1940 onward.

By the late 1950s, however, it was becoming increasingly clear to many scientists that those attributes that made DDT so effective—that is, its toxic effect on insect nervous systems and its persistence in the environment—were double-edged swords. First, its lethality affected not only harmful insect populations but also beneficial ones, specifically those that fed off other insects or those needed in pollination. At the same time, its persistence meant that it accumulated in larger quantities as it went up the food chain; that is, those animals that ate bugs showed higher levels of DDT in their systems and those animals that ate bug-eating animals had higher levels still. In particular, it was noted that certain birds of prey, including the very symbol of American sovereignty, the bald eagle, were accumulating so much in their systems that they could not reproduce young effectively—DDT made for paper-thin eggshells that were easily broken—thereby threatening the species with extinction. The 1962 publication of the best seller *Silent Spring* by American conservationist Rachel Carson brought the subject to widespread public attention and is credited as a major factor in the birth of the modern environmental movement.

Other scientists and activists pointed out the dangers posed by pesticides to the farmworkers who applied them to crops or were exposed to them in large amounts in the course of their labor. Along with wages, pesticide toxicity was one of the key grievances that inspired the farmworkers' movement in the United States in the 1960s and similar movements around the world since. Although exposed to far smaller amounts, the consuming public also grew concerned about the health implications of pesticide residues on food and in groundwater, and their role in rising cancer rates in the postwar era.

Meanwhile, the use of artificial fertilizer also began alarming scientists and environmentalists around the world. Beginning in the 1980s, analyses of waters in the Gulf of Mexico near the Mississippi Delta revealed depleted levels of oxygen, a condition known as hypoxia, resulting in the mass die-offs of fish and other marine organisms and creating what became known as the Gulf Dead Zone. By 2008, a UN Environment Programme study had revealed more than 400 dead zones around the world, including the largest, a 27,000-square-mile (70,000-square-kilometer) area in the Baltic Sea of

Post–World War II Pesticides Determined to Be Hazardous by the World Health Organization

Active ingredient	Type and how used	WHO classification	Health and environmental effects
Aldicarb	Carbamite; used on citrus, peanuts, vegetables	Extremely hazardous	Highly toxic to workers and wildlife
Aldrin	Organochlorine insecticide	Highly hazardous; widely banned for agricultural use	Potentially cancerous, affects reproductive system
Chlordane	Organochlorine insecticide used on crops and termites	Moderately hazardous	Persistent in environment
Chlordimeform	Insecticide once used on cotton	Moderately hazardous; banned	Potentially cancerous
DBCP	Fumigant and insecticide	Extremely hazardous	Potentially cancerous, causes sterility, contaminates groundwater
DDT	Organophosphate insecticide now used on mosquitoes	Highly hazardous, widely banned for agriculture	Negative effects on health and environment
Dieldrin	Organochlorine insecticide used on fruit, soil, seeds	Highly hazardous; widely banned for agricultural use	Birth defects, cancers, serious environmental impact
Endrin	Organochlorine insecticide	Highly hazardous	Toxic to fish, bees, wildlife
Heptachlor	Organochlorine insecticide used for soil, pests, mosquitoes, fire ants	Moderately hazardous; widely banned for agricultural use	Persistent in environment, causes cancer in mice
Hexachlorobenzene	Organochlorine fungicide widely used in past	Extremely hazardous	Adverse effects on humans and environment
Lindane	Insecticide used in agriculture and to treat head lice	Moderately hazardous; banned in a few countries	Persistent in environment, with cancerous, endocrine-disrupting effects in humans and animals
Paraquat	Organophosphate insecticide used on citrus, cotton, other crops	Extremely hazardous	Poisonous in small quantities
Parathion-Methyl	Organophosphate insecticide	Extremely hazardous	Poisonous in small quantities
Pentachlorophenol	Fungicide used on cereals, mushrooms	Extremely hazardous	Toxic; dangerous to fish
Toxaphene	Insecticide used on cattle, grain, fruit, vegetables	Moderately hazardous; banned	Extremely toxic to fish, harmful to other animals
2,4,5,T	Phenoxyacetic acid herbicide	Moderately hazardous; banned	Harmful to fish, humans, environment

Source: World Health Organization.

northern Europe. The cause of these dead zones is the growth of certain oxygen-consuming one-celled organisms, which feed on the nitrogen and phosphorous of artificial fertilizers washed down to the sea in rivers.

Responses

Farmers, farmworkers, industry, governments, and the public at large have taken a number of measures to reduce the impact of pesticide and artificial fertilizer use on human health, wild plant and animal populations, and the environment generally.

One such measure has been the spread of organic farming, which, to meet both governmental standards and public expectations, must be undertaken without the use of synthetic pesticides and fertilizers. Globally, by 2009, 0.84 percent of the world's 5.3 million square miles (13.7 million square kilometers) of arable land was being farmed organically, though the figure varied widely between the developed and developing worlds.

Although organic and traditional farming are growing trends, the United States remains the world's largest consumer of synthetic pesticides, accounting for 20 percent. The Rotterdam Convention of 1998 set standards for global trade in hazardous chemicals. *(Yasuyoshi Chiba/ AFP/Getty Images)*

For Europe, the figure was 1.9 percent; for Africa, it was 0.1 percent.

Far more widespread has been the adoption of traditional farming methods that require less use of pesticides. So-called integrated pest management methods include four key components: (1) the planting of crop varieties that are more resistant to pest infestation or that can thrive in the presence of more weeds; (2) the use of new types of pesticides that have short lifespans or that biodegrade; (3) the use of hormones that interfere with the life or reproduction cycles of pests; (4) the release of sterile insects, with which fertile insects cannot breed; and (5) the modification of farming practices. This latter category includes mixing crops to prevent infestation by pests attracted to one variety, altering water usage and amount, and crop rotation. These methods not only lessen the impact of pesticide use on the environment, farmworkers, and the consuming public, but also they save farmers money, since they require reduced amounts of often expensive pesticides. At the same time, they require extensive education and training for the farmers and those who work for them.

Finally, the relatively new science of genetics and techniques employing genetic engineering and modification are having a growing impact on farming methods and are likely to alter the way artificial fertilizers and pesticides are used into the future. Among the earliest and most successful of the trends has been the adoption of transgenic Bt crops, such as Bt cotton. "Bt" refers to the bacterium *Bacillus thuringiensis*, which produces a toxin deadly to certain pests, such as the bollworm, long the scourge of cotton farmers. For decades, solutions containing Bt were sprayed on crops as a pesticide. Beginning in the 1990s, scientists began genetically reengineering cotton with those elements of Bt that produce the toxin, making the plant itself toxic to the bollworm. Other crops, such as soya beans, have been modified to thrive on fewer nutrients. Because they have higher resistance to pests or require fewer nutrients, say advocates, the planting of Bt and other genetically modified (GM) crops allows for less use of pesticides and artificial fertilizers. But critics point to an opposite trend. Some GM crops, they note, are designed to be resistant to certain herbicides, allowing the latter to be used in larger amounts. Beginning in the 1990s, the chemical giant Monsanto began to introduce a variety of GM crops that it called Roundup Ready crops because they were highly resistant to the company's patented wide-spectrum herbicide Roundup.

More generally, the use of GM crops presents several problems going into the future. One is their capacity to breed with nearby organic crops, thereby spoiling the latter's claims to being "natural," a major selling point that enhances their value. Second, advocates for agriculturalists, particularly in the developing world, worry that farmers will become too reliant on GM seeds, leaving them at the mercy of the multinational corporations that own the patents on these seeds and can then set higher prices. And, finally, there are unknown environmental consequences. Just as early adopters of pesticides such as DDT were unaware of its environmental consequences, particularly its negative impact on beneficial insect populations, so today's adopters of GM crops may be sowing the seeds, as it were, of environmental catastrophes to come. Such talk of unknown consequences has met with differing receptions in various parts of the world. In the European Union, it has led to widespread rejection of—and bans on—GM crops and even food products that contain GM crops from elsewhere. In the United States, on the other hand, GM crops have been widely accepted, a trend that appears to be being followed in those areas of the developing world that can afford such crops.

James Ciment

See also: Biodiversity and Extinction; Environmental Illnesses; Farm Policy; Fishing and Fish Stocks; Genetically Engineered Crops and Foods; Mosquito-borne Disease; Parasitic Disease; Pollution, Water.

Further Reading

Carson, Rachel. *Silent Spring.* Boston: Houghton Mifflin, 1962.

Hond, Frank den, Peter Groenewegen, and Nico M. van Straalen, eds. *Pesticides: Problems, Improvements, Alternatives.* Malden, MA: Blackwell Science, 2003.

Horlick-Jones, Tom, et al. *The GM Debate: Risk, Politics, and Public Engagement.* New York: Routledge, 2007.

Kendall, Ronald J., Thomas E. Lacher, George C. Cobb, and Stephen Boyd Cox, eds. *Wildlife Toxicology: Emerging Contaminant and Biodiversity Issues.* Boca Raton, FL: CRC, 2010.

Levine, Marvin J. *Pesticides: A Toxic Time Bomb in Our Midst.* Westport, CT: Praeger, 2007.

Matthews, G.A. *Pesticides: Health, Safety and the Environment.* Ames, IA: Blackwell, 2006.

Sideris, Lisa H., and Kathleen Dean, eds. *Rachel Carson: Legacy and Challenge.* Albany: State University of New York Press, 2008.

Wargo, John. *Green Intelligence: Creating Environments That Protect Human Health.* New Haven, CT: Yale University Press, 2009.

Wheeler, Willis B. *Pesticides in Agriculture and the Environment.* New York: Marcel Dekker, 2002.

Web Sites

International Council of Chemistry Associations: www.icca-chem.org

Pesticide Action Network: www.panna.org

UN Environmental Programme: www.unep.org/hazardoussubstances/UNEPsWork/Pesticides/tabid/298/Default.aspx

UN Food and Agriculture Organization: www.fao.gov

U.S. Environmental Protection Agency: www.epa.gov/pesticides

Documents

Document 1: Rotterdam Convention on the Prior Informed Consent Procedure for Certain Hazardous Chemicals and Pesticides in International Trade, 1998

Signed in 1998 and taking effect in 2004, the Rotterdam Convention is an international treaty promoting standards in the trade of hazardous chemicals, including pesticides and the component agents of pesticides. By signing the treaty, chemical-exporting states agreed to provide—or enforce measures to make companies operating under their jurisdiction provide—more information to importers and to improve the labeling of hazardous chemicals, including the provision of more effective handling instructions. The treaty came about in response to concerns that the developed nations that dominate the international chemical industry were shipping dangerous pesticides and other hazardous chemicals, already banned at home, to poor countries.

www.pic.int/TheConvention/Overview/Textofthe
Convention/tabid/1048/language/en-US/Default.aspx

Source: UN Rotterdam Convention.

Document 2: *Chemical Trespass: Pesticides in Our Bodies and Corporate Accountability,* Pesticide Action Network, 2004

Published by the Pesticide Action Network, an activist organization critical of synthetic pesticides and the chemical industry that manufactures and markets them, the 2004 report Chemical Trespass *offers a relatively objective synthesis of findings about pesticides and human health from the Centers for Disease Control. The report concludes that the dangers inherent in the use of chemical pesticides make it important for farmers and the food industry to move to "sustainable" agricultural methods that eschew "bioaccumulative and pervasive pesticides found in people's bodies."*

www.panna.org/issues/publication/chemical-tresspass-english

Source: Pesticide Action Network.

PHARMACEUTICALS: AVAILABILITY, COST, EFFICACY, AND SAFETY

Pharmaceuticals are chemical compounds manufactured for use as medicine. Their molecular structure can be based on naturally occurring compounds, entirely synthetic compounds, or a combination of the two.

Pharmaceuticals are of ancient origin, with pharmacologies, or lists of medical compounds, dating back to the beginnings of recorded history. Modern pharmaceuticals date largely to the late nineteenth century, a result of advances in the fields of medicine and chemistry.

The main issues associated with pharmaceuticals today can be divided into two general categories: medical and economic. The former concerns the efficacy and safety of pharmaceuticals; the latter revolves around their availability and cost.

In the future, pharmaceuticals are likely to be an even more important part of health-care professionals' arsenal against chronic and communicable diseases and medical conditions, though cost and availability problems are likely to remain acute, especially in the developing world.

History

People have employed pharmacological substances, usually found in plants, since prehistoric times, as archaeologists analyzing the preserved bodies of prehistoric people have discovered. With the rise of civilization came specialized pharmacologists, often priests or other religious figures, and written pharmacologies (lists of compounds and naturally occurring medicines), or *materia medica*, as they were once known. Such listings have been found from before the Common Era in ancient Egypt, India, Mesopotamia, China, and elsewhere. Non- and preliterate peoples also developed their own pharmacologies, which were passed on orally.

The Western pharmacological tradition begins with ancient Greece, though pharmacologists there often borrowed from Egypt. The first-century C.E. physician and botanist Pedanius Dioscorides compiled much of this into a five-volume pharmacological encyclopedia, which became the basis for European pharmacology through the Middle Ages. Also building upon the Greek tradition—but adding many new compounds of their own as well as new methods of delivering them, such as the syringe and various kinds of liquid elixirs—were the pharmacologists of the medieval Arab world. Indeed, it was Greco-Arab tradition that dominated European pharmacological traditions through the Renaissance and into the Enlightenment.

Regardless of the place or era, virtually all traditional pharmacologies were based on the notion that all people possessed essential energies and elements and that when they fell out of balance, disease ensued. In the Western tradition, the force, known as the "vital force," was affected by the four elements of the body, each corresponding to one of the essential elements of creation: blood, which was associated with air; black bile, or earth; yellow bile, or fire; and phlegm, or water. Pharmacological substances, which contained the vital force of the plants or animal parts from which they were derived, were then used, internally or externally, to rectify that imbalance.

Only in the nineteenth century did this millennia-old understanding give way to more modern notions of how the human body works and how pharmacological substances affect it. Of critical importance was the synthesis of effective drugs from inorganic sources, which finally proved that there was no vital force at work in pharmacology. By the late nineteenth and the early twentieth century, pharmacological scientists—by then, a distinct specialty—in Europe and North America were synthesizing numerous drugs. An understanding of genetics had advanced the development of new pharmacological substances by the late twentieth century even as ever more powerful computers allowed for the processing of the enormous quantities of data made possible by genetic sequencing. Because of such breakthroughs in genetics and biotechnology, previous approaches, which usually involved finding the active ingredient in traditional plant-based remedies, were replaced with an analysis of metabolic pathways and how certain molecules affected them.

Meanwhile, efforts were made to ensure the safety and efficacy of these drugs. Beginning with the United States in 1906, most major industrialized countries established regulations and agencies to prohibit dangerous drugs, ensure that drugs were not adulterated with harmful substances, and provide information to consumers and health-care providers about the ingredients in drugs and their proper dosage. Such regulations—rules about providing information on contraindications with other drugs and possible side effects were added later—helped to turn a business that was often populated with charlatans and peddling questionable patent medicines into a professional industry dominated by large companies, accredited professionals, and scientifically researched and tested drugs.

Costs and Availability

Much about the cost and availability of drugs is subject to dispute between the pharmaceutical industry and its many critics. One thing beyond dispute is that drug research and development are becoming more expensive and time consuming, as the easily discovered compounds have already been found, leaving only the more complex ones. Aside from the high cost of facilities, equipment, and professionals required, there is a high risk. It is estimated that roughly one in 5,000 to 10,000 compounds developed by pharmaceutical companies—sometimes after much time and money have been expended—ends up as a marketable drug, usually after a period of seven to 10 years. Although estimates vary widely, the new drug typically costs about $1.4 billion to develop.

Estimated Average Cost of Developing a New Drug, United States, 1975–2010

Year	Cost (constant 2010 dollars, in millions)
1975	175
1987	400
2000	1,000
2010	1,400

Source: PhRMA.

Cost of Standard Antiretroviral Fixed Dose Combination for AIDS Treatment, Pre-Generic Availability and Post-Generic Availability (U.S. dollars, not adjusted for inflation)

Pre-generic availability, 2001	Post-generic availability, 2011
$10,000	$87

Source: Médecins sans Frontières/Doctors Without Borders.

Pharmaceutical companies claim that this is why new drugs are so expensive and why rigorous patent protections need to be enforced internationally. That means investigating and prosecuting illegal producers of patented drugs—a major problem in some developing countries, such as India—but also legitimate companies, many of them in Brazil and India as well, that seek to make generic versions of drugs available at a far lower cost. Without that protection, the industry argues, research into new life-saving drugs cannot be done. As the industry also points out, as expensive as new drugs are, they are still competitively priced, in the sense that many provide treatment for conditions that once required far more costly surgery, hospital care, and convalescence.

Critics of the commercial pharmaceutical industry break down into two groups. Some argue that life-saving drugs are too important to people's health to leave to profit-making corporations. Thus, patent restrictions that drive up costs—particularly for people in developing countries, with life-threatening conditions such as AIDS—should not take precedence over providing low-cost drugs. Others argue that prescription drug companies overstate publicly what research and development really cost them as a proportion of revenue and that, in fact, they spend far more on promoting profitable drugs in developed countries or paying hefty dividends to stockholders and pay to executives. It is indisputably the case that pharmaceutical companies are some of the most profitable corporations of any sector of the economy.

Estimated Promotional Costs vs. Research and Development Costs, Percentage of Sales, U.S. Pharmaceutical Companies

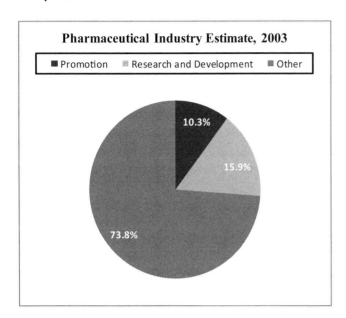

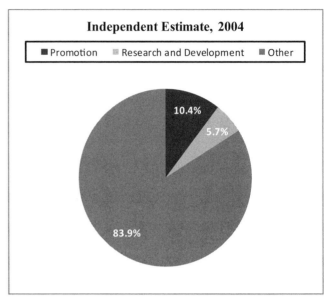

Source: "The Cost of Pushing Pills: A New Estimate of Pharmaceutical Promotion Expenditures in the United States," PLoS Medicine, January 3, 2008; PhRMA.

Aside from costs, the issue of availability also relates to what kinds of drugs pharmaceutical companies develop—that is, vaccines to prevent the spread of communicable diseases prevalent in developing countries or drugs to treat medical conditions affecting people in developed countries. The pharmaceutical industry claims that it invests heavily in vaccines, even though they are often marketed at a loss. Critics argue that the industry spends too much of its resources on profitable "lifestyle pharmaceuticals" for people in wealthy countries, such as those for erectile dysfunction or mild depression, or on developing "me-too" drugs, that is, pharmaceuticals that mimic successful ones already on the market with just enough molecular adjustment to avoid patent conflicts. They also argue that drug companies spend too much money adjusting existing drugs and then heavily marketing the new drugs as far more improved than they really are, in the interest of extending patents. Drug companies insist that the improvements are real and that innovation comes not from new blockbusters but from steady improvements in existing drugs.

Although it does not influence cost directly, another aspect of pharmaceutical industry practice significantly affects people in developing countries. As noted earlier, biotechnology and genetic sequencing have allowed companies to phase out earlier approaches based on synthesizing plant-based rem-

edies. This method continues, however, often taking advantage of the rich potential pharmacopeia of tropical forests and the traditions of the indigenous people who live there. Many advocates for indigenous peoples contend that drug companies fail to pay adequate—or sometimes any—compensation for the profitable drugs that they synthesize from tropical plants. The drug companies defend what they pay, or do not pay, indigenous peoples and their governments with two arguments: first, the plants are in the public domain, so any payments made are purely out of altruism; and, second, the companies themselves spend enormous amounts of money to convert such plants and remedies into safe and effective pharmaceuticals and so deserve the lion's share of revenues from them.

Safety and Efficacy

Testing for the safety and efficacy of new drugs is a major part of the expense of developing a new drug. Testing usually begins under laboratory conditions, such as when a potential new antibiotic is tested against bacteria grown in cultures. In more recent years, computer simulations also are used to determine effectiveness. If a compound proves effective, it is then given to test animals, to reaffirm its efficacy and confirm that it is safe. A new drug is then approved for clinical trials only after regulatory officials determine that, compared with existing drugs, it is likely to be more therapeutic, safer, or both. Clinical trials follow, in several stages, first with healthy test subjects to determine dosage levels and monitor for side effects and then with successively larger groups of subjects who suffer from the disease or condition that the drug is meant to treat.

Despite the rigorous testing and elaborate regulatory environment that have developed around drug manufacturing and marketing since the early twentieth century, dangerous pharmaceuticals have been marketed from time to time. In the late 1950s, for example, Thalidomide, a sedative given to pregnant women to treat morning sickness—approved by drug regulatory agencies throughout Europe, though not in the United States—was later found to have caused serious birth defects in thousands of babies. In response, many agencies around the world instituted new rules requiring trials for safety during pregnancy before granting approval to market a drug.

A more recent high-profile case arose regarding the anti-inflammatory arthritis drug rofecoxib, better known by its main brand name, Vioxx. Approved in the United States in 1999, the drug was withdrawn in 2004 after it became associated with a variety of cardiovascular events among people taking it. In the many lawsuits related to use of the drug—including class-action suits on behalf of thousands of litigants—numerous failures in the testing and regulatory phases of the drug's development were cited, including

that the drug had failed to prove it was a significant improvement on existing—and, thus, theoretically safer—drugs.

Without discounting the suffering caused by these examples of insufficient testing and regulation, it should be said that such drugs nevertheless affect relatively small numbers of people. Far more dangerous, say experts, are two other issues affecting the pharmaceutical industry in recent decades. The first is the manufacturing and distribution of counterfeit drugs. According to the World Customs Organization, about $200 billion of the world's $900 billion in pharmaceutical sales, or 22 percent, are of counterfeits, about 75 percent of which come from India, home to the world's largest generic drug industry. Although these drugs might be considered counterfeits legally, not all of them are actually fakes; that is, while not produced under patents, they nevertheless are chemically identical to those which are produced legally under patents. Still, the fakes are numerous enough that millions of people not only lose their money buying them but also risk their health and even life when the dosages prove incorrect, the compounds contain dangerous adulterants, or the drugs simply prove worthless in fighting a serious disease or treating an acute medical condition.

The second safety and efficacy problem relates to corruption, particularly in developing countries. It comes in many forms. For example, pharmaceutical manufacturers or marketers might bribe officials to purchase a particular drug for a government

HIV/AIDS patients in India protest a law that would prohibit the generic manufacture of patented drugs, which would drive up prices. The lack of patent protection helped make India's pharmaceutical industry one of the world's largest by keeping down production costs. (Raveendran/AFP/ Getty Images)

pharmacy program even though better or cheaper equivalents are available. Or it might simply take the form of officials stealing drugs in order to sell them for personal profit. In either case, government health budgets in developing countries, which are usually small, being measured on a per capita basis, are wasted or misspent, depriving citizens of needed drugs or medical care.

The Future

The same issues that have confronted the pharmaceutical industry in recent years, and the vast majority of the people who rely on its products—or potentially could rely on them—are likely to continue: high development costs, availability problems, safety and efficacy concerns, and counterfeiting and corruption problems.

At the same time, observers point to some hopeful signs as well. Although high development costs are unlikely to abate, what they pay for is likely to improve, as further advances in biotechnology promise not only better and safer pharmaceuticals but also ones targeted for unique genetic profiles. Such benefits are likely to accrue to wealthy countries and the affluent in poorer countries. But for the countries and people who are less well-off, the burgeoning pharmaceutical industry in developing countries promises at least to offer less-expensive generics.

James Ciment

See also: Drug Resistance; Food and Drug Safety; Health Care; Public Health; Vaccination.

Further Reading

Attaran, Amir, and Brigitte Granville. *Delivering Essential Medicines.* Washington, DC: Brookings Institution, 2004.

Burch, Druin. *Taking the Medicine: A Short History of Medicine's Beautiful Idea and Our Difficulty Swallowing It.* London: Vintage, 2010.

Burger, Alfred. *Drugs and People: Medications, Their History and Origins, and the Way They Act.* Charlottesville: University of Virginia Press, 1988.

Cox, Stan. *Sick Planet: Corporate Food and Medicine.* Ann Arbor, MI: Pluto, 2008.

Liska, Ken. *Drugs and the Human Body: With Implications for Society.* 8th ed. Upper Saddle River, NJ: Pearson Prentice Hall, 2009.

Quirke, Viviane, and Judy Slinn, eds. *Perspectives on Twentieth-Century Pharmaceuticals.* New York: Peter Lang, 2009.

Weatherall, M. *In Search of a Cure: A History of Pharmaceutical Discovery.* New York: Oxford University Press, 1990.

Williams, Simon J., Jonathan Gabe, and Peter Davis, eds. *Pharmaceuticals and Society: Critical Discourses and Debates.* Malden, MA: Wiley-Blackwell, 2009.

Web Sites

Health Action International: www.haiweb.org
Medecins sans Frontieres/Doctors Without Borders: www.msf.org
U.S. Food and Drug Administration: www.fda.gov
World Health Organization, Pharmaceutical Products: www.who.int/topics/pharmaceutical_products/en/

Documents

Document 1: Pure Food and Drug Act, United States (excerpt), 1906

The U.S. Pure Food and Drug Act, signed into law in 1906, was one of the first efforts by any country to regulate the safety and efficacy of commercially sold drugs. (As its name implies, the law also regulated foods.) Until this legislation, purveyors of pharmaceuticals were not required to label the ingredients that went into their medications or to tell the consumer the proper dosage to be taken. In addition, the law laid the foundation for the Food and Drug Administration, among the first government agencies in the world created to regulate the manufacture and distribution of pharmaceuticals.

Section 3. That the Secretary of the Treasury, the Secretary of Agriculture, and the Secretary of Commerce and Labor shall make uniform rules and regulations for carrying out the provisions of this Act, including the collection and examination of specimens of foods and drugs manufactured or offered for sale in the District of Columbia, or in any Territory of the United States, or which shall be offered for sale in unbroken packages in any State other than that in which they shall have been respectively manufactured or produced, or which shall be received from any foreign country, or intended for shipment to any foreign country, or which may be submitted for examination by the chief health, food, or drug officer of any State, Territory, or the District of Columbia, or at any domestic or foreign port through which such product is offered for interstate commerce, or for export or import between the United States and any foreign port or country.

Section 4. That the examinations of specimens of foods and drugs shall be made in the Bureau of Chemistry of the Department of Agriculture, or under the direction and supervision of such Bureau, for the purpose of determining from such examinations whether such articles are adulterated or misbranded within the meaning of this Act; and if it shall appear from any such examination that any of such specimens is adulterated or misbranded within the meaning of this Act, the Secretary of Agriculture shall cause notice thereof to be given to the party from whom such sample was obtained. Any party so notified shall be given an opportunity to be heard, under such rules and regulations as may be prescribed as aforesaid, and if it appears that any of the provisions of this Act have been violated by such party, then the Secretary of Agriculture shall at once certify the facts to the proper United States district attorney, with a copy of the results of the analysis or the examination of such article duly authenticated by the analyst or officer making such examination, under the oath of such officer. After judgment of the court, notice shall be given by publication in such manner as may be prescribed by the rules and regulations aforesaid.

Section 5. That it shall be the duty of each district attorney to whom the Secretary of Agriculture shall report any violation of this Act, or to whom any health or food or drug officer or agent of any State, Territory, or the District of Columbia shall present satisfactory evidence of any such violation, to cause appropriate proceedings to be commenced and prosecuted in the proper courts of the United States, without delay, for the enforcement of the penalties as in such case herein provided.

Section 6. That the term "drug," as used in this Act, shall include all medicines and preparations recognized in the United States Pharmacopoeia or National Formulary for internal or external use, and any substance or mixture of substances intended to be used for the cure, mitigation, or prevention of disease of either man or other animals. The term "food," as used herein, shall include all articles used for food, drink, confectionery, or condiment by man or other animals, whether simple, mixed, or compound.

Section 7. That for the purposes of this Act an article shall be deemed to be adulterated:

In case of drugs:

First. If, when a drug is sold under or by a name recognized in the United States Pharmacopoeia or National Formulary, it differs from the standard of strength, quality, or purity, as determined by the test laid down in the United States Pharmacopoeia or National Formulary official at the time of investigation: Provided, That no drug defined in the United States Pharmacopoeia or National Formulary shall be deemed to be adulterated under this provision if the standard of strength, quality, or purity be plainly stated upon the bottle, box, or other container thereof although the standard may differ from that determined by the test laid down in the United States Pharmacopoeia or National Formulary.

Second. If its strength or purity fall below the professed standard or quality under which it is sold . . .

That for the purposes of this Act an article shall also be deemed to be misbranded:

In case of drugs:

First. If it be an imitation of or offered for sale under the name of another article.

Second. If the contents of the package as originally put up shall have been removed, in whole or in part, and other contents shall have been placed in such package, or if the package fail to bear a statement on the label of the quantity or proportion of any alcohol, morphine, opium, cocaine, heroin, alpha or beta eucaine, chloroform, cannabis indica, chloral hydrate, or acetanilide, or any derivative or preparation of any such substances contained therein. . . .

Section 10. That any article of food, drug, or liquor that is adulterated or misbranded within the meaning of this Act, and is being transported from one State, Territory, District, or insular possession to another for sale, or, having been transported, remains unloaded, unsold, or in original unbroken packages, or if it be sold or offered for sale in the District of Columbia or the Territories, or insular possessions of the United States, or if it be imported from a foreign country for sale, or if it is intended for export to a foreign country, shall be liable to be proceeded against in any district court of the United States within the district where the same is found, and seized for confiscation by a process of libel for condemnation. And if such article is condemned as being adulterated or misbranded, or of a poisonous or deleterious character, within the meaning of this Act, the same shall be disposed of by destruction or sale, as the said court may direct, and the proceeds thereof, if sold, less the legal costs and charges, shall be paid into the Treasury of the United States, but such goods shall not be sold in any jurisdiction contrary to the provisions of this Act or the laws of that jurisdiction: Provided, however, That upon the payment of the costs of such libel proceedings and the execution and delivery of a good and sufficient bond to the effect that such articles shall not be sold or otherwise disposed of contrary to the provisions of this Act, or the laws of any State, Territory, District, or insular possession, the court may by order direct that such articles be delivered to the owner thereof. The proceedings of such libel cases shall conform, as near as may be, to the proceedings in admiralty, except that either party may demand trial by jury of any issue of fact joined in any such case, and all such proceedings shall be at the suit of and in the name of the United States.

Section 11. The Secretary of the Treasury shall deliver to the Secretary of Agriculture, upon his request from time to time, samples of foods and drugs which are being imported into the United States or offered for import, giving notice thereof to the owner or consignee, who may appear before the Secretary of Agriculture, and have the right to introduce testimony, and if it appear from the examination of such samples that any article of food or drug offered to be imported into the United States is adulterated or misbranded within the meaning of this Act, or is otherwise dangerous to the health of the people of the United States, or is of a kind forbidden entry into, or forbidden to be sold or restricted in sale in the country in which it is made or from which it is exported, or is otherwise falsely labeled in any respect, the said article shall be refused admission, and the Secretary of the Treasury shall refuse delivery to the consignee and shall cause the destruction of any goods refused delivery which shall not be exported by the consignee within three months from the date of notice of such refusal under such regulations as the Secretary of the Treasury may prescribe: Provided, That the Secretary of the Treasury may deliver to the consignee such goods pending examination and decision in the matter on execution of a penal bond for the amount of the full invoice value of such goods, together with the duty thereon, and on refusal to return such goods for any cause to the custody of the Secretary of the Treasury, when demanded, for the purpose of excluding them from the country, or for any other purpose, said consignee shall forfeit the full amount of the bond: And provided further, That all charges for storage, cartage, and labor on goods which are refused admission or delivery shall be paid by the owner or consignee, and in default of such payment shall constitute a lien against any future importation made by such owner or consignee. . . .

Approved, June 30, 1906.

Source: U.S. Statutes at Large, 59th Cong., 1st sess., 3915: 768–772.

Document 2: A Framework for Good Governance in the Pharmaceutical Sector, World Health Organization (excerpt), 2009

As part of an overall effort by the United Nations to push for good governance in member countries, the World Health Organization in 2009 established a framework for the pharmaceutical sector, citing it as one of the largest and most critical industries in the world, as well as one with great potential for corruption. The framework, excerpted below, calls on member governments to be vigilant as to bribery, theft, extortion and other corrupt practices in the procurement, marketing, distribution and sale of pharmaceuticals.

5. The Specific Case of the Pharmaceutical Sector

Globally more than US$3 trillion is spent on health services each year. The value of the global pharmaceutical market is estimated at over US$600 billion. Such large amounts of money are an attractive target for abuse, making the pharmaceutical sector highly vulnerable to corruption and unethical practices. For instance, Transparency International estimates that 10 to 25% of public procurement spending is lost to corruption, and in some countries up to two-thirds of often scarce medicine supplies at hospitals are lost through corruption and fraud.

This is in part due to the high market value of pharmaceutical products as described above. Also, the pharmaceutical sector is highly regulated. Poorly defined and documented processes, lack of checks and balances, as well as lack of transparency will increase vulnerability to corruption. Equally, if institutional checks are too cumbersome and slow down processes, clients may be tempted to offer a bribe or a gift "to get things done." Another factor making the pharmaceutical sector particularly vulnerable to corruption is the information imbalance between the various players, such as manufacturers, regulators, health-care providers and consumers. Information is not shared equally and not all players have the necessary information to make informed judgments and independent assessments of the quality, safety and efficacy of medicines.

5.1 Types of unethical behaviour

The pharmaceutical sector is a wide and complex sector—also referred to as the 'medicines chain'—and includes many different steps, beginning with the research and development of new medicines or chemical entities and ending with the consumption of medicines by the patient and pharmacovigilance. Each step is vulnerable to corruption and involves different professional expertise, such as the medical profession (nurses, pharmacists, physicians, etc.), economists, lawyers and researchers. These can serve in governments, private pharmaceutical companies, academia, or civil society organizations.

The medicines chain includes the following steps:

1. Research and development of new medicines or chemical entities
2. Conducting clinical trials
3. Filing patents
4. Manufacturing
5. Registration
6. Price fixing
7. Licensing of professionals and establishments
8. Selection of essential medicines
9. Procurement
10. Distribution

11. Inspection of establishments
12. Prescription
13. Dispensing
14. Pharmacovigilance
15. Medicines promotion

Management of conflicts of interest

Conflicts of interest are often the motivating force generating unethical behaviour. Three types are frequently encountered in public institutions that tolerate corrupt behaviour, namely when a public servant:

- has vested personal interests in a particular company
- practices nepotism or cronyism when hiring personnel
- receives post-employment benefits from a contracted company.

When a government official or an expert serving on a government committee, for example for the registration of medicines, or the selection of essential medicines or tender committee, has a conflict of interest, he/she may put undue pressure and influence on the final decision of that committee to favour a particular company, instead of basing the decision on scientific evidence. Such practices include:

- special interest groups offering "incentives" to individuals or pressurizing public officials to include particular medicines on lists of medicines that may be procured or using misinformation to influence decision-making on procurement
- falsifying safety/efficacy data resulting from clinical trials.

Public institutions often limit their concern about unethical practices to these three forms of corrupt behaviour, by establishing policies and procedures that attempt to prevent these types of conflict of interest. Unfortunately other forms of corrupt practices exist that are sometimes ignored by public institutions, and which become part of the unofficial institutional culture. The following list represents the types of unethical behaviour that are at the heart of corruption in the management of pharmaceuticals.

Accepting or extorting bribes, kickbacks and/or gifts:

Bribery and gift giving are probably the most common forms of corruption in any sector and the pharmaceutical sector is no exception. They can be proactively offered to or extorted by public servants, for speeding up services or simply for making some services happen, for ignoring some information or the omission of other important information, or falsifying data.

Bribes or gifts can be offered at any step of the medicines chain, for example:

- Registration:
  - by suppliers to government officials to register medicines even though the required information has not been provided
  - by suppliers to government officials to speed up the process of drug registration
  - government officials will slow down registration procedures in order to pressurize suppliers into paying a bribe.
- Selection of essential medicines:
  - by suppliers to selection committee members to include the medicines they manufacture or import on the national essential medicines list.
- Inspection:
  - not including findings on medicines quality in inspection reports
  - certification of a manufacturer that is not compliant with good manufacturing practices.
- Medicines promotion:
  - offering of bribes by suppliers to government officials to approve, for example, an unethical promotion campaign or materials
  - offering of bribes by companies to government officials to gain authorization for "pseudo" clinical trials that are a cover for marketing.
- Procurement:
  - bribery of public officials by suppliers to gain a monopoly position at the tendering stage or providing procurement contracts
  - not holding accountable suppliers who fail to deliver
  - gratuitous payment made to a person for referral of business.

Other forms of corruption or unethical practices

Mismanagement of conflict of interest and bribery are unethical practices that can be found throughout the medicines chain. Other abuses in pharmaceutical systems are also reported, which are in fact more specific to some steps of the chain, including:

- Theft in the distribution chain:
  - theft of medicines for personal use or diversion for private sector resale
  - pocketing money from the sale of medicines that were supposed to be supplied free of charge.

- Collusion in procurement and price fixing:
  - collusion in bid rigging during procurement by providing vendors with confidential and privileged information relating, for example, to price.

- Favouritism:
  - officials may favour the recruitment and/or promotion of family members (nepotism) or friends (cronyism) instead of basing their decision on professional merit
  - the same favours can be applied to selecting experts on committees.

- State capture
  - as in any other sector, outside interests can "bend" pharmaceutical laws, policies and regulations to their financial benefit through corrupt transactions with public officers and politicians. These laws and regulations can be extremely detrimental to public health objectives and outcomes.

Obviously these types of corrupt behavior are not limited to the governance and management of pharmaceuticals. Unfortunately, all sectors of society are vulnerable to some degree to such unethical practices. The development of an ethical framework for the governance and management of the pharmaceutical sector may be relevant for other sectors, just as the experience gained in other sectors in addressing ethical issues may provide important inputs in the area of pharmaceuticals.

5.2 Impact on the health system and health status

As stated, the pharmaceutical sector is particularly vulnerable to corruption and unethical practices. Determining the extent of this corruption is difficult, especially at the global level but some studies reveal figures at the national level. A study carried out in 2005 in one European country revealed that up to 9.5% of national expenditures on health care are estimated to be lost due to corruption. Resources that could otherwise be used to buy medicines or recruit much-needed health professionals are wasted as a result of corruption, which reduces the availability of essential medicines and can cause prolonged illness and even deaths.

Corrupt and unethical practices in the pharmaceutical sector can have a significant impact on the health system and the health status of the population:

- a health impact as the waste of public resources reduces the government's capacity to provide good-quality essential medicines, and unsafe medical products proliferate on the market; it also leads to an increase in the irrational use of medicines
- an economic impact when large amounts of public funds are wasted. It is estimated that pharmaceutical expenditure in low-income countries amounts to 25–65% of total health-care expenditures, representing potentially major financial loss
- an image and trust impact as inefficiency and lack of transparency reduce public institutions' credibility, erode the trust of the public and donors, and lower investments in countries.

Source: World Health Organization.

PIRACY, MARITIME

A crime as ancient as maritime trade itself, piracy is generally defined as attacks on ships, and more recently aircraft, outside of national jurisdictions, for monetary gain. Better maritime security and improved governance led to piracy's decline through much of the twentieth century. Collapsed states, increased poverty, and growing maritime traffic have led to its resurgence in recent decades, particularly around Africa and in Southeast Asia. Over the centuries, states, private shippers, and the international community have taken various steps to address the problem.

Historical Background

Maritime piracy has a long history, including off the Horn of Africa and in Asian waters, where it is currently of much concern. Piracy was manifest in the Mediterranean Sea of ancient Greece and Rome, and can be found throughout later world history with the activities of Viking raiders from Scandinavia; Asian pirates who raided and pillaged for many years throughout the seas of East Asia; the Barbary corsairs, the "enemies of God and Man" who terrorized parts of the Mediterranean from the sixteenth to the nineteenth century; and the infamous pirates of the Caribbean in the seventeenth and eighteenth centuries, who preyed upon the Spanish ships conveying precious metals from the Americas to Europe.

Many stories of heroism in the U.S. Navy and Marine Corps have their origins in American operations against the Barbary pirates, who attacked American and other ships from bases in North Africa in the late eighteenth and the early nineteenth century, as reflected in the opening lines of the Marine Corps anthem:

> *From the Halls of Montezuma*
> *To the Shores of Tripoli;*
> *We fight our country's battles*
> *In the air, on land and sea . . .*

More recently, the coast of China was notorious for pirate attacks up until the mid-twentieth century, and merchant vessels working along that coast normally had barricaded bridges and physical defenses to prevent attacks similar to those now used by ships off the Horn of Africa. In Southeast Asia, the word "bogyman," meaning a frightening apparition scaring children, originated with the Bugis men, the traditional seafaring people and "pirates" from Sulawesi in the Indonesian archipelago.

Definition

The strict legal definition of "piracy" is provided in Article 101 of the 1982 UN Convention on the Law of the Sea (UNCLOS), which states:

Piracy consists of any of the following acts:

(a) any illegal acts of violence or detention, or any act of depredation, committed for private ends by the crew or the passengers of a private ship or a private aircraft, and directed:
  (i) on the high seas, against another ship or aircraft, or against persons or property on board such ship or aircraft;
  (ii) against a ship, aircraft, persons or property in a place outside the jurisdiction of any state;
(b) any act of voluntary participation in the operation of a ship or of an aircraft with knowledge of facts making it a pirate ship or aircraft;
(c) any act of inciting or intentionally facilitating an act described in sub-paragraph (a) or (b).

This definition establishes piracy as a crime subject to universal jurisdiction against which all states might take action. Key words are "high seas" and "for private ends." Any incident elsewhere than on the high seas, and in an exclusive economic zone (EEZ), is not an act of piracy, because it is under the jurisdiction of the coastal state and no other state has a right to intervene. Piracy under international law cannot occur within the territorial sea, archipelagic waters,

Somali pirates prepare a small vessel for new attacks on commercial shipping in the Gulf of Aden and Indian Ocean in 2010. Hijacking, for the purpose of extracting ransom from ship owners and insurance companies, is the usual goal of Somali pirates. *(Mohamed Dahir/AFP/Getty Images)*

or internal waters of a state—that is, the maritime zones under the full sovereignty of a coastal state. The expression "for private ends" excludes acts of terrorism from the definition of piracy, as terrorism is not normally conducted for "private ends."

Another prerequisite of piracy is that two ships (or aircraft) need be present. If the piratical act is committed by the crew, passengers, or even stowaways of one ship or aircraft against that same ship or aircraft, then it is not piracy under international law. Such an act remains under the jurisdiction of the flag state of the vessel.

To overcome the limitation of the narrow definition of "piracy" under international law, the International Maritime Organization (IMO) and the International Maritime Bureau (IMB) have introduced a separate definition for "armed robbery against ships." This means "any illegal act of violence or detention, or any act of depredation, or threat thereof, other than an act of piracy, committed for private ends and di-

rected against a ship or against persons or property onboard such a ship, within a State's internal waters, archipelagic waters and territorial sea; or any act of inciting or of intentionally facilitating an act described above."

This definition includes not only acts against vessels during passage, but also acts against vessels in port or at anchor, and regardless of whether they are inside or outside territorial waters when attacked. It has no weight in international law. Piracy and armed robbery against ships are really separate crimes: piracy occurs on the high seas, whereas armed robbery against ships occurs only elsewhere, in the territorial sea, in port, or in an anchorage.

The strict definition of "piracy" exists in law to establish piracy as a universal crime against which all states may take action. Crimes such as armed robbery, mutiny, and other acts of violence onboard ship remain under the jurisdiction of the flag state or coastal state as appropriate.

Causes

The prime causes of piracy lie in the lack of economic opportunity, employment, and good governance onshore. Many contemporary pirates and sea robbers come from coastal fishing communities that have suffered from the decline in fish stocks and overfishing, particularly by commercial fishing interests. It is often claimed that illegal, unreported, and unregulated (IUU) fishing by fishing vessels from Europe and Asia is one of the root causes of the current situation off Somalia.

Economic problems may cause political insecurity and internal security problems leading to a higher risk of illegal activity. Lack of good governance and policing onshore leads to a similar situation offshore, with illegal activity flourishing in adjacent waters, including smuggling in all its forms and piracy. Corruption among police, maritime officials, and shipping companies may also be a factor, as pirates may be well informed about shipping movements and cargoes, and sometimes appear to enjoy some protection from law enforcement authorities. Marine police and naval personnel have sometimes been accused of complicity in piratical activities in Indonesian waters.

Global Piracy

The number of acts of piracy and armed robbery against ships (actual and attempted) worldwide reported by the IMB in 2011 was 439, a decline of 6 from 2010, but 146 more than in 2008. By far the greatest concentration of these incidents (237) was off Somalia and in the Gulf of Aden; the increased number of attacks globally since 2008 is mainly due to a deterioration of the situation there and in Southeast Asia.

There are marked differences in the types of attacks that occur in the three main "hot spots" for piracy—the Horn of Africa, the Gulf of Guinea and Southeast Asia (which had 237, 51, and 80 attacks, respectively, in 2011, representing over 80 percent of the total global attacks during that year). The nature of piracy in these three areas varies considerably.

Horn of Africa

The situation off the Horn of Africa remains serious, with 151 attacks on ships reported in 2011, compared with 127 in 2010. The pirates reportedly earned $146 million from these raids. As of the end of May 2012, Somali pirates were holding eight large ships with a reported 235 hostages, demanding tens of millions of dollars in ransom. Although the number of shipping attacks by Somali pirates increased in 2011 over the previous years, the number of successful hijackings continued their downward trend. Of the 151 ships reporting attacks in 2011, 25 were actually hijacked, down from 47 in 2010. The decline in the number of successful attacks may be attributed to increased awareness by ships, the use of citadels (secure areas) by crews if attacked, and the actions of international naval forces.

Initially, attacks occurred mainly off Puntland, the most lawless part of Somalia, but then the pirates appreciated more opportunities in the Gulf of Aden. However, as security arrangements became more effective there, they began to operate hundreds of miles out to sea into the Indian Ocean, even as far out as the Seychelles, using a larger craft and even a vessel hijacked earlier and with crew still aboard, as "mother ships." This tactic is difficult for naval forces to counter, as not only does it vastly increase the area in which attacks might occur, but it also means that security forces are hesitant to engage the mother ship for fear of endangering its crew members.

Responses to piracy off the Horn of Africa include multinational naval patrols; the establishment of a Maritime Security Patrol Area in the Gulf of Aden with secure shipping lanes protected by international shipping patrols; improved arrangements for surveillance and information sharing between participating navies; and a series of IMO meetings that have developed a Code of Conduct between littoral countries covering matters such as the prosecution of offenses.

The pirates are well organized, and their "business plan" involves the hijacking of ships and crews for ransom, with the ransom paid for a large vessel and its crew now averaging around $5.4 million—or $9.5 million in the case of the large oil tanker *Samho Dream*, hijacked in 2010. The attackers understand that ship owners and insurance companies will pay the ransom and that once a ship has been successfully hijacked, patrolling navies will likely not use force to recover it due to the risk of casualties among the warship's crew and hostages. The pirates are not interested in a ship's cargo or in using the ship for further service, unless as a mother ship.

Somali pirates get away with their actions because they operate in unpoliced waters off a lawless land. They have secure anchorages to hold hijacked ships and are well supported by infrastructure on land.

Actual and Attempted Piracy Attacks, 2006–2011

Location	2006	2007	2008	2009	2010	2011
Southeast Asia	87	78	65	68	113	80
Indian subcontinent	53	30	23	30	28	16
Americas	29	21	14	37	40	25
Horn of Africa*	20	44	111	218	219	237
Gulf of Guinea**	25	49	56	47	38	51
Other Africa	16	27	22	7	4	2
Rest of world	9	14	2	3	3	28
Total, world	239	263	293	410	445	439

* Horn of Africa includes attacks in the Gulf of Aden, Red Sea, Arabian Sea, and Indian Ocean and off Oman and Somalia—all believed to be carried out by Somali pirates.

** Gulf of Guinea includes Benin, Cameroon, Congo, Democratic Republic of Congo, Equatorial Guinea, Ghana, Guinea, Ivory Coast, Nigeria, and Togo.

Source: International Maritime Bureau (IMB) Piracy Reports.

While just 10 or so pirates might actually conduct an attack, they subsequently have the assistance of many more people, in fact, whole villages, to help guard a hijacked ship and look after its crew. All share in the spoils.

Gulf of Guinea

The situation is rather different around the Gulf of Guinea, where attacks are usually more violent, with frequent loss of life. Vessels, particularly those associated with the offshore oil and gas industry, are attacked in coastal waters, anchorages, and rivers, and crew members are held for ransom. Unlike the Somali pirates, the pirates on the west coast of Africa are unable to hold a vessel securely while ransom negotiations take place, so they focus on kidnapping crew members, usually more senior or highly skilled technical people who may attract higher ransoms. The situation off Nigeria has improved recently (19 attacks in 2010, compared with 29 in 2009) but has deteriorated off Benin, where there were 12 attacks in the first half of 2011, as compared with only one in the previous five years.

Southeast Asia

Southeast Asian waters were a major area of concern in the early 2000s, but there was steady improvement until 2009, when the situation deteriorated again. The number of attacks in these waters increased from 68 in 2009 to 113 in 2010, mainly due to increased attacks in the South China Sea and in and around ports in Indonesia and Vietnam. Vessels at anchor in the eastern approaches to Singapore Strait have also

been robbed. This is an area where many ships are laid up with skeleton crews as a consequence of the downturn in international shipping associated with the global financial crisis.

The situation in Southeast Asian waters initially improved in the mid-2000s for several reasons. The disastrous tsunami in December 2004 reduced attacks off Sumatra, particularly near the port of Belawan and in the Malacca Strait. The peace agreement between the Indonesian government and the Gerakan Aceh Merdeka (GAM) movement also helped, as GAM rebels had been attacking ships to raise funds. National and regional responses, including increased patrolling and surveillance, have been important. As a consequence, few attacks now occur in the Malacca Strait and the ones that do occur are relatively minor.

Tighter government control and local policing onshore have also contributed to the decline in attacks, as well as greater security awareness in the shipping industry following the introduction of the International Ship and Port Facility Security (ISPS) Code by the IMO in 2002. The Regional Cooperation Agreement on Combating Piracy and Armed Robbery Against Ships in Asia (ReCAAP) is a major regional measure to counter piracy. The ReCAAP organization is also contributing its expertise to regional capacity building to counter piracy off the Horn of Africa.

Most attacks in Southeast Asian waters consist of opportunistic petty theft from vessels at anchor, in port, or entering or leaving harbor. This type of piracy is especially rife in and off ports in Indonesia, Vietnam, and the Philippines. It is countered by active patrolling of the port or anchorage by marine police and greater vigilance on the part of ships' crews.

Another type of piracy occurs when ships are under way. Ships in regional waters may be vulnerable due to their proximity to shore and the presence of numerous other shipping and fishing vessels, which can hide the approach of small craft. In this situation, pirates board vessels to steal cash and valuables. Notable features of this type of piracy are the skills demonstrated by the pirates in making their attack, and the fact that violence is not normally used unless resistance is offered. Numerous attacks of this nature have occurred recently in southernmost parts of the South China Sea near Pulau Tioman off Malaysia and near Anambas and Natuna islands in Indonesia.

Smaller ships, such as tugs and barges, are occasionally hijacked in Southeast Asia with the intention of recycling them for service under another name. These incidents are partly due to the increased tug and barge traffic across the South China Sea, with Singapore now importing much of the sand and gravel required for construction and reclamation from Cambodia and Vietnam.

Elsewhere

Elsewhere around the world, piracy has been on the decline, including off the Indian subcontinent, where acts of armed robbery against ships have been prevalent over the years. These attacks were all in or off ports and anchorages, mainly in Bangladesh. The drop in the number of attacks may be attributed to increased port security and harbor patrolling.

Vulnerability of Ships

The vulnerability of ships to piratical attack and sea robbery depends on the type of ship; its size, speed, and freeboard (height above water level); and the type of voyage it is undertaking. Substandard ships are more vulnerable than well-operated and -maintained vessels with well-trained and efficient crews. The latter vessels are much more likely to take all the precautions against attack recommended by the IMO and shipowner associations, such as the Best Management Practice guidelines produced by the shipping industry in consultation with the combined naval forces operating against piracy off the Horn of Africa. Unfortunately, however, there are still ships that do not follow these guidelines.

While it is not always the case, a large merchant vessel traveling at its normal operating speed, and taking all appropriate precautions, should not be successfully attacked unless it slows down or stops.

Pirates understand this, of course, and will do what they can with the intimidating use of weapons to persuade a vessel to slow down or stop.

Armed Security Guards

The use of armed security guards is a vexing issue. The IMO Maritime Safety Committee has approved interim guidance to shipowners and ship managers covering the use of privately contracted armed security guards onboard ships in the Gulf of Aden and Indian Ocean. This guidance points out that employing armed guards is not an alternative to best management practices and should be considered only following a risk assessment. While slow, vulnerable, and valuable vessels, such as some crude oil tankers, may require armed protection, many vessels using these waters, such as large and fast container ships, do not.

Having armed security guards onboard a ship certainly helps prevent a hijacking; however, there are strong legal and practical arguments against firearms onboard a commercial vessel. The use and handling of lethal weaponry requires special training and precise rues of engagement, normally practiced only by disciplined forces acting under proper authority. The use of firearms onboard oil tankers, gas carriers, and other vessels with volatile cargoes is especially dangerous.

The carriage of firearms onboard merchant ships poses difficult legal questions. Many countries have legislation preventing ships from having weapons onboard in their territorial waters. The carriage of weapons and the use of deadly force by armed guards should be covered under legislation of the flag state, but few flag states have such legislation. It is also essential that armed guards be appropriately trained and experienced. Many guards being used off the Horn of Africa come from army backgrounds and may not be familiar with conditions at sea.

Piracy in Perspective

Piracy off the Horn of Africa is serious, but it needs to be kept in perspective. In economic terms, the impact of piracy is relatively small. News reports and other sources often cite costs in the billions of dollars, but these figures are invariably based on "worst case" scenarios and overestimates of the costs. Only a small proportion of the ships passing through the area are successfully hijacked, and those that are tend to be at the lower end of the spectrum in terms of the value and standard of the ship and its cargo.

As well as the pirates themselves, many entities, particularly private security companies offering the services of armed guards, have an interest in the risks of piracy remaining high. Responses need to be measured to ensure that the level of violence does not escalate and more innocent seafarers are not hurt or killed. The shipping industry itself has a responsibility to ensure that best management practices are followed and ships are properly prepared to meet possible threats.

Piracy and armed robbery are just one form of criminal activity at sea and will likely continue in one form or another in various parts of the world. However, there are optimistic indications that the situation off the Horn of Africa may have started to improve and become more manageable. Measures such as improved governance onshore, better enforcement by local security forces, international support for capacity-building assistance to these forces, enhanced cooperation between the foreign navies engaged on counter-piracy operations, and greater vigilance by the crews of merchant ships all provide support for this optimistic assessment. Improved governance onshore is the vital factor, but it is also the most difficult to achieve.

Sam Bateman

See also: Crime, Organized; Failed States and Nation-Building; Kidnapping and Hostage-Taking; Terrorism.

Further Reading

Eklöf, Stefan. *Pirates in Paradise—A Modern History of Southeast Asia's Maritime Marauders.* Copenhagen: Nordic Institute of Asian Studies, 2006.

Elleman, Bruce A., Andrew Forbes, and David Rosenberg, eds. "Piracy and Maritime Crime—Historical and Modern Case Studies." *Naval War College Newport Papers 35.* Newport, RI: Naval War College Press, 2010.

Kraska, James. *Contemporary Maritime Piracy: International Law, Strategy, and Diplomacy at Sea.* Santa Barbara, CA: Praeger, 2011.

Murphy, Martin N. "Contemporary Piracy and Maritime Terrorism: The Threat to International Security." *Adelphi Paper 388.* London: International Institute for Strategic Studies, 2007.

———. "Dire Straits: Taking on Somali Pirates." *World Affairs* (July/August 2010).

———. *Piracy, Terrorism and Irregular Warfare at Sea: Navies Confront the 21st Century.* Cass Series: Naval Policy and History. London: Routledge, 2011.

———. *Somalia: The New Barbary? Piracy and Islam in the Horn of Africa.* New York: Columbia University Press, 2011.

One Earth Future. "The Economic Cost of Maritime Piracy." *One Earth Future Working Paper*, December 2010.

Web Sites

International Chamber of Commerce Commercial Crime Services (Piracy Statistics): www.icc-ccs.org/piracy-reporting-centre

International Maritime Organization: www.imo.org/MediaCentre/HotTopics/piracy/Pages/default.aspx

Oceans Beyond Piracy: www.oceansbeyondpiracy.org

Documents

Document 1: UN Convention on the Law of the Sea (excerpt), 1982

For centuries, rules governing the "high seas"—that is, waters not subject to national jurisdiction—were unwritten ones, generally accepted by all maritime nations but not formally agreed to or binding. As the seas became more widely exploited in the twentieth century, various UN conventions came into force, culminating in the 1982 Convention on the Law of the Sea. Among other things, it committed signatory nations to fighting piracy. The following are the articles of the convention pertaining to piracy.

Article 100
Duty to cooperate in the repression of piracy
All States shall cooperate to the fullest possible extent in the repression of piracy on the high seas or in any other place outside the jurisdiction of any State.

Article 101
Definition of piracy
Piracy consists of any of the following acts:

(a) any illegal acts of violence or detention, or any act of depredation, committed for private ends by the crew or the passengers of a private ship or a private aircraft, and directed:

(i) on the high seas, against another ship or aircraft, or against persons or property on board such ship or aircraft;

(ii) against a ship, aircraft, persons or property in a place outside the jurisdiction of any State;

(b) any act of voluntary participation in the operation

of a ship or of an aircraft with knowledge of facts making it a pirate ship or aircraft;

(c) any act of inciting or of intentionally facilitating an act described in subparagraph (a) or (b).

Article 102
Piracy by a warship, government ship or government aircraft whose crew has mutinied
The acts of piracy, as defined in article 101, committed by a warship, government ship or government aircraft whose crew has mutinied and taken control of the ship or aircraft are assimilated to acts committed by a private ship or aircraft.

Article 103
Definition of a pirate ship or aircraft
A ship or aircraft is considered a pirate ship or aircraft if it is intended by the persons in dominant control to be used for the purpose of committing one of the acts referred to in article 101. The same applies if the ship or aircraft has been used to commit any such act, so long as it remains under the control of the persons guilty of that act.

Article 104
Retention or loss of the nationality of a pirate ship or aircraft
A ship or aircraft may retain its nationality although it has become a pirate ship or aircraft. The retention or loss of nationality is determined by the law of the State from which such nationality was derived.

Article 105
Seizure of a pirate ship or aircraft
On the high seas, or in any other place outside the jurisdiction of any State, every State may seize a pirate ship or aircraft, or a ship or aircraft taken by piracy and under the control of pirates, and arrest the persons and seize the property on board. The courts of the State which car-

ried out the seizure may decide upon the penalties to be imposed, and may also determine the action to be taken with regard to the ships, aircraft or property, subject to the rights of third parties acting in good faith.

Article 106
Liability for seizure without adequate grounds
Where the seizure of a ship or aircraft on suspicion of piracy has been effected without adequate grounds, the State making the seizure shall be liable to the State the nationality of which is possessed by the ship or aircraft for any loss or damage caused by the seizure.

Article 107
Ships and aircraft which are entitled to seize on account of piracy
A seizure on account of piracy may be carried out only by warships or military aircraft, or other ships or aircraft clearly marked and identifiable as being on government service and authorized to that effect.

Source: United Nations.

Document 2: UN Security Council Resolution 2015, 2011

Recognizing the ongoing threat of piracy off the Horn of Africa, the UN Security Council issued Resolution 2015 on October 24, 2011. While calling on member states to take additional measures to combat the problem, the resolution also recognized that an effective and permanent solution required the input of the Somali authorities and people.

http://oceansbeyondpiracy.org/sites/default/files/unsc_res_2015_2011.pdf

Source: UN Security Council.

POLICE CORRUPTION AND BRUTALITY

Police corruption occurs when a member of a governmental domestic security organization, usually a police force, uses his or her position to commit an act, for personal gain or the gain of another, that violates the rights of another party or runs counter to officially prescribed duties.

There are many forms of police corruption, from the petty act of a traffic officer taking a small bribe to quash a ticket to the commission of capital crimes. Police corruption may be motivated by money, a desire for power, a belief that police sometimes have to act outside the law, or simply animus, the latter typically involving ethnic or other prejudices. Such animus is often evinced as brutality, that is, the application of unreasonable and unlawful force, or threat of such force, against suspects, arrestees, and even innocent bystanders. Police corruption is sometimes committed by rogue officers but can also be endemic to an entire department.

The type of corruption and its pervasiveness within a police force is often a reflection of the society in which it occurs. At the same time, the existence of police corruption has a debilitating effect not only on police organizations, whose effectiveness is reduced, but on societal attitudes and behavior as well, as it generates a sense of social insecurity and undermines respect for the law. Ever since the establishment of modern police forces in the nineteenth century, there have been efforts—both internal and external—to combat corruption, though most experts agree it can never be fully eliminated, given the nature of police work and corruption in society generally.

Types

Just as there are numerous crimes that police are hired to combat, so there are dozens and dozens of different acts of corruption that police can engage in. Police officials and experts, however, outline several basic categories of corruption, each of which tends to occur among different members of police departments or police departments in different kinds of societies. These include bribery, extortion, evidentiary suppression or distortion, brutality, and criminal activity.

Bribery is among the most common and pervasive acts of police corruption and can be found in both the more disciplined and effective departments of the developed world and the poorly paid and less trained departments in the developing world. In most cases, bribery is engaged in by uniformed police officers who interact with the public, and it usually involves ignoring or overlooking violations of the law in exchange for money or special favors. Sometimes this can be a petty matter, such as not issuing a traffic ticket, but at other times it can involve overlooking more serious crimes. While never completely accepted in any society, bribery, particularly of the petty type, may be so pervasive in a society as to be the operative norm. For instance, drivers in many countries know to include some cash with the license they present to officers when being stopped for a traffic violation, the expectation being that the officer will then let the driver off with a warning rather than a ticket.

Extortion is, in most experts' opinions, a higher order of corruption than bribery. Whereas the latter is a largely passive act in that the officer does not necessarily solicit a bribe—though sometimes police are known to pull drivers over even when they have not disobeyed traffic laws, to create a situation in which a bribe is likely to be offered—extortion is initiated by police officers themselves. As with bribery, it usually involves uniformed police officers who interact with the public. In addition, most police extortion is connected with so-called victimless crimes, such as drug dealing, illegal gambling, and prostitution. In such instances, police officers may demand that those engaging in these illegal enterprises turn over part of their illicit earnings in order to avoid arrest and prosecution. Extortion may take the form of payment in cash or in kind, as when officers demand sexual favors from prostitutes. Related to extortion is the act of taking kickbacks, or demanding payment for providing protection, which police should be doing as part of their jobs. In such cases, officers may inform legitimate business owners that they will receive a more prompt response should they need police protection if they pay money to the police officers. While extortion is endemic in all societies, kickbacks are more typical of developing-world societies where the provision of government services is more spotty, overall corruption is more endemic, and there is less respect for the law.

Evidentiary suppression or distortion is endemic to police departments in all parts of the world and engaged in by both uniformed officers and plain-clothes detectives. Typically, uniformed police officers may lie under oath, either to protect a guilty person or, more often, to convict an innocent suspect or a suspect whose guilt an officer is not entirely certain of. Investigating detectives may destroy or misplace evidence that incriminates a suspect or, conversely, fabricate evidence to incriminate a suspect.

Brutality is also a problem found among both uniformed police officers and detectives, and it ranges from beatings to the unauthorized use of nondeadly force to shootings. Uniformed police officers may engage in brutality in the arrest of suspects, in dealing with interfering bystanders, or in crowd control situations. There is substantial statistical evidence from many countries, particularly those with diverse populations and a history of discrimination and tense relations among sectors of the population, that brutality is often inflicted by officers who are members of the dominant population against those who belong to a minority or repressed group. Detectives engage in brutality when interacting with suspects once they have been arrested, although here there is less of a correlation between ethnic background and the likelihood of brutality.

The most egregious form of police corruption—but, arguably, also the least common, particularly in societies with more professional police forces—is when officers or detectives engage in activities that are criminal in and of themselves and not necessarily connected with their duties as police. These run the gamut of victimless, property, and violent crimes. Such criminal police may engage in drug dealing—sometimes with drugs stolen from evidence lockers—the stealing of property at crime scenes, and even murder.

Finally, most of the police corruption outlined in this section is of a type experts refer to as internal corruption, that is, acts engaged in by department personnel on their own initiative. But corruption can also involve external players. Police officers in both developed and developing countries have been known to work with organized crime in the carrying out of criminal activity. In countries with less developed democratic institutions, police may work with politicians or military rulers to illegally suppress members of the political opposition. In places torn by civil conflict, such as Colombia in the late twentieth and the early twenty-first century, police may work with paramilitary death squads to fight rebels or murder political opponents.

Motivations and Causes

Police engage in corruption for any number of reasons. Monetary gain, of course, is the primary motivation, but there are many aggravating circumstances beyond the greed of corrupt police officers. One factor is low pay, particularly in poorer countries. As experts point out, where officers do not earn enough money to take care of themselves and their families, they may resort to corruption, and where pay is poor, there is less fear of losing one's job for getting caught engaging in corruption.

Moreover, many poorer countries have gross inequalities in wealth or are plagued with corruption at all levels of society, creating a sense of injustice among officers who see themselves as either underpaid for the kind of dangerous work they do or as tools of a corrupt ruling class. In either case, they may rationalize the gains from corrupt behavior as their just due. In addition, general corruption breeds a general contempt for the law among all members of society, an attitude to which police are not immune. But even in relatively just societies where wealth is broadly distributed, police are put in situations where the opportunities for corruption abound. First, they are often in the company of criminals, who have few moral scruples and every interest in corrupting a police officer if that will get them out of trouble with the law. Police officers often work autonomously in the field, with little oversight, and with all kinds of opportunities to pilfer evidence, take bribes, or engage in extortion. Police are also often engaged in efforts to fight victimless crimes, such as gambling, drug dealing, and prostitution, which generate a lot of cash and are crimes with less stigma attached to them, allowing police to rationalize their own participation in them.

Finally, while individual officers may start their career with no intention of engaging in corruption, that commitment becomes harder to stick to if they are surrounded by other corrupt officers. This last factor leads to situations in which police engage in corruption for nonpecuniary reasons. Officers who fail to engage in endemic departmental corruption might be ostracized by other officers, given poor assignments, not receive backup in the field should harm threaten them, or even be fired from their jobs.

Another nonpecuniary factor behind police corruption, particularly where brutality is involved, is animus toward a given individual or category of individuals, such as an ethnic minority. Sometimes, however, police engage in brutality and other forms of intimidation simply to demonstrate their power over others. As some sociologists have pointed out, police work often attracts individuals with that propensity, while the work itself provides all kinds of opportunities to express it.

There is, in the words of British criminologist Maurice Punch, "noble cause" corruption, or, as it is sometimes referred to in the United States, the "Dirty Harry" factor, after the famous movie police character who engages in vigilante behavior. Here the motivating factor is a belief that the system for catching and successfully prosecuting criminals is flawed, giving the police officer the right to go around the rules—planting evidence, roughing up suspects, even extra-judicially punishing them to enforce the law and impose justice. This, say some criminologists who have studied police propensity to lie under oath during trials, may be the most pervasive form of corruption of all. Related to such behavior, but on a much broader scale, are fundamental ideological factors. If a police officer or department feels that society generally is corrupt or heading in the wrong direction ideologically, that individual or department may—on its own or in collusion with political authorities—justify the suppression of political dissent.

History

Corruption, of course, has been endemic to all societies throughout history and thus to all individuals and institutions aimed at protecting society against criminal behavior. Indeed, the creation of modern metropolitan police forces in nineteenth-century Europe and America was not simply due to the rising criminality of growing urban areas and the ineffectiveness of the ad hoc system of constables that had existed prior to these police forces, but also to the corruption of the former. By recruiting top candidates, training them well, and paying them adequately, it was expected that these new forces would be less likely to engage in the kind of brutality, corruption, and even criminal behavior that had marked earlier, more informal systems of policing, whereby constables and others were often paid by those whose persons and property they protected, opening up all kinds of opportunities for corruption.

Despite this innovation, both corruption and various forms of brutality persisted in police departments into the twentieth century. With the rise in illicit drug use in many countries after World War II came an increase in organized crime activity. In response, many governments initiated campaigns to interdict supplies and arrest users and dealers, as part of the so-called war on drugs. Many police departments found themselves so corrupted that they were forced to undergo outside investigations, many of which exposed the corruption and led to the institution of reforms that helped to stem the problem. But, as many criminologists noted, the opportunities for corruption led to many police officers finding ways around the reform procedures put into place.

At the same time, some police departments came to the conclusion that the best way to reduce corruption was to reduce the opportunities for it, which, reformers assumed, came from too close contact between police officers and the communities they served. This led to bribery of cops on the beat as well as those same police officers running extortion rackets. Regular foot patrols were replaced by car patrols and the use of police from outside the policed community. Such was the approach taken by the Los Angeles Police Department (LAPD), which, in the first half of the twentieth century was among the most corrupt in the developed world. But the separation of cops from the community led to other problems, particularly an us-against-them mentality of cops versus the communities, especially where the latter were composed of African Americans or Latinos. By the latter part of the century, the LAPD had become one of the least corrupt departments in America, by traditional measures, but also one of the most prone to police abuse and brutality against citizens. This, along with persistently high crime rates, led the LAPD, though it followed other departments' leads, to institute a new emphasis on community policing, so as to create better relations between officers and the communities they served. Whether this approach has been responsible for driving down crime rates is much debated among experts, but most agree that it has certainly improved police–community relations.

Ramifications

The existence of police corruption and brutality has immediate bearing on police effectiveness, as well as ramifications for society at large. Corruption reduces efficiency, as police spend their time on illegal activities rather than enforcing the law. Corruption also undermines morale, particularly of those personnel who try to remain clean. Moreover, when individual police or, worse, whole departments are seen as brutal and corrupt, people's confidence in the police is undermined, reducing their willingness to cooperate with police, an essential element in effective crime control. Police corrupted by outside forces, such as organized crime, are less willing and able to stop the crimes committed by those organizations and to arrest and help in the prosecution of criminals.

Farther afield, corrupt and brutal police forces undermine respect for the law and for government generally. When the public comes to believe, rightly or wrongly, that the police do not respect the law, then they see little reason to do so themselves. Incidents of police brutality have been the cause of numerous riots, with all of the looting and other general lawlessness that goes with them, since the 1960s in both North America and Europe. But the ramifications of corruption and brutality, say experts, is even more acute in developing countries, where governments and civil society are already weak. Making the problem worse is the perception that police are merely there to do the bidding of political or economic elites, rather than to uphold the law fairly.

FBI agents escort Puerto Rican police officers after arresting 89 of them in October 2010 for allegedly aiding drug dealers and smuggling illegal firearms. FBI officials called it the largest police corruption investigation in the agency's 102-year history. *(AP Photo/El Nuevo Dia, Angel M. Rivera)*

The series of political uprisings that swept across the Arab world beginning in late 2010 are an example of what can happen when the public perceives the police as corrupt or politically controlled. The so-called Arab Spring began in Tunisia when a street merchant set himself on fire—and later died from his burns—to protest the constant harassment he was getting from police as he tried to make a modest living. As the video of the event went viral on the Internet, the Tunisian public, as well as those in neighboring countries, responded with demonstrations, many of which were attacked by police, leading to the overthrow of the government in Tunis and several other Arab capitals. Notably, in Egypt, many protesters did not trust the police to maintain order around the demonstrations but accepted presence of the army, which they saw as less brutal and corrupt.

Combating Corruption

Fighting corruption and brutality in police departments is not an easy task, as attested to by the fact that numerous successful reforms tend to come undone over time. Part of the problem is that police departments do not exist in a vacuum. If a society or government is rife with corruption, then it is highly unlikely that its police officers or departments remain untainted. Similarly, a society divided by ethnic hatred is highly unlikely to find itself with a police department immune to such attitudes. Moreover, as noted earlier, there are intrinsic aspects of policing, such as the autonomy of officers, the close contact with criminal elements, and the handling of illicit gains, that provide opportunities and motivations for corrupt behavior. Finally, policing is an inherently dangerous activity very different from most civilian occupations, creating a high degree of solidarity in many departments. This has its benefits, of course, but it can also lead to a culture of insularity and protectiveness that shields corrupt or brutal police.

Still, experts cite a number of things that can be done to reduce corruption and brutality. It starts, they say, with proper recruitment and the utilization of psychological and sociological experts and methodologies to make sure corruption-prone or brutal individuals are kept off forces in the first place. Proper training is critical as well, making cops more sensitive to community values and thereby reducing brutality. A well-designed training program can foster a culture of high standards as well. Decent pay is also important, particularly in poorer countries, as it makes police less susceptible to bribes and more likely to stay honest as the cost of losing one's job becomes higher.

All of these things are, of course, preventive measures; departments also have to deal with corruption as it occurs. To that end, most large departments have set up internal affairs units to investigate corruption and brutality and discipline offending members. Such units operate on the assumption, widely held in much of the developed world, that corruption is a matter of a few "bad apples" and that the vast majority of police are honest and hardworking. This is true in most cases, but there is the matter of corrupt departments, particularly in poorer and more weakly governed societies. Here the task of cleaning up the corruption entails wholesale political reform at all levels of government.

More radical efforts to clean up corruption have also been bruited about by experts and even some policy makers. Some have called for the recruitment of more women, as studies and experience have shown that they are less brutal and less prone to corruption. Others argue for the use of new technologies, such as the videotaping of traffic stops, to prevent bribes. More controversial are calls for external, or civilian, review boards to monitor police brutality and corruption, though these are often vehemently opposed by police officers, unions, and departmental management. Still others have called for the legalization and regulation of victimless crimes such as drug possession, gambling, and prostitution in order to reduce general lawlessness, which feeds contempt for the law by police and the public, and to eliminate the opportunities for police corruption that come with efforts to fight these crimes.

Finally, some say that the best way to fight brutality and corruption is already here and need not await government action—new technologies. Over the past several decades, beginning with portable consumer video cameras in the 1980s and evolving into the ubiquitous cell phone with camera in the 2000s, technology has given ordinary citizens the means to monitor police corruption and brutality on their own. And the ability to spread damaging images of such actions over the Internet has made it more difficult for corrupt and brutal police officers and departments to act with impunity, as the uprisings of the Arab Spring have made clear.

James Ciment

See also: Government Corruption and Transparency; Human Rights; Prisoners and Prisoner Rights; War Crimes.

Further Reading

Amir, Menachem, and Stanley Einstein, eds. *Police Corruption: Challenges for Developed Countries. Comparative Issues and Commissions on Inquiry.* Huntsville, TX: Office of International Criminal Justice, Sam Houston State University, Criminal Justice Center, 2004.

Avery, Michael, David Rudovsky, and Karen M. Blum. *Police Misconduct: Law and Litigation.* St. Paul, MN: Thomson/West, 2008.

Claussen-Rogers, Natalie L., and Bruce A. Arrigo. *Police Corruption and Psychological Testing: A Strategy for Pre-Employment Screening.* Durham, NC: Carolina Academic, 2005.

Gottschalk, Peter. *Police Management: Professional Integrity in Policing.* New York: Nova Science, 2010.

Ivkovic, Sanja Kutnjak. *Fallen Blue Knights: Controlling Police Corruption.* New York: Oxford University Press, 2005.

Klockars, Carl B., Sanja Kutnjak Ivkovic, and M.R. Haberfeld. *Enhancing Police Integrity.* Dordrecht, Netherlands: Springer, 2006.

Kuhns, Joseph B., and Johannes Knutsson. *Police Use of Force: A Global Perspective.* Santa Barbara, CA: Praeger, 2010.

Miller, Seumas, ed. *Police Ethics.* Burlington, VT: Ashgate, 2006.

Palmiotto, Michael J., ed. *Police Misconduct: A Reader for the 21st Century.* Upper Saddle River, NJ: Prentice Hall, 2001.

Prenzler, Tim. *Police Corruption: Preventing Misconduct and Maintaining Integrity.* Boca Raton, FL: CRC, 2009.

Punch, Maurice. *Police Corruption: Deviance, Accountability and Reform in Policing.* Portland, OR: Willan, 2009.

Web Sites

Amnesty International: www.amnesty.org
Human Rights Watch: www.hrw.org
International Association of Chiefs of Police: theiacp.org
Police Crimes.com: www.policecrimes.com
Transparency International: www.transparency.org
United Nations Office on Drugs and Crime: www.unodc.org

Documents

Document 1: UN Code of Conduct for Law Enforcement Officials, 1979

Recognizing that ethical police conduct is an essential component to good governance and the effective rule of law, the United Nations General Assembly established a model Code of Conduct for Law Enforcement Officials in 1979. While acknowledging the difficulties facing law enforcement officials as they go about their work, the code emphasized the potential for abuse and the ramifications of that abuse for both police force effectiveness and social cohesion and harmony generally.

www2.ohchr.org/english/law/codeofconduct.htm

Source: United Nations High Commissioner for Human Rights.

Document 2: City of New York Commission to Investigate Allegations of Police Corruption and the Anti-Corruption Procedures of the Police Department (Mollen Commission) Report, 1994

Responding to a series of high-profile shootings and other abuses by police in the 1980s and 1990s, New York City mayor David Dinkins in 1992 established the City of New York Commission to Investigate Allegations of Police Corruption and the Anti-Corruption Procedures of the Police Department, better known as the Mollen Commission after its head, former judge Milton Mollan. The commission, set up some 20 years after the Knapp Commission had highlighted extensive corruption in the department in the 1960s and 1970s, showed how police misbehavior was endemic despite the best efforts of reformers. It also demonstrated how corruption reemerges in new forms when reforms are put into place. Rather than a culture of bribery, extortion, and general collaboration between police and criminals, as revealed by the Knapp Commission, the Mollen Commission report noted widespread brutality and abuse of authority.

www.parc.info/client_files/Special%20Reports/4%20-%20Mollen%20Commission%20-%20NYPD.pdf

Source: Police Assessment Resource Center.

POLIO

Polio is an ancient virus that, unlike most other ancient diseases, has become more frightening and deadly in the past century. Known by a variety of names through history, polio's significance long paled in comparison to that of many more lethal diseases that have plagued mankind.

In the 1910s, however, sporadic outbreaks of what was most commonly called "infantile paralysis" began to affect many people, far more than ever before. This new intensity of an old disease baffled physicians. The modern understanding of the link between hygiene and good health seemed to promise the eventual eradication of disease, yet here was an illness that was becoming more prevalent and more devastating. During these twentieth-century epidemics, increasing numbers of victims were left partially or entirely paralyzed. If the paralysis spread to the muscles necessary for respiration, the victim either died or, after the invention of the iron lung, faced the possibility of a lifetime struggling to breathe.

Today, polio has been virtually eliminated in the United States and Europe thanks to the development of effective vaccines, but the threat continues in Africa, Asia, and South America, as inoculation programs have not yet reached full coverage in these regions. The fight against polio is one of the greatest success stories of modern medicine, and most immunologists are confident that, given the resources to vaccinate all populations, the time will come when it will be completely eradicated. However, that time has not yet arrived.

History

A 3,500-year-old Egyptian carving seems to show a man whose leg has been partially paralyzed in a way that doctors recognize as being strongly associated with polio's aftereffects. Ancient Greek and Roman physicians described a condition that caused partial paralysis, which also seems to suggest polio. For centuries, however, this disease received only scant notice, as it was rarely associated with epidemics, paralysis, or death.

Polio is most commonly spread through fecal matter, usually because of improper handling of food or unwashed hands, though it can also be spread mouth-to-mouth. The virus then travels via the bloodstream to the nervous system. The disease was endemic through most of human history. Until the dawn of modern sanitation techniques, nearly everyone was exposed at a very young age, when polio tends to be less severe. Most of those who contracted polio in infancy or very young childhood had a case so mild that they did not exhibit any symptoms. Others showed symptoms that were easily mistaken for a cold or mild case of the flu, from which they quickly and fully recovered. Although some were left with permanent deformity or weakness in one or more limbs, few felt the devastating effects that became common in recent periods. Consequently, the disease was poorly understood and haphazardly diagnosed; for most of human history, it did not even have a single, agreed-upon name. By the late 1700s, polio was most often referred to as "debility of the lower extremities" and classified as a disease of children.

In the late 1800s, polio became more prevalent, with occasional outbreaks in various places, such as Sweden and Vermont. By this point, the disease was most commonly known as infantile paralysis or poliomyelitis. By the late nineteenth century, polio was recognized as a disease that most affected industrialized countries, where modern sanitation was expected to bring an end to epidemic outbreaks of the disease.

In the early twentieth century, European and American outbreaks in the summer—when polio thrives—became more frequent, with more cases some years than others. Sporadic outbreaks occurred in Germany, France, and England. Scandinavian countries seemed especially vulnerable; a major outbreak in Sweden in 1911 killed nearly 3,840. Australia also had occasional epidemics. The United States, too, began to see a rise in polio cases. Not only were such epidemics becoming more common, but the disease also began to be contracted by older populations. Adolescents and young adults who came down with polio were more likely to suffer a severe case and to be paralyzed or even die; as a result, these new outbreaks not only were more frequent but also left more devastation in their wake.

In 1916, a polio epidemic spread to 26 states in the United States, with some 27,000 cases reported and 6,000 deaths nationwide. The outbreak was at its most virulent in New York City, where 9,000 cases were reported and approximately 2,400 people died. Doctors scrambled to stop it, but because they did not understand how the disease was spread, their efforts were based on little more than guesswork and they disagreed as to which measures were likely to be effective. They were baffled by the fact that polio had become more common, and more deadly, even as other diseases abated with the advent of improved hygiene. Campaigns were launched for the eradication of flies. Rumors circulated that cats carried the disease, and so thousands of stray cats and family pets were rounded up and destroyed; as many as 70,000 cats were killed in New York City in a single week in July. Travel was restricted in some areas to try to stem the epidemic's spread. Many summertime entertainments were canceled, or attendance by children was prohibited. Officials frequently cited urban immigrants and their crowded, dirty environments as the point of origin of the disease, although, inexplicably, fewer and less-devastating cases were found in immigrant neighborhoods than in other areas.

It was only in the mid-twentieth century that scientists began to understand that improved hygiene was actually a factor in making the disease more prevalent and devastating. Better sanitation ended the centuries-long pattern in which polio was generally contracted in infancy and thus had mild effects. Now, people were exposed to and came down with the disease at a later age, when the effects were much more serious. One of the most famous polio victims made this late-onset threat abundantly clear: In 1921, Franklin Delano Roosevelt, a wealthy and well-known New York politician (and later, president of the United States), contracted "infantile paralysis" at the age of 39. His struggle with polio brought the disease heightened public awareness, and his efforts to help sufferers eventually led to the founding of the March of Dimes, an organization that played a pivotal role in the eventual development of viable vaccines.

Polio outbreaks continued to fluctuate but took a dramatic turn in 1943, when the number of cases again began to climb, along with the ages of those affected, as did the severity of the infection. For example, in 1916, roughly 80 percent of polio cases in the U.S. outbreak were in children ages four and under. In 1949, by contrast, just 20 percent of cases affected this young age group, while 40 percent were among those more than 10 years old.

Little could be done at the time to preserve muscle use for those who suffered a severe case of polio. Doctors used splints to try to keep tightened muscles from contorting limbs, but beyond that, they were helpless. This changed when a new method for the treatment of polio's typical muscle contractions was introduced by the Australian nurse Sister Elizabeth Kenny. Using compresses of hot, damp wool, her method aimed to relax the muscles. In addition, physical therapy exercises were done to stretch the limbs and keep them flexible. These techniques greatly improved the outcome for those whose muscles were affected.

By the mid-twentieth century, the development of an effective polio vaccine had become one of the most pressing goals of medical professionals. The American physician and epidemiologist Jonas Salk developed a vaccine made with killed, or inactive, poliovirus, which was licensed in 1955. Although this was an important breakthrough, complications arose when batches of the vaccine produced by Cutter Laboratories actually caused paralysis in approximately 100 recipients. Meanwhile, the American physician and virologist Albert Sabin developed a vaccine containing live poliovirus. It was tested in the Soviet Union and was licensed for use in the United States in 1961. Huge public campaigns to inoculate children were put in place as soon as these vaccines were available.

Polio Today

Both types of polio vaccine are used today in the effort to eradicate the disease worldwide. After its efficacy was proven, Sabin's live oral polio vaccine (OPV) replaced Salk's inactivated polio vaccine (IPV) for general use in the United States, though concerns about complications from OPV led the United States to change back to the use of IPV in 2000. Some countries never adopted the use of OPV, preferring to continue the use of the inactivated vaccine. Large-scale vaccination efforts in the developing world, however, generally rely on the use of OPV.

Each vaccine type has advantages. The live oral

vaccine is easier to administer, seems to give somewhat greater protection, and gives some protection to those in close contact with the recipient. But because it must be kept refrigerated, it poses some difficulties for use in remote areas. It also can cause vaccine-induced paralysis (about four cases per million recipients), and, rarely, epidemics have been linked to the use of the live vaccine. The inactivated vaccine is more expensive and must be given through inoculation, so it also poses challenges for massive vaccination campaigns in less-developed areas; however, IPV has almost no side effects. Eradication efforts now sometimes use the oral and inactive vaccines in combination, given in either three or four doses in the first months of life. Through the use of these two vaccines, polio has been largely eliminated in the developed world.

Poliovirus comes in three distinct strains: types 1, 2, and 3. The last reported case of type-2 polio was in 1999; this strain is now considered to have been eradicated. Types 1 and 3 continue to be problematic, occasionally even flaring up in areas previously thought to be polio-free. Overall, vaccination efforts have proven to be extremely effective. The World Health Organization (WHO) estimated in 2010 that since vaccination for polio became routine in the United States, more than a million cases of polio and 160,000 polio-related deaths have been avoided. Although the cost of vaccinations in the United States in that period totaled $1.7 billion, the cost of care and treatment of the patients who would otherwise have contracted polio would have been some $180 billion. Vaccination efforts have therefore proven to be cost effective.

In 1988 WHO, buoyed by polio-eradication success in Europe and the United States, began efforts to eliminate polio globally. That year, an estimated 350,000 children were left paralyzed by polio. Pointing to the successful total elimination of smallpox, scientists were cautiously optimistic that tackling polio could be equally successful. Polio, however, poses more challenges. Carriers of the virus are not always easy to identify. Some people refuse vaccination on religious or other grounds, and so a small portion of the population, even in developed regions, lacks protection. Areas that have poor sanitation and hygiene standards are breeding grounds for polio. These factors combine to make transmission from less-protected to more-protected regions possible. Widespread modern transportation also allows the disease to travel easily. To combat this ongoing problem, WHO recommendations include polio boosters for those who travel from developed regions to areas where polio remains endemic, as well as a full series of vaccinations for those traveling from polio-endemic areas to more-developed countries.

In addition to wild poliovirus transmission, health officials also have to guard against vaccine-derived poliovirus (VDPV), a possible outcome of the use of the live oral vaccine. In fact, in many developed countries, VDPV is now considered a greater threat than wild poliovirus. For this reason, the inactivated vaccine has continued to gain favor. In areas where polio is still endemic, however, and their near neighbors, the oral vaccine is usually recommended, sometimes in combination with IPV.

Even if the epidemics can someday be eradicated, polio will have a lasting effect for some time to come. Scientists and physicians in countries long thought to be essentially free of the disease have more recently had to deal with the long-term effects of polio for those who contracted it decades ago. Although aftereffects of the disease have been described since the late 1800s, it was not until the 1980s—when polio patients from the European and American outbreaks of the 1930s and later, especially those who had severe cases, reached advanced ages—that post-polio syndrome was widely recognized and studied. Post-polio syndrome is marked by both mental and physical fatigue, even exhaustion. It is more prevalent in women than in men, but can strike both sexes. In some cases, those who had polio in their youth but recovered the use of their limbs with only minor impairment find many years later that they are suddenly confronted with a return of the more debilitating aspects of their earlier paralysis. Older post-polio patients are also at higher risk of osteoporosis (low bone density that increases the chance for fractures).

The Future

WHO estimates that wild polio cases declined by 99 percent between 1988 and 2005. However, it is too soon to declare polio's extinction. Four countries still have significant endemic polio: Pakistan, Afghanistan, Nigeria, and India. Other countries have suffered recent outbreaks due to transmission from these countries. As long as some populations are still unprotected, the risk of contracting polio will continue. Scientists are also well aware that as long as live poliovirus is used in vaccines, with its potential for vaccine-derived polio cases, the disease will not be truly wiped out. Eventually all vaccination is likely to be of the inactivated type; for now, though, the oral vaccine still offers the best chance of reaching those who are not yet protected.

One continuing obstacle to final eradication of this disease is funding. Vaccination efforts require a large amount of money, especially as they attempt to penetrate further into less developed, sparsely populated regions or, conversely, impoverished, overcrowded areas. Countries such as Germany, the United Kingdom, and the United States have contributed large sums toward the effort, but budget shortfalls and economic pressure in these countries have had a ripple effect on immunization programs. Rotary International has long helped in the effort to rid the world of polio but does not have the resources necessary for total eradication. The American billionaire Bill Gates also has given generously toward this goal through the Bill and Melinda Gates Foundation.

Other roadblocks to wiping out polio are ideology and political instability. People in some less-developed nations are reluctant to allow what they perceive as U.S. or European medical interference in their society and culture. Some extremist Muslim clerics in Pakistan and Nigeria, for example, have denounced vaccination. Concerns about U.S. and European tampering occasionally fuel rumors about vaccine dangers and international conspiracies, reducing compliance even further. Pakistan and Afghanistan, moreover, have many areas that are considered too risky for vaccination teams due to war and unrest.

Nigeria continues to be a trouble spot for polio eradication efforts. Political instability, corruption, and a general opposition to and distrust of vaccination programs have combined to slow progress in fighting the disease there. In 2007, Nigeria had a substantial increase in polio rates, and transmission of the virus from the country subsequently resulted in cases in at least 15 countries that had at that point been polio-free for some time. Many experts consider Nigeria's continuing opposition to vaccination efforts one of the most difficult obstacles to worldwide eradication of this disease. The 2007 outbreak, along with increased pressure from the UN and WHO, has resulted in some increased acceptance of vaccination and some success in lowering Nigerian polio rates, with the number of cases considerably lower in 2010.

A handful of experts question the goal of eradication itself, pointing out that efforts have been ongoing for decades but the war against polio may in fact be impossible to completely win. They argue that although 99 percent of polio has been eliminated, eradication of that last 1 percent has been remarkably elusive. They suggest that control of the disease, not total eradication, should be the goal. Organizations such as WHO, along with many immunology experts, hold out hope that as long as funding continues to be available, eventually all pockets of wild poliovirus will be targeted and that one day soon polio will be eliminated.

Julie Turner

See also: Neurological Disease; Public Health; Vaccination.

Further Reading

Aylward, Bruce, and Tadataka Yamada. "The Polio Endgame." *New England Journal of Medicine* 364:24 (June 16, 2011): 2273–2275.

Daniel, Thomas M., and Frederick C. Robbins, eds. *Polio.* Rochester, NY: University of Rochester Press, 1997.

Gould, Tony. *A Summer Plague: Polio and Its Survivors.* New Haven, CT: Yale University Press, 1995.

Kluger, Jeffrey. *Splendid Solution: Jonas Salk and the Conquest of Polio.* New York: Putnam, 2004.

Larson, Heidi, and Isaac Ghini. "Lessons from Polio Eradication." *Nature (International Weekly Journal of Science)* 473:7348 (May 26, 2011).

Oshinsky, David. *Polio: An American Story.* New York: Oxford University Press, 2005.

Rogers, Naomi. *Dirt and Disease: Polio Before FDR.* New Brunswick, NJ: Rutgers University Press, 1992.

Silver, Julie, and Daniel Wilson. *Polio Voices: An Oral History from the American Polio Epidemics and Worldwide Eradication Efforts.* Westport, CT: Praeger, 2007.

Wilson, Daniel J. *Living with Polio: The Epidemic and Its Survivors.* Chicago: University of Chicago Press, 2005.

Web Sites

Centers for Disease Control and Prevention: www.cdc.gov

National Library of Medicine, National Institutes of Health: www.nlm.nih.gov

United Nations Foundations, Polio Eradication Initiative: www.unfoundation.org/what-we-do/campaigns-and-initiatives/polio-eradication-initiative

World Health Organization: www.who.org

Documents

Document 1: *Infantile Paralysis, and Its Attendant Deformities* (excerpt), by Dr. Charles Lafayette Taylor, 1867

Characteristic of the nineteenth century, this selection from an 1867 book by Dr. Charles Lafayette Taylor, resident surgeon at New York Orthopaedic Dispensary, demonstrates a clear lack of understanding of polio's causation. The author is aware that polio seems to target the middle and upper classes more frequently than the lower classes, but he flails in efforts to find an explanation as to why this would be the case.

Probable Cause.

Modern, and especially American, civilization is characterized by peculiar activity of the brain, and this is often carried to great excess.

The motive-force of American progress is brain-power. It is the ceaseless activity of directing mind that, in two centuries, has subdued the wilderness and peopled the continent; that has built vast cities whose commerce reaches the remotest regions of the globe; and that has proved itself capable of solving the most difficult political problems. The creative energy of the distinctively American intellect is recognized everywhere. But such vast results of this creative intelligence have not been accomplished without some sacrifices. It has diminished our physical endurance. As a people, we are dyspeptic, and weak in bodily vigor in the inverse ratio of over-activity of brain. Our laborers have to be imported. We are predisposed to nervous derangements. As a people, we are overworked. The nervous system becomes exhausted, and a constitution less strong than our own, but more excitable and impressive, is transmitted to our children.

Why Vigorous Parents Produce Sickly Offspring.

It is often asked, "How is it that, when both parents are well and vigorous, the children are often puny and nervous?" The reply must be, that the offspring partake of the parents' condition at the time they were begotten. A man who is thoroughly engrossed in business calculations and cares, or even in the pleasures of society, will beget children with physical powers correspondingly subordinated to the nervous. To ensure a perfect plant, it is not only requisite that the seed be produced by a strong and vigorous tree, but no drought must have absorbed its sap or untimely frosts have chilled it while the seed was maturing. We have imperfect grapes if an accidental cut lets the juice of the vine leak out.

How, then, can even naturally vigorous persons expect to bear children of equal vigor if begotten while they themselves are exhausted with intense mental labors and excitements? It is a physiological impossibility. Hence our children are born with a surprising degree of nervous irritability; just the temperament for the production of infantile paralysis when favorable circumstances combined to produce it.

Most Common Among The Rich.

And, as may be supposed, this disease occurs most frequently in the families of active business men. Indeed, while strumous diseases abound in the lower classes, I have seen but very few cases of infantile paralysis among them. My whole experience has led me to regard infantile paralysis as being almost confined to the families of active, intelligent men, as above indicated.

Source: Charles Lafayette Taylor, *Infantile Paralysis, and Its Attendant Deformities* (Philadelphia: J.B. Lippincott, 1867).

Document 2: "Citizens Threaten to Wreck Paralysis Hospital" (excerpts), *The New York Times,* August 27, 1916

The following article from The New York Times *in 1916, which describes the violence that occurred upon the opening of a polio hospital for children on Long Island, reflects the fear engendered by the disease in the years before it was fully understood.*

THREATEN TO WRECK PARALYSIS HOSPITAL; Citizens of Woodmere, L.I., Angered by Building of Institution There. ARMED GUARDS DEFEND IT Appeal Made to Governor by Rich Promoters; Epidemic Still Wanes in This City

Public and private armed forces opposed each other last night and the night before at Woodmere, L.I. [Long Island], where wealthy Summer residents of Rockaway Peninsula have built an isolation hospital for infantile paralysis patients. . . .

The present situation developed from the efforts of the Committee for the Control of Infantile Paralysis on the Rockaway Peninsula to provide scientific medical treatment and adequate housing of poliomyelitis patients. . . .

But before the hospital was completed the residents of Woodmere had stirred themselves. The committee maintained that it selected a site for the hospital on a neck of land almost entirely surrounded by water and nearer the large estates, where there was no congestion, than the homes of the citizens of Woodmere. The citizens, however, resented the idea of receiving infantile paralysis patients in their village, and, according to report, they were aided and abetted by a number of Summer residents, whose estates are from one to two miles from the hospital.

The protest of citizens was voiced at a mass meeting held on Thursday night. . . . The result was an order that no infantile paralysis cases should be sent to the hospital except such as had their origin in the villages of Woodmere and Hewlett.

There is only one case in Woodmere and none in Hewlett, so the hospital, as matters stand now, has been built for a single child who will be moved into it today. There are about six other cases on the Peninsula. . . .

Because the populace feared an attempt would be made to take the six cases to the hospital on Friday night, they gathered about it, some 500 or 600 strong, and threatened to burn the buildings. The committee employed half a dozen detectives from New York to guard the property, and last night this force was increased to twenty. Deputy sheriffs joined the crowd about the hospital and barricaded the approaches with rakes and other implements to prevent the dashing in or out of automobiles.

The deputy sheriffs threatened to shoot anyone who attempted to take a patient into the hospital, and the detectives threatened to shoot anyone who attempted to approach the buildings without permission. . . .

Source: The New York Times, August 27, 1916, p. 12.

POLLUTION, AIR

The contamination of the earth's atmosphere is the result of human activity—most of all the burning of hydrocarbon-based fuels, such as coal and oil. The conflict between the need to use fuels and the negative consequences of air pollution on health, building materials and infrastructure, and the ecosystem has meant that solutions to the problem of air pollution have often developed slowly.

The Emerging Problem

Although seen as a largely contemporary issue, air pollution is in fact a scourge going back to ancient times. Various ancient Egyptian, Sumerian, and Babylonian texts have comments about smoke and odor. The relationship between air quality and human health was recognized in the Hippocratic Corpus of Greek medicine, but it was in Roman times that pollution first became an administrative matter, to be regulated by the state. Urban air pollution issues also arose in the Middle Ages, most notably in London, as urban dwellers switched from wood sources of fuel, which were rapidly disappearing, to coal in the thirteenth century. The unfamiliar and noxious smell of coal smoke spawned health fears, which led authorities to relocate sources of offensive odors beyond city walls, specify chimney heights, and regulate the type of fuel that could be burned.

Pollution regulation of the late Middle Ages focused on very local pollution sources, but over time industrial activities began to evince similarities across localities, especially as the steam engine and coal furnace became ubiquitous in industrializing regions and countries. Regulation of these new industrial sources emerged in Europe in the opening years of the 1800s. In Britain, pollution by hydrochloric acid, a substance produced in the manufacture of caustic soda for soap production, led to the Alkali Act of 1863, a key example of a law applied to an entire country and administered by a scientist, in this case Robert Angus Smith. In Germany, by the end of the

nineteenth century, intense debate and scientific research focused on the smelter smoke of the Ruhr Valley. In the United States, the Bureau of Mines took the lead in researching the causes and effects of early coal-based air pollution.

The problem of air pollutants and their health impact in urban areas was addressed as part of the broad reforms in sanitation that typified much of Europe and North America in the late nineteenth and the early twentieth century. This change brought a need for new skills that paralleled the professionalization of the Victorian period. Sanitation inspectors and a smoke inspectorate emphasized the increasingly specialized skills needed to improve the state of the urban environment.

The twentieth century became dominated by the emerging problems related to the automobile. A specific example of research into this subject was that of U.S. public health expert Alice Hamilton, whose studies of how lead is metabolized in humans triggered concern over the impact of leaded fuels developed in the 1920s. By the end of the century, the problems of acid rain, a hole in the ozone layer, and the carbon dioxide–driven greenhouse effect also had a wide political impact.

Sources

In its simplest sense, the air pollution problem can be seen as relating to fuel. Fuels are usually hydrocarbon based, so when they are burned, they yield carbon dioxide and water. However, an engine or a furnace often does not have enough oxygen, so carbon monoxide, which is a toxin, is produced instead of carbon dioxide. In the presence of even less oxygen in the burning process, the fuel is not converted to an oxide, so the result is the emission of carbon or soot. This black soot can be seen in the exhaust of a badly tuned diesel vehicle while mounting a hill. The engine is being fed sufficient fuel, but not enough oxygen to convert it to carbon dioxide. Less visible problems result as the organic compounds in the fuel are pyrolyzed—subjected to temperatures so high that they lead to decomposition—in the engine, forming polycyclic aromatic hydrocarbons such as benzopyrene, a carcinogen.

However, it is not simply the hydrogen and the carbon in fuel that gives rise to pollutants. Fuels are normally burned in air, not pure oxygen. Air contains 80 percent nitrogen, and the combustion process can split molecular nitrogen into highly reactive nitrogen atoms, which enter chain reactions with oxygen and rapidly produce nitrogen oxide in exhaust. In addition, fossil fuels, especially coal, contain large amounts of sulfur, released as sulfur dioxide during combustion. This is a key pollutant in coal-burning cities, creating much of the air pollution in Victorian-era cities, including the dense smoke fog (smog) that caused respiratory illnesses, such as bronchitis, and rising death rates due to the state of medical treatment of such conditions at the time. As electricity and gas gradually replaced coal as the predominant source of heating in homes and businesses in the developed world after World War II, the level of sulfur dioxide and soot in urban air began to fall, as exemplified by figures for Paris, France.

Atmospheric Sulfur Dioxide and Soot, Paris, 1955–2009

Month/Year	Sulfur dioxide*	Soot*
January 1955	398	312
July 1955	62	68
January 1959	345	174
July 1959	56	61
January 1964	462	207
July 1964	73	45
January 1969	214	87
July 1969	49	39
January 1974	137	52
July 1974	53	26
January 1979	224	73
July 1979	65	30
January 1984	58	33
July 1984	40	26
January 1989	60	32
July 1989	39	21
January 1994	24	14
July 1994	9	16
January 1999	15	18
July 1999	5	14
January 2004	11	11
July 2004	4	10
January 2009	7	21
May 2009	2	14

* Micrograms/per cubic meter of air.
Source: Department for Environment, Food and Rural Affairs, France.

The twentieth century was a time of momentous changes in the source and composition of air pollution as well as its study. A key notion was the understanding of secondary versus primary pollutants, which developed in midcentury. Earlier, air pollution was seen as merely the material that came from chimney stacks or the exhaust of vehicles. A greater understanding of the pollution in Los Angeles showed that this view was not accurate—air pollution problems were not a result merely of source pollution but of photochemical reactions in the atmosphere.

Photochemical Smog

Beginning in the early twentieth century, Los Angeles developed as a city in which the car was the dominant method of transportation. The air over the city also became very polluted. Indeed, by World War II, air pollution had become so extreme that spectators reported being unable to view baseball games from the stands. Many suspected that local industries, such as a major artificial rubber plant near downtown, were responsible, but objections were muted because artificial rubber was such an important strategic material. Moreover, some observers noted that the smog episodes were bad even when the plant was not operating. In the immediate postwar years, there was great pressure to improve air quality, and although experts spent much time proposing solutions, none seemed effective. It was not until the 1950s that Arie Haagen-Smit, a biochemist at the California Institute of Technology, noted the air pollution damage to the lettuce crop that could not have been the product of traditional sulfur dioxide. He realized that the offending pollutant was ozone, which was largely a product of the interaction of sunlight and volatile organic material. Those volatile materials came from evaporating or unburned automotive fuel, creating the city's unique form of smog. Naturally, as this newer form of pollution was the result of the volatility of liquid fuel for motor vehicles, it rapidly began to spread to other cities with large numbers of automobiles.

This novel form of air pollution was gradually understood to derive from a complex sequence of reactions involving fragmented organic molecules (from the evaporated fuel), which promote the conversion of nitric oxide to nitrogen dioxide, a brown-colored gas. Nitrogen dioxide reacts in sunlight to produce the ozone that characterizes modern smog. The process produces oxidized compounds that irritate the eyes and lungs. These secondary pollutants arising from chemical reactions in the atmosphere are not closely linked to their immediate sources in the way that smoke might be identified as coming from a factory chimney. This created a new problem for regulators, and even in the 1950s it became evident that managing this form of pollution required a detailed understanding of the chemistry of the atmosphere, rather than a simple identification of a single pollutant source. Regulators began to fund scientific investigations of atmospheric chemistry and promoted modeling as a tool to allow the development of regulatory strategies such as air quality management. This approach accounted for the subtlety of the transformations that take place among the mixture of precursor pollutants.

The complexity also prevented easy victories in the fight against smog, and Los Angeles and its environs still have significant problems with air pollution, though it is much improved since the mid-twentieth century. The measures that led to this improvement involved a reduction in the emission of nitrogen oxides and carbon-containing compounds—carbon monoxide and hydrocarbons from evaporating and unburned fuel. The key to reducing these automotive emissions was the addition of three-way catalytic converters to car exhaust systems, which removed all three compounds—nitrogen oxides, carbon monoxide, and hydrocarbons. However, it soon became apparent that this was not enough and hydrocarbon emissions were higher than anticipated because it came from two sources: leakages of vehicle fuel directly as it evaporated from the engine and spilled fuel. Further organic compounds came from paints and other architectural materials. In some parts of the world, the large amount of organic material evaporating from forests made a significant addition to the reactive hydrocarbons in the atmosphere.

Although this type of pollution was first recognized in Los Angeles, it is now seen in most urban areas, particularly in the burgeoning cities in developing countries. In many cities, an evolution has taken place from primary coal-burning pollution to the secondary pollution that accompanies the use of automotive fuels. This pattern of change seems to be found everywhere, at varying rates. The changes that took almost 700 years in London seem to have occurred in about 50 years in Beijing, as it has accelerated its industrial development, though much of it is still powered by dirty coal, and moved toward the widespread use of automobiles.

Regional and Global Issues

It is not only urban air pollution that has typified the twentieth century's air-quality problems. Acid rain was a key environmental issue in the 1980s, although its origins date much earlier, including observations of the transport of pollutants that cause acid rain in Scandinavia in the nineteenth century. According to detailed studies, the deposition of materials on land surfaces, which had accumulated through the 1960s, showed that the deposits were large enough to interfere with ecosystems. Fish were most vulnerable, as the hatchlings were especially sensitive to the acidity of the streams in which they developed.

In both Europe and North America, declining fish stocks and forest die-outs became serious problems in the 1970s; by the 1980s, these consequences of acid rain began to receive wide public attention. The key driver of these effects was the large amount of sulfur dioxide from coal that traveled long distances and was deposited as sulfuric acid, usually caused by the burning of coal by public utilities (e.g., for electricity). A transition was already under way there, as coal use had begun to decline because new exploitation methods came into use that made gas a less-expensive energy source, and it has the additional benefit of being lower in sulfur. Gradually, very large power stations were obliged, at some expense and with great political reluctance in certain countries, such as the United Kingdom, to reduce the sulfur content of their stack emissions.

The improvements in the North Atlantic have made it easy for politicians to believe that the acid rain problem has gone away. Emissions of sulfur dioxide are now much reduced in this part of the world, thanks to the lower sulfur content of fuels, and thus so is the amount of sulfur deposited in rain there. The decline in some parts of the United Kingdom and Germany has been so large that crops such as oats and oilseed rape have shown signs of sulfur deficiency, necessitating its addition as a fertilizer. However, the decreases in deposited sulfur are not always matched by equivalent improvements in the amount of acid brought down in rain. Lower sulfur emissions have not always been accompanied by lower emissions of the nitrogen oxides that lead to nitric acid. Broadly, much of the acid rain problem has moved, along with sulfur emissions, to Asia, where vast quantities of coal are burned during the current period of rapid economic development.

In the late twentieth century, concerns mounted

A coal-fired power plant in the Mongolian capital of Ulan Bator produces electricity for export and local consumption but contributes to a serious air-pollution problem. The WHO has identified Ulan Bator as one of the most air-polluted cities in the world. *(Danfung Dennis/Bloomberg via Getty Images)*

over the depletion of the ozone layer over the poles, which is critical to protecting the planet from solar radiation. The depletion was caused by the use of CFCs (chlorofluorocarbons or Freons) as refrigerants. These stable compounds traveled to the stratosphere, where the intense radiation broke them down and the liberated chlorine atoms enhanced the chemical cycles that destroy ozone. The problem was a relatively narrow one that arose from a rather restricted group of compounds. Although they were widely used, they were also amenable to international regulation, and national leaders rapidly agreed to the Montreal Protocol of 1987 and subsequent amendments that promoted the use of less dangerous compounds, initially HCFCs (hydrochlorofluorocarbons) and then FCs (fluorocarbons). The reduction in emissions of these compounds raises hopes for closing the ozone hole by 2040–2050, although the regulations started by addressing compounds that were easier to reduce. More difficult issues may lie ahead, say experts.

Even as ozone depletion faded as a popular concern, the media and public attention focused on global issues such as the buildup of carbon dioxide in the atmosphere, which drives the greenhouse effect and brings about climate change. This problem is less tractable than the ozone hole because of the multiplicity of sources of carbon dioxide and because there is no simple replacement, as there is for CFCs. (This problem is more thoroughly discussed in the chapter on climate change.)

Some pollutants do not derive directly from human activity, as events in recent decades illustrate. The ash caused by volcanic eruptions, for example, can erode and damage the turbine blades of jet engines. The most significant eruption in recent years was that of Eyjafjallajökull in Iceland, which reduced air traffic over the North Atlantic for several days in the spring of 2010. In Asia, one regular problem in springtime is the windblown dust that originates in the deserts of northwestern China. The dust is driven eastward, affecting the coastal cities as well as Korea and Japan. Pollutants from the cities can attach to the dust particles, so they are no longer simply windblown crustal material and can present greater health risks.

Forest fires are also a major source of air pollutants. The smoke haze episodes of the past 20 years have had a particular impact in Southeast Asia, but the problem occurs in all parts of the world with large forests. One interesting question is whether the pollutants from forest fires are natural, as the fires may be deliberately set by farmers as the result of agricultural practice. The same can be asked about the dust blown from deserts, which can be exacerbated by overgrazing or nonsustainable farming activities.

Human Health and Social Problems

From the earliest times, air pollutants were believed to affect human health adversely. Although the nature of this harm was not well understood, in the seventeenth century some statistical evidence emerged that coal smoke increased mortality in cities and many began to believe that ingredients such as arsenic and sulfur in the coal were responsible for the damage. The first pollutant to be properly understood was carbon monoxide. In the late nineteenth century it was discovered that it binds with hemoglobin in the blood. This direct biochemical link made the development of health standards clearer than for other pollutants for which the biochemical explanation was not as obvious.

In the first half of the twentieth century, deadly smoke-laden fog in the Meuse Valley in Belgium and northern France, Donora in the coal country of Pennsylvania, and then London created awareness of the epidemiological impact of the air pollution from coal. In each of these incidents, intensive studies attempted to evaluate the observations and set sensible goals for pollution reduction. It was apparent from the beginning that the links between pollutants and health outcomes are confounded by a range of social variables: personal behavior, individual health status, age, and so on. For most of the twentieth century, the health impacts of airborne pollutants of various kinds were seen as respiratory, with pollutants inducing bronchitis or, over the long term, leading to carcinogenesis in the form of lung cancer.

By the end of the twentieth century, our understanding had changed as it became increasingly clear that concentrations of fine particles in the atmosphere had implications beyond the respiratory system. These finer particles, had diameters of 10, 2.5, and even 1 micron. Such particles, especially those of 2.5 microns or less, can penetrate deep into the lungs, where they enter the alveoli, or air sacs, and are often engulfed by alveolar macrophages in a process known to be a key mechanism for removing bacteria and other particles from the lungs. The interaction between the macrophages and the particles releases cytokines, coagulant factors that cause a loss of deformability in the finer microtubules of the circulatory system, making the blood more likely to clot and increasing the risk of heart attacks and strokes. The importance of this observation was that air pollutants could have health outcomes related to the circulatory system in addition to the respiratory system.

Air pollutants had other effects. It had long been evident that smoke blackened urban buildings, but by Victorian times this damage was so severe when combined with the sulfuric acid that came from burning coal that the facades of buildings were often damaged before they were even completed. The concomitant deposition of soot on building surfaces led to thick and disfiguring black gypsum crusts. Blackened buildings typified the coal-burning cities of fin-de-siècle Europe, not only leading to a century of scientific concern and a range of interventions but also influencing the nature

of modern architecture, as architects often responded by changing the design of buildings. This may have been the reason neo-Gothic architecture, with its highly detailed moldings cut in soft limestone, was abandoned so quickly. It was extremely vulnerable to soot and acidic pollutants. Architects began to adopt neoclassical designs, in which simpler lines created a style that was less affected by pollutants. Later in the twentieth century, the issue of acid rain sensitized people to the effects of pollutants on buildings and led to extensive cleaning programs.

A big change in urban life and habits also occurred in the twentieth century. As people spent more time indoors, they became exposed to a range of indoor pollutants, such as the by-products of smoking, cleaning, and cooking. New materials used indoors run the risk of releasing pollutants indoors. Formaldehyde from glue and insulating foam has been a key concern, especially as some scientists came to consider it a carcinogen. Some indoor air pollution problems, such as "sick building syndrome," raise important sociological issues. Sick building syndrome is characterized by a combination of ailments experienced by people who occupy or work in certain interior spaces. It is most often associated with poor ventilation. Yet while the syndrome has at times been attributed to pervasive odors, the sufferers are often linked as much by social interconnections—that is, by traditional person-to-person infection—as by the ventilation system.

Changing family structure in the late twentieth century has also had consequences. As younger generations move away, the elderly are increasingly left to fend for themselves. During the Paris heat wave of 2003, elevated ozone levels severely affected the elderly and were exacerbated by the absence of younger relatives and members of the medical profession, who were away from the city for the long summer holidays, leaving their elders with little support.

Technological Change and the Future

The nature of air pollution has changed enormously in the past 100 years. This has altered the health outcomes and approaches to regulation. In general, air quality has improved in many cities in terms of the burden of pollutants, though mostly in developed countries. However, the complexity of the problem and the advent of newer pollutants remain a challenge. Air pollution is a global problem, and its effects have accelerated as lifestyles have converged between the developed and developing worlds. This has some advantages, for example, allowing generic responses that may offer speedier recovery in cities that continue to have low air quality. Modern lifestyles also have an impact as well. The spread of high-speed access to the Internet allows people to work from home, which reduces pollutants related to driving to a place of employment. In addition, breakthroughs in battery and other technologies could lead to the replacement of internal combustion engines with electric ones, although air pollution will remain if the electricity for these engines is generated by coal-burning plants.

Peter Brimblecombe

See also: Climate Change; Environmental Illnesses; Oil, Environmental and Health Aspects; Respiratory Disease.

Further Reading

Ayres, J., R. Maynard, and R. Richards. *Air Pollution and Health*. London: Imperial College Press, 2006.

Brimblecombe, Peter. *The Big Smoke*. 2d ed. London: Routledge, 2011.

———. "The Clean Air Act After Fifty Years." *Weather* 61 (2006): 311–314.

DuPuis, E. Melanie. *Smoke and Mirrors: The Politics and Culture of Air Pollution*. New York: New York University Press, 2004.

Ho, Mun S., and Chris P. Nielsen. *Clearing the Air: The Health and Economic Damages of Air Pollution in China*. Cambridge, MA: MIT Press, 2007.

Jacobs, Chipo, and William J. Kelly. *Smogtown: The Lung-Burning History of Pollution in Los Angeles*. Woodstock, NY: Overlook, 2008.

Jacobson, Mark Z. *Atmospheric Pollution: History, Science, and Regulation*. New York: Cambridge University Press, 2002.

Lovett, G.M., et al. "Effects of Air Pollution on Ecosystems and Biological Diversity in the Eastern United States." *Annals of the New York Academy of Sciences* 1162 (2009): 99–135.

Thorsheim, Peter. *Inventing Pollution: Coal, Smoke, and Culture in Britain Since 1800*. Athens: Ohio University Press, 2006.

Web Sites

Environmental Protection Agency:
    www.epa.gov/urbanair/
European Environment Agency:
    www.eea.europa.eu/themes/air/
United Nations Environment Programme: www.unep
    .org/urban_environment/issues/urban_air.asp
World Health Organization:
    www.who.int/topics/air_pollution/en/

Documents

Document 1: "FUMIFUGIUM: or The Inconveniencie of the Aer and Smoak of London Dissipated. Together with some Remedies humbly Proposed" (excerpt), 1619

An early architectural critic, England's John Evelyn was particularly concerned about what he considered the sorry state of London's rapidly growing and congested urban landscape in the early seventeenth century. While particularly critical of architects, he also noted that the putrid state of the city's atmosphere, most notably its abundance of coal smoke, was corroding and defacing building exteriors. Not just one of the first texts on the effects of urban pollution on architecture, Fumifugium *also was among the first texts in English to note the impact of such pollution on human health, particularly of the lungs.*

TO THE KINGS MOST SACRED MAJESTY—

SIR,

IT was one day, as I was Walking in Your MAJESTIES Palace at *WHITE-HALL* (where I have ſometimes the honour to refreſh my ſelf with the Sight of Your Illuſtrious Preſence, which is the Joy of Your Peoples hearts) that a preſumptuous Smoake iſſuing from one or two Tunnels neer *Northumberland-houſe*, and not far from *Scotland-yard*, did ſo invade the Court; that all the Rooms, Galleries, and Places about it were fill'd and infeſted with it, and that to ſuch a degree, as Men could hardly diſcern one another for the Clowd, and none could ſupport, without manifeſt Inconveniency. It was not this which did firſt ſuggeſt to me what I had long ſince conceived againſt this pernicious Accident, upon frequent obſervation; But it was this alone, and the trouble that it muſt needs procure to Your Sacred Majeſty, as well as hazzard to Your Health, which kindled this Indignation of mine, againſt it, and was the occaſion of what it has produc'd in theſe Papers.

Your Majeſty who is a Lover of noble Buildings, Gardens, Pidures, and all Royal Magnificences, muſt needs defire to be freed from this prodigious annoyance ; and, which is ſo great an Enemy to their Luſtre and Beauty, that where it once enters there can nothing remain long in its native Splendor and PerfeSion : Nor muſt I here forget that Illuſtrious and divine Princeſſe, Your Majeſties only Siſter, the now Dutcheſſe of Orleans, who at her Highneſſe late being in this City, did in my hearing, complain of the Effects of this Smoake both in her Breaſt and Lungs, whilſt She was in Your Majeſties Palace. I cannot but greatly apprehend, that Your Majeſty (who has been ſo long accuſtomd to the excellent *Aer* of other Countries) may be as much offended at it, in that regard alfo ; efpecially fince the Evil is fo Epidemicall; indangering as well the Health of Your SubjedS as it fullies the Glory of this Your Imperial Seat.

Sir, I prepare in this fhort Difcourfe, an expedient how this pernicious Nuifance may be reformed; and offer at another alfo, by which the Aer may not only be freed from the prefent Inconveniency; but (that remov'd) to rendernot only Your Majefties Palace, but the whole City likewife, one of the fweeteft, and moft delicious Habitations in the World . . .

Source: Openlibrary.org.

Document 2: Health Aspects of Air Pollution with Particulate Matter, Ozone, and Nitrogen Dioxide, World Health Organization (excerpt), 2003

Recognizing that an effective understanding of the health effects of particulate matter in the atmosphere was critical for setting clean air standards, the World Health Organization (WHO) of the United Nations established air quality guidelines for Europe. In this report, WHO's Working Group determined that particulate matter measuring 2.5 microns is of particular concern for human health, as particles of this size can penetrate deep into lung tissue and cause pulmonary and cardiovascular health problems. Since this report was issued, the 2.5-micron measurement has become the standard for most air quality management agencies throughout the world.

1 Introduction

In most countries in Europe, ambient air quality has improved considerably in the last few decades. However, there is a large body of evidence suggesting that exposure to air pollution, even at the levels commonly achieved nowadays in European countries, leads to adverse health effects. In particular, exposure to pollutants such as particulate matter and ozone has been found to be associated with increases in hospital admissions for cardiovascular and respiratory disease and mortality in many cities in Europe and other continents. Recent studies have also tried to quantify the health effects caused by ambient air pollution; e.g., within the "Global Burden of Disease" project of the World Health Organization (WHO) it has been estimated that worldwide, close to 6.4 million years of healthy life are lost due to long-term exposure to ambient particulate matter.

In the 1990s, WHO updated its Air quality guidelines (AQG) for Europe to provide detailed information on the adverse effects of exposure to different air pollutants on human health. The prime aim of these guidelines was to provide a basis for protecting human health from effects of air pollution. The guidelines were in particular intended to provide information and guidance for authorities to make risk management decisions.

2 Scope and Purpose

Since the most recent update of the WHO AQGs, there have been many new studies published that have investigated the effects of air pollution on human health. In order to provide (European) policy makers with state-of-the-art knowledge on the effects of air pollution on human health, it was considered necessary to review the new evidence systematically. At this stage, the review concentrated on the following pollutants: particulate matter (PM), ozone (O_3) and nitrogen dioxide (NO_2). In particular, the question under discussion was whether there was sufficient new evidence to reconsider the current WHO guidelines. . . .

5 Particulate matter (PM)
5.1 Introduction

Airborne particulate matter represents a complex mixture of organic and inorganic substances. Mass and composition in urban environments tend to be divided into two principal groups: coarse particles and fine particles. The barrier between these two fractions of particles usually lies between 1 μm and 2.5 μm. However, the limit between coarse and fine particles is sometimes fixed by convention at 2.5 μm in aerodynamic diameter ($PM_{2.5}$) for measurement purposes. The smaller particles contain the secondarily formed aerosols (gas-to-particle conversion), combustion particles and recondensed organic and metal vapours. The larger particles usually contain earth crust materials and fugitive dust from roads and industries. The fine fraction contains most of the acidity (hydrogen ion) and mutagenic activity of particulate matter, although in fog some coarse acid droplets are also present. Whereas most of the mass is usually in the fine mode (particles between 100 nm and 2.5 μm), the largest number of particles is found in the very small sizes, less than 100 nm. As anticipated from the relationship of particle volume with mass, these so-called ultrafine particles often contribute only a few % to the mass, at the same time contributing to over 90% of the numbers.

Particulate air pollution is a mixture of solid, liquid or solid and liquid particles suspended in the air. These suspended particles vary in size, composition and origin. It is convenient to classify particles by their aerodynamic properties because: (a) these properties govern the transport and removal of particles from the air; (b) they also govern their deposition within the respiratory system and (c) they are associated with the chemical composition and sources of particles. These properties are conveniently summarized by the aerodynamic diameter, that is the size of a unit density sphere with the same aerodynamic characteristics. Particles are sampled and described on the basis of their aerodynamic diameter, usually called simply the particle size.

Source: World Health Organization.

POLLUTION, WATER

Water pollution is any contamination of water with chemicals or other foreign substances that are detrimental to human, plant, or animal health. These pollutants include fertilizers and pesticides from agricultural runoff; sewage and food-processing waste; lead, mercury, chromium, and other heavy metals; chemical wastes from industrial discharges; and contamination from hazardous waste sites. Worldwide, nearly 2 billion people drink contaminated water that could be harmful to their health, and water pollution and contamination are the two largest causes of sickness and death in the world.

The sources of water pollution fall into two general categories: point and nonpoint. Point sources refer to identifiable and discrete conveyances, such as pipes, ditches, and tunnels. Nonpoint sources have diffuse origins, and the pollution occurs when rainfall or snowmelt move over and through the ground. As the runoff moves, it picks up and carries away natural and human-made pollutants, finally depositing them into lakes, rivers, wetlands, coastal waters, and groundwaters. Return flows from irrigated agriculture and urban storm water runoff are two widespread examples of nonpoint water pollution.

Many factors, such as increasing urbanization, climate change, mining, forest and wetland destruction, the expanding geographic extent of energy exploration, and many other direct and indirect anthropogenic activities, pose significant threats to our water resources. Since water is one of the three primary requirements for life on Earth (energy and organic molecules being the others), failure to properly understand and manage water pollution has severe consequences for civilization.

Earth's Water—A Vital Resource

Water is unique because it is the only substance on Earth found in all three states (liquid, solid, and gas) within the planet's temperature range. Liquid water is essential to life, as it composes approximately 60 percent of the human body by weight and 70 percent of the human brain. Some organisms are 90 percent liquid water by weight. Each day, humans must replace 0.63 gallons (2.4 liters) of water, some through drinking and the rest taken by the body from the foods consumed.

Without water humans would not exist. The ability of water to dissolve so many different substances allows cells to use the nutrients, minerals, and chemicals in biological processes. In natural systems, wherever water goes—the air, the ground, streams and lakes, biota, or through our bodies—it takes valuable chemicals, minerals, and nutrients picked up along the way. Globally, the movement of water is cyclical and is called the hydrologic cycle, or water cycle. This movement of water is initiated by solar energy, which evaporates surface water into the atmosphere. Much of this water vapor condenses and falls as some form of precipitation on a distant land surface, where it either evaporates, flows back into the oceans through rivers and streams, is taken up by vegetation and slowly released into the atmosphere as evapotranspiration, or infiltrates into the ground. Groundwater also migrates back to the oceans.

Today, there are immense challenges facing humans with respect to securing water for their basic needs and long-term quality of life. Although almost three-fourths of Earth's surface is covered by water, most of this water is not potable; a high percentage of the fresh water is either frozen, underground, or in a gaseous phase. In addition, water on Earth is very unevenly distributed, from the deserts where it is scarce to the rainforests where it is plentiful. Moreover, the precipitation so critical to replacing our surface and groundwater reservoirs is highly variable and unpredictable.

The transport ability of water also means it can carry substances harmful to humans and the environment. If these contaminants are present at a sufficient concentration and the exposure is long enough, harm-

Earth's Water by Source, Volume, and Type

Water source	Water volume (cubic miles)	Percentage fresh water	Percentage total water
Oceans, seas, and bays	321,000,000	—	96.5
Ice caps, glaciers, and permanent snow	7,773,000	68.7	1.74
Groundwater (total)	5,614,000	—	1.7
Groundwater (fresh)	2,526,000	30.1	0.76
Groundwater (saline)	3,088,000	—	0.94
Soil moisture	3,959	0.05	0.001
Ground ice and permafrost	71,970	0.86	0.022
Lakes (total)		—	0.013
Lakes (fresh)	42,320	0.26	0.007
Lakes (saline)		—	0.006
Atmosphere	3,095	0.04	0.001
Swamps	2,752	0.03	0.0008
Rivers	509	0.006	0.0002
Biological water	269	0.003	0.0001
Total, World	332,500,000	—	100.0

Source: I. Shiklomanov, "World Fresh Water Resources." In *Water in Crisis: A Guide to the World's Fresh Water Resources*, ed. P.T. Gleick, pp. 13–24. New York: Oxford University Press, 1993.

ful effects can occur. The damage can be immediate and obvious—as when oil is washed up on a beach and kills waterfowl—or slow developing and silent, such as the leaking of gasoline from an underground storage tank into a drinking water well.

Protecting the oceans is especially critical, since all water on Earth and any residual contaminants present will eventually cycle through this reservoir. The necessity of reducing wastes before they are released into the environment, and decreasing their quantity and toxicity, underscores the close relationship between water quantity and water quality. For example, when the amounts of urban runoff contaminated by sediment, heavy metals, and pesticides are reduced, the quality of the receiving water bodies generally improves.

All these characteristics of water make protecting it for human use very complex, so a successful and sustainable effort will require a combination of political, sociocultural, economic, and technological factors that are guided by science-based planning.

Human Development and the History of Water Pollution

With the domestication of plants and animals about 12,000 years ago, humans made the transition from nomadic to settled societies. Many of the early human settlements began near a water source in large river valleys, such as the Tigris-Euphrates, Indus, and Nile. Soon, rivers and other water bodies became useful for transportation, water supply (both potable and for agriculture), and as a receptacle for human waste.

During the first 11,000 years in which agricultural societies developed and subsequently began to dominate our planet, the importance of clean water was not understood. For example, in ancient Rome, sewers carried human waste into the Tiber River. About 2,300 years ago, this river became so polluted the Romans had to construct aqueducts to obtain clean drinking water. The pollution of water by raw sewage acted as the catalyst for subsequent typhoid and cholera outbreaks in many parts of the world.

After the establishment of sedentary agriculture, human population grew slowly. Indeed, it was not until the early 1800s that population reached 1 billion. Improvements in medicine, public health, and living standards spawned by the Industrial Revolution resulted in a population explosion. Yet the connection between water pollution with human waste and the outbreaks of diseases such as cholera was not understood until the 1850s. In 1854, a devastating cholera outbreak occurred in the Soho section of London, centering around the Broad Street well. A physician named John Snow deduced through statistical maps that the cause of the outbreak was contamination of the well. Since no one believed him, Snow suggested taking off the well pump's handle. Once the well was not in use, the epidemic ended. The cause was later traced to washing a sick baby's dirty diapers in a cesspool that seeped into the well. Unfortunately for the people of Soho, calls for eliminating cesspools from the vicinity of wells in that area went unheeded for quite some time.

Human population has now reached 7 billion people. Over the past 200 years, this impressive quantitative growth in population has been accompanied by rapid urbanization, which has influenced the distribution of people on Earth. As the population living in cities increased, the waste released was directed into streams and landfills without adequate pollution regulations or the infrastructure necessary to minimize its impact on the environment. To make matters worse, after World War II, the type of pollutants involved changed significantly. Industries within the industrialized nations of Asia, North America, South America, Europe, and Australia began manufacturing and using synthetic materials such as plastics, polychlorinated biphenyls (PCBs), and inorganic pesticides, including the notorious dichlorodiphenyl trichloroethane, better known as DDT. These materials are toxic, accumulate in the environment, and take a long time to biodegrade. Many of these chemicals and other industrial waste by-products found their way into the water, either through direct dumping or through leaching into groundwater from landfills or dumps.

Current Effects of Water Pollution

About 2 billion people worldwide still lack access to potable water. The World Health Organization estimates that 78 percent of the people in developing nations do not have clean water supplies, and up to 85 percent of those people live in areas with inadequate sewage treatment. In these areas, cholera outbreaks are an ongoing concern. In New Delhi, for instance, a third of the water supply is lost through cracks in an antiquated delivery system, and much of the sewage from the city is being discharged untreated back into local waterways. A recent United Nations report noted that some 3 billion people globally can be expected to be without clean water and adequate sanitation by the year 2025. Globally, the lack of sanitation and clean water has made diarrhea the second leading cause of child mortality, with most of these deaths occurring in Africa and Asia.

The most prevalent water quality problem worldwide is eutrophication, a result of high nutrient loads (mainly phosphorus and nitrogen), which substantially impairs beneficial uses of water. Major nutrient sources include agricultural runoff, domestic sewage (also a source of microbial pollution), industrial effluents, and atmospheric inputs from fossil fuel burning and bush fires. Lake Erie (U.S.-Canada border) and the Baltic Sea (northern Europe) provide two notable examples of this problem.

Other widespread consequences of water pollution include accelerated species mortality and the reduction of biodiversity. A primary example of these ecosystem impacts is seen in many of the world's coral reefs, which have become "bleached." Coral reef bleaching is the whitening of the organisms that live symbiotically within the corals and results from anthropogenic and natural variations in the reef environment. Coral-bleaching events have been increasing in both frequency and extent worldwide in the past 20 years, with all of the world's major coral reef regions (Caribbean/western Atlantic, eastern Pacific, central and western Pacific, Indian Ocean, Arabian Gulf, Red Sea) experiencing some degree of this process. Two of the primary human-induced factors are sedimentation from accelerated land erosion and the input of excess organic nutrients from fertilizers.

Until only a few decades ago, the oceans had been viewed as limitless and unaffected by human actions. Throughout the world, coastal countries have used the oceans as receptacles for all types of waste, from sewage and sewage sludge, to industrial and radioactive wastes, to munitions and other warfare agents. As a result, harmful red tide events have become more frequent and widespread since the 1980s. A red tide occurs when huge volumes of algae are produced and discolor coastal waters. The algae may deplete oxygen in the waters and/or release toxins that cause illness in humans and other animals. Major factors influencing red tide events include warm ocean surface temperatures, low salinity, high nutrient contents within agricultural runoff, calm seas, and rain followed by sunny days during the summer months. Countries affected by red tide events include Argentina, Australia, Brazil, Canada, Chile, Denmark, England, France, Guatemala, Hong Kong, India, Ireland, Italy, Japan, the Netherlands, New Guinea, New Zealand, Norway, Peru, the Philippines, Romania, Russia, Scotland, Spain, Sweden, Thailand, the United States, and Venezuela.

Plastics, other nonbiodegradable materials, and oil spills have also besieged the oceans. Many experts believe that the ocean floor has essentially become a vast underwater dump. In the Pacific Ocean alone, an area the size of the state of Texas has been affected. The occurrence of several large oil spills annually

Population of Megacities Dependent on Groundwater, 2010 (millions)

City	Population
Mexico City	25.8
Calcutta	16.5
Tehran	13.6
Shanghai	13.3
Buenos Aires	13.2
Jakarta	13.2
Dhaka	11.2
Manila	11.1
Cairo	11.1
Bangkok	10.7
London	10.5
Beijing	10.4

Source: United Nations Environment Programme (UNEP), *Groundwater and Its Susceptibility to Degradation: A Global Assessment of the Problem and Options for Management.* Nairobi, Kenya: UN Division of Early Warning and Assessment, 2003.

is also a concern, since oil damages the water and marine life for at least a decade.

Besides the oceans, other major reservoirs of the water on Earth also suffer the extensive impact of pollution. Every day, 2 million tons (1.8 million metric tons) of human waste is disposed of in rivers. Consequences of this pollution include water-borne illness, water shortages, and lowered property values. Groundwater—the largest supply of accessible fresh water—is also at risk. Since groundwater usually flows more slowly than surface water, the pollution within this reservoir stays around longer and can potentially affect the health of more people. As a result, the direct, or hydraulic, connection between groundwater and surface water has become increasingly important as a global issue because larger urban areas are seeking out subsurface supplies for their growing populations.

The increase in groundwater withdrawals in urban areas has placed the pollution of groundwater front and center. For example, in the industrial Midwest of the United States, the highly toxic compound hexavalent chromium has been detected in groundwater. Across the world in Ho Chi Minh City, Vietnam, heavy use and contamination have caused groundwater levels to fall. As a result, high concentrations of iron and nitrate have developed, and the groundwater has become brackish near the coast from saltwater intrusion.

Responses

For most of the years following the Industrial Revolution, the prevailing attitude toward pollution was that the "solution to pollution is dilution"; that is, the volume of the nearby water body—and especially the oceans—was sufficient to handle whatever pollution it received. This view held up until several high-profile events, such as the major oil spill off the coast of California in 1969, and the inundation of major lakes such as Erie (North America) and Biwa (Japan) with phosphates spurred social action against pollution. Coordinated international action to address ocean pollution began in 1972 with the Convention on the Prevention of Marine Pollution by Dumping of Wastes and Other Matters. This convention was established to control pollution of the sea by dumping of wastes, which could create hazards to human health or harm living to resources and marine life, damage amenities, and interfere with other legitimate uses of the sea. The convention encourages supplementary regional agreements. It calls on parties "to promote measures to prevent pollution by hydrocarbons, other matter transported other than for dumping, wastes generated during operation of ships etc., radioactive pollutants and matter originating from exploration of the sea bed."

To address pollution, many nations have adopted the "Polluter Pays Principle," which states that the party responsible for producing pollution is responsible for paying for the damage done to the natural environment. This framework has been adopted by most Organisation for Economic Co-operation and Development and European Community countries.

To date, efforts to limit the sources of transboundary pollution, such as acidic precipitation (United States, Canada, and Northern Europe) and groundwater contamination have stalled, as have comprehensive protection measures for groundwater in South America, Africa, and Asia. On a smaller geographic scale, however, the response has been more noticeable, with numerous watershed-level organizations on every continent working to reduce pollution within their regions.

Challenges and Solutions

Climate change will continue to worsen already scarce water resources, from the western United States and cities like Las Vegas, to countries in Africa, which the UN has designated as one of the "most vulnerable continents," primarily because of its dry climate and inadequate infrastructure. In China, severe declines in some river and groundwater basins have occurred as a result of rapidly melting Himalayan glaciers, and coastal areas are rapidly experiencing saltwater intrusion as a result of overpumping existing groundwater

An estimated 4.9 million barrels of crude oil gushed into the Gulf of Mexico after the April 2010 explosion of BP's Deepwater Horizon oil rig and the rupturing of a wellhead a mile underwater. It was considered the worst marine environmental disaster in history. *(AP Photo/Gerald Herbert)*

wells. Climate change is also affecting South America. For example, Peru depends upon meltwater from high mountain glaciers and ice fields for its fresh water supply and hydroelectric power. But because of the rapidly shrinking glaciers emanating from the Quelccaya ice cap, Peru could face a water crisis in the coming decade. This crisis would directly impact Lima, Peru's capital on its arid Pacific coast, where officials are already piping water directly from the mountains.

As the global population becomes more concentrated in urban areas, energy consumption will increase. The need to expand energy supplies to meet this rising demand will expand the extent of fossil energy exploration, at least in the short term. Techniques such as offshore drilling, hydraulic fracturing, and tar sand recovery each pose unique contamination risks to significant portions of the world's water resources. For instance, the spent drilling fluids used in hydraulic fracturing and the unpredictable flow of liberated methane gas could contaminate large quantities of groundwater. In addition to the environmental challenges posed by these newer technologies, increasing regional tensions

over dwindling natural resources could limit the effectiveness of water pollution control efforts.

Sustainable outcomes that prevent further pollution and improve the state of the world's water are not possible without preventing further land contamination and land degradation. Knowing how the land was formed and how it functions as a landscape is critical to managing it properly, and this principle underscores the value of the earth sciences in watershed management. Managing the land properly will help to reduce the pollution loads transported by eroded sediment and storm water and protect drinking water supplies in surface water and aquifers.

Unfortunately, the effective use of science alone cannot attain sustainable water for the planet. Comprehensive watershed management and the attainment of sustainable watersheds also depend on the success of institutional reforms. The mismatches between landscape process and institutional reforms will have to be resolved, and all levels of government, the private sector, and the public will need to share a common vision.

Watersheds represent a high level of complexity that operates through a variety of systems, incorporating an array of hydrologic, ecologic, and geologic, and climatic processes. Nature has organized these systems, and society now has the opportunity to create institutional organizations to work with these natural structures and manage air and land to prevent further water pollution. Inter-watershed cooperation is a necessity to protect local watersheds and their ultimate destinations—the oceans of the world.

Experts believe that 80 percent of the pollution in the oceans is due to the activities of humans. This fact, and the nature of the hydrologic cycle, indicate that a great deal of our existing water pollution could be reduced through source control—preventing pollution from entering the environment. Some of the ways to achieve source control are improving urban planning techniques; banning the use of certain chemicals; improving wastewater systems; using renewable energy; and involving more environmental scientists in the land-planning process.

Education is critical to the success of any of these efforts, say experts, whether they involve one or more of the health, ecological, social, or political arenas. In terms of simple measures, a recent study by the United Nations found that hand washing with soap at critical times can reduce the incidence of diarrhea by up to 47 percent. At a more complex social and political level, a majority of the nations in the world still do not have basic laws that protect groundwater and recognize its interaction with surface water. Broadening public education about water, watersheds, and the interactions between humans and their environment is a constructive step to help initiate and sustain the necessary political and legal reforms for curbing water pollution.

Finally, successful water pollution control will require improved engineering, better infrastructure, and the political will to implement sustainable long-term solutions rather than economically attractive short-term fixes.

Martin Kaufman

See also: Environmental Illnesses; Fishing and Fish Stocks; Oil, Environmental and Health Aspects; Pesticides and Artificial Fertilizers; Toxic Waste; Waste Disposal; Water Supply and Access; Wetlands.

Further Reading

Allsopp, M., S.E. Pambuccian, P. Johnston, and D. Santillo. *State of the World's Oceans*. Heidelberg: Springer, 2009.

Gleick, P.H. *The World's Water 2008–2009*. Washington, DC: Island, 2008.

Jones, J.A. Global Hydrology: Processes, Resources, and Environmental Management. London: Longman, 1997.

Kaufman, M.M., D.T. Rogers, and K.S. Murray. *Urban Watersheds: Geology, Contamination, and Sustainable Development*. Boca Raton, FL: CRC, 2011.

Markham, Adam. *A Brief History of Pollution*. New York: St. Martin's, 1994.

United Nations Environmental Program (UNEP). *Groundwater and Its Susceptibility to Degradation: A Global Assessment of the Problem and Options for Management:* Nairobi, Kenya: Division of Early Warning and Assessment, 2003.

World Health Organization. *World Health Statistics 2011*. Geneva: WHO, 2011.

Web Sites

UNESCO World Water Assessment Program: www.unesco.org/water/wwap/facts_figures/basic_needs.shtml

United Nations International Decade for Action, Water for Life 2005–2015: www.un.org/waterforlifedecade/background.html

Documents

Document 1: The 3rd UN World Water Development Report (excerpts), 2009

The World Water Assessment Program (WWAP), founded in 2000, is a program of UN-Water. Hosted and led by UNESCO, WWAP is a United Nations systemwide effort to develop the tools and skills needed to achieve a better understanding of the processes, management practices, and policies that will help improve the supply and quality of global freshwater resources. The principal objective of the WWAP is to assess and report on the state, use, and management of the world's freshwater resources and the demands on these resources, define critical problems, and assess the ability of nations to cope with water-related stress and conflict. Its primary product, the United Nations World Water Development Report, is published every three years and launched in conjunction with the World Water Forum.

Urban sewage treatment still limited mainly to high-income countries

To achieve pollution mitigation objectives for the environment and human health, improved sanitation must be accompanied by sewage treatment. Sewage treatment is the removal of physical, chemical and biological contaminants from wastewater, both surface drainage and domestic, using physical, chemical and biological processes. The objective is to produce a treated waste stream (or treated effluent) and solid waste or sludge suitable for discharge or reuse back into the environment. Data on the rates and levels of collection and treatment of sewage are limited and often difficult to compare.

Sewage: a problem to manage?

More than 80 percent of sewage in developing countries is discharged untreated, polluting rivers, lakes and coastal areas. Even in some developed countries treatment of urban wastewater is far from satisfactory. The OECD online environmental compendium finds a broad range of applications of tertiary waste treatment, from 3.6 percent in Turkey to 90 percent in Germany.

In most low- and middle-income countries wastewater is discharged directly into the sea or rivers without treatment. Urban wastewater constitutes a significant pollution load and is particularly hazardous when mixed with untreated industrial waste—a common practice. Many large cities still have no treatment plants or plants quickly become undersized as urban population growth outpaces investments. A nationwide survey in Pakistan found that only 2 percent of cities with a population of more than 10,000 had wastewater treatment facilities and that less than 30 percent of wastewater receives treatment in these cities. Some 36 percent of wastewater is used in agriculture: (2.4 million m³ a day directly for irrigation and 400,000 m³ a day is disposed of in irrigation canals), and 64 percent is disposed of in rivers or the Arabian Sea. In many developing countries waterborne sanitation systems and pollution mitigation facilities may not be the most sustainable option; other improved facilities may be more suitable (for example, using lagoons for collective units and ecosanitation units for rural households). In developed countries wastewater is progressively coming under control. Over the last 20 years Europe's Urban Wastewater Treatment Directive has resulted in significant improvements in treatment capacity, with more advanced wastewater treatment becoming increasingly common. Continuous progress is being made. Belgium, for example, put in operation a mega-treatment plant, which has improved its situation since 2006.

Source: UNESCO.

Document 2: World Water Quality Facts and Statistics (excerpts), The Pacific Institute, 2010

The Pacific Institute conducts interdisciplinary international research with stakeholders to produce solutions that advance environmental protection, economic development, and social equity. Topics of interest include water shortages, habitat destruction, global warming, and environmental injustice. Founded in 1987, the institute has become known for independent, innovative thinking that cuts across traditional areas of study, and its interdisciplinary approach brings opposing groups together to forge effective real-world solutions. Currently, the institute is focusing on four initiatives: International Water and Communities, Water Use in Business, Climate Impacts and Adaptation, and Integrity of Science.

Global Water Pollution

• Every day, 2 million tons of sewage and industrial and agricultural waste are discharged into the world's water (UN WWAP 2003), the equivalent of the weight of the entire human population of 6.8 billion people.

• The UN estimates that the amount of wastewater produced annually is about 1,500 km³, six times more water than exists in all the rivers of the world. (UN WWAP 2003)

Human Waste

• Lack of adequate sanitation contaminates water courses worldwide and is one of the most significant forms of water pollution. Worldwide, 2.5 billion people live without improved sanitation. (UNICEF WHO 2008)

• Over 70 percent of these people who lack sanitation, or 1.8 billion people, live in Asia.

• Sub-Saharan Africa is slowest of the world's regions in achieving improved sanitation: only 31 percent of residents had access to improved sanitation in 2006.

• 18 percent of the world's population, or 1.2 billion people (1 out of 3 in rural areas), defecate in the open. Open defecation significantly compromises quality in nearby water bodies and poses an extreme human health risk. (UNICEF WHO 2008)

• In Southern Asia, 63 percent of rural people—778 million people—practice open defecation.

Human Health Impacts

• Worldwide, infectious diseases such as waterborne diseases are the number one killer of children under five years old and more people die from unsafe water annually than from all forms of violence, including war. (WHO 2002)

• Unsafe or inadequate water, sanitation, and hygiene cause approximately 3.1 percent of all deaths worldwide, and 3.7 percent of DALYs (disability adjusted life years) worldwide. (WHO 2002)

• Unsafe water causes 4 billion cases of diarrhea each year, and results in 2.2 million deaths, mostly of children under five. This means that 15 percent of child deaths each year are attributable to diarrhea—a child dying every 15 seconds. In India alone, the single largest cause of ill health and death among children is diarrhea, which kills nearly half a million children each year. (WHO and UNICEF 2000)

Pollution from Agriculture

• In a recent comparison of domestic, industrial, and agricultural sources of pollution from the coastal zone of Mediterranean countries, agriculture was the leading source of phosphorus compounds and sediment. (UNEP 1996) Nutrient enrichment, most often associated with nitrogen and phosphorus from agricultural runoff, can deplete oxygen levels and eliminate species with higher oxygen requirements, affecting the structure and diversity of ecosystems.

• Nitrate is the most common chemical contaminant in the world's groundwater aquifers. (Spalding and Exner 1993) And mean nitrate levels have risen by an estimated 36 percent in global waterways since 1990 with the most dramatic increases seen in the Eastern Mediterranean and Africa, where nitrate contamination has more than doubled. (GEMS 2004)

• According to various surveys in India and Africa, 20–50 percent of wells contain nitrate levels greater than 50 mg/l and in some cases as high as several hundred milligrams per liter. (cited in FAO 1996)

Source: Pacific Institute.

POPULATION GROWTH AND DEMOGRAPHIC ISSUES

Human populations are in constant flux, usually growing, at specific times and places shrinking, but very rarely static. And even stable populations, while remaining roughly the same size overall, experience internal compositional change in their age, gender, class, immigrant, and ethnic cohorts. Many factors—resources, technology, economics, health care, education, government policy, migration, and more—play a role in population change. And, of course, this change affects all matters of the natural and human world, from environmental quality to economic well-being to social order and national security.

Studying Population

Given its centrality to the nature and quality of existence, the study of population and population characteristics—or demographics—has been a preoccupation of humankind throughout its history. Governments have attempted to count population since at least ancient Egypt, usually to enhance taxation and conscription. In modern times, counts have been conducted to allow governments to better represent and serve their people, such as the decennial census mandated by the U.S. Constitution. As old as efforts to count populations have been debates over how human numbers affect society. Plato and Aristotle, for example, argued that republics were best suited for states with small populations while monarchies best served states with large populations.

Over the centuries, other thinkers grappled with how population size affects state power and geopolitical relations, generally leaning toward the idea that a bigger population confers more power and wealth, and that governments should encourage population growth. Such ideas were upended by English political scientist Thomas Malthus. In his *Essay on the Principle of Population* (first published in 1798),

arguably the most influential treatise on population in history, Malthus maintained that while populations grew geometrically, agricultural output expanded arithmetically. In other words, societies inevitably outstripped their food supplies, leading to famine.

Writing at the dawn of the Industrial Revolution, Malthus underestimated technology's capacity to expand food supply. In addition, he failed to anticipate that social modernization would lead many families to limit offspring. This led to fears in Europe and America that whites and the more educated middle and upper classes—that is, those most likely to limit family size—would be swamped by the nonwhites and the lower classes of the world. Such thinking produced the eugenics movement—persuading or coercing supposedly inferior people to have fewer, or no, children. In addition, immigration restrictions were placed on people from poorer or nonwhite countries, and government incentives encouraged middle-class or native-born couples to have more children.

Largely discredited by the mid-twentieth century, such population ideas were superseded by a school of thought known as neo-Malthusianism. Popularized by Stanford University biologist Paul Ehrlich and his wife, Anne, in their 1968 best seller, *The Population Bomb*, neo-Malthusianism translated the eighteenth-century English thinker's ideas to a twentieth-century world, where rapid population growth—made possible by advances in public health—once again threatened famine, as well as environmental collapse. As did Malthus, the Ehrlichs argued for more government birth control efforts. Challenged on many fronts—most notably, the Catholic Church—neo-Malthusian ideas remain the dominant thinking about population issues in the early twenty-first century, though some economists point out that rising consumption levels are more threatening to the environment than rising population.

Demographic History of the World

For most of human existence, population grew very slowly. Prior to the development of agriculture approximately 10,000 years ago, hunter-gatherer societies were constrained by their environment's carrying capacity, or ability to support a given number of people. Expansion across the globe allowed population to grow to about 5 million. The development of agriculture and centralized civilizations acted as population accelerants, and by about 1750 global population had grown to roughly 900 million.

Of course, this growth has not been even or steady geographically or over time. Major historical events—such as the introduction of highly productive and nutritious crops from the Western Hemisphere after 1492, including corn, potatoes, and manioc—would also accelerate population growth, in this case in the Eastern Hemisphere. At the same time, Europe's "discovery" of the Americas produced demographic catastrophe in the latter, as economic exploitation and new diseases wiped out up to 90 percent of Amerindian populations. Meanwhile, the slave trade and the social chaos it engendered stunted Africa's population growth for centuries.

The industrial and commercial revolutions of the late eighteenth and the nineteenth century allowed societies to better discover, exploit, and distribute resources while medical and public health advances lowered mortality rates. The result was rapid population rises in those areas of the world where these events first occurred, notably North America and Europe. In 1750, their combined population of 170 million represented about 20 percent of humanity; by 1900, their 500 million constituted one-third. Over the course of the twentieth century, these economic and health advances spread—if unevenly—to the developing world, accelerating global population growth at a phenomenal pace. Whereas it took humanity all of prehistory and history to 1800 to reach 1 billion, a second billion was reached by 1927, a doubling to 4 billion by 1974, the 6 billion mark by 1999, and the 7 billion in 2011.

By the early twenty-first century, the world could roughly be divided into three zones, as far as population growth was concerned, with major exceptions in each. The first zone, comprising the developed world of Europe, North America, and parts of Oceania and East Asia, has seen population stabilize and begin to contract. While mortality rates in all of these regions

Historical Global Population, 10,000 B.C.E. to 2100 C.E.

Year	Range (millions)*
10,000 B.C.E.	1–10
5,000 B.C.E.	5–20
1 C.E.	170–400
500 C.E.	190–206
1000	254–345
1100	301–320
1200	360–450
1300	360–432
1400	350–374
1500	425–540
1600	545–579
1700	600–679
1800	813–1,125
1900	1,550–1,679
1950	2,400–2,557
2000	6,000–6,200
2050**	7,400–10,800
2100**	5,500–14,000

  * Ranges based on a summary of major studies.
 ** Projected by the United Nations.
Sources: U.S. Census Bureau; United Nations Population Division.

have fallen, fertility rates, or the number of births per woman, have fallen even more dramatically, to below the replacement rate. This decline is due to several factors. In East Asia, economic growth, rising levels of education, the emergence of a broad middle class, and urbanization have all led people to postpone marriage and opt to have fewer children. In Europe, there is more debate over the decline, though most experts cite cultural factors and stagnant economic opportunities for young people. In the former Soviet bloc, population contraction is due to both declining fertility rates and high mortality rates since the collapse of Communist-era health-care systems. The great exception to population decline in the developed world is the United States, where fertility rates remain at roughly those needed to replace population. Thus, with its high immigration numbers, the United States is one of the few developed world countries expected to experience significant population gain this century.

The second zone comprises those countries of the developing world, including parts of East, Southeast and South Asia, as well as Latin America, that have experienced sustained economic growth in recent years. The same factors apply here. Improved public health has lowered mortality rates, but economic growth; better education, particularly for girls and women; and urbanization have led people to restrict family size, though not quite to the same extent as their counterparts in Europe or Japan. In this trend, wealthier parts of Southeast Asia tend to set the pace ahead of South Asia and Latin America. In the latter region, the influence of the anti–artificial contraception doctrines of the Catholic Church, while declining, remains significant. In terms of population growth, the great exception to these poorer but expanding economies is China. There, a government policy punishing families for having more than one child, instituted in 1979, led to dramatic declines in fertility rates and, despite lowering mortality rates, a population growth rate of roughly zero.

The final population growth region is the Middle East and Africa, where fertility rates remain extremely high, even as better public health measures have lowered mortality rates. There, economic growth rates remain slow or stagnant, the middle class small, and education lags behind that of the first two population regions. Perhaps, even more importantly, the status of women in both regions remains low, and where women are poorly educated and powerless, they cannot control their reproductive destinies. Such factors keep fertility rates high despite two countertrends, urbanization in both regions and the AIDS pandemic in sub-Saharan Africa, which most severely affects the population cohort of reproductive age. Finally, this region, too, contains a great exception—the oil-rich states of the Persian Gulf. While most of these are middle- and high-income urbanized countries, with greatly improved educational systems since the 1970s, they continue to experience very high fertility rates. Experts cite the low status of women and government policies, which continue to encourage large families as a way to provide a native labor force to take over from foreign nationals.

Percentage of Global Population, by Region, 1800–2050*

Region	1800	1900	2000	2050**
Africa	10.9	8.1	13.4	21.7
Asia	64.9	57.4	60.5	57.3
Europe	20.8	24.7	11.9	7.2
Latin America/Caribbean	2.5	4.5	8.5	8.4
North America	0.7	5.0	5.2	4.8
Oceania	0.2	0.4	0.5	0.5

* Some percentages do not add up as percentages are rounded off to nearest tenth.
** Projected.
Source: United Nations Population Division.

Impact of Population Change

The impact of population change—both growth and decline—is a multifaceted one, affecting virtually every aspect of human society and the natural world. This survey will focus on the most salient aspects: environment, resources, economics, politics, social policy, and national security.

Environment and Resources

Human beings alter their environment in two basic ways: in what they extract—land, minerals, forests, and so forth—and in what they put back as waste. This has always been the case, but only with the rise of densely populated civilizations in the third millennium B.C.E. was it possible for humans to radically transform local ecosystems, or communities of organisms, and the environments they inhabit. With the Industrial Revolution, humanity has become an ecological force of global proportions. Since 1800, world population has risen sixfold, as have consumption rates, meaning that humanity's impact on the environment has increased by a factor of more than 30.

It is almost impossible today to find an ecosystem anywhere that has not been transformed by human activity. On the extraction side of the equation, vast forests have been felled, plains plowed under for agriculture, mountaintops reduced by mining, rivers dammed and diverted for irrigation and energy, and lands of all types consumed by urban sprawl. As for what human beings put into the environment, the list is almost endless—sewage, solid waste, toxic chemicals, air pollutants, radiation, heat—all of which alter and degrade environments. Meanwhile, the vast expansion of population and consumption has accelerated human civilization's carbon output, a phenomenon that has been linked to climate change on a global scale. This change is altering virtually every ecosystem on the planet, from melting arctic ice to dying temperate forests to desertification in the tropics. And when ecosystems are altered, or disappear, so do plant and animal species, leading to a loss of biodiversity and an increased rate of extinction. Scientists estimate that current extinction rates are roughly 100 to 1,000 times the normal "background rate" of extinction (since most extinctions go unnoted, estimates vary widely). Noted biologist Edward O. Wilson has predicted that if current population growth and consumption patterns persist, humanity will have eliminated roughly one-half of all higher life forms on Earth by the year 2100.

Tragic as this ongoing destruction of species is, it does not necessarily threaten human populations or civilizations. But a related phenomenon—resource depletion—may. Rapidly growing population and consumption levels are eating up the world's resources at an accelerating pace. To take just one example—arguably, the most important one—oil consumption has increased eightfold between 1950 and 2012, from 11 million barrels per day to 88 million, a result of human population growth from 2.5 to 7 billion and rising gross domestic product (GDP) from $6.4 trillion to $69.1 trillion (in constant 2010 dollars). These numbers illustrate the explosive growth in demand created when rapidly expanding population numbers are multiplied by rising income, and thereby consumption, levels.

Meanwhile, estimates put global oil reserves at between 900 billion and 1.3 trillion barrels, meaning that even if current consumption rates continue, the world will go through those reserves sometime between the year 2040 and 2060. But, of course, consumption rates are not going to remain the same. While falling populations in much of the developed world—along with energy efficiencies and a shift from manufacturing—will reduce oil consumption there, such drops will be more than offset by rising populations and, more importantly, consumption levels in the developing world. By 2020, for example, it is estimated that world oil consumption will grow by roughly one-fourth, to 112 million barrels per day, perhaps outstripping the growth in production.

Finite resources, such as oil, always run out eventually, of course. But what alarms many environmentalists and policy makers is that population and consumption growth are straining and even destroying renewable resources as well. Aquifers around the world are being depleted faster than they are replenished. According to one estimate, at current rates of population growth the average person in 2050 will have about one-fourth as much water as his or her counterpart in 1950. Of course, this will vary enormously as fresh water resources are unevenly distributed. Despite the use of tree plantations, forested areas are expected to shrink from their current level of about 1.25 acres (0.5 hectares) to about 0.9 acres (0.36 hectares) per person. Global fishing resources are declining fast as well, as competing national fleets harvest at rates unmatchable by natural reproduction rates, not to mention the impact climate change is having on ocean acidity and oxygen levels, both necessary for the survival of many fish species.

As for agriculture, by the late twentieth century, it appeared as if food production could keep pace with rapid population growth, as new lands and new advances in the horticultural sciences, many of them made possible by the Green Revolution, allowed more food to be grown in a given area of land. Countries such as Vietnam and China that had once been net food importers became exporters. At the same time, those parts of the world with rapidly rising populations and stagnant economies, such as the Middle East and Africa, became large-scale importers. Exacerbating such trends is climate change, which is suspected of having disrupted the monsoons of South Asia and increased drought in the Sahel region of sub-Saharan Africa.

Thus, while global food supplies have grown dramatically since the 1960s, they have also become more prone to disruption, leading to widespread malnutrition, regional famines, and spiking food prices, which tend to hit the poorest members of affected societies the hardest. By the early twenty-first century, signs had emerged—in the form of food riots and political unrest in places as far afield as Haiti and Algeria, both nations with exceptionally high fertility rates and stagnant economies—that production was lagging behind demand. Adding to the strain, paradoxically, are rising income levels in the more economically dynamic parts of the developing world, such as East Asia, which have led to increased meat consumption. Compared with nutrition from plants, nutrition from meat requires more water, land, and energy to produce—as staple crops are fed to animals rather than people—thereby putting further strains on world food production. Still, many agricultural experts insist the problem is not one of food production—which, given scientific advances could easily feed a much larger human population, even with higher consumption rates—but distribution.

Society: Economics, Politics, Social Issues, and National Security

As recent history reveals, economic development usually produces lower fertility rates and slower—or even negative—population growth. When people become wealthier, they also become better educated and more urbanized, leading them to choose smaller families. South Korea provides a particularly extreme example of this. In 1960, the country was among

Traffic, strain on basic services, and sheer human congestion are worsening problems in Lagos, Nigeria, the largest city in Africa and one of the fastest-growing in the world. Africa itself is the fastest-growing continent; Asia is by far the largest. *(AP Photo/Lekan Oyekanmi)*

the poorest in Asia, with a GDP per capita of just $104 ($750 in 2010 dollars), and a near six-births-per-woman fertility rate. By 2010, the nation's GDP per capita stood at $20,200 while the fertility rate had dropped to 1.2, below the rate necessary for maintaining a stable population.

Just as economic development affects population, so population size and, perhaps more importantly, age cohort composition, affect virtually every aspect of human society. Most economists agree that, to a certain extent, population growth is a positive force for various reasons. First, an expanded population allows for economies of scale. Even population growth that puts pressure on resources can have a positive effect. While Malthus saw catastrophe in such a development, many economists argue that it spurs innovation. Still others have pointed out that expanding populations increase human capital; in other words, the more people there are, the more human ingenuity and imagination. There have also been naysayers. Economists influenced by neo-Malthusianism argue that rising populations lead to resource depletion

and hence inflation, undermining economic growth. They also argue that rising populations increase current consumption—as families and governments spend more on children—at the expense of savings and investment.

This latter point brings up the importance of age cohort composition as it affects economic growth and development. Theoretically, the current income invested in children pays dividends when those children become more productive adults. Scholars of the subject speak of a "demographic gift" where high birth rates, followed by a period of declining fertility—the post–World War II "baby boom" era in the developed world or the post-1980 rapid growth era in East Asia—lead to a huge cohort of people of an age at which they produce the most and demand the least in terms of education and health care. Such rosy scenarios, however, are only possible where there are jobs, which is not the case in many developing world economies.

Then there is the opposite scenario, in which continuing declines in fertility lead to population shrinkage, even as improved health care extends life, the case in much of Europe, Japan, and even newly developed countries like South Korea. A shrinking population leads to lower demand, which can result in deflation. Seemingly a happy scenario—more resources to go around, lower costs—this can actually be detrimental economically, as people defer consumption and businesses defer investment, one anticipating lower prices and the other lower demand. Moreover, an expanding cohort of older people places greater burdens on pension programs and health-care systems just at the moment when the cohort of people in their productive years—those whose taxes and insurance premiums pay for such social services—is shrinking.

Both scenarios—the rising proportion of old people in the developed world and the rising numbers of unemployed young people in parts of the developing world—create economic conditions that can lead to political turmoil. In the former, demographers speak of generational conflict, as older citizens, who vote more consistently than persons in their economically productive years, insist that more resources be devoted to health care and pensions rather than education. The robust democracies of developed world economies have thus far kept such disputes peaceful and within existing political structures.

That has not been the case in the developing world, where democratic institutions are weak, though there is some evidence that even tentative democratization promotes lower fertility rates, as democracies tend to invest more in education and health care than do authoritarian states. Still, in much of the developing world the bulging cohort of idle young people—a result of high fertility and low economic growth rates—has created an explosive political situation, as the revolutions in the Middle East in 2011 attested. Many of the young men who participated in the protests lacked economic prospects in countries with corrupt dictatorships, where opportunities were confined to the politically well connected. Without jobs, these young men could not move out of their parents' homes and start their own families, leading to a loss of dignity and sexual frustration.

In China, where nearly one-fifth of humanity lives, a different demographic variant plays out, albeit one with potential for the same politically explosive results. As a result of the one-child policy and improved pre-birth gender-determination methods, many couples chose to abort female fetuses, since males traditionally not only are more highly valued but also have the

socially prescribed role of supporting their parents in their dotage, an important factor in a country with a weak social safety net. This has led to an excess of males over females—roughly 108 to 100—meaning that many of the former will never have the opportunity to marry and start families, a situation leading to further social and political tensions.

Potentially, all of these forces—resource depletion, ecosystem degradation, economic stagnation, and political turmoil—raise issues of social conflict, war, and national security. History provides numerous examples in which states have gone to war because of overcrowding and declining resources. But while there are examples of civil conflict over declining resources in the contemporary world—some scholars argue that disputes over land contributed to the 1994 genocide in densely populated Rwanda—resource wars are relatively rare today. For example, even states with rising population and consumption levels have sought to negotiate over water rather than go to war.

Indeed, scholars are reluctant to assign blame for conflict to demographic causes alone, though broad surveys have shown that countries with denser populations experience more civil unrest and are more likely to be involved in international wars, as are countries with higher proportions of males in their late teens and early twenties. Domestically, demographers have argued that the drop in U.S. fertility rates in the 1970s corresponded to the drop in crime rates a generation later, when persons born in that decade entered their most crime-prone years. The problem, say demographers, is the classic one of separating cause from mere correlation. Virtually every country in sub-Saharan Africa, for example, contains large cohorts of males between the ages of 15 and 24, yet some have remained at peace while others have been wracked by internal warfare, despite having equally dismal economic records.

The Future

Demographers offer different population scenarios through the end of the twenty-first century. These have been collated by the United Nations into three projections: a high one in which growth follows at its current pace, creating a global population of 14 billion; a medium one whereby population stabilizes midcentury at about 9 billion; and a low one where population begins to decline after 2040, falling to about 5.5 billion, a full 1.5 billion below its current level. Most demographers say the middle scenario is

Fertility Rate, Life Expectancy, and Population, Selected Countries, 2010; Projected Population in 2050

Country	Fertility rate (births per woman)	Life expectancy, in years at birth*	GDP per capita in US$	Population 2010 (in millions)/ ranking	Population 2050 (in millions)
Africa, Sub-Saharan					
Ethiopia	6.07	52.9	364	88	186
Kenya	4.38	54.1	888	40	55
Nigeria	4.82	46.9	1,324	152	279
South Africa	2.33	49.3	7,101	50	47
Asia, East and Southeast					
China	1.54	73	4,520	1,330	1,462
Indonesia	2.28	70.7	2,963	243	311
Japan	1.2	82.6	42,325	127	109
Philippines	3.23	71.7	2,011	100	128
South Korea	1.22	78.6	20,165	49	52
Vietnam	1.93	74.2	1,032	90	124
Asia, South and Central					
Afghanistan	5.5	43.8	560	29	72
Bangladesh	2.65	64.1	640	158	265
India	2.68	64.7	1,176	587	1,572
Kazakhstan	1.87	67	8,326	16	15
Pakistan	3.28	65.5	1,049	177	344
Europe, Eastern and Former Soviet Bloc					
Czech Republic	1.25	76.5	18,721	11	8
Poland	1.29	75.6	11,521	38	33
Romania	1.27	72.5	7,390	21	18
Russia	1.54	65.5	10,521	139	104
Europe, Western					
France	1.97	80.7	40,591	65	62
Germany	1.42	79.4	40,512	82	71
Great Britain	1.92	79.4	36,298	61	59
Italy	1.32	80.5	33,828	58	43
Latin America/Caribbean					
Argentina	2.33	75.3	8,663	41	55
Brazil	2.19	72.4	10,471	201	247
Cuba	1.61	78.3	n/a	11	11
Guatemala	3.36	70.3	2,839	14	27
Mexico	2.31	76.2	9,243	112	147
Middle East/North Africa					
Algeria	1.76	72.3	4,477	35	51
Egypt	3.01	71.3	2,771	80	114
Iran	1.89	71	4,484	67	121
Saudi Arabia	4.5	72.8	16,641	29	60
North America					
Canada	1.58	80.7	45,888	34	40
United States	2.06	78.3	47,132	310	397
Oceania					
Australia	1.78	81.2	54,869	23	27
Fiji	2.65	68.8	3,544	1	1

* Data for 2008.
Sources: World Bank, IMF, UN Population Division; UN Population Fund.

most likely. Economic prosperity is spreading, and with it educational levels; the status of women seems to be improving around the world; and urbanization is also spreading.

All of these factors lead to lower fertility rates. Latin America is just the latest example of a phenomenon that began in Europe and North America in the late nineteenth century and spread to Asia in the latter third of the twentieth. Fertility rates there have dropped from more than 6 children per woman in 1950 to fewer than 2.8 by 2010 even as GDP per capita has risen from just over $4,200 to more than $7,500 in constant 2010 dollars. It is probable, say most population experts, that such trends will reach the remaining areas of rapid population growth. Still, problems loom in the middle future, between now and 2050. Because there are so many young people in these regions today, the absolute rate of population growth will accelerate for a time, even with lower fertility rates. At the other extreme, this period presents a dangerous transition for economies with shrinking populations, as the growing cohort of elderly people strains the capacity of people of productive age to support them, until the population pyramid, or age cohort balance, recalibrates through attrition at a more sustainable setting.

Then there is the problem of rising consumption levels. While economic growth may lead to lower fertility rates and a stabilized global population, it creates greater strains on resources and the environment, especially as the effects of climate change intensify. While a warmer world may make temperate lands more productive, it is also likely to make the tropics less so through increased drought, heat, and flooding. And this is where population growth rates remain highest. For that reason, virtually all scholars who study the subject emphasize the need for a global shift to sustainable economic development, particularly in terms of water and renewable and non- or low-carbon-emitting energy sources. Only by making this transition, they say, can the planet and human institutions support the twin phenomena of rising populations and rising standards of living.

James Ciment

See also: Hunger and Malnutrition; Infant Mortality; Public Health; Reproductive Issues; Urbanization.

Further Reading

Boserup, Ester. *The Conditions of Agricultural Growth: The Economics of Agrarian Change Under Population Pressure.* New Brunswick, NJ: Aldine Transaction, 2005.

Connelly, Matthew. *Fatal Misconception: The Struggle to Control World Population.* Cambridge, MA: Belknap Press of Harvard University Press, 2008.

Demeny, Paul, and Geoffrey McNicoll, eds. *The Political Economy of Global Population Change, 1950–2050.* New York: Population Council, 2006.

Dyson, Tim, Robert Cassen, and Leela Visaria, eds. *Twenty-First-Century India: Population, Economy, Human Development, and the Environment.* New York: Oxford University Press, 2004.

Ehrlich, Paul. *The Population Bomb.* New York: Ballantine Books, 1968.

Fishman, Ted C. *Shock of Gray: The Aging of the World's Population and How It Pits Young Against Old, Child Against Parent, Worker Against Boss, Company Against Rival, and Nation Against Nation.* New York: Scribner, 2010.

Harris, P.M.G. *The History of Human Populations.* Westport, CT: Praeger, 2003.

Lee, Ronald D., and David S. Reher, eds. *Demographic Transition and Its Consequences.* New York: Population Council, 2011.

Malthus, Thomas. *An Essay on the Principle of Population.* New York: Oxford University Press, 1999.

Mazur, Laurie, ed. *A Pivotal Moment: Population, Justice, and the Environmental Challenge.* Washington, DC: Island, 2010.

Meadows, Donella H. *Limits to Growth: A Report for the Club of Rome's Project on the Predicament of Mankind.* New York: Universe Books, 1972.

Sen, Amartya. *Development as Freedom.* New York: Oxford University Press, 2001.

Simon, Julian. *The Ultimate Resource 2.* Princeton, NJ: Princeton University Press, 1996.

Weiner, Myron, and Sharon Stanton Russell, eds. *Demography and National Security.* New York: Berghahn Books, 2001.

White, Tyrene. *China's Longest Campaign: Birth Planning in the People's Republic, 1949–2005.* Ithaca, NY: Cornell University Press, 2006.

Web Sites

Office of Population Research, Princeton University: http://opr.princeton.edu

Population Council: www.popcouncil.org

Population Institute: www.populationinstitute.org

Population Reference Bureau: www.prb.org

United Nations Department of Economic and Social Affairs, Population Division: www.un.org/esa/population

United Nations Population Fund: www.unfpa.org

United Nations Population Information Network: www.un.org/popin

U.S. Census Bureau: www.census.gov

Zero Population Growth: www.zpg.org

Document

Document 1: *An Essay on the Principle of Population,* **Thomas Malthus, 1798**

Arguably the most influential treatise ever published in the field of demographics, Thomas Malthus's Essay on the Principle of Population *proposed that human population growth inevitably outpaces the agricultural capacity, resulting in periodic famines. Malthus's thesis, while revolutionary, failed to take into account technological progress, which allowed humans to produce more food with less effort and land.*

www.econlib.org/library/Malthus/malPlong.html

Source: Library of Economics and Liberty.

POVERTY

Poverty can be defined in two ways. Basic poverty is the inability of a person or a household to obtain the basic necessities of life—food, water, clothing, and shelter—on an ongoing and secure basis. Beyond an ability to meet those basic needs, poverty is also socially determined by the time and place in which the person lives or the household exists. In other words, a person deemed poor in a wealthy country today might be seen as well-off in a poor one. Meanwhile, a poor person living in a developed country today enjoys luxuries unknown to the wealthy of that society in centuries past. Poverty can also be applied to communities and even entire countries. In the last two cases, the term usually refers to such collectives where a large portion of persons or households are living in poverty.

An inability to meet basic needs has been part of the human experience since the species evolved. Most economists agree that poverty can exist only where inequalities arise in income and wealth among members of those societies or residents of those countries. In other words, you cannot have poverty where there is no wealth. Thus, poverty emerged only after people settled into stable, sedentary societies, which allowed for differentiation in economic well-being. For the most part, the industrialization of the past several centuries has lifted huge numbers of people out of poverty, but this effect has not been evenly distributed globally or even within specific communities and countries.

In the early twenty-first century, poverty remains a significant problem in most developed countries even though it affects a relatively small portion of the population. In developing countries, poverty is far more endemic and exerts far more of a brake on economic development even as that lack of development contributes to poverty levels.

The strategies for dealing with poverty vary widely, with approaches often shaped by ideological convictions. Those at the liberal end of the political spectrum typically advocate a bigger role for government and international nonprofit institutions, while those at the conservative end more often believe that free markets, if left to themselves, are the best force for alleviating poverty. There is room for consensus, as recent trends toward economically empowering the world's poorest citizens have made clear.

Globalization is likely to continue to have a major impact on poverty rates in the coming years. Continued rapid economic growth in the developing world is likely to lift more people out of poverty, but, as in the past, this effect will not be felt evenly. At the same time, there is the potential for modest upticks in poverty in developed countries, a result of growing inequalities in wealth and income and uncertain economic fortunes for those entering retirement.

History

Periods when the resources necessary for survival are lacking is the fate of all life on Earth. Indeed, the ability—or inability—to survive such periods of dearth is a driving force behind the evolution of species. It may very well be the reason our apelike ancestors left the forests for the savannahs hundreds of thousands of years ago and early *homo sapiens* ventured out of Africa tens of thousands of years ago. The hunting-and-gathering societies that have dominated human existence experienced many periods of want, and these have continued through the thousands of years since humanity settled into stable agriculture-based communities some 10,000 years ago.

But, as has been noted, poverty must be socially defined to have any real contextual meaning. Mere want alone does not make for poverty if all suffer from it. It was the emergence of large-scale civilizations, with their various classes of people, that, in a sense, gave birth to poverty—that is, the situation in which some people have the basic necessities or, if socially defined, additional amenities, while others do not.

For much of human history, the vast majority of people who lived in the largely agriculturally based societies with great differences in wealth and income could be said to be living in poverty, though this varied from place to place, depending on social conditions and the fertility of the local environment. Indeed, societies where poverty was more or less prevalent were widely distributed, even as late as the beginning of the eighteenth century. It is estimated, for example, that the difference in per capita wealth between the richest country at the time—Britain—and the poorest societies of Asia and Africa was measured only by a factor of five or 10. In other words, poverty was not so much a matter of difference among countries but within countries, as class differences in wealthier societies could be quite stark. One historical study of Spain in the 1700s estimated a Gini coefficient for income of about .5, more typical of developing countries today, and far higher than the .32 for Spain today. (A Gini coefficient is a ratio of inequality with 0 representing perfect equality—all people have exactly the same income—and 1 representing perfect inequality—one person makes all the income.)

The early industrial and commercial revolutions—first in Britain in the late 1700s and then spreading to North America and continental Europe in the nineteenth century—changed this picture in two ways. First, while it provided more wealth for nearly all members of society, it tended to reward the middle and upper classes more, thereby accentuating inequalities of income and wealth and thereby poverty, as socially defined; that is, expectations of what made for a decent lifestyle rose, thereby defining more people as impoverished. More important, it exaggerated the differences between societies that were undergoing industrialization and those that were not, especially as many of the latter came under the political control of the former, who directed their economies to benefit their own. Thus, by the turn of the twentieth century, the differences in wealth between the richest country in the world—now, the United States—and the poorest was a factor of 20 or more. Today, the differences are even starker, with a factor of 100 or more.

Over the course of the nineteenth and, especially, twentieth centuries, poverty diminished significantly in the developed world, typically down to about 10 to 15 percent of the population, whereas in the eighteenth century well over half the population in most countries lived in poverty, as defined by the time and place in which it existed. And, of course, poverty is relative geographically as well. A poor person in a rich country today rarely faces starvation, as in the past, and is most likely to enjoy access to basic health care, education, clothing, shelter, and a few luxuries, such as basic household appliances. These lower poverty rates have come about for two historical reasons. Economic growth has meant a larger pie of income and wealth to distribute, even if the slices are unequal. And, especially since the early twentieth century, governments have instituted a number of antipoverty measures, including more widespread public education, social welfare programs, and income transfer policies, all of which have alleviated poverty, most experts agree. For example, the large-scale antipoverty programs instituted by U.S. president Lyndon Johnson as part of his Great Society agenda of the 1960s allowed the U.S. poverty level to decline from 22.4 percent in 1959 to 11.1 percent by 1973, though certainly the great economic expansion of those years contributed to the decline as well.

A host of factors have caused a different picture of poverty in the developing world since the nineteenth century, which has not only led those countries to remain far poorer than developed-world countries but to have far higher levels of poverty within those countries and far higher gaps in income and wealth distribution. One of these historical developments was imperialism—and, in the case of Africa, the trans-Atlantic slave trade—which redirected the wealth and economic development of those countries outward, toward countries that had colonized them. In addition, the development of extractive economies—whether in agricultural or mineral products—left a legacy of underdevelopment and a ruling elite that took over from colonial authorities upon independence that benefited from those extractive industries. Thus, elites saw no need to invest in the capital improvements necessary to economically develop and diversify or in the human resources of the country through better education and health care. To do so would diminish their own share of the wealth and would create competition for the extractive industries or would produce an unruly populace that might challenge the gross inequalities in wealth and high levels of poverty.

Not all developed countries remained mired in this trap. Particularly in East Asia, and most particularly in countries that lacked extractive industries, elites and the government that they controlled perceived it as in their interest to forward the economic development measures and investments in human capital that allow for more broad-based prosperity and thus lower levels of poverty. Thus, even as literacy rates in South Korea rose from 22 percent in 1945 to 99 percent in 2011, GDP per capita rose from $100 a year to $31,400 (not adjusted for inflation). Meanwhile, many African countries that were dependent on extractive industries stagnated, and their GDP per capita today is barely above where it was at independence in the 1960s, even if literacy rates and educational levels have improved somewhat.

Numbers and Distribution

The world today is roughly divided into four groups of countries: low-income, medium-income, upper-medium-income, and high-income. By World Bank measurements, low-income countries have per capita income of about $1,000 a year or less, according to purchasing power parity (that is, accounting for the fact that income goes farther in poorer countries because of lower prices); medium-income countries have per capita income from $1,000 to roughly $4,000; upper-middle-income countries, with a per capita income range of $4,000 to about $12,300; and high-income countries have a per capita income above that level. The World Bank also defines abso-

Percentage of Population Living Below Global Poverty Levels, Selected Countries, 2009

Country*	Percent living in extreme poverty (on $1.25 or less per day)**	Percent living in moderate or extreme poverty (on $2 or less per day)**
Angola (M)	54.3	70.2
Argentina (H)	0.9	2.4
Bangladesh (M)	49.6	81.3
Bolivia (M)	14.0	21.9
Brazil (UM)	3.8	9.9
Cambodia (M)	25.8	57.8
China (UM)	15.9	36.3
Egypt (UM)	under 2.0	18.5
Ethiopia (L)	39.0	77.6
Haiti (L)	54.9	72.1
India (M)	28.1	54.0
Kyrgyzstan (M)	3.4	27.5
Mexico (UM)	0.8	8.1
Pakistan (M)	22.6	60.3
Philippines (M)	22.6	45.0
Romania (UM)	under 2.0	4.1
Rwanda (L)	76.6	90.3
Uzbekistan (M)	46.3	76.7
Vietnam (M)	21.5	48.4
Yemen (M)	17.5	46.6
World	20.0–30.0	30.0–55.0

* L = low-income country; M = middle-income country; UM = upper-middle-income country; H = high-income country.
** by purchasing power parity (PPP).
Source: World Bank.

Gini Coefficient of Income Inequality, Selected Countries, Selected Years

Country	Year	Gini coefficient*	World ranking**
High income			
Canada	2005	.321	105
Poland	2008	.342	93
South Korea	2010	.310	111
United States	2007	.450	40
Upper-middle income			
Albania	2008	.345	91
Brazil	2009	.539	13
China	2007	.415	53
Egypt	2001	.344	92
Middle income			
Bolivia	2009	.582	10
Cambodia	2007	.444	43
Guatemala	2007	.551	12
Kenya	2008	.425	49
Low income			
Afghanistan	2008	.294	119
Haiti	2001	.592	8
Madagascar	2001	.475	29
Zimbabwe	2006	.501	25

* On a scale of zero to one, from least to most unequal.
** World rankings are listed in order of inequality; a lower ranking means more unequal.
Source: CIA World Factbook.

lute levels of global poverty. Those who live on less than $2 per day, or about $730 a year, are said to be living in absolute poverty, while those living on less than $1.25 a day, or about $450 annually, are said to be living in extreme poverty.

Of course, such numbers indicate the median income, meaning half the people live above the figure and half below. But they do not explain how well distributed that income is. In other words, two high-income countries might have very different amounts of poverty, depending on how that income is distributed. This is where the Gini coefficients come into play. For example, Canada and the United States have roughly comparable income levels—in fact, income in the United States is slightly higher—but their Gini coefficients are very different. Canada's is far lower than that of the United States—.321 versus .450. Not surprisingly Canada's poverty rate of 11 percent is nearly 25 percent below that of the 15 percent rate in the United States. In general upper-middle- and high-income countries tend to have more equal distributions of wealth than middle- and low-income countries.

In general, poorer countries are clustered in tropical regions, with the very poorest largely in sub-Saharan Africa and South Asia. Middle- and upper-income countries are more widely distributed—many of these countries are in East and Southeast Asia and Latin America. Finally, high-income countries tend to be in Europe or Europe settler-state offspring in Oceania and North America, such as Australia, Canada, New Zealand, and the United States. A long-standing exception to this rule is Japan, which in recent decades has been joined by other East and Southeast countries, such as Singapore, South Korea, and Taiwan. Finally, oil wealth has thrust some Persian Gulf countries, particularly those with small populations, such as Kuwait, Qatar, and the United Arab Emirates into the category of high-income countries.

Within countries, poverty tends to be somewhat more prevalent in rural areas, though majorities of people in the larger metropolises of the developing world often live in poverty as well. In countries with ethnic minorities—particularly those that have suffered a history of discrimination—these groups tend to have higher poverty rates. In addition, women on average tend to have higher poverty rates than men, and children have higher rates than adults. Among adults, the highest rates are seen among the young and the elderly, and those in their thirties, forties, and fifties generally have the lowest rates.

Causes and Impact

Aside from the historical causes outlined above—colonialism, slavery, and past discrimination—economists point to a number of factors that lead to higher levels of poverty, though, of course, all of these are rooted in history to some extent. By far, the most important factor is the productivity level of workers. Where the value added to products and services is low, so is income. Low productivity levels have two basic causes: a lack of capital equipment that might make them more productive and a lack of investment in the workers—that is, workers with less education are less productive, as are those who suffer from diseases because of a lack of health-care services.

Corruption is also critical; poorer countries tend to have higher levels of corruption. In corrupt systems, not only are the poor extorted by officialdom and better-off citizens but corruption undermines investment, both domestic and foreign, as those with money shy away from putting it into countries where laws are not obeyed and property rights are not protected. Farther down the list are such things as an inadequate resource base and overpopulation, though both can play a factor in a country's level of poverty, or wealth, if they are evident to extreme

degrees. Finally, all these underlying causes present the classic chicken-and-egg riddle; that is, how much do low levels of literacy and poor health care contribute to national poverty levels and how much are they the result of them?

As to why certain cohorts of a population within a country tend to be more impoverished than others, the reasons vary. Rural areas tend to have larger percentages of poor people, particularly in developing countries, because there are fewer job opportunities in the countryside than the city. Also, farming without modern equipment and methods produces little income. Women tend to be poorer because women typically earn significantly less than men and because they are often burdened with caring for children, which bring down the per capita income level of female-headed households. Child poverty rates are higher because many of them live in female-headed households, and many live on the streets as well, where they earn very small sums of money. As for the elderly, their diminished capacity for work and their deteriorating health undermine their ability to secure adequate incomes. Making things worse for the elderly in many countries is a breakdown in older social norms in which children traditionally care for their elderly parents, usually because they are poor or because they are forced to leave their parents behind in poor villages while they go to cities to earn money. And for minorities, lingering discrimination

Corruption Perception Index, Selected Countries, 2011

Country	Index*	World ranking
High income		
Canada	8.7	10
Poland	5.5	41
South Korea	5.5	43
United States	7.1	24
Upper-middle income		
Albania	3.1	95
Brazil	3.8	73
China	3.6	75
Egypt	2.9	112
Middle income		
Bolivia	2.8	118
Cambodia	2.1	164
Guatemala	2.7	120
Kenya	2.2	154
Low income		
Afghanistan	1.5	180
Haiti	1.8	175
Madagascar	3.0	100
Zimbabwe	2.2	154

* Scale of 1–10, from most to least corrupt.
Source: Transparency International.

often prevents them from obtaining better jobs and education. In some cases, many end up living in areas, such as U.S. inner cities or the suburbs of European metropolises, where there are fewer good-paying jobs.

Antipoverty Strategies and the Future

Only in the post–World War II era, when economic conditions allowed great abundance, have governments set themselves the task of alleviating poverty itself. During the first several decades after the war ended, governments in most developed countries devised ambitious social welfare and income redistribution schemes, the former to provide for the basic health, education, and other needs of the poor and the latter to redistribute wealth from the more affluent to the economically disadvantaged. During these decades, poverty in the developed world diminished noticeably.

Those on the liberal side of the political spectrum maintained that such programs were responsible; conservative critics argued that the economic dynamism of this era had much more to do with the dramatically falling poverty rates. In fact, they insisted, such welfare and income redistribution plans hampered the progress of bringing the economically disadvantaged into the mainstream by creating dependency on government handouts and creating labor market distortions, as unemployment and welfare allowed people to forgo low-paying employment. As many developed-world governments became more politically conservative, means-tested welfare programs gave way to programs that required recipients to work in order to receive government aid.

In the developing world, different approaches were attempted. Most governments implemented economic modernization schemes in an effort to play catch-up with the West by developing large-scale manufacturing. Many countries, however, overemphasized industrialization at the expense of agriculture, impoverishing the countryside and sending millions into cities, where there were few jobs, creating large cohorts of urban poor. At first, many multilateral institutions, such as the U.S.-led World Bank, also emphasized large-scale infrastructure projects, only to see them succumb to decay, as local populations had little invested in them and did not have the expertise to maintain them. In addition, many developed-world governments allowed their fiscal situation to deteriorate as they tried to industrialize their way out of poverty. Multilateral institutions, spearheaded by the U.S.-led World Bank, then emphasized privatization schemes and rollbacks in government services, the latter to ease these governments' problematic macroeconomic situations. The result, in some parts of the developed world, such as Latin America, was a decade or more of stagnation and continued poverty.

Some countries, particularly in Asia, were able to escape this cycle of poverty by emphasizing the development of human resources, particularly in the form of large expenditures on education and health care, as well as carefully targeted government spending on and direction of some private sector industries. This approach helped lift South Korea and Taiwan out of poverty and, in somewhat modified form, helped China make the transition from a low-income country to an upper-middle-income one. Such governments also worked to root out corruption, which can help enhance economic growth. By the twenty-first century, globalization's impact on poverty was also being felt, as foreign and domestic investment in export-oriented industries helped millions of the poor join the middle class, though in some cases by further widening the disparities in wealth between the very well-off and the very poor.

Many experts in the field of poverty argue that the best way to advance poverty alleviation might lie in a combination of philanthropy and private enterprise, as practiced by microlending institutions, such as Bangladesh's Grameen Bank. Such institutions provide tiny loans to small entrepreneurs who would never be able to secure financing from banks and other regular commercial lenders—the philanthropic part—but then demand strict repayment and operate on a for-profit basis as do regular financial institutions.

James Ciment

See also: Homelessness; Inequality, Income and Wealth; Social Welfare.

Further Reading

Banerjee, Abhijit V., and Esther Duflo. *Poor Economics: A Radical Rethinking of the Way to Fight Global Poverty.* New York: PublicAffairs, 2011.

Bauman, Zygmunt. *Collateral Damage: Social Inequalities in a Global Age.* Malden, MA: Polity, 2011.

Beaudoin, Steven M. *Poverty in World History.* New York: Routledge, 2007.

Gilbert, Geoffrey. *World Poverty: A Reference Handbook*. Santa Barbara, CA: ABC-CLIO, 2004.

Jones, Gareth Stedman. *An End to Poverty?: A Historical Debate*. New York: Columbia University Press, 2004.

Karlan, Dean, and Jacob Appel. *More Than Good Intentions: How a New Economics Is Helping to Solve Global Poverty*. New York: Dutton, 2011.

Landes, David S. *The Wealth and Poverty of Nations: Why Some Are So Rich and Some So Poor*. New York: W.W. Norton, 1999.

Milanovic, Branko. *The Haves and the Have-nots: A Brief and Idiosyncratic History of Global Inequality*. New York: Basic Books, 2011.

Mohan, Brij. *Development, Poverty of Culture, and Social Policy*. New York: Palgrave Macmillan, 2011.

Thurow, Roger, and Scott Kilman. *Enough: Why the World's Poorest Starve in an Age of Plenty*. New York: PublicAffairs, 2009.

Williamson, Jeffrey G. *Trade and Poverty: When the Third World Fell Behind*. Cambridge, MA: MIT Press, 2011.

Web Sites

Global Poverty Project: www.globalpovertyproject.com

United Nations Development Programme: www.undp.org

United Nations, Millennium Development Goals: www.un.org/millenniumgoals/

World Bank: www.worldbank.org

Documents

Document 1: Speech to the Sanitary Commission of London, Charles Dickens, May 10, 1851

Nineteenth-century British novelist Charles Dickens wrote eloquently and passionately in his many novels about the living conditions of the poor in Victorian England, poverty he had experienced in his own youth. While primarily a writer, Dickens occasionally turned his hand to social reform. Of particular concern to him were the unsanitary conditions in which the poor of London lived. As he notes in this after-dinner speech to the Metropolitan Sanitary Commission in 1851, more sanitary conditions should come before even education as a priority for reformers hoping to lift the urban masses out of their poverty. More than 150 years later, many antipoverty advocates agree, citing better public health as a prerequisite for economic growth, as it increases worker productivity.

There are very few words for me to say upon the needfulness of sanitary reform, or the consequent usefulness of the Board of Health. That no man can estimate the amount of mischief grown in dirt, that no man can say the evil stops here or stops there, either in its moral or physical effects, or can deny that it begins in the cradle and is not at rest in the miserable grave, is as certain as it is that the air from Gin Lane will be carried by an easterly wind into Mayfair, or that the furious pestilence raging in St. Giles's no mortal list of lady patronesses can keep out of Almack's. Fifteen years ago some of the valuable reports of Mr. Chadwick and Dr. Southwood Smith, strengthening and much enlarging my knowledge, made me earnest in this cause in my own sphere; and I can honestly declare that the use I have since that time made of my eyes and nose have only strengthened the conviction that certain sanitary reforms must precede all other social remedies, and that neither education nor religion can do anything useful until the way has been paved for their ministrations by cleanliness and decency.

I do not want authority for this opinion: you have heard the speech of the right reverend prelate this evening a speech which no sanitary reformer can have heard without emotion. Of what avail is it to send missionaries to the miserable man condemned to work in a foetid court, with every sense bestowed upon him for his health and happiness turned into a torment, with every month of his life adding to the heap of evils under which he is condemned to exist? What human sympathy within him is that instructor to address? what natural old chord within him is he to touch? Is it the remembrance of his children? a memory of destitution, of sickness, of fever, and of scrofula? Is it his hopes, his latent hopes of immortality? He is so surrounded by and embedded in material filth, that his soul cannot rise to the contemplation of the great truths of religion. Or if the case is that of a miserable child bred and nurtured in some noisome, loathsome place, and tempted, in these better days, into the ragged school, what can a few hours' teaching effect against the ever-renewed lesson of a whole existence? But give them a glimpse of heaven through a little of its light and air; give them water; help them to be clean; lighten that heavy atmosphere in which their spirits flag and in which they become the callous things they are; take the body of the dead relative from the close room in which the living live with it, and where death, being familiar, loses its awe; and then they will be brought willingly to hear of Him whose thoughts were so much with the poor, and who had compassion for all human suffering.

The toast which I have to propose, The Board of Health, is entitled to all the honour which can be conferred upon it. We have very near us, in Kensington, a transparent illustration that no very great thing can ever be accomplished without an immense amount of abuse being heaped upon it. In connexion with the Board of Health we are always hearing a very large word which is always pronounced with a very great relish the word centralization. Now I submit that in the time of the cholera we had a pretty good opportunity of judging between this so called centralization and what I may, I think, call "vestrylisation." I dare say the company present have read the reports of the Cholera Board of Health, and I daresay they have also read reports of certain vestries. I have the honour of belonging to a constituency which elected that amazing body, the Marylebone vestry, and I think that if the company present will look to what was done by the Board of Health at Glasgow, and then contrast those proceedings with the wonderful cleverness with which affairs were managed at the same period by my vestry, there will be very little difficulty in judging between them. My vestry even took upon itself to deny the existence of cholera as a weak invention of the enemy, and that denial had little or no effect in staying the progress of the disease. We can now contrast what centralization is as represented by a few noisy and interested gentlemen, and what centralization is when worked out by a body combining business habits, sound medical and social knowledge, and an earnest sympathy with the sufferings of the working classes.

Another objection to the Board of Health is conveyed in a word not so large as the other, "Delay." I would suggest, in respect to this, that it would be very unreasonable to complain that a firstrate chronometer didn't go when its master had not wound it up. The Board of Health may be excellently adapted for going and very willing and anxious to go, and yet may not be permitted to go by reason of its lawful master having fallen into a gentle slumber and forgotten to set it a going. One of the speakers this evening has referred to Lord Castlereagh's caution "not to halloo until they were out of the wood." As regards the Board of Trade I would suggest that they ought not to halloo until they are out of the woods and forests. In that leafy region the Board of Health suffers all sorts of delays, and this should always be borne in mind. With the toast of the Board of Health I will couple the name of a noble lord (Ashley), of whose earnestness in works of benevolence, no man can doubt, and who has the courage on all occasions to face the cant which is the worst and commonest of all the cant about the cant of philanthropy.

Source: The Dickens Project.

Document 2: *Millennium Development Goals Report 2011,* on Poverty, United Nations

In 2000, the United Nations established the Millennium Development Goals to improve human livability and en- *vironmental indices by 2015. The first of the eight main goals was to halve the proportion of people living on less than $1 per day, defined by the World Bank as living in extreme poverty, from the 1990 level. The 2011 update report—excerpted below—noted great progress, concluding that the goal of reducing the proportion of people in poverty to 23 percent would likely be met. However, it cautioned that the progress was uneven, with most of the drop in poverty levels attributable to China and several other East Asian countries.*

GOAL 1: ERADICATE EXTREME POVERTY AND HUNGER

Target. Halve, between 1990 and 2015, the proportion of people whose income is less than $1 a day

Sustained growth in developing countries, particularly in Asia, is keeping the world on track to meet the poverty-reduction target

Robust growth in the first half of the decade reduced the number of people in developing countries living on less than $1.25 a day from about 1.8 billion in 1990 to 1.4 billion in 2005. At the same time, the corresponding poverty rate dropped from 46 per cent to 27 per cent. The economic and financial crisis that began in the advanced countries of North America and Europe in 2008 sparked declines in commodity prices, trade and investment, resulting in slower growth globally.

Despite these declines, current trends suggest that the momentum of growth in the developing world remains strong enough to sustain the progress needed to reach the global poverty-reduction target. Based on recently updated projections from the World Bank, the overall poverty rate is still expected to fall below 15 per cent by 2015, indicating that the Millennium Development Goal (MDG) target can be met. . . .

The fastest growth and sharpest reductions in poverty continue to be found in Eastern Asia, particularly in China, where the poverty rate is expected to fall to under 5 per cent by 2015. India has also contributed to the large reduction in global poverty. In that country, poverty rates are projected to fall from 51 per cent in 1990 to about 22 per cent in 2015. In China and India combined, the number of people living in extreme poverty between 1990 and 2005 declined by about 455 million, and an additional 320 million people are expected to join their ranks by 2015. Projections for sub-Saharan Africa are slightly more upbeat than previously estimated. Based on recent economic growth performance and forecasted trends, the extreme poverty rate in the region is expected to fall below 36 per cent. . . .

Target. Achieve full and productive employment and decent work for all, including women and young people

Economic recovery has failed to translate into employment opportunities

More than three years have passed since the onset of the fastest and deepest drop in global economic activity since the Great Depression. While global economic growth is rebounding, the global labour market is, in many respects, behaving as anticipated in the middle of the crisis: stubbornly elevated unemployment and slow employment generation in developed economies, coupled with widespread deficits in decent work in even the fastest-growing developing countries.

In the developed regions, the employment-to-population ratio dropped from 56.8 per cent in 2007 to 55.4 per cent in 2009, with a further drop to 54.8 per cent in 2010. Clearly, many developed economies are simply not generating sufficient employment opportunities to absorb growth in the working-age population. Again, this reflects an ongoing lag between economic recovery and a recovery in employment in this region. This contrasts with many developing regions, some of which saw an initial decline in the employment-to-population ratio but where, with the exception of the Caucasus and Central Asia and Eastern Asia, the estimated employment-to-population ratio in 2010 has changed little since 2007.

Progress in reducing vulnerable employment stalled following the economic crisis

In developing regions overall, the majority of workers are engaged in "vulnerable employment," defined as the percentage of own-account and unpaid family workers in total employment. Vulnerable employment is characterized by informal working arrangements, lack of adequate social protection, low pay and difficult working conditions.

On the basis of available data, it is estimated that the vulnerable employment rate remained roughly the same between 2008 and 2009, both in developing and developed regions. This compares with a steady average decline in the years preceding the economic and financial crisis. Increases in the vulnerable employment rate were found in sub-Saharan Africa and Western Asia.

Worldwide, one in five workers and their families are living in extreme poverty

A slowdown in progress against poverty is reflected in the number of working poor. According to the International Labour Organization, one in five workers and their families worldwide were living in extreme poverty (on less than $1.25 per person per day) in 2009. This represents a sharp decline in poverty from a decade earlier, but also a flattening of the slope of the working poverty incidence curve beginning in 2007. The estimated rate for 2009 is 1.6 percentage points higher than the rate projected on the basis of the pre-crisis trend. While this is a crude estimate, it amounts to about 40 million more working poor at the extreme $1.25 level in 2009 than would have been expected on the basis of pre-crisis trends.

Source: United Nations.

PRESS, FREEDOM OF

Freedom of the press is the ability of individuals and organizations to publish and disseminate information and ideas openly through media outlets. Press freedom can play important roles in the promotion of liberty and the right of self-determination, including (1) providing citizens with the information that they need to make decisions regarding voting and running for office; (2) encouraging debates and allowing the public to learn about different perspectives; (3) inviting citizens to express their opinions about national affairs; and (4) serving as a watchdog by monitoring and reporting government's unethical or criminal behavior.

Although press freedom is considered fundamental in a democracy, all governments have legislation that regulates the press. The level of censorship used by government authorities has changed throughout history and varies widely among countries today. Some governments censor information because of their need to ensure national security and the citizens' right to privacy and justice. For example, most Western democracies have laws that prevent journalists from distributing inaccurate and damaging statements against an individual, a country's secrets, and pornography.

By contrast, dictatorships tend to focus their efforts on censoring information that can lead the public to rise against those in power. Indeed, due to the immense influence that the media can have over public opinion, authoritarian governments, terrorist groups, and some criminal organizations have developed aggressive methods to stop journalists from properly informing the public. This includes physical and electronic censorship, as well as various forms of assault against journalists, among them forced exile, imprisonment, sexual assault, and murder. Many organizations have as their goal to resist these tactics. At the same time, the rise of the Internet and other new technologies has made it more difficult than ever before for governments to control the information that their citizens obtain and share.

Historical Background

The notion of press freedom began to emerge in the 1600s. At that time, monarchs controlled the number and the content of the publications that were allowed to circulate. Moreover, monarchs used the press to promote themselves and their regimes. In England, authors were required to obtain licenses and to submit their work to the king before publishing. Books and papers could not contain any information that questioned those in power. Authors, editors, and publishers who did not comply with the rules were subjected to different penalties, including physical attacks and imprisonment.

Poet John Milton was the first author to publicly condemn the licensing and censoring system in England. In 1644, he wrote *Areopagitica, a Speech of Mr. John Milton for the Liberty of Unlicensing Printing to the Parliament of England*. Although Milton did not immediately receive the support that he was expecting from his peers, their discontent over the monarchy's unlimited power grew over time. It was this discontent that led English citizens to the "Glorious Revolution" and the English Bill of Rights, which severely restricted the monarchy's authority. Years later, the philosopher John Locke continued the argument for freedom of speech, placing even more pressure on the government to end the licensing law. In 1694, these efforts finally bore fruit when the licensing law was eliminated.

During the eighteenth century, France and the United States incorporated the concept of press freedom into their constitutions. On August 26, 1789, the French Revolution promulgated Article 11 of the Declaration of the Rights of Man and of the Citizen, with the objective of protecting every citizen's right to "speak, write, and print freely." The First Amendment of the U.S. Constitution, which mandates that "Congress shall make no law . . . abridging the freedom of speech, or of the press," was added in 1791.

In the nineteenth century, "freedom of the press"

remained both a celebrated and a fairly unchanging concept, at least in democracies. At the beginning of the twentieth century, however, the Western idea of press freedom was criticized by the Marxist Russian revolutionary Vladimir Lenin. In 1917, Lenin argued that in capitalist societies, press freedom entailed "freedom for the rich . . . to deceive, corrupt and fool the exploited and oppressed mass of the people, the poor." Thus, he proposed "declaring private press advertisement a state monopoly" with the objective of allowing individuals' access to the press. Lenin believed press freedom meant that "all opinions of all citizens may be freely published." His idea was originally implemented in the Soviet Union. However, individual citizens' participation decreased over time until any attempt to use the media to criticize the government became illegal in the Soviet Union.

During the 1930s and 1940s, Adolf Hitler established the Reich Ministry for People's Enlightenment and Propaganda, which was directed by Joseph Goebbels. This ministry had the objectives of suppressing any publication against Hitler's dictatorship and creating and disseminating Nazi ideals through the media. Goebbels understood that the press has an enormous power to influence public opinion. He stated, "We advertise for our own ideal, and therefore we fight using all good means to make good propaganda to win the soul of our people."

The crimes of the Nazi regime and the experience of World War II led numerous countries to develop a common document that would forbid governments from committing abuses while protecting the rights of every citizen. On December 10, 1948, the UN General Assembly adopted the Universal Declaration of Human Rights, in which Article 19 states: "Everyone has the right to freedom of opinion and expression; this right includes freedom to hold opinions without interference and to seek, receive and impart information and ideas through any media and regardless of frontiers."

Despite efforts by the United Nations and numerous nongovernmental organizations (NGOs) to ensure press freedom, violations and abuses continued. In order "to evaluate press freedom around the world, to defend the media from attacks on their independence and to pay tribute to journalists who have lost their lives in their exercise of their profession," the United Nations Educational, Scientific, and Cultural Organization (UNESCO) declared May 3 World Press Freedom Day. Every year on May 3, a journalist is awarded the UNESCO/Guillermo Cano World Press

Freedom Prize, which is given to "a person, organization or institution that has made notable contribution to the defense and/or promotion of press freedom anywhere in the world, especially if this involved risk." Guillermo Cano was a Colombian journalist who was assassinated in front of his office in 1986 because he publicly argued for regulations against drug traffickers.

Press Freedom Around the World

Consistent with the principles espoused by UNESCO and in the Universal Declaration of Human Rights, a number of different NGOs monitor the level of press freedom around the world and report their findings to the public. Reporters Without Borders (RWB) publishes a Freedom Index every year that ranks countries based on (1) the number of journalists who were forced into exile, tortured, threatened, or murdered; (2) the monopolization of media outlets; (3) the prevalence of censorship and self-censorship; (4) the degree of media's independence; and (5) the obstacles that foreign journalists have to overcome in order to report from the country in question. In 2010, RWB rated Finland, Iceland, Norway, the Netherlands, Sweden, and Switzerland as the countries that provide the maximum level of press freedom. At the other end of the scale, the countries that were found to be the most oppressive toward journalists included Eritrea, North Korea, Turkmenistan, Iran, Myanmar (Burma), Syria, Sudan, and China.

RWB highlighted in its 2010 Freedom Index that the European Union is no longer the leader in press freedom that it once was, with France (44th), Italy (49th), Romania (52nd), and Greece and Bulgaria (tied for 70th) all receiving middling rankings. The main problems in these countries include the monopoly of the media, the harassment of journalists, and the pressure on journalists to reveal their sources.

Several countries in Asia obtained low rankings in the Freedom Index because of their constant suppression of the media. For example, in Myanmar, North Korea, China, Laos, and Vietnam, the government exercises total or near-total control over the press. In China, the government uses the media to circulate propaganda while also directing journalists as to which materials should not be published. Reporters who disobey these orders are subjected to imprisonment. In the Philippines, the 2009 Ampatuan massacre resulted in the deaths of 32 reporters and workers employed by the press. Even though the number of journalists killed declined in 2010, the Philippines remains a dangerous place for reporters.

During the 1970s and 1980s, many Latin American countries were led by military dictatorships that severely punished reporters who challenged their regimes. Hundreds of journalists were murdered, tortured, or forced into exile. Although most countries in Latin America are now democratic, press freedom is still threatened by drug lords, paramilitary organizations, and some governments. In Mexico, for example, more than 60 reporters have been murdered since 2000, as drug-trafficking rings have increased their power over the media by harassing, torturing, and executing journalists. This has gone beyond the elimination of negative coverage and now includes the placement of stories and other items that celebrate and justify the activities of drug traffickers.

The press freedom in other countries in Latin America is also constrained by government ownership of media outlets, sanctions against reporters, harassment, threats, and the closure of news organizations. In some cases, the government restrictions are imposed in direct retaliation to the press attempts to criticize or remove someone in authority. For example, media outlets that were privately owned organized a coup d'état in Venezuela with the objective of overthrowing President Hugo Chávez in 2002. The coup was unsuccessful, and Chávez remained in power. In order to prevent being ousted, Chávez began to make aggressive use of Article 192 of the Organic Telecommunications Act, which establishes that government officials can use the media to disseminate messages for free. Chávez later proceeded to create new legislation placing numerous restrictions on what can be broadcast or reported, limiting the media's ability to inform the public.

In the Middle East, the most notable obstacles to a free press have been the compulsory dissemination of government propaganda and the censoring of any dissenting reports. In 2010, Iraq's press freedom deteriorated, as the government implemented rigorous measures to regulate reporters' work and even established a specific court to deal with press-related offenses. It has been estimated that 96 percent of people who live in the Middle East and North Africa do not enjoy press freedom. Rigid laws regarding blasphemy, defamation, and the inability to make any negative statements against monarchs and public officials restrict journalists' right to work.

Press Freedom in the United States

The case of the United States illustrates that press freedom can be elusive, even in long-standing democracies. Government officials in the United States, including President Barack Obama and Secretary of State Hillary Clinton, have spoken openly in support of freedom of expression and against any restrictions in access to the Internet. They have also advocated for the rights of protesters and bloggers in Asia, Latin America, and the Middle East. However, the organizations whose work focuses on protecting civil and human rights have repeatedly accused the U.S. government of failing to protect the very rights they claim to defend. The most recent cases in which the violation of these rights have been alleged include the Wikileaks case, the killing of journalists in Iraq and Afghanistan, and the subpoenas against New York Times journalist James Risen.

The Wikileaks case raised a variety of issues—freedom of expression, freedom of the press, war crimes, and the need to keep certain government information confidential. Wikileaks is a Web site that was created to encourage transparency by allowing individual users to submit secret information from governments and corporations. Bradley Manning, a U.S. Army private, allegedly used the site to disseminate U.S. diplomatic cables and other materials, including a video showing a helicopter attack by the U.S. Air Force. This attack took place in Baghdad in 2007 and resulted in the deaths of 12 people, including two employees of the Reuters news agency. Manning was accused of treason and violating defense secrets; held in solitary confinement for eight months; charged on 22 counts, including aiding the enemy; and, if convicted of the most serious of the charges, faces a sentence of life in prison.

Similarly, the high number of murders of American journalists in Iraq and the lack of prosecution of the perpetrators has led some human rights organizations to question the U.S. commitment to press freedom. It has been reported that the majority of the journalists who have died in Iraq and Afghanistan were not victims of war-related bombings but of homicides. One of the most publicized cases involved the shooting of Reuters cameraman Mazen Dana, which took place in August 2003 in front of the Abu Ghraib prison. Dana was filming a U.S. tank when a soldier inside the tank shot the cameraman in the chest, having mistaken his camera for a rocket launcher. The soldier was later cleared of wrongdoing by the U.S. military.

Organizations that seek to protect press freedom often argue for journalists' right to maintain their sources' confidentiality. The United States often objects to this point of view, particularly in cases that involve secret government information. When James Risen, a *New York Times* reporter and two-time Pulitzer Prize winner, published a series of stories based on leaked government information, he was subpoenaed by a federal court to reveal his sources. Risen has fought the subpoena—which expired in 2009 and was renewed in 2010—aggressively, explaining, "I will continue to fight the government's effort because I believe that this case is a fundamental battle over freedom of the press in the United States. If I don't fight, the government will go after other journalists."

Threats

According to Freedom House, an NGO that publishes a Freedom Index similar to the one produced by RWB, only 15 percent of the world's population has access to complete press freedom—reporters are safe and can work without being constrained by oppressive legal or monetary burdens, the government avoids involvement in press-related work, and political information is covered extensively. For the other 85 percent, freedom of the press is constrained in many ways, from censorship to murder.

The Committee to Protect Journalists (CPJ) found that 72 percent of the 831 reporters who were killed around the world from 1992 to 2010 were targeted and murdered in retaliation for their work. In at least 89 percent of these murders, little or no effort has been made to prosecute the perpetrators. It has been estimated that terrorist and antigovernment organizations were responsible for 30 percent of the murders, while government officials and progovernment organizations combined were responsible for 38 percent. The CPJ reported that the countries with the highest number of murders of journalists were Honduras, Indonesia, Iraq, Mexico, and Pakistan. In addition, to avoid being beaten or murdered, hundreds of reporters have fled their home countries. The countries with the highest number of reporters who live in exile for these reasons are Sri Lanka, Eritrea, Guinea, Afghanistan, Pakistan, Mexico, Colombia, and Ethiopia.

Incarcerating journalists is another method that some governments use to control the media. For 11 consecutive years, China imprisoned more journalists than any other country, until Iran displaced it in 2009. Other countries known for detaining reporters in direct retaliation for their work include Cuba, Eritrea, Kyrgyzstan, Myanmar, and North Korea. Reporters who publish their materials online are often regarded as particularly "dangerous" because of their ability to reach millions of people, and about half of the jailed journalists are incarcerated for their activities online.

Journalists are also at risk of sexual assault. For example, one case that attracted international attention was the rape of Jineth Bedoya, a Colombian reporter. Bedoya was attacked by several men who raped her while she was attempting to collect information about right-wing paramilitary groups. The CPJ indicates that the majority of sexual assaults against journalists fall into one of three categories: (1) sexual attacks against reporters who have been targeted because of their work; (2) sexual assaults during demonstrations, marches, or other events where a large number of people are congregated; and (3) sexual assaults of reporters who have been arrested, abducted, or imprisoned. The majority of journalists who are sexually assaulted do not disclose this information to the authorities, either because their culture would condemn them rather than condemning the perpetrators or because they do not believe that their attackers will ever be brought to justice. Many victimized journalists choose not to inform their superiors about the attacks so as to avoid being seen as fragile or unable to do certain types of work.

Censorship is one of the most common tools used by governments to restrict the information that can be disseminated to the public. In Russia and Venezuela, the governments have exercised control over the media by denying or suspending the licenses of press outlets that were critical of the government. Iran and Egypt temporarily interrupted satellite television transmission and Internet access during moments of protest and turmoil. In China, South Korea, Syria, Thailand, and Vietnam, Facebook and thousands of other Web sites cannot be accessed by the public. North Korea prohibits its citizens from accessing the Internet at all.

To combat these restrictions, RWB created an online anticensorship shelter to allow online reporters and activists to use the Internet freely by having their identities protected while posting content on the Web. The shelter allows visitors to use encrypted e-mail and Web access and provides them with USB flash drives that can be used anywhere to anonymously connect to the Internet and use secure networks. RWB informs

Demonstrators in Paris express their outrage at the deaths of three journalists covering the Syrian Uprising of 2011–2012. Foreign media were barred from the country and forced to report under cover. Freedom of the press remains the enemy of government repression. *(Mehdi Fedouach/AFP/Getty Images)*

the public about cases regarding assaults against journalists and forced exiles and provides financial support to reporters who face emergencies (fleeing a country, loss of funds due to high monetary sanctions, loss of work equipment due to vandalism or robbery, and so forth). Other organizations that promote press freedom and provide assistance to reporters include the CPJ, the International Press Institute in Vienna, and the Federation of Journalists.

Effects of Press Freedom

The presence or the absence of press freedom can have a profound impact on individual lives as well as on the development of societies, cultures, and economies. Press freedom allows citizens to receive accurate information about social, political, and economic issues around the world. Citizens can use this information to form opinions and make decisions when buying and selling products, when supporting a candidate, voting, running for office, and when making their government officials accountable.

In countries where a free press is limited or nonexistent, people can be manipulated to believe that an oppressive political system is preferable to others, that corrupt politicians are innocent, that excessive prices of products or services are fair, or that their country is safer than it really is. Lack of press freedom can prevent people from using the media to exchange ideas, from demanding meaningful changes in their government, and from offering suggestions as to how to improve their country.

Throughout history, authoritarian governments have used different methods to control the information that people are allowed to obtain and disseminate with the objective of preventing uprisings. However, the widespread use of the Internet has created enormous challenges to governments all around the world, particularly those that want to exercise total control over the media. Although just over one-third of the world's population in 2012 reads newspapers in hard copy to be informed, the proportion of those who obtain the news on the Internet is growing dramatically. It has been reported that BBC.com, for example, had nearly 60 million monthly visitors in 2011. In addition to accessing Web sites of well-known media outlets, people read blogs to obtain information gathered by citizen journalists. In many countries, such blogs report information that is not available in other media because of censorship and self-censorship. Global Voices Online, for example, is a network of more than 300 bloggers and translators who publish articles in 15 different languages.

A major problem that governments face when trying to prevent people from using the Internet is that reducing its use can affect the country's economy. The inability to use the Web can be detrimental for businesses that wish to sell products or services, for companies that promote tourism, and for organizations that need to facilitate and lower the cost of communications and financial transactions. Thus, even governments that are aware that the number of their opponents might grow because of access to the Internet are forced to permit access, however limited. This situation has allowed people to obtain and disseminate information against their government and to organize social movements such as the Arab Spring.

The Arab Spring began in Tunisia, where people united to protest unemployment, poverty, and corruption after seeing a video of the self-immolation of Mohamed Bouazizi, a college-educated street vendor who found it impossible to make a living because of poverty and injustice in his country. The video went viral and represented the frustration shared by many in the region; thereafter, Facebook, Twitter, and other Web sites played a central role in allowing protestors to contact and organize supporters. This ultimately led the country's ruler, Zine el-Abidine Ben Ali, to step down, ending his 23-year dictatorship and allowing for the development of more democratic institutions. This event and others like it across the Arab world and elsewhere demonstrate that a new citizen-driven, social networking form of journalism, if that is even an accurate word for the term, has come to supplement traditional forms of journalism in educating the citizenry about events in their own countries.

The events in Tunisia inspired people in Egypt to follow their example in organizing their own revolution, which lasted 18 days. Again, Web sites such as Facebook and Twitter were used to speak out against torture, inequality, and injustice and to promote massive protests. In an attempt to stay in power, President Hosni Mubarak disconnected Egyptians' access to the Internet. However, his actions simply caused more outrage among the people in Egypt and contributed to his downfall.

People who are organizing social movements around the world are also using cell phones to disseminate relevant information. In the Philippines, for example, citizens sent over 7 million text messages during a single week to coordinate demonstrations, voice their disapproval of President Joseph Estrada, and ensure that key evidence against Estrada would be presented at his impeachment trial. Estrada was successfully removed from the government.

Other recent movements organized with the help of technology were unsuccessful in bringing the changes that activists were expecting to see. Such was the case of protests in Belarus in 2006 that eventually led to an increase in Internet control. Protesters in Iran in 2009 and in Thailand in 2010 were also silenced by severe repression and violence from the government.

The Future

Press freedom is fundamental for the development and strengthening of self-determination. Through the media, people can obtain the information they need to make decisions regarding voting, supporting, or withdrawing their support for certain public officials, or running for office. An independent media can inform the public about irregularities in the government and lead people to hold officials accountable for their actions.

The arrival of new technology has expanded the role of the media even further as it has changed the way people obtain, produce, and disseminate information. Now, individuals have the opportunity to record images on a cell phone, post blogs on the Internet, and communicate information via social media, which has a wider reach than any hard copy newspaper. The new wave of citizen journalism has been critical in advancing revolutions and social movements. Although not all of these movements have been successful in the short term, it is clear that the nature and definition of press freedom cover broader ground now than ever before.

Maria Espinola

See also: Digital Divide; Secrecy, Government.

Further Reading

Cohen-Almagor, Raphael. *The Scope of Tolerance: Studies on the Costs of Free Expression and Freedom of the Press.* New York: Routledge, 2005.

Dizard, Jake. "Fragile Progress, Rising Threats: Press Freedom and Politics in Latin America." *Harvard International Review* (Fall 2010).

Giles, Robert. "An Emergent Neo-Journalism: The Decline and Renewal of News Media." *Harvard International Review* (Fall 2010).

LaMay, Craig L. *Exporting Press Freedom.* New Brunswick, NJ: Transaction, 2009.

Lippman, Walter. *Liberty and the News.* New Brunswick, NJ: Transaction, 1995.

Lisosky, Joanne M., and Jennifer R. Henrichsen. *War on Words: Who Should Protect Journalists?* Santa Barbara, CA: Praeger, 2011.

Riaz, Saqib. "Role of News Media in a Democratic Society." *FWU Journal of Social Sciences* 4:2 (2011): 89–98.

Stevenson, Robert L. "Freedom of the Press Around the World." In *Global Journalism: Topical Issues and Media Systems,* 4th ed., ed. John C. Merril and Arnold de Beer. New York: Allyn & Bacon, 2003.

Trappel, Josef, and Werner A. Meier, eds. *On Media*

Monitoring: The Media and Their Contributions to Democracy. New York: Peter Lang, 2011.

Warf, Barney. "Geographies of Global Internet Censorship." *GeoJournal* 76 (2011): 1–23.

Zeno-Zencovich, Vincenzo. *Freedom of Expression: A Critical and Comparative Analysis.* New York: Routledge-Cavendish, 2008.

Web Sites

Amnesty International: www.amnesty.org

Committee to Protect Journalists: www.cpj.org

Freedom House: www.freedomhouse.org

Human Rights Watch: www.hrw.org

Reporters Without Borders: www.rsf.org

United Nations Educational, Scientific and Cultural Organization (UNESCO), Communication and Information: www.unesco.org/new/en/communication-and-information/

Documents

Document 1: *Areopagitica* (excerpt), John Milton, 1644

John Milton's Areopagitica, *a tract published at the height of the English Civil War in November 1644, protested the Licensing Order of 1643, by which the English Parliament allowed for the censorship of books and newspapers. Milton's polemical essay, subtitled "A Speech for the Liberty of Unlicensed Printing to the Parliament of England," was one of the first published defenses of the freedom of the press and is still regarded as one of the most eloquent.*

Where there is much desire to learn, there of necessity will be much arguing, much writing, many opinions; for opinion in good men is but knowledge in the making. Under these fantastic terrors of sect and schism, we wrong the earnest and zealous thirst after knowledge and understanding which God hath stirred up in this city. What some lament of, we rather should rejoice at, should rather praise this pious forwardness among men, to reassume the ill deputed care of their religion into their own hands again. A little generous prudence, a little forbearance of one another, and some grain of charity might win all these diligences to join and unite in one general and brotherly search after truth, could we but forego this prelatical tradition of crowding free consciences and Christian liberties into canons and precepts of men. . . .

And if the men be erroneous who appear to be the leading schismatics, what withholds us but our sloth, our self-will, and distrust in the right cause, that we do not give them gentle meetings and gentle dismissions, that

we debate not and examine the matter thoroughly with liberal and frequent audience; if not for their sakes, yet for our own?—seeing no man who hath tasted learning but will confess the many ways of profiting by those who, not contented with stale receipts, are able to manage, and set forth new positions to the world. And were they but as the dust and cinders of our feet, so long as in that notion they may yet serve to polish and brighten the armoury of Truth, even for that respect they were not utterly to be cast away. But if they be of those whom God hath fitted for the special use of these times with eminent and ample gifts, and those perhaps neither among the priests nor among the Pharisees, and we in the haste of a precipitant zeal shall make no distinction, but resolve to stop their mouths, because we fear they come with new and dangerous opinions, as we commonly forejudge them ere we understand them; no less than woe to us, while thinking thus to defend the Gospel, we are found the persecutors.

Good and evil we know in the field of this world grow up together almost inseparably; and the knowledge of good is so involved and interwoven with the knowledge of evil, and in so many cunning resemblances hardly to be discerned, that those confused seeds which were imposed upon Psyche as an incessant labour to cull out and sort asunder, were not more intermixed. It was from out the rind of one apple tasted that the knowledge of good and evil, as two twins cleaving together, leaped forth into the world. And perhaps this is that doom which Adam fell into of knowing good and evil, that is to say of knowing good by evil. . . .

And how can a man teach with authority, which is the life of teaching, how can he be a doctor in his book as he ought to be, or else had better be silent, whenas all he teaches, all he delivers, is but under the tuition, under the correction of his patriarchal licenser, to blot or alter what precisely accords not with the hidebound humour which he calls his judgment?—when every acute reader, upon the first sight of a pedantic license, will be ready with these like words to ding the book a quoit's distance from him: "I hate a pupil teacher; I endure not an instructor that comes to me under the wardship of an overseeing fist. I know nothing of the licenser, but that I have his own hand here for his arrogance; who shall warrant me his judgment?" "The State, sir," replies the stationer, but has a quick return: "The State shall be my governors, but not my critics; they may be mistaken in the choice of a licenser, as easily as this licenser may be mistaken in an author; this is some common stuff." And he might add from Sir Francis Bacon, that "Such authorized books are but the language of the times." For though a licenser should happen to be judicious more than ordinary, which will be a great jeopardy of the next succession, yet his very office and his commission enjoins him to let pass nothing but what is vulgarly received already.

Source: John Milton, *Areopagitica,* Vol. 3, Part 3. The Harvard Classics. (New York: P.F. Collier & Son, 1909–1914).

Document 2: Declaration of Principles on Freedom of Expression, Organization of American States, 2000

The Inter-American Commission on Human Rights of the Organization of American States approved this declaration of principles on October 19, 2000. It was and remains one of the most sweeping and most important statements of the freedom of expression (including freedom of the press) ever put to paper.

1. Freedom of expression in all its forms and manifestations is a fundamental and inalienable right of all individuals. Additionally, it is an indispensable requirement for the very existence of a democratic society.

2. Every person has the right to seek, receive and impart information and opinions freely under terms set forth in Article 13 of the American Convention on Human Rights. All people should be afforded equal opportunities to receive, seek and impart information by any means of communication without any discrimination for reasons of race, color, sex, language, religion, political or other opinions, national or social origin, economic status, birth or any other social condition.

3. Every person has the right to access to information about himself or herself or his/her assets expeditiously and not onerously, whether it be contained in databases or public or private registries, and if necessary to update it, correct it and/or amend it.

4. Access to information held by the state is a fundamental right of every individual. States have the obligation to guarantee the full exercise of this right. This principle allows only exceptional limitations that must be previously established by law in case of a real and imminent danger that threatens national security in democratic societies.

5. Prior censorship, direct or indirect interference in or pressure exerted upon any expression, opinion or information transmitted through any means of oral, written, artistic, visual or electronic communication must be prohibited by law. Restrictions to the free circulation of ideas and opinions, as well as the arbitrary imposition of information and the imposition of obstacles to the free flow of information violate the right to freedom of expression.

6. Every person has the right to communicate his/her views by any means and in any form. Compulsory membership or the requirement of a university degree for the practice of journalism constitute unlawful restrictions of freedom of expression. Journalistic activities must be guided by ethical conduct, which should in no case be imposed by the State.

7. Prior conditioning of expressions, such as truthfulness, timeliness or impartiality, is incompatible with the right to freedom of expression recognized in international instruments.

8. Every social communicator has the right to keep his/her source of information, notes, personal and professional archives confidential.

9. The murder, kidnapping, intimidation of and/or threats to social communicators, as well as the material destruction of communications media violate the fundamental rights of individuals and strongly restrict freedom of expression. It is the duty of the state to prevent and investigate such occurrences, to punish their perpetrators and to ensure that victims receive due compensation.

10. Privacy laws should not inhibit or restrict investigation and dissemination of information of public interest. The protection of a person's reputation should only be guaranteed through civil sanctions in those cases in which the person offended is a public official, a public person or a private person who has voluntarily become involved in matters of public interest. In addition, in these cases, it must be proven that in disseminating the news, the social communicator had the specific intent to inflict harm, was fully aware that false news was disseminated, or acted with gross negligence in efforts to determine the truth or falsity of such news.

11. Public officials are subject to greater scrutiny by society. Laws that penalize offensive expressions directed at public officials, generally known as "desacato laws," restrict freedom of expression and the right to information.

12. Monopolies or oligopolies in the ownership and control of the communication media must be subject to antitrust laws, as they conspire against democracy by limiting the plurality and diversity which ensure the full exercise of people's right to information. In no case should such laws apply exclusively to the media. The concession of radio and television broadcast frequencies should take into account democratic criteria that provide equal opportunity of access for all individuals.

13. The exercise of power and the use of public funds by the state, the granting of customs duty privileges, the arbitrary and discriminatory placement of official advertising and government loans, the concession of radio and television broadcast frequencies, among others, with the intent to put pressure on and punish or reward and provide privileges to social communicators and communications media because of the opinions they express threaten freedom of expression, and must be explicitly prohibited by law. The means of communication have the right to carry out their role in an independent manner. Direct or indirect pressures exerted upon journalists or other social communicators to stifle the dissemination of information are incompatible with freedom of expression.

Source: Organization of American States.

PRISONERS AND PRISONER RIGHTS

A prison is a place of confinement for those in legal detention, known as prisoners. Prisoners can either be awaiting trial or, after trial, be serving out a sentence whose length of time has been determined by a judge or jury at a trial. In some cases, people who are not awaiting trial or have not undergone a trial also can be held in detention, some of them under emergency security laws and others under extralegal conditions, often political prisoners, and prisoners of war.

Although various forms of imprisonment have existed since ancient times, using it solely as a punishment is largely a phenomenon of modern penal policy, which shifted the purpose of prisons from a place where one waited for punishment, in the form of a physical penalty, to a place where the detention itself for a fixed period constituted the punishment, by denying the prisoner the ability to enjoy society's rights and benefits.

Rates of imprisonment rise and fall based on a number of factors, including crime rates, public attitudes toward crime and punishment, government finances and other economic factors, and prison capacity. In general, rates of imprisonment have increased around the world in the past couple of decades; this applies not only to the dominant population of prisoners—that is, adult males—but also to juveniles, usually defined as persons under the age of 18, and women.

Conditions of imprisonment vary widely around the world, with those in developing countries and authoritarian states often times lagging behind those in democracies and developed countries. Prison conditions include the following issues: health care, both physical and mental; levels of violence and security; crowding; opportunities for rehabilitation, including education and substance abuse treatment; and labor.

Prisoners are entitled to some rights, by either custom or law, including both national and local statutes and international treaties and conventions. These rights basically fall into two categories: decent conditions, including the aspects named earlier, and, for those in pretrial detention, the right to a fair trial within a reasonable time and, for those who have been tried, the right to appeal convictions or sentencing and to appeal conditions of imprisonment.

History

Historically, prisons, in this case more accurately called jails, were simply temporary housing for the accused who were awaiting trial and convicted criminals awaiting sentencing. In addition, they served as confinement for those unable or unwilling—or so their creditors claimed—to pay their debts. In some cases, prisoners were held by authorities for political crimes, often without formal trial or sentencing. Typically, criminals were punished by other means—they were compelled to pay restitution to victims or their families (or, in the case of slaves, the masters); to suffer various forms of corporal punishment; to serve as forced labor, as in the case of galley slaves in the Roman and other empires of antiquity; to be transported to penal colonies, most famously the British colony in Australia; and, of course, to pay the ultimate price, execution.

From Corporal Punishment to Imprisonment

The rise of urban populations in Europe and elsewhere in the eighteenth and nineteenth centuries led to increases in crime and the need to detain criminals and the accused on a large scale, both before and after trial. In addition to these practical concerns were changes in attitudes. Increasingly, reformers began to argue that corporal punishment was a barbaric practice that had no place in a modern society. Some thinkers, notably French philosopher Michel Foucault, have theorized a more nuanced and complex set of reasons for the shift from corporal punishment to imprisonment, including humanitarianism, changing views about the power of the state, the nature of modern society, the sanctity of the human body, and the malleability of the human character. The founders of the United States, for example, codified these changing attitudes in the Eighth Amendment to the Constitution, banning "cruel and unusual" punishment, which, at the time, largely proscribed corporal punishment of various kinds.

At the time, jails were dismal and chaotic places—dank and dark, unhealthful, overcrowded, and dangerous. All kinds of prisoners were thrown in together, regardless of sex, age, and the offense of which they had been convicted. Pickpockets, murderers, and insolvent debtors were thrown into the same establishments, even into the same cells, sometimes bringing their destitute family with them. Many jails did not provide for prisoners, forcing them, or their family on the outside, to obtain their food, clothing, or medicine. A prisoner with significant resources could live quite well, while the impoverished might actually die from lacking those basic provisions. Jails existed for three reasons: to protect society by keeping dangerous people off the streets; to force debtors or those sentenced to pay restitution to victims to come up with the money owed; and to punish those being confined. Little thought was given to, and even less interest was expressed in, rehabilitation.

Rise of the Penitentiary and Other Reforms

Such attitudes began to change in the early nineteenth century, in Britain and, in particular, the northern United States. Reformers such as Jeremy Bentham in Britain and various evangelical and Quaker politicians in New York and Pennsylvania began to develop the idea of the penitentiary, clean, healthful, and, most important, orderly places where prisoners would be gradually inured to a disciplinary regimen that would inculcate in them the self-discipline they would need to become productive and moral citizens after they were released. In New York's Auburn Prison, founded in 1816, and Pennsylvania's Eastern State Penitentiary, founded in 1822, inmates were kept in isolation—at Auburn, they were held in isolation only at night; during the day, they worked with others—and enforced silence, the better to contemplate what

they had done wrong and cultivate penitence (hence the name of the Pennsylvania institution and those modeled after it).

By the late nineteenth century, new thinking about criminality, including changing ideas about categorizing crimes according to their seriousness and the degree of criminal culpability, led to differentiation of prison types to house violent and nonviolent criminals, women, juveniles, and those with mental illness. In addition, beginning in the early twentieth century, new ideas developed about the rehabilitation of criminals—for their own sake as well as that of society, which would eventually have to cope with them after they were released. This rethinking led to educational programs and, with new attitudes after World War II regarding the need to rehabilitate those suffering from substance abuse, drug treatment programs. As noted above, many of these reforms were largely confined to the more advanced democracies of Europe, North America, and elsewhere. In much of the rest of the world, prisons remained poorly managed and short of resources, prisoners were largely left to their own devices, guards had near-impunity in imposing order, and all those confined were thrown together regardless of their crime, their age, and their propensity to violence.

Trends in the larger society contributed to the development of improved prison conditions and reconsideration of their mission. Economic growth and increased taxation allowed governments to spend more money on prisons; at the same time, falling crime rates and levels of violence in the first half of the twentieth century—in the United States, homicide, the best documented crime, declined by more than half, from 9.7 per 100,000 in 1933 to 4.5 in 1958—led popular opinion and policy making to take a more humane attitude about and treatment of prisoners, especially in developed democracies. By the 1960s, many sociologists and criminologists, and the liberal-leaning policy makers who accepted their conclusions, began to see criminals not as inherently prone to crime or morally flawed but as victims of social circumstances—for example, poverty or racism—which added further impetus to efforts aimed at improving prison conditions and providing opportunities for prisoner rehabilitation.

Backlash

Surging crime rates beginning in the 1970s, however, put a brake on such reformist impulses. In

Growth in Imprisonment Rate, Selected Countries, 1992–2010 (per 100,000 population)

Country	1992	1995	1998	2001	2004	2007	2010
Brazil	74	92	102	133	183	220	253
China	109	109	115	112	122	124	122
India	n/a	n/a	27**	29	31**	32	31**
Russia	487	622	688	636	588	613	609
Saudi Arabia	n/a	n/a	114***	110***	n/a	178***	160***
South Africa	285	301	349	386	403	339	331
United Kingdom*	90	100	126	127	141	149	153
United States	501	592	655	685	725	758	730

* England and Wales only.
** for 1999, 2005, and 2009 respectively.
*** for 2000, 2002, 2009, and 2011 respectively.
Source: International Centre for Prison Studies.

the United Kingdom, for example, the homicide rate more than doubled, from .68 per 100,000 in 1965 to 1.41 in 1997. These rising crime rates led to harsher attitudes toward criminals among the public and policy-making circles, which in turn led to harsher punishments handed down by courts and tougher sentencing statutes by legislatures, and thus rising incarceration rates. In the United Kingdom, for example, incarceration rates rose from roughly 63 per 100,000 in 1970 to about 153 in 2010. In addition, prisons became harsher places, as rehabilitation and educational programs were cut back—due in part to overall government austerity measures—and facilities became more crowded, reducing the quality of life in prison and sparking higher levels of violence there. Since the 1990s, despite generally falling crime rates in much of the developed world, harsher sentencing rules have remained in effect, as have policies that lead to harsher prison conditions. The reasons for the reduction in crime rates are not universally agreed on. Conservative commentators credit harsher sentencing, while more liberal opinion makers point to a number of other factors, including better policing and changing demographics (that is, proportionately fewer young men in the population with a high propensity for crime). Lawmakers see few political benefits in easing criminal statutes, fearful that their opponents will accuse them of being "soft on crime."

Patterns and Numbers

Prisoners can be divided into four categories and several subcategories. The first category and by far the most numerous comprises "common" criminals, those accused or convicted of having committed or-dinary crimes, ranging from minor violations, such as petty thievery, to premeditated murder. This group is subdivided into those in pretrial detention and those serving sentences after having been found guilty at trial. The second category is political prisoners. They are often technically guilty of breaking a country's laws but, by the standards set by the international community, they are guilty only of opposing those in power. Some countries have vaguely worded laws that allow governments to arrest and try anyone suspected even remotely of endangering national security or unity. Such political prisoners are subdivided into pretrial detainees, those found guilty of breaking national security laws, and those held extrajudicially, that is, they will not undergo a trial in a reasonably defined time frame or even have the promise of one. The third category is prisoners of war, including those more or less formally held by the government or military of the parties to the conflict. The fourth category includes informal prisoners, those held by rebel groups in civil conflicts.

Worldwide, it is estimated that there are approximately 10 million people now in penal institutions, either pretrial or posttrial, or roughly 143 per 100,000 population. In the United States, roughly 20 percent of the total are in pretrial detention. Numbers and rates vary widely. Just three countries—the United States, China, and Russia—have about one-quarter of the world's population but almost half of all prisoners. The United States and Russia have by far the highest proportion of their populations incarcerated—730 and 525 per 100,000, respectively. In general, most developed countries have higher levels of incarceration, simply because they have the resources and capacity to pursue, prosecute, and punish common criminals. The United States incarcerates far

Number of Prisoners and Rate of Imprisonment, Selected Countries

Country	Year	Number of prisoners	Rate of imprisonment (per 100,000 population)
Brazil	2011	513,802	261
China	2010	1,650,000	122
India	2009	376,969	31
Russia	2012	749,600	525
Saudi Arabia	2011	45,000	160
South Africa	2011	157,375	310
United Kingdom*	2012	87,002	155
United States	2010	2,266,832	730

*England and Wales only.
Source: International Centre for Prison Studies.

more people than other developed countries, while, among developing countries, higher rates are noted in Latin American and Caribbean countries and the former Soviet Union. Not unexpectedly, as in the United States, these countries tend to have higher rates of crime.

How many of these people are political prisoners is hard to determine, as most are detained or punished under the statutes of their country. Moreover, governments are reluctant to reveal how many political prisoners they are holding. China, for example, claims it holds but 50 political prisoners, while international human rights monitors put the likely figure in the thousands. Per capita, it is believed that Sri Lanka, which has some 12,000 political prisoners in a population of 20 million, has the highest proportion of political prisoners, a consequence of emergency detention legislation enacted during the nearly three-decade-long civil war with Tamil separatists. The number of prisoners of war has declined dramatically since the 1970s, along with the decline in international conflicts. During conflicts, however, the numbers can swell. For example, allied forces held some 175,000 Iraqis prisoner during the First Gulf War in 1991.

The rise of international terrorism in the 1990s, especially since the al Qaeda terrorist attacks on the United States on September 11, 2001, has been accompanied by indefinite detention of terrorist suspects by the United States and its allies. Such detainees can number in the thousands, and many of them were captured by U.S. forces and then turned over to countries where international rules about detention are not honored. U.S. authorities argue that holding them indefinitely without trial is neces-

sary in an age of a new kind of warfare, in which the enemy is a nonstate actor and therefore there is no government with which to negotiate a transfer, nor is there any requirement they will abide by international laws regarding human rights, even of prisoners. The overriding rationale is that indefinite detention is warranted because they pose an ongoing threat if released. Moreover, it has been argued that because of the nature of terrorism ordinary courts cannot adequately determine their guilt, there is no way to effectively prosecute them.

As for those held by rebel groups, it is impossible to determine accurately how many prisoners are held at a given time because such groups operate outside the law and in the fog of war; it is also difficult to determine what constitutes a prisoner of war in such a conflict. Did, for example, the term apply to the hundreds of thousands of Hutu refugees held against their will in the Democratic Republic of Congo by Hutu extremists after the Rwandan genocide of 1994?

Prisoner Rights

Prisoner rights fall into two broad categories: those concerning the conditions under which the prisoner is held, including the right to appeal such conditions, and those that offer prisoners certain legal rights concerning their case and their imprisonment—both during the pretrial detention and posttrial punishment phases—including the right to a fair and speedy trial; the right to know the charges against them and to confront their accusers; the right, in some cases and places, to post bond for pretrial release; and, in the posttrial phase, the right to appeal a verdict or sentence. In addition, certain rights apply to special categories of prisoners, most notably juveniles and those suffering from mental illness.

International organizations, such as the United Nations, have issued a number of conventions, treaties, and documents pertaining to the treatment of prisoners. The first, and most important, one is the 1955 Standard Minimum for the Treatment of Prisoners, a nonbinding set of rules on the treatment of prisoners and the management of penal facilities. These call for decent accommodation, clothing, bedding, food, and labor conditions, as well as basic levels of personal hygiene and security. The standard also calls for minimal physical restraint; contact with friends, family, and others in the outside world; freedom to practice religion; and mechanisms and procedures

Amnesty International issued a report in 2011 singling out Liberia for its "appalling" prison conditions, citing overcrowding, lack of sanitation, and inadequate food and water. Several international conventions protect prisoner rights, but conditions remain dire for millions. *(AP Photo/Rebecca Blackwell)*

for prisoners to have violations of these minimum standards brought to the attention of authorities and to be addressed by authorities. Separate conventions, such as the 1985 Convention Against Torture, ban inhumane treatment of prisoners, though there is much dispute over what constitutes inhumane treatment. (For a more thorough discussion of the topic, see the chapter on torture.) In many countries, particularly in democratic states, statutes require appropriate educational facilities and rehabilitation programs, such as substance abuse programs, though these are often in short supply due to limited funds.

Among the leading problems facing prisoners in many countries today is overcrowding. Most countries in the world have prison populations that exceed their official prison capacity, which leads to inhumane, unhealthful, and dangerous conditions. For example, Kenya, the worst offender in this respect, has a prison population more than three times its official capacity. Even wealthy countries like the United States and the United Kingdom have prison populations exceeding capacity—at about 110 percent for each. In the United

States, the rate of overcapacity varies widely among states and municipalities. In 2011, for example, the U.S. Supreme Court ordered the state of California—after an appeal of an earlier decision by a panel of three federal judges—to either add more prison capacity or release some 46,000 prisoners, as the state's prison population was at 137 percent of capacity, thereby violating the Eighth Amendment of the Constitution.

Prison Capacity and Occupancy, Selected Countries

Country	Year	Prison capacity	Occupancy rate (%)
Brazil	2011	303,993	165.7
China	—	n/a	n/a
India	2009	307,052	122.8
Russia	2012	955,421	91.6
Saudi Arabia	—	n/a	n/a
South Africa	2011	118,154	133.2
United Kingdom*	2012	77,749	111.2
United States	2008	2,093,021	110.1

* England and Wales only.
Source: International Centre for Prison Studies.

The second set of rules applying to prisoners concern the rights to challenge their detention and the verdict at trial and the subsequent sentence dictating their imprisonment term. The 1966 UN International Covenant on Civil and Political Rights, which almost all UN members—except China, Saudi Arabia, and Myanmar—have ratified, also calls on states to guarantee detainees and others the right to due process of law, a fair trial within a reasonable time, and the right to appeal a verdict or a sentence to a higher tribunal.

Finally, the 1955 document on Standard Minimum Treatments also requires that juveniles and women be imprisoned in separate facilities from those of adult males and that pretrial detainees be jailed separately from convicted criminals. Of course, as is so often shown by the violations of internationally agreed upon standards and rights for prisoners in various countries, such standards and rights are adhered to in varying degrees. A lack of finances, internal conflict, political discord, rising crime rates, racism or ethnic divisions, and other factors lead countries to fail to live up to their treaty obligations.

The Future

Looking to the future, several factors, including economic growth in many developing countries, seem to be pulling much of the world toward both more humane treatment of prisoners and a decrease in the detention of prisoners for violations of what most of the world agrees are strictly political offenses. Although having more resources can lead to higher rates of imprisonment, as the judicial and penal systems become more effective, they can also provide the financial resources to improve the lot of those being imprisoned.

There is also the spread of democracy. As noted, democratic states typically hold fewer political prisoners and provide prisoners with better conditions and more legal rights. Even some nondemocratic states, such as Myanmar, where the ruling junta agreed to release thousands of political prisoners, appear to be moving in this direction. The virtual end to international conflict has lessened the numbers of prisoners of war, and the gradual cessation of civil conflict in much of the world is reducing the numbers of those held by non-state actors.

Some notable countertrends are evident. Imprisonment rates have been rising around the world since the 1990s, a result of rising crime rates in some countries, more effective prosecutions in other countries, and hardening attitudes toward crime. In addition, the austerity measures forced on many developed countries, as a result of rising levels of sovereign debt, might trigger cutbacks in prison budgets, which can undermine the quality of life for prisoners, their ability to appeal verdicts and sentences, and programs that will help them readjust to civilian life after release.

At the same time, budget cuts, combined with higher rates of incarceration, have led many countries to experiment with noncustodial sentences for nonviolent, first-time offenders, including community service, electronic monitoring that allows for work and home release, and off-site facilities where prisoners are confined at night but allowed to work outside the facility during the day. Much of this is motivated less by humane impulses than a desire to save money.

Finally, many states emerging from civil conflict, such as a number of sub-Saharan African countries, are attempting transitional justice programs for those who committed crimes in wartime, whereby those found guilty confess their crimes in front of Truth and Reconciliation Commissions—pioneered by South Africa after its 1990s transition from apartheid—pay restitution to victims or society at large, and take other measures meant to punish and rehabilitate the guilty party outside traditional prisons.

James Ciment

See also: Human Rights; Police Corruption and Brutality.

Further Reading

Ahn-Redding, Heather. *The "Million Dollar Inmate": The Financial and Social Burden of Non-Violent Offenders.* Lanham, MD: Lexington Books, 2007.

Beaumont, Gustave de, and Alexis de Tocqueville. *On the Penitentiary System in the United States, and Its Application in France.* Trans. Francis Lieber. Philadelphia: Carey, Lea & Blanchard, 1833.

Brown, Michelle. *The Culture of Punishment: Prison, Society, and Spectacle.* New York: New York University Press, 2009.

Easton, Susan. *Prisoners' Rights: Principles and Practice.* New York: Routledge, 2011.

Foucault, Michel. *Discipline and Punishment: The Birth of the Prison.* Trans. Alan Sheridan. New York: Vintage, 1977.

Hirsch, Adam Jay. *The Rise of the Penitentiary: Prisons and Punishment in Early America.* New Haven, CT: Yale University Press, 1992.

Othmani, Ahmed, with Sophie Bessis. *Beyond Prison: The Fight to Reform Prison Systems Around the World.* Trans. Marguerite Garling. New York: Berghahn, 2008.

Ross, Jeffrey Ian. *Special Problems in Corrections.* Upper Saddle River, NJ: Pearson/Prentice Hall, 2008.

Rusche, Georg, and Otto Kirschheimer. *Punishment and Social Structure.* New Brunswick, NJ: Transaction, 2003.

Scott, David. *Penology.* Los Angeles: Sage, 2008.

Useem, Bert, and Anne Morrison Piehl. *Prison State: The Challenge of Mass Incarceration.* New York: Cambridge University Press, 2008.

Wener, Richard E. *The Environmental Psychology of Prisons and Jails: Creating Humane Spaces in Secure Settings.* New York: Cambridge University Press, 2012.

Web Sites

American Civil Liberties Union: www.aclu.org

Amnesty International: www.amnesty.org

Human Rights Watch: www.hrw.org

International Centre for Prison Studies: www.prisonstudies.org

Office of the United Nations High Commissioner for Human Rights: www.ohchr.org

Documents

Document 1: "On the Penitentiary System in the United States and Its Application in France" (excerpt), Alexis de Tocqueville and Gustave de Beaumont, 1833

In the early nineteenth century, the United States was a pioneer in penal reform. In 1831, the new government of France sent political theorist Alexis de Tocqueville and his friend, prison reformer Gustave de Beaumont, to the United States to study the reforms. Of particular interest to French reformers was the new penitentiary systems in New York (the Auburn System) and Pennsylvania (the Pennsylvania System); both aimed at rehabilitating criminals by inculcating in them self-discipline and reflection of their crimes. But they differed in one important way, the degree of solitude suffered by the prisoners. In the following passage from their 1833 report, Tocqueville and Beaumont argue in favor of the less isolating Auburn system.

This separation, which prevents the wicked from injuring others, is also favourable to himself. Thrown into solitude he reflects. Placed alone, in view of his crime, he learns to hate it; and if his soul be not yet surfeited with crime, and thus have lost all taste for anything better, it is in solitude, where remorse will come to assail him. Solitude is a severe punishment, but such a punishment is merited by the guilty, [American jurist] Mr. [Edward] Livingston justly remarks, that a prison, destined to punish, would soon cease to be a fearful object, if the convicts in it could entertain at their pleasure those social relations in which they delighted, before their entry into the prison. Yet, whatever may be the crime of the guilty prisoner, no one has the right to take life from him, if society decree merely to deprive him of his liberty. Such, however, would be the result of absolute solitude, if no alleviation of its rigours were offered.

This is the reason why labour is introduced into the prison. Far from being an aggravation of the punishment, it is a real benefit to the prisoner. But even if the criminal did not find in it a relief from his sufferings, it nevertheless would be necessary to force him to it. It is idleness which has led him to crime; with employment he will learn how to live honestly. Labour of the criminals is necessary still under another point of view: their detention, expensive for society if they remain idle, becomes less burthensome if they labour. The prisons of Auburn, Sing-Sing, Wethersfield, Boston, and Philadelphia, rest then upon these two united principles, solitude and labour. These principles, in order to be salutary, ought not to be separated: the one is inefficient without the other. In the ancient prison of Auburn, isolation without labour has been tried, and those prisoners who have not become insane or did not die of despair, have returned to society only to commit new crimes.

Source: Internet Archive, www.archive.org

Document 2: Standard Minimum Rules for the Treatment of Prisoners, United Nations, 1955 (amended 1957 and 1977)

In 1955, the United Nations Congress on the Prevention of Crime and the Treatment of Offenders adopted the Standard Minimum Rules for the Treatment of Prisoners, later approved by the Economic and Social Council. Although not binding, the standard established a model set of rules for the treatment of prisoners and the management of penal institutions.

www2.ohchr.org/english/law/treatmentprisoners.htm

Source: Office of the United Nations High Commissioner for Human Rights.

PRIVACY

Little of certainty can be said about the concept of privacy other than the fact that it has been discussed and debated for centuries—perhaps even millennia. The exact meaning of the word, as well as the circumstances under which privacy is important; the appropriate means for safeguarding privacy; and whether privacy is even possible or desirable are all the subject of much disagreement, particularly as the world grows both more interconnected and more computerized.

History

Looking back, and with the benefit of modern understandings of the term, many scholars detect the first instances of "privacy" in documents that date back thousands of years. The Jewish Talmud decrees that individuals have the right to avoid being watched, the New Testament describes several different individuals who attempt to foil eavesdroppers, and the Koran includes various passages such as this one from Surah 24:

> O ye who believe! Enter not houses other than your own until you have asked leave and saluted the inmates thereof. That is better for you, that you may be heedful. And if you find no one therein, do not enter them until you are given permission. And if it be said to you, 'Go back,' then go back; that is purer for you. And Allah knows well what you do.

The ancient Greeks, ancient Chinese, Romans, and medieval Britons also had statutes protecting individuals from one sort of trespass or another. Some guarded an individual from being spied on in his residence; others forbade the sharing of certain types of personal information.

Each of these laws and texts speaks to very specific circumstances, and none actually utilizes the term "privacy." Indeed, it was not until 1534 that the word first found its way into print in an English-language text, and it slowly achieved wider currency thereafter. William Shakespeare mentions privacy in two of his plays—*Merry Wives of Windsor* (1602) and *Troilus and Cressida* (1609)—and John Milton does the same in his 1649 tract *Eikonoklastes*. Alexander Pope decided that Homer was referring to privacy several different times when he translated the *Iliad* in 1715, and Henry Fielding made extensive use of the word when he authored *Tom Jones,* one of the first English-language novels, in 1749.

Starting in the latter part of the eighteenth century, privacy issues began to find their way into the realm of law. In a groundbreaking 1765 decision, the British jurist Lord Camden (Charles Pratt) ruled in *Entick v. Carrington* that three men in the employ of the king had violated the law when they forcibly entered the residence of writer John Entick and seized his private papers. Member of Parliament and future prime minister William Pitt applauded the ruling, declaring, "The poorest man may in his cottage bid defiance to all the force of the Crown." When the British colonies of North America rebelled and became the United States, they made a point of incorporating protections against unlawful search and seizure into their constitution.

France also took steps to enshrine privacy rights into law during the eighteenth and nineteenth centuries. The Declaration of the Rights of Man and of the Citizen (1789), which launched the French Revolution, recognized property rights in much the same manner as the U.S. Constitution. Several decades thereafter, in 1858, the French legal code was expanded to include prohibitions against publishing private information. This new law was put to a high-profile test just five years later, when the author Alexandre Dumas, the elder, posed for pictures with his mistress Adah Isaacs Menken. The photographer published the images, which touched off a scandal. Dumas sued for violation of privacy, won his case, and was awarded damages.

In the nineteenth century, intellectuals and philosophers also began to grapple with privacy in a serious way. In 1854, Henry David Thoreau published *Walden, or, a Life in the Woods,* detailing his two-year experiment living in relative seclusion in a cabin near Walden Pond, in northeastern Massachusetts. The account is a kind of privacy manifesto. "I have never found a companion that was as companionable as solitude," Thoreau observed. In 1859, the British political theorist John Stuart Mill published *On Liberty,* which takes privacy as one of its central themes. In an influential 1890 article for the *Harvard Law Review,* lawyers Louis D. Brandeis (later a U.S. Supreme Court justice) and Samuel Warren famously defined privacy as "the right to be let alone."

By the twentieth century, privacy was well established as a right nearly worldwide and had been enshrined in most constitutions. In nations whose constitutions do not specifically recognize privacy rights—India and Ireland, for example—court decisions have generally affirmed the privilege instead. The right to privacy is also included in dozens of international declarations and conventions, including the Universal Declaration of Human Rights (1948), Convention for the Protection of Human Rights and Fundamental Freedoms (1950), European Convention on Human Rights (1952), International Covenant on Civil and Political Rights (1966), UN Convention on the Rights of the Child (1989), and UN Convention on Migrant Workers (1991).

Meaning

While privacy is widely regarded as desirable—indeed, essential—across much of the world, there is little consensus about what exactly it means to have privacy. The Universal Declaration of Human Rights, for example, asserts:

> No one shall be subjected to arbitrary interference with his privacy, family, home or correspondence, nor to attacks upon his honour or reputation. Everyone has the right to the protection of the law against such interference or attacks.

This is regarded as a particularly important and influential statement of privacy rights. It is also exceedingly vague, leaving unstated most dimensions of the concept.

In fact, when an activist, jurist, or scholar speaks of privacy, he or she may be referring to one or more of several different types of privacy. First among these is informational privacy—the right to keep details about one's personal activities, finances, and life from public view. This includes bank account numbers, credit records, grades and test scores, medical information, and anything that can be used to verify—or steal—identity, such as one's address, birth date, or phone number.

A related concern is privacy of communications—the right to keep one's interactions with other human beings shielded from outsiders. This embraces older technologies such as postal mail and telephones as well as such newer tools as electronic mail and other Internet tools. Because of the growing importance and ubiquity of the latter types of communication, this sort of privacy is presently a hot-button issue. Indeed, when some individuals and organizations refer to privacy, they exclusively mean it in the context of the Internet.

A third type of privacy is bodily privacy—the sanctity of one's person. This includes protection against unwanted medical procedures, for instance, drug screens and genetic tests, as well as prohibitions on cavity searches, unwanted touching, and so forth. Some individuals also regard compulsory immunization programs as a violation of bodily privacy, though this position is controversial and not mainstream in any culture.

Yet another category of privacy is territorial privacy. Just as individuals generally have the right to the sanctity of their body, so too do they have the right to sanctity of their domicile or workplace. Violations can include trespasses on private property, unlawful government searches, and unwanted video surveillance.

It should be noted that these categorizations are all widely used, but neither the general breakdown nor the specific catalog of concerns within each category is universally agreed upon. Some analysts, for example, prefer to speak of privacy of the person, of personal behavior, of personal communications, and of personal data. It is also not uncommon to see organizational or corporate privacy included on some lists. Similarly, some scholars regard the collection of data about Internet usage as a violation of informational privacy, while others see it more as an affront to privacy of communications.

Challenges

However the conceptual deck may be shuffled, no form of privacy is absolute, even in nations where privacy rights are most zealously guarded. In most jurisdictions, for example, a spouse may have access to medical information about a wife or husband without securing permission. It is generally legal for an employer to require drug tests as a condition of employment. Criminals—or, suspected criminals—may be compelled to yield all manner of rights: Their telephone calls may be monitored, their houses invaded, their e-mails seized, and their bodily cavities searched.

The fact that there are exceptions to every rule presents the first challenge with which privacy advocates must contend. Who, precisely, decides the exceptions? And on what basis? For example, many nations use biometrics systems to verify identity—France, Germany, Jamaica, Russia, and Spain all require fingerprint validation for various purposes, while Canada, Germany, the United States, and the United Kingdom are all working to build DNA databases. Some analysts find this to be an accurate and convenient means for people to identify themselves and to avoid being defrauded; others believe it is an unacceptable violation of bodily privacy.

To provide another example, privacy rights in the workplace are hotly debated within and between nations. Many countries—the United States and United Kingdom, for example—allow employees' activities to be recorded by cameras while they are at work. Others—Austria, Norway, and Sweden, for example—strictly forbid the practice. Even more controversial are "keystroke capture" programs, which allow employers to document what users type while working at their computer. This software is presented as a tool both for keeping workers efficient and honest and for detecting fraudulent use of company time for personal purposes. But what if the programs capture personal information that is highly sensitive and has the potential for abuse—banking information, login names, passwords, and so forth? There have been few answers to this question.

Wherever the line may be drawn between acceptable and unacceptable invasions of privacy, there are always individuals and organizations willing to cross that line for their own gain, even when doing so is a criminal offense. For example, it is commonplace for businesses to collect credit or marketing information about individuals (this is often called "data mining") and to use that data to target their sales efforts or to sell the information to other businesses. Often, such efforts are barely within the bounds of the law; in other instances, they are clearly outside the law. Even more damaging is identity fraud—the acquisi-

tion and use of an individual's personal information by someone wishing to impersonate that individual. This might be done to avoid blame for a crime, to gain access to a person's assets, to kidnap a child, or to get access to medical care.

The advent of the Internet and the computer age has made both of these offenses—data mining and identity fraud—vastly more common than ever before. A great many companies have access to massive amounts of data about their customers or users and have proven willing to use it. Apple, Facebook, Google, Microsoft, and Yahoo! have all been sued or fined at one point or another for their overly aggressive data mining. Similarly, countless individuals have enriched themselves with phony e-mails or Web sites that are designed to trick a person into yielding up logins, passwords, and other sensitive information (a practice called "phishing").

The threats do not stop at the individual or corporate level, however, since many governments violate their citizens' privacy rights on a regular basis. For quite a few national leaders, a constitutional promise of privacy is little more than empty words on a piece of paper. China, Cuba, Iran, Kyrgyzstan, North Korea, Pakistan, Saudi Arabia and a host of other countries regularly monitor their citizens' Internet use, access personal records and other data, and violate the sanctity of both persons and domiciles. Not all governments are quite as aggressive as this, but studies indicate that more than 90 nations engage in illegally monitoring the communications of human rights workers, journalists, labor organizers, and political opposition movements. Included among those nations are Colombia, Italy, the Philippines, Russia, South Africa, Sudan, and Venezuela.

In addition to the challenges of safeguarding privacy against individual, corporate, and government intruders, it should be noted that not all individuals or cultures see this right as valuable or useful. To start with, there are a number of languages—Chinese, Indonesian, Italian, Japanese, and Russian among them—that do not have a word that exactly corresponds to "privacy," which implies a certain lack of interest in the concept. And in some cultures, particularly those that tend toward collectivism (anti-individualism), privacy may actually be seen as harmful. The Chinese author Xiaolu Guo, for example, writes that, "privacy makes people lonely. Privacy makes families fall apart."

A handful of intellectuals and cultural critics also have spoken disdainfully of privacy. Some legal scholars, such as Robert Bork and Judith Jarvis Thomson, argue that privacy rights need not be safeguarded, because the term is simply a synonym for other rights—such as property rights—that are already well protected by law. A few feminists, such as Catharine MacKinnon, argue that privacy is antithetical to women's equality because it allows for abuse and other exploitative behaviors to be hidden from public view. And some analysts argue that privacy is no longer achievable in the face of globalization and technical progress. Scott McNealy, Sun Microsystems cofounder and former CEO, is among those who feel this way. "You have zero privacy anyway, get over it," he famously observed.

Protections

Governments that desire to protect privacy tend to embrace one of three approaches, each problematic in some way. The first is known as the regulatory model, wherein a legislature adopts a broad-ranging privacy law and then appoints an official or a bureaucracy to interpret and enforce the law as specific cases arise. The regulatory model is utilized, to a greater or lesser extent, in Australia, Canada, Hong Kong, much of Europe, and New Zealand. The difficulties with this approach are that enforcement apparatuses tend to be fairly weak or nonexistent and individuals or corporations accused of privacy violations can challenge the charge and keep the matter tied up in court for many years.

A second approach is to avoid vaguely defined laws meant to be applied broadly in favor of more precise legislation addressed to specific issues—theft of financial information over the Internet, for example, or police searches of automobiles. This is called the sectoral approach, and the most prominent nation to employ this strategy is the United States. The downside to such a piecemeal approach is that new laws must be written, debated, and passed each time a new issue or technology or loophole arises. As such, nations that use the sectoral approach typically lag years behind the latest and most pressing issues in privacy protection.

A third option, and one that can be combined with the other two, is to utilize the power of the free market by encouraging private companies to regulate privacy. The notion is that consumers will abandon a Web site that takes liberties with people's personal information, a bank that is careless about combating identity fraud, or a corporation that is known to spy on its employees. The difficulty with the free market approach is that there is little evidence that it works. Indeed, it often encourages fraud and dishonesty, because many companies claim they are taking privacy-protecting steps, when in fact they are not.

In part because of the issues outlined above, many privacy activists argue that the power to protect privacy rights lies mostly with the individual. They suggest that steps such as carefully protecting one's personal information, vigilantly monitoring bank accounts, and installing firewalls and other computer tools are the very best ways to fight the war against incursions on individual privacy. To take but one example, universal use of e-mail encryption using a technology called Pretty Good Privacy (PGP) would all but end nearly all forms of e-mail fraud.

Unfortunately, putting the onus on the individual has actually proven to be the least effective way of protecting privacy rights. The difficulty is that privacy, like free speech or good health, is not truly valued until it is taken away. In other words, people overwhelmingly assert that they value privacy, but they rarely do anything to put that sentiment into action. In the United States, for example, 60 percent of people say they fear the "loss of privacy" and 80 percent express support for more aggressive steps to protect online privacy—however, only 7 percent of Americans have actually done anything at all to safeguard their privacy.

Indeed, the individuals who say they value privacy not only fail to protect their rights, but also they are often quite reckless in giving away their right to privacy. For example, one study found that people were generally willing to yield up all of the necessary information to apply for and receive credit in exchange for a coupon valued at a mere 50 cents. Similarly, members of shopping clubs regularly hand over their contact information and copious amounts of data about their spending habits in exchange for better prices on the goods they need—or even the ones they do not need.

To take yet another example, more than 500 million users have signed up for the Web site Facebook, the vast majority dismissing any and all documents put before them that outline the terms and conditions of their usage. From that point forward, they contribute to the 25 billion photos, personal details, and other pieces of information that the site collects each day. By the terms of the user agreement that nobody reads, Facebook owns all of this private information in perpetuity. Much the same holds true for the millions or billions of people who use Baidu,

Bing, Blogspot, Gmail, Google, LinkedIn, Myspace, Twitter, Yahoo!, and YouTube.

The Future

There is a clear disconnect, then, between the way people think about privacy and the way in which they act when confronted with privacy issues. This has allowed governments, corporations, and individuals to grow ever more bold in infringing on individuals' privacy in the past decade. Perhaps most troubling is that the governments speaking most loudly in favor of privacy are often some of the worst perpetrators; the USA PATRIOT Act is often cited as an example. While there may still be time for change, and certainly a great deal of energy is still being spent by legislators and activists on the fight for privacy rights, it is, without question, easy to see why Scott McNealy feels that privacy is a concept whose time will soon be past.

Christopher Bates

See also: Cybercrime; Human Rights; Identity Fraud; Secrecy, Government.

Further Reading

Alderman, Ellen, and Caroline Kennedy. *The Right to Privacy.* New York: Alfred A. Knopf, 1995.

Andrews, Lori. *I Know Who You Are and I Saw What You Did: Social Networks and the Death of Privacy.* New York: Free Press, 2012.

Diffie, Whitfield, and Susan Landau. *Privacy on the Line: The Politics of Wiretapping and Encryption.* Cambridge, MA: MIT Press, 2010.

Lane, Frederick S. *American Privacy: The 400-Year History of Our Most Contested Right.* Boston: Beacon, 2010.

Solove, Daniel J. *The Digital Person: Technology and Privacy in the Information Age.* New York: New York University Press, 2004.

———. *Understanding Privacy.* Cambridge, MA: Harvard University Press, 2008.

Wacks, Raymond. *Privacy: A Very Short Introduction.* New York: Oxford University Press, 2009.

Web Sites

Electronic Frontier Foundation: www.eff.org/issues/privacy

Electronic Privacy Information Center: http://epic.org/privacy

Global Privacy and Information Quality Working Group: www.it.ojp.gov/gpiqwg

International Association of Privacy Professionals: www.privacyassociation.org

Privacy International: www.privacyinternational.org

Privacy Rights Clearinghouse: www.privacyrights.org

UNESCO Chair in Data Privacy: http://unescoprivacychair.urv.cat

Documents

Document 1: "The Right to Privacy" (excerpt), *Harvard Law Review,* Louis D. Brandeis and Samuel Warren, 1890

The Harvard Law Review *article of December 1890 in which attorneys Louis D. Brandeis and Samuel Warren tackled the burgeoning body of law on privacy rights stands as one of the seminal texts on the issue, and as such is quoted widely in both American and international court decisions.*

That the individual shall have full protection in person and in property is a principle as old as the common law; but it has been found necessary from time to time to define anew the exact nature and extent of such protection. Political, social, and economic changes entail the recognition of new rights, and the common law, in its eternal youth, grows to meet the new demands of society. Thus, in very early times, the law gave a remedy only for physical interference with life and property, for trespasses vi et armis. Then the "right to life" served only to protect the subject from battery in its various forms; liberty meant freedom from actual restraint; and the right to property secured to the individual his lands and his cattle. Later, there came a recognition of man's spiritual nature, of his feelings and his intellect. Gradually the scope of these legal rights broadened; and now the right to life has come to mean the right to enjoy life,—the right to be let alone; the right to liberty secures the exercise of extensive civil privileges; and the term "property" has grown to comprise every form of possession—intangible, as well as tangible.

Thus, with the recognition of the legal value of sensations, the protection against actual bodily injury was extended to prohibit mere attempts to do such injury; that is, the putting another in fear of such injury. From the action of battery grew that of assault. Much later there came a qualified protection of the individual against offensive noises and odors, against dust and smoke, and excessive vibration. The law of nuisance was developed. So regard for human emotions soon extended the scope of personal immunity beyond the body of the individual. His reputation, the standing among his fellow-men, was considered, and the law of slander and libel arose. Man's family relations became a part of the legal conception of his life, and the alienation of a wife's affections was held remediable. Occasionally the law halted, as in its refusal to recognize the intrusion by seduction upon the honor of the family. But even here the demands of society were met. A mean fiction, the action per quod servitium amisit, was resorted to, and by allowing damages for injury to the parents' feelings, an adequate remedy was ordinarily afforded. Similar to the expansion of the right to life was the growth of the legal conception of property. From corporeal property arose the incorporeal rights issuing out of it; and then there opened the wide realm of intangible property, in the products and processes of the mind, as works of literature and art, goodwill, trade secrets, and trademarks.

This development of the law was inevitable. The intense intellectual and emotional life, and the heightening of sensations which came with the advance of civilization, made it clear to men that only a part of the pain, pleasure, and profit of life lay in physical things. Thoughts, emotions, and sensations demanded legal recognition, and the beautiful capacity for growth which characterizes the common law enabled the judges to afford the requisite protection, without the interposition of the legislature.

Recent inventions and business methods call attention to the next step which must be taken for the protection of the person, and for securing to the individual what Judge Cooley calls the right "to be let alone." Instantaneous photographs and newspaper enterprise have invaded the sacred precincts of private and domestic life; and numerous mechanical devices threaten to make good the prediction that "what is whispered in the closet shall be proclaimed from the house-tops." For years there has been a feeling that the law must afford some remedy for the unauthorized circulation of portraits of private persons; and the evil of invasion of privacy by the newspapers, long keenly felt, has been but recently discussed by an able writer. The alleged facts of a somewhat notorious case brought before an inferior tribunal in New York a few months ago, directly involved the consideration of the right of circulating portraits; and the question whether our law will recognize and protect the right to privacy in this and in other respects must soon come before our courts for consideration.

Of the desirability—indeed of the necessity—of some such protection, there can, it is believed, be no doubt. The press is overstepping in every direction the obvious bounds of propriety and of decency. Gossip is no longer the resource of the idle and of the vicious, but has become a trade, which is pursued with industry as well as effrontery. To satisfy a prurient taste the details of sexual relations are spread broadcast in the columns of the daily papers. To occupy the indolent, column upon column is filled with idle gossip, which can only be procured by intrusion upon the domestic circle. The intensity and complexity of life, attendant upon advancing civilization, have rendered necessary some retreat from the world, and man, under the refining influence of culture, has become more sensitive to publicity, so that solitude and privacy have become

more essential to the individual; but modern enterprise and invention have, through invasions upon his privacy, subjected him to mental pain and distress, far greater than could be inflicted by mere bodily injury. Nor is the harm wrought by such invasions confined to the suffering of those who may be the subjects of journalistic or other enterprise. In this, as in other branches of commerce, the supply creates the demand. Each crop of unseemly gossip, thus harvested, becomes the seed of more, and, in direct proportion to its circulation, results in the lowering of social standards and of morality. Even gossip apparently harmless, when widely and persistently circulated, is potent for evil. It both belittles and perverts. It belittles by inverting the relative importance of things, thus dwarfing the thoughts and aspirations of a people. When personal gossip attains the dignity of print, and crowds the space available for matters of real interest to the community, what wonder that the ignorant and thoughtless mistake its relative importance. Easy of comprehension, appealing to that weak side of human nature which is never wholly cast down by the misfortunes and frailties of our neighbors, no one can be surprised that it usurps the place of interest in brains capable of other things. Triviality destroys at once robustness of thought and delicacy of feeling. No enthusiasm can flourish, no generous impulse can survive under its blighting influence.

Source: Harvard Law Review 4:5 (December 15, 1890).

Document 2: "Privacy Principles," Personal Information Protection and Electronic Documents Act (Canada), 2000

Canada has taken a leading role in developing the international body of law on privacy. In 2000, the nation's legislature adopted the Personal Information Protection and Electronic Documents Act, which includes this list of Privacy Principles.

Principle 1—Accountability
An organization is responsible for personal information under its control and shall designate an individual or individuals who are accountable for the organization's compliance with the following principles.

Principle 2—Identifying Purposes
The purposes for which personal information is collected shall be identified by the organization at or before the time the information is collected.

Principle 3—Consent
The knowledge and consent of the individual are required for the collection, use, or disclosure of personal information, except where inappropriate.

Principle 4—Limiting Collection

The collection of personal information shall be limited to that which is necessary for the purposes identified by the organization. Information shall be collected by fair and lawful means.

Principle 5—Limiting Use, Disclosure, and Retention

Personal information shall not be used or disclosed for purposes other than those for which it was collected, except with the consent of the individual or as required by law. Personal information shall be retained only as long as necessary for the fulfilment of those purposes.

Principle 6—Accuracy

Personal information shall be as accurate, complete, and up-to-date as is necessary for the purposes for which it is to be used.

Principle 7—Safeguards

Personal information shall be protected by security safeguards appropriate to the sensitivity of the information.

Principle 8—Openness

An organization shall make readily available to individuals specific information about its policies and practices relating to the management of personal information.

Principle 9—Individual Access

Upon request, an individual shall be informed of the existence, use, and disclosure of his or her personal information and shall be given access to that information. An individual shall be able to challenge the accuracy and completeness of the information and have it amended as appropriate.

Principle 10—Challenging Compliance

An individual shall be able to address a challenge concerning compliance with the above principles to the designated individual or individuals accountable for the organization's compliance.

Source: Office of the Privacy Commissioner of Canada.

PRIVATIZATION

Privatization is the process by which state-owned or state-operated business or industries are transferred to private ownership or put under private operation. It is the inverse of nationalization, in which private assets are put under public ownership or control. While sometimes motivated by ideological considerations—a general belief that productive assets belong in private as opposed to state hands—privatization is usually undertaken for economic reasons, frequently either to rid the public sector of unprofitable industries or to make industries more efficient and competitive. Corruption can also play a factor, as in Russia and some of the other countries formed out of the former Soviet Union, where former officials and others were able to gain control of state assets for prices below the market value, either through personal connections, government positions, or bribery. Privatization has become increasingly common over the past several decades and, while frequently undertaken in capitalist countries, is also a policy of many nominally socialist and communist countries, such as China and Vietnam.

Throughout the past four decades, governments in both the developed and developing worlds have used the privatization of state assets as a key tool of economic policy. This privatization process involves state-owned industries such as telecommunications, airlines, banking, turnpikes, and even state lotteries. Yet even after a wave of privatizations, state-controlled companies account for 80 percent of market capitalization in China and more than 60 percent in Russia. So it appears that state-controlled companies will continue not only to exist but to thrive. For experts and policy makers, then, the question becomes when is it appropriate to privatize a firm, or an entire industry?

History and Theory

Privatization can be defined as any movement toward a market-driven economy or any increase in private ownership and control. Today, elements of privatization and free market orientation can be seen in almost every economy in the world, from the mixed markets of Europe and the United States, to the formerly communist economies of Eastern Europe, as well as even Communist China, which is gradually opening up to private enterprise. But privatization is no longer considered a panacea for economic problems. During the post–World War II period, state-controlled industry protected socialist and mixed-market economies from foreign investors and interests, especially in the oil industry. In the case of newly independent colonies, state companies were often formed in an attempt to sever the influence of a resented colonial power. With the prevalence of the state-controlled industries, politicians quickly found that control of the economy gave them control of the political process, securing their power. Consequently, state companies began to be influenced by politicians in the name of public welfare—padding payrolls, for example, to assure low unemployment or to provide jobs for political supporters—which took an eventual toll on competitiveness and economic efficiency. By the 1970s, many state companies had become synonymous with bloated bureaucracies, wasteful and costly inefficiencies, and corruption.

According to advocates of privatization, competition is the key to economic efficiency and long-term growth. Evidently, that was the thought process of countries around the world as the 1980s approached and a need to address stagnant economic growth became increasingly pressing. Thus, the push for privatization was strong in the 1980s, sweeping across countries whose governments ranged across the spectrum of political ideology and whose economies operated at varying levels of development. The inefficiencies of state ownership had been exposed and economies globally were suffering, both of which weakened faith in national governments. The skeptical public turned to the private sector for the solution.

A whirlwind of conditions set the stage for privatization during this time period. Historians of the process cite two broad forces: the rise of a managerial class and changes in market structures. The former refers to the arrival of managerial and technical knowledge that did not exist before, accompanied by financial resources, which would allow those in the private sector to take over and successfully manage a recently divested industry. The latter refers to developments in technology that allowed for the growth, in the words of scholar Raymond Vernon, of "an international capital market in which developing countries could raise capital for the financing of their public enterprises."

Case for Privatization

The fundamental argument in favor of privatization is that privatization breeds economic efficiency and ultimately leads to more potential for long-term economic growth than nationalization. The driving force that brings about this efficiency is competition. It is easy to see why competition is so vital when examining what occurs when it is absent. Critics contend nationalized industries often become privileged "deadbeats" of national economies, allowing for gross incompetence by management, padded payrolls, and even outright looting, especially in nationalized oil industries. Corruption is common because the state has nobody else to regulate it and decisions are often made for purely political reasons. Bureaucracy is problematic, too, because it often translates into a government's unwillingness to improve or advance a good or service unless the industry's performance is so poor that it reflects negatively on the administration. Competition, as the argument goes, eliminates these drawbacks of public ownership.

Competition under privatization also typically yields a greater revenue stream. Managers of a privatized industry may be more specialized or better equipped to run the industry than their government-appointed counterparts, thus enhancing competiveness and profitability. Also, state-owned enterprises do not exist solely to generate profits, whereas privately held corporations do. Consequently, state-owned enterprises are often wasteful when it comes to spending money. For example, nationalized companies typically employ many more workers than their private sector counterparts (which explains why labor unions traditionally favored nationalization), but this means that the workers are less productive, making the real cost of the good or service higher. Additionally, the government can raise taxes or issue debt in order to fund a failing industry, even if it does not make economic sense to let the industry survive in public hands. A private company, on the other hand, must fund its operations by either attracting private investors or using its own internal funding; therefore, a private company has a greater incentive to create high-quality goods and services. Finally, the revenues generated by private enterprises are taxed, and hence the public treasury will still benefit from the business or industry after it has been privatized.

State governments do have alternatives that allow them to enjoy the benefits of privatization without completely privatizing an industry. One common alternative is governmental outsourcing of a particular good or service to the private sector, as is often the case in the day-to-day operations of government-owned airports. Another example of a service that has been contracted to the private sector around the globe is garbage collection. This allows for a more efficient team of managers and employees to manage the trash collection, while the service is still "publicly owned" and funded by the government. Outsourcing

Top 10 Privatizations, Non-Chinese, 2000–2007

Country	Company	Sector	Year	Proceeds (billions of US$)
Russia	Rosneft	Energy	2006	10.700
Russia	Sberbank	Financial	2007	8.800
Russia	Vneshtorgbank	Financial	2007	8.000
Turkey	Turk Telecom	Communications	2005	6.550
Ukraine	Kryvorizhstal	Steel	2005	4.800
Romania	Banca Comercial Romania	Financial	2006	4.700
Poland	Telekomunikacja Polska (TPSA)	Telecommunications	2000	4.300
Brazil	Petrobras	Energy	2000	4.233
Turkey	Tupras	Energy	2006	4.140
Mexico	FARAC Highway Concession Package	Infrastructure	2007	4.030

Source: World Bank.

Top 10 Privatizations, China, 2000–2007

Company	Sector	Year	Proceeds (billions of US$)
Industrial and Commercial Bank of China	Financial	2006	22.041
Bank of China	Financial	2006	13.714
PetroChina	Energy	2007	9.154
China Shenhua Energy	Energy	2007	9.124
China Construction Bank	Financial	2007	7.955
China Pacific Insurance	Financial	2007	7.700
China CITIC Bank	Financial	2007	6.051
China United Communications	Telecommunications	2000	5.653
Ping An Insurance Group	Financial	2007	5.327
China Life Insurance	Financial	2007	3.881

Source: World Bank.

to the private sector can be especially important when the good or service to be produced requires extensive managerial or technical knowledge, in which case the private sector can often bring to bear better resources than can the government.

Another effective alternative to privatization is to allow private firms to enter into competition with the public enterprises. An example of this would be allowing a private airline to enter into direct competition with a state-owned airline. Alternatively, the government could allow for multiple state-owned companies to compete against one another, as was the case in the 1980s in China, when the government allowed for the creation of a new state-owned airline when another state-owned air transport company already existed. The bottom line is that all of these options allow for competition, which in turn allows for the benefits of privatization to be realized.

It is generally acknowledged that not all industries are more effective when privatized. The most noteworthy example of this is one in which the industry represents a natural monopoly, such as a utility, where economies of scale and the importance of avoiding duplication of infrastructure mean that one company will be more efficient than several in providing the good or service. A utility is often a natural monopoly because the principal cost is the setup cost. It is typically more efficient for one firm to dominate the market, as this keeps the average cost to the customer lower. In a situation such as this, the enterprise is often publicly owned.

Evaluating the Privatization Process

A framework for evaluating privatization involves a four-step process. The framework evaluates the eco-

Framework for Evaluating Privatization

	Short-run	Long-run
Economic	1 Business efficiency increased	3 Corporate options increased
Political	2 Gains by various stakeholder groups	4 Stakeholder options increased

Source: Richard McGowan and John Mahon. "A Framework for Evaluating Privatization Policy." *Business and the Contemporary World* 6:1 (1994): 44.

nomic and political effects of privatization, over the short and long term, forming a two-by-two matrix.

Those evaluating the privatization process ask various questions that correspond to the cells in the above figure: Has privatization enabled a newly privatized firm to develop business strategies that lead to increases in market share and/or profits? Is that firm better able to achieve operating economies and to reduce its overall cost structure? The privatization of a previously "public good" will permit it to pursue a number of business strategies that were unavailable throughout its recent history, because of financial or political restrictions. For example, privatization of a lottery or a turnpike allows government to rid itself of excess employees and outsource many of the maintenance functions. Obviously, governments receive a huge windfall in revenue when private operators purchase these state-owned operations.

The key questions addressed in the second cell are: Do customers of the previously state-owned firm still have access to the product and service? Does the increase in quality of the service or product provided justify the price increase that private firms impose after they take over a state-owned enterprise? Were unions and other interested parties satisfied that their interests were not discounted when short-term policy decisions were made for the newly privatized firm? Usually the primary political consideration at this stage of the privatization is whether the price paid for the state-operated enterprise has enabled government to provide needed services without raising taxes.

An example of a situation in which short-run political expectations overwhelmed the revenue benefits was Chicago's attempt to sell off its parking meters in 2009. In March of that year, the city privatized parking meters. Rates were immediately raised so that the cost to park a car for two hours in the Loop area rose to $7. In exchange for a 75-year lease, the city got $1.2 billion to help plug its budget holes. But by handing over municipal parking meters to a private company, the city has given its citizens a colossal case of sticker shock, as the cost of most meters will quadruple by 2013. In response, citizens started to organize a boycott of the parking meters. The privatization was termed a fiasco and is said to be one reason why the incumbent mayor, Richard Daley, bowed out of any reelection plans. It also forced the shelving of other privatization plans of Daley's, including the privatization of Midway Airport. So while the privatization of the parking meters was an economic success, its political failure made future Chicago privatizations or outsourcing less likely, at least in the short run.

The key questions addressed in the third cell concern whether privatization aided in the development of a corporate strategy, which ensures continued profitability of the privatized firm. Can the firm pursue a diversification strategy so that it is no longer dependent on just one source of revenue? Has privatization enabled the firm to compete in new markets outside those in which it has traditionally been present? Can newly privatized firms take the risk to use the economies of scale that government has in some ways bestowed to establish economies of scope? Notice that the concept of "risk" was not one that nationalized firms had to contend with. On the other hand, if a newly privatized firm is going to be considered a success in the long run, it will have to take risks in new markets as well as develop new products.

An example of a privatization that allowed previously state-owned firms to expand globally is

With the end of Soviet communism in the early 1990s, the Russian government privatized the landmark GUM department store in Moscow, along with factories, oil producers, and other successful concerns. In some cases it sold partial shares, in other cases full shares. *(AP Photo/ Liu Heung Shing)*

Altadis. Altadis was the result of a 1999 merger between Spain's Tabacalera and France's Seita, both government-owned tobacco firms. The merged privatized firms created a very wide and deep product line. Altadis became one of the leading players in the European retail tobacco market, as well as in the wholesale distribution sector. By 2008, according to imperial-tabacco.com, it ranked third in Western Europe in the sale of cigarettes, first in the world in cigars, and was "one of the foremost distributors to convenience outlets in southern Europe and South America." The structure of the product line of Altadis can best be divided into three complementary core businesses that include blond and dark cigarettes, cigars, and distribution.

Altadis was also a great success for both the Spanish and French governments. Its establishment permitted both governments to exit the controversial tobacco industry, allowing them to enact more stringent antismoking laws, as well as raise excise taxes on cigarettes by significant amounts. Overall, both governments actually raised more annual revenue after the privatization of their cigarette industries.

Yet while Altadis had been able to expand into some markets, it was clear that it did not have the resources to enter many global markets. The 2008 acquisition of Altadis by Britain's Imperial Tobacco's put the latter in a great position to be a dominant factor in the tobacco industry. Already strong in areas such as the Netherlands, Belgium, Ireland, and France, Imperial Tobacco increased its dominance in France, Spain, and other Spanish-speaking countries through the purchase of Altadis. Today, Imperial Tobacco has almost total control of these markets and has gained the power to dictate the prices for the tobacco products in those areas. What was once a primarily Spanish- and French-run company is now part of a global powerhouse. Overall, the purchase of these two companies allowed Imperial Tobacco to challenge Philip Morris as the leader in the tobacco industry.

In the fourth cell of the 2 x 2 matrix, the emphasis is on the long-term role that government will play in the conduct of a privatized firm. There are two types of long-term political involvement. The first involves regulation. What type of regulation will government impose on a privatized firm? For example, when utilities such as water and electricity are privatized, will government permit the firm to set rates or will any rate increase have to be approved by a government commission? Another example would be outsourcing the operations of an airport. Will new airport operators determine which airlines receive additional slots, or will government be able to favor a local or nationalized airline?

The other long-term political worry for a privatized firm is that governments will renationalize the firm. One industry in which this has repeatedly occurred is the oil industry. An outstanding example of this is the oil industry in Argentina, where oil was discovered in the 1930s. Throughout the history of this industry, Argentina has lacked a fundamental political consensus about how to exploit its oil resources. The result is that the status of Argentina's oil industry has constantly swung between state ownership and private ownership. Those arguing in favor of privatization maintain that private investment is needed to allow for the full development of Argentina's oil resources. Meanwhile, those who favor a state-operated oil industry are highly suspicious of the motives of foreign oil companies. They would prefer an oil industry where the profits would be purely directed toward Argentina's interests, even if it meant an inefficient oil industry.

Argentina's government has demonstrated that under political or economic pressure, it will try to meddle with the privatization process by raising taxes on the oil industry and by increasing regulation on the oil monopoly it helped create, as well as by simply renationalizing the industry. Currently, Repsol-YPF is Argentina's largest private oil firm. It is unique in Latin America, where oil resources are typically monopolized by state companies. Repsol-YPF's perceived success in building a relationship with the Argentine government will undoubtedly serve as a model to encourage, or discourage, oil privatization in the rest of Latin America, say experts. The firm's continued economic success will depend on its ability to develop a lasting, mutually beneficial political relationship with the Argentine government. Without cultivating a wider base of political support over the long term, Repsol-YPF will find its earnings and market share used as a political football. If the firm wishes to benefit from Argentina's historically "national" oil resources, it must take steps to develop its public image as more national than foreign.

Larger Considerations

Firms and industries that governments are likely to privatize or nationalize vary depending on the specific economic conditions of the firm and industry in question, or of the national economy as a whole. But there is also the overriding factor of ideology. In some countries privatization is considered outside the political mainstream, while in others nationalization is equally unlikely. For example, it is nearly inconceivable that the U.S. government would nationalize the oil industry, while in Venezuela it would be equally unlikely to see the government privatize the oil industry. But ideology alone is not always the deciding factor.

Economic factors play a major role in whether or not an industry will be privatized, particularly in countries where ideological considerations are more ambivalent. The first question asked is whether a firm is thought to be economically viable on its own. If it is not economically viable, and it is thought to be in the national interest to keep the firm in operation, then that firm will remain in governmental hands. If the firm is economically viable, however, the situation becomes much more complex, leading to the question of how much revenue a privatized firm will be able to contribute to government and, if the firm/industry remains nationalized, what resources will government need to spend in order to keep the firm/industry viable. There is no one "successful" privatization or nationalization strategy, say experts, unless all the stakeholders in a firm/industry are willing to make necessary sacrifices.

Richard McGowan

See also: Deficits and Sovereign Debt; Protectionism and Free Trade; Regulation, Business and Financial; Traffic and Mass Transit.

Further Reading

Crew, Michael, and David Parker, eds. *Developments in the Economics of Privatization and Regulation.* Northampton, MA: Edward Elgar, 2008.

Hodge, Graeme, ed. *Privatization and Market Development: Global Movements in Public Policy Ideas.* Northampton, MA: Edward Elgar, 2006.

Likosky, Michael B., ed. *Privatising Development: Transnational Law, Infrastructure, and Human Rights.* Boston: Martinus Nijhoff, 2005.

McDonald, David A., and Greg Ruiters, eds. *Alternatives to Privatization: Public Options for Essential Services in the Global South.* New York: Routledge, 2011.

McGowan, Richard. *Privatize This?* Santa Barbara, CA: Praeger, 2011.

McGowan, Richard, and John Mahon. "A Framework for Evaluating Privatization Policy." *Business and the Contemporary World* 6:1 (1994).

Pint, E.M. "Nationalization and Privatization: A Rational-Choice Perspective on Efficiency." *Journal of Public Policy* 10 (July–September1990).

Schipke, Alfred. *Why Do Governments Divest? The Macroeconomics of Privatization.* New York: Springer, 2001.

Vernon, Raymond. *The Promise of Privatization: A Challenge for U.S. Policy.* New York: Council on Foreign Relations, 1988.

Vickers John, and George Yarrow. *Privatization: An Economic Analysis.* Cambridge, MA: MIT Press, 1988.

Yergin, Daniel, and Joseph Stanislaw. *The Commanding Heights: The Battle for the World Economy.* New York: Simon & Schuster, 2002.

Web Sites

International Monetary Fund: www.imf.org
New Rules Project: www.newrules.org/governance/rules/antiprivatization-initiatives
United Nations Economic and Social Council: www.un.org/en/ecosoc
World Bank: www.worldbank.org
World Economic Forum: www.weforum.org
World Trade Organization: www.wto.org

Documents

Document 1: "We Can Develop a Market Economy Under Socialism" (excerpts), Comments of Deng Xiaoping, Chairman of the Chinese Communist Party, 1979

Taking over the reins of power in mainland China in the late 1970s, Communist Party chairman Deng Xiaoping launched a radical transformation of the nation's economy. While maintaining Communist Party control of the political apparatus and retaining state control over critical industries, he launched a massive experiment with market forces, including the privatization of many businesses and industries. The reforms have transformed China, creating a massive middle class and a world-beating export industry, but also gross inequities in wealth, speculative bubbles, and potential political discord. The comments that follow are from an interview with Chairman Deng by several North American China experts in 1979, just as the great experiment of "socialism with Chinese characteristics" was commencing.

Modernization does represent a great new revolution. The aim of our revolution is to liberate and expand the productive forces. Without expanding the productive forces, making our country prosperous and powerful, and improving the living standards of the people, our revolution is just empty talk. We oppose the old society and the old system because they oppressed the people and fettered the productive forces. We are clear about this problem now. The Gang of Four said it was better to be poor under socialism than to be rich under capitalism. This is absurd.

Of course, we do not want capitalism, but neither do we want to be poor under socialism. What we want is socialism in which the productive forces are developed and the country is prosperous and powerful. We believe that socialism is superior to capitalism. This superiority should be demonstrated in that socialism provides more favourable conditions for expanding the productive forces than capitalism does. This superiority should have become evident, but owing to our differing understanding of it, the development of the productive forces has been delayed, especially during the past ten-year period up to 1976. In the early 1960s, China was behind the developed countries, but the gap was not as wide as it is now. Over the past 11 or 12 years, from the end of the 1960s through the 1970s, the gap has widened because other countries have been vigorously developing their economies, science and technology, with the rate of development no longer being calculated in terms of years, not even in terms of months, but in terms of days.

For a fairly long period of time since the founding of the People's Republic, we have been isolated from the rest of the world. For many years this isolation was not attributable to us; on the contrary, the international anti-Chinese and anti-socialist forces confined us to a state of isolation. However, in the 1960s when opportunities to increase contact and cooperation with other countries presented themselves to us, we isolated ourselves. At last, we have learned to make use of favourable international conditions.

. . .

It is wrong to maintain that a market economy exists only in capitalist society and that there is only "capitalist" market economy. Why can't we develop a market economy under socialism? Developing a market economy does not mean practising capitalism. While maintaining a planned economy as the mainstay of our economic system, we are also introducing a market economy. But it is a socialist market economy. Although a socialist market economy is similar to a capitalist one in method, there are also differences between them. The socialist market economy mainly regulates interrelations between state-owned enterprises, between collectively owned enterprises and even between foreign capitalist enterprises. But in the final analysis, this is all done under socialism in a socialist society. We cannot say that market economy exists only under capitalism. Market economy was in its embryonic stages as early as feudalist society. We can surely develop it under socialism. Similarly, taking advantage of the useful aspects of capitalist countries, including their methods of operation and management, does not mean that we will adopt capitalism. Instead, we use those methods in order to develop the productive forces under socialism. As long as learning from capitalism is regarded as no more than a means to an end, it will not change the structure of socialism or bring China back to capitalism.

Source: China.org.cn.

Document 2: World Bank, Sample Laws on Privatization

Founded in 1944 under U.S. leadership, the World Bank is an international financial institution that receives funds from member countries, largely in the developed world, and provides loans to other member countries, largely in the developing world. Its main aims are to reduce poverty and assist economic development. To these ends, the World Bank has been one of the leading promoters of privatization of state industries and assets. To do this, the bank has sometimes made privatization a condition for receiving loans. It also offers advice on how countries can achieve privatization, including sample laws. The Law on Privatizing, prepared by the World Bank, is a nonbinding

composite—for illustration purposes only—of a number of examples of privatization laws from civil law systems, such as those that operate in most continental European countries and the many countries colonized or influenced by them.

Article 15

(1) The [appropriate authority] may, by decree: (a) convert a State owned enterprise eligible for privatization, which is not a public company, into a public company in accordance with the provisions of the Companies Act; and (b) retain a share in the capital of a State owned company and convert such share into a golden share.

(2) The [appropriate authority] shall by notice in writing to a State owned company appoint from time to time the board of directors of the company. The board shall be accountable to the [appropriate authority] for the operation of the company.

(3) The shares in a State owned company shall be allotted to the State represented by the [appropriate authority].

(4) The decree referred to in paragraph (1) shall vest in or impose on the State owned company any asset or liability, or any class of such asset or liability, specified in such decree.

(5) Any asset or liability of the State may be vested in or imposed on a State owned company whether or not any Act or agreement relating to the asset or liability permits such vesting or imposition or requires any consent.

(6) Where a transfer of the kind described in paragraph (4) takes place—

(a) the transfer shall not entitle any person to terminate, alter, or in any way affect the rights or liabilities of the Government or the State owned company under any Act or agreement;

(b) the Government shall remain liable to any third party as if the asset or liability had not been transferred; and

(c) any contract relating to the activities carried on by the State owned company shall, from the publication date of the notice described in paragraph (1) of this Article, be deemed to be a contract entered into by the State owned company.

Article 16

The [appropriate authority] may, by decree, initiate the liquidation of a State owned enterprise, or a State owned company in accordance with the provisions of the Companies Act. The Director of the Agency shall be appointed as the liquidator of the enterprise or company. . . .

Article 18

The Agency may employ the following modes of privatization:

(a) public offering of shares;

(b) sale of shares through negotiated or competitive bids;

(c) sale of the assets and business of a State owned enterprise;

(d) management or employee buyouts by management or employees of a State owned enterprise;

(e) lease, management or concession contracts; or

(f) any other method the Agency may consider appropriate.

Source: World Bank, Legal Department.

PROTECTIONISM AND FREE TRADE

Protectionism and free trade represent polar positions along a continuum that describes the facility with which international states exchange goods and services. Toward the protectionist pole (in the real world these polar points are seldom realized), states erect barriers to trade. This protectionism can take many forms. The most common is the tariff, which is simply a tax on imports that has the effect of raising the production cost (and presumably therefore the price) of imported goods relative to domestically produced goods. However, other forms of import protection, collectively referred to as nontariff barriers (NTBs), are often used in addition to, or instead of, tariffs. One common NTB is a quota, whereby only a certain amount of a particular commodity may be imported into a country in a given year. Another is an import license, whereby foreign producers are required to purchase, often at exorbitant cost, a license permitting them to import goods into a country. A third is a voluntary export restraint, whereby an exporting country voluntarily limits its penetration of a particular commodity into another country as a means of forestalling imposition of import duties or NTBs. Toward the free trade pole, states can employ a number of arrangements, discussed in more detail later on.

Studying Protectionism and Free Trade

Generally speaking, students of trade politics argue that countries' trade policies are dedicated to the pursuit of one or more of three objectives: maximization of wealth; realization of security; or institutionalization of justice.

States that seek to maximize wealth are better off under free trade regimes than protectionist ones. Eighteenth-century British economist Adam Smith held that free markets are efficient because they encourage self-interested producers to allocate resources in an optimal fashion. David Ricardo, a British economist of the nineteenth century, extended the logic internationally, suggesting that free trade serves to rationalize countries' economies such that producers shift resources toward the production of goods for which their country is most suited. This logic of comparative advantage is analogous to a social division of labor whereby individuals perform tasks for which they have the most aptitude (such as, for example, the practice of law) and contract with others to perform tasks for which they are less suited (e.g., health care).

For states that seek to realize security, wealth is important, but only to the extent that it increases a state's relative power in the international system. These so-called realists see trade as a zero-sum game, whereby one party's gains come at the expense of the other party. Free trade is to be preferred, therefore, only to the extent that it makes a country wealthier relative to those it trades with. To the extent that realists are free traders, they tend to seek a favorable balance of trade, as measured by weighing total imports against total exports. One manifestation of this free trade realism is seen in so-called hegemonic stability theory, which holds that hegemons, the dominant states in a system or subsystem, coerce others into one-sided trade arrangements. Thus, for realists free trade emerges from coercion whereby strong powers use their strength to coerce weaker powers into trade agreements to the relative advantage of the stronger powers.

Finally, in the case of states that seek to institutionalize justice, free trade is seen by some as a means to exploitation of developing nations by developed ones. For so-called dependency theorists, free trade arrangements are manifestations of neocolonialism. Instead of undertaking the costs of classical imperialism, developed nations achieve similar benefits through open markets for trade and investment. Commonly, this is perceived as multinational corporations taking advantage of rich natural resources and cheap labor in the periphery to generate large profits, very little of which are reinvested in developing nations. In order to facilitate this exploitation, developed governments use their superior power to construct one-sided free trade agreements, often agreed to by corrupt indigenous elites, government officials who compromise the greater good of their own nations in exchange for personal considerations.

History

Throughout most of modern history, states have practiced protectionist trade policies. The reasons are easy to understand if we consider that frequent warfare between the major powers made all states mindful of the danger of empowering potential rivals through trade. Import protection was not only prudent, but also attractive for other reasons. An obvious one was that free-trading nations essentially commit to contracting out production of certain types of goods to foreign producers. This is fine if such goods are not of military or strategic importance. However, state security often demands that many vital products, such as foodstuffs, heavy industry, high-tech goods, and so on, be produced domestically to ensure self-sufficiency in times of war. Another reason is that by distorting market prices, protectionism creates rents—profits earned in excess of market rates—upon which many (often politically powerful) domestic producers come to rely. Finally, particularly in times before internal revenues were generated through mechanisms such as income taxes, import duties were important sources of government revenue.

As international commerce began to pick up during the Renaissance, countries adopted protectionist policies that we traditionally group under the heading of mercantilism. Mercantilism was a form of realism; trade was understood instrumentally as a means to the larger end of (depending on the size and power of a state) imperialism or national defense. It was not until Britain's repeal of the Corn Laws in 1846 that a sustained movement away from protectionism and toward liberalization of trade began to emerge. With repeal, Britain became the world's hegemonic power and hence had the capacity and motivation to maintain an open trading system, which Britain

accomplished for much of the remainder of the nineteenth century.

By the early twentieth century, however, British hegemony was a spent force. Britain's natural successor was the United States. However, still in the thrall of Splendid Isolationism following World War I, the United States failed to assume the mantle, instead preferring an insular foreign economic policy highlighted by the enormous and comprehensive Smoot-Hawley Tariff of 1929. As the world sank deeper into the Great Depression, however, the Franklin Roosevelt administration undertook significant economic reforms. In abandoning the "beggar-thy-neighbor" policy of protectionism and currency devaluation, Roosevelt laid the groundwork for the General Agreement on Tariffs and Trade (GATT).

In the aftermath of World War II, the trading world was increasingly divided between the industrial North and preindustrial South. For the North, the most significant development was the creation of GATT. GATT (now the World Trade Organization, or WTO) is a multilateral regime dedicated to the elimination of obstacles to trade. It operates according to a series of "rounds," negotiations dedicated to a discrete agenda of trade liberalization. In its early years, GATT dedicated itself only to liberalization of trade in industrial goods. Each round was concerned with reduction of tariffs on a commodity-by-commodity basis. Beginning with the Kennedy Round (1964–1967), however, GATT adopted the so-called Swiss Formula, which proposed a large reduction of tariffs on all industrial goods. The success of that round was followed by the Tokyo Round (1973–1979), dedicated to the elimination and reduction of NTBs on industrial goods, to the extent feasible. The Uruguay Round (1986–1993) was dedicated to the elimination of agricultural subsidies (where it achieved but minimal success) and the liberalization of trade in goods and services.

World Trade Organization

Distrust of the WTO runs deep in the developing world. Prior to the Uruguay Round, GATT (as it was known then) focused on liberalization of the sort of capital-intensive industrialized goods that only wealthier nations were able to produce efficiently. By contrast, agricultural goods, which were efficiently produced in less developed countries, were excluded. The Doha Round, technically still in formulation but essentially moribund politically, was

Protesters demonstrate outside the 2007 Aid for Trade Forum near Manila, the Philippines, aimed at boosting trade for poorer countries. The protesters picketed against the WTO, the Doha Round of trade talks, and protectionist trade policies benefiting rich countries. *(AP Photo/Bullit Marquez)*

designed to facilitate that transition by making the WTO more economically beneficial for developing nations. In order to accomplish this, the WTO will have to overcome distrust of the developed nations by developing ones and the logistics of getting 153 independent and very differently situated nations to agree on what in some cases would be politically controversial agreements.

The issue of agricultural subsidies reinforces distrust. One of the enduring policies of the New Deal was a series of agricultural subsidies that have persisted as entitlements into the twenty-first century. The effects of the persistence of U.S. farm subsidies have been enormous. Perhaps the most important has been to create incentives for other countries and regimes, the European Union (EU), in particular, to maintain their own entrenched system of agricultural subsidies. Farm subsidies in the developed world have made it very difficult for developing countries, many of which have comparative advantage in agricultural production, to export their products into developed markets. Finally, because part of the subsidy program has mandated the restriction of agricultural production, artificial restrictions on supply have inflated the price of foodstuffs to the detriment of poorer nations.

As of 2012, Doha appears to be dead in the water. Talks broke down in 2008 over the issue of agricultural subsidies, and it appeared unlikely that any agreements would be reached any time in 2012, when the U.S. electoral cycle promised to put trade on the back burner in the United States. Talk of a Doha Plan B is gaining some purchase, however, among many in the developed world who feel the imperative to make the international trade system more attractive to developing nations. Plan B would provide greater access for exports from developing nations into the markets of industrialized countries, as well as possibly eliminate or reduce subsidies for industries in developed nations that compete with exports from the developing world.

Regional Trading Blocs

While the WTO represents the overarching global free trade regime, its rules do not preclude the construction of regional free-trading blocs. Generally speaking, there are two types of trading blocs. The first type is the regional free trade area, exemplified by the trilateral (three-country) North American Free Trade Agreement (NAFTA), which came into effect in 1994. Regional free trade areas typically are designed to promote economic growth and prosperity in definable geographic regions and represent trade concessions among member states above and beyond those provided under the WTO. Other prominent free trade areas exist for nations in East Asia, Central America, Central Europe, and Arab states.

The second type of trade bloc is the customs union. A customs union creates a common market in which member countries maintain a common set of external barriers to imports while allowing for free trade within the union. Although they are free-trading agreements, there is a whiff of protectionism surrounding many customs unions, which oftentimes are constructed for defensive purposes as a means of protecting regional economies against the rest of the world, even as these regional economies engage in free trade among themselves. An excellent example is the Southern Cone Common Market (known by its Spanish-language acronym MERCOSUR). Not all customs unions are designed with trade protection. The European Union, for example, began as a means of maintaining peace in Western Europe. Over time, administration of its common market has led to the construction of common political institutions and a common currency, the euro.

Ramifications of Free Trade

Is free trade desirable or undesirable? That, say experts, is a very tricky question. Generally speaking, one's position on trade is informed by the sorts of values one privileges. Thus, if you consider wealth maximization to be of prime importance, chances are you will find free trade to be a good thing. If you value social justice over wealth maximization, you are likely to consider it a bad thing. And if you subordinate both of these values to peace and state security, you could probably go either way.

One of the most attractive things about free trade, according to Ricardo, is that it creates an incentive for producers to allocate their productive resources most efficiently. To use Adam Smith's famous metaphor, in any well-regulated market, resources are allocated with optimal efficiency, as if by an invisible hand. As the table shows, contracting parties to a free trade deal benefit in absolute terms, meaning that participating countries generate more wealth for themselves with free trade than they did before. And because wealth, say some economists, tends to trickle down, if not directly then indirectly through better social infrastructure, increased jobs, and so forth, most citizens will benefit economically to some extent.

Free trade is also good because it tends to generate innovation and rationalization. Innovation occurs when producers have an incentive to create products of better quality for less money. Competition provides this incentive, such that the more intense the competi-

tion, the greater the incentive to innovate. Rationalization occurs when firms that produce inferior and/ or costlier goods are forced out of the marketplace. Under conditions of innovation and rationalization, consumers enjoy greater choice, higher-quality goods, and lower prices for those goods.

In the view of its proponents, free trade creates and maintains peaceful relations among countries. Voluntary free trade is a manifestation of cooperation. This cooperative ethos at the state level is reinforced by inter-firm linkages, or ties based on mutual advantage between firms in participating countries. Similarly, producers and consumers forge cross-border relationships as companies establish export markets. Because all commercial enterprises come to rely on a stable base of customers and suppliers, free trade binds nations together in a complex network of alliances at the societal level. Furthermore, countries that trade with one another typically conform to (or develop) similar principles with respect to open markets, individual liberty, property rights, and civil rights. Put differently, free trade often serves to develop, maintain, and reinforce liberal democratic values.

International cooperation creates three critical obstacles to warfare: states can extract benefits from one another without resorting to conquest, free trade creates a dedicated constituency for cross-border trade on the part of both producers and consumers, and free trade helps forge and reinforce common political values. So successful has this been that the so-called democratic peace theory holds that historically, liberal republics have never fought an international war against one another.

One of the least desirable aspects of free trade is that it tends to exacerbate the gap between wealthy countries and poor countries. We have already seen through the logic of Ricardo that when two countries engage in trade, both are made better off in *absolute* terms. But by definition, both cannot be made better off in *relative* terms. In almost all cases, one country's gains are higher, often a lot higher, than another's. If your comparative advantage lies in production of high-tech consumer goods, and mine is in agricultural production, the odds are pretty good that you will earn a good deal more profit by specializing in your area of comparative advantage than I will by specializing in mine.

For many people, it is unfair that rich countries earn more from free trade than do poor countries. When the standard of living in developed countries is so much greater than it is in developing countries,

Ricardo's Theory of Comparative Advantage

	Country	Labor hours	Commodity	Earnings	Total earnings	Net gain
Protectionism	Portugal	100	Wine	12,000.00		
		100	Cloth	10,000.00	22,000.00	
Free trade	Portugal	200	Wine	24,000.00		
		0	Cloth	0.00	24,000.00	2,000.00
Protectionism	England	100	Wine	8,000.00		
		100	Cloth	9,000.00	17,000.00	
Free trade	England	200	Wine	0		
		0	Cloth	18,000.00	18,000.00	1,000.00

Source: David Ricardo, *On the Principles of Political Economy and Taxation* (1817).

it is hard for citizens of the latter not to feel a sense of injustice. No one wants to be the proverbial hewer of wood and drawer of water whose natural and physical resources go toward creating fabulous wealth for others. This sense of injustice is amplified if we consider that the industrial production creating so much wealth for the citizens of developed countries also generates a hugely disproportionate share of pollution, something that affects the world as a whole.

For many in the developing world, it is also unjust that the rules governing international trade tend to favor the wealthier, developed countries at the expense of poorer, underdeveloped or developing ones. From this perspective, it is no accident that the GATT/WTO was so efficacious in the liberalization of trade in industrial goods (in which developed countries have comparative advantage) and so reluctant to liberalize trade in agricultural goods and textiles. Thucydides was correct when he famously said, "The strong do what they can and the weak suffer what they must." But he was making an empirical statement, not a normative one.

Finally, free trade may be considered unjust insofar as any time there are fundamental social, economic, or political changes, there are differential effects on people. Some will win and some will lose. Free trade creates many losers, at least in the short term, before the longer-term benefits discussed above kick in. (Economists call this the J-curve phenomenon: things get worse before they get better.) Indeed, just because a country is made wealthier in the aggregate, it is well to remember that not all within that country will be enriched. Typically, short-term losers from free trade include those who cannot easily transfer their

productive resources (labor, land, or capital) from inefficient sectors of the economy to efficient ones. For example, owners of immobile capital—capital that has been sunk into a physical structure such as a farm or factory—whose property is significantly devalued through the shifting production patterns that typically accompany significant changes in trade policy are likely to see their investments damaged. Skilled workers in high-wage economies might find themselves suddenly far less employable if the industry that values their skill-set shifts its production offshore. And in the developing world, in cases where free trade creates opportunities for commercial farming, often known as agribusiness, a renewed emphasis on efficiency and technology-based farming practices can have the effect of displacing farmworkers from their jobs.

The Future

In the middle of the 1990s, free trade appeared to be the wave of the future. The European Union was more tightly integrated than ever, and the United States appeared to be firm in its resolve to use soft power, such as economic leadership, to craft a new world order in the wake of the Cold War. The wave peaked when President Bill Clinton hosted a summit for all leaders of American governments (North, South, and Central) except Cuba in Miami in 1994. At that summit, all 34 leaders agreed in principle to a hemispheric trade agreement known as the Free Trade Area of the Americas. By further integrating the economies of these nations, U.S. leaders believed, closer political ties, including an institutionalization of democracy, would follow.

It did not work out that way. The initial enthusiasm that swept through Latin America in the 1990s has given way in many countries to the sorts of concerns associated with dependency theory. As such, MERCOSUR, led by Brazil, has become increasingly wary of the potential for U.S. dominance of the South American economy. In other countries—Venezuela is a good example—populist anti-Americanism has precluded international cooperation. Large stumbling blocks, including agricultural subsidies, developing countries' distrust of industrialized nations (the United States, in particular) and the U.S. focus on the War on Terror, have conspired to slow the momentum of trade liberalization in the twenty-first century. However, patterns of liberalization tend to follow cycles, and the common long-term interest that all states have in the international economy suggests that over the medium term momentum will move once again in favor of free trade.

Michael Lusztig

See also: Fair Trade; Farm Policy; Regulation, Business and Financial; Self-Determination and Sovereignty; Unions and Workers' Rights.

Further Reading

Barton, John H., Judith L. Goldstein, Timothy E. Josling, and Richard H. Steinberg. *The Evolution of the Trade Regime: Politics, Law, and Economics of the GATT and the WTO*. Princeton, NJ: Princeton University Press, 2006.

Cohen, Benjamin J. *International Political Economy: An Intellectual History*. Princeton, NJ: Princeton University Press, 2008.

Findlay, Ronald, and Kevin H. O'Rourke. *Power and Plenty: Trade, War, and the World Economy in the Second Millennium*. Princeton, NJ: Princeton University Press, 2007.

Hufbauer, Gary Clyde, Jeffrey J. Schott, and Woan Foong Wong. *Figuring Out the Doha Round*. Washington, DC: Peterson Institute for International Economics, 2010.

Keohane, Robert O. "The Old IPE and the New." *Review of Political Economy* 16:1 (2009): 34–46.

Milner, Helen V. *Resisting Protectionism: Global Industries and the Politics of International Trade*. Princeton, NJ: Princeton University Press, 1988.

Peterson, Wesley E. *A Billion Dollars a Day: The Economics and Politics of Agricultural Subsidies*. Chichester, UK: John Wiley & Sons, 2009.

Ricardo, David. *On the Principles of Political Economy and Taxation*. New York: Dutton, 1960.

Valenzuela, J. Samuel, and Arturo Valenzuela. "Modernization and Dependency: Alternative Perspectives in the Study of Latin American Underdevelopment." *Comparative Politics* 10:4 (1978): 535–557.

Winham, Gilbert R. *The Evolution of International Trade Agreements*. Toronto: University of Toronto Press, 1992.

Web Sites

International Chamber of Commerce: www.iccwbo.org

United Nations Conference on Trade and Development: www.unctad.org

World Bank: www.worldbank.org

World Trade Organization: www.wto.org

Documents

Document 1: *On the Principles of Political Economy and Taxation* (excerpt), David Ricardo, 1817

David Ricardo's great contribution to political economy was to show that independent of what other countries do with regard to tariffs, a country is always economically better off if it produces that which it is efficient at producing (referred to as producing to its comparative advantage) and importing that which it is inefficient at producing. As such, even where one country is large (like England) and another is small (like Portugal) both countries benefit from free trade with one another. The argument is summarized in the accompanying table on Ricardo's Theory of Comparative Advantage.

Under a system of perfectly free commerce, each country naturally devotes its capital and labour to such employments as are most beneficial to each. . . . It is this principle which determines that wine shall be made in France and Portugal, that corn shall be grown in America and Poland, and that hardware and other goods shall be manufactured in England. . . .

England may be so circumstanced, that to produce the cloth may require the labour of 100 men for one year; and if she attempted to make the wine, it might require the labour of 120 men for the same time. England would therefore find it her interest to import wine, and to purchase it by the exportation of cloth. . . . To produce the wine in Portugal, might require only the labour of 80 men for one year, and to produce the cloth in the same country, might require the labour of 90 men for the same time. It would therefore be advantageous for her to export wine in exchange for cloth. This exchange might even take place, notwithstanding that the commodity imported by Portugal could be produced there with less labour than in England. Though she could make the cloth with the labour of 90 men, she would import it from a country where it required the labour of 100 men to produce it, because it would be advantageous to her rather to employ her capital in the production of wine, for which she would obtain more cloth from England, than she could produce by diverting a portion of her capital from the cultivation of vines to the manufacture of cloth.

Source: David Ricardo, *On the Principles of Political Economy and Taxation* (1817).

Document 2: Joint Statement on the Doha Round by the Heads of the IMF and World Bank (excerpt), October 29, 2005

As the two preeminent world lending institutions, the International Monetary Fund (IMF) and the International Bank for Reconstruction and Development (IBRD, or World Bank) are charged with a global mandate to ensure the soundness of the world's financial situation. Often this necessitates balancing the interests of the developed countries that provide the lion's share of the lending/funding with those of developing countries, which rely on the IMF for currency stabilization and the World Bank for longer term development loans.

WTO member governments have the chance to move collectively toward more open markets, lifting millions of people in developing countries from poverty and boosting growth in rich and poor countries alike. This opportunity may be lost in the coming days unless key governments face down interest groups that would perpetuate high trade barriers benefiting relatively few

at a cost to many. Failure would cast a shadow over the multilateral trading system and further embolden protectionists, at a time when the world needs cooperation rather than conflict.

It is clear what needs to be done. At the heart of the Doha Round lies agriculture, and appropriately so. The sector remains riddled with trade distortions that penalize consumers everywhere and the many poor in developing countries who earn their living from it. Comprehensive and sharp reduction of tariffs in the largest countries will deliver the greatest development gains. Trade-distorting subsidies must also be cut, however, and not simply through technical maneuvers.

Agriculture, important as it is, should not have a monopoly on this Round. The growth potential in other sectors is at least as large. All countries stand to make real gains from removing high tariffs that sap their competitiveness, and from reforming the inefficient services that act as brakes on their own development. Active and fruitful negotiations in services and manufactures are not simply a question of self-interest; they are essential to maintaining the balance of all countries' interests in the negotiations.

Ambitious market opening in agriculture, services and manufactures must be accompanied by significantly increased aid for trade to help the poorest countries take advantage of new opportunities and cope with any adjustment costs. The Bank and Fund are working with donors and beneficiaries to make sure that more and more effective aid for trade is ready to support a Doha outcome.

We urge all Doha participants to remember that trade reform is not a zero-sum game. It is a step toward enhanced opportunity and productivity that benefits all, and that can make a durable contribution to poverty reduction around the world.

Source: International Monetary Fund.

PUBLIC HEALTH

Public health is a wide-ranging field of health care that involves numerous policies, medical specialties, and efforts, all aimed at understanding, preventing, and managing disease and promoting better health outcomes among individuals, communities, population cohorts, nations, global regions, and the entire world.

Recognition that human environments and behavior can have a major impact on people's health has led societies to attempt public-health measures for thousands of years. But only with the resources made available by the Industrial Revolution were sustained and effective public health-care initiatives undertaken, based on the germ theory of disease, which gave public-health officials a better understanding of how diseases spread and how that spread could be prevented or managed.

By the early twenty-first century, such public-health measures and expenditures have alleviated most basic public health-care problems in the developed world and large swaths of the better-governed and economically advancing developing world. But a lack of resources, as well as a lack of education among local populations, has prevented the benefits of public-health efforts from reaching the very poorest countries, which still suffer from communicable diseases and public-health problems largely eliminated in the rest of the world.

Looking to the future, public-health officials have reason for both optimism and concern. Continued economic growth in the developing world, along with medical advances, is expected to spread the benefits of public-health measures more widely. At the same time, population growth, political turmoil, and climate change, which can alter disease vectors, will present new challenges.

What Is Public Health?

Technically speaking, because every individual is a member of the public, every effort to improve health and health care falls under the rubric of "public health"—from a personal visit to a doctor to the taking of an aspirin. But to give the term practical meaning, most experts narrow it down to measures taken by public authorities on behalf of the population to improve the health of those populations small and large, geographically confined or dispersed, and homogenous by identity (ethnic, gender, age) or diverse.

Public-health measures can be broken down into two basic categories: gathering and analyzing information about the state of the public's health (or lack thereof) and using that data, through establishing measures to improve the state of a population's health.

The gathering and analyzing of data is further divided into two interdependent branches: epidemiology and biostatistics. Epidemiology is the study of the causes and influences of diseases and health events, including the study of disease vectors, human behavior, and environmental factors. The category known as health events is broad and can include an array of nondisease events, from automobile accidents to violent crime to occupational injuries—anything that affects the overall health of the population. The tools of epidemiologists include disease surveillance, screening, biomonitoring, and clinical trials. Biostatisticians gather and analyze the statistical data that epidemiologists need to develop their theories and reach their conclusions about the cause and spread of diseases and other health events. Two points should be made here: Epidemiologists and biostatisticians are often one and the same person, and both epidemiologists and biostatisticians can be researchers and clinicians—that is, they can develop new theories and methods and work in the field implementing existing methods and procedures.

Epidemiology and biostatistics are the two most important fields associated with public health, but other fields significantly overlap with it, including environmental health (the study of the impact of the natural and built environments on human health), behavioral health (how human behavior and actions, both individual and collective, affect human health), community health (the study of environments, behaviors, and other factors of specific communities of individuals), and occupational health (the study of how workplace environments, production methods and materials, and other factors affect the safety and health of workers). In addition, the gathering and analysis of data about the causes and effects of disease and other health events can also require examination of public policies and socioeconomic factors.

All of this gathering and analysis of information is aimed at instituting measures to improve the health of a given population—that is, public health is ultimately a clinical science. Such measures effectively break down into three basic categories: those that in some way alter environmental and other factors that contribute to the incidence, spread, and severity of disease outbreaks and other health events; those that modify human behavior to lower the incidence, spread, and severity of diseases and other health events; and those that provide the infrastructure, tools, and medicines necessary to achieve these ends. Public-health measures require the input of professionals from a host of disciplines, many of them specialists in public health, including physicians, nurses, dentists, psychologists, nutritionists, social workers, health officials and inspectors, engineers, and even veterinarians, as many issues that affect human health overlap with those among domesticated and wild animals.

The first category comprises measures that are typically capital and labor intensive and include installing or upgrading public infrastructure, such as sanitation and water systems, or environmental engineering projects, such as draining or filling bodies of standing water, in which disease-carrying insects can proliferate. Because public health also includes measures to combat nondisease events, it can be argued that efforts beyond what is normally associated with the field of public health might, in fact, be closely related to it, such as improving highway safety or providing better public safety services so as to lower the incidence of violent crime.

The second category of public-health measures mentioned above, behavioral modification, can also be subdivided into two general categories: communication and education measures. Communication involves the development of effective methods to convey messages about how behavioral changes can affect individual and public health, while education

The World Health Organization (WHO), based in Geneva, Switzerland, was founded in 1948 as a special agency of the United Nations responsible for directing and coordinating public-health programs. WHO employs 8,500 people in nearly 150 countries. *(AP Photo/Keystone/ Salvatore Di Nolfi)*

includes the provision of information about such measures. Together, communication and education measures comprise persuading people to use condoms to prevent the spread of sexually transmitted diseases, to stop smoking, or to use mosquito nets while sleeping. One of the biggest communications and education campaigns undertaken by the World Health Organization (WHO) in recent years is simply to get people to wash their hands more frequently, which experts say can be the most cost-effective public measure, though in poorer areas it might require an infusion of capital to improve sanitation and water facilities. A more indirect way of getting people to change their behavior is to use economic incentives by imposing or raising taxes and fines on products or behaviors with a negative impact on public health, such as cigarettes, alcohol, or driving above the speed limit.

Finally, there is the third category of measures, which relates to the infrastructure, personnel, and materials needed to improve public health. Such measures include the building of hospitals and clinics, the training and paying of public-health professionals, and the provision of medicines and other products, which comprise the development, production, and distribution of various prophylactics against disease.

Such measures encompass the research that goes into developing new pharmaceuticals, usually vaccines, aimed at arresting the spread of communicable disease and their effective distribution or sometimes simply better distribution of existing vaccines. But this involves more than medicines, since the distribution of simpler items, such as the above-mentioned mosquito nets and condoms, can do much to halt the spread of disease and improve public health.

Historical Background

Public-health concerns and public-health measures are nothing new. People have always taken measures to prevent disease and unpleasant living conditions, even if those came down to accepted rules and customs about not defecating where one eats and sleeps. Many religions have imposed restrictions on foods and behaviors that were seen as detrimental to human health, such as Jewish proscriptions against eating pork or shellfish or the Muslim prohibition on alcohol consumption. Religions also have rules about how to dispose of the dead, including doing so quickly and in ways that prevent their decay from affecting populations of the living.

Early urban civilizations, which had an increased population density, had an even greater need for public-health measures. For example, the Romans, recognizing that a failure to remove human waste impinged on public health, even if they did not exactly understand why, built elaborate sewage systems. The first efforts at public inoculation campaigns go back even farther, to the early years of the first millennium B.C.E., when people in China were encouraged to take deep breaths around the infected lesions of smallpox sufferers, as a means of inoculating them. By the middle of the last millennium the practice had evolved into injecting tissue infected with smallpox under the skin of healthy persons, a practice that spread outward from Persia to the Ottoman Empire and ultimately Europe, North America, and other parts of the world by the late eighteenth century.

Epidemic diseases resulted in other measures to protect public health. The bubonic plague, or Black Death, which wiped out a third of Europe's population in the fourteenth century, led to quarantines against travelers from infected regions, enforced burning of dead sufferers' effects, and even setting aflame entire affected neighborhoods. The growth of international sea trade, slave trafficking, and migration beginning in the sixteenth century led to the routine practice of quarantining ships with infected passengers.

Modern public-health measures—those based on the systematic gathering and analysis of health data and official efforts taken based on those data—date back to mid-nineteenth-century Britain and came in response to a cholera outbreak. As a result of increased international trade and movement of peoples, this waterborne disease—endemic to the Indian subcontinent—ravaged Europe over the course of the nineteenth century. It had long been suspected that cholera was somehow connected to tainted water sources. After an exhaustive mapping of the 1854 cholera outbreak in London, physician and pioneering epidemiologist John Snow, a leading advocate of the then nascent germ theory of disease, provided scientific proof for that theory and for public health by demonstrating that a particular public street pump, located near a cesspit, was directly responsible for a cluster of infected persons. Unfortunately, although city leaders responded by removing the offending pump, they failed to make the larger effort of inspecting and fixing the city's water system, as this would have been prohibitively expensive and might have offended Victorian society's prudish views about bodily functions.

By the second half of the nineteenth century, attitudes began to change. First, as a result of the pioneering work of French chemist and microbiologist Louis Pasteur, the germ theory became the dominant scientific paradigm on how communicable diseases were spread, displacing older notions about bad air and miasmic vapors. By the end of the century, most physicians had come to recognize the need for sterilization of wounds, operating instruments, and hospital environments generally. Second, the rapid growth of cities in Europe and North America had created a new urgency for public-health measures, even as economic growth—and the revenue that it earned for government and private utilities—allowed for investments in major public sanitation and water supply projects. Laws were passed and efforts made to provide more open space in cities, in recognition that fresh air and exercise contributed to public health. Finally, by the early twentieth century, reformers had helped policy makers and the public overcome residual squeamishness about addressing matters directly related to bodily functions. Social workers, initially working for philanthropic organizations and later government agencies, fanned out to inform people about the need for sanitary facilities and practices, proper nutrition, and effective hygiene. Mothers were given scientific advice on prenatal and neonatal care, while women generally, and controversially, were given advice and prophylactics for family-planning purposes.

Such public-health measures, along with medical advances, including new serum antibody vaccines against such scourges as typhoid, cholera, plague, and diphtheria, led to quantum drops in morbidity and mortality rates among the general population as well as declines in infant and childhood mortality rates. Further advances, particularly in the development of antibiotics after World War II, added to the momentum, as did efforts to clean up environmental pollutants. The results were rapidly growing populations, even with falling birth rates; improved worker productivity; overall improvements in health and well-being; and lengthening life expectancies.

Such advances were largely confined to the industrialized world—Europe, North America, Japan, and so on. The Communist government of the Soviet Union also made public health a major priority, with similar outcomes. There were some advances made in the developing world at this time, particularly where colonial governments recognized the economic benefits that would accrue from improved public health. But for the most part, public health was not a major priority in developing countries in the first half of the twentieth century. Most people there still lived in rural areas and so did not benefit from the measures taken, which were largely confined to urban areas.

With independence in the first decades following World War II, which coincided with the discovery and distribution of antibiotics, many new governments committed themselves to public-health measures. Unfortunately, many chose to pursue what development experts call "prestige projects," such as major hospitals in the capital that offered the latest in Western-style medicine but only to the small proportion of the population that lived near them or could afford to take advantage of them. Little effort was made to establish networks of small clinics and people trained in basic health-care procedures that experts agreed were critical to providing better care in the rural areas, where most people in the developing world still lived. Nonetheless, new medicines and better nutrition slowly improved the health outcomes of many people in developing countries, particularly the more advanced ones in East Asia and Latin America.

Several events in the late twentieth and the early twenty-first century allowed the spread of public-health gains, especially economic development. As countries grow richer, they gain the financial resources to implement public-health measures. The increase in the population living in urban areas, a result of economic development, allowed public health education to reach more people. At the same time, encouraged by international nongovernmental organizations (NGOs) and multilateral lending institutions, as well as an improved understanding among local policy makers, new emphasis was placed on developing the kinds of basic health-care systems appropriate to countries with a large number of poor. Finally, improved literacy helped public-health officials to achieve one of their most essential goals: communicating and educating people to change their health-related behaviors. The result of all these changes has been rising health indices in much of the world, including lower infant mortality rates and longer lifespans, with the exception of parts of sub-Saharan Africa where the AIDS epidemic reversed many of the gains made at the end of the twentieth century.

Global Profile, Early Twenty-First Century

A picture of the state of public health in the world today requires an examination of three interrelated questions: How much is being spent on health care, what kinds of infrastructure are being put into place, and what kinds of outcomes are being achieved?

It is difficult to determine what governments, NGOs (both local and international), and private businesses expend on public-health measures, as opposed to health care in general. The most complete data from WHO's statistical arm grouped all of them together, but it is reasonable to assume that the total amount spent on health care—in absolute and per capita terms—bears some relation to the amount spent on public-health measures specifically.

Not unexpectedly, there is a general correlation between a country's overall wealth and productivity and its expenditures on health, despite major differences within all four national income categories: low-income countries with an annual per capita income below about $1,000 in purchasing power parity (PPP, which accounts for the fact that goods and services in poorer countries are generally cheaper than in richer countries); middle-income countries, $1,000 to $4,000; upper-middle-income countries, $4,000 to $12,000; and high-income countries, above $12,000. (All of the following figures are for 2008, the latest available from WHO.)

Health Care Expenditures, Selected Country by Income Level, 2000 and 2008

Country	Total expenditure on health care, 2000 (% of GDP)	Total expenditure on health care, 2008 (% of GDP)	Per capita expenditure, 2000 (at PPP*)	Per capita expenditure, 2007 (at PPP*)
Low income				
Afghanistan	6.2	7.4	$16	$57
Congo**	2.1	2.7	$59	$108
Ethiopia	4.3	4.3	$20	$37
Liberia	9.3	11.9	$39	$46
Middle income				
Mongolia	4.9	3.8	$87	$131
Nicaragua	7.0	9.4	$129	$251
Philippines	3.4	3.7	$79	$129
Uzbekistan	5.7	4.9	$81	$134
Upper-middle income				
China	4.6	4.3	$107	$265
Egypt	5.4	4.8	$180	$261
Jamaica	5.5	4.8	$313	$364
Serbia	7.4	10.0	$313	$867
High income				
France	10.1	11.2	$2,535	$3,851
Japan	7.7	8.3	$1,969	$2,817
Russia	5.4	4.8	$379	$985
United States	13.4	15.2	$4,703	$7,164

* At purchasing power parity.
** Democratic Republic of Congo.
Source: World Health Organization.

Low-income countries on average devoted about 5.4 percent of GDP to health care, or about $74 per person, 16.4 percent of which came from external sources. Middle-income countries spent about 4.3 percent of an admittedly larger GDP on health care, or about $197 per person, with just 1 percent coming from external sources. Upper-middle-income countries spent 6.3 percent on health care, or about $830 per person, with just 0.2 percent coming from external sources. And high-income countries spent 11.1 percent on health care, about $4,246 per person, with negligible amounts coming from external sources. In all categories, except middle-income countries, perhaps because their overall GDP expanded rapidly, there was an increase in health-care expenditures between 2000 and 2008: 4.6 percent to 5.4 percent in low-income countries, 4.4 percent to 4.3 percent in middle-income countries, 5.9 to 6.3 percent in upper-middle-income countries, and 10 to 11.1 percent in high-income countries.

Expenditures on health care pay for a number of things, including buildings and their maintenance, health-care professionals, and various goods, such as medicines and equipment. Again, the extent and quality of this infrastructure is generally a direct reflection of how much is spent on it, which, in turn, is a reflection of the country's overall economic

Health-Care Infrastructure, Selected Countries by Income Level, Averages for 2000–2010

Country	Physicians per 10,000 population	Hospital beds per 10,000 population
Low income		
Afghanistan	2.1	4
Congo*	1.0	16
Ethiopia	0.2	2
Liberia	0.1	7
Middle income		
Mongolia	27.6	59
Nicaragua	3.7	9
Philippines	11.5	5
Uzbekistan	26.2	48
Upper-middle income		
China	14.2	41
Egypt	28.3	57
Jamaica	8.5	17
Serbia	20.4	54
High income		
France	35.0	71
Japan	20.6	138
Russia	43.1	97
United States	26.7	31

* Democratic Republic of Congo.
Source: World Health Organization.

performance. On average for the period 2000–2010, low-income countries have approximately 2.8 physicians and 13 hospital beds for every 10,000 people; middle-income countries have 10.1 and 22; upper-middle-income have 22.4 and 36; and high-income countries have 28.6 and 59.

Other than health care, sanitation and water supply and other areas have a major impact on public health. A country's income level usually determines how extensive these non-health-care infrastructure networks are. In developing regions of the world, about 84 percent of the population had access to safe drinking water in 2008 (up from 71 percent in 1990), compared with 100 percent of the population in developed regions. Meanwhile, the percentage of the population with access to modern sanitation hovered at about 50 percent for the world's poorest countries in 2008, between two-thirds and 100 percent in middle- and upper-middle-income countries, and 100 percent in virtually all high-income countries. All these figures are averages. As noted earlier, there are great variations within countries; typically, middle- and upper-income households have better access to public-health infrastructure than their lower-income counterparts, and urban dwellers have better access than rural dwellers.

Health outcomes typically reflect both expenditures and infrastructure, meaning that as income level falls, so do health indices, such as infant mortality rates and heart disease mortality, though such indices are also affected by such non-health-care factors as diet and prevalence of smoking. Since the early 1990s, however, increased health-care spending and public-health measures have lifted various indices for all income groups. For example, between 1990 and 2009, in low-income countries life expectancy at birth rose from 50 to 55 years, in medium-income countries from 61 to 66, in upper-middle-income countries from 64 to 68, and in high-income countries from 72 to 77. Meanwhile, neonatal mortality rates fell from 47 to 36 per 1,000 live births in low-income countries, 36 to 26 in middle-income countries, 21 to 11 in upper-middle-income countries, and 6 to 4 in high-income countries.

Impact and Responses

Aside from the human misery it causes, lack of public-health expenditures, infrastructure, and measures can have a detrimental effect on a country's economy and social well-being. Workers in ill health are less productive, either becoming so impaired that they cannot perform their job effectively or by being forced to quit because of that low performance. Workers can also become less productive because of the need to care for sick family members.

Ironically, improving public health care can, at least temporarily, place a burden on a society and

Health Care Outcomes, Selected Countries by Income Level, 1990, 2000, 2009

Country	Life expectancy at birth, 1990	Life expectancy at birth, 2000	Life expectancy at birth, 2009	Neonatal mortality rate, 1990 (per 1,000 live births)	Neonatal mortality rate, 2000 (per 1,000 live births)	Neonatal mortality rate, 2009 (per 1,000 live births)
Low income						
Afghanistan	44	46	48	60	56	53
Congo*	54	51	53	32	34	36
Ethiopia	44	48	54	52	43	35
Liberia	37	50	56	57	51	37
Middle income						
Mongolia	62	64	69	27	20	11
Nicaragua	68	73	74	25	18	12
Philippines	65	69	70	23	16	15
Uzbekistan	66	66	69	29	26	17
Upper-middle income						
China	68	71	74	23	19	11
Egypt	62	68	71	33	21	11
Jamaica	73	72	71	13	13	12
High income						
France	77	79	81	4	3	2
Japan	79	81	83	3	2	1
Russia	69	65	68	12	11	6
United States	75	77	79	6	5	4

* Democratic Republic of Congo.
Source: World Health Organization.

its economy. Typically, where a poor public health infrastructure leads to high infant and child mortality rates, families have more children in order to provide enough hands to work on farms or take care of aging parents in countries that lack old-age pension plans. But as the health-care system improves, these mortality rates go down, leading to burgeoning population growth for a period that can last decades and overwhelming a developing country's capacity to provide enough jobs. This, in turn, can sow political discord, as evidenced by the Arab uprisings of 2011 and 2012. Burgeoning populations can also have detrimental effects on local environments.

Various entities have long been involved in the development of public-health infrastructure and the provision of public-health services including governments and nonprofit organizations—the Bill & Melinda Gates Foundation is one prominent example—as well as international organizations, such as WHO, and multilateral lending institutions, the most prominent of which is the World Bank. For many years, such organizations took an essentially top-down approach to public health care, funding large-scale sanitation projects, hospitals, clinics, health-care professional education and financing, and communications and educational efforts. These efforts have led to great strides in providing public health care and in improving overall health outcomes.

More recently, two new approaches have emerged. The first is a market-based approach, such as recent initiatives to provide mosquito netting in the world's poorest countries, an effective low-cost prophylactic against mosquito-borne diseases like malaria and dengue fever. Traditionally, international aid organizations simply distributed mosquito nets gratis to people in low-income countries who needed them. But this led to problems, as many either failed to use them properly or remained unserved by the networks set up by such organizations. Public-health professionals have argued that providing in-country entrepreneurial networks with low-cost nets for resale improves distribution, as the number of small vendors in such areas exceeds that of public-health workers, and increases use, as people tend to utilize things more effectively when they have paid for them, even if the price is very modest.

The second approach involves the use of new technology, most notably the Internet and, in developing countries, mobile phones. These tools can be used in a top-down approach, with government and other organizations providing information to the public. But they can also be used by ordinary people to communicate public health information to authorities and to other people, allowing everyone to respond more quickly and effectively to public-health emergencies, especially those following natural disasters.

As these innovations make clear, the future of public health in developing countries where it remains woefully inadequate does offer cause for optimism. In addition, rapid economic growth in many middle- and upper-middle-income countries will generate more resources for public-health efforts and lead to a more literate population that can make use of the information about health-care behaviors taught by public-health workers and agencies.

At the same time, public-health experts point to looming problems. Burgeoning populations in many parts of the developing world will strain public-health professionals and infrastructure unless both are increased in necessary proportions. Improving health outcomes is especially problematic in regions experiencing ongoing conflicts, especially in sub-Saharan Africa. It is no coincidence, say experts, that countries that are undergoing internal conflict, such as Afghanistan, South Sudan, and Pakistan, are also where polio—the target of one of the most aggressive international efforts at mass immunization in recent years—remains endemic. In addition, public health can be expected to be affected by climate change, which can result in diminishing water supplies and the spread of disease-carrying insects to newly warming regions where they were once rare or unknown.

James Ciment

See also: AIDS/HIV; Environmental Illnesses; Food and Drug Safety; Gastrointestinal Disease; Health Care; Hepatitis; Hunger and Malnutrition; Infant Mortality; Mosquito-borne Disease; Obesity and Eating Disorders; Parasitic Disease; Pharmaceuticals: Availability, Cost, Efficacy, and Safety; Tobacco; Tuberculosis; Vaccination; Water Supply and Access; Waterborne Disease.

Further Reading

Ady, Lu Ann, ed. *Reinventing Public Health: Policies and Practices for a Healthy Nation.* San Francisco: Jossey-Bass, 2005.

Beracochea, Elvira, Corey Weinstein, and Dabney P. Evans, eds. *Rights-Based Approaches to Public Health.* New York: Springer, 2011.

Green, Judith, and Ronald Labonté, eds. *Critical Perspectives in Public Health.* New York: Routledge, 2008.

Hofrichter, Richard, ed. *Health and Social Justice: A Reader on the Politics, Ideology, and Inequity in the Distribution of Disease.* San Francisco: Jossey-Bass, 2003.

Kunitz, Stephen J. *The Health of Populations: General Theories and Particular Realities.* New York: Oxford University Press, 2007.

Mooney, Gavin. *Challenging Health Economics.* New York: Oxford University Press, 2009.

Navarro, Vicente, ed. *Neoliberalism, Globalization, and Inequalities: Consequences for Health and Quality of Life.* Amityville, NY: Baywood, 2007.

Schneider, Dona, and David E. Lilienfeld, eds. *Public Health: The Development of a Discipline.* 2 vols. New Brunswick, NJ: Rutgers University Press, 2008–2011.

Sheard, Sally, and Helen Power, eds. *Body and City: Histories of Urban Public Health.* Burlington, VT: Ashgate, 2000.

Waitzkin, Howard. *Medicine and Public Health at the End of Empire.* Boulder, CO: Paradigm, 2011.

Webster, Charles, ed. *Caring for Health: History and Diversity.* Philadelphia: Open University Press, 2001.

Web Sites

Centers for Disease Control and Prevention, Public Health Information Network: www.cdc.gov/phin/

European Commission, Public Health: http://ec.europa.eu/health/index_en.htm

What Is Public Health?: www.whatispublichealth.org

World Health Organization, Public Health and Environment: www.who.int/phe/en/

Documents

Document 1: "Report . . . from the Poor Law Commissioners on an Inquiry into the Sanitary Conditions of the Labouring Population of Great Britain" (excerpt), Edwin Chadwick, 1842

As head of the Royal Commission inquiring into the operation of Britain's Poor Laws, legislation for poverty relief with origins in medieval times, social reformer Edwin Chadwick conducted an investigation of sanitary conditions in the country's main urban and industrial centers. Among the most important of his conclusions were that built-up environments in which the working classes of Britain lived were chiefly responsible for their health problems.

After as careful an examination of the evidence collected as I have been enabled to make, I beg leave to recapitulate the chief conclusions which that evidence appears to me to establish.

First, as to the extent and operation of the evils which are the subject of this inquiry:—

That the various forms of epidemic, endemic, and other disease caused, or aggravated, or propagated chiefly amongst the labouring classes by atmospheric impurities produced by decomposing animal and vegetable substances, by damp and filth, and close and overcrowded dwellings prevail amongst the population in every part of the kingdom, whether dwelling in separate houses, in rural villages, in small towns, in the larger towns—as they have been found to prevail in the lowest districts of the metropolis.

That such disease, wherever its attacks are frequent, is always found in connexion with the physical circumstances above specified, and that where those circumstances are removed by drainage, proper cleansing, better ventilation, and other means of diminishing atmospheric impurity, the frequency and intensity of such disease is abated; and where the removal of the noxious agencies appears to be complete, such disease almost entirely disappears.

The high prosperity in respect to employment and wages, and various and abundant food, have afforded to the labouring classes no exemptions from attacks of epidemic disease, which have been as frequent and as fatal in periods of commercial and manufacturing prosperity as in any others.

That the formation of all habits of cleanliness is obstructed by defective supplies of water.

That the annual loss of life from filth and bad ventilation are greater than the loss from death or wounds in any wars in which the country has been engaged in modern times.

That of the 43,000 cases of widowhood, and 112,000 cases of destitute orphanage relieved from the poor's rates in England and Wales alone, it appears that the greatest proportion of deaths of the heads of families occurred from the above specified and other removable causes; that their ages were under 45 years; that is to say, 13 years below the natural probabilities of life as shown by the experience of the whole population of Sweden.

That the public loss from the premature deaths of the heads of families is greater than can be represented by any enumeration of the pecuniary burdens consequent upon their sickness and death.

That, measuring the loss of working ability amongst large classes by the instances of gain, even from incomplete arrangements for the removal of noxious influences from places of work or from abodes, that this loss cannot be less than eight or ten years.

That the ravages of epidemics and other diseases do not diminish but tend to increase the pressure of population.

That in the districts where the mortality is greatest the births are not only sufficient to replace the numbers removed by death, but to add to the population.

That the younger population, bred up under noxious

physical agencies, is inferior in physical organization and general health to a population preserved from the presence of such agencies.

That the population so exposed is less susceptible of moral influences, and the effects of education are more transient than with a healthy population.

That these adverse circumstances tend to produce an adult population short-lived, improvident, reckless, and intemperate, and with habitual avidity for sensual gratifications.

That these habits lead to the abandonment of all the conveniences and decencies of life, and especially lead to the overcrowding of their homes, which is destructive to the morality as well as the health of large classes of both sexes.

That defective town cleansing fosters habits of the most abject degradation and tends to the demoralization of large numbers of human beings, who subsist by means of what they find amidst the noxious filth accumulated in neglected streets and bye-places.

That the expenses of local public works are in general unequally and unfairly assessed, oppressively and uneconomically collected, by separate collections, wastefully expended in separate and inefficient operations by unskilled and practically irresponsible officers.

That the existing law for the protection of the public health and the constitutional machinery for reclaiming its execution, such as the Courts Leet, have fallen into desuetude, and are in the state indicated by the prevalence of the evils they were intended to prevent.

Secondly. As to the means by which the present sanitary condition of the labouring classes may be improved:—

The primary and most important measures, and at the same time the most practicable, and within the recognized province of public administration, are drainage, the removal of all refuse of habitations, streets, and roads, and the improvement of the supplies of water.

That the chief obstacles to the immediate removal of decomposing refuse of towns and habitations have been the expense and annoyance of the hand labour and cartage requisite for the purpose.

That this expense may be reduced to one-twentieth or to one-thirtieth, or rendered inconsiderable, by the use of water and self-acting means of removal by improved and cheaper sewers and drains.

That refuse when thus held in suspension in water may be most cheaply and innoxiously conveyed to any distance out of towns, and also in the best form for productive use, and that the loss and injury by the pollution of natural streams may be avoided.

That for all these purposes, as well as for domestic use, better supplies of water are absolutely necessary.

That for successful and economical drainage the adoption of geological areas as the basis of operations is requisite.

That appropriate scientific arrangements for public drainage would afford important facilities for private land-drainage, which is important for the health as well as sustenance of the labouring classes.

That the expense of public drainage, of supplies of water laid on in houses, and of means of improved cleansing would be a pecuniary gain, by diminishing the existing charges attendant on sickness and premature mortality.

That for the protection of the labouring classes and of the ratepayers against inefficiency and waste in all new structural arrangements for the protection of the public health, and to ensure public confidence that the expenditure will be beneficial, securities should be taken that all new local public works are devised and conducted by responsible officers qualified by the possession of the science and skill of civil engineers.

That the oppressiveness and injustice of levies for the whole immediate outlay on such works upon persons who have only short interests in the benefits may be avoided by care in spreading the expense over periods coincident with the benefits.

That by appropriate arrangements, 10 or 15 per cent. on the ordinary outlay for drainage might be saved, which on an estimate of the expense of the necessary structural alterations of one-third only of the existing tenements would be a saving of one million and a half sterling, besides the reduction of the future expenses of management.

That for the prevention of the disease occasioned by defective ventilation and other causes of impurity in places of work and other places where large numbers are assembled, and for the general promotion of the means necessary to prevent disease, that it would be good economy to appoint a district medical officer independent of private practice, and with the securities of special qualifications and responsibilities to initiate sanitary measures and reclaim the execution of the law.

That by the combinations of all these arrangements, it is probable that the full ensurable period of life indicated by the Swedish tables; that is, an increase of 13 years at least, may be extended to the whole of the labouring classes.

That the attainment of these and the other collateral advantages of reducing existing charges and expenditure are within the power of the legislature, and are dependent mainly on the securities taken for the application of practical science, skill, and economy in the direction of local public works.

And that the removal of noxious physical circumstances, and the promotion of civic, household, and personal cleanliness, are necessary to the improvement of the moral condition of the population; for that sound morality and refinement in manners and health are not long found co-existent with filthy habits amongst any class of the community.

Source: Victorianweb.org

Document 2: "Poliomyelitis: Intensification of the Global Eradication Initiative" (excerpt), Report by the Secretariat, 2011

In 1988, the World Health Organization, UNICEF, and the Rotary Foundation inaugurated the Global Polio Eradication Initiative, one of the greatest public health-care initiatives since the successful effort to eradicate smallpox (which achieved its goal in 1977). Polio, a disease that often leaves its victims paralyzed, is a waterborne communicable disease for which effective vaccines have been available since the early 1950s. But poverty and a lack of public health infrastructure prevented the use of such vaccines in many developing-world countries, hence the need for the initiative. By the time of the 2011 World Health Organization Progress Report, polio had been effectively isolated to a few countries in South Asia and sub-Saharan Africa, most of them countries that are currently experiencing or have recently experienced civil conflict.

1. In 2008, the Sixty-first World Health Assembly in resolution WHA61.1 requested the Director-General to develop a new strategy to reinvigorate the fight to eradicate poliomyelitis. The ensuing Global Polio Eradication Initiative Strategic Plan 2010–2012 was subsequently launched in June 2010 and, in keeping with the guidance from the Executive Board, an Independent Monitoring Board was established to monitor the situation by reference to the milestones in the Strategic Plan. This report provides an update, at mid-November 2011, on progress towards—and challenges to reaching—the Strategic Plan's milestones, summarizes the Independent Monitoring Board's concerns regarding the risks to completing eradication, and proposes next steps for the Global Polio Eradication Initiative.

2. As at 8 November 2011, cases of paralytic poliomyelitis due to wild polioviruses had declined by 34% in 2011 compared with the same period in 2010 (505 cases compared with 767 cases). Cases due to the serotype 1 wild poliovirus declined by 35% (444 cases compared with 692), and cases due to the serotype 3 wild poliovirus declined by 18% (61 cases compared with 75 cases).

3. Among the four countries with endemic transmission of wild poliovirus, only India was on track to meet its end-2011 milestone of stopping virus circulation, with its most recent case having onset of paralysis on 13 January 2011. In Nigeria, 2011 saw a fourfold increase in cases compared to the same period in 2010, with new cases in a number of northern states, especially Kano, Kebbi and Borno (42 cases compared with 10 cases for the same period in 2010). Equally as alarmingly, Afghanistan and Pakistan suffered a 135% and 22% increase in cases, respectively, between the same periods in 2010 and 2011 (20 cases compared

with 47 cases, and 111 cases compared with 136 cases, respectively). Of the four countries or areas with "re-established" poliovirus transmission, only southern Sudan was on track to meet the end-2010 goal, with its most recent case having onset of paralysis on 27 June 2009. Although Angola has seen a substantial decrease in new cases in 2011 compared with 2010, the country missed the end-2010 milestone and its most recent case had onset of paralysis on 7 July 2011. In Chad and the Democratic Republic of the Congo, however, intensive transmission continues, complicated by major outbreaks due to new importations of wild poliovirus in 2010.

4. Since January 2010, 19 countries have had outbreaks of poliomyelitis due to ongoing or new importations of wild poliovirus. One such outbreak, on the border between Kenya and Uganda, has continued for more than 12 months since confirmation of the index case. Twelve of the 19 outbreaks were stopped within six months of confirmation of the index case. Six outbreaks were continuing, but for less than six months at end-October 2011: the Central African Republic (2 cases), China (18), Côte d'Ivoire (35), Guinea (2), Mali (8) and Niger (1). All recent imported polioviruses in countries in the African Region were genetically linked to virus originating in northern Nigeria. The virus detected in China originated in Pakistan.

5. ... [I]n April 2011, the Independent Monitoring Board assessed the goal of global eradication by end-2012 to be "at risk," warning that "polio eradication will not be completed if it is in any sense a secondary priority." The Independent Monitoring Board underscored that "the Global Polio Eradication Initiative needs greater priority focus of leaders. Completing the eradication of polio is a global health emergency." It recommended that "the World Health Assembly in May 2011 considers a resolution to declare the persistence of polio a global health emergency." The Regional Committee for Africa in August 2011 adopted resolution AFR/RC61/R4, in which it urged Member States to declare any continued circulation of poliovirus or new infection a national public health emergency.

6. In October 2011, the Independent Monitoring Board re-affirmed that "polio eradication needs to be treated as a global health emergency," and that "polio simply will not be eradicated unless it receives a higher priority—in many of the polio-affected countries, and across the world." ...

9. To accelerate the overall eradication effort, a new, more efficient strategy is being examined, which would combine the eradication of residual wild poliovirus transmission with the polio "endgame" strategy that had been designed to deal with vaccine-derived polioviruses, but only after certification of wild poliovirus eradication. The new strat-

egy is based on new diagnostic tests for vaccine-derived polioviruses, the availability of bivalent oral poliovirus vaccine, and new low-cost approaches for the use of inactivated poliovirus vaccine. The Strategic Advisory Group of Experts on immunization endorsed the central premise of the new strategy: in summary, the removal of Sabin polioviruses from immunization programmes should be phased, beginning with the particularly problematic Sabin type 2 poliovirus in the near term, followed by the remaining serotypes after certification of wild poliovirus eradication globally. . . .

Action by the Executive Board

10. The Executive Board is invited to consider the following draft resolution:

The Executive Board,

Having considered the report on poliomyelitis: intensification of the Global Polio Eradication Initiative, RECOMMENDS to the Sixty-fifth World Health Assembly the adoption of the following resolution:

. . .

1. DECLARES the completion of poliovirus eradication a programmatic emergency for global public health, requiring the full implementation of current and new eradication strategies, the institution of strong national oversight and accountability mechanisms for all areas infected with poliovirus, and the application of appropriate vaccination recommendations for all travellers to and from areas infected with poliovirus;

2. URGES Member States with poliovirus transmission to declare such transmission to be a "national public health emergency," requiring the development and full implementation of emergency action plans, to be updated every six months, until such time as poliovirus transmission has been interrupted;

3. URGES all Member States:

(1) to maintain very high population immunity against polioviruses through routine immunization programmes and, where necessary, supplementary immunization activities;

(2) to maintain vigilance for poliovirus importations, and the emergence of circulating vaccine-derived polioviruses, by achieving and sustaining certification-standard surveillance for polioviruses;

(3) to urgently make available the financial resources required for the full and continued implementation through end-2013 of the necessary strategic approaches to interrupt wild poliovirus transmission globally, and to initiate planning for the financing to the end of 2018 of the polio endgame strategy;

4. **REQUESTS the Director-General**:

(1) to plan for the continued implementation through 2013 of the approaches for eradicating wild polioviruses outlined in the Global Polio Eradication Initiative Strategic Plan 2010–2012 and any new tactics that are deemed necessary to complete eradication;

(2) to strengthen accountability and monitoring mechanisms to ensure optimal implementation of eradication strategies at all levels;

(3) to undertake the development and rapid finalization of a comprehensive polio eradication and endgame strategy that exploits new developments in poliovirus diagnostics and vaccines, informs Member States of the potential timing of a switch from trivalent to bivalent oral poliovirus vaccine for all routine immunization programmes, and includes budget scenarios to the end of 2018;

(4) to continue mobilizing and deploying the necessary financial and human resources for the strategic approaches required through 2013 for wild poliovirus eradication, and for the eventual implementation of a polio endgame strategy to the end of 2018;

(5) to report to the Sixty-sixth World Health Assembly and the subsequent two Health Assemblies, through the Executive Board, on progress in implementing this resolution.

Source: Global Polio Eradication Initiative.

There are no entries for letter Q.